OTHER BOOKS BY STANLEY WEINTRAUB

*Private Shaw and Public Shaw*

*Journey to Heartbreak*

*Aubrey Beardsley: Imp of the Perverse*

*Whistler: A Biography*

*Four Rossettis: A Victorian Biography*

*The London Yankees*

*A Stillness Heard Around the World: The End of the Great War*

*Victoria*

*Disraeli: A Biography*

*Shaw's People: Victoria to Churchill*

*The Last Great Victory: The End of World War II, July/August 1945*

# UNCROWNED KING

## The Life of Prince Albert

STANLEY WEINTRAUB

THE FREE PRESS

*New York London Toronto Sydney Singapore*

THE FREE PRESS
A Division of Simon & Schuster Inc.
1230 Avenue of the Americas
New York, NY 10020

THE FREE PRESS and colophon are trademarks
of Simon & Schuster Inc.

Manufactured in the United States of America

10   9   8   7   6   5   4   3   2   1

**Library of Congress Cataloging-in-Publication Data**

Weintraub, Stanley
          Uncrowned king : the life of Prince Albert / Stanley Weintraub.
                    p.          cm.
          ISBN 0–684–83486–3
          1. Albert, Prince Consort of Victoria, Queen of Great Britain,
          1819–1861.   2. Great Britain—History—Victoria, 1837–1901.
          3. Princes—Great Britain—Biography.   I. Title.
          DA559.A1W45      1997
          941.081'092
          [B]—DC21                                          96–37752
                                                            CIP

*To my children*
*Mark and Judith*
*David and Carie Lee*
*Erica and Bruce*

*Prince Albert in his last years, an engraving by William Holl from a photograph by O.G. Reylander*

'The Prince is become so identified with the Queen,
that they are one person, and as he likes and she dislikes
business, it is obvious that while she has the title he is
really discharging the functions of the Sovereign.
He is King to all intents and purposes.'

Charles Greville,
Clerk to the Privy Council


'He was part of my dream, of course –
but then I was part of his dream, too!'

Lewis Carroll,
*Through the Looking Glass*

# *Contents*

# Illustrations

The author and publishers gratefully acknowledge the following for permission to reproduce illustrations: Plates 1, 6, 8, 9, 26, 27, The Royal Collection © Her Majesty Queen Elizabeth II; 2, Verwaltung de staatl. Schlosser, Garten u. Seen, Museumabteilung, München; 3 and 4, Herbert Appeltshauser, Coburg; 21, 24, The Royal Archives © Her Majesty Queen Elizabeth II; 17, Collection of Charles W. Mann; 28, *Illustrated London News*; 30, © English Heritage. Plates 5, 7, 22, 23 and 25 are from the collection of the author. The original of Plate 27 is untraced; photographic reproductions are held by the Wellcome Institute for the History of Medicine, and the Royal Collections.

The illustration reproduced on p.iv. is gratefully reproduced with the permission of The Royal Collection © Her Majesty Queen Elizabeth II.

# *Preface*

H IS ROYAL DIADEM was a crown of thorns. Having come to an alien country to sire the succession, he remained always the alien. His ways were not English ways, and although he arrived at twenty with much to learn – and learned it, and more – he never adapted successfully to English society and culture, and his adopted people never fully accepted him. Yet the mark he left upon England as merely the Queen's husband was far greater than that of most monarchs, and his marriage, arranged as it was and as stormy as at times it could be, remains one of the most memorable of love stories.

Although his achievements were political and constitutional, scientific and economic, social and cultural, his life was also a romance. His biography opens almost as musical comedy in a feudal backwater that might have anticipated Ruritania, and closes as grand opera on an imperial stage. Nevertheless it is authentic history, not far removed in time from the memories of our great-grandparents, and taking place in the era of steamship, railway, telegraph and photograph.

Despite that sense of the near-present, his life possesses the makings not only of myth but of a complete mythology. At the beginning, one finds the boy from the bucolic village destined for transplantation to the great, sophisticated – and even wicked – city. The minor princeling in a place bypassed by time and destined to inherit nothing would become uncrowned king of the greatest empire on earth. Before that, however, he will be a child devastated when his beautiful mother is driven away by a villainous and dissolute father, for whom the son must thereafter feign affection. To fill the void he will become a Homeric Telemachus, finding, in a physician turned sage, his Mentor.

Here, too, as in many myths of East and West, is the pilgrimage of suitors from foreign lands for the hand of a young queen who rejects them all. Or, conversely, the sovereign summoning, and choosing, a spouse – only the throne is occupied by a woman and the supplicant is a man. Like others celebrated in song and story, the hero is a foreigner in a strange land who must struggle for acceptance by powerful figures whom he despises and whose values he rejects. Beset by enemies, he will best them all.

Also echoing myth, he has a principal heir who brings him little but grief, and a radiant and devoted daughter who is his greatest joy – but whom he must sacrifice. And, although a paragon of all the known virtues, and a seeker after a Utopia he has helped to formulate and which he can see in the near distance, he finds that fate will deny him entrance. Inevitably, a fatal flaw strikes him down at the pinnacle of his hard-won power and prestige.

Born, like Queen Victoria, in 1819, Prince Albert of Saxe-Coburg and Gotha was, from his marriage in 1840 until his death in 1861, the uncrowned king of England. The English had tolerated, uneasily, their fill of German occupants of Windsor Castle, both sovereigns and their spouses, before Albert became the last of them. The first George could not even speak English; even the fourth George, like his brother, William IV, was simultaneously king of a German state – Hanover, from which the first had been imported. Only the accident of Victoria's sex kept her, too, from being a German monarch. No one then alive could recall a regal personage of English descent on the British throne. That was handicap enough for Albert as royal immigrant, but the disability would be emphasized by each of his many public addresses. He could never abandon his heavy German accent, however eloquent or wise or persuasive was the English he spoke.

Albert also had to labour, from the beginning, under the handicap of being required to exercise virtues that were completely negative and went against the grain of his character. As the Queen's husband, he was not to act, but was instead to abstain from action and perform his role as royal cipher with exemplary tact and gravity. Passive excellence and regal inoffensiveness were expected to characterize him – yet whatever his intended public posture, a life of dignified unemployment could not be sustained in the man. He was no drone in a royal hive.

One of the myths that reflected his role as if in a distorting mirror materialized for Albert with a shock of recognition he almost certainly did not explain to anyone, let alone Victoria. In the legend of Omphale, Queen of Lydia, the queen bought the enslaved Hercules as a lover, and to father her sons. Reports would reach Greece that he was to be entirely ornamental while she ruled. Allegedly, he discarded the warrior's lion pelt that was his badge as well as his aspen wreath, and wore, in their place, jewelled necklaces and golden bracelets – even a woman's turban, rather than a crown. While Omphale issued commands, he sat with her Ionian maids and spun thread, outwardly displaying no shame. Hercules would in time, after siring three sons, reject his servitude and go on to perform the feats for which he was destined.

Early in his marriage, Albert encountered – and purchased – a large painting, by a German artist now otherwise forgotten, of Hercules in submission to Omphale (see chapter VIII). By the time of the acquisition Albert had already begun breaking out of his confines as mere consort. The queenly pregnancies which he had been imported to ensure were creating the conditions which enabled him to transform his role. Style would give way to substance. The picture, duly hung where the Prince could see it, remains, still, where he placed it.

With the sundered bondage to a queen, the mythic parallels strikingly intersect Albert's experience. Well aware of the situation awaiting him in England, he realized nevertheless that his alternatives made the risk worth taking. Rather than being mere succession insurance or ceremonial appendage, *Macmillan's Magazine* would later concede, he was 'a man of acute and strong intelligence, as capable as any within the whole circle of British aristocracy of acting a well-reasoned part, and as likely, if there were occasion, to act it resolutely. One even fancied that, at the [a]rouse of some not impossible juncture of affairs, that brain and head [of his] might turn out, in some less reversed manner than hitherto [expected], to be of some importance to the nation.'

Whether or not that reflected largely unspoken speculation as he arrived on the scene during an abyss in esteem for the Crown, it mirrored his own confidence. And so it would work out, although not without hazards and anxieties sufficient for a five-act drama. Barred from holding office or sitting in Parliament or signing an official paper, the Queen's husband created a role for himself above rank or office, and used himself up in its performance. The painting of Omphale and Hercules remained a picture rather than a prophecy.

Because Albert was much more than the Queen's husband – a reality that would cause him considerable misery as well as gratification – there has been no shortage of biographies. Since Theodore Martin's massive five-volume authorized life of 1875–1880, produced with Victoria's co-operation but also with Sir Theodore's sense of his sovereign looking over his shoulder, nearly every decade has seen the publication of another biography of the Prince Consort. Yet even now he emerges as a much more complex figure than we knew. As we look back at the decades since his premature death, we can perceive the potential for a far different history for his sceptred isle had the uncrowned king, as he had certainly become, lived out a biblical span of years.

That this volume parallels the first half of my *Victoria* is inevitable. The Queen and Prince shared lives as well as families, and lines from the distaff life will be echoed here. Events will also, inevitably, parallel and overlap, but from an Albertine perspective. Further, new sources have been exploited, and earlier documentation rediscovered. Clues have turned up in archives previously untapped, even in the sale catalogues of dealers and auction houses. Memoirs, letters and newspapers have been mined, even the scandalmongering press. Gossip and innuendo have value as an index to perception or reputation.

Further, aspects of Albert have been found in sources to which biographers of the Prince have never turned. No previous limner of his life has explored, for example, the American dimension. Although he travelled abroad very little after his marriage – only to France, Belgium, and Germany – an unceasing queue of people with royal business sought out the Prince. (Also, he was a public figure who endured the reality of the adage that a cat may look at a king.) Americans who encountered him included diplomats like Edward Everett and George Dallas, writers like Herman Melville and Washington Irving, artists like G.P.A. Healy, businessmen like George Peabody. Their pens preserved the moment.

Access to sources is not always by design. Some doors were opened by the publication of my *Victoria* and *Disraeli*. A biographer's mail may include happy and opportune leads and tips – even several of the illustrations reproduced here – as well as cranky observations and corrections of past inaccuracies for the next printing, 'if there is one'.

Someone, certainly, will deplore the loss of material from earlier lives of Albert. To create the illusion of a life, the biographer cannot replicate all the seemingly major events in it, let alone the everyday minutiae. In the course of reducing the Prince to a single volume of readable size, I have omitted particulars for which readers may wish to return to earlier biographies. Much must be left out to evoke the essentials of the man.

With changing times, there is also much that illustrates a life that seemed beyond the biographer in a more reticent day. One's subject may evidence vindictiveness as well as valour, obtuseness as well as foresight. One's subject is permitted a sex life, and may experience the unpleasantness of disease. His parents, both an allegedly revered father and a beautiful and beloved mother, may prove to be less than paragons. It diminishes none of his admirable qualities if he is also human enough to be spiteful at times, petty at others; or if he squabbles with his wife or, on occasion, arrogates to himself authority or perquisites not actually his, for power is a potent addiction, even to those who feel that they are eschewing it. That Albert spoke English in public and German in private in the edifice that, more than any other, symbolized monarchical England – Windsor Castle – would have caused royal embarrassment if revealed in the contemporary press, but that reflected a division of soul that was part of his personality. There were other such paradoxes in what was a distinguished and productive life which, however abbreviated, marks him still as the greatest of royal spouses. Tennyson got close to Albert's achievement, yet saddled him with a benign malediction in the form of a compliment when he wrote, in broad Laureate generosity, of a Prince

> Beyond all titles, and a household name,
> Hereafter, thro' all times, Albert the Good.

However well intended, the accolade did the Prince's posthumous reputation some harm. It suggested only gentility and passivity. On his record, Albert required an active, forceful adjective. The pages which follow illustrate why.

Stanley Weintraub

# I

# *Leaving for Good*

## *1839–1840*

T HE DEPARTING PRINCE, if his circumstances were more believable, could have been the hero of a romantic play of 1898, *Alt Heidelberg*, later a long-running operetta with music by Sigmund Romberg. Much like the Karl Franz of venerable but mythic Sachsen-Karlsberg in *The Student Prince* (1924), the authentic prince, tall and handsome, with a light moustache and flashing eyes, had to forgo the remainder of his university days, including boon companions, singing clubs and *gemütlich* inns, to join his betrothed in an arranged marriage. The Saxon duchy was as minuscule as the fictional one, and the university was Bonn, but the bride was too august for credible operetta. Theatre requires some suspension of disbelief.

Prior to doing his marital duty, Prince Albrecht of Saxe-Coburg and Gotha,* like his stage counterpart, would even return to the scene of his student days for a nostalgic farewell. Yet for him, *Abschiednehmen* – leavetaking – was a month-long rite of passage from Coburg to Gotha and from youth-beneath-notice to person-of-consequence. The inner town of Gotha – the Frankish settlement of Gotaha founded in 775 – was already old when the imposing palace of Friedenstein was begun in 1643 by Duke Ernest the Pious on the site of the razed castle of Grimmenstein. Franz Albrecht August Karl

---

* In the bygone world of German dukedoms, baronies and petty principalities, the sons and daughters of Serene – rather than Royal – Highnesses were styled princes and princesses.

Emanuel, the twenty-year-old second son of Ernest I, the far-from-pious reigning duke, was departing from Gotha to become husband of Victoria of Great Britain and Ireland, the queen of the mightiest empire on the globe.

Home for the Prince had been a day's carriage journey to the south, in Coburg, known to history only since the tenth century. From 1353 it was the seat of the margraves of Meissen, descendants of the ambitious Wettin family, who elevated their titles to dukes as they accumulated castles and estates through marriages and inheritances. Franz Albrecht had been born a princeling of Saxe-Coburg-Saalfeld, but in a redivision of family lands after a death without male issue in 1826, Duke Ernest relinquished Saalfeld, to the north-east, for the larger province of Gotha, on the northern edge of the Thüringer Wald. More familiar to the Duke's sons was his Coburg country seat, once the round-towered residence of Adam Alexander von Rosenau, where Albert was born in 1819; and the Ehrenburg Palace, just off the market square, in the town, converted in 1543, early in the Reformation, from a dilapidated Franciscan monastery. In 1540 Martin Luther himself had resided in Coburg, in the Veste, a once-fortified hilltop castle that withstood sieges in the Thirty Years' War.

For all its venerable history and its happy commercial situation on the toll-road between Leipzig and Frankfurt, the Duchy of Coburg was only 201 square miles, half the size of the Isle of Wight, and had only 41,000 inhabitants, nine thousand of them in the town itself. Gotha and its detached principality to the east, Altenburg, added 596 square miles and sixty thousand subjects to Ernest I's domains, ranking him twelfth in the German Diet and requiring him to furnish a contingent of eight hundred soldiers – half his standing army – for the service of the German confederation.

Gotha boasted a population of 13,874 in the capital, by far the largest of twelve towns in the principality. Fifty miles north of Coburg, it was the last family destination on Albert's farewell journey toward England, and matrimony. Although he had not yet left the hourglass frontiers of Coburg and Gotha, he had already relinquished his German name, and understood that on his arrival on English soil he would be naturalized an English subject of the Queen. Nonetheless he vowed solemnly to his former University of Bonn companion, Prince William von Löwenstein-Wertheim-Freudenberg, 'Whilst striving and working

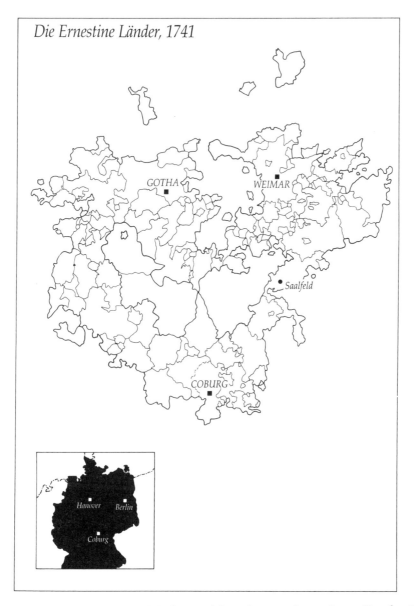

*The Ernestine principalities, dukedoms and dependencies in Saxony in pre-Napoleonic times. Coburg is to the south, Gotha to the north-west. By accretion they gradually expanded towards each other. Saalfeld, once a Coburg dependency, is to its north-east.*

indefatigably for the country to which I shall belong in future and in which I shall be called to occupy a high position, I shall not cease to be a loyal German, Coburger, Gothaner.'

On the instructions of Victoria and with his father as her proxy in Gotha, on 23 January, 1840 her husband-to-be had been invested with the Order of the Garter in his new English guise. The Queen had been unable to invest him as well with an English peerage – a confirmation of the low esteem into which the monarchy had fallen – and he would be leaving Germany with only a bejewelled blue ribbon and an anglicized name.

In his last letter to Victoria from Coburg – each took seven or eight days by courier across Germany, Flanders and the Channel – Albert had written, having it both ways, 'I strongly approve of your method of writing to me in English when you feel you must express yourself very clearly, and I beg you continue your habit of writing partly in German and partly in English, a method I shall likewise follow, and by which we shall not only be enabled to understand each other fully, but by which also my dearest Victoria will become the most amiable and useful language master I can possibly have.' It was dated three days before Christmas, his last at home among the German table-top evergreen trees bright with candles.

The formal declaration of Albert's betrothal had been made in Coburg two weeks earlier, in ceremonies on a scale that would have amused the English. The Court, he had explained the day before to Victoria, would gather 'in full dress to hear the Word of God; then it assembles in the Throne Room along with members of the Chamber, Delegates from the towns, chiefs of Colleges, the Army, the Clergy, etc., and, before Papa and myself, Minister von Carlowitz (after Saxon custom, the Ruler never speaking in Person) will read the Declaration, which will then be printed and sent throughout the country in a special newspaper issue. Then a Court [levée] for congratulations . . . and then a state Banquet.' But solemnity was limited to the Saxon élite. Public reaction in Coburg was less restrained than in London, and dramatized the gulf between the two cultures. 'The joy of the people was so great', Albert wrote to Victoria on 10 December, two days after the official ceremonies in the duchy, 'that they went on firing in the streets with guns and pistols during the whole night, so that one might have imagined that a battle was taking place.'

Events affecting Coburg, a backwater even in fragmented Germany, created few ripples in relatively somnolent, post-Napoleonic Europe. A very young husband for a reigning queen seemed likely to have no impact other than to promise continuity for the royal line. In Britain, where the Whig grip on government had been slackening, strengthening the succession was a triumph for a party electorally imperilled since the coronation.

In London, Victoria had done no more, formally, than to read a paper – composed by Melbourne – to the Privy Council. Once the sovereign's private consultative body, it had lost most of its political powers to the Prime Minister's Cabinet as the Crown's powers declined, but membership remained a sought-after distinction although the Council met largely to formalize decisions already taken.* Victoria's assured presence before it, however, allayed concerns about the young queen's mishandling of her role, which had disquieted both government and opposition almost since her succession. Whatever common folk thought about the importation of a young and inexperienced foreigner to be her consort, the party in power saw in him a check on her more deplorable tendencies. As for the Tories, Sir James Graham wrote to the Conservative leader, Sir Robert Peel, 'no change can well be for the worse; and in such circumstances almost any change becomes desirable.'

On Christmas Day in London, after dining with the dowager queen, Adelaide, at Marlborough House, Lady Wharncliffe returned to her town residence in Curzon Street, Mayfair, and penned a gossipy letter to her daughter, Caroline Talbot. The former queen – she was only forty-seven, a quarter-century younger than the late William IV – was a favourite of Victoria, who liked her aunt far better than her own mother, the ambitious Duchess of Kent. The fondness had long been mutual. Unable to carry a child beyond stillbirth or early infancy, Adelaide had loved the young Victoria, destined by biology to be William's successor, as if she were their child. A Christmas parcel from Victoria had arrived, and Adelaide opened it in Lady Wharncliffe's presence. It contained a bracelet enclosing, in the custom of the day, a cutting of the giver's hair.

'She was much pleased with it', Lady Wharncliffe wrote of the dowager queen. Before her arranged marriage, Adelaide had been a

---

* The cabinet office of Lord President of the Council linked the two bodies.

princess of Saxe-Coburg-Meiningen – as Victoria's own mother had been a princess of neighbouring Saxe-Coburg-Saalfeld (and Albert's aunt). Protestant princesses of childbearing age had been much sought after by George III's sons after the death in childbirth of Princess Charlotte, the only child of the unadmirable Prince of Wales – who soon after became George IV.

Adelaide was charmed by the letter which accompanied Victoria's Christmas gift, 'which was in German & in German characters, & then told me that when she was at Windsor she had said to the Queen she should like much to get a German letter from her *some day*. She said it was very well written' – although Victoria afterward deplored her own early attempts at German as 'shocking bad' – '& that she now writes in German to Prince *Albert*. Of *him*, she' – Adelaide – 'gives a very favourable report, from all she has heard, & told us that he not only loved music – how lucky! – but *composed* very well indeed.' The young queen had even asked Adelaide to visit at five on an afternoon and listen to some of the Prince's songs. 'Accordingly she went, & I think it was in the Duchess of Kent's apartment – and there she remained singing her Albert's compositions till seven.' Lady Wharncliffe was weak on pronoun references but it was evident that Victoria's pride in her future husband was already substantial.

Reactions were very different elsewhere in London. The gutter press had quickly dampened the euphoria about the Queen's betrothal to a handsome and talented young prince. One broadside sold and sung in the streets, Charles Dickens alleged to the young MP Richard Monckton Milnes, not only emphasized Albert's foreign origins, but suggested a local pronunciation for his name that emphasized the Queen's own Saxon, and Hanoverian, origins:

> So let 'em say, whate'er thay may
> Or do whate'er they can;
> Prince Hallbert he will always be
> My own dear Fancy man.

Before the old year was out, even the Prime Minister was suggesting to the Queen that Albert was, in character and upbringing, alien to English ways, repeating to her a concern voiced by a lady in Melbourne's worldly circle that the Prince's German university traits would be made fun of by English university men, whose experience was less of learning than of license, and who emerged as gentlemen rather than as professors. 'Any attention to morality in universities [here] was ridiculed, which I said was too shocking', Victoria confessed in her diary on 31 December. 'I said funnily I thought Lord M. didn't like Albert so much as he would if he wasn't so strict. "Oh! no, I highly respect it," said Lord M. I then talked of A.'s saying I ought to be severe about people. "Then you'll be liable to make every sort of mistake. In this country all should go by law and precedent," said Lord M., "and not by what you hear." '

Two weeks later, Melbourne seemed concerned, in talking with the Queen, about 'Albert's indifference about Ladies'. He appeared innocent of female entanglements, too inexperienced to be a husband. 'A little dangerous, that's all it is', Melbourne explained. 'It's very well if that holds, but it doesn't always.'

Victoria was shocked. 'I said [to Lord M.] this was very wrong of him, and scolded him for it.'

The Saxon mini-states had furnished more than their share of spouses for English royalty, including Victoria's – and Albert's – uncle Leopold, who was Princess Charlotte of Wales's widower, but Gotha had not identified itself with the English royal house until its linkage with Coburg. The duchy's population of 96,000 – about five per cent of metropolitan London's two million in 1839 – was ecstatic about the rise of their own princeling to as high an estate as there was in the world. A new traffic count in London had tabulated seven thousand vehicles passing the intersection of Oxford Street and Newman Street in Soho daily. There were not that many carriages in all of Gotha. Now someone who otherwise at best would have been only a *Herzog zu Sachsen*, would, through marriage to a Wettin cousin for whom German was a foreign language, sit next to, if not upon, the throne of England.

Albert was under no illusions about his likely powerlessness. Still, the brilliant role in life arranged for him was better than life as a younger son in a third-class German statelet. Gotha had principally been known for the publishing house of Justus Perthes, which since 1753 had issued the *Gothaische Hofkalender*, better known as the *Almanach de Gotha*, the genealogical, diplomatic and statistical annual to which one referred for such information as the heads of ruling houses. This marriage would assure Albert a prominent place in it.

The high dignitaries converging upon Gotha for their farewells – a *Landgrave*, a *Landesherr*, a *Herzog* – were as nothing compared to those soon to crowd Albert's appointment book. For the visiting *Grossherzog* – Grand Duke – of nearby Weimar, a shooting party was arranged in the gross fashion of *Mitteleuropa*, a *battue* in which masses of game were driven into firing range. 'I took part,' Albert boasted to Victoria – he would be somewhat more cautious in England – 'and was so lucky as to kill 105 hares with my own gun.'

A few days before the colourful Garter ceremony, festive Gotha was plunged into mourning when Herr von Carlowitz, Duke Ernest's minister of state for eighteen years and his only intimate friend (three privy councillors completed the Lilliputian government), died suddenly of a stroke. Mourning had to be brief. The wedding at Windsor could not be postponed, and travel by the ducal entourage would not be easy.

No one told Albert, amid the festivities, that London rumour had it that the marriage might have to be postponed because of fears of revolution. Parliament had scorned a Chartist bill of rights for redress of grievances. (Much of it would be legislated piecemeal over the years.) A violent reaction was feared – even the Thames, it was rumoured, would be set on fire, and churches torched. The worst incident turned out to be a meeting in Bethnal Green which was broken up by the police.

While the outlook for order was improving, for Albert nothing good was happening in London. Despite Albert's origins in the duchy that had sheltered Luther, the Duke of Wellington, conservative even by Tory standards, moved in the Lords that a reference to Prince Albert be prefaced by the word 'Protestant', to protect England from Papist contamination. After all, members of his family, to rise in the world, had married Catholics, and Albert himself might have 'papistical leanings'. The amendment, Charles Greville, clerk to the Privy Council, observed in his diary, was 'a sop to the silly'. He was 'grieved' to see the elderly, doddering Wellington 'descend to such miserable humbug'. It was party posturing, with Albert as pawn.

Albert himself would have been grieved had he read in *Hansard* the debates in Parliament about granting him anything, from rank or title to an allowance befitting his station. 'Did the noble Lord', the Radical MP Joseph Hume taunted Viscount Melbourne's Chancellor of the Exchequer, Lord John Russell, 'know the dangers of setting a young man down in London with so much money in his pocket?' Laughter drowned out the difference between an annuity for the consort of the Queen and a pocketful of golden sovereigns carried down to Soho by a well-born blade from the country. As a further indignity, the bill as passed on 27 January would commence payment to Albert only on the day of the wedding, with the first instalment not due before Easter. Albert would have staff appointed for him and no means of paying them, a prospect which compelled him to plead, vainly, that he should have foisted upon him 'only enough gentlemen for appearance's sake'.

Through January the issue of his purse had been debated in print as well as in Parliament. 'Little Vic is in a dreadful stew', the irreverent weekly *The Satirist* reported, 'for ever since the prepayment system had been adopted she has got no letter of advice from Albert, as the Grand Duke of Saxe-Coburg refuses to sell his Duchy in order to enable the poor young man to prepay his letters.' (The Penny Post had just gone into effect in England.)

The Queen had been fearful of such stipulations when she formally opened Parliament on 16 January, but she went through her address with grace and dignity, breaking down only after Melbourne informed her, after eleven in the evening on the twenty-seventh, that the resolution on the Prince's status as proposed by Sir Robert Peel and his Tories had beaten the divided Whigs by 104 votes. The opposition had made every matter concerning Albert's perquisites a party question and Peel had sternly commanded Tory loyalty. 'We smashed the Government', the Tory MP from Maidstone, Benjamin Disraeli, gleefully reported to his sister, Sarah.

The royal earful which the Prime Minister received must have been much like the grievance which Victoria registered in her diary. The 'vile, confounded, infernal Tories' had aimed at embarrassing the shaky Whig government, and the Queen's marriage happened to be in the way, but Victoria took personally what Disraeli called 'a war to the knife'. 'As long as I live, I'll never forgive those infernal scoundrels, with Peel at their head . . . for this act of personal spite!!'

Since the Duke of Wellington had insisted upon diminishing Prince Albert's allowance, Victoria declared to Melbourne that she would not extend the expected invitation to her wedding to the venerable hero of Waterloo. 'I really couldn't ask the Duke.' Only days before Albert's entourage clattered on toward Calais, Wellington remained intractable in the Lords, also objecting to a clause in the marriage act assigning

Albert precedence over all members of the royal family after the Queen. The royal dukes, Victoria's uncles, had objected and the Queen had even tried bribery, offering to give the Duke of Sussex's illegal wife (under the Royal Marriage Act) the title of Duchess of Inverness, and to have him give the bride away at the wedding. The Duke of Cambridge offered consent so qualified that Wellington interpreted it as an implicit rejection despite the Queen's public thanks. The Duke of Cumberland, now King Ernest Augustus of Hanover, would not hear of a mere princeling preceding him. On the twenty-sixth, a Sunday, Lord Clarendon intervened with Wellington, explaining in vain that Albert was marrying a queen, and that the precedents of Leopold and Charlotte, and – a century earlier – of Prince George of Denmark and the future Queen Anne, then a princess, did not apply. Wellington would not be budged, and Melbourne patiently counselled Victoria to give up the losing battle.

'I was perfectly frantic', the Queen confessed in her diary, '– this wicked old foolish Duke, these confounded Tories, oh! may they be well punished for this outrageous insult! I cried with rage . . . Poor dear Albert, how cruelly they are ill-using that dearest Angel! Monsters! You Tories shall be punished. Revenge! Revenge!'

Since anything less would have scandalized a still-adoring country, the avuncular Melbourne succeeded in obtaining for Wellington an invitation to the wedding. The Queen remained adamant about the wedding breakfast. The Duke intended no disrespect, Melbourne cajoled vainly: 'It's his conscience.' Still, Victoria had to inform Albert of his eroded position before his packet docked at Dover. Albert had lost on every issue, material and symbolic. Even before his round of farewells in Germany had begun, he had relinquished any hope of appointing his own Household other than for inferior servants. For private secretary and controller of his purse he had already accepted George Anson, the Prime Minister's secretary. It seemed almost as if Melbourne had arranged for a spy at Court. Albert's protest that he should remain outside 'party politics', earned him a wry history lesson from the Prime Minister. 'To compose your Household of persons who are neither themselves nor by their relations connected with political parties is impossible. So many neutral persons fit for the purpose do not exist and would form a strange assemblage if they could be found.' Rather, Melbourne saw the necessity for the appointment of 'persons of rank and character . . . with a decided leaning to the opinions of the present government.' Otherwise, he warned, the appearance would be created 'that Your Serene Highness is adverse to Her Majesty's ministers, and you will find yourself, in spite of yourself, taken up by the party in opposition . . .'

Unwilling to surrender easily, Albert had appealed from Gotha on 12 January 1840 that 'a mixed household of Whigs and Tories' would establish 'that I will belong to no party'. It was high-minded, but the Prime Minister was interested in perquisites rather than in principle, and although Albert sent copies of his exchanges to Victoria with the vow, 'I declare calmly that I will not take Mr Anson nor anybody now', he would have to back down. Melbourne left it to the Queen to appoint Anson. Too embarrassed to insult Albert directly by telling him what she had been required to do, having reaped the whirlwind of past political blunders, Victoria insulted him even further by leaving it to her confidante, Baroness Lehzen. Yet the Prince was trapped. 'I am leaving my home,' he had already objected to Victoria, 'with all its old associations, all my bosom friends, and going to a country in which everything is new and strange to me – men, language, customs, modes of life, position. Except yourself I have no one to confide in.'

The narrow streets of Gotha were dense with well-wishers as the Prince's carriages passed for the last time. In one was Colonel Charles Grey, who, to take a place in the Royal Household, had relinquished the parliamentary seat at High Wycombe he had first won in a contest with an ambitious upstart named Benjamin Disraeli. Grey had travelled to Gotha with Lord Torrington bearing the Queen's patent for emptily honouring Albert with the Garter. Torrington, the 7th Viscount and a young gentleman still in his twenties, was a favourite of the Queen but, unknown to her, a compulsive gossip who would soon feed hurtful stories about Albert to the press, particularly to *The Times*, as 'your Windsor special'. Yet at Court he would outlast the Prince. Another favourite whom Albert would shortly encounter, since he had been instructed to escort him across the Channel, was Lord Clarence Paget, one of the six sons of the Marquess of Anglesey, several of whom held Household posts. His brother, Lord Alfred Paget, was once rumoured as a possible mate for Victoria. Gossip referred to them as the 'Paget House Club' – but the youngest brother, Lord George, would confound expectations by distinguishing himself in the Crimea and rising later to general.

Torrington and Grey were to accompany Albert overland to the Channel in three carriages sent by Victoria. They had been among the 180 guests at Gotha who had celebrated the Garter investiture at an elaborate dinner that had included toasts, trumpet flourishes, the band of the Coldstream Guards brought over for the occasion to play 'God Save the Queen', and a salute by 101 cannons in the square. At the third and last toast, the windows were flung open as a signal to the artillery and the breeze blew the thin muslin curtains into the candle flames. In an instant they blazed to the tops of the tall windows. The dinner guests, already standing, were trapped between the crowded tables, but the fragile curtains flamed out in seconds. The panelled dining-room survived almost unscathed. Postprandial coffee in the Duchess's apartments was served almost as if nothing had happened, after which the company reassembled to go in state to the new opera house. (It had opened three weeks earlier with a gala production of Giacomo Meyerbeer's *Robert le diable*.)

In Carl Maria von Weber's *Der Freischütz*, the staged operatic shooting seemed anticlimactic. 'With the opera', Grey understated in his journal, 'ended a most exciting and interesting, if somewhat fatiguing, day, but the hours kept are so much better than those in England, that all was over between ten and eleven.'

A plethora of luncheons, dinners and state balls filled the final week. On the Monday evening before Albert's departure, the last banquet was followed by a concert. At its close, as the musicians put away their instruments, the ladies and gentlemen of the duchy, and invited German guests, many of them in tears, passed before the Prince to bid him *auf Wiedersehen*. On Tuesday morning, 28 January, the journey began. 'Every window', Grey recalled, 'was crammed with heads, every housetop covered with people, waving handkerchiefs and crying with each other in demonstrations of affection.' At the home of the dowager duchess of Gotha, the late Duchess Louise's aged stepmother, the carriages halted long enough for her to come to her own window to raise her arms and, weeping, twice shout Albert's name. Too frail to descend and join the family in still another farewell, Duchess Caroline permitted her attendants to help her away. Others, in twenty carriages, gathered at The Last Schilling, a small tavern just north of Gotha, where there were further embraces and handshakes. Finally, in the snow beneath an arch of fir trees erected at the ducal frontier, garlanded girls in white dresses, accompanied by a band, sent him off with a farewell hymn which steamed into the frosty air.

With the Queen's carriages were five of Duke Ernest's, carrying his own entourage that was to attend Albert at the wedding on 10 February. At one o'clock the party stopped by arrangement at Birschhausen for lunch, and at eight they put up at an inn at Kassel for the night; but before dining, the duke and his sons paid a courtesy visit to the Elector of Hesse, whose seat it was. The following morning at nine the carriages clattered east to Arnsberg, arriving at ten in the evening and going on the next day to the Rhine, which they had to cross near Köln (Cologne) by ferry in cold, heavy rain. By three in the afternoon the sodden, exhausted party reached Aachen (Aix-la-Chapelle), where messages awaited Albert, among them the disagreeable news that Parliament had refused to vote him a stipend equal to that secured by his uncle in 1816 as husband of Princess Charlotte, whose death in 1817 had opened the succession to the yet-unborn Victoria.

Having turned down the new throne of turbulent Greece, Leopold had been made King of the Belgians when the nation was formed from the secessionist lower provinces of the Netherlands in 1831. Yet, to the outrage of the House of Commons, he had failed to relinquish his lifetime parliamentary grant of an annual £50,000; and Albert was the second Coburger consort for whom funds had been requested by the Court in little more than two decades. The allegation was at least in part unfair. On the day Leopold left London for Brussels, 16 July 1831, he renounced his full £50,000 stipend. He continued to deduct from it, however, the upkeep of his English estate, Claremont; of the horses and carriages and servants he retained in England; his donations to English charities and subscriptions to English clubs; and the funds he diverted for a time to his nearly penniless sister Victoire for the upkeep of her establishment, including Princess Victoria. These English expenses he computed as about £20,000. The £30,000 he returned was, perhaps not by coincidence, the amount offered by Parliament to his nephew Albert. A younger brother to Duke Ernest, Leopold had been a prince of Saxe-Coburg-Saalfeld, the title into which Albert was born, three months after his cousin Victoria, on 26 August 1819. Leopold at twenty was in the Russian army fighting Napoleon. By Waterloo he had become a senior officer, and had met Princess Charlotte when in London after the war in the suite of the Tsar. To Parliament, Albert was little more than a child, a university student called from his class-room in Bonn.

To Albert, his parliamentary rebuffs suggested that England was now weary of foreign spouses for royalty – especially Coburgers. Parliament had been forced after the death of Charlotte and her stillborn child to pay the debts of, and provide stipends to, George III's spendthrift and often dissolute sons, some already in illegal marriages, to press them into begetting legal heirs. Leopold's stipend now seemed to MPs an expensive anachronism.

It was into the Belgian domains of his uncle that Albert arrived by early evening on the last day of January. By ten his entourage was ready, wearily, to settle down in Liège for the night. Instead, they found the provincial governor and his party waiting to escort them in state to the Pavilion Anglais, where a brass band assaulted the tired travellers until midnight. 'Nor was it all quiet when they ceased', Grey wrote. 'About one o'clock a large company of peasants took their place, and serenaded the Prince with vocal music till nearly two in the morning.'

The next day Albert reported from Brussels via the courier that he had arrived safely in the capital that afternoon. To his 'Dear Beloved Victoria' he poured out his frustration that their ill-treatment was coming not only from the lesser classes elected to the lower house, but from the peers who might rather have applauded the dynastic stability his presence would promise. 'You can imagine how annoyed I am at the news of the really most indecent vote in the Commons about my income,' he wrote. 'We saw it in the paper when we dined at Aix. Even in the House of Lords they are making themselves unnecessarily unplea-sant. I must stop, and only can tell [you] that if your love remains, they cannot make me unhappy.'

Awaiting Albert in Brussels was Thompson, the Queen's tailor, with the uniform that the Prince was to wear at the altar. He had left his Coburg court dress at Windsor to be used as a pattern, and the fitting would take place in a third court – Leopold's. (Innocent of military experience, Albert would be caricatured in his field marshal's regalia astride a rocking-horse.) A letter from Victoria also awaited him in Brussels, cautiously making no mention of the pared stipend, which Albert continued to see as an index to his likely status in England. He was too innocent of the world to be restrained about it, even to the bride to whom he would owe everything but his few Ernestine florins. 'I am surprised', he confessed on 4 February, 'that you have said no word of sympathy to me about the vote of the 28th, for those nice Tories have cut off half my income (that was to be expected), and it makes my position no very pleasant one. It is hardly conceivable that anyone could behave as meanly and disgracefully as they have to you and me. It cannot do them much good, for it is hardly possible to maintain any respect for them any longer.'

Alarmed by the resentment Albert found no reason to conceal during his pause at Brussels, Leopold rushed a letter the same day, 4 February, to the Queen at Windsor. The wedding was only six days away. Albert was 'much irritated', Leopold warned. 'He does not care about the money, but he is much shocked and exasperated by the disrespect of the thing.' He was 'pretty full of grievances'. Albert would have been even more outraged had he known that the Queen had given in to the army of old men in the Privy Council and in Parliament without much of a fight, but the royal cachet had sunk as close to worthlessness as it seemed able to fall, and she was hardly more than a girl.

Albert still assumed that royal regard meant something to a Parliament that had been exasperated by the worthless sons of George III, two of whom had succeeded to the throne, and had been further disillusioned by the young queen, child of another of the embarrassing royal dukes. Victoria had disappointed expectations by her personal failings and appeared flighty and foolish – in need of a mature, sophisticated husband at her side. Yet Albert was even three months younger than the Queen.

Overruled earlier about the staff of his own Household, Albert, already in Belgium, discovered yet another rebuff, this time from his future spouse. Victoria's letter awaiting him had responded to Albert's appeal for a honeymoon, even if only at Windsor Castle, long enough to afford some privacy. He hardly needed to remind Victoria that they had been permitted little experience of each other by Court etiquette. The Queen admonished him loftily, her affectionate interpositions notwithstanding,

You have written to me in one of your letters about our stay at Windsor, but, dear Albert, you have not at all understood the matter. You forget, my dearest Love, that I am the Sovereign, and that business can stop and wait for nothing. Parliament is sitting, and something occurs almost every day, for which I may be required, and it is quite impossible for me to be absent from London; therefore two or three days is already a long time to be absent. I am never easy a moment, if I am not on the spot, and see and hear what is going on, and everybody, including all my Aunts (who are very knowing in all these things), says I must come out after the second day, for, as I must be surrounded by my Court, I cannot keep alone. This is also my own wish in every way.

Whatever Albert's ambitions for himself, marriage with an obscure but appropriately born lesser heiress from Hesse or Saxony or Württemburg may have seemed, then, an opportunity for which he should have waited. He could have completed his university degree or, like Ernest, apprenticed himself to a military career in Saxony. At twenty he would have, at Victoria's order, the uniform of a field marshal, but it would only be a costume in which to be wed.

In London, balladeers hawked broadsheets, mocking 'Saxe-Coburg's pauper prince' and 'the dozen cowboys who compose his court'. In another, the Prince proclaimed, in card-playing metaphor,

> They say I'm a ninny,
> and not worth a ginny,
> But Vic, she declares
> I'm a trump.

The Coburg delegation was to leave Brussels for Calais, Albert wrote to Victoria, early on the fifth – 'and then there awaits us that sad time on the sea, which, I fear, will be bound up with great sacrifices! The public, who will probably be assembled at Dover, will obtain a pleasant vision of me!' Melbourne's view of Albert remained unsatisfactory, but not because of his susceptibility to seasickness. On the same day, at a dinner for the Cabinet given by Lord Palmerston, Melbourne had remarked that the Queen was 'very angry' with him, and the Earl of Clarendon asked why. 'The Queen was talking with him about Prince Albert', Lady Clarendon reported, 'and remarking that one thing that pleased her very much was that he never paid any attention to any other woman. Lord Melbourne *inadvertently* (as he called it) answered, "No; that sort of thing is apt to come later"; an odd remark to make to any woman on the eve of marriage – let alone *the Queen*. She said, "I shan't soon forgive you that!" Lord Melbourne rubbed his hands…and chuckled over it amazingly.'

Registry of Albert's marriage and his exchange of vows with Victoria would lift him on 10 February from Serene Highness to Royal Highness. Their essential preliminary, the Naturalization Bill, cost the Queen and Prince agonies of waiting. It passed on 4 February, the day before he left Brussels by the new railway for Ostend *en route* to Calais. Embarrassingly, the bill guaranteed him no precedence after the Queen. The seemingly harmless precedence clause had been withdrawn in order to get it by its third reading.

All that Melbourne had managed was to prevent Colonel Sibthorp, the architect of the Prince's reduced stipend, from amending the bill in the Commons to cease Albert's annuity if the Queen should die and he did not afterwards remain at least six months every year in England. It was an unveiled slap at King Leopold, and even the Leader of the Opposition, Sir Robert Peel, asked the cranky colonel to withdraw his paragraph. At five in the morning after four nights of debate the Government's slender majority was only twenty-nine. Albert was on his way to becoming a subject of his Queen.

Leaving Buckingham Palace, Albert's emissary Baron Stockmar encountered Melbourne. Long confidential agent for the Coburgers, especially for Leopold, now King of the Belgians, the prematurely wizened Stockmar, by profession a medical doctor, had become a physician of souls, a discreet counsellor to the next generation of ambitious Ernestine princes. He observed unhappily that some members of the Whig Cabinet had evaded voting on the bill. 'The Prince will doubtless be much irritated against the Tories', the Prime Minister conceded. 'But it is not the Tories alone whom the Prince has to thank for the curtailment of his appanage. It is the Tories, the Radicals, and a good many of our own people. I hope you will yourself say this to the Prince.'

Stockmar penned his memorandum, which would reach Albert as he disembarked in England, on 6 February. Stockmar understood that Melbourne felt too weak as minority Prime Minister to demand party loyalty, and did not want misplaced rancour to make a political partisan of the Prince. The problems in accepting the young and inexperienced foreigner as consort to a young and wilful queen were more complicated than simple loyalty to the sovereign.

Albert's party reached Calais on the evening of 5 February and remained overnight. Channel crossings were rightly dreaded, especially in winter, and they were to sail in the morning, to cross in daylight. The two best vessels in the service had been ordered to Calais by the Queen, the steam packets *Ariel* and *Firebrand*, but the wind was at half gale force as the party arrived at dockside on the sixth. It was impossible to board the pitching *Firebrand*. Everyone crowded aboard the *Ariel*, and as the packet weighed anchor at noon, the *Firebrand* followed, nearly empty. Helpless on deck was Victoria's personal representative, Lord Clarence Paget.

Buffeted by high seas, the packets struggled across the Channel, His Serene Highness hanging on to a staircase rail below for most of the voyage. At 4.30 p.m. the white cliffs hove into view. As the ships docked, awaiting crowds shouted, 'God save the Queen!' and 'Hurrah for the Prince!' Weak with seasickness, the tottering Coburgers, accompanied still by Lord Torrington and Colonel Grey, wanly received salutes from a guard of honour from the 90th Regiment, which guided them in the drizzle to open carriages-and-four. The crowds parted to let them through to Payne's York Hotel, where the mayor of Dover and his delegation were to offer a formal address of welcome. Albert was too seasick to receive it. The mayor, magistrates and town councillors offered to return in the morning.

On the banks of the Thames beyond Barking Reach in the direction of London, gawkers and greeters remained waiting for some sign of the Prince's party. People had gathered at Woolwich and Greenwich on the basis of mistaken information in the afternoon papers, expecting Albert to disembark at the docks near the Royal Arsenal rather than at Dover. With disappointment and frustration increasing, the crowds thinned. Some die-hards set off, as dusk fell, toward Shooters Hill overlooking Woolwich Common and the town of Greenwich. They were still hoping to catch a glimpse of the Prince if indeed he were taking the road to London. Instead, at seven the party dined, cautiously under the circumstances, upon a repast on which the landlord of the York had spared little expense. Wobbly, Albert postponed writing to Victoria until the next morning.

Early on Friday a courier took his message to the Queen, anticipating the following day – the eighth – when 'I shall be looking into your dear eyes'. The crossing, Albert confessed, had been 'terrible', with the decks of the *Ariel* 'crammed with sick people'. He could not recall ever 'having suffered so long or so violently. Papa and Ernest too were in miserable condition. When we landed our faces were more the colour of wax candles than human visages.' Yet he saw their tumultuous reception as recompense for the shabby treatment by Parliament. 'Thousands were standing on the quay, and greeted us with loud and continuous cheering.'

Effectively now an Englishman as he set foot on Kentish soil, he awaited the reappearance of the Dover dignitaries and his next leg of the ceremonial journey to London. 'Papa and Ernest lay themselves at your feet', he closed in the courtesies of the occasion. 'I lay myself higher – right up to your heart, hoping to find it open to me, and remain with unchanging love and attachment, my own dear bride's ever faithful, ALBERT.' Thus ended the first full day of the lifetime vocation to which he had been born and bred.

# II

## *Silver Spoon*

### *1819–1831*

I N  T H E  S C H L O S S  called the Rosenau in Coburg, a 'Pumpernickel State', W.M. Thackeray would joke anonymously in *Punch* in 1845, was exhibited the actual silver spoon, embossed with the English royal arms, which Prince Albert had in his mouth when he was born. Awed, 'the correspondent of the *Morning Herald* fainted when he saw this admirable relic'. The notion that Albert's birth as a younger son to the ruler of a small Saxon duchy might place him in line to be consort to the queen of a great world power could not have been held by many on 26 August 1819. Still, a connection existed. His first cousin, Alexandrina Victoria, had been assisted into life at Kensington Palace three months earlier via the services of the same *accoucheuse*, Dr Marianne Heidenreich von Siebold. The Princess's mother, the Duchess of Kent, born a Coburger herself, was a sister to Duke Ernest, the boy's father.

For years there would be little likelihood that the infant princess would be queen in England. She was merely the first in her generation to be born after the death of Princess Charlotte of Wales, heiress to the future George IV. The corpulent 'Royal George', who would succeed to the throne early the next year, was the eldest of a brood of odious brothers each eligible by accident of death or birth of an heir to be, or to sire, the next king – or queen. Several of the ageing royal dukes would jettison ineligible mistresses and illegal wives to marry and beget, hoping to find in the sorry lottery a means, at worst, of having a grateful Parliament reward such duty to the succession by paying off their substantial debts. Only as the Princess survived what was almost a royal tontine did she appear in political need of a husband, and there were greater princes in Europe than one whose father reigned over what seemed hardly larger than a royal park in England.

Aside from his dubious prospects as little more than an insurance policy upon his elder brother, Ernest, born a year earlier, on 21 June 1818, Albert's life looked cloudless. The little dukedom on an edge of the sprawling Thüringer woods was peaceful and idyllically beautiful. Albert's ducal father was secure in the rule of his mini-state, one of the less significant of the thirty-nine sovereignties in the jerrybuilt jigsaw of the German Confederation. Albert's mother, formerly Princess Louise of neighbouring Saxe-Gotha-Altenburg, born on 21 December 1800, was young, clever and beautiful. No silver spoon of English design was in sight.

Sixteen at her marriage to the worldly thirty-three-year-old Duke Ernest, Albert's mother was eighteen at his birth. Although her elder son had been born in Coburg itself, at the sooty yellow, sham-Gothic Ehrenburg Palace, her *Alberinchen* arrived at the Rosenau, four miles north of the walled town. Unpretentious but for its squat round tower and set amid rolling green hills, its remodelling, with added English gardens, had been financed by Ernest I after the Napoleonic armies receded, through credit advanced by the Frankfurt Rothschilds. Albert's elaborate christening ceremony there, utilizing water from the Itze, which flowed below the rise of the Rosenau, may have been the last happy public event in the doomed marriage. Proudly, the publishers of the *Almanach de Gotha* issued for 1818 a Wedding Edition, with frontispiece portraits of the ducal pair. Since sovereigns awarded each other gaudy Orders as compliments, Ernest's high-collared uniform was weighted down with them, and the young Princess of Gotha, now a duchess, wore her hair in coils atop her head, crowned by a diadem of pearls. There were also views of Gotha and of Coburg, and an ornate dedication, inevitably in French. No king or queen could have been better served by the modestly sized but magisterial book of blue bloods.

On the arrival of the couple in Coburg after the wedding in Gotha, their greeting punctuated by the booming of thirty-six guns, happy townspeople unharnessed the horses from the couple's coach-and-four and in a traditional demonstration of enthusiasm pulled the carriage the rest of the way to the castle. That evening at a concert in their honour a choir sang, 'Hail, Duke! Hail, Duchess! Soon you will be rocking princes in your lap!' Louise was enchanted, but not for long. After the first post-nuptial sermon in the royal chapel, she carped to Augusta von Studnitz, her closest friend in Gotha, she heard only praise of Duke Ernest, and 'not one religious thought'. Her life, with few responsibilities other than to fulfil the hopes of the Coburg choristers, would become one of ordering Paris fashions, accompanying Ernest to the chase with wives of the other huntsmen 'to hear the calling of the stags', and entertaining neighbouring serene highnesses.

An early shadow over the marriage was Louise's visit with her 'beloved husband' to the fortress of Leutenburg, east of Saalfeld, where seventeenth-century Duke Johann Casimir of Coburg had kept his wife, whom he accused of adultery with a young knight, Ulric von Lichtenstein, and whom he had had imprisoned and divorced. She had died in captivity in 1613. A portrait of Duchess Anna and another of her vengeful husband still hung in the gloomy vaults, and were pointed out to Louise by the Duke in the manner of a dramatic monologue by Robert Browning yet to be written, 'My Last Duchess'.

'I thought I could still hear the weeping of the unhappy Anna, and see the flowing blood of the perfidious Lichtenstein', Louise confided to Fräulein Augusta. 'I clutched the Duke's arm and looked anxiously to see if there was, perhaps, any likeness in his beautiful dark-brown eyes to this terrible ancestor, but I don't believe it. Anna was miserable because she was unfaithful. Posterity will never be able to say that about me.'

In Louise's own marriage, the infidelities at first had all been Duke Ernest's, but Louise had no knowledge of his profligate past, nor that he had not relinquished wenching when he pledged his vows. Early in their union, it seemed to the Duchess, they were seldom apart for long. They were together in Vienna, their children left with nursemaids, when, on 23 January 1820, the Duke of Kent, the infant Victoria's father and Ernest's brother-in-law, died suddenly in England. When the dread news reached Ernest's shocked entourage, Louise wrote, 'We . . . became ill, all of us.' That distant thunderbolt was as nothing, however, to the damaging gossip of her stepmother's lady-in-waiting. Charlotte von Bock claimed to *Grossmutter* Gotha – to whom one had to shout, as she was very deaf – that a courtier, Count Solms, was in love with the flirtatious Duchess Louise. Alexander Solms, a chamberlain, Louise confided to Augusta, laughed at the canard, but also 'felt quite proud, because of the honour of such a likelihood'. It was much less of a lark when the 'boundless stupidity' was brought to the Duke. 'If he had been sensible', Louise explained, 'he would have laughed also, but he took it seriously and was angry with me. Finally, we had it out; all ended in [my] tears. Now he watches me, which he never used to do, and he misconstrues everything.'

Yet for the moment, with an heir in place and another in reserve, and 'well and jolly', Duke Ernest was content, and Louise's stepmother, the Dowager Duchess of Gotha, kept the children's Coburger aunt in London apprised of happier developments. Albert 'looked like a little squirrel with large black eyes', but soon they had become blue and he was 'pretty as an angel'. Duke Ernest's own mother Augusta, *Grossmutter* Coburg, also kept her twice-widowed daughter in England informed that *Alberinchen*, while 'not a strong child', before he was two (21 July 1821) could 'say everything'. Although 'too slight for a boy', unlike his sturdy elder brother, he was 'lively, very funny, all good nature, and full of mischief' (11 August 1821).

Albert and Ernest were not the Duke's only sons, but Coburgers were cautious about open references to his illicit amorous life, even after Pauline Panam, one of his discarded mistresses, published her *Mémoires d'une jeune Grecque* in Paris in 1824. At fifteen she had been slipped into Coburg dressed as a boy. (Among the paintings which had been commissioned for the refurbishment of the Rosenau, Louise would note, was one 'of a Knight who has discovered that his supposed page is really a beautiful girl'.) At sixteen, in March 1809 – Ernest had been Duke since his father, Francis Frederic, had died in 1806 – Pauline had given birth to his son, an earlier Ernst, in Frankfurt, where she had been sent. Leopold had given her some money, and the Dowager Duchess offered her a pension if she refrained from identifying herself with the Duke and named her child Pauline if a girl, and eschewed Ernest if a boy. She ignored the injunction. The Duke's adjutant, Johann Maximilian von Szymborski, offered a settlement if she 'quit' Saxe-Coburg territory. In Dresden and Frankfurt, she received small sums grudgingly given, then went to Vienna and, finally, Paris, where – as *la belle Grecque* – she somehow supported herself, very likely through the 'special protection' of titled admirers and further blackmail of the Duke. The illegitimate Ernst led a dissipated manhood, and persisted in calling himself a Prince of Coburg until his death at thirty.*

Long before Pauline Panam's tell-all book, Louise had become aware of the Duke's proclivities, which may have justified her enjoyment of undisguised male admiration at the tiny court, if at first nothing more. Louise wrote anxiously to her friend Augusta when the *Landgraf* of Hesse-Cassell was expected for a visit that he would be accompanied by his young sister. 'She will make a sensation with her beauty', the Duchess explained. 'I am frightened for the Duke when he sees her.' Once, taking the waters at Franzensbad, she confided to Augusta about the eighteen-year-old Countess Marie of Klebelsberg that she was 'loved by all'. She had accompanied Louise as lady-in-waiting, 'and God knows what will come of it!' Yet her own admirers at the time ranged from *Kammerherr* Thankmar von Munchhausen, twenty-eight, who was 'hopelessly in love' with her, to 'good-looking Baron Stillfried', a Cherubino at only seventeen, who climbed apple trees to look into her windows, and 'did a thousand pretty, amorous things, which amused me'. There was even 'an Austrian *Rittmeister*' who 'lay at my feet, sighed and languished like a turtle dove'. Mozart might have made an opera of it.

At least into the first months of 1823 Louise shut her eyes to Ernest's straying and pretended as well that her own flirtations were harmless acknowledgements of her charms as an adornment to the duchy. Court life had its quota of make-believe, and some small price had to be paid to sustain it. On 16 December 1822, the Duke held a masked ball, with participants garbed as characters from Sir Walter Scott's *Waverley*, an enormous success on the Continent as well as in Britain. Louise came as the beautiful heroine Flora MacIvor, who ominously retires to a convent at the end of the novel. On the twenty-first was another ball, concluded by a sleigh-ride, and the festivities of the holiday season continued into the new year with scarcely a thought for young Ernest and Albert, who were better cared for in any case by their *Kindermädchen*.

---

* Just as Ernest and Albert had a half-brother with a familiar name preceding them, so Victoria had an illegitimate half-sister unknown to her and carrying her name. Adelaide Victoire was the product of the Duke of Kent's early wild oats, born to a Frenchwoman who died in childbirth in Geneva in 1789. He supported her indirectly via Coutts Bank until 1832, when she faded from history.

Balls, especially masked ones, furnished transparent cover for trysts, and Louise appeared guilty only of evoking ducal jealousy. A later invention, a pamphlet of 1915, however, alleged her involvement with yet another court chamberlain, Baron Ferdinand von Meyern, claiming that 'without contradiction' the affair made Albert 'a half-Jew'. In his bitchy fashion, Lytton Strachey in 1921 would repeat this canard as true. The baron's daughters, Bertha and Malvina, were close friends of Louise. But while the posthumous allegation had no substance, at least one obvious relationship seemed to go too far for the Duke. In 1822 Louise had met Lieutenant Alexander von Hanstein, but she did not mention the 'good-looking' officer with 'black, curly hair' and 'shining bright eyes' to Augusta until March 1824. 'Now comes the worst', she finally confessed; 'don't damn me completely . . . I have sacrificed everything, but don't also let me lose your friendly heart.'

Expecting the worst, Louise was not surprised when it came. With sanctimonious hypocrisy, given his own lifestyle, the Duke had a letter delivered to her insisting that henceforth they were to live apart. 'You have dreadfully deceived me. I can affirm before God that you have had my heartfelt love . . .' And he went on about her 'blackest betrayal and ingratitude'. She was ordered to remain at the Rosenau until he received a letter he had requested from her stepmother recalling her to Gotha 'or wherever else she wants to send you'. He was too affected, he closed, by his sense of hurt to continue the letter further. 'We shall hardly see each other again. May you not become so unhappy as you have made me.'

Hanstein was later identified in the Duke's formal petition for legal separation. Ernest sent Szymborski, now a colonel, with stipulations for the Duchess. She was to sign away any remaining rights in Gotha, then leave quietly or be expelled. 'If you will have a divorce,' Ernest wrote, 'I will not withhold my consent for a complete parting.'

The news surfaced quickly. Coburgers, she would claim to Augusta on 24 September 1824 (the last letter that has survived), thought she had been betrayed, and gathered at the Rosenau to wish the Duchess well as she departed into exile on the last Sunday in August. As Louise emerged to step into her carriage, townspeople burst through the hedges, unharnessed her horses, and with choruses of loyalty to her, 'pulled me from the Rosenau, through the town to the [Ehrenburg] Schloss, cheering and shouting all the way.' Cries of '*Die Herzogin kommt!*' echoed through the narrow streets, '*die Burger und die Bauern*' – the towns-people and the farmers, as she put it – joining each other.

'At each village a fresh lot took up the harness. Everywhere was black with people. Their love was touching, but very frightening, too, for they were all armed.' When they reached the castle the throng, which had been increasing all the way, discovered that the Duke was away at his mother's residence. From the balcony of the schloss Duchess Louise offered her gratitude to the crowd 'for their love'. They cheered her, sang 'Now thank we all our God', and set out for Ketschendorf to find the duke, 'and brought him and my children here. They wanted to unite us by force. Poor deluded people!...They felt themselves to be power-ful, and rushed wildly into the Schloss, demanding that Szymborski should be given up.' Thousands cried for ousting of 'the foreigner', assuming that the alleged 'grinder of peasants' was the real authority in the duchy. Intervening, a courtier sympathetic to Louise, Moritz von Thümmel, kept the peace, but not without threats from the Duke, who vowed to summon Austrian cavalry to disperse them by force.

It was an empty threat. A villager, recalling the scene nearly forty years later, remembered that Ernest, in white top hat and long green coat fastened up to the neck, rushed down to reprimand the obstrep-erous Coburgers, then hastened inside. The ducal regiment, com-manded by Major Wilhelm von Wangenheim – his son was a playmate, at the Rosenau, of the princelings – had already been called for assistance, but Wangenheim had objected to using the military against the people. Execrations of Szymborski were becoming more violent, and several clergymen, summoned to pacify the crowd, appeared in their vestments, exhorting their parishioners to go home. They were met with insults. Then the throng saw a closed chaise drawn by four horses arrive at a gate of the Ehrenburg. They rushed toward it, assuming that Szymborski was trying to escape, but a castle functionary appealed to them to make way for the Dowager Duchess. Respectfully, the people moved back, and Szymborski leaped in and was driven away at a rapid gallop. By then the Duke had succeeded in summoning the municipal fire brigade and the ceremonial company of archers to shore up the castle entrances. The crowd dispersed, and Louise was sent back to the Rosenau.

In her last surviving letter to Fräulein von Studnitz, Louise wrote, 'I stayed several [further] days in Coburg...I signed the deeds of separation...I often went for drives, being greeted with shouts and hurrahs.' On Friday, 4 September, two days after she had signed away everything, she left Coburg 'at the stroke of midnight' – to evade more loyal demonstrations. Coburgers still knew nothing about her expulsion. Louise's carriage went westward toward Brückenau, on the high road half-way to Frankfurt. She was permitted to take 'a Court Household of my own choosing, and go to a Schloss belonging to my uncle'. The arrangement with the Duke of Gotha would not work out – he would lend her nothing – but she had with her, temporarily, the von Thümmels and a few others, and settled at St Wendel, Ernestine property in the Saar.

'Parting from my children', she wrote to Augusta, 'was the worst thing of all. They have whooping-cough, and they said, "Mamma is crying because she had to go away while we are ill." The poor little mice, may God bless them!' Ernest was six and Albert five. 'Oh, misery!' she wept by letter to Augusta. 'Oh, measureless misfortune!' Louise may never have seen her sons again.

An official notice was printed in the Coburg newspaper: 'On September 2, 1824' – the day she had signed away her rights – 'Duchess Louise left for St Wendel in the Lichtenberg jurisdiction.' It would be a hermitic existence. Propriety kept Hanstein distant. To her sister-in-law Sophie Mensdorff-Pouilly she lamented, 'I live here lonely as ever; each day resembles the last, so that I have no idea of the passage of time.'

In responding to the divorce action, which took eighteen months before it became final – and was never acknowledged in the *Almanach de Gotha* – she neither admitted nor denied the charge of adultery, but on 31 March, 1826 she married Hanstein, who three months earlier had been created Count von Polzig-Baiersdorf by the sympathetic Duke Frederick of neighbouring Saxe-Hildburghausen. 'Speak sometimes with Prince Leopold about me,' she appealed in a letter to Baron Stockmar, Coburg physician and confidant to all the brothers, Ernest included. 'I would not like him to forget me completely.'

Leopold and Stockmar, she guessed correctly, could be conduits to the children. And her stepmother, who had not been without guilt in harming the Duchess's reputation, would once (31 July 1831) write to Duke Ernest of the 'sad condition' of 'poor' Louise. 'The thought that the children have quite forgotten her worries her deeply. She wishes to know if they talk about her. I told her that it was impossible for them to forget their mother, but they were not told how much she suffered, as that would make them suffer too.' A tale almost too poignant to be true, told by Max Müller, is that Louise caught a glimpse of her sons only once, when she heard that they would be at a harvest festival, and slipped into the crowd in the guise of a peasant woman.

Louise was indeed in a sad condition, and on 16 February 1831, she went with her husband to Paris to consult the eminent gynaecologist Dr Antoine Dubois. On 6 March, while watching the celebrated ballerina Maria Taglioni at the Opera, she haemorrhaged and was carried unconscious from the theatre. She was suffering from uterine cancer. On 8 August she dictated her will to her maid, Anna Metz, asking that she be buried in Germany unless her husband chose to live elsewhere. 'If death is going to part us, I want my body at least to be near him.'

In November 1822 she had experienced in Coburg what may have been a miscarriage, described to Augusta von Studnitz only as constant stomach pains and an 'inflammation of the bowels', leading to a haemorrhage. She may have experienced then the first signs of cancer. Still in Paris on 30 August 1831, she collapsed and died before her husband, in the next room, could rush in. On 13 December 1832, she was reburied in the churchyard at Pfesselbach, near St Wendel. Fourteen years later, after their father's death, Ernest and Albert, flouting her will, had Louise's body removed to the ducal tomb in the Church of St Moritz in Coburg where Duke Ernest lay, violating her spirit but satisfying Coburgers as well as the marital ideal that had eluded both their parents.*

By the time of the divorce, the duchy and the princelings had acquired new names, as the deaths of Louise's father, Augustus of Saxe-Gotha-Altenburg, and then his brother, both without male issue, had required a rearrangement of Thüringian mini-states. Duke Ernest added Gotha in exchange for non-contiguous Saalfeld, which went to the Duke of Meiningen, creating the hyphenated title by which Albert was known thereafter. Since ducal dignity was often a reflection of the size of the state, Ernest had achieved, just before the breakup of his marriage might have made the accession of territory impossible, the opportunity for the grander style his children would know, but Albert –

---

* Count Polzig had by then remarried. His second wife died in 1845 but he lived on to become Personal Adjutant to Frederick William IV of Prussia.

unlike his brother – would always prefer countrified Coburg to bourgeois Gotha.

Other than for their visits to one or another of the fond *Grossmutterin*, no female presences replaced the vanished Louise in the boys' lives. Despite the circumstances of her departure and the void left in his life, Albert never doubted his mother's affection, and he would name one of his daughters after her. The very years in which his formal learning began were melancholy ones. Education in real life had already preceded the tutors and the books. Certain things, both boys understood, were unmentionable, and certain questions were not to be asked.

Immediately following the exile of the Duchess, the self-indulgent Ernest left on a shooting holiday with his still-footloose brother Leopold. As late as the Duke's birthday, on 6 January 1825, an event celebrated locally since his accession, he had not returned to Coburg. It was a desolating time for the children, but his heir later imagined a humane and heroic father. The second Ernest wrote of 'the earnest mildness' of the Duke, of his 'delicacy of feeling' and his unfeigned 'attention to custom of every kind'. Albert's brother could not recall, forty years later, ever hearing 'a harsh or ugly word from his lips', and 'never saw an action of his which would not have satisfied every idea[l] of good breeding'. As children, he and Albert 'looked upon him – and with right – as the ideal of perfection, and although he never spoke a stern word to us, we felt for him not only love and adherence, but a degree of respect which bordered on fear'.

The Duke, Ernest contended, 'seldom blamed, [or] praised unwillingly', yet 'we exerted ourselves more than if we had been blamed or praised'. When asked – possibly by Leopold – whether the boys studied diligently and were well behaved, the Duke allegedly answered, 'My children cannot misbehave, and they know of themselves that they must learn something in order to become able men, so I don't trouble myself further about them.' Yet he did, although seldom about learning from books. 'He never allowed a negligence in dress or carelessness of demeanour; any transgression was punished by a look alone, but a look that was so grave that it said more than a long lecture.' The portrait of Duke Ernest as a genial, loving and indulgent father seems largely fiction, not only from what emerges between the lines of purported memory, but from the record itself.

From the start, Albert and Ernest were schooled together as if twins. Intellectually ahead although fourteen months younger, Albert was physically and emotionally less mature. As Ernest would put it, 'His physical development did not keep pace with the quick unfolding of his remarkable mental powers; he . . . had the physical leaning of the weaker toward the stronger.' He was only three – in May 1823 – when the duke assigned Christoph Florschütz of Coburg, an experienced tutor although only twenty-five, to educate both boys. Ernest, whose marriage was already under strain, was eager to remove the boys from the care of their mother and nursemaids and put them under male supervision. Summoned for advice, Count Stockmar recommended young Florschütz.

Christoph Florschütz was the tutor of Alexander and Arthur Mensdorff, the younger sons of Ernest's sister Sophie and her husband, the Count of Mensdorff-Pouilly. Relinquished to the Duke's sons, Florschütz would remain with them for fifteen years. Albert was 'so young and little', Florschütz recalled, that at the start he willingly allowed his tutor to carry him up and down the stairs of the Rosenau, which became schoolroom as well as home for the boys. Set in unspoiled forested hills, it came to be what Albert would recall as 'the paradise of our childhood'.

Well aware of the manly and female-free regimen that the Duke intended for his sons, Florschütz loyally deplored the deficiencies of their upbringing prior to his summons to rectify it. 'Endowed with brilliant qualities, handsome, clever and witty, possessed of an eloquence and a lively, fervid imagination,' he conceded, 'Duchess Louise was wanting in the essential qualifications of a mother. She made no attempt to conceal that Prince Albert was her favourite child. He was handsome and bore a strong resemblance to herself . . . The influence of this partiality upon the minds of the children might have been most injurious.'

However 'sad' the expulsion of the Duchess was, Florschütz claimed, it remained a 'satisfaction' to him that it did not 'interfere permanently with the happiness of my beloved pupils', who retained 'the cheerfulness and entire innocence of childhood. Deprived of a mother's love and care, the children necessarily depended more entirely on that shown by their tutor.'

Often in his early years with Florschütz, Albert cried, his own record of the melancholy time contradicting nostalgic memories he found appropriate to relate afterwards of a childhood Utopia. In the candour of a precocious early boyhood he confided in a journal he kept from January to May 1825, when he was only five, the ups and downs of his unsteady emotions only months after his mother had gone. (In the evenings, before prayers, he and Ernest would write in their obligatory diaries.) On 21 January he was happy. 'Dear Papa' – who had finally returned to Coburg – fetched them for breakfast and took them after lunch on a shooting party. On 23 January Albert awakened ill, with a cough. 'I was so frightened that I cried.' He left his bed only at three in the afternoon – to draw, to build a castle, to do his lessons, to paint a picture and to play with a Noah's Ark. On the 26th he cried because he could not repeat his lessons to Florschütz, 'for I had not paid attention'. When his punishment for crying was a ban from play after dinner he cried yet again, and was permitted to draw with 'black chalk' – probably charcoal. Ordered by 'the *Rath*' – Florschütz was officially a Coburg councillor – to put away lesson books he had left lying about, Albert again dissolved into tears. One detects more tutorial impatience than ingenuity in Albert's notation that February, 'I cried at my lesson today, because I could not find a verb: and the *Rath* pinched me, to show me what a verb was. And I cried about it.'

At first Albert fled from strangers, often retreating into the arms of his brother, who shared an affection not reciprocated by a cold, aloof father. His summons to share breakfasts and dinners, always at the wrong time of day for children and an intrusion into study or play times, were stiff occasions. Even before the illness and death of Louise, about which he knew little, Albert was obsessed by thoughts of sickness and death. He also rejected other women brought into the household, and Theodore Martin, who later wrote a five-volume official biography under Queen Victoria's supervision and with her recollection of Albert's memories, noted cautiously that the Prince had 'even as a child shown a great dislike to be in the charge of women'. In a memorandum to her aide, Charles Grey, in 1864 when he was writing at her assignment *The Early Years of HRH the Prince Consort* (1867), the Queen observed that her husband 'spoke with much tenderness and sorrow of his poor mother, and was deeply affected in reading, after his marriage, the accounts of her sad and painful illness'. In his childhood journals and letters, however, Albert very likely felt too vulnerable to mention his mother at all.

Florschütz was to supervise the studies of both boys in ducal residences in which their father was often absent. Sometimes he took them, at Baron Stockmar's suggestion, for lengthy stays with a *Grossmutter*. With the physician's art of making bad news palatable, the shrewd Coburger never let their father suspect that his sons were being removed, as often as possible, from the contaminated ambience of the ducal court.

The references to a kindly, caring father in the boys' journals reflect their awareness that he had access to them through Florschütz. While complaints about 'the *Rath*' abound in the daily entries – he was expected to ensure discipline – there was not a hostile murmur about the feared, authoritarian Duke. On a good day in April 1826, for example, the boys visited *Grossmutter* Coburg at Ketschendorf, where, with 'dear Papa', they 'drank beer, and ate bread and butter and cheese'. Soon, however, accounts involving their father dealt with tests of manliness more arduous than acquiring a taste for beer.

Some of the early journal entries confess to unremarkable fights with Ernest, or report sequences of lessons or excursions for rock collecting – a favourite teaching device for Florschütz. Albert also reported going to see a play, Friedrich Schiller's *Wallenstein's Camp* – where 'they carried out a monk'. Florschütz was extremely wary at what he recalled in writing, as he remained in the service of the duchy all his active life, yet he remembered escorting the boys to breakfasts with the Duke at so many locations – 'the Hof Gardens, at the Festung, the Kallenberg, at Ketschendorf, or in the Rosenau – and from Gotha in like manner at various places – [that] the greater part of the forenoon was inevitably wasted, to the interruption of useful studies . . . The Duke, however, was indifferent to this, and we can only wonder that the Princes, notwithstanding, retained their love for study.'

Albert's distaste for his father, whom he had good reason to blame for a lonely and insecure childhood, was blunted by time, as were his impressions of his severe upbringing and his feelings toward Florschütz, who became, as Albert grew up, a kind companion and devoted teacher. Dinner (until the boys were much older) was invariably with their tutor in the early afternoon. If the Duke were in residence, or either grandmother, appearances before them were required later in the afternoon, followed by supper with Florschütz at seven, after which Albert 'was glad to retire to bed as soon as possible. An irresistible feeling of sleepiness would come over him in the evening, which he found difficult to resist . . . and even his most cherished occupations, or the liveliest games, were at such times ineffectual to keep him awake.' Despite his often staying out, and awake, beyond ten, and his beginning each day at six, Albert remembered later only the childhood urge to sleep. So did Florschütz, recalling his earliest days with the boys. 'If prevented from going to bed', he wrote about Albert, who was kept on the regimen of his elder brother, 'he would suddenly disappear, and was generally found sleeping quietly in the recess of the window . . . On one occasion – the first time I was present at his supper – the young Prince suddenly fell asleep and tumbled off his chair, but he was not hurt, and continued to sleep quietly on the ground.' Albert was three.

Early in their acquaintance with books, Albert discovered one with pictures that explained to him his name. 'Our boys', the Dowager Duchess had written to her daughter Victoire in London, 'are called after the sons of the Elector Frederick the Gentle, who were stolen by Kunz von Kaufungen: Ernest and Albert.' Each prince had a handful of baptismal names, but she meant the names by which they would actually be known, and most Coburg schoolboys knew the story of the brothers from whom two lines of Saxon sovereigns would come. The Chamberlain of the Elector of Saxony, von Kaufungen, seeking revenge after a lost dispute over property rights, had kidnapped the boys, on the night of 8 July 1455, from Schloss Altenburg. Albert almost evaded abduction by hiding under his bed, and the Chamberlain's henchmen snatched another boy by mistake. Kaufungen, however, recognized the error, went back himself, and found Albert.

Because of the delay, the kidnappers had taken different routes into the forest. It was day, and the sun was hot, when Albert had begged for a drink and the Chamberlain dismounted to find water. When a charcoal-maker unexpectedly appeared with his dog, Albert cried for help. The labourer went after Kaufungen with his staff while the dog barked excitedly, attracting other charcoal-burners, and the culprit was overpowered. The kidnapper holding Ernest hid in a cave on hearing of the capture, but soon surrendered on condition that his life be spared. It was, but Kunz von Kaufungen was executed and his nemesis, the charcoal-maker, was rewarded with a farm – perhaps one confiscated from Kaufungen.

The story suggested something told by the brothers Grimm, to whose stories Ernest and Albert were introduced early in their schooling. Jacob and Wilhelm Grimm, writing their tales in Kassel, had produced the first volume of *Kinder- und Hausmärchen* in 1812, and in ten years added two more, and Ernest and Albert could recognize settings in Grimm much like their own villages of ornately decorated, steeply gabled wooden houses and small farms ploughed by plodding oxen. Happenings resembling Grimm tales could still occur in the little-populated but tradition-laden duchies. Although the Coburg princes did not know their own mother's history, that too could have been written by Jacob and Wilhelm Grimm.

The great event of Albert's early childhood was the formal accession to Coburg of Louise's home duchy late in 1826. After her father's death, in his late forties, Louise's bachelor uncle Frederick, the last male heir, became Duke of Gotha, and, shopping for a wife who might bear a successor, lighted upon Augusta von Studnitz, who refused him. After Frederick's own death, childless, in 1825, Gotha went to Louise's heirs. Her divorce was still pending. The redivision of the Thüringian *Staaten* had required some petty diplomacy, none of it leaving Coburgers content, as Gotha would become, immediately, the major political factor within the reconstituted borders. Despite the relative insignificance of Coburg, Duke Ernest was determined to receive the homage of his new subjects with all due ceremony. The younger Ernest recalled in his memoirs 'the two cold November days on which we journeyed from Coburg to Gotha, my father in front with the Prince of Leiningen,* and my brother, myself, and Florschütz in the second carriage'. To demonstrate permanency of occupation, Ernest's entire household was moving north to take possession of ducal properties, the carriages assembling below the city, at Siebleben, for a grand procession into the capital. 'My father was on horseback [now]; my brother and I drove in an open carriage, drawn by six horses, with Chamberlain [Ferdinand Hartmann von] Erffa and Councillor Florschütz, while a second empty six-horse conveyance followed behind.' Two further carriages held courtiers, and to further give the impression of substance, mounted gendarmes, post office officials, postilions, minor officeholders, militia volunteers and ducal huntsmen followed, with soldiers closing the ranks. Hardly a male of any status had been left in Coburg.

---

* Emich Charles of Leiningen was a cousin, the son by her first husband of Victoire, Duchess of Kent and mother of Victoria.

'My monarchical principles', Gotha-born historian Frederick Perthes, of the *Almanach* family, remarked, 'have gained new followers, for everything suddenly devolves to the new Prince; he is indeed, like King Saul, a head taller than everybody else.' Everyone, he thought, was 'enchanted' with Ernest, and even republican-minded Gothaners 'have acquired a ducally inclined heart overnight'. To make certain of that, the Duke's festivities lasted a week, with Ernest prominent at all of them, uniformed and impressive, the very model of a magistrate.

After the week of homage and the wintry ride back to the Rosenau, the tutorial regimen resumed with little sign of the duke. Florschütz in any case had relative freedom to plan a course of study for the brothers that included French and English – and eventually Latin – as well as German. As the hours of instruction expanded with their years, the princes were introduced to basic mathematics (through a visiting teacher) and rudimentary natural science – especially geology.

And as always, the instructional schedule was subject to summonses to leisurely ducal breakfasts and dinners. Further, the Duke did more than encourage outdoor play. Even his meals taken with his sons were often *im Freien*. The November ride to Gotha in an open carriage had been part of the disciplined toughening of body expected of Saxons as well as Prussians. 'Hunting, fishing, riding, driving', the younger Ernest recalled, 'were allowed us' – perhaps *required* would have been more accurate – 'from our ninth year. On the other hand, he would never tolerate the least complaint of bodily inconvenience, even of pain; we were hardened in every way. I remember that we once rode in the depth of winter over the mountain road from Coburg to Gotha, and suffered fearfully from the intense cold. On such an occasion my father expected us to show the self-command of grown men, and we had to behave in a manly way in every such uncomfortable situation.'

Through precept and chronicle, story and ceremony, Ernest and Albert acquired the essentials for adult behaviour. Their cousin Arthur Mensdorff remembered, more than thirty years later, playing at the Rosenau with other boys, some of them Coburg cousins,

> and some of us were to storm the old ruined tower on the side of the castle, which the others were to defend. One of us suggested that there was a place at the back by which we could get in without being seen, and thus capture it without difficulty. Albert declared that 'this would

be most unbecoming in a Saxon knight, who should always attack his enemy in front', and so we fought for the tower so honestly and vigorously that Albert, by mistake, for I was on his side, gave me a blow upon the nose, of which I still bear the mark. I need not say how sorry he was for the wound given me.

Albert also learned to temper magnanimity with pragmatism. Mensdorff once saw him 'give a beggar something by stealth'. He wondered why, until Albert explained that it was prudent to avoid being overwhelmed by seekers after money. 'When you give to the poor, you must see that nobody knows of it.' Once he was voted a stipend by Parliament, however beneath his expectations, it was clear that he had a guaranteed income, and even his father, extravagant and selfish in his ways, would attempt to cadge money from his son. A few months after his arrival in England, Albert had to write to his brother, 'If you could restrain Papa from constantly asking for money I should be grateful.' Sometimes charity did not begin at home.

Despite Albert's looking back nostalgically at his earliest years in letters to Ernest, Vicky, the Princess Royal, remembered her father saying 'that he could not bear to think of his childhood [as] he had been so unhappy and miserable, and had many a time wished himself out of this world'. Yet always the exception, the Rosenau seemed to Albert a place apart – remote from the selfish, sordid reality. On a knoll above small villages, woods of poplar and pine, and the winding Itze, and out of sight of Coburg, it was school and dormitory and refuge from court and city. There Florschütz lived with his charges, shared meals with them, and kept vigil at night as well. He had no other life than that of the princes.

Their study schedule, which on paper appeared relentless, was often dislocated by the Duke's whim, and broken for play, which Florschütz called exercise. For the less studious Ernest, the regimen had a purpose – to prepare him as heir. For Albert, purpose unfolded less easily. He was a younger son without guaranteed occupation. In the back of the Duke's mind may have been a future for Albert as husband for Victoire, his first cousin and daughter of Ferdinand, Ernest's younger brother by a year, and his wife, Antoinette, heiress of Prince Joseph of Kohary, Chancellor of Hungary, who possessed vast Hungarian estates. For Albert, purpose manifested itself more slowly. The year of change was 1831, in the

*Prince Albert and Prince Ernest in Coburg, 1831. Drawing by Sebastian Eckhardt. (From the Veste, Coburg)*

crowded months before his twelfth birthday. Prince Leopold, the youngest of his uncles and the one he knew best, had been searching for a role in life since his opportunity to be consort to a queen had vanished with the death of Princess Charlotte of Wales. As one of the candidates proposed by the great European powers, he had been in the running to become king of tumultuous and leaderless Greece, independent from Turkey only since the mid-1820s. Then an alternative opportunity emerged, to be first king of the Belgians, who possessed a precarious small state wrested from the lower provinces of the Netherlands, which had misruled them. First considering Greece, but realizing that the situation might turn out badly for him, Leopold had made his terms unacceptable. Belgium was more civilized, less remote, possessed of a workable constitution and at least a promise of secure borders.

British governments disliked the ambitious, avaricious Leopold, but heading off the French candidate for Belgium, the duc de Nemours, appeared as useful an aim as getting Leopold out of England for good. As soon as Leopold was settled in Brussels, he invited his ducal brother and nephews to visit. Albert had written in his journal at eleven, 'I intend to train myself to be a good and useful man.' Brussels would afford him both reason and purpose for what was still a vague, if worthy, goal. That Leopold could become a king suggested that there could again be a gilded future for younger Coburg sons.

# III

# *The Student Prince*

## *1832–1838*

COBURG BOASTED THE *Gymnasium Casimirianum*, an academy which furnished a curricular model for Ernest and Albert, but Florschütz dispensed with its studies in Greek, substituting mathematics and the natural sciences. Latin was taught almost as a second language, but only German was spoken in their father's presence. French and English came later. Florschütz also honed their debating skills. Unenthusiastic but dutiful about 'the business of shooting', which required 'going out for the whole day', Albert preferred riding his English pony into the woods among the larch and pine trees, and searching for geological specimens to add to their cabinet at the Rosenau. Proud of their outdoors hardiness, on 30 January 1831 he wrote to his father, who claimed to be spending long periods in grander Gotha although he may have been wenching elsewhere, 'It snowed without stopping for three or four days, and the snow is very deep. The drifts are six feet high at the Festung, as we found out ourselves yesterday. We walked to Ketschendorf, and thence through the snow, by an unbeaten track through von Schauroth's garden, [back] to the Festung, and sank several times up to our middle...'

Since they were granted student privileges at the Academy, Albert added that he was offering a poem to the Academy poetry competition '[so] that I may get the prize this afternoon'. He radiated confidence in his abilities. Later in the year – in July – he wrote to his still-absent father that both boys had driven to the Gymnasium for its summer fête 'and heard a beautiful speech from Professor Troupheller. I am sure it would have pleased you.' The brothers strained to please the Duke. Albert would have been horrified, later, by the thought that his attitudes were already being formed by quiet rebellion against everything his father was, for his responses on the surface seemed lovingly dutiful. He was a month short of twelve. Although he would not learn of it then, that was the month his mother died.

Since July was the natal month of their *Grossmutter* Coburg, the boys rode to Ketschendorf to offer the Dowager Duchess Augusta 'two little poems that we made for her'. It was the last time they would see her. She died that November, but had lived long enough to visit her son Leopold, King of the Belgians, in Brussels.

In the summer of 1832 the young princes, accompanying their father and overseen by Florschütz, had the opportunity to visit their uncle and bask in the pride of his new status. Brussels, with a population of a hundred thousand, was the seat of government and focus of intellectual life in the new kingdom. It was the grandest city the princes had yet encountered, sophisticated beyond anything in the duchies. At Baron Stockmar's suggestion – he kept a house and family in Coburg but spent most of his time as confidential secretary to Leopold in Belgium – the boys were offered a return visit, to widen their world and (a private understanding between the King and the Baron) to separate them from the contamination of their father's life, about which they knew nothing.

The Duke remarried late in 1832. The event came as a surprise to Albert. In a letter to him – his father was again, ostensibly, in Gotha – on 21 September 1832, the Prince made no allusion to the imminence of a stepmother, who would have been offered, if the betrothal were known, a dutiful closing greeting. The new duchess was Duke Ernest's own niece, the Princess Mary of Württemberg, daughter of Ernest's sister Antoinette. At thirty-three she was fifteen years younger than the Duke. The boys travelled with their father to the Castle of Thalwitz in Saxony to await the arrival of their new stepmother and to accompany her to the duchies, but they saw little more of her. The marriage proved quickly to be less than a success, and the Duchess lived largely apart from their father, who was himself seldom at the Rosenau, where the boys remained. From the letters of Albert to Duchess Mary, one would not guess the emotional and physical distance, as, diplomatically, the prince always addressed his letters to 'Dear Mama', and closed them as effusively as they began.

When the boys were confirmed together on Palm Sunday 1835 in Coburg, the Duchess wrote that the weather remained too inclement for her to attend. She was not close to their affairs any more than she was, but for the title, part of the Duke's life. Still, it was a major occasion for the princes, who were nearly seventeen and sixteen. They had determined to make their ceremonial profession of faith together although Albert was the younger – and the fact of jointly lived lives would even be legislated later when the Hereditary Prince came of age at eighteen. Later it became diplomatic for Florschütz to stress, in his memoir for Victoria, the 'singularly earnest and thoughtful' preparation Albert made for his confirmation, and Charles Grey, in his early life of Albert written for the Queen, emphasized Albert's 'conviction of the great truths of Christianity'. For English publication, such professions were essential.

A worldly Coburg clergyman, Karl Gottlieb Bretschneider, fifty-six, was, to the younger Ernest, 'like a friend of the family. His extraordinary learning and ... his important scientific services, as well as his easy, companionable ways, shielded both him and us from the reproach of taking too light a view of religious things and the historical puzzles of dogmatics; but our Christianity lay in Bretschneider's hand ...' Although he enabled the brothers 'to look forward cheerfully to our confirmation, being neither too alarmed by the indiscoverable ... nor too much hemmed in by the ideas of a bigoted church', the rote preparation was overseen by a very different breed of theologian, a Revd Jakoby, Court preacher at Coburg and former director of the Gymnasium at Rinteln, who had an 'encyclopaedic' knowledge of church history.

For the public in the duchies on 11 April 1835, assembled in the Giants' Hall in the castle in Coburg, the ceremony that Saturday, with each prince responding to theological questions with a scrupulous correctness coached by a local cleric, was a satisfying event, reinforcing the pieties. 'St Paul's doctrine was kept here', Albert's brother wrote, looking back on their confirmation, 'as in an impregnable fortress. People took an interest in the often unspeakably prosaic and sometimes absurd explanations of the biblical wonders.'

Ernest recalled his pleasure that 'no formula' or 'strict confession of faith' was forced on them: they responded to their examiner, instead, 'with a surprising amount of familiarity with church questions'. As for the 'natural piety' ascribed later to Albert, his brother noted wryly, 'it was probably on account of the English public, for this description suited him certainly even less than it me'. The rite required closing with the question as to whether the confirmants intended to remain true to the Evangelical Church, which meant the Augsburg Confession of 1530, endorsed by Martin Luther. 'I and my brother', Ernest declared for both, 'are determined to remain faithful to the acknowledged truth.'

On Palm Sunday the princes celebrated their success in the Cathedral of Ehrenburg, where, in 1818, with the benedictions of the same Pastor Genzler, the Duke of Kent had married Ernest's and Albert's aunt Victoire. The next day at a banquet in the Giants' Hall, *Rath* Florschütz was presented with a diamond ring to acknowledge service to the princes that was not yet over, although Ernest was nearly seventeen and Albert approaching sixteen.

Since his presence would have been inappropriate as king of a largely Catholic state, their uncle Leopold wrote from Brussels to congratulate them, adding that he had 'a fatherly affection' for the brothers and felt that their 'home education' had gone far enough – that it was time 'to prepare for the affairs of life'. The invitation to continue their studies in Belgium would be repeated – and accepted. First, however, came a Saxon version of the traditional Grand Tour offered well-born young men on the brink of adulthood. Duke Ernest was to initiate a tour of central Europe.

Their first journey was to Mecklenburg, to visit the venerable Grand Duke of Mecklenburg-Schwerin, grandfather of their late mother, on the fiftieth anniversary of his accession as *Grossherzog*. Then they went on to Berlin, where, once they were again presented, Duke Ernest left them to Florschütz for the remainder of the itinerary – Dresden, Prague (where their uncle, Count Mensdorff, now commanded the Austrian garrison), Vienna and Budapest. From Berlin, Albert wrote to his stepmother, with the tour hardly begun, 'It takes a giant's strength to bear all the fatigue we have had to undergo. Visits, parades, *déjeuners*, dinners, suppers, balls and concerts follow each other in rapid succession, and we have not been allowed to miss any of the festivities.' Travel was difficult enough by horse-and-carriage on rutted, often muddy if not dusty, post roads on which moving five miles in an hour was expeditious. It was exhausting then to march through a formal schedule in appropriate garb. Yet following the circuit came another required visit, to *Grossmutter*

Gotha for her birthday, after which Florschütz, unwilling to have their studies further interrupted, returned them to the Rosenau.

As a transition to external education they were soon transplanted to Gotha, but from a distance their studies were now overseen as well by Dr Seebode, the director of the Gymnasium at Coburg, to whom they sent completed papers for review. Albert worked on a naïvely ambitious essay on German philosophy concluding, he explained, with 'a retrospect of the shortcomings of our time, with an appeal to everyone to correct those shortcomings in his own case and thus to set a good example to others'. By March 1836 he was also working on a history of German literature which 'gets on but slowly, owing to our Gotha engagements'. (Seebode would later respond to Albert that he had omitted Friedrich Gottlieb Klopstock, an epic and lyric poet who had influenced Goethe and the *Sturm und Drang* movement as well as song cycles by Gluck, Beethoven and Schubert. Albert in turn would write from Brussels – where Leopold's educational programme for him was about to begin – 'It is painful to see the mean idea which the French and Belgians, and even the English, have of our German literature.')

The world began to open to Albert in May 1836. Earlier in the year, King Leopold sent Stockmar to furnish a confidential assessment of Albert. Ernest's place was assured. He would, when of age, be commissioned into the army of Saxony or Prussia to mature and to wait out his inheritance of the duchies. Albert's prospects as he passed sixteen were less clear, yet whatever they were depended upon his suitability as future mate for some desirable aristocratic or noble heiress. Earlier, his father and Leopold had contemplated a Kohary cousin. Although her Roman Catholicism was a technical obstacle to a professed Lutheran, Victoire Kohary was heiress to a Hungarian fortune and, even as early as 1831, when the Kohary children resided temporarily at the Rosenau in refuge from a cholera outbreak at home, she was on her way to becoming a beauty.

By 1836 other alternatives had appeared. It seemed then certain that another Victoire in the Coburg cousinhood – Princess Victoria of England – would, if she lived into her own inheritance as child of the eldest, though deceased, royal duke, become Queen. Her aunt Adelaide, William IV's queen, had suffered a succession of miscarriages and deaths in infancy. The King was seventy-one and seriously ailing. Adelaide and William loved Victoria almost as a daughter, but Victoria's ambitious mother (she was, after all, a Coburger) and her even more ambitious aide, Sir John Conroy, whom no one but the Duchess trusted, were anathema to the King, who hoped to remain alive until Victoria was of age if only to forestall a regency under the Duchess.

To Victoria, fatherless before her first birthday, Leopold was the '*dearest* of uncles', a paternal figure she relied upon, if only as occasional visitor and regular correspondent. Might Albert be up to the role of consort to a future queen? Leopold asked Stockmar to report to him. If the potential existed, their mutual uncle would attempt to educate Albert into the role and commit Victoria to the arrangement. Let in on the secret, Florschütz was enthusiastic, but conceded his charge's diffidence and unsophistication. Leopold's agent arrived to check for himself. At sixteen the young prince, Stockmar reported, was handsome and 'tolerably developed' for his age. With maturity, he would acquire a 'distinguished bearing', and was likely to be attractive to women. 'It may also be considered a fortunate circumstance that he has already a certain English look about him.'

Albert, Stockmar advised, had little understanding of contemporary European affairs but was otherwise well educated for his years. The Florschütz regimen excluded post-Napoleonic history, and the relapse into eighteenth-century authoritarianism that ignored the cautionary lessons of the French Revolution and its aftermath. Classical Greece and Rome were studied, as well as a sentimentalized national history that glossed over German fragmentation. Beyond the limitations of tutoring, Stockmar saw Albert as painfully prudent – in need of a seminar in striving from his uncle Leopold, who had vaulted from Coburg to serve a Tsar, wed (however tragically) a likely queen, and become a king. Wits and wariness were 'not enough. He must not only have great capacity but true ambition, and a great strength of will. To pursue so difficult a political career a whole life through requires more than energy and inclination.' It required, he thought, a readiness 'to sacrifice mere pleasure to real usefulness. If simply to fill one of the most influential positions in Europe doesn't satisfy him, how often will he feel tempted to regret what he has undertaken?' Further, Stockmar saw nothing in the late Duchess Louise's flightiness or in Duke Ernest's amorality to suggest that Albert might have inherited any strength of character. But nor had Albert acquired anything negative from 'such a father and such a brother, both equally unprincipled'.

What Stockmar had already perceived in the younger Ernest to worry him was left unsaid, but Leopold apparently understood. There was mettle in Albert to be cultivated – and protected. Besides, young Victoria might be coerced into an early marriage by courtiers not susceptible to Leopold's influence. His sister, the Duchess of Kent, might seek someone she and Conroy could control, while English politicians might want a much older husband who could control the future queen for them.

Leopold also worried that further immersion in Coburg and Gotha would tarnish the Prince as well as impair his chances. Stockmar agreed that 'an endless amount of good can be done, and an equal amount of evil be prevented. The Prince ought to receive the education which the consort of an English Queen requires.' He could not be sent to England, and the 'petty circumstances' of the duchies were 'impossible'. Limiting the alternatives to the universities at Berlin, Vienna and the smaller German states, the Baron ruled out Vienna as 'not at all a suitable school for a German prince'. The only subjects about which Albert would 'gain anything' in the Prussian capital were 'political administration and military organization'. In Berlin, the Prince would 'hear everything about politics but the truth', and 'a certain dissoluteness is as epidemic in Berlin as the influenza'. Stockmar would look into a more advantageous arrangement while both brothers, he suggested, should pursue preparatory studies under Leopold's 'superintendence' in a 'constitutional country' – Belgium.

On 16 April 1836, Stockmar suggested that the immediate essential was a letter from the Duchess of Kent, as Duke Ernest's sister, suggesting that he and his sons visit Kensington Palace as her guests. 'If the first favourable impression is now made, the foundation stone is laid for the future edifice. But it must be a *conditio sine qua non* that the real intention of the visit should be kept secret from the Princess as well as the Prince, that they may be perfectly at their ease with each other.'

Leopold quickly arranged for the invitation – and a further one made on his own. After the stay in England, both princes would remain in Brussels under tutelage that would lead to matriculation at a German university. To preserve the necessary ambiguities of purpose, the strategies had to involve, at every stage, Ernest as well as Albert.

Duke Ernest began the journey to England separately from his sons, possibly to revisit his former Rhenish principality – actually on the

Nahe – of Lichtenberg, just incorporated into the Prussian district of Trier. Once in the Napoleonic department of the Sarre, it had been awarded by the Congress of Vienna to Ernest for services rendered in the war, and included St Wendel, where the body of Duchess Louise lay. Named for an old Palatine castle, the territory, distant from Coburg, was useless to the Duke, who had tried for years to trade it for detached Prussian properties in Saxony. Germany was a patchwork of *Kleinstaaterei*. In 1833 he thought he had succeeded, and reported as much to Prince Clemens Metternich in Vienna, as Austria dominated the confederation, but the wily foreign minister retorted that governments had difficulty in keeping order in 'far removed territories, especially when they lie in a bad tract of land as on the left bank of the Rhine'.

What Metternich reported to Berlin is unknown, but Ernest, assuming the exchange as settled, 'made the mistake', his elder son recalled, 'of inspecting the domains in ... Saxony which he thought would be his, and thus arousing [local] attention'. The arrangement lapsed, and the next year Ernest transferred his burdensome sovereignty to Prussia for a landless annuity of 80,000 thalers. Every hectare added in the Rhineland shifted the fulcrum of Prussian power in Germany further toward France, exacerbating the problems created by the Congress of Vienna in expanding Prussia substantially westward. Ernest's acres were few, but they would contribute to Prussia's future hegemony, and to concerns inherited by his sons.

Jolting overland day and night, Albert claimed to his stepmother from Rotterdam on 17 May 1836 that he and Ernest – without Florschütz – had made the carriage journey from the duchies to Mainz, on the Rhine, in twenty-two hours. At Koblenz they boarded a Rhine steamer. Having conducted business or assignations, or both, the Duke met the boat at Rüdesheim. At Cologne they changed for another steamer to Rotterdam, where they waited impatiently for a North Sea packet. 'We have to thank some Dutch speculators', Albert fumed, 'whose object it is to detain travellers as long as they can.'

On board the Rhine steamer he practised his English on several returning Londoners, to whom they remained 'incognito, which succeeded perfectly, till the chamberlain of the Princess of Orange, saluting us with a malicious smile, unmasked us'. Only then did it occur to Albert that he had been entered, rather prematurely, in a matrimonial competition for which the stakes were high. It was already news in the Netherlands that the Prince of Orange and his two eligible sons* and the young Duke William of Brunswick had been invited by an ill-tempered William IV at the same time. The King intended to foil the Coburgers, a family he detested and had not summoned. Before Ernest and Albert had even embarked for England, to the Prince's embarrassment everyone knew why they were coming, although ostensibly it was to visit 'Aunt Kent'. As far as her brother Leopold was concerned, only one of them – and he hadn't told that one as much – was fit for the office of royal consort, and he had every intention of bringing off the betrothal. Victoria knew very well why, as she approached seventeen, young men of high birth were being pressed upon her. Understanding King Leopold's wary game, Victoria responded with cautious indirection until he sent her a warning in a letter of 13 May delivered via confidential messenger. Was she aware, he asked, that she was being imposed upon by the King?

> Really and truly I never heard or saw anything like it, and I hope it will a *little rouse your spirit*; now that slavery is even abolished in the British Colonies, I do not comprehend *why your lot alone should be to be kept, a white little slavey in England,* for the pleasure of the Court, who never bought you, as I am not aware of their having gone to any expense on that head, or the King's even having *spent a sixpence for your existence.* I expect that my visits in England will also be prohibited by an Order in Council...
>
> I have not the least doubt that the King, in his passion for the Oranges, will be *excessively rude to your relations*; this, however, will not signify much; they are *your guests* and not *his*, and will therefore *not* mind it.

Victoria knew of the schemes to attach her to someone, and had already entertained her own ideas, soon discovering that they were not permitted. Knowing that the Duchess of Kent read her daughter's diaries every evening, Victoria does not mention John Elphinstone, the thirteenth Lord Elphinstone in the Scottish peerage (1807–1860), since 1826 in the Royal Horse Guards. He rose to captain by 1832 and then

---

* The elder, two-and-a-half years older than Albert, would become King of the Netherlands in 1849, reigning until 1890.

became Lord-in-Waiting to King William, affording Victoria the opportunity to make his acquaintance. The Princess, so Court gossip had it (and it was repeated by Robert Browning), was 'bent on marrying nobody but Lord Elphinstone'. Suddenly, just before the parade of potential suitors began arriving in England, Lord Elphinstone was posted, at twenty-nine, to India, to become governor of Madras, a remarkable appointment for a young man.

If his removal was to distance him from contention, his exile to India hardly improved Victoria's estimate of her supplicants. Early among them were the two sons of Duke Ferdinand of Saxe-Coburg-Kohary. The ineligible one, also a Ferdinand, and twenty, was on his way to Lisbon to marry Queen Maria da Gloria, sixteen, whom he had never met. The other, Prince Augustus, only eighteen, Victoria noted in her diary on 17 March, 'is a dear good young man, and is very handsome', but 'extremely quiet and silent'. What remained unspoken was the Kohary religious disability. Uncle Ferdinand had married wealth and property, but a Roman Catholic ceremony had made his opportunities possible. The throne of Portugal also required a Roman marriage. Augustus, his father assumed, would accept whatever benedictions were required for proximity to a throne. The Coburg clan's religion seemed to be simple pragmatism.

The next day Victoria described – and dismissed – Augustus as 'a dear boy . . . so extremely good, kind and gentle'. When the brothers left, she was sorry only to see the balls and other entertainments arranged for her cease. She was starved of companionship from her own generation, but her professions of affection for the Kohary brothers suggested little more. Uncle Leopold in any case had another brace of Coburg nephews ready.

King William's instructions to Palmerston were to 'turn back' Ernest and Albert, and the Foreign Secretary did send Leopold a message that it would be 'highly desirable' that the princes put off their visit for another year. But the Coburgers were not travelling through Belgium, and Leopold would not see them until the return leg of their journey. Given the subtleties of Palmerston's machinations, it is at least possible that the delay in Rotterdam may have been occasioned by some discreet bribes which made a clear field possible for the Dutch aspirants.

On 13 May 1836, William gave a ball in honour of the Princes of Orange, William and Alexander. Since her cousin Prince George of Cambridge, Victoria's own age and heir to Augustus Frederick,

George III's seventh son, was also present, three aspirants for espousal were on view. ('She must marry somebody', Palmerston would urge the King. 'Why not the Prince of Cambridge? He has been educated here and we know him.') Leopold was relieved when Victoria wrote on 17 May, 'The [Netherlander] boys are very plain and have a mixture of Kalmuck' – Mongol – 'and Dutch in their faces, moreover they look heavy, dull and frightened and are not at all prepossessing. So much for the *Oranges*, dear Uncle.'

The confident dismissal of the Dutch princes belied her concern that a husband might be imposed upon her. The unspoken pressure she sensed, Victoria recalled nine years later, was so intense that she felt 'extremely crushed and kept under, and hardly dared say a word'.

For two frightening days in turbulent waters, the Dutch paddle-wheeler ploughed across from Rotterdam. His stomach churning with the swells, Albert declared 'a disgust of the sea'. Unsteady on English soil, the Coburgers arrived on the eighteenth to a surfeit of levées, balls and other after-dark entertainments originally arranged for the disappointed Netherlanders, who had left earlier than planned, and into whose schedule Ernest and Albert were introduced. (Once her cousins arrived, the Dutch aspirants were of increasingly diminished interest to Victoria.) Albert struggled at first to stay awake, then to keep down the heavy English meals always served too late.

Recording their first meeting, at a quarter to two in the afternoon, Victoria wrote, 'Ernest is as tall as Ferdinand and Augustus; he has dark hair, and fine dark eyes and eyebrows, but the nose and mouth are not good; he has a most kind, honest and intelligent expression in his countenance, and has a very good figure.' Clearly she was assessing the genetic as well as the companionable qualities in her possible suitors. 'Albert, who is just as tall as Ernest but stouter,' she noted, 'is extremely handsome; his hair is about the same colour as mine; his eyes are large and blue, and he has a beautiful nose and a very sweet mouth with fine teeth; but the charm of his countenance is his expression, which is most delightful.' He also seemed 'full of goodness and sweetness, and very clever and intelligent'.

Further, the brothers spoke English competently, and she could converse as easily with them as she could with her sophisticated uncle Ernest. To her delight, he brought as a gift 'a most delightful Lory' – a brightly plumaged parrot – 'which is so tame that it remains on your hand, and you may put your finger into its beak, or do anything with it, without its ever attempting to bite'. Had the duke brought a symbol of what her future husband should be like?

A formal dinner at St James's Palace, following a royal levée and preceding a concert that ran until two in the morning, left Albert barely able to remain on his feet. Before long, he was running what he described in a letter to his stepmother as a 'bilious fever'. Summing up his dilemmas he explained unhappily, 'The climate of this country, the different way of living, and the late hours, do not agree with me.'

The afternoon following, he and Ernest had to be upright for a drawing-room reception with a receiving line of nearly four thousand guests, which itself was only a prelude to another long night. On 23 May, at a grand dinner at Kensington Palace hosted by the Duchess of Kent, Albert, having reached the end of his endurance, excused himself and went to bed. The next day, Victoria's seventeenth birthday, was occasion for a state ball hosted by the King at St James's Palace. Albert could not miss it without damaging his prospects, for he understood that he was only one of many to be set before the future queen. 'Poor, dear Albert', Victoria sympathized in her diary '... looked very pale and felt very poorly.' After two quadrilles he 'turned pale as ashes; and we all feared he might faint; he therefore went home' [to Kensington Palace].

Again Albert recovered. 'We took them to the Opera on Friday,' Victoria wrote to Leopold, 'to see the *Puritani* [by Vincenzo Bellini], and as they are excessively fond of music, like me, they were in perfect ecstasies...' Both brothers also played the piano, composed, and drew 'very well' ('especially Albert'). Exhaustion then left Albert with what Victoria described in her journal as 'a smart bilious attack', but after a day in bed, and 'by dint of starvation, he is again restored to society, but looks pale and delicate'.

A few days of lessened activity brought the Prince around. He played piano duets with Victoria and managed to stay up 'until 10 minutes past 10'. He told Victoria about his plans to be prepared at Brussels, under their uncle's guidance, for university studies, and to travel with Ernest to Italy to see more of the world. He had no idea that Victoria already knew – from Leopold – more than he did of his future.

Despite King William's objections, she had been well prepared, Leopold having written on 1 May to her one-time nurse and tutor, and now confidante, Louise Lehzen, 'I talk to you at length and through you speak to Victoria.' Though the Princess and her cousin had never before met, Leopold was now certain that the small and rather plain future queen would see her best possible destiny in Albert. However, any 'immediate alliance' was impossible as Victoria was not yet in control of her future. At her eighteenth birthday, he explained, 'the possibility of a Regency vanishes like an evil cloud'. And no potential consort of 'riper years' existed 'to whom we could entrust the dear child without incurring the gravest risk'.

On the last day of May, Albert felt up to an evening of dancing at Kensington Palace, but quickly pleaded illness. Victoria left with him until he was able to return, and she recalled, half a year later, in a letter to Leopold, 'The last ball *I* was at was our own, and I concluded that very ball at half-past three in the morning with a country dance, Albert being my partner.' At the time she noted that it was 'broad daylight when we left the room', and, as she confided to her uncle early the next year, 'I *often* think of that night'.

When only a few more days remained before the princes were to leave, Victoria called their father in for a private meeting at which she gave him a letter to Leopold, whom they would visit *en route* home.

By the time of the princes' departure, even King William had warmed to Albert, yet the King was in such failing health that he was given only a small chance of surviving until Victoria's eighteenth birthday. Conroy and the Duchess still loomed – Leopold's 'evil cloud'. Victoria hoped for the best in a letter to Leopold which she framed carefully to evade any direct commitment:

> I must thank you, my beloved Uncle, for the prospect of *great* happiness you have contributed to give me, in the person of dear Albert. Allow me, then, my dearest Uncle, to tell you how delighted I am with him, and how much I like him in every way. He possesses every quality that could be desired to render me perfectly happy. He is so sensible, so kind, and so good, and so amiable too. He has, besides, the most pleasing and delightful exterior and appearance you can possibly see.
>
> I have only now to beg you, my dearest Uncle, to take care of the health of one, now *so dear* to me, and to take him under *your special*

protection. I hope and trust that all will go on prosperously and well, on this subject of so much importance to me.

On 10 June, Victoria breakfasted with the princes for the last time before they departed by carriage to Dover. She could not restrain her tears. 'I feel this separation ... deeply', she told her diary, but, after the pressure of earlier princely attentions – they had begun when she was barely fourteen – the tension had eased. Her nerves had not been as 'strong' as they now were. 'I can bear more now.'

Duke Ernest could not put off his need for less genteel entertainment, delaying the family visit to Brussels and Leopold until he could sample the pleasures of Paris. Prince Ernest was already under his tutelage, and as early as the post-confirmation Grand Tour, to Albert's horror and shame, had sampled the underside of Berlin with his father. Kept awake at the Hôtel des Princes in the rue Richelieu by the noise that seemed never to leave Parisian streets, and worn by illness and exhaustion after his introduction to English court life, Albert indulged, when he could, in sleep.

A month later, dandy and failed merchant Thomas Raikes, distant from his creditors in Paris, was told by the Dutch Minister to France, General Fagel, that the chances of the princes of Orange were nil – 'fine young men, but stiff and formal'. The Coburg brothers, Fagel and Raikes recognized, had the advantages of an aunt at Kensington Palace, yet that might not produce results at Buckingham Palace. 'The son of the Duke of Cambridge would be the most popular match ... in the eyes of the English people.'

The life of the court of Louis-Philippe meant nothing to Albert, although his father and brother were delighted by invitations to meet the King and the younger generation of the House of Orléans. The Queen of the Belgians, Marie-Louise, was a daughter of the French sovereign, and the Coburgers found that their uncle Leopold was also a guest at the Tuileries. Later, in Belgium, Ernest learned that he had been looked over in Paris as a possible husband for Louis-Philippe's daughter Clementina, a union that would have required his conversion to Rome. Seven years later the Princess would marry his Kohary cousin Augustus. To his stepmother, Albert reported that they had been received by the royal family 'with the greatest kindness and civility', but he was more interested in the places in which history had been made – Versailles, the Trianon, Meudon, Neuilly. He was also in a quiet panic arising from his naïvety when in England. He had little idea then how seriously he was being considered as Victoria's consort, although he was not yet seventeen. In Paris, his father explained that the Duchess of Kent accepted the family strategy that 'some time in the future' the sixteen-year-old Albert would marry the future queen. Victoria had been privately warned that her uncle William was trying to treat her like a white slave; Albert now realized that his Coburg aunts and uncles were not seeking his permission to offer *him* into a possibly splendid foreign slavery.

Brussels emerged as an oasis for Albert. His father left almost immediately, although Leopold had not yet returned to his capital from Paris. The King, however, had arranged everything. 'Nothing disturbed us', Ernest recalled; 'everything seemed formed to help us to gain the end in view' – which was preparation for an appropriate German university. They occupied a house with garden that was, Albert wrote to his stepmother with relief, 'perfectly insulated from the noise of the streets' although just off the bustling Boulevard de l'Observation. There they were overseen by the ubiquitous Florschütz and, for logistical matters, Baron von Wiechmann, a colonel who had served under Wellington at Waterloo in the German English Legion.

No tutor, however eminent, was likely to turn down a royal request to furnish expertise. Among the visitors to offer instruction was the director of the Royal Observatory, the mathematician and astronomer Laubert Adolphe Jacques Quételet, who became a godlike figure to Albert. Quételet was a founder of the science of statistics – what Albert would call 'governing laws...which can only be approached by the accumulation and reduction of statistical facts'. The Prince's orderly mind responded gratefully to what Quételet offered, and as Ernest would put it, the Belgian's influence upon Albert 'was one which formed his whole manner of viewing the world. During his entire lifetime he preserved the statistically mechanical grasp of social and political questions.' Quételet himself later quipped that Albert never thought enough of his own talents, while the King of the Belgians never forgot his.

As tutors in economics and politics, Leopold assigned Charles and Henri de Broukere, Members of Parliament and men of ability. Charles de Broukere had already been Minister of the Interior and Minister for

War, and was a future prime minister. For instruction in French and English literature, Leopold chose Dr Pierre Bergeron, Professor of Rhetoric at the University of Brussels, and Dr Henry Drury, a minor poet once a friend of Lord Byron. Sir Henry Lytton Bulwer, Secretary of the English legation, then at the beginning of a distinguished diplomatic career, was brought in for history and foreign affairs. Leading Belgian painters invited the princes to their studios for instruction, and Leopold's Cabinet Secretary visited to explain governmental administration.

Since the Dutch had refused to sign the Treaty of London under which the Belgian provinces were detached as a separate nation, both countries remained on a war footing. With Leopold's army actively mobilized, in early August the King took Ernest and Albert to the plain of Beverlo where his troops were encamped overlooking the southern finger of Holland at Maastricht, and both young men were assigned as staff officers to generals for manœuvres. The experience would lead, later, to Albert's proposal for a permanent English site for military exercises. The outcome would be Aldershot.

In mid-October, as another break from studies, Colonel von Wiech-mann took the young men to Waterloo, where, Albert wrote to his father, they 'went on foot all over the field of battle'. Other explorations opened more of the real world. Politicians and thinkers of every persuasion, even exiled revolutionaries from other countries, were permitted entry at the cul-de-sac off the Boulevard de l'Observation. In turn Ernest and Albert even visited the house in the Brussels suburbs where Italian fugitives involved in the secret society of the *Carbonari* awaited their call to action. In Coburg the Duke worried about what sympathies his sons would ingest in the heady atmosphere of Brussels, and invited – commanded – them home for an extended Christmas stay. Unhappily, Albert brought the letter to his uncle, who recommended a 'reasoned and calm' explanation why returning would be unwise.

'We should be so glad to accept your invitation', Albert responded on November 29, 1836, ' . . . But if we are to profit from our stay here, I am afraid we must deny ourselves that pleasure. Such an expedition would require five or six weeks, and our course of study would be quite disturbed by such an interruption. We told dear uncle the purport of your letter, and he said he would write to you on the subject.'

The King duly wrote, and the brothers remained until matriculation time neared at a university chosen for them. Consulting Stockmar further, Leopold had ruled out Munich ('formal and priggish'), Göttingen, Jena (although founded by the early Ernestines), and Heidelberg, settling upon the newer University of Bonn, already recognized for the quality of its professoriate. To alleviate Duke Ernest's anxieties that university life would reduce his sons to the level of ordinary Germans, they were to be enrolled as noblemen rather than as normal students. Leopold even offered to pay half the fees.

Although, as the younger Ernest explained, 'the Head of no reigning house would be too willing to see his sons allowed to follow a public course of study at a university', German princelings were beginning to sample higher learning, and the Duke pronounced himself satisfied. From London, Victoria wrote to her uncle Leopold that she missed 'both young gentlemen'.

In April 1837 Ernest and Albert left Brussels for Berlin, where they were to meet their father, then return with him to the duchies before leaving for Bonn, on the Rhine fifty miles south of Cologne. With the new term to begin on 3 May, thoughts of Victoria were put aside.

The number of princelings, overt and covert, out to win Victoria during what would prove to be the last year of William IV's reign would have been far higher had the King and the Duchess of Kent not discouraged some of them and forbidden others. Warding them off required every means from diplomacy to lies. On the very day that Albert was beginning studies at Bonn, the English Minister in Berlin, Lord William Russell, appealed to the Duchess of Kent, 'Would it be agreeable to your Royal Highness that Prince Adalbert of Prussia, the son of Prince William, should place himself on the list of those who pretend to the hand of HRH the Princess Victoria?'

Five days later, on 8 May 1837, the Duchess parried the plea by recommending that Prince Adalbert, who was twenty-six, apply to William IV: 'But if I know my duty to the King, I also know my maternal ones, and I will candidly tell your Lordship that I am of opinion that the Princess should not marry till she is much older.' When Russell explained the Duchess's objections, the King of Prussia withdrew his request for a visit, and Russell apologized to Kensington Palace, commenting it was 'only proposed to admit Prince Adalbert to the list of suitors for the hand of Princess Victoria, to which he was to

*The Electoral Palace (*Residenz*) was given to the University of Bonn for its new site. Albert knew it in this form.*

win his claim by his character and personal attractions'. The Prussian prince hoped only for a place on a rumoured but non-existent roll, yet Victoria's mother admitted neither Adalbert nor the list. Nor, in future years, would the suits of the duc de Nemours, Louis-Philippe's second son, or Prince Christian of Schleswig-Holstein, the future Christian IX of Denmark, or other serene or royal highnesses, be entertained.

Bonn had boasted a university as early as 1786. It had been suppressed by Napoleon, remaining, however, the seat of many learned societies. In 1818, awarded the buildings which had belonged to the Electors of Cologne, the university reorganized, and under the rectorship of Wilhelm Wutzer was, for Germany, a liberal institution with eighty professors and seven hundred students.* At the head of the *Sommerhalbjahr* matriculation register, in rigid aristocratic tradition, was Friedrich Wilhelm, the young Grand Duke of Mecklenburg-Strelitz, followed by August Ernst, Hereditary Prince of Saxe-Coburg-Gotha, and Albrecht Franz, identified as a duke of Saxe-Coburg-Gotha, all listed as studying jurisprudence. Lesser students pursued medicine, agriculture, theology (Catholic or Evan-

---

*At the same time Göttingen also averaged seven hundred students, while Heidelberg had five hundred.

gelical), philosophy, classics, natural science. Almost all were from the German states, but one, Gustav Ferreira Bandeira, listed his home as 'Bahia in Brasilien'.

In Bonn, Florschütz remained in attendance, assisted by the brothers' valet, Cart, while Baron von Wiechmann continued in charge of non-academic matters. (A French-speaking Swiss also fluent in German, Isaac François Daniel Cart had been with the boys since Ernest was eight and Albert seven.) The entourage required for Ernest and Albert ruled out common undergraduate digs. Other minor nobility resided apart as a matter of course, and in the case of the Coburgers there was the matter – left unspoken but hardly unknown – of what was fitting for the rumoured consort of the Queen of England. Despite their rented, semi-detached house, with servants and a major-domo, the princes tried valiantly to mix with other university students. That they managed to blend in, although Bonn did not subscribe to the forced equality of academic dress, made Albert's experience, even when interrupted, an idyll.

During their first *Sommerhalbjahr*, the brothers attended lectures by Moritz Arndt von Bethmann-Hollweg on Roman and on Prussian civil law, Clemens Perthes on German law, Johann Wilhelm Loebell on ancient history, Peter Kaufmann on finance, and Edward d'Alton on art history. 'With all our conviviality,' Ernest recalled, 'we were all nevertheless very diligent and possessed a kind of reading rage, which caused us to devour a huge quantity of books.' At lectures they filled their 'beloved notebooks' – which they then reviewed 'with the greatest conscientiousness'. Some professors held '*conversaziones*, in which there was a great deal of ardent discussion'.

Six weeks into the term came the news from England that William IV had died and Victoria was queen. She was one month past eighteen. Albert wrote to his 'dearest cousin' on 26 June to offer his 'sincerest felicitations on that great change which had taken place in your life'. It was a difficult letter to compose. Now that she was 'Queen of the mightiest land of Europe', he went on, 'the happiness of millions' lay in her hands, and he trusted that Heaven would assist her in 'that high but difficult task'. He hoped for a long and happy – and glorious – reign, in which she would achieve the 'thankfulness and love' of her subjects. He wished neither to be indiscreet nor to 'abuse' her time, but, he closed, 'May I pray you to think likewise sometimes of your cousins in Bonn, and to continue to them that kindness you favoured them with till now.' And he signed it as 'your Majesty's most obedient and faithful servant, Albert'.

Further bulletins came from his aunt in London and his uncle in Brussels, keeping him informed, and he wrote to his father in Coburg, 'Cousin Victoria is said to have shown astonishing self-possession. She undertakes a heavy responsibility, especially at the present moment, when parties are so excited, and all rest their hopes on her.' Leopold continued to furnish news, which seemed to picture England in the new reign as 'a network of cabals and intrigues', with political parties arrayed against each other 'in the most inexplicable manner'. Knowing almost nothing of the English party system, and of the mysteries of the English unwritten constitution, for which there was no parallel in Germany, the young prince was mystified.

With Victoria now queen, rumours circulated that Albert would soon be marrying her. Deflating them, Victoria announced, both to deflect matchmakers and to furnish herself with time to enjoy her elevated new status without domestic hindrance, that she had no present interest in matrimony. That put no quietus on the rumours in Britain and abroad. One circulating across the Atlantic was that the widower President of the United States, Martin Van Buren, who was the same age as Viscount Melbourne, 'thinks seriously of making an offer' to the young queen. Commenting on the report in the Salem, Massachusetts *Register*, the Boston *Daily Advertiser* observed that Victoria was 'at liberty to marry whom she chooses, *except a Papist*'. Since Van Buren passed that test although 'everything by turns and nothing long', the *Daily Advertiser* saw 'no reason why he should not *offer*, or why he may not stand as good a chance as the namby-pamby princes and kinglings of Europe'.

Albert's situation in Bonn was compromised by the reports and the gossip, and Leopold advised him to 'disappear' into unpublicized but useful travel. Albert concurred that the reasons were 'imperative and conclusive'. Leaving Bonn at the close of term on 28 August 1837, Ernest, Albert and Florschütz journeyed south into Switzerland, Austria and Italy, going as far as Venice and returning to Coburg through Munich. Whatever their condition, many roads required payment of tolls. In pre-railway days – and there was little trackage then, only between a few industrial sites – travel without one's own conveyance and horses was by stage from inn to inn. It would be four years before the first international line for steam locomotives was operating, from Strasbourg to Basel. In Germany the first line had already opened in December 1835, between Nuremberg and Fürth.

In days of large families and dynastic marriages, hardly a place in Europe was without a Coburg relative, and in the grand Elfenau *Gut* (Estate) overlooking the Aar in the suburbs of Bern, Ernest and Albert found their aunt Julia, known in Russia still as Grand Duchess Anna Feodorovna although she had been divorced fourteen years earlier from the dissolute second son of Tsar Paul, Grand Duke Constantine, who had died in a cholera epidemic in St Petersburg in 1831. (Contrasting his huge country with Julia's native duchy, Constantine had once scoffed that her brother 'reigns over six peasants and two village surgeons'.) Leaving their aunt on 9 September, Ernest and Albert set out on foot. As much as was possible – and it was often necessary in Alpine terrain – they walked. Beginning in incessant rain along the Rhine, they trudged into the Swiss cantons as far as Lucerne, took a boat across the lake, and saw the next sunrise from a snow-covered mountain-top, descending then on foot to the glacier of the Rhone. Ponies accompanied the party through the Alps, but wherever possible Albert refused them, intending to keep to his purpose of a walking tour. They crossed through the Simplon Pass into Italy, then through the lakes region into Milan, and, by 12 October, across the top of the boot to Venice. 'Milan, and still more, heavenly Venice', Albert wrote to his father, 'contain treasures of art that astonish me'.

Once home, Albert prepared a small album of scenes he had drawn on the journey, a dried '*Rose des Alpes*', and a scrap of Voltaire's handwriting he had obtained from an old servant of the philosopher at Verney, and posted the souvenir to Victoria. Years later she attested it was 'one of her greatest treasures', but her acknowledgement at the time only expressed envy that he could travel to such places while she – as Victoria innocently assumed – could no longer, as monarch, go abroad. 'I fear now I shall never do so.'

The brothers returned to Bonn in early November to resume studies while Albert, as he wrote to his father, began to contemplate 'the arrangement of my mode of life'. He was only nineteen, and whatever arrangement had been contemplated for him with Victoria now seemed uncertain at best. 'The last term really ended before we had time to collect our thoughts about it', he explained in a letter to Duke Ernest on 12 November. 'We have already plunged into the midst of the new one.'

In the *Winterhalbjahr* they were 'overwhelmed with lectures, papers, exercises . . .' As before, they studied Roman law, German law, political science, the principles of finance and, with d'Alton, the art of ancient Greece. They also attended lectures on literary history by A. W. von Schlegel, and on anthropology as well as philosophy by Immanuel Hermann von Fichte. Schlegel was privately derided by students for his vanity and his pandering to nobility. When Schlegel learned, Ernest wrote, that the Hereditary Prince of Lippe-Bückeburg would be present, he had a beadle set apart a chair for the Prince, and, as Friedrich Wilhelm of Mecklenburg arrived, 'the Professor opened his address by solemnly welcoming the Grand Duke, and then turned to the rest of the audience', and 'an unexampled uproar ensued, so that Schlegel had trouble in making himself heard'.

Still, Ernest conceded, 'old Schlegel' was 'brighter than all the star professors', and Bonn had a distinguished faculty. In Schlegel's own house 'we shared in the . . . pleasure of hearing him read Shakespeare. His clever and brilliant delivery made one forget his incredibly senile manner and problematical character. His delineation in his "History of Literature" of modern German poetry since Schiller, in which he enlarged particularly on the romantic style, forms one of the most unfading impressions which I ever received. These lectures were public, and immensely sought after. My brother and I attended them like other students, and were looked upon as such by everyone.' But not by Schlegel, who told the equally elderly William Wordsworth in Bomal, a Belgian town east of Brussels, of Albert's 'promising habits and dispositions, wh[ich] he was prompted to do by the then already talked of probability that the Prince would become the husband of our young Queen'.

More than lectures occupied the princes. Museums, a riding school, botanical gardens, and a well-stocked library of 150,000 volumes were attached to the university. Bonn offered fencing, theatricals, singing and drinking clubs, and the shops that enabled Albert to begin an art collection. In walks down the Rhine to nearby towns, he bought a Dürer drawing and a portrait by Van Dyck, and sketched landscapes and riverscapes. When lectures began to bore, he drew heads of teachers and students. He composed music for the university organ and bought a cheap piano that seemed to require the continuous services of a tuner. It was a vain attempt by Albert to put at bay, by activity, speculation about a future over which he had little control.

On 17 November Ernest and Albert were asked – in effect, commanded – to spend Christmas week, when there would be no lectures, with King Leopold in Brussels. 'We shall then have an opportunity', Albert explained to his grandmother in Gotha, 'of learning more distinctly what Uncle thinks of the coming separation, next spring, of our hitherto united lives, and also of giving him . . . our own views of it'. (The plans set out for them had been to leave the university after the *Sommerhalbjahr* of 1838, with Ernest becoming an apprentice officer in the Saxon army at Dresden.) But Albert injured a knee just before Christmas when a horse from the riding school refused to take a jump and crashed into a wall. He broke no bones but would retain a deep scar. The holiday in Brussels was cancelled, and Albert limped about Bonn into the new year.

The delay in consulting with Leopold meant a trip to the Belgian summer palace at Laeken for Easter. By then, Stockmar had visited Victoria and found her rejecting all thoughts of marriage, even startling the Baron with the remark that she was unsure whether Albert was experienced enough for the role they had contemplated for him. For her coronation scheduled for June, an elaborate event with thousands of guests, she had invited Duke Ernest but not his sons – possibly a signal to Albert. At Laeken, the King explained that he would consult Victoria confidentially, but continued to find it awkward to be in England and would absent himself from the coronation festivities. He advised Albert to keep a low profile and to use his time in waiting for study and travel. Explaining the situation to Stockmar, Leopold wrote, 'He looks at the question from a most elevated and honourable point of view; he considers that troubles are inseparable from all human positions and that, therefore, if one must be subjected to plagues and annoyances, it had better be for some great and worthy object rather than for trivial and paltry ends.'

Leopold followed up his understanding with Albert with a letter to Victoria so blunt and businesslike as to suggest that it must have been hand-carried by Stockmar who, she had written to her uncle, 'knows best my feelings and wishes on that subject'. Both uncle and niece had been discussing Albert as a commodity for which the Queen was not ready to accept delivery. She referred to 'the finishing of Albert's education' as equivalent to the finishing of a painting in oils or a piece of cabinetry – and as if he were not far better educated than she. Victoria was Queen: formal learning seemed now superfluous.

'Concerning the education of our friend Albert', Leopold wrote to Victoria on 13 April 1838, 'it has been the best plan you could have fixed upon, to name Stockmar your *commissary-general*; it will give *unité d'action et de l'ensemble*, which otherwise we should not have had.' Stockmar, he agreed, would be their joint intelligence agent, reviewing the finishing of Albert, which would include, at the Baron's recommendation, further guided travel, 'as nothing enlarges the mind so much'. (Victoria herself had journeyed only to a few country houses of the aristocracy in the Home Counties, and as a child had visited the seaside at Ramsgate.) 'On one thing you can rely', their uncle promised, 'that it is my *great anxiety* to see Albert *a very good and distinguished young man*, and *no pains will be thought too much* on my part if this end can be attained . . .'

While the prince was being packaged, with no guarantee that something might intervene to preclude acceptance of the finished product, Albert knew that Victoria continued to receive aspirants for her hand, including elevated and dashing ones like the Grand Duke Alexander of Russia, a year older than Victoria and a future Tsar. As Mary I had discovered with Philip of Spain, becoming the bride of a reigning monarch of a great nation – the Grand Duke would become Alexander II – was a practical impossibility. The hospitality which the Queen continued to offer to suitors suggested that Victoria was resisting Coburger matchmaking. 'My intentions are still the same', she would assure her uncle, Duke Ernest, when he came for the coronation, 'but that could not happen before two or three years'. Albert could only do the possible, which was to begin the new *Sommerhalbjahr* and to occupy himself in student pursuits. He practised with the broadsword, won a fencing match, and emptied cartridge cases in target-shooting.

As the Queen readied herself for her coronation, Albert walked his black greyhound, Eos, along the banks of the Rhine, and had long, impassioned talks with one of the serene highnesses who had been attending the same lectures, Paul Wilhelm, Prinz von Löwenstein-

Werthheim-Freudenberg, with whom he had been close since the winter term. Without Ernest, who had other preoccupations, they hiked into the nearby Siebengebirge, and along the valley of the Aar to the Walportzheimer vineyards. Perhaps because he was a crucial year younger as a child when his mother was banished, perhaps because he was always under strain to keep up physically and intellectually with his more mature brother, Albert was a very different young man as he neared seventeen than was Ernest at eighteen. Brought up like twin brothers, they might have developed, but for such formative contrasts, in the same ways.

Professions of intimacy with his brother would remain vocal and zealous, and Albert remained excessively loyal all his life, but Ernest was busy demonstrating his own maturity, which went well beyond Albert's in seductions of servant girls and other evidences of manliness that recalled his father's lifestyle. Leopold's careful housing arrangements failed to deter Ernest. The brothers were lodged in a house rented from Dr Bischof, a professor of medicine at Bonn. On a slope overlooking the Rhine, it was set in a small courtyard enclosed by an iron railing. Until their household, from tutor and *Stallmeister* to domestics, was complete, meals were sent in from the Star Hotel, Bonn's best establishment. Still, Albert and Ernest attempted to blend in as much as did the other young noblemen whose lives were set apart by rank. Somewhat stiffly, Albert would recall to Prince William later in the year, when Löwenstein remained at Bonn but his Coburger crony had gone, 'I believe that the pleasant days which we spent together, partly in useful occupations, partly in cheerful communion, will ever appear to me as the happiest of my life ... How pleasant were our winter concerts – our theatrical attempts – our walks to the Venusberg – the swimming-school – the fencing-ground!'

The useful occupations were the lectures on Roman law, German civil law, public administration, modern history, property law, finance, policy studies, fine arts theory and the archaeology – to be revised by Schliemann – of Homeric Greece. Curiously, given Albert's great interest in music, he attended no lectures on music theory, although studies in music were available. He may not have had time.

Few anecdotes exist about Albert at Bonn. He recognized the necessity for a low profile. Even if apocryphal, one suggests his personality. A student with whom he had become friendly came from Andernach, on the Rhine below Bonn. When his mother, a well-to-do widow, remarried, and the new husband drastically curtailed the free-spending ways of his stepson, three undergraduates on a river ramble who recognized the 'old gentleman' embarrassed him with a public tirade about his miserliness. Angered, the man from Andernach offered money to some passing peasants if they would pursue the students, give them a thrashing, and throw them into the river. Overpowering the boys, the farmhands performed their office and boasted about who had paid them to do it.

Drenched and soiled, the undergraduates returned to the campus and recruited volunteers to avenge them. As they gathered on the riverbank, still in their academic gowns, to plot stern punishment at least equal to the offence – retaliation which they failed to realize might prompt their expulsion – Albert turned up. Moving to the head of the mob, he exhorted them to behave with moderation. 'The circumstances connected with this affair', he reportedly said, 'require some particular mark of our determination to defend and avenge each and every one who had been abused; but I hope that in chastising the offenders no one will overstep the bounds of prudence, or use any uncalled-for violence. Remember, we belong to Bonn University, and any misdeeds of ours will throw odium upon one of the finest institutions in the kingdom. Convince the aggressors that you will not let them escape with impunity, but do so in a manner that will be equally creditable to yourselves as it will be efficient in its object.'

The students cheered, then went off to hunt down the culprits, whom they 'paraded through Andernach amid deafening shouts'.

At his Easter tête-à-tête with Leopold, Albert had been spared none of the realities of his position, which remained awkward both publicly and privately. At best, no rival had materialized. Enjoying power, status and the freedom both afforded, Victoria appeared to have no intention of marrying, and had even begun to complain coldly that uncle Leopold was attempting to rule her 'roost'. The Prince's situation as he was completing what was to be his final term in Bonn was precarious. His inherited income was small. Even his potential as Protestant spouse in a lesser court was hostage to his marital limbo in England. He had agreed that Leopold could confide to Victoria after the coronation that he – Albert – was willing to submit to reasonable delay 'if I have only some assurance to go upon'. If, after waiting for three years, 'I should find that the Queen no longer desired the marriage, it would place me in a very ridiculous position, and would, to a certain extent, ruin all the prospects of my future life'.

As the *Sommerhalbjahr* came to a close, Albert returned to Coburg without even a tourist's look at the coronation. His student years were over, and perhaps his useful life. He had no status and no role. In the Queen's letters to his family he went unmentioned. His few cautious letters to her went unanswered. To his grandmother in Gotha he would confess, in boredom, a few months later, 'when a man is sunk in idleness, it is difficult to get out of it'. He was crammed with facts, but having gone to the University of Bonn with the half-promise of Windsor Castle to follow, his life as a student had to be more guarded and more remote from scandal than the ordinary playboy prince. Not that it was in his nature to follow the profligate examples of his father and, now, brother. As a later observer would put it, 'His virtue was, indeed, appalling; not a single vice redeemed it.'

# IV

## *Courting a Husband*

### *1838–1839*

FOLLOWING THE CORONATION to which he was not invited and the close of the final *Halbjahr* which the brothers were to spend at Bonn, Albert expected his life to be one of waiting for something to happen. What happened first was a fire. The ducal palace at Coburg was heated by wood stoves. While Ernest and Albert were at the Ehrenburg Palace overnight, a servant lit a fire in a seldom-used stove that was piled high with books and prints and against which were more maps and prints. They awakened to billowing smoke and darting flames. Albert shouted 'Fire! Fire!' and with the aid of Ernest and their valet, Cart, battled the blaze with two jugs of water and another of camomile tea. 'Ernest took my cloak and his own', Albert wrote to their grandmother in Gotha the next day, 18 October, 1838, 'and threw them upon the flames, while I dragged all my bedding there, and pressed the mattresses and large counterpanes against the burning wall. Cart lifted a marble table with incredible strength and threw it against the bookcase enveloped in flames, causing it to fall down...The heat and smoke were so powerful that all the windows had fallen out; even the glasses of the framed pictures [on the walls] were cracked, and the pictures shrivelled, and the paint of the doors is quite charred.'

Aside from the material damage, Albert and Cart scorched the soles of their feet by repeated barefoot dashes into the cinders. 'The only picture that is not injured', he summed up to Dowager Duchess Caroline, 'is the one of the fire at the Palace of Gotha.'

Two partings altered Albert's life in the closing months of 1838. Florschütz became betrothed to the daughter of Pastor Genzler, ending his close association as the princes' *Rath*, and Ernest took up his military apprenticeship in Dresden. The Duke and Albert travelled north-east from Coburg to meet the younger Ernest at Lobenstein for another round of farewells, driving, in the Duke's hardy manner, in an open carriage in freezing late-November weather.

Stockmar had recommended that Albert, who had sampled Italy only from Milan to Venice, spend the winter and early spring in Florence and Rome absorbing history and the arts – that it would be a more pleasant atmosphere than Berlin or Vienna or Brussels in which to wait out the winter, and Victoria's hoped-for change of mind about matrimony. With Florschütz no longer available as mentor, the Duke offered to conduct Albert as far as Munich, and then leave him to such arrangements as Stockmar might work out. The *Rath* had become suspect in any case as possibly a bad influence, the Duke's militia chief, von Wangenheim, having reported on 11 April 1838, 'as a faithful Gothaner', his suspicions that the Prince had 'imbibed liberal principles' from Florschütz. Both he and the Prince admired Leopold's constitutional monarchy. The sooner Albert was distant from such influences the better.

In early December the ducal party set off southwards. The fiftyish physician was not the ideal companion. Stockmar suffered from chronic indigestion and general hypochondria, and could not manage many miles each day, but at least he preferred travelling in a closed carriage. In bitterly cold weather, often on snow-covered roads, they jolted through Innsbruck, the Brenner Pass, Verona, Mantua, Modena, Bologna, Conigliano and, finally, Florence, which they reached on 29 December. 'The whole of north Italy', Albert wrote to his father, 'is covered with snow three feet deep. We found so much snow in the Apennines that we took five hours to accomplish what should have been less than three, though we had six horses and two oxen to the carriage.' Just short of Florence they had to be dug out of a snowdrift and move at walking pace. On 9 January 1839, he wrote again, confirming that they had established themselves in a 'well situated' house belonging to the Marquis Cerini. Albert would remain in Florence with Stockmar until early March.

Life for well-placed expatriates in Florence was crowded with balls, concerts, exhibitions, dinners and sightseeing, all opportunities for Albert to become more socially sophisticated – yet there is no hint of any involvement with young women of his class. For diplomatic reasons, perhaps, he did attend a ball given by Henry Fox, Minister Plenipotentiary in Florence, in January, to celebrate Her Britannic Majesty's forthcoming coronation. Fox was the son of Lord and Lady Holland, social lions and great friends of Viscount Melbourne. Very likely Albert understood that his presence would be reported to London, and indeed Fox wrote to his mother that young Prince Albert was handsome and pleasing, 'and so unaffectedly gay and amused'.

It would take some weeks, until the atmosphere of Florence altered in anticipation of Carnival, for Albert to feel its contagion. To Florschütz he wrote, 'Every morning by five o'clock I sit down by my little student's lamp' – and he did study English and French most mornings, and practise on the organ and piano in the early afternoons, after which he often took long walks round what had been, since medieval days, a city with attractive architecture and striking views along the Arno and from the nearby hills. To Prince William, a far different audience for his activities, he wrote, 'I am often quite intoxicated with delight when I come out of one of the galleries... I have lately thrown myself entirely into the whirl of society. I have danced, supped, paid compliments, have been introduced to people, and had people introduced to me; have spoken French and English – exhausted all remarks about the weather – have played amiable... You know my passion for things, and must therefore admire my strength of character, that I have never excused myself – never returned home till five in the morning – that I have emptied the carnival cup to the dregs.' If true, during Carnival week at the least, he was not burning his student's lamp at the usual pre-dawn hour.

On 10 March, he and Stockmar left for Rome, where they expected to remain for three weeks and then go on to Naples until the heat of late spring would drive them back toward the Alps, and home. From the cultural standpoint he enlarged his view beyond German, Dutch and Flemish painting and Romanticism in general, thanks largely to young Ludwig Gruner, brought along by Stockmar, who knew little about such things. Gruner was especially drawn to the accomplishments of the early Renaissance, then little appreciated in England.* Albert wrote to Florschütz with cautious understatement that he had made his peace 'with the Antique'. He would also learn to love Italian 'primitives' like Giotto in the most convincing way of all – by purchase.

In Florence one of his friends had been the duc de Nemours. Another was Lieutenant Francis Seymour of the English 19th Regiment, who joined the Prince early in February on leave of absence from his unit. Seymour, like the crotchety but well-meaning Stockmar, was there at the behest of King Leopold, to rein in any possible defection from the straight and narrow by Albert – hardly a real concern in his case – and to be Leopold's, and therefore Victoria's, spy. (Seymour's parents lived in Brussels and were known to Leopold.) Seymour continued with the party into Rome for Holy Week, and the Prince – six years his junior – was delighted to have a young companion. Seymour – later Lieutenant General Sir Francis, and a future Crimean War hero – would have links with the English Court that outlasted Albert, and a daughter, Victoria, to whom the Queen would be godmother. Seymour wrote home that Easter, 'The Prince danced the Cottilion with Lady Augusta Fox,[†] which lasted until five o'clock in the morning... Tuesday went to the Bal Masqué with the Prince...'

Even in Italy, Seymour reported, the Prince, who 'has grown very handsome and distinguished in his appearance... is talked of in public... as the husband of our young Queen. I accompany him everywhere, because the Baron is too unwell to go out...' Regularly, however, Stockmar would report to the Queen about their progress, to remind her that Albert's education on her behalf was progressing favourably; and from Naples on 16 April, once they had left Rome, he sent her what he described as 'a further account of our crusades'. Of the visit to Gregory XVI he said little more than 'We paid our respects to the Holy Father.' Albert, he added, made an 'admirable' sketch of the Pope.

---

* Ludwig Gruner, who became Lewis in England, would advise Albert on art matters from 1841 to 1856. Beginning as an architectural historian, he became an expert on northern Italian terracotta and ornamental art with books to his credit which he dedicated to Albert and to the Princess Royal. The Italianate aspects of Osborne House would owe much to Albert's consultations with him, and he would design the Royal Mausoleum at Frogmore, Windsor, in 1862.
[†] Wife of Sir Henry Fox.

On 31 March they had gone to observe the Pope's Easter blessing of the crowds in St Peter's Square 'from the balcony, amidst the ringing of bells, firing of cannon, and military music'. It was, Albert wrote to Lowenstein, 'really a most imposing scene', although it 'savoured strongly of idolatry'. Nevertheless he arranged an interview with Pope Gregory, and 'The old gentleman was very kind and civil. I remained with him nearly half an hour, shut up in a small room. We conversed in Italian on the influence the Egyptians had on Greek art, and...on Roman art. The Pope asserted that the Greeks had taken their models from the Etruscans. In spite of his infallibility I ventured to assert that they had derived their lessons in art from the Egyptians.' In the arrogance of youth, bolstered by scraps of newly acquired knowledge, the nineteen-year-old foreigner, new to Tuscany (pre-Roman Etruria), had committed the high solecism of challenging the Pope. And although only partially correct, Albert was less wrong than the venerable Gregory XVI. Much of Etruscan art seemed of Greek origins, while its funerary culture, with tomb provision for ultra-terrestrial life, appeared linked to the Egyptians. Some Etruscan writings would be found with mummy wrappings.

His Lutheran training at odds with Roman ritual and trappings, Albert also thought – so he wrote to Florschütz – that the Pope looked 'like a Pagoda'. Another German who had obtained an audience, a Herr Plattner,* Albert reported irreverently, flung himself on his knees to kiss the Pope's foot. 'He had already brought his lips within reach of the shoe when the Pope took a step backwards and turned round to pull the bell for the door to be opened to us. Thereupon P[lattner] lost his balance and fell on his face. Nevertheless he crawled after His Holiness on his stomach and grasped his raised foot. The Pope, a very stout, heavy man whom one foot only could not support, began to stagger and made violent efforts to free himself, which made him kick Plattner's mouth, outstretched to kiss, ten times at least.' In the background, struggling to keep from laughing, were Seymour and Stockmar, who

---

* The obsequious German who shared Albert's audience was very likely Ernst Zacharias Platner (1773–1855), an art historian from Leipzig who had painted piously biblical subjects before settling in Rome, and turning to art criticism, in 1804. He doubled as the King of Saxony's agent, then chargé d'affaires, to the Holy See. (Only *hearing* the name, Albert apparently doubled the 't'.)

pushed Plattner out the door as he mumbled thanks to the Pope for his 'graciousness'.

Later the Prince would be faulted for failing to evidence a sense of humour, but his public manner had to conform to his aspirations. Even now, with his unconfirmed future accepted as fact wherever he went, he was cautious to a fault. A public embarrassment might doom his chances. Stockmar reported as much to Leopold, observing that Albert, however amiable to everyone, showed no interest in women, and that the Prince, who had a passion for ideas, nevertheless did not discuss politics. (Earlier, Stockmar had noted that in Coburg Albert seldom looked at any newspaper other than the *Augsburger Allgemeine Zeitung.*) 'On the whole,' the Baron concluded, 'he will always have more success with men than with women, in whose society he shows too little *empressment,** and is too indifferent and retiring.' Since the public world in which Albert hoped to move was entirely male, and the only woman whose favour he required was Victoria, the Prince appears to have been aware of his priorities.

That he needed to project a maturity and sagacity beyond his few years was becoming evident as his Italian experience was coming to a close. The Queen at twenty – her birthday in May was in the month that Albert returned home – had become a problem even to herself. Dazzled by her position and inadequately trained for her role, she was imperious, unsophisticated and wilful. With the suave, widowed Prime Minister, who had already weathered extra-marital scandal, at her side afternoon and evening, mentoring her in his easy, avuncular manner, Victoria's obstinacy about being limited by a husband intensified. Malicious gossip reached her only through the rude crowds that occasionally jeered 'Mrs. Melbourne!' as she cantered in London parks with him or showed herself to the public in her carriage. All such signals were ignored, although much later she confessed, 'I was very young then, and perhaps I should act differently if it was all to be done again.' Charles Greville confided to his diary that the young queen's feelings toward Melbourne were 'sexual though she does not know it'.

That Victoria was queen of the Whigs rather than sovereign of England was a perception seemingly confirmed by the 'Bedchamber

---

* Eagerness.

Crisis' in which she was adamant about retaining her 'ladies' after a confidence defeat in the Commons had apparently unseated Melbourne. 'They wished to treat me like a girl,' Victoria exploded indignantly to Melbourne, 'but I will show them that I am Queen of England.' Largely the wives and daughters of leading Whigs for whom the appointments were political perquisites, they were, Peel patiently pointed out, holding public offices with stipends authorized by Parliament. But when Victoria insisted, in a misunderstanding of constitutional principle, that Peel was deviously attempting to dominate her Household, which she claimed was exempt from ministerial control, he refused office, restoring Melbourne's untenable government – exactly what the Queen wanted.

The embarrassing Lady Flora Hastings affair had already shown Victoria as petty and precipitate. In her haste to worsen the none-too-good reputation of Sir John Conroy, who she privately suspected was her mother's lover, Victoria had accused Lady Flora, a sister of the Tory Marquess of Hastings and lady of the bedchamber to the Duchess of Kent, of being pregnant out of wedlock, and hinted that Conroy had been responsible. The questionable swelling proved to be cancer, and the innocent Lady Flora died. The press fanned public outrage, revealing the Queen to be much in need of counsel she did not have. And looming over the North Sea was her allegedly wicked uncle, the Duke of Cumberland, and also now, since a provision much like Salic Law* prevented her own succession there, King Ernest Augustus of Hanover. Should the young queen die without issue, the Hanoverian king would wear the English crown as well, as had his brothers George and William.

Someone with an appropriate bloodline, preferably of mature years, was needed to rescue the girl-queen from herself – and sire the succession. Early in 1839 the problem was to persuade Victoria, who now preferred to put off marriage, that a consort was preferable sooner rather than later. Into that breach – and in Albert's interest – Leopold

---

* Since George I had succeeded Queen Anne in England, the sovereigns of Hanover also reigned in England. The Electorate of Hanover had been raised to kingdom status in 1814 after the post-Napoleonic powers decided not to restore the dismembered Holy Roman Empire. Salic Law eliminated females altogether from succession. A woman could not succeed in Hanover as long as male members on the paternal side of the family survived.

directed Stockmar to negotiate not with the Queen, but with Louise Lehzen. Daughter of an Hanoverian clergyman, Lehzen had come to England in 1818 as governess to Victoria's half-sister, Princess Feodora of Leiningen, transferring her functions to Victoria in 1824, when she was five. To afford Lehzen some status, Princess Sophia, the elderly unmarried daughter of George III who, like Victoria's family, had apartments in sprawling Kensington Palace, persuaded her brother, George IV, to raise Lehzen to Hanoverian baroness. As such, she performed Household administrative duties for Victoria, and was Stockmar's conduit for strategies to bring Albert and Victoria together. Stockmar wrote to Lehzen in the direct language of one private secretary to another, and neither showed their texts to the person for whom each was acting. The conspiratorial method would prove its necessity.

Late in May Albert's entourage began returning northward through Pisa, Leghorn, Genoa and Milan, crossing through the St Bernard Pass to Lausanne and then to Bern. At Milan he was met by his father and his cousin Count Hugo Mensdorff. Stockmar returned home to his family, and to covert correspondence with Brussels and Windsor. From Geneva, where Lieutenant Seymour parted company for London, Albert and the Duke began their return to Coburg, where, by act of its assembly on 21 June, the coming-of-age day of Prince Ernest, both brothers were declared, simultaneously, to be of legal age. Albert was still two months short of twenty.

On 13 July, Albert accompanied Ernest to Dresden, planning to remain for two weeks. 'Then', he wrote to his friend Löwenstein, 'I must go to a place that I hate mortally, that charming Karlsbad, where Papa is taking the waters, and much wishes me to be with him. I hope this campaign will be over by the middle of August.' Albert had dreaded the Duke's plans for months, and hoped they would fade away. His father wanted him to 'accustom himself more to society', and 'pay more attention to the ladies', which 'as an occupation' Albert disliked. The fashionable Bohemian spa, frequented by females among whom might be some who would see to it that the Prince came of age in other ways then by legislative fiat, seemed to the Duke the appropriate place to further Albert's education. 'I had, on the contrary', Albert recalled, 'formed the finest plans for the study of the English language and history, for which the quiet of the Rosenau would have been particularly well suited.'

As far as Victoria was concerned, Albert's immersion in things English was premature. In her diary for 12 June she recorded a discussion with Lord Melbourne in which she 'talked of my cousins Ernest and Albert coming over – my having no great wish to see Albert, as the whole subject was an odious one, and one I hated to decide about; there was no engagement between us, I said, but that the young man was aware that there was no possibility of such a union; I said it wasn't right to keep him [hanging] on and not right to decide before they came; and Lord M. said I should make them distinctly understand anyhow I couldn't do anything for a year.' Privately, she felt that she could think of no marriage at all for at least four years. In the meantime she wrote to Albert rather coldly that although she looked forward to seeing both brothers at Windsor again, she hoped that neither would be ill as he had been in their only previous visit nearly three years earlier.

Melbourne, who preferred matters as they were, without unpredictable spousal intrusion, offered no objection. He seldom said 'no' to Victoria. Since it was her pushy uncle in Brussels who kept reminding her of Albert, she wrote to Leopold three days later as if nothing were happening in England to erode public confidence in her as queen. Airily, she assumed – and she appeared to have the Prime Minister's concurrence – that she could go on indefinitely in her wilful independence, and that 'the young man' could be kept waiting, or perhaps fobbed off on someone else. Most surprising of all to Leopold, who knew that she did not want to be reined in, was that she had no sense of the dissatisfaction about her. No one close to the Court was willing to tell her the truth.

She was sending her letter by courier, she began, as the content was sensitive. Talk of a visit by Ernest and Albert was to cease: 'I am desirous [it] should not transpire.' Further, she went on, imperiously,

I wish to know if *Albert* is aware of the wish of his *Father* and *you* relative to *me*? Secondly, if he knows that there is *no engagement* between us? I am anxious that you should acquaint Uncle Ernest, that if I should like Albert, that I can make *no final promise this year*, for, at the *very earliest*, any such event could not take place till *two or three years hence*. For, independent of my youth, and my *great* repugnance to change my present position, there is *no anxiety* evinced in *this country* for such an event, and it would be more prudent, in my opinion, to wait till some such demonstration is shown, – else if it were hurried it might produce discontent.

Though all the reports of Albert are most favourable, and though I have little doubt I shall like him, still one can never answer before-hand for *feelings*, and I may not have the *feeling* for him which is requisite to ensure happiness. I *may* like him as a friend, and as a *cousin*, and as a *brother*, but not *more*; and should this be the case (which is not likely) I am *very* anxious that it should be understood that I am *not* guilty of any breach of promise, for *I never gave any.*

As Leopold paused to wonder what he could do, Albert was writing to Stockmar about his premature – but legal – majority, 'I am now my own master, as I hope always to be, and under all circumstances.' Yet even then he was not, as the Duke was bent upon keeping him away still longer from the Rosenau. He was 'almost dying of boredom' in Karlsbad, he wrote to Ernest; 'yesterday I nearly hanged myself in desperation when I heard that the reward for all my sufferings is to be a stay at Reinhardsbrunn.' The Thür-inger Wald family castle was certain to be even more dull than Karlsbad. But his father had given up on Victoria and was eager to make connections for Albert although the benefactor of his industry showed no enthusiasm for the scheme.

Without warning, the Duke's plans were altered and a reprieve won for his son. Leopold had summoned Ernest to England. Unable to spurn a delegation of her Coburg uncles, Victoria had conceded, with some exasperation, to a visit. In the last days of August, Duke Ernest travelled to Windsor with Prince Ferdinand of Saxe-Coburg-Kohary. On 6 September, King Leopold, who had pressed for the meeting, arrived with Queen Louise, whom Victoria considered a friend. The business was briefly dispatched. The Queen again declared her misgiv-ings about marriage but agreed, so long as no understanding was read into their presence, to see the princes.

Duke Ernest returned to Coburg to report that the Queen had insisted that she had settled on no spouse, had no intention of marrying very soon, and was quite content the way things were – and that the lax Prime Minister, whose Downing Street lease had been extended by the Bedchamber fiasco, was of similar disposition. Victoria's subjects felt otherwise, the Duke conceded. She enjoyed entertainments that went on into the small hours, and then sleeping late. She loved pomp and display, and was more stubborn than ever. She 'might as well marry George of Cambridge, since no one else will have her'. And the Duchess of Cambridge, the former Princess Augusta of Hesse-Cassel, imagining such chances, was unsubtle in pressing the claims of her son, whose bad complexion, at nineteen, was concealed by fresh whiskers. 'Infamous woman', Victoria snapped in her journal.

Twenty on 26 August, Albert had written to his brother, as Ernest was hurrying to Windsor, 'Our childhood is over ... yet I can say that I retain my childlike soul, and this is the treasure that everyone should take with him into his future life.' Ordered about by his peremptory father, he may have felt more of the powerlessness of the child than the ideal of innocence and wonder he fantasized. The days leading up to his birthday, for example, had to be spent, unwillingly, in Gotha, in which he never felt at home. But he was back in Coburg to read Victoria's invitation which reopened the question of his future yet left him in the position of a child. His life was still being discussed and determined without even his presence.

To make her position clear, Victoria had drawn up an invitation that was little short of a cold dismissal. Its language suggests that she intended to evoke either an outright rejection or a humble acceptance of conditions set by a sovereign understood as having her way then and thenceforth. Ernest and Albert were each to bring only one accompanying person, neither of whom was to be the suspect Stockmar, and they were to arrive by 28 September. Albert's move in the chess game of wills was to make the tactless Queen wait. The King of Saxony planned a state visit to Coburg beginning on September 30, and the presence of both brothers, Albert claimed, was mandatory. Ernest was, after all, serving in the Saxon army.

When Leopold urged that one didn't keep the queen of a great nation waiting, Albert, intending exactly that, explained to his uncle, 'We really have no option, and we shall not be able to leave before the fourth [of October].' It would take nearly a week after that, by carriages overland and then by the wretched Channel boat, to make it to England. He hadn't lost interest in being consort to a queen, but he was having gloomy second thoughts about the price. (In a letter dated 6 December, Albert would confide to Prince William of Löwenstein that he had determined to go only 'with the quiet but firm resolution to declare, on my part, that I also, tired of the delay, withdraw entirely from the affair'.)

Since two could play the stalling game, Victoria rushed off a request to Leopold that he hold the brothers in Belgium longer than their planned overnight stay. 'You will think', she told her uncle, 'I only mean to employ you in *stopping* my relations at Brussels', but she alleged need for a delay to afford her ministers, who were coming to Windsor 'on affairs of great importance', time to leave – as, if Ernest and Albert arrived before the Cabinet departed, 'people would say – it was to *settle matters*'. Besides, she added, with more than a little arrogance, 'I think indeed a day or two at Brussels will do these young gentlemen good, and they could be properly fitted out there for their visit.' The ungracious aside suggested that 'these young gentlemen' from the forests of Thüringia (otherwise 'my relations') might be planning to arrive in *Lederhosen.*

On October 1 she pouted to Leopold, 'The *retard* of these young people puts me rather out...I had a letter from Albert yesterday saying they could not set off, he thought, before the 6th. I think they don't exhibit much *empressement* to come here, which rather shocks me.' But she would send 'a gentleman and carriages to meet my cousins, either at Woolwich or the Tower, whichever place you inform me they land at.'

Sailing from Antwerp, Ernest and Albert – and the uninvited four-legged Eos – arrived at the Tower of London dock in the Thames on 10 October, a Thursday. Since the rough overnight voyage had left both brothers in agonies of seasickness, they failed to notice that their trunks were not stowed onto their carriages, which guaranteed that whatever they had been fitted out with, they would begin the visit without acceptable clothes.

At Windsor the day had mellowed into a beautiful autumn evening before the sound of hooves and wheels sent a servant scurrying to report that the princes were arriving. The Queen had been walking with her guests on a terrace edged by what Lady Granville described as an 'embroidered garden'. Returning indoors, Victoria awaited Ernest and Albert at the top of the broad stairs in the upper quadrangle. She had lost the pounds she had put on when, to allay her gathering anxieties, she had eaten and drunk to excess, and Harriet Granville thought she appeared 'lovely, much more delicate without looking ill'. Victoria had chosen her vantage to suggest a height she did not have. Just under five feet, she intended to look queenly.

As the brothers ascended, erotic lightning struck. 'It was with some emotion', Victoria confided to her journal, 'that I beheld Albert – who is beautiful. I embraced them both and took them to Mamma.'

Amid the initial presentations, Victoria learned that they had arrived not with inappropriate clothes but with no trunks at all. Although protocol demanded formal attire for dinner, the Queen failed to recall the lines which Shakespeare had given to Henry V in wooing Katherine of France – that 'nice customs curtsy to great kings', who are 'the makers of manners'. Dining apart, the princes joined Victoria in her spacious drawing-room '*in spite of their negligé* ', as she would write, and she presented them to Melbourne, who sat with her on a sofa as usual. Albert was offered a chair opposite the Queen, who found it difficult to keep her eyes off him. 'Lord M.' took due note, and when Victoria managed to turn away to ask him in a whisper whether he saw any family resemblance, the Prime Minister answered gallantly, 'Oh! yes. It struck me at once.'

The Queen's postprandial guests sat through the evening, Lady Granville wrote to the Duke of Devonshire, 'with much to look at . . . Prince Albert the youngest is charming. Ladies Sandwich, Clanricarde and I are won. It remains to be seen who else will be.'

As was customary, they broke up into small groups, and Albert chose chess over cards. The emotional pitch was high. Lady Clanricarde commented, *sotto voce*, 'The trial is too great; if he wins he has a master mind.' He lost. Her Majesty bent over the velvet-gowned Lady Clanricarde to ask, 'Do you think my cousin [looks] like me?' 'Yes', she said.

Harriet Granville and the other transfixed ladies, having had 'all our eyes on', came away thinking that the Queen evidenced 'much attention but no liking', which if so, demonstrated the Queen's public manner as more disciplined than her pen. She was besotted. Her journal for the next day included as much of a physical description of Albert as clothing permitted. He was 'quite charming, and so excessively handsome, such beautiful blue eyes, and exquisite nose, and such a pretty mouth with delicate moustachios and slight but very light whiskers; a beautiful figure, broad in the shoulders and fine waist; my heart is quite going . . . '

On the twelfth she wrote to Leopold in terms that made clear that the uncles' strategy had worked. She and Albert rode into Windsor

Forest together, danced after dinner, played at cards, and as Eos stretched and yawned, talked into the night. In her journal for the thirteenth her cousin was now 'dearest Albert', and she confided to Lord M. that she had changed her opinion about marrying and felt that she had to decide 'soon'.

'You could take another week', said Melbourne, agreeing in effect that little further consideration was necessary. Albert, he conceded, was

*Victoria's proposal to Albert on 15 October 1839, in a contemporary lithograph.*

'a very fine young man'. The next day – the fourteenth – she told Melbourne that she had made up her mind, and the Prime Minister wrote to Lord John Russell, 'I do not know that anything better could be done.' To the Queen he ventured, 'I think it'll be very well received; for I hear there is an anxiety now that it should be; and I'm very glad of it; for a woman cannot stand alone for long, in whatever situation she is.'

They discussed how 'such things were done' when the gender situation was reversed, and Victoria decided to send Baroness Lehzen to Albert's equerry, Captain Buffo von Alvensleben, to inform him that a personal declaration from the Queen was forthcoming.

On the fifteenth, a half hour after noon, Victoria sent for Albert. She was alone and tried to restrain her trembling. 'I said to him', she wrote in her journal, 'that he must be aware *why* I wished [him] to come here, and that it would make me *too happy* if he would consent to what I wished (to marry me); we embraced each other over and over again, and he was so kind, so affectionate. Oh! to *feel* I was, and am, loved by such an *Angel* as Albert was *too great a delight to describe!* he is *perfection*; perfection in every way – in beauty – in everything! I told him I was quite unworthy of him and kissed his dear hand – he said he would be very happy "*das Leben mit dir zu zubringen*" and was so kind and seemed so happy, that I really felt it was the happiest brightest moment of my life, which made up for all I had suffered and endured. Oh! *how* I adore and love him, I cannot say!! *how* I will strive to make him feel as little as possible the great sacrifice he has made; I told him it was a great sacrifice, – which he wouldn't allow . . . '

It would be a sacrifice in many ways, Albert knew, but at the moment he was loved, and he was on the verge of being extricated from the claustrophobic court of Coburg, where he was a superfluous son in a statelet of little consequence. He had been offered the career for which he had been groomed.

Returning to his rooms to get his emotions under control, Albert penned a note to Victoria, in effect to confirm the betrothal. 'How is it that I have deserved so much love, so much affection?' And he signed it, 'In body and soul ever your slave, your loyal Albert'. In circles where courtship followed the engagement rather than created the conditions for it, they were about to begin the next phase of their lives.

Later in the day Victoria hurried a message to Leopold completely at variance with the chilly hostility her uncle had learned to expect. 'My feelings are a *little* changed, I must say, since last Spring,' she confessed. Her mind was 'quite made up' – and she had told Albert as much.

'*If you love him, and are kind to him,*' the King responded, 'he will easily bear the burden of the position.' It would be a burden; the career of consort to a reigning queen at any time or place had seldom, if ever, been a source of satisfaction. For the next few weeks, however, as Ernest and Albert lingered on at Windsor at Victoria's request, the couple were in a state of complete bliss. Alone, they kissed 'again and again', and Albert called her '*vortrefflichste*' – superb one. Still, Albert was uneasy in England. He was uncomfortable with the language, the climate, the food, the prospect of alienation, the likely frustrations of his occupation. To Stockmar he wrote, nevertheless, with deep feeling, lines from Schiller's *Lied von die Glocke,*

> *Das Auge sieht den Himmel offen,*
> *Es schwimmt das Herz in Seligkeit –*

One's eye sees heaven open, the heart floats on a sea of blessedness.

Yet the announcement, Albert warned, was to be withheld, for reasons of state, until Parliament met in mid-November. What particularly grieved him, he confided, was that Victoria's mother – his own aunt – 'is not to know of it. But as everyone says, she cannot keep her mouth shut and might even make bad use of the secret if it were entrusted to her.'

Secrets were difficult to keep at Windsor, where servants blended into the furnishings. Having been present when the princes arrived, and with lines of communication to Windsor open, it was only the day after Victoria's proposal that Harriet Granville reported to the Duke of Devonshire the latest gossip from the Dowager Lady Sandwich – that 'Prince Albert has been flirting the last two days, she was not sure, but thinks with Miss Cocks. An odd distraction I think.' Lady Caroline Somers-Cocks was a maid of honour to the Queen, and it is quite possible that a young Saxon prince, bored with inactivity, was distracting himself in his habitual manner. But it would have been Ernest – a case of mistaken identity which at least kept the betrothal under wraps a little longer.

Two days after Victoria and Albert became engaged, they attended a musical evening at Windsor. His standard for music being high, and bored by the waltzes and galops, Albert covered his handwritten programme with doodles and caricatures. The Queen treasured it, keeping it all her life.

The fleeting days before the public announcement of the engagement were spent in work and play. With Albert her imperious surface vanished, and she was the vulnerable young woman who had craved affection all her life. Having arrived to be interviewed by his prospective employer, the Prince succumbed to her passion. She asked for a cutting of his 'dear hair' to wear in a locket, and gave him a ring 'with the ever dear to me 15th engraved in it'. Radiant in her new happiness, she understood, nevertheless, that she was no beauty, and Albert confided his impatience with society beauties. Alone, afterward, with Lord Melbourne she innocently told him of the exchange and he grumbled, disapprovingly, with what he thought was political wisdom, 'Ought to pay attention to the ladies'.

Between kisses in the Queen's blue sitting-room one day, Victoria signed a sheaf of papers and warrants, Albert at her side, 'and he was so kind as to dry them with blotting paper for me'. It was symbolic of the official role intended for him, but such concerns remained far from his mind. His life had taken on an unexpected emotional dimension, and the couple returned to reality only when such business as setting a wedding date came up – it would be 10 February 1840 – and what other arrangements had to be made for Albert – an income, a staff, a rank or title, even such an essential as citizenship.

With much to do to wind up his affairs in Germany and to proclaim the nuptials there officially, he soon had only eight weeks left for all of it, including the journeys back and return. He left with Ernest, via Belgium, on 14 November. 'We kissed each other so often, and I leant on that dear soft cheek, fresh and pink as a rose . . .', Victoria gushed in her journal for the day. 'It was ten o'clock and the time for his going . . . I gave Albert a last kiss, and saw him get into the carriage – and drive off. I cried much, felt wretched, yet happy to think that we should meet again so soon. Oh! how I love him, how intensely, how devotedly, how ardently! I cried and felt so sad. Wrote my journal. Walked. Cried.'

Since Albert had been secluded at Windsor, few knew but many guessed at the outcome. Ordinary visits, however important the guest, did not lengthen into weeks. Even so, Victoria's mother – Albert's aunt Kent – had not been called in to be told of the betrothal until 10

*Victoria's watercolour sketch of Albert made at Windsor when he was twenty shows far more honestly than the idealized portraits by Court painters how young he was. (Royal Collections)*

November. Although she wept then with happiness, second thoughts quickly intervened. The next day, to consolidate her position at Court she began urging upon Albert appointments of her friends, and insisting that she would live with the couple after their marriage – 'which we agreed *never* to do', Victoria noted. Once Albert left, the Duchess began complaining about her imminent separation from her daughter, who offered no consolation. Instead, Victoria consulted with Melbourne, who urged that her mother be moved 'out of the house. There must be no harshness, yet [be] firm.'

Albert's departure was only hours old when Victoria began, in her sudden physical loneliness, to pour out her passion for him in letters interspersing English and German, the first sent via her uncle, so that the Prince would receive it *en route* home. Confident that Melbourne, as he guaranteed in his usual accommodating manner, could fix all the details of the marriage to mutual satisfaction, Victoria promised to have Albert invested with the Order of the Garter before he left Coburg, to have him made a field marshal, and to have a simple marital declaration approved by Parliament. 'Everything will be very easily arranged.' Yet even in the very first of many messages to be exchanged between November and February a dark foreshadowing of difficulties emerged: '*Lord Melbourne told me yesterday that the whole Cabinet are strongly of opinion that you should not be made a Peer.*' The crucial word was 'yesterday'. She had known that Albert would have to be married in his trivial and un-English title of Prince of Saxe-Coburg and Gotha, but could not bring herself to tell him and spoil their leavetaking.

Because of winds and tides, the Channel crossing to Calais had to be delayed until 2.30 in the morning. Even then the *Firebrand* could not dock at the quay and passengers had to go ashore in a small boat just after dawn. The entire party, Albert wrote to Victoria, was fearfully ill. 'I have hardly recovered yet.' But his letter closed with all the endearments she could have wished for. 'Your image fills my whole soul. Even in my dreams I never imagined that I should find so much love on earth.'

After Brussels they travelled by way of Aix la Chapelle and Bonn, where the brothers hosted 'a great luncheon for one of the professors, who was our old tutor', and met their father, the Duke, at Wiesbaden, for a formal escort home. It was there that Albert answered, with tact and shrewdness, his future mother-in-law's parting request to give her as a token something he had worn. 'I send you the ring which you gave me at Kensington [Palace] on Victoria's birthday in 1836. From that time it has never left my finger. Its very shape proclaims that it has been squeezed in the grasp of many a manly hand. It has your name upon it: but the name is Victoria's too . . .'

At Coburg, Albert met Stockmar, whom he would send to England as his representative in negotiations about his status. Awaiting him from Victoria was a book never part of his law studies at Bonn – Sir William Blackstone's *Commentaries* (1765–69) on the laws of England. He promised that the volumes would receive 'a thorough study', but it was much later before he discovered that the unwritten English Constitution, a body of precedent, conceded him 'just as much space as I could stand upon'. Although English marriage laws left a wife as little more than a chattel of her husband, the Constitution was 'silent as to the Consort of the Queen; – even Blackstone ignores him'. But that was years afterward. Legal English was a more complex matter than ordinary language, which was trying enough despite his schooling. He should have responded in English, he conceded, 'but German runs more easily with me, and as we always spoke in German together during that heavenly time together at Windsor, it does not sound right to me at all to address you in English'. Their private interchanges in all the years of their marriage would follow the same pattern. In public an English prince, at home he and Victoria spoke German.

By the time that Albert informed his friend Prince William, in early December, of the royal engagement, difficulties were emerging about his English status. He expected to be happy in his marriage, he confided, 'for Victoria possesses all the qualities which make a home happy', but his role beyond that of husband was another matter. 'My future lot is high and brilliant, but also plentifully strewed with thorns.' Frank, too, was his assessment to the Duchess of Kent, to whom he described, the same day (6 December 1839), the 'multitude of emotions' that overwhelmed him as he prepared to leave Coburg – 'hope, love for dear Victoria, the pain of leaving home, the parting from very dear kindred, the entrance into a new circle of relations... prospects most brilliant, the dread of being unequal to my position, the demonstrations of so much attachment on the part of the loyal Coburgers, English enthusiasm on the tip-toe of expectation, the multiplicity of duties to be fulfilled, and to crown all, so much laudation on every side that I could sink to earth with very shame. I am lost in bewilderment.'

The praise in England, except from those close to Victoria, was already diminishing as others were redefining him as alien and parasite. It would be impossible for Victoria to keep that from him. Meanwhile, he told his aunt, while outside the countryside was deep in snow and he struggled with a heavy cold, 'I pack, arrange, give directions about pieces of property, settle contracts, engage servants, write an infinitude of letters, study the English Constitution, and occupy myself about my future.'

The formalities for that future, social as well as legal, were far more complex than either had anticipated. Before the Privy Council, and Parliament, knew, the Queen had to inform, confidentially, if the delicious confidences could be kept, Queen Adelaide, her royal uncles, and those of the Cabinet not already knowledgeable. On 18 November she invited the Cambridges – including Prince George – to acquaint them with her betrothal. Her cousin, she told Melbourne, was 'evidently happy to be *clear* of me'. Melbourne's sister, Emily Cowper, long Palmerston's mistress and now that she was widowed, to be married to him in a month – which amused Victoria, since the elderly lovers were in their fifties – had been to Windsor to meet Albert. 'Nothing openly stated', Lady Cowper wrote to Dorothea de Lieven in Paris, but 'with a good figure and well built'. Albert possessed 'everything which is likely to engage a young girl's affections'. Marriage, the future Lady Palmerston predicted, would come 'sooner or later, and I do not think she could find anyone more suitable. They say he is as sensible as his uncle [Leopold] and has great learning.'

Soon after Albert returned to Coburg a letter arrived from Victoria, dated 22 November, with more disconcerting news. Melbourne had been asked in the Cabinet about confirming the Prince's Protestantism. He had assumed that it was understood and had not been necessary in the Declaration. Now Victoria required a history of the ducal house and its religious ties, '*for a few stupid people* here *try* to say you are a Catholic...'

Her next letter to Albert would describe the ordeal of announcing her own betrothal. As Lord Holland put it in his diary, 'A modest girl of twenty, unaccompanied by any one of her own sex, had to announce to a grave and observant assembly of 85 men her *determination* to take as bedfellow a young man who had lately left her palace.' Asked afterwards by the Duchess of Gloucester if the prospect of the ceremony alarmed her, Victoria said, 'A little, but not much, for I had to propose it to Albert himself and had gone thro' that much more awkward ceremony before I mentioned it to the Privy Council.'

The Privy Council met in Buckingham Palace at two in the afternoon on 23 November. Victoria had come in from Windsor for the session, and a crowd had begun gathering, recognizing that the marital rumours were about to be confirmed. When the folding doors of the council chamber were swung open, the Queen entered alone, wearing a simple morning gown. Her only jewellery was a bracelet containing Albert's portrait in profile – a miniature by Sir William Charles Ross. 'I had to read the Declaration,' Victoria wrote to Albert. '*It was rather an awful moment, to be obliged to announce this to so many people, many of whom were quite strangers.*' Charles Greville, as Clerk of the Council, saw her hands quiver as she held the folded sheet with the statement composed by Melbourne, but, Tory stalwart John Wilson Croker wrote to Lady Hardwicke, 'I cannot describe to you with what a mixture of self-possession and feminine delicacy she read the paper. Her voice, which is naturally beautiful, was clear and untroubled; and her eye was bright and calm, neither bold nor downcast, but firm and soft.'

As the Queen's carriage passed through the gates *en route* back to Windsor on the cold, overcast day, smoke as usual hanging low over London, crowds, now larger and aware of the news, cheered Victoria lustily. 'Radiant and bowing' according to press accounts, she responded happily. The public, however, appeared more delighted with the betrothal than would Parliament, already less than enthusiastic about providing a purse for yet another penniless German princeling, especially as political agitation burgeoned. Farms and factories were both subject to market forces, and machines also seemed to take jobs from the able-bodied. When consumption declined, the work-force fell even further, although not the fertility of the exploding population. Since Parliament feared that economic distress would increase discontent, which in turn would feed revolutionary fervour, its members, more middle-class since the Reform Act of 1832 enlarged the electorate, sought expenditures for police and poorhouses and public works. The unemployed got little help indeed from Parliament, and its largesse towards Albert seemed, if anything, overly generous. Looking back at precedent, Victoria complained to Melbourne that the 'very stupid and insignificant' Danish prince who became Queen Anne's husband was made Lord High Admiral and presented with a £50,000 stipend. Yet their failure to assure the succession – no child survived infancy – had brought the despised Hanoverians to England, including the uncles of the Queen, Princes of the Blood Royal, who even now disputed raising a mere Serene Highness to precedence over them. Albert's hypothetical sons – the very reason for his importation – would be born to precedence over their father, a problem of little concern to the people in the streets, but of great moment to the rank-ridden classes that still ruled.

Lord Shaftesbury recalled nearly forty years later being told by Melbourne that the Queen was eager to have Albert made, by parliament, King Consort upon his marriage. Cautiously evading a direct answer, the Prime Minister was very pressed for one, and determined that it was his duty to be 'very plain' about it. 'For God's sake', he said to Victoria, 'let's hear no more of it, ma'am; for if you once get the English people in the way of making kings, you will get them into the way of unmaking them.'

Whether on religious or national grounds, the undercurrent of hostility towards another imported sovereign or consort was real. England had endured five Hanoverian kings and their German brides. Also forgotten was Leopold. And now, a malicious broadsheet, *The German Bridegroom*, mocked,

> Saxe-Coburg sends [Albert] from its paltry race,
> With foreign phrases and a moustachio'd face,
> to extract treasure from Parliament by wooing
> The hoyden Sovereign of this mighty isle[, who]
> Welcomes her German with enraptured smile.

Debate on the Naturalization Bill had thrown Victoria's precedents back at her. Prince George of Denmark had been awarded all the pocket money the Queen had claimed, but it had come from the future Queen Anne's own pockets, and the Coburger Leopold had indeed received a parliamentary stipend, yet on departing for another throne had continued taking Parliament's money. The climate for German bridegrooms had changed.

Since Parliament was determined that Albert should play no political role, he was also to have no rank in the army, and no English peerage. 'It needs but the stroke of your pen to make me a peer and to give me an English name,' Albert had appealed from Wiesbaden *en route* home. He had no idea what an unpopular and even illegal act that would have been. From status-conscious Vienna, Prince Metternich would scoff that one could no more make a man royal who was not so, than make him eight feet tall. Victoria was furious at the outcry. Parliament was not merely legislating, mean-spiritedly, the lives of two twenty-year-olds about to be married; it was attempting to diminish the powers of the sovereign. Was Albert, she asked Melbourne, worth less than Queen Anne's consort, 'stupid old George of Denmark'?

The votes against comparable arrangements for Albert were actually less a rebuff to Victoria than to the weak Melbourne Ministry that she had, through her own wilfulness, kept too long. Albert was paying the price. It did not augur well that his only legal position in England was to be that of a minor foreign princeling who happened to be the Queen's husband. Even his arms were to be quartered with the royal arms in the inferior position, as if he were a woman. As for his role in politics, he could continue to wield the blotting paper. The functions for which he was imported from Coburg would have to be performed in bed.

# V

# *Serene Highness to Royal Highness*

## *1840–1841*

A T NOON ON 7 February 1840, now recovered from seasickness, the Coburgers departed Dover for Canterbury. Despite the cold February rain they rode in open carriages under darkened skies to accept loyal English cheers. Exposure to the elements was a hazard of rank Albert had experienced at home.

The escort changed as they clattered closer towards Canterbury. Now it was the crack 11th Dragoons, commanded by James Thomas Brudenell, 7th Earl of Cardigan, a lieutenant-colonel who had inherited a peerage and vast income in the year Victoria succeeded to the throne. Spoiled beyond efforts at discipline from his superiors, at forty-two he had already been the beneficiary of a commission and a seat in the Commons, both purchased for him; and he used his private purse to promote the swagger of his men and mounts. Only the best equine breeds were good enough for the 11th. On a costly Arab charger, Cardigan greeted the Prince's party at the head of two files of just over one hundred smartly accoutred troops. As cathedral bells pealed, the Dragoons accompanied the future consort into Canterbury.

Following divine service, the weary Saxons dined at the Royal Hotel with Cardigan and two majors from his regiment. Canterbury was illuminated as never before. Defying the drizzle, crowds outside the hotel shouted for the Prince and hailed him when he appeared on a balcony. Learning about the enthusiasm the next day, Melbourne advised Albert wryly not to become intoxicated by adulation.

*A contemporary lithograph, by G.F. Bragg, of Albert's carriage being escorted from Dover early in February 1840, by the Earl of Cardigan's 11th Light Dragoons.*

On Saturday morning – it was now the eighth, with the nuptials set for Monday – the entourage set out for London, the Dragoons leading the way along the road toward Sittingbourne, on the south bank of the Thames. The balding, bewhiskered Earl was in his glory. His men were in their finest plumage and efficiently doing what he had trained them to do while garrisoned in Cork. Even his enemies, of whom there were many, conceded that he had the makings of an excellent sergeant-major.

Young Albert was impressed. Not long after the wedding Cardigan was informed by the Adjutant-General, Sir John Macdonald, 'My Lord, I have the honour to acquaint you . . . that Her Majesty has been graciously pleased to direct that the 11th regiment of Light Dragoons shall be armed, clothed and equipped as Hussars, and styled the "Eleventh" or "Prince Albert's Own Hussars".' A dragoon in the British army was a mounted infantryman armed with a short musket; a hussar – a term originally in use in Hungary for a light cavalryman, and a variant of the Italian *corsaro*, or corsair – was the same soldier decked out in flamboyant uniform, exactly to the taste of the Earl. Cardigan, who spent at least £10,000 a year of his personal fortune on tack and tailoring for his troops, quickly employed fifty fitters to fashion brilliant new plumage. It was more appropriate to *Mitteleuropa* than to an army that needed to learn all over again, long after Waterloo, how to fight. The Earl was a patrician parader of post troops, unable to hear above the splendid din of drum and trumpet any orders from nominal superiors. Blundering in 1854 at Balaclava, he would inspire a poem by Tennyson.

Albert's personal escorts were rewarded in a different manner. Lord Seymour, a companion in Italy, would spend much of his subsequent career as a courtier, as would George Byng, the 7th Viscount Torrington, who would be Lord-in-Waiting to Albert and then to Victoria, while Charles Grey would rise to general in the royal administrative retinue.

The escort of the Prince brought him to London by mid-afternoon on the eighth, using a route again different from advance prognostications in the press. Albert offered no complaints but his brother, peeved at the futility, recalled, 'The bridegroom, in the most incomprehensible manner, was driven through side streets, while people vainly awaited him in another part of the city.'

At four-thirty the Prince's carriage and escort arrived at Buckingham Palace through the centre gate. 'I stood at the very door,' Victoria wrote, evidencing her eagerness; '1st stepped out Ernest, then Uncle Ernest, and then Albert, looking beautiful and so well; I embraced him and took him by the hand and led him up to my [sitting] room...' No privacy was possible; her mother, uncle, cousin and the Prime Minister followed them. Gifts were exchanged – the Star and Badge of the Garter in diamonds for Albert, a sapphire brooch set round with diamonds for Victoria. Within half an hour the Lord Chancellor had administered the formal oath of naturalization to Albert. He had now left Germany legally as well as physically.

At dinner Albert claimed to be still giddy from seasickness, but the ailment was more likely the tension that was inevitable in his situation. The next day, a Sunday, was left to him to recover, but by early afternoon he was again in Victoria's sitting-room, this time to accept, however sulkily, the staff appointed for him, including George Anson as his private secretary and treasurer. What confidentiality was he to have if Melbourne's own secretary were to become his? 'We had some little misunderstandings', Victoria understated in her journal, 'and he was so dear and *ehrlich*' – honest – 'and open about it; he will appoint him. I embraced him again and again.' They went over the wedding responses, and even practised placement of the rings.

When Albert drove away toward Kensington Palace, his guest quarters, the Queen saw throngs out in welcome – Londoners caught up in the romance and unimpressed, if aware at all, about higher-level misgivings that Victoria needed a more experienced, more mature, spouse at her side.

Upper-class concerns about the Prince often followed party lines. The Tory John James Ruskin, a prosperous wine merchant (and father of the critic), carped that the Queen's choice augured badly for Britain: 'I wish the Boy may grow into something better. It is a poor prospect for the Country.' The Earl of Aberdeen, a Peelite Tory and future Prime Minister, expressed no enthusiasm to Princess Lieven, whose lover, French politician François Guizot, was about to move to London as ambassador. 'The affair had excited no great interest', he scoffed, seeing Victoria as queen only of the Whigs; '... the Government have been unwise in giving a party character to the proceedings. It is said that the Duke of Wellington has only been invited at the last moment, and after much difficulty.' Assuming that it was Melbourne's decision to snub the Tory icon, rather than Victoria's, Aberdeen offered a scenario that suggested a more authoritarian Melbourne than was the case. 'Had they persevered in the omission, I really believe that publick indignation would have been so strong as to have endangered their places.' Still, 'Everything we hear of Prince Albert is favourable; he will have much in his power, and if he possesses sense and discretion he may be eminently useful to the country.'

Monday began miserably. Gusts of rain made travel unpleasant for the hundreds of wedding guests in elaborate finery. Since the venerable Chapel Royal, St James's Palace, could not seat everyone required by rank, relationship or diplomatic representation, invitees were seated everywhere some glimpse of the royal couple was possible, even on the staircase. As carriages queued up, Victoria – who had to travel to the chapel like the others – saw Albert 'for the last time alone, as my Bridegroom' – a flouting of tradition. The sky was clearing as the Prince, in his field marshal's uniform, left for St James's. As Victoria, accompanied by the Duchess of Kent and the Mistress of the Robes, the Duchess of Sutherland, who had become the Queen's closest friend, squeezed her satin gown with its lace flounces into her carriage, the rain persisted. It was twelve-thirty. A guard of honour opened a path for the short distance across Green Park: 'I never saw such crowds of people as there were in the Park', Victoria wrote, 'and they cheered most enthusiastically'.

Victoria's revenge upon the Tories for their treatment of the Prince was observable in the presence of only two Conservative peers, Lord Liverpool and the Duke of Wellington, both former Prime Ministers, and the Duke would not be invited to the wedding breakfast. Albert entered with his father as the organist played, incongruously, 'See the Conquering Hero Come'. The Queen's procession included twelve train-bearers. She was led in by the Lord Chamberlain and given away by her uncle the Duke of Sussex, who was 'always ready to give away', *John Bull* quipped, 'what does not belong to him'. The most awkward moment in the ceremony came, according to Sallie Stevenson, wife of the American Minister, when Albert had to profess endowing Victoria with all his worldly goods, yet he responded strongly when asked whether he would take 'this woman' for his wife – and the Queen looked into his eyes as he said 'I will'.

'The idle portion of the Town', Thomas Carlyle wrote crankily the next day, 'was in a sort of flurry owing to the marriage of little Queen Victory. I had to go out to breakfast with an ancient Notable of this place, one named Rogers, the Poet and Banker; my way lay past little Victory's Palace, and a perceptible crowd was gathering there even then, which went on increasing till I returned (about one o'clock) . . . ' The sage of Chelsea had been on his way to 22 St James's Place, to which the elderly bachelor banker and sometime poet, bald, gnomelike Samuel Rogers, now seventy-seven, had retired in 1803 to cultivate his muse and the art of conversation. 'Streams of idle gomerils' – Carlyle was employing an obscure Scots word for *simpleton* – '[were] flowing from all quarters, to see one knows not what – perhaps Victory's gilt coach and other gilt coaches drive out, for that would be all! It was a wet day, too, of bitter heavy showers and abundant mud.'

Over breakfast, Rogers had defended the Queen against Carlyle's acerbities – 'her fooleries and piques and pettings' – and the Sage withdrew into ironic sympathy for the royal couple. 'Poor little thing, I wish her marriage all prosperity too . . . As for him they say he is a sensible lad; which circumstance may be of much service to him; he burst into tears on leaving his little native Coburg, a small, quiet town, like Annan [in south-west Scotland], for example; poor fellow – he thought, I suppose, how he was bidding adieu to *quiet* there, and would probably never know *it* more, whatever else he might know.'

The bridal party and guests had to return through the rain for the wedding breakfast at Buckingham Palace. Although chroniclers have written of 'Queen's weather' – sunshine – breaking through, Lady Charlotte Guest, future translator of the *Mabinogion* and wife of a Welsh ironmaster, noted in her diary (she was in a carriage directly behind Victoria's party), 'The rain was pouring in torrents, but it did not damp the hearty expression of feeling which burst from the enthusiastic crowd.' Few of the drenched onlookers had missed seeing newspaper descriptions of the wedding cakes, but the confections would elude ordinary Londoners although over a hundred were ordered. Gunter's of Berkeley Square baked fourteen – for royals and the Cabinet. One was for a banquet for élite guests after the bride and groom had departed. The primary wedding cake was a nine-foot circle on which another layer rested on pedestals, with Britannia observing the royal pair pledging their vows, Cupid apparently recording it on tablets, watched over by masses of turtle doves.

At twenty minutes to four – the couple were to leave for Windsor on the hour – Melbourne came to bid farewell to the Queen, who had changed into white silk travelling clothes. 'Nothing could have gone off better,' he crowed. Wearing a dark coat, Albert joined her, and as their carriage departed they again accepted the cheers of what Sallie Stevenson called 'her sight-loving subjects who took the rain as quietly as if it had been a passing April shower'. Fashionable London then separated into smaller celebratory parties – Lord Palmerston gave a diplomatic dinner for forty – while the newly-weds clattered toward Windsor in what Charles Greville called 'a very poor and shabby style. Instead of the new chariot in which most married people are accustomed to dash along, they were in one of the old travelling coaches, the postilions in undress liveries.'

Not only was it to be an inelegant wedding trip; it would be more abbreviated than that of many lesser folk. Albert had appealed from Gotha for some private time with Victoria at Windsor. 'It is usual in England, is it not, for newly married people to stay up to four to six weeks away from the town and society...?' He had been willing to settle for 'at least a fortnight – or a week'. Even then he had been rebuffed, the Queen having declared that her presence when Parliament sat was needed 'after the second day'. In reality their absence would encompass the working week, with the couple departing for Buckingham Palace on Friday after arriving at Windsor on Monday evening. Victoria could well have remained into Sunday, but then would not have had her way. As one lampoon put it,

> She's lovely, she is rich
> But they tell me when I marry her
> That she will wear the *britsch*.

It seemed an inauspicious beginning, and the first months of marriage would be a roller-coaster of emotions for Albert, but he saw some positive signs. The Queen, not Parliament, signed army commissions, and he had become before the wedding a field marshal with no duties, but formally more than a wearer of a dress uniform. Leaving the Palace, the couple were followed by three coaches as escort, and Albert was surprised and pleased to discover as they continued on towards Windsor that they picked up an informal additional escort of well-wishers on horseback and in gigs and carriages which scattered happy throngs in their path. Approaching Windsor in early evening darkness, they saw homes brightly lit in welcome and crowds out with lanterns.

Almost in the shadow of the Castle, masters and students at Eton waited impatiently to receive the royal couple, and the boys followed the carriage up the hill, cheering and shouting. As Victoria and Albert alighted at the quadrangle, Etonian merriment echoed off the venerable walls.

While elsewhere in the town three public banquets, one of them chaired by the mayor, celebrated the wedding, in their private suite in the Castle the Queen ordered dinner brought but could not touch it. She blamed 'such a sick headache', and was 'quite deaf' from the lusty cheering over the route from London. With Albert at her side, she spent the evening on a sofa, 'and his excessive love and affection gave me feelings of heavenly love and happiness I could never have *hoped* to have felt before. He clasped me in his arms, and we kissed each other again and again. His beauty, his sweetness and gentleness – really how can I ever be thankful enough to have such a *Husband*!' In her journal she confided that 'to be called by names of tenderness I have never heard used to me before – was bliss beyond belief!'

*'Counting the Chickens'. Broadside cartoon, 1840, in which Victoria expounds to Albert on possible names for their future children, largely compliments for their uncles and aunts, from Leopold to Sophia. The Prince's shocked reaction shows in his posture. (Collection of the author)*

A London cartoonist, in a broadside sold on the streets, depicted the newly-wed couple 'Counting the Chickens' at their dining-table, perhaps the morning after. 'I have decidedly made up my mind, Al', says Victoria, 'to have our first Boy named after my much respected Uncle Leopold, the next in honour of my Uncle Cambridge, Adolphus Frederick; then we must have one [named] Augustus Fred for Uncle Sussex; and then, Al, in case of twins, Albert and Edward, we will call them; there's my cousins of Hanover and Cambridge [both named George]; we mustn't forget them, you know...' In case of girls, she adds, they might use Mary, Caroline, Sophia, Wilhelmina, Louisa, and Adelaide. Albert is given no response.

'When day dawned (for we did not sleep much)', Victoria wrote of her first night as a bride, 'and I beheld that beautiful angelic face by my side, it was more than I can express! He does look so beautiful in his shirt only, with his beautiful throat seen.' Greville got it wrong when he guessed that the relationship at the start, especially on Victoria's part, was not passionately physical. 'It was much remarked', he noted, 'the Queen and the Prince...were up very early on Tuesday morning walking about, which is very contrary to her former habits. Strange that a bridal night should be so short; and I told Lady Palmerston that this was not the way to provide us with a Prince of Wales.' To Melbourne that morning after, Victoria scribbled an ecstatic message about her 'most gratifying and bewildering night'. She never thought she 'could be so loved'.

The Queen's frankness was as nothing to the *risqué* 'club wit' going the rounds about the marriage of that rare pairing among the high-born, two virgins. Richard Monckton Milnes, MP, littérateur and collector of pornography, would receive a letter from his Scottish crony Robert Monteith acknowledging 'notelets from you containing the last indecencies on the subject of Royal venery; I burn with chaste and loyal indignation, shout with laughter & end by showing the documents right and left'. In contrast was the 'simple provincial spirit' of the folk on his demesnes, Monteith gibed. 'How sincere was the mighty bonfire I raised on a hill top – how spontaneous the gush of ale & porter which it cost 9 men's toil to distribute, how cordial the vibrations of the [fiddle] catgut to which 800 people danced & reeled like Baal wor-shippers round the blazing summit...How our poor villagers lit their windows – every pane in a glow!' At the same time, he scoffed, Milnes's people in England, 'with your hearts shrivelled with meanness and envy & hate & ...debauchery[,] could only make bawdy charades on this solemn sowing of a new Royal [family] tree. Do you mean to insinuate he has dared to touch her?'

At polar opposite were Elizabeth Barrett's chaste verses, 'The Crowned and Wedded Queen', in the *Athenaeum* of 15 February 1840. Sentimentally the future Mrs Browning looked beneath the regal pageantry and celebrated 'uncrowned womanhood':

> SHE vows to love who vowed to rule –
>     (the chosen at her side)
> Let none say, 'God preserve the queen!'
>     – but rather, 'Bless the bride!'
> ...She is a *woman*, and *beloved*! – and 'tis
>     enough but so.

> Count it enough, thou noble prince, who
>     tak'st her by the hand,
> And claimest for thy lady-love, our lady
>     of the land!

From the start, tables were set up in the Queen's room so that they could work side by side, but the work was Victoria's. Albert could make small talk or write personal letters. Sometimes she involved him enough to record a journal entry like 'rested and read Despatches – some of which I read to Albert'. What she wanted during the first days of marriage was closeness to Albert. She would watch him shave – an occasion dramatized with great charm by Laurence Housman in his play *Victoria Regina* (1934). 'How strange it looks!' Housman had his Victoria exclaim, '...and how interesting! – fascinating!...Is it dangerous?'

'Not if you don't talk to me,' says Albert.

When Victoria dressed, in those first idyllic days, Albert would help her put on her stockings – assistance unstageable in days when the Lord Chamberlain's censor guarded theatrical propriety so rigidly that even Housman's most circumspect scenes were first forbidden because 'her near kin' were alive.

Victoria's own reaction is clear enough from a letter she would write to their cousin 'Victo' (Victoria Augusta Antoinetta). The daughter of Uncle Ferdinand was about to marry the duc de Nemours. Only weeks after her own wedding, Victoria rushed to offer such advice as 'Love him with all your heart always and then you will be happy. YOU CANNOT IMAGINE HOW DELIGHTFUL IT IS TO BE MARRIED. I COULD NOT HAVE DREAMED THAT ANYONE COULD BE SO HAPPY IN THIS WORLD AS I AM.'

Eager to show Albert off to her contemporaries, Victoria ordered Lord Clarence Paget to organize a dance for her second evening at Windsor, and had high-spirited young people in for galops and quadrilles. Privacy was in any case impossible. By their second day as husband and wife, the Duchess of Kent, Duke Ernest, the younger Ernest and their attendants had come to Windsor. Another ball followed, and on the fourteenth the Court returned to London so that the Queen could receive, with Albert, formal addresses from both Houses of Parliament, and begin a series of levées at Buckingham Palace which introduced the Prince to the many who counted in government, business and society left out of the limited list for the wedding. On each occasion Albert led in the Queen at her left hand, the place he would continue to occupy. Every visit to the theatre or to divine services became an event, as Londoners vied to glimpse the royal couple.

For Albert, a melancholy post-wedding inevitability was the departure of his father – and soon after his brother – his last links with home. Yet he knew that the tender family feelings which he professed concealed realities he could not confide to Victoria. 'He said to me', the Queen told her journal, 'that I had never known a father, and could not therefore feel what he did. His childhood had been very happy.' If she continued to love him, he added, 'I could make up for it all'. He 'never cried', he insisted, but Coburg aides who had to part from him 'had cried so much that he was quite overcome. Oh, how I did feel for my dearest, precious husband at this moment! Father, brother, friends, country – all he has left, and all for me. God grant that I may be the happy person, the *most* happy person, to make this dearest, blessed being happy and contented! What is in my power to make him happy I will do.'

Some things the Queen could not do, and others at which she hesitated tore at older if now less tenacious loyalties. Albert was immediately lonely in an environment where no one else spoke English in his heavy, accented fashion, and it helped little that Victoria continued in the privacy of their domestic suite to speak in German, which kept his English more that of the written or printed page. As Ernest left for Dresden, Albert was compelled to recognize that the Saxon officer and Hereditary Heir (in the German usage) who had been almost a twin brother would not only be living a very different life, but had already done so. The symptoms of venereal infection had emerged, and Albert felt unable to speak to Ernest about his anxiety for him. At court, Victoria seemed too imprisoned by her veteran courtiers to initiate changes in her husband's favour. Louise Lehzen even questioned Albert's right to ride with the Queen in the State Carriage. Appointees through Melbourne's influence seemed to share the Prime Minister's indefinite tenure, and socialite courtiers appeared to encompass entire families, like the Pagets or the FitzClarences – the illegitimate but titled brood of William IV.

The Prince began discovering his silken bonds immediately on return from the non-honeymoon, and was not always assisted by the persistent intrusions of Stockmar, who seemed nearly as ubiquitous as Lehzen.

His bureaucratic and domestic advice, hammered at Albert in long Teutonic memoranda, urged boldness where caution was called for, and offered inapplicable remedies to peculiarly English problems. For Albert it was nevertheless not enough that his cage was gilded. Buckingham Palace had been sumptuously decorated for Victoria when she became Queen, and early in 1840 many of the rooms were equipped with gaslight. The modern lighting eased paperwork, but there was still no work for Albert to do. Making fun of his apparent uselessness, a spoof Court Circular would announce the appointment of a Toothbrush in Ordinary and a Shaving-pot in Waiting to his Royal Highness, adding, 'There is no foundation for the report that there is to be a Lord High Clothes-brush.' At first Melbourne, characteristically cynical, approved. 'The Prince is indolent,' George Anson noted Lord Melbourne as remarking, '& it would be better if he was more so, for in his position we want no activity.'

Already loyally taking the Prince's side, Anson countered that there was 'no scope' for Albert's energy. 'If you required a cypher in the difficult position of Consort of the Queen you ought not to have selected the Prince; having got him you must make the most of him, & when he sees the power of being useful to the Queen he will act.' In the early months of the marriage the Queen still confided in him only after she had consulted with Melbourne and Lehzen. Lehzen even retained her private passage into the couple's bedroom, and controlled the Queen's personal expenditures, no bill being authorized for payment until the Baroness had signed.

How the public viewed Albert's status was evident in dozens of sardonic jingles and verses making the rounds. When a paper reported that sometimes at Windsor the Queen drove her husband out in their pony carriage, another joked,

> *Why* Vic drives the Prince is plain
> To any common view –
> The Sovereign who holds the rei[g]n
> Should have the whip hand too.

Melbourne predicted to Greville, although it did not appear that way at the start, that the Prince would acquire 'boundless influence'. Possibly because he did not want the next – almost certainly Tory – Prime Minister to have his own influence with the Queen, Melbourne urged

Victoria to show her husband all the state papers he wished to see. Albert, he knew, would be above party. To help the process along, Melbourne began discussing public matters with Albert, and since Albert's background suggested that his interest might lie in foreign affairs, the Prime Minister urged that the Prince forward his views. 'He seldom answers me', Albert would write to his father, 'but I have often had the satisfaction of seeing him act entirely in accordance with what I have said.' For Albert, any discussion with someone as easy with words as Melbourne was painful, as his own English was awkward, and that realization, combined with his natural shyness, left the impression of a frigid reserve. Newspapers made the most of it. Victoria corrected his spelling in drafts of his letters, but even there his prose retained a rigidity that paralleled his public persona.

Albert's initiation into public life progressed slowly. When François Guizot dined at Windsor, he was looking forward to more than a social call. Palmerston was present, and Guizot, a power in the July Monarchy of Louis-Philippe, wanted to gain assistance for Turkey against the ambitions of Russia. Guizot was left to a postprandial chat with Lady Palmerston. The Queen sat on a sofa, sewing, while others gossiped round her small table. Albert played chess. Guizot was glad to be recalled in a few months to become foreign minister.

On 21 March the Queen awoke feeling unwell; recognizing the symptoms as possibly the first signs of pregnancy, she cried bitterly. Two months before the wedding she had confided to her journal how much she looked forward to marriage, and how little to childbearing – 'the ONLY thing I *dread*'. Years later she would describe pregnancy to her firstborn as 'an unhappy condition' that replaced 'happy enjoyment'. She was then, she confessed, 'furious'.

Whether or not Victoria blamed Albert, the satiric papers, even before the news was out, printed tales that she had begun directing her virago temper against him. One allegation was that he had, at tea, contradicted her on a trivial matter, whereupon 'the Queen sprinkled the contents of her cup over his face, which led to an estrangement for the whole evening'. Another report had Albert admiring a bouquet brought in by a pretty Maid of Honour. Allegedly Victoria dismissed Miss Pitt, then 'seized the bouquet and scattered its fragments over the room'. Whatever the truth of such gossip, the gutter press relished rumoured quarrels, common to all newlywed couples and difficult to conceal in a palace atmosphere where there was very little privacy. 'Is your Queen so much in love with her husband as to be already jealous of him?' Princess Lieven asked Lady Palmerston from Paris. 'What is to become of Prince Albert; will he always remain at his wife's side? It will be a dreary situation.' Such canards quickly crossed the Channel, as did the intelligence that the Queen was expecting, which seemed to reach Dorothea Lieven immediately after Victoria's consultation with her physician. 'Is the Queen pregnant?' she queried Lady Palmerston on April 5. 'And is her husband attempting to acquire some political influence?'

An inquiry about Albert's relations with the Queen even came, hardly more than a month after the marriage, from as far away as Rome, from the Scottish wife of the Comte de Flahault, the former Margaret Elphinstone, 'The Queen and Prince', Emily Palmerston protested, 'are very happy in their marriage, and there is no truth in any of the foolish stories that have been invented to the contrary. He is very good looking and amiable and charming, and pleases every body that approaches him. Even the mob, who are much taken with his looks and agreeable expression . . . ' Royals, however, seemed to create gossip merely by existing – almost, to the mob, a reason for their existence.

Victoria's frustrations about her pregnancy and its discomforts were for Albert's ears alone, and since she appeared to be in glowing health, the reason first went unsuspected. Lord Melbourne's advice, when the Queen confirmed that she was expecting, was to eat and drink heartily, for which she needed little prompting. Albert tried to reduce her involvement in public business, but she insisted that she was Queen, and had responsibilities uniquely her own. While shut out of her working routine and seeking things to do on the fringes of official life, he remained the focus of gossip very likely gleaned from, or invented by, Household staff. 'They say', Disraeli would prattle to his sister, Sarah, 'that Prince A[lber]t does nothing but eat[,] sing, and learn to ride* – speaks little and never but on the most trifling subjects, – very bored by his wife who is fearfully jealous. This is a Whig acc[oun]t – the Tories on the contrary maintain that he is a good Conserv[ativ]e and will make [out] all right. Fudge.'

That May, Albert wrote to Löwenstein that in his home life he was 'very happy and contented', but that he had difficulty outside it in

---

* In the English fashion, as opposed to German equestrian style.

finding any dignified role for himself. 'I am only the husband, and not the master in the house.' It was an awkward business to approach Victoria directly about his being left out of things, especially as he realized that her pregnancy, which she despised, would in time limit her independence, but he was only twenty, and impatient. He left it to Stockmar to approach Melbourne, who saw the Queen daily, and the two men met with Anson on 28 May after the Prime Minister brought up the subject with Victoria. The Queen conceded, Anson minuted, that Albert had complained of 'a want of confidence' both in 'trivial matters' and in 'matters connected with the politics of this country'. She blamed her own 'indolence', then confessed her belief 'that domestic harmony is more likely to follow from avoiding subjects likely to create difference'.

Albert, she did not need to say, had little knowledge of domestic English politics and had come only recently to any interest in Continental matters. Three months of residence on the other side of the Channel had not made him an expert in either realm. Still the Prince, Melbourne understood, intended to apply himself with Germanic discipline to both tasks, and he suggested tactfully that Victoria 'by degrees impart everything to him' and discuss with her husband 'any subject she pleased'.

Suspecting that Victoria's withholding royal business from Albert arose at least in part from Lehzen's attempts to retain what she recognized as a fading influence, Melbourne spoke, as he told the Queen, 'most seriously' to the Baroness, warning her that if she created dissension between husband and wife she would 'draw down ruin on herself'. Biology was against her. It was a power rivalry which Lehzen could not win. The Queen's condition not only drew husband and wife closer emotionally, but inevitably, as Victoria gradually relinquished more of the day-to-day details she had always insisted upon knowing, she threw more responsibility on to the husband. The red dispatch boxes arrived whether or not the Queen was up to them, and Albert read the contents, often to Victoria. As pregnancy increased the Queen's lassitude and the selection from the red boxes became his, Albert's informal authority and influence grew.

Without official status – he was only a recently naturalized subject of the Queen, although married to her – he had to become formally useful in other ways. One of his first ventures was to accept the presidency of the Society for the Extinction of the Slave Trade and for the Civilization of Africa. 'Civilizing' Africa meant Christianizing the continent: slavery was already illegal in the Empire. Ending the slave trade was far more difficult so long as there were markets for working bodies. France would permit slavery in its colonies until 1848; it remained lawful in the United States. Still, the international meeting was high-minded, with dozens of impassioned American abolitionists, especially women, setting the tone.

Albert found his role in the chair in keeping with the public posture he wanted to display. He wrote his own brief address – only about two hundred words – in German, then translated it with Victoria's help. Nervously he memorized it, trying out on Victoria his ringing phrases about the slave trade as 'repugnant to the spirit of Christianity' and 'the blackest stain upon civilized Europe'. Then, on 1 June 1840, he spoke before 'five or six thousand people' (in his estimate), at Exeter Hall in the Strand. Propping his remarks on the brim of his upturned hat, he opened the proceedings in his halting English, distracted only a little when his papers fell into the crown of the hat. On his conclusion, he reported to Victoria, there was 'great applause'. To attempt the address at all was an act of courage for a twenty-year-old to whom English was a foreign tongue.

'All the world has been this morning to Exeter Hall to see Prince Albert in the chair,' Disraeli wrote to Sarah. After the address Sir Robert Peel moved a vote of thanks to the Prince, and went on to describe emotionally how two slave ships in a recent storm on the high seas had battened down their hatches and caused seven hundred slaves to die from suffocation. He called for action to suppress the trade in humans. Disraeli observed 'a great effect on his Highness'. But after two hours of orations Albert slipped out, as he would learn to do on hundreds of occasions when he represented the Crown, often several times on a single day. (The chair was taken by the Earl of Ripon.)

One outcome was to support the fitting out of three vessels – one christened the *Albert* – to make contacts with the inhabitants of inland West Africa, and induce them to cease co-operation with slave traders. On 14 April the expedition sailed off, eventually to probe three hundred miles up the Niger. Of the 301 crewmen, forty-one, including one of the captains, would die of fever. The well-intentioned enterprise ended in failure.

Another gesture of Albert's would be to become a patron of the newly established London Library, which Carlyle called 'a democratic institution... where all men, on payment of a small annual sum, can now borrow Books... which in such a city as London, appetite growing by what it feeds on, may well become by and by one of the best Libraries extant... Prince Albert, good youth,' he added to Karl Varnhagen von Ense in Germany with unaccustomed if condescending praise, 'is Patron, by his own free offer; has given 50 pounds of money, and promises "a stock of German books".'

Ten days after the Exeter Hall baptism into public life, as the Queen and Prince drove up Constitution Hill, just above the Palace, beginning an early evening outing in the long summer light, 'a little mean-looking man' (in Albert's description), a pistol in each hand, fired a shot at them from about six paces away. Although the open phaeton made them an easy mark, the gunman missed. As he fired again, Albert drew Victoria down out of view. His reaction would have been too late for an accurate marksman, but young Edward Oxford, a waiter in a 'low inn', was slow-witted and equally slow of foot. (He would be judged guilty but

EDWARD OXFORD FIRING AT THE QUEEN AND PRINCE ALBERT ON CONSTITUTION HILL, JUNE 10ᵗʰ 1840.

*A lithograph printed in June 1840 to celebrate the escape of the Queen and Prince from an assassin near Buckingham Palace.*

insane.) Onlookers who had cheered the Queen and Prince seized him, and the royal couple called to the postilions to go on. They visited 'Aunt Kent' – who had been moved to Ingestre House, Belgrave Square – and took a drive through Hyde Park, Albert wrote, 'to show the public we had not . . . lost all confidence in them'.

The attack had no adverse effect on Victoria's pregnancy, then four months along, and now common knowledge. As the news of the attempted shooting spread across London, crowds gathered on horseback, in carriages and on foot, to hail the Queen as her carriage made its way back through the gates and Marble Arch, then still before the Palace. For days afterwards, wherever the couple went they were applauded enthusiastically, with special cheers for Albert, whose coolness was much admired in the newspapers. Spontaneous choruses of 'God Save the Queen' were common, even at the opera, where formality usually prevailed.

Addicted since her teens to opera and ballet, Victoria under Albert's tutelage also began regular playgoing, with an emphasis on Shakespeare that Professor Schlegel would have applauded. Covent Garden, under the direction of Madame Lucy Elizabeth Vestris and her husband Charles James Mathews, was then producing Shakespeare with Charles Kemble as leading actor. With Albert devoted to music, Victoria had begun going to concerts of more serious fare then heretofore. She first heard Mozart's *The Magic Flute* on 12 June 1840, when excerpts were performed at an amateur palace concert arranged by the Prince, at which he and Victoria sang a duet from Luigi Ricci's opera *Il disertore de amore*, 'Non funestar, crudele' ('Don't afflict me, cruel one!'). Luigi Lablache also took part – Albert knew he was one of the Queen's favourites – as did Battista Rubini and a lesser-known singer, Michael Costa, whom Victoria later knighted for his eminence as a conductor; and other roles were taken by the ladies and gentlemen of the Court. Even earlier, in March 1840, Albert had become a director of the Ancient Concerts, which attempted to keep alive such neglected composers as Handel.

Albert was only twenty-one that August, and too inexperienced to promote his larger ambitions. Nevertheless, he was exploiting the cultural opportunities that came his way, and Parliament registered its confidence before his birthday came, and with it his legal majority in England. He was designated Regent in the event of Victoria's death while their child was still a minor. Stubbornly, the old Duke of Sussex, the King of Hanover's brother, cast the only negative vote in the upper house. Until then, every parliamentary division had served to diminish him, as had the measure just before his marriage which stipulated that he could not possess any property that had been acquired by the Queen.

Stockmar's political efforts had made the Regency Bill possible, and on that success he quietly returned to Coburg (where he spent his summers with his family), briefing Anson before departure. The Baron's concerns about the royal couple's immaturity were still acute, but he realized that every German at Court after Albert was one too many, and that both he and Lehzen had to go. She was the conspicuous presence, relishing her Palace perquisites. Stockmar had kept a low profile from his earliest days in England, slipping in and out of Court and maintaining a residence few could locate. Albert labelled Lehzen 'the House Dragon'. He saw her removal – at minimal pain to Victoria – as his personal priority. But he had to work imperceptibly, increasing his pressure by degrees.

Lehzen even arranged who sat at dinner with Albert, for she controlled Household affairs, and Albert intervened fruitlessly with Melbourne to suggest that the Queen might be educated indirectly about practical matters by having men distinguished in scientific and cultural pursuits invited to the palace. The Prince had been bored by the courtiers, socialites, and occasional diplomats at the table, and the Prime Minister's 'She'll come round to it by and by' prompted Albert to consult Leopold. The result was that Sir John Cam Hobhouse, an MP who had been friendly with the Belgian king in his London years, came for dinner at Victoria's invitation, and through Hobhouse, once a crony of Lord Byron, Albert was able to invite Englishmen who could improve the quality of conversation as well as furnish him with useful contacts.

Altering the pool of dignitaries for whom 'covers were laid' at the Queen's table would often be a futile effort, and the Prince had to meet the people he wanted separately, and at other times. While much was made of the occasional intellectual at dinner, most guests were 'illustrious by courtesy' rather than 'illustrious by deeds', as *Punch* put it, inventing 'covers laid for forty', including authors, astronomers, sculptors, painters, geologists – 'princes of the realm of thought' – in a mock Court Circular that included authoress Joanna Baillie, painter Edwin Landseer, architect (of the new Houses of Parliament) Charles Barry, playwright Sheridan Knowles, physicist Michael Faraday, and Astronomer Royal George Airy.

A symbolic political success came when on 10 July Albert could write to Palmerston, 'The Queen thinks you might like to see the accompanying letter from the King of Portugal giving an account of proceedings at Lisbon...' It was a beginning of his personal involvement in world affairs – which was not to the foreign minister's liking – and a beginning, as well, of his acting for Victoria. There were now, also, dinners and meetings for the Prince outside the Palace, including his involvement with the medieval survival of membership in a company or guild, which had become a distinction precious to Londoners. In the City on 28 August 1840, according to the goatskin-bound New Testament on which he was sworn, His Royal Highness was 'admitted to the Freedom of the Fishmongers' Co[mpany]...the oath administered to him in their Hall on this book. A copy of the Freedom was presented in a Gold Box.'

Unfortunately, some honours recognizing the Prince's position were complicated by the rankling issue of royal precedence that failed to vanish and which Victoria and Albert felt they could not ignore. Both were furious that August when, at a banquet given for Victoria by the dowager queen, Adelaide, the Duchess of Cambridge – before her marriage only a Serene Highness herself, as the third daughter of the Landgrave of Hesse-Cassel – remained seated when Albert's health was toasted. The Queen retaliated at her next ball, when no Cambridge was invited – a marked public insult. Then Albert was invited to receive the Freedom of the City of London, the ceremony to be followed by a banquet at the Guildhall. The venison and turtle soup, the Lord Mayor promised, 'would be such as to startle the company'. But the Duke of Cambridge was present, and rather than, by protocol, sit next to him, Albert announced that he could not remain for dinner because of the illness of the Queen's aunt, the Princess Augusta. (She died on 22 September, a month later.)

Augusta, the Duke observed loudly, was his own sister, and he had heard no news so urgent. If he could stay, the Prince could also. But Albert left anyway, which meant that the Duke had to reply to the toast to Albert, the absentee that the company had assembled to honour. That the illustrious Prince could not remain, the Duke declared, was everyone's disappointment, but he thought that all would understand the validity of His Royal Highness's excuse. 'The Prince had lately married a very fine girl, and they were somehow or other very fond of each other's society.' There was loud cheering. Then the Duke added broadly that he thought that no one present would deny the Prince credit for his 'performances' to date – a smirking reference to Victoria's pregnancy that provoked more laughter and cheers.

The Queen read, to her outrage, an account of her uncle's response in the newspapers the next day. Someone had fed it to the press. Her relatives, Victoria later told her eldest daughter, 'behaved shockingly to dearest Papa. . . . I was always in a state of feud about it.' Still, the elderly dukes of the Blood Royal were taken less and less seriously. As was the Baroness Lehzen. When Parliament was to be formally closed for the session that August, Albert boasted to his brother, 'In spite of Lehzen and the Master of the Horse, I shall drive *with* Victoria in a carriage to the House of Lords, and sit beside her, on a throne especially built for me. As Lord Albemarle will not feed all the horses sent by the Shah of Persia, Imam of Muskat, Princes in India, etc.,* Arabian, Persian and Indian horses (which cannot be ridden) at his expense, I induced Victoria to make me a present of them. So I will have a stud at Windsor. V. will give me the money to keep them and I shall have the sole control over them.'

As Victoria's pregnancy advanced, Albert's control of other aspects of their lives was enhanced. At a Privy Council meeting on 11 September at Windsor, the Queen introduced Albert, implying an active role for him now that the Regency Bill had afforded him status, and Palmerston began to receive letter after letter from the Prince on the subject of confronting French ambitions in Syria and Egypt. He began to look into the ways in which Lehzen ran the Household, and the Queen's life. And an apparent prudery began to take hold at Court that observers attributed to the Prince's rigid imported morals. Yet Albert had brought with him from Germany only a distaste for what he saw, which coincided with the expansion of Wesleyan Methodism in Britain. 'Nobody is gay now', Melbourne had mourned to Victoria in the year of her accession; 'they are so religious'.

---

* Wedding presents to the pair. Albemarle, Master of the Horse, was a Whig appointment.

Evangelical religion emphasized religious revival, but also seriousness of behaviour, respectability and the work ethic. Since the human
body was the temple of the spirit, looseness in sexuality was deplored
despite the awareness that economic need drove women into prosti-
tution, couples into irregular unions and children into working
naked deep in dark sweltering mines. Methodism was especially
tainted among the upper classes by its attractiveness to the lower
ones, but that appeal was strong, and the first Reform Parliaments
included more and more of its adherents and sympathizers. Albert's
un-English seriousness and strictness had found its time and place as
the balance of political power was beginning to shift away from the
ruling classes of the Regency.

People welcome at Court began to bear different histories than
heretofore. The Prince's prudery, if it was that, represented what he
wanted the public's perception of Victoria's court to be. He knew
what it had been during the raffish reign of the Queen's uncles. And
he knew the sleazy sexuality of the Coburg court under his own father,
and what had happened to his mother – and what appeared to be
happening to his brother. Albert had only to look around him every
day for evidence of what he had escaped. Soon he would have with
him not only Isaac Cart, who had been with him since childhood, but
a second personal attendant, Rudolf Löhlein. The Queen later
described Löhlein as the son of a forester of Füllbach, near Coburg,
but her courtiers were convinced that he was a by-blow of Duke
Ernest, whom he closely resembled. If so, Albert had imported his
unacknowledged half-brother. He appealed to his brother to marry,
and soon, without regard for the prestige or wealth of the bride –
although the elder Ernest was seeking a match with the Grand
Duchess Olga of Russia, rank and riches having more to do with the
choice than religion or nation. Such an elevated alliance, the younger
Ernest suggested, envying his brother's new prestige, would mean that
he would hardly feel his marital chains.

'Chains you will have to bear in any case,' Albert warned, 'and it will
certainly be good for you . . . The heavier and tighter they are, the better
for you. A married couple must be chained to one another, be inseparable, and they must live only for one another. I wish you could be here
and see in us a couple united in love and unanimity.' Each, he said with
evident pride, gave up things for the other, and he was ready 'to give up

everything for her sake'. But, he insisted, he was not leading 'a submissive life'. He was, in the marriage, in 'the lawful position of the man'.

Ernest was offended and so was their father, as both their responses made clear. Albert, his junior, was issuing orders to the heir to the duchy, and even advising him – although Ernest had brought up the subject – not to move from Coburg to more sophisticated Gotha when his military apprenticeship to Saxony ended. Aside from the expense of 'building new houses', Albert explained, 'I should consider it a sin'. Meanwhile he recognized that both his father and brother wanted hand-outs from their rich relative, who, despite Parliament's penurious-ness, had access to Victoria's capacious purse.

Victoria's love, however angry she was with herself for her pregnancy, was at least as capacious. She and Albert, whatever their lack of sexual experience, had quickly discovered a compatibility between the sheets that would last. Despite carping from outsiders about the Queen's plainness, Albert would write to his brother (22 August 1840), 'Victoria has changed much to her advantage. . . . She was lovely to look at yesterday at dinner. She had a very low-necked dress, with a bunch of roses at her breast which was swelling up from her dress.' Some of the change was the radiance of her despised pregnancy, and the bust enlargement which resulted, but Albert's pleasure was obvious.

Whether the press guessed from the results, or learned from Court gossip, the assumption was that Victoria, at least, had a Hanoverian libido. Circumstances failed to inhibit it. The Queen required a maid or dresser to sleep nightly on a sofa outside her bedroom. 'I never do otherwise', she later confided to her eldest daughter, ' . . . wherever I go – even if Papa is with me.' Further, she confessed, Albert, who was always as cold as Victoria was warm, slept 'in long white drawers, which enclosed his feet, as well as his legs, like the sleeping suits worn by small babies'. Whatever the conjunction of opposites, a published rhyme early in the marriage suggested only marital bliss, with the royal pair sipping nightcaps

> Before, like honest man and wife,
> Withdrawing into private life,
> Or, in the phrase we often hear,
> Retiring into *Bed*-fordshire . . .

With her pregnancy uneventful and Parliament prorogued, the couple remained at Windsor as long as Victoria's doctors permitted, returning on 13 November to what Albert called 'the smoky town'. Labour began in the morning darkness of 21 November, three weeks early, and lasted twelve less-than-difficult hours. The Queen remembered, forty-four years later, 'a dark, dull, windy, rainy day with smoking chimneys, and . . . Papa's great kindness and anxiety'. When Dr – later Sir Charles – Locock had first examined her and asked about her likely need for sedatives, she had insisted, 'I can bear pain as well as other people.' On his way out, he also asked Albert, who scoffed and predicted 'a great *Rompos*'.

With a shifting population of Cabinet ministers and clergy in the next room as potential witnesses by tradition, Victoria was determined to be queenly to the end, and was. 'Oh, Madam,' the dignitaries could hear Locock say before the naked baby was brought out for their inspection, 'it is a Princess.'

'Never mind', said the Queen, 'the next will be a Prince.' But her husband wrote to his brother in Dresden, sheepishly, 'Albert, father of a daughter; you will laugh at me'. Both parents, Lord Clarendon wrote to Lord Granville in Paris, 'were much disappointed at not having a son . . . but what the country cares about is to have a life more, whether male or female, interposed between the succession and the King of Hanover'.

On one of Locock's visits after the delivery, the Queen asked whether Prince Albert might read to her. When the doctor objected that a novel would be too exciting in her condition, she explained, 'No, he would read to me the lessons for the day, and as he has done so ever since we were married, it would be particularly gratifying to me now.' In an age when religion permeated the home, from morning prayers to bedtime, Locock found no way to refuse.

For the celebratory banquet following the christening on 10 February 1841, Albert composed a chorale. After writing songs as a student – a '*Reiterlied*', a '*Winterreise*', and '*Abendruhe*', and more than a dozen others – and music for piano, organ and violin, he would find less time now for composition and produced little following his marriage. But his firstborn was something special: she remained alert during the ceremonies and her father concluded proudly that she was 'very intelligent and observing'.

From the beginning, Albert was as devoted to the Princess Royal as he was to the Queen, and a rapport would grow between them unlike that with any of the later children. But Albert's solicitude for his wife was tender beyond anything she could have expected, and as she indulged in the lassitude of postnatal recovery, which physicians then preferred to prolong, she became more and more dependent upon him than she had intended. As her pregnancy had progressed, she had approved setting up writing-tables side by side in Buckingham Palace, like those in use at Windsor, and from there Albert began sending almost daily notes to Melbourne, as well as Palmerston, usually on foreign questions. Mehmet Ali, Ottoman viceroy in Egypt, had used the death of the Sultan and the succession of his sixteen-year-old son, Abdul Mejid, to attempt to break away from Turkey, exacerbating great power rivalries in the Middle East. Albert argued for the politics of conciliation rather than confrontation with France and Russia. Melbourne and Palmerston did much as they wished, but were pulled back into more temperate language by the Prince's intervention. Carefully, however, Melbourne's messages went to Victoria, with reference to 'the Prince's observations'. More and more, even the letters in Victoria's hand would be based on Albert's 'observations'.

The Court returned to Windsor for Christmas, which was celebrated in German fashion. Gifts were placed on tables under small Christmas trees, with each table and tree, decorated with candles, sweetmeats, and cakes hung by ribbons and paper chains, intended for a different recipient. Introduced from Germany earlier in the century, credit for their popularity is sometimes given to Queen Adelaide, and even to George III's Queen Charlotte, who had set up a tree of yew branches at Windsor. But Albert imported small trees from Coburg, and turned the royal family's Christmases into semi-public events. The fashion caught on, popularized by the new illustrated papers.

Not intended as a Christmas present to Albert, but timed almost as such, was Albert's own key to the prized red boxes in which Cabinet papers were delivered. During the last weeks of Victoria's pregnancy he had handled all her business, and become, as Anson put it, 'in fact, tho' not in name, Her Majesty's Private Secretary'. Since authority gravitates to its user, Albert quickly took advantage of an incident several weeks before Christmas when 'the Boy Jones' was discovered lolling about in Buckingham Palace. Edmund Jones had climbed a wall and crept through a window, 'sat upon the throne', he said, 'saw the Queen and heard the Princess Royal squall'. Home Office interrogation revealed that he was seventeen, stunted in growth, and the son of a tailor in Cannon Row. A chronic intruder, he had been declared insane the first time, and discharged; this time he was sentenced to three months for vagabondage, after which he returned once more, and following three more months on the treadmill at Tothill Street he was sent to sea.

The royal couple had known little about the lax security that had encouraged the curiosity of 'Boy Jones' and an even earlier 'Boy Cotton'. Now, Albert had a reason to reform the slipshod administration of the palace. To accomplish that meant removing the stewardship reins that Lehzen had been accumulating from her hands, but Albert was determined to end the palace inefficiencies as well as the Baroness's powers. For both he needed some further pretext, and he began to look for one.

One area of the Queen's life he could begin to organize was the business of the Duchy of Cornwall, which furnished hereditary income in 1840 of £36,000. One-third of that, Albert discovered, disappeared in administrative costs. He began cutting expenses and raising revenues, furnishing the royal couple with more discretionary funds. He also began organizing the Queen's day, which before marriage had begun so late that much of it was wasted. They began to breakfast regularly at nine, then took a walk, and worked on incoming and outgoing correspondence immediately after. Relaxing after their business, they drew or etched together.

When at Windsor or at Buckingham Palace, they would lunch together at two, after which Victoria, often now accompanied by Albert, would meet with one or more of her Ministers, usually Melbourne. (When the Queen was at Windsor, 'Lord M.' usually lived there unless Parliament was sitting.) Then the royal couple would drive in the park in a pony phaeton, the Prince at the reins. (If the Prince was away on his own or the Queen's affairs, as became increasingly frequent, she went for a drive with her ladies-in-waiting, or her mother.) Dinner was at eight, usually with guests. Before or after dinner one often read to the other, Albert reading 'serious' works, Victoria reading fiction.

Sometimes they went over albums of their own drawings, or of engravings and etchings they had begun to purchase. The Prince's art interests had been quickly recognized in London, and later in the new year Peel would appoint him chairman of a royal commission (at first a select committee) 'to take into consideration the Promotion of the Fine Arts of this Country, in connexion with the Rebuilding of the Houses of Parliament'. At the studio of John Lucas, a portrait painter and engraver for whom Albert would sit, Elizabeth Barrett visited and talked, she wrote to her friend Miss Mitford, 'of Prince Albert & his talents', quoting Lucas as saying, 'If he had studied five years under Raffael, his remarks could not have been acuter.' Lucas, she added cattily, thought the Prince 'very handsome, & the Queen charmless if you except the pleasant countenance & youthful freshness'.

At Windsor during the holidays Albert received a letter informing him of his brother's 'severe illness' – a recurrence of a venereal infection, he realized. 'I am deeply distressed and grieved . . .' he wrote to Ernest on New Year's Day. 'I have to infer that it is a new outbreak of the same disease which you had here.' As a 'loving brother', he urged Ernest to give up thoughts of marriage until his health was restored, as 'to marry would be as immoral as dangerous . . . for you. If the worst should happen, you would deprive your wife of her health and honour.' Further, he might sire 'a sick heir'. Neither prudery nor shame got in the way of Albert's candour. 'For God's sake,' he appealed, 'do not trifle with matters which are so sacred.'

Returning to Buckingham Palace early in January for the resumption of Parliamentary business, the royal couple learned of a controversy about them in Paris that had already reached London – yet which afterwards vanished from history. Lord Granville, Palmerston's envoy to France, had objected to a farce due to open on 9 January at the Théâtre de Renaissance, *Il était une fois un roi et une reine* – 'Once upon a time there was a king and queen'. Rejected seven times by the Board of Censorship of the Department of Fine Arts, it had been finally approved for performance in 'mutilated' form (according to the Paris press). The author, Léon Gozlan, was a novelist whose only previous play had been a failure. His new work was set in the English court, and Granville objected vigorously to its alleged slanders on Victoria and Albert, who according to the play was 'a husband who is not a king'.

Granville's charges of questionable references to the Crown had been lodged before, and the sanctioned text allegedly contained no identification of the rulers or nation, yet the two principal characters were still in positions equivalent to that of Queen and husband. On the day before the opening, with handbills distributed and posted, the censorship office learned that political radicals, many of them students, planned to fill the theatre, cheer every reference that could be construed as anti-English (as Palmerston's policies were considered hostile to French interests), then exit toward the British embassy, where they intended to break all the windows. Guizot, now Minister of the Interior, consulted with King Louis-Philippe and decided against risking a rupture with London. At four o'clock on the afternoon of the ninth, a few hours prior to performance, a police commissioner with his deputies ordered the playbill removed and replaced with an *affiche* reading '*Relâche par ordre*'.

The opposition French press was apopleptic about the slight 'to the honour of France'. *The Times* responded with an attack on the mob spirit of Paris, and praised the French government's 'desire not to subject a young Queen and the Prince her consort to allusions, and perhaps to ridicule'. Although rebuffed, Gozlan briefly became a local hero. Prudently, some months later, he transferred his locale to Sweden and on 24 December 1842, the play began a run of sixty performances, after which it was never heard of again.

A month to the day after the suppression of Gozlan's farce, Albert had a more local embarrassment. Winter temperatures had been bitter, and the pond in Buckingham Palace Gardens had frozen over enough to tempt him into ice skating, an accomplishment in which he took pride. 'I was making my way to Victoria, who was standing on the bank with one of her ladies,' Albert wrote to *Grossmutter* Gotha, '... when within some few yards of the bank I fell plump into the water, and had to swim for two or three minutes in order to get out. Victoria was the only person who had the presence of mind to lend me assistance; her lady [in waiting] being more occupied in screaming for help.' The shock from the chill was 'painful', as he had gone in over his head, but he had no more than a cold thereafter, which fortunately held off until after the christening of Victoria Adelaide Mary Louisa the next day.

Recognizing the imminence of political change and attempting to keep the Court above politics, Albert prevailed upon Victoria to invite the old Duke of Wellington, so recently considered her bitter enemy, to stand in at the christening for the designated godfather, Albert's ailing brother Ernest. 'The Duke is the best friend we have', Victoria assured herself in her journal. Albert was pleased that the infant's heraldic device would bear the Saxon arms 'in the middle of the English'.

The Saxon 'in the middle of the English' suggested something of Albert's trials with his adopted tongue, although he worked at it assiduously, writing his English in large, almost childish, hand to get it right. Carlyle, never happier than when dispraising someone, would refer to him (to Monckton Milnes on 9 March) as 'His Serene Highness the Incarnate-Solecism Prince Albert'. Almost at the same time Albert was writing to his brother to anticipate more christenings: 'It will interest you to hear that we are expecting an increase of our family. Victoria is not very happy about it.' The Queen had herself, as well as the state of medicine, to blame. Since the only respectable method of birth control was abstinence, the passionately fond young couple, both only twenty-one and even more ignorant of contraception than their doctors, had to take for granted that biological roulette was the mandate of Divine Providence. Artificial methods of birth control were condemned by the Church; and most nineteenth-century physicians who had the temerity to recommend the semi-abstinence of a rhythm method (would a Queen's gynaecologist have had the courage?) were confused about the menstrual cycle. Assuming that women were like animals in heat, many recommended against intercourse immediately after the menses and considered it safe in mid-month.

Seventeen years later Victoria would write to her eldest daughter, 'I had constantly for the first 2 years of my marriage...aches – and sufferings and miseries and plagues – which you must struggle against – and enjoyments etc. to give up – constant precautions to take...' It was 'the yoke of a married woman' that no queen who desired a spouse could evade – yet 'certainly it is unbounded happiness – if one has a husband one worships! It is a foretaste of heaven.' Albert's solicitude in her pain was enormous, leading the insensitive Stockmar to warn that the Prince could be setting an inescapable pattern of docility that would erode the powers already accruing to him. A change of ministry was inevitable, and Stockmar wanted Albert to gain by it as Victoria was certain to lose the personal relationship she had enjoyed with the avuncular Melbourne. 'Be you, therefore,' Stockmar enjoined Albert, 'the Constitutional genius of the Queen.'

Stockmar's letter from Coburg was dated 18 May. On 8 May, Albert had already sent Anson to Peel, who seemed certain to succeed Melbourne, to consult about the Queen's ladies. Sir Robert's 'doggedness', Melbourne had warned Anson, might cause the Bedchamber once more to become a battleground of principle. Albert felt that both sides had to yield. Without informing Victoria, he had Anson recommend a compromise whereby the Queen would announce the 'resignations' of her three most politically visible ladies.

A stickler for protocol, perhaps because he was born into the acquired purple of manufacturing wealth rather than the aristocracy of land, Peel countered that Albert should furnish him with a list of ladies acceptable to the Queen from whom he would make, and announce, a selection. The appointments were to be perceived as his. Victoria was furious. Peel could select and *she* would appoint. Seeing that his future in political accommodation required some sort of initial success, Albert sent Anson back. This time the Prince's formula was that Peel could inform the ladies of the Household as to the Queen's intentions for them, while Victoria would offer each personally the actual appointment. Consulting Wellington, Peel discovered a convert to the Crown. 'The truth is,' he wrote to Peel, 'that all I desire is to be as useful as possible to the Queen's service – to do anything, to go anywhere ... '

Although the compromise was settled, Melbourne's fall did not take place in May, or even in June. Division after division in the Commons went against the Whigs, with a vote of no confidence on 4 June – actually three in the morning on 5 June – failing by only one vote. Change was certain, however, and both Albert and Peel understood that they would get along but that it would take Albert to bring along the Queen.

As the elections approached to which Melbourne looked forward as his only hope of remaining in office, the Queen agreed to a round of Whig country house visits to help prop up the party's chances. Unhappily, Albert accompanied the Queen as was essential, visiting the Palmerstons at Pansanger and Woburn, and Melbourne at Brocket. Emily Palmerston described the multitude of Victoria's subjects looking on at Brocket (where she was also hostess for her brother) as 'an ampitheatre of heads' while Melbourne 'with his grey hair floating in the wind and the Queen on his arm ... walked her round the lawn'. Afterwards there was a dinner for thirty-six in the ballroom. 'Albert', she added in her letter to Elizabeth Huskisson, widow of the one-time Colonial Minister, 'is like the Prince of a fairy Tale, all perfection'.

*

The royal reception was very different when the Prince's turn at centre stage came at Oxford, where he was awarded an honorary doctorate. In the Sheldonian Theatre the Queen was cheered, as was Albert, but, Greville wrote, 'her Ministers, individually and collectively, were hissed and hooted with all the vehemence of Oxonian Toryism. Her Majesty said she thought it very disrespectful to the Prince to hiss her Ministers in his presence; but she must learn to bear with such manifestations of sentiment, and not fancy that these *Academici* will refrain from expressing their political opinions in any presence, even her own.'

Unused to the electoral system, Albert observed the turmoil with amusement. He had heard the Whig arguments for Free Trade and the rejectionist arguments for Protection from the conservative wing of the Tories, yet realized that seats in the House of Commons were being won less on the price of bread than on the price of a vote. He was less amused on learning that Lehzen, an outspoken Whig, had given £15,000 of the Queen's money to the party coffers. When Albert confided his horror to Melbourne, the Prime Minister shrugged off the complaint, observing that the few thousands were nothing compared to what George III used to spend on elections. Bribery and corruption were widespread; the Reform Bill, despite its merits, had also increased the number of new voters whose ballots candidates, inured to bribery, attempted to purchase, and many non-voters also expected something for their vocal support, something that Albert – and the Queen – did not realize when they were greeted at Ascot with prearranged cheers and loud cries of 'Melbourne for ever!' Even so, it was clear that the Whigs were unpopular and that the Tories would get their chance.

Victoria dissolved Parliament on 29 June. The Whigs were smashed, and despite second thoughts about resignation by the Duchess of Bedford, she and two other ladies were replaced. Victoria's initial feeling (according to Anson) 'that she had been hurried and compromised by the Prince and Lord Melbourne', was quickly over, but not before a scene that Anson watched with dismay. 'The Q[ueen] ... burst into tears which could not be stopped for some time – & said that she could Not force the Duchess [of Bedford] to resign – they could not make her do that & she would never appoint any Tories...'

'The P[rince] said, in this moment all shd be done to quiet you & get you over difficulties & it was shameful on the part of those who attempted to convert her mind...'

Albert was clearly accusing Lehzen, behind the scenes, but the Queen's summons to Peel on the evening of 29 August was Whiggishly frigid. Still, he understood that Albert and Anson would prevent the embarrassments of 1839. At half past twelve noon the next day, the new Prime Minister kissed hands and spent twenty minutes assuring Victoria that he was anxious to do whatever was agreeable to her, and would not even press ministerial recommendations upon her on their first interview.

The three principal Whig ladies at Court had already offered their resignations, as recommended; and Albert, the Queen learned, had asked his two leading Household officers, both Whigs, to resign. Anson remained the intermediary for Albert in choreographing mutual concessions, and on 1 September Peel told Lord Ellenborough, who was riding in a carriage with him from the railway station at Slough, 'Prince Albert is altogether with us'. It was already evident, even outside officialdom, that the Prince, who had just passed his twenty-second birthday, was an assiduous planner and did not intend to be a political cipher. Writing to the actor William Macready on 24 August, Charles Dickens observed of one of their friends that he had 'gone into his case as if he were Prince Albert, laying down all manner of elaborate projects...' For better or worse, Albert had established that reputation.

Victoria had remained prone to depression through her entire second pregnancy. She was in her seventh month when she had to preside over the ceremonial changes of the ministries on 4 September 1841. The Privy Council was summoned to Claremont, Leopold's former estate near Esher, where Victoria and Albert had retreated for privacy. Greville, the Council's secretary, found the Queen there 'with the Prince, and the table covered with bags and boxes' – the seals of office just relinquished by outgoing Whig ministers, and their dispatch boxes. Recognizing Victoria's emotional and physical burdens, the new Tory appointees praised her dignity and fairness in the proceedings. 'This struck me', Greville wrote, 'as a great effort of self-control, and remarkable in so young a woman. Taking leave is always a melancholy ceremony, and [those] whom she thinks are attached to her, together with all the reminiscences and reflections which the occasion was calculated to excite, might well have elicited uncontrollable emotions.' Peel told Greville that she had behaved 'perfectly'.

What Peel did not know at the time was that at her emotional parting with Melbourne she had asked him, unwisely, to continue contacts. Their emotional bonds were too great to be severed at once, and it would require both Anson and Stockmar to ensure that Melbourne kept his political distance. Sensing his opening, Albert also urged Melbourne, through Anson, to suggest to the Queen that her husband be her future guide on political questions. Melbourne duly wrote that he had 'formed the highest opinion of HRH's judgement, temper and discretion', and that the Queen 'cannot do better than have recourse to it'. That, too, was a changing of the guard as great as the ministerial one, and it would be even longer-lasting. While the Queen was lying-in for the birth of her second child, Peel sent Albert nightly reports of debates in the Commons and discussions in the Cabinet. A year earlier, Albert had not even had his own key to the boxes.

# VI

## *Taking Hold*

### *1841–1843*

A 'PRIVATE LETTER' FROM Hanover, *Punch* joked, revealed that 'precisely at twelve minutes to eleven in the morning on the ninth of the present November, his majesty King Ernest was suddenly attacked by a violent fit of blue devils. All the court doctors were immediately summoned, and as immediately dismissed, by his Majesty, who sent for the Wizard of the North (recently appointed royal astrologer), to divine the mysterious cause of this so sudden melancholy. In a trice the mystery was solved – Queen Victoria "was happily delivered of a prince"!...There are now two cradles between the Crown of England and the White Horse of Hanover. We have a Prince of Wales!'

'From some crotchet of Prince Albert's,' Greville complained, 'they put off sending intelligence of her Majesty being in labour till so late that several of the Dignitaries, whose duty it was to assist at the birth, arrived after the event had occurred, particularly the Archbishop of Canterbury and the Lord President of the Council.' The actual reason was a series of earlier false alarms, but it was now predictable that the young father of the newborn prince would be blamed for anything that made bureaucrats unhappy. Yet it did not displease male officialdom that Albert had accrued authority as Victoria had relinquished it to childbearing. The Queen's womanly role better suited her sex, and Albert was unexcitable and businesslike.

The Queen and Prince fitted the figurehead conception many in government had of post-Reform Bill constitutional monarchy. John Stuart Mill would visualize the system as one in which 'the so-called sovereign does not govern, ought not to govern, is not intended to govern; but must yet be held up to the nation, be addressed by the nation, and even address the nation, as if he or she did govern'. On the day of the birth of Albert Edward, the future Prince of Wales, the crowds that enthusiastically sang 'God Save the Queen' wherever Victoria's subjects gathered, were acclaiming a sovereign who reigned rather than ruled. But behind the royal façade Albert would seek a more influential activist role for the sovereign and, indirectly, for himself.

Recognizing that some powers required position and opportunity rather than parliamentary sanction, Albert acted for the Queen during her lying-in and even beyond the christening on 25 January. His relationship with Peel flowered, and the Prime Minister, eager to have the Palace friendly rather than frosty, accepted Albert almost as a surrogate son. They discussed German literature, which Peel admired, and the Prince presented him with a lavish new edition of the *Nibelungenlied*, warmly inscribed. They discussed Dutch paintings, and the state of the arts in England. They hunted for pheasant and hare in Windsor Great Park on mornings when the Prime Minister was in residence, Peel in his town clothes and with borrowed gun. And Peel and his foreign minister, Lord Aberdeen, condoned Albert's communications in the Queen's stead with Continental monarchs.

Once Parliament resumed its sittings in February 1842 Peel began sending Albert confidential memoranda on proposed amendments to the Poor Law of 1834 that had established coldly economical workhouses separating even spouses by sex, and to the Corn Laws establishing import duties on grain, which the Prime Minister, despite fierce opposition from die-hard Tories, hoped to eliminate. If the Prince were interested, he would continue the practice. Albert, it appeared, was interested in everything. He began signing his letters to Peel 'always, my dearest Sir Robert'. The tall, commanding, workaholic Peel was something new for Albert – an English father-figure who sought the role and fitted the Prince's needs. Rarely able to expose his emotions – Irish MP Daniel O'Connell described Peel's forced smile as 'like the silver plate on a coffin' – he was honest, honourable and businesslike, with an encyclopaedic grasp of past legislation and parliamentary studies. Between Peel and the Prince the smiles were genuine.

With assistance in drafting responses from Anson and Stockmar, who shuttled between Coburg and London, Albert put further distance between Victoria and her out-of-office father-figure, the amiable Melbourne. The Duke of Kent had died when his daughter was eight months old. Only Leopold had replaced him – until Melbourne. A quiet contest for power was inherent in the move, but Albert insisted that continued political contacts with the former Whig leader might injure her relations with the Tory ministry. Both Melbourne and the Queen were peeved, but the former Prime Minister kept to friendly gossip and Peel was appreciative.

Claiming postpartum fatigue, Victoria argued that some levées could be conducted with Albert and without her, but the experiment was not a success. However curious her subjects were about Albert, they wanted only to *see* him, but to kiss the ringed hand of their Queen. Actress Fanny Kemble recalled a drawing-room reception in 1842 at which the Queen presided, and where, 'in great uncertainty of mind' as to whether she should look at Victoria, she lowered her eyes and kissed 'a soft white hand which I believe was hers'. Eyes still down 'I saw a pair of very handsome legs, in very fine silk stockings, which I am convinced were not hers, but am inclined to attribute to Prince Albert'.

Victoria would suffer from more than postpartum fatigue following each accouchement. As her pregnancies would advance, and into the months following each birth, she resented her condition, however unavoidable, and would lash out at her husband, who could no more prevent the circumstances than could the Queen. And their turbulent exchanges could not be private where servants were ubiquitous. Pained, Albert learned to respond quietly, in handwritten notes.

Taking control in the Household became easier for Albert after the birth of the Prince of Wales. Without consulting Lehzen, he appointed Lady Lyttelton in April to take charge of the royal children. Born Lady Sarah Spencer, she was well connected and a widowed mother of five. Her appointment accelerated the erosion of Lehzen's domination, which the Baroness herself hurried on by proposing that she oversee the Duchy of Cornwall revenues, usually linked with the Prince of Wales, and that nursery expenses be drawn from them. Since Anson's authority came in part from being comptroller of the Duchy's revenues, he and Albert perceived Lehzen's bid as a test of strength.

Whatever the Baroness's credits with the Queen, and they were many and well-earned, she had outlived her role. Victoria, in her lack of experience, had depended upon Lehzen. Although the Baroness had

CUPID OUT OF PLACE.

Punch *in 1843 observing Albert's apparent lack of any employment but his siring of the succession.*

no official title, and was innocent of administrative detail, she had been given a proliferation of duties and responsibilities. While her interests were focused upon the Queen, sinecures and perquisites flourished. Courtiers, from titled officials to humble attendants, lived and dined on Victoria's purse; tradesmen furnished supplies that went elsewhere than Buckingham Palace or Windsor; and horses and carriages were ordered by anyone willing to sign someone else's name. While few of the figures presented for inspection were verifiable, no one had ever been concerned about that before.

Unsophisticated about the costs of anything, Victoria entertained often and lavishly, and gave expensive gifts. In 1839 alone – her last year without Albert – she spent £34,000 from her Privy Purse on pensions and charities, and £600 on her box at the opera. In the first three months of 1840, when royal guests had come for the wedding, inflating normal expenditures, 24,600 dinners were served at Buckingham Palace. At Windsor Castle the year before, 113,000 dinners were served, not including the grand ball suppers. Even when the Court was not in residence, more than a dozen large joints of meat were roasted daily for the servants permanently present. The statistics also included people who elected to dine at the Queen's expense because it was easy to do. Many of the meals billed for may have never been served, with someone pocketing the funds. The christening of the Prince of Wales cost the Queen's purse £4,991 16s. 5d. Yet this was an age when the pound sterling was so sturdy and inflation so low that a shilling – a twentieth of a pound – could purchase a dinner, and a penny – a twelfth of a shilling – could post a letter.

Laurence Housman's stage-Albert explains to Victoria, 'One of the things I discovered was that anything once ordered always goes on being ordered. The thing is sent in and paid for, but it is not used.' It was very nearly like that. In the palaces, Albert observed, hundreds of candles were placed in chandeliers and candelabras daily, then replaced even if never lighted. He discovered – the Queen had never noticed – that since Queen Anne's day the privilege of selling 'Palace ends' for pocket money had been that of the servants. Similar sinecures existed at Windsor Castle, such as the thirty-five shillings that a half-pay officer received annually for 'Red Room wine' meant for a captain of the guard last on duty in the reign of George III.

Getting Court management under control would be a slow process. Too many absentee authorities officially oversaw such matters. In Lehzen, however, Albert had someone to blame for at least part of the chaos. He had already enlisted Stockmar to do research on the problems and possible solutions, all of which would make many more besides the Baroness unhappy. Still, consolidating administrative functions and powers, as much as he could within existing traditions and regulations, in his own hands and those of George Anson as his deputy, required pushing Lehzen aside. Since all her powers were informal, Albert needed only Victoria's acquiescence. He confronted the Queen with a litany of Household waste and inefficiency detailed in Stockmar's memorandum. When Victoria refused to see Lehzen as obsolete, or the relationship with the Baroness as dangerous, Albert explained to Stockmar, Victoria 'has never been away from her, and like a very good pupil, [she] is accustomed to regard her governess as an oracle. Besides this, the unfortunate experience they went through together at Kensington had bound them still closer, and Lehzen, in her madness, has made Victoria believe that whatever good qualities she possesses are due to her.' He saw 'the welfare of my children and Victoria's existence as sovereign' at stake if Lehzen remained, and through the first weeks of 1842 there were bitter words exchanged between husband and wife, each writing to Stockmar in Coburg as intermediary.

'Victoria is too hasty and passionate...' Albert explained. 'She will not hear me out but flies into a rage and overwhelms me with reproaches of...want of trust, ambition, envy, etc., etc. There are, therefore, two ways open to me: (1) to keep silence and go away (in which case I am like a schoolboy who has had a dressing down from his mother and goes off snubbed); (2) I can be still more violent (and then we have scenes...which I hate, because I am sorry for Victoria in her misery, besides which it undermines the peace of the home)...'

The Queen insisted to Stockmar that Albert exaggerated the Baroness's influence. 'I have often heard Albert own that everybody recognized Lehzen's services to me and my only wish is that she should have a quiet home in my house and see me sometimes...about papers and *toilette* for which she is the greatest use to me...Dearest Angel Albert, God only knows how I love him. His position is difficult, heaven knows, and we must do everything to make it easier.' In a later letter to Stockmar, on 20 January 1842, Victoria acknowledged that she was 'so passionate when spoken to', an impulse she feared was 'irremediable', and made her say 'cross and odious things which I don't myself believe and which I fear hurt A., but which he should not believe'. Their position was 'very different to any other married couples. A. is in my house and not I in his. – But I am ready to submit to his wishes as I love him so dearly.'

Submission came when the Princess Royal became seriously ill and Albert blamed 'Pussy's' condition on Victoria's toleration of Lehzen's mishandling of the nursery and Sir James Clark's continuing incompetence. Dr Clark, Albert told the Queen in a note, 'has mismanaged the child and poisoned her with calomel, and you have starved her. I shall have nothing more to do with it; take the child away and do as you like, and if she dies you will have it on your conscience.'

The war was over, although more battles would be fought – delaying actions by Lehzen. Had she made any conciliatory gestures toward Albert, she might have rescued her place in the palace. Instead, the Baroness discovered that her departure was the price of the Queen's future happiness. As with Peel and the ladies of the Court, Albert took the initiative when he saw his opportunity. By then, anticipating her expulsion, she had quietly passed on her responsibility to make copies of Victoria's outgoing correspondence in a letter-press to the Queen's loyal dresser, Marianne Skerret. The niece of Queen Charlotte's subtreasurer, she had entered Victoria's service in 1837, and would remain into 1862, largely writing letters to tradespeople.

On 25 July, Albert informed Victoria that Lehzen had decided to retire because of her health. Since the Baroness was a vigorous fifty-six, Victoria understood that it was a move 'for our & her best'. Lehzen was presented with a carriage and a pension of £800, an annual income which would enable her to live in comfort in Germany. At the end of September she slipped out of London without any farewells – a gesture to spare Victoria's tears – and went to Bückeburg, a quiet town west of Hanover. Lehzen's sister, with whom she intended to live, died unexpectedly three months later. The Baroness remained alone, in a house filled with royal memorabilia, until her own death at eighty-six, in 1870.

It was Lehzen, Albert claimed to Anson, who was responsible for the Queen's fears of intellectual inadequacy. She had overseen Victoria's education and had kept it at an inferior level. It was true that Victoria knew little about science and technology, Albert's chief passions, and was reluctant to bring them into her conversation. She knew more about art and music, interests he shared, but her tastes were rather conventional. She knew still more about history and politics, and understood their direct importance to her; but Albert saw that as only a beginning, and had set to work to become her Stockmar as well as her university. When she began to lean more and more on her husband's competencies, and later, when she would have to work alone, her ministers would confront a shrewd mind and a sharp writing style. At twenty-three, Victoria did not have some of the sophistication that might have been useful during country-house weekends, but she had survived her upbringing well. Further, few people would dominate her intellectually, if only because as Queen she could select her conversation topic or dismiss it.

Whatever the external frustrations in his own position, Albert could see growth in Victoria's grasp of her role, and could preen himself for having added a dimension to it. When Victoria was having her hair done, she read *Cornwallis on the Sacrament* or Guizot's *Révolution de l'Angleterre*. When Felix Mendelssohn came to England in June 1842 to conduct a performance of his new A minor (*Scottish*) Symphony, Victoria invited him and his wife Cécile to Buckingham Palace. On June 20, the composer, thirty-three but small and boyish under a mass of curly black hair, arrived to play for the royal couple, giving them a recital of his *Songs Without Words*. Afterwards, he and Cécile were taken to tea in the Grand Gallery. Before they left, Albert invited the Mendelssohns back the following Saturday so that Felix could try the palace organ; and he returned to play 'How Lovely Are the Messengers' from his *St Paul*, with Albert assisting with the stops.

The musical capacities of Victoria and Albert, Mendelssohn discovered, went beyond any social requirements. First, Albert played a chorale, 'by heart, with the pedals, so charmingly, clearly and correctly, that it would have done credit to any professional . . . and then all the music sheets going all over the floor, and being picked up by the Queen'.

Finding the pages she wanted, Victoria sang the lyrical '*Italien*', and then with Mendelssohn at the piano she tried his '*Lass dich nur*' – 'really quite faultlessly, and with charming feeling and expression', the composer wrote to his mother.

Then the Prince sang the '*Erntelied*', also from the *Pilgerspruch*, and finally Mendelssohn improvised happily on the piano from musical themes the couple recognized, then took his leave. It seems likely that in conversation the forthcoming royal trip to Scotland came up, for once back in Germany Mendelssohn wrote to the Queen to obtain her permission to dedicate his symphony, inspired by Scottish airs and dances, to her.

For royal travel, the Great Western Railway Company had designed a State carriage, short (even by 1840s standards) and ornate, with a small crown on the roof, its interior suggesting a small but opulent parlour. On 14 June 1842, the Queen and Prince made a trial journey in it, on the new line from Slough, near Windsor, to Paddington Station in London. The Queen announced herself 'quite charmed', but Albert worried about dangerously excessive speed – fifty miles an hour. (It was the year that J. M. W. Turner was painting his brilliantly impressionist 'Rain, Steam and Speed – the Great Western Railway'.)

For the trip to Scotland the Court proceeded on 29 August, in a convoy of carriages, to Slough, where they boarded a special train of engine, luggage tender, royal saloon, and two carriages for attendants and railway officials. (Twenty-seven royal horses and five carriages went on in advance.) The party would change to carriages at Paddington, crossing the city to Woolwich, where they embarked on the antiquated yacht *Royal George*.

The voyage was unpleasant. The *Royal George* had ferried the eight-months-pregnant Duchess of Kent from Calais to Dover in 1819 and was a cumbersome sailing ship in the new age of steam. Lurching to Scotland, it was towed by two steamers, and the uneven strain on the tow ropes, combined with the North Sea swells, left the royal party severely seasick. The planning had been meticulous, except for the obsolescence of the *Royal George*.

Yet the royal tour went well. 'The Highlands and the mountains are too beautiful', Victoria wrote to Melbourne from Taymouth on 10 September, 'and we *must* come back for longer another time.' (She was still corresponding with Melbourne, but neither Peel nor the Prince was concerned any more, as the letters now exchanged felicities and trivialities.) Besides, Peel had accompanied her on the voyage, and was working at winning her confidence. He was 'very nervous', Peel later told Greville, for the tour went through 'disturbed districts' where there had been unrest among the working class, but the outpouring of loyalty to the Crown impressed Victoria and Albert.

Scottish devotion remained high for the full fourteen days. Few English sovereigns spent any time north of the Tweed. For Scots, the Prince had been little more alien than the Queen. Accompanying newspapermen leaped at Albert's failure to comprehend the Scottish 'Ben' (from the Gaelic *beann*) for 'peak'. An equerry had observed that

Ben Lomond held his head particularly high during their visit. 'Benjamin who, did you say?' asked the Prince.

'Ben Lomond,' explained the equerry.

'Oh, Benjamin Lomond,' Albert insisted with studious Germanic formality

Recognizing, however, their forests that reminded Albert of Thuringia, the *Caledonian Mercury* predicted happily 'no long absence of the royal pair; and perhaps . . . the formation of a more permanent tie with Scotland'. It might have been initiated even then, as they refused to return on the heaving *Royal George*, waiting instead for the steamship *Trident*. A paddle-wheeled royal yacht would be ordered for future progresses by sea. 'Utilitarianism must prevail over the Romantic and Picturesque even in the case of Royal Voyages', Peel would explain to the Earl of Haddington at the Admiralty. 'Towing, after all, is but an ignoble process.' He had been aboard, and he knew.

Once back with their red boxes, the Queen and Prince recognized the extent of the foreign policy concerns that their domestic affairs had put out of mind. The press made much of disputes with the United States, a major unfriendly power, over Canada's border with Maine and over the Admiralty's right to search ships suspected of slave trading; and new British interventions in Afghanistan, India, Persia and China – where Hong Kong had been seized as a base for trade. From Paris, the government of the bourgeois monarch, Louis-Philippe, was intriguing in adjacent Spain, where England supported the weak regency of a child queen under her mother, Maria Cristina. The Regent, Victoria wrote to Aberdeen, 'is thoroughly attached to England'. That would always be the index to her policies. After reading a draft of a message to her ambassador in Portugal, she returned it to Aberdeen with the suggestion 'to *soften* the words under which she has drawn a pencil line'. The matter was not as important as the conciliatory intent and the continuing intervention with her ministers. It made no difference that Albert may have drafted the original of a memorandum that Victoria then rewrote in her own hand. It was in the Queen's name that both then insisted on being informed, and on making their views known.

Among Albert's appointments, arranged by Peel, was to preside over the committee to oversee the internal decoration of the new Houses of Parliament. Such chairmanships were usually honorific, but the Prince went to the meetings, Lady Holland wrote on 19 April, and 'shews not only taste but considerable knowledge. One great question is how the walls are to be treated. Fresco paintings are proposed.' The subjects suggested were incidents from British history and from works by major poets, and when Milton was named, Albert turned to Lord John Russell, a widower who had recently remarried, asking, 'Perhaps you would approve of passages from *Paradise Regained*?' Lady Holland was impressed. 'This was very well for a Royal joke, & in a foreigner.'

Three weeks later, Albert presided over the annual dinner of the Literary Fund, his willingness surprising Irish poet Tom Moore, who observed in his journal, 'this is indeed meeting the spirit of the times more than half-way – the King-Consort taking the chair at a Free-Mason* Tavern Dinner!' On 11 May Albert duly arrived, and his remarks, Moore noted, 'were delivered with much grace and in what the ladies call "very pretty English".' Washington Irving, a London Yankee, returned the company's thanks, and Scottish poet Tom Campbell, doddering at sixty-six, followed with an oration, Moore noted, that broke down 'from sheer tipsiness in the middle...' Yet it was a 'grand show', and everyone left late, in pelting rain.

The next day promised a more stately occasion. 'Your *fête* I believe', King Leopold would write to his niece, was 'probably one of the most splendid *ever* given. There is hardly a country where so much magnificence exists; Austria has some of the means, but the Court is not elegant from its nature.' Even the most high-minded intentions can have contrary results, however, and the Plantagenet Ball on 12 May was a painful example. Since Sir Robert Peel had emerged from a wealthy cotton-spinning family in the Midlands, his background had helped focus the royal couple's minds on the vast and crucial English textile industry, then beset by foreign competition and falling demand. Why not, Victoria and Albert thought, create what would be described more than a century later as a 'media event' to focus attention upon English goods? Specifically, they had the Spitalfields silk-weavers in mind in planning a ball in fourteenth-century guise, and after some research they determined to dress as Edward III and Queen Philippa, in costumes copied from their effigies in Westminster Abbey. Intended as a

---

* The name of the tavern.

tribute to English history as well as to domestic industry, the ball fell victim to a practical joke.

Richard Monckton Milnes sent the *Morning Chronicle* what he purported was the text of a debate in the Chamber of Deputies in Paris about the intentions of the *bal masqué* to reawaken 'the long-buried griefs of France' about their defeats by the English at Crécy, Poitiers and Calais. The Home Secretary rushed to Sir Robert Peel, crying, 'There's the devil to pay in France about this foolish ball!' And in Paris a newspaper suggested holding a similar ball at which the duc d'Orléans should attend, costumed as William the Conqueror.

Controversy increased interest in the ball but twisted its focus. The display of the Queen's gown in Hanover Square drew crowds to gaze at its magnificence, but also caused London newspapers to decry the extravagance at a time when the unemployed were hungry. *Punch* published verses in which aristocratic 'revellers', in 'purple dress'd', were contrasted with the poor, whose 'only swathing was The cere-cloth of the dead.' Instead of promoting the weaving industry, the Plantagenet Ball created discord, but the Queen stubbornly commissioned Edwin Landseer to paint her and Albert in their regalia. By a stroke of good luck, it was only days later that John Francis tried to assassinate them; the attempt stirred a new wave of public good feeling. The royal pair would regularly ride the roller-coaster of rejection and acclaim.

On 29 May, they had been shot at again while out in an open carriage near Buckingham Palace. When the gunman was not apprehended, Victoria worried over being 'shut up for days' because of the threat of a renewed attempt. Such fears were not empty. Peel's private secretary, Edmund Drummond, had been killed early in 1843 by a gunman who thought he had shot Peel. Some shootings were the work of political radicals targeting a scapegoat for hard times; others were copycat crimes committed by the mentally deranged. Attacks on political figures had been a hazard of office since Spencer Perceval, the Prime Minister who was the younger William Pitt's successor, was assassinated in 1812.

As if nothing had happened, the royal couple drove out again the next afternoon, this time without a lady-in-waiting but with their usual 'gentlemen', to try to draw the gunman's fire. 'You may imagine', Albert wrote to his father, 'that our minds were not very easy. We looked behind every tree, and I cast my eyes round in search of the rascal's face.' From five paces, Francis fired again and missed; this time he was arrested. (John Francis was condemned to death; then, on 1 July 1842, hardly a month after the incidents, he was reprieved.) Two days later, John William Bean, a stunted young man barely four feet tall, fired a pistol at the Queen. When it proved to be loaded with more tobacco than gunpowder, he was released as insane. The public applauded the royal couple's courage. A later age may marvel at their youthful folly. The Queen's birthday had just passed. She had already reigned for nearly five years, and was just twenty-three. Albert was still twenty-two.

The Prince's responsibilities were staggering for a young and inexperienced man, and his status was only what he could make of it. Fortunately for Victoria, he submerged much of his ego in tireless work behind the scenes to extricate her from the intermittent despair that had overtaken her euphoric first years as Queen. The Bedchamber imbroglio, the battles over Conroy, the Lady Flora embarrassment, the defeats over Albert's position and stipend, the loss of Melbourne, the expulsion of Lehzen, the unwanted pregnancies (with fear of more), had proved Victoria to be less than she seemed. With her ministers she was assured; in her correspondence she was confident; at Court ceremonials she was queenly. Yet Anson had already written at Christmas 1841 that 'Her Majesty interested herself less and less about politics' – because, he knew, Albert was discreetly maintaining the monarchy's business while Victoria struggled through a prolonged depression about which few were aware.

Albert bore his matrimonial trials with patience and grace, but he realized that if he did not assert himself as husband, Victoria's Hanoverian hauteur could unravel the monarchy as well as their marriage. Sallie Stevenson recalled a tedious evening at Buckingham Palace when, after she complimented Albert on his English and he said, realistically, 'Oh, no; it is just tolerable. I hope to improve', a group sat down at tables with the Queen to play whist, as usual. The Prince, who despised cards, sat separately with several others over four-handed chess, a curious nineteenth-century version of the game, played with partners and two sets of chessmen of different colours on a board of 160 squares. Finally the whist players rose, at the Queen's lead, to retire. Since the Prince 'was still intent on his game', the Queen 'leaned over to him and said in the softest, sweetest tones, "Albert!" But as His Royal Highness was too much employed to hear these soft and silvery accents, she repeated his name again and again, each time modulating her voice to greater earnestness, without losing any of its sweetness or tenderness. They do say, however, that, Queen though she be, he will not allow himself to be, in matrimonial phrase, "managed", – that when it is necessary, he resists her firmly, though kindly, and I think it is the best security for their future happiness.'

The painter E.M. Ward remembered one such moment when the Prince had gone to dine with the Council of the Royal Academy. Before dinner had proceeded very far, a messenger arrived to announce that the Queen desired Albert's presence at Buckingham Palace. The Prince nodded, and sent the messenger off. Soon a second messenger turned up with a message that the Queen was still waiting. Albert again nodded and waved the emissary off, only to find a third messenger at the door with a peremptory 'The Queen *commands* your Royal Highness's immediate return to the Palace'.

Dismissing the servant, the Prince remained with the company the rest of the evening. When Ward escorted him to his carriage he heard the coachman instructed to drive to Claremont, where, undoubtedly, Albert slept soundly while Victoria learned once more that even sovereigns made up only half of a marriage.

Albert's assertiveness and Lehzen's departure combined to bring stability to the marriage. It did not take Victoria long to recognize that. The night following Lehzen's exit, Victoria dreamed that the Baroness had come back to say good-bye, and the Queen awakened only to the reality of her loss. The next day she pulled down some of her old diaries, perhaps to recall Lehzen's part in her life, and came to a passage in 1839 where she had written of her 'happiness' with Melbourne. Now, with both Melbourne and Lehzen gone, she noted, '1st October. Wrote & looked over & corrected my old journals, which do not now awake very pleasant feelings. The life I led then was so artificial & superficial, & yet I thought I was happy. Thank God! I now know what real happiness means.'

On 13 December 1842, musing over the departure from their lives of Melbourne and Lehzen, Victoria and Albert wondered what had caused her 'unbounded admiration and affection' for Melbourne, which already was beginning to seem puzzling, given their satisfaction with each other and the rapid emergence of their confidence in Peel. In her journal, Victoria blamed her 'very warm feelings', which had nowhere else to go, but, she added, 'Albert thinks I worked myself up to what really became, at last, quite foolish.'

After the discordant notes recorded by Anson at the close of 1841, the ending of 1842 echoed with harmonies that Victoria and Albert hardly dared anticipate only a few months earlier. Even the Queen's less than welcome third pregnancy caused little alarm, and she could respond to Leopold's congratulations, 'My poor nerves, tho' thank God! nearly *quite* well *now* were so battered last time that I suffered a *whole year* from it...Still those nerves were incidentals and I am otherwise so strong and well, that if only my happiness continues I can bear anything else with pleasure.' At the same time – actually 27 December 1842 – Albert was writing to Stockmar, again in Coburg, that when he had left his parting words had been, 'When you really want me, write, and I will come.' Again Albert wanted him. Having managed 'a host of trifles', he wanted to deal with 'higher and graver things'.

It was no trifle, however, that Albert had furnished the nation in less than two years with two heirs to the throne and a third on the way. The fact lent itself to much punning in the press, especially after Albert, so *Bell's Life* reported, secured 'a large number of hares' from the Earl of Leicester's game preserve for his own at Norfolk Farm, 'to be let loose for breeding against the ensuing season'. *The Satirist* had Albert explain the acquisition to Victoria as a method to improve the breeding stock, and the Queen responds,

> If clever, thus, in the *hare* line,
> Why not, Albert, improve mine?

Determined 'to outstrip all competition', *Punch* forecast 'the Royal Family ten years hence', listing further, one a year, Augustus Leopold (Duke of Brompton), Sophia Maria, Elizabeth Leonora Jane, Henry Philip William (Duke of Lambeth), Mary Alexandrina, John Charles Peter (Duke of Chelsea), Timothy Theobald Thomas (Duke of Kensington), Matilda Seraphina, Richard Stephen (Duke of Deptford), Ethelred Guthrum (Duke of Battersea), and Seraphina Susan Cecilia. 'The above will be thought by any reasonable person enough for the present.'

Under Peel's ministry and with Lehzen's departure, and abetted additionally by royal confinements, Albert had become Victoria's unofficial private secretary and confidant, acquiring the informal power possessed by all efficient private secretaries. Everything the Queen was to see passed through his hands, and papers that went on to her usually bore comments and in some cases a draft reply, which she would revise, improving his English into something more Victorian. With Germanic thoroughness, he organized and filed documents, kept minutes of the Queen's conversations with ministers – which he attended – and gave each record a subject title in red ink. He read newspapers she would not see, cut out and marked articles for her attention, and prepared memoranda on topics he deemed of current or future importance. While simplifying her work, he was carefully forming Victoria's mind. He also hoped that the volumes of paperwork he was compiling would some day be of use as reference to the Prince of Wales, whom he viewed not as a pretty child just learning to walk, but as a future Albertine king.

Victoria's relationship with Peel, thanks to Albert and to her own maturity, was very different from that with Melbourne. She was less malleable, more inquiring, and willing to accept, or assent to, ministerial decisions once Peel had given her (and Albert) an opportunity to register their reactions. Theoretically unfettered by a written constitution, the Queen was nevertheless bound by the unwritten one of legislative precedent and the accumulating restraints of Cabinet democracy. She had the right to be informed – a right that she and Albert insisted upon – and to be heard. The sovereign, as the continuing instrument of government, possessed moral authority beyond that of elected officeholders, and technically, royal assent was needed for a host of government appointments and operations; nevertheless, an expanding electorate had left few initiatives to the monarch and little more than what Walter Bagehot would describe, in the later years of Victoria's reign, as the right to be consulted, the right to encourage, and the right to warn. Used shrewdly and cautiously, these 'rights' remained powers that could make the sovereign more than a symbol. And not only the sovereign but, in Victoria's case, her consort. However he effaced his traces from her official actions, she knew how much of her authority emanated from Albert's preparation and from his reshaping of her personality. She recorded in her journal how she once told the Prince, 'It is you who have entirely formed me.' The sweeping adverb was far from accurate, as she was too strong a personality to be so diminished, but Lord Brougham, once a Whig Lord Chancellor and a combative law reformer and parliamentary debater, recognized the reality and called her privately 'Queen Albertine'.

Henry Brougham had always been short on civility, and his acerbic aside was gossiped about until it got to Albert, who made sure that pamphlets which the noble lord had sent to Buckingham Palace – his miscellaneous publications alone would number 133 – were acknowledged cordially by both Queen and Prince. To Brougham's surprise, he was entrusted to carry some important Court documents to Paris – he travelled often to Nice, where he resided out of session. Albert explained to his brother, 'A little attention towards a man like Brougham is never thrown away.'

# VII

# The Goldfish-bowl

## 1843–1844

I N THE EARLY years of her reign, Victoria had enjoyed the goldfish-bowl of public attention in which she lived from morning to night. Royal levées and drawing-rooms remained the formal entrée into Society; levées held on an occasional morning to introduce gentlemen to Court, drawing-rooms in the afternoon for ladies. Rigid in dress and protocol, emotionally arid and only momentary in contact, the opportunities to brush one's lips upon the sovereign's hand and to exchange fleeting words with the Queen and Prince were, nevertheless, essential credentials for the privileged. Yet the first years with Albert saw a gradual withdrawal by the Queen, as much as was possible, into reserved hours of privacy. Since Albert was uncomfortable with the demands and preoccupations, as well as the denizens, of upper-class society, Victoria soon disappeared as the focal point of high life in London. As the monarchy became more bourgeois, in public as well as in private, it would lose much of its attractiveness to the aristocracy, traditionally a counterweight to the fickle public mood. Although peerages and perquisites remained in the sovereign's gift, in the diminished modern monarchy these were far more often her Prime Minister's selection than her own.

Change came at first imperceptibly. The most private part of their lives, apart from the large bed in which Victoria and Albert slept, was their morning. The romantic pair of writing-tables, side by side, had soon given way to the more efficient practice of using separate rooms. At the close of the morning's work the Prince would come to the Queen to discuss business, or they would read to each other from books as various as Hallam's *Constitutional History* and Scott's *The Lay of the Last Minstrel.*

After a luncheon, usually with guests, appointments often filled their afternoons. When there was leisure time, they still played piano duets, sketched, or painted. Despite Albert's seriousness in public, a result of his continued grappling with English language and manners, when he was with Victoria, as with his young children, he was playful and eager to shed restraints, crawling about the floor with Pussy and Bertie, delighting Victoria by making her an 'April Fool'. Only their walks and their guests would make the uninformative Court Circular offered to the press.

All of the Princess Lieven's visitors in Paris, she wrote to Lady Palmerston, reported 'that Prince Albert is exceedingly unpopular, the Queen also, and that both of them are extremely rude'. They were not so much rude as ungracious – the acquired arrogance that often came with elevated position. Whatever small courtesies Victoria had been taught as a child, protocol, even among the most privileged, limited her intimacies as Queen. Albert bore himself stiffly and shook hands awkwardly – more, perhaps, a sign of insecurity than *Hochmut.* At Court there were murmurs of resentment that the pair, for privacy, often exchanged comments in German. Albert even made comments in English that suggested unweaned loyalty to Germany. His 'No tailor in England can make a coat' caused as much outrage on one island as his 'The Poles are as little deserving of sympathy as the Irish' did on the other.

Early in the royal marriage the Boston artist G.P.A. Healy, newly married to an English girl, Louisa Phipps, and struggling to make a living, petitioned for permission to copy several portraits at Windsor for King Louis-Philippe. Healy was already at work before the much admired Sir Thomas Lawrence canvas of Earl Bathurst when the Queen and Albert happened upon the Yankee painter, only a few years their elder. Citizen of a socially egalitarian realm, he did not realize that what happened next was a result of a young sovereign's training that one spoke to the lower orders only indirectly. Wondering what Healy was doing, Victoria turned to her husband and said, 'Ask Mr Healy if – ', and the Prince put her questions to him 'as though he had been translating from a foreign tongue' and the Queen were somewhere in another dimension.

The interrogation over, she exclaimed, looking at Healy's copy rather than at him, 'It is extremely like!' – and with an almost imperceptible 'bend of the head' strode off with Albert, neither offering another word. 'I own', Healy recalled with indignation decades later, 'that my American blood boiled in my veins.' However unkind he thought the royal couple were, in their rarefied sphere they were merely being, as always, correct.

The public prudery by which they continued to protect the Court reflected a similar unworldliness, a rule-book reign. But Albert had little need to persuade Victoria that her Court, its recent past tarnished, had to earn respect by example and be impenetrable to scandal. 'On the Queen's accession,' Albert noted in a memorandum in 1852, 'Lord Melbourne had been very careless in his appointments, and great harm had resulted in the Court therefrom. Since her marriage I had insisted upon a closer line being drawn, and though Lord Melbourne had declared that "damned morality would undo us all", we had found great advantage in it and were determined to adhere to it.' Albert recorded an instance that year when Lord Derby, as Prime Minister, appealed unsuccessfully to have the wife of the new Lord Chancellor, Lord St Leonards, presented at Court 'although she had run away with him when he was still at school, and was now nearly seventy years old'. The transgression had occurred a half-century earlier, and the couple had since lived respectable lives, but the Queen 'said it would not do to receive her now...although society might do in that respect what it pleased; it was a principle at Court not to receive ladies whose characters are under stigma.'* With the most succulent gossip barred from conversation, Victoria ran out of things to say after family talk and empty pleasantries, even with her closest friend in the Household, the Duchess of Sutherland. Almost the only time the Prince came alive at

---

* The highest society deplored the strict morality as out of touch with reality. Even the cautious Albert was caught up in early 1843 as a sponsor of the Society for Ancient Music. The 'prudish ladies' who attended, Lady Holland (who did not) wrote acidly to her son in Naples in May 1843, 'are scandalized at the *immoral* life of [Giulia] Grisi; & have remonstrated with Prince Albert & [the] Duke of Wellington at her singing here. Can you believe such canting folly?' The soprano, then thirty-two, was famed for her roles in operas by Bellini and Donizetti, but would not marry tenor Giuseppe Mario, with whom she travelled and performed, until 1856. Yet the concert-going ladies kept to the double standard and deplored only his partner.

dinner was when he could discuss problems of drainage and heating, or the royal farm animals.

Dinner for Victoria and Albert, whether in London or at Windsor, was often solemn and seldom private. With rare exceptions, courtiers, however much they dreaded the duty, were present, even when no formal evening entertainment was scheduled. The cycle of ladies-in-waiting and gentlemen-in-waiting might change the names of the company at the table, but each was expected to remain in nominal attendance until the Queen and Consort elected to retire for the night. The Queen was, by protocol, last to arrive at dinner, Albert preceding her but first looking in at her preparations. Then came Victoria, often a quarter of an hour later, her doors opened by two courtiers who bowed deeply as the bejewelled Queen made her entrance with a nod or a smile at the Prince.

Dinner was over as soon as the Queen finished her portion. Since she was served first, and never toyed with her food, small talk could leave a guest hungry. The knowledgeable kept their remarks animated but brief. An intimate family meal with a rare German visitor was more relaxed, Victoria noting how her husband was 'always so merry' on such occasions. To King Frederick William IV of Prussia, who had come to London to be godfather at the Prince of Wales's christening, Albert wrote of the 'deep pleasure' he had felt when his 'old friend' from Bonn University, 'Fritz Strelitz' – then, as since, the Grand Duke of Mecklenburg-Strelitz – visited; and he was delighted to entertain 'Uncle Mensdorff' and talk over old times. When Frederick sent an aide to study English agricultural practice, Albert took him round the parks and public gardens, 'which we may say without exposing ourselves to a just reproach of Anglomania, are more numerous and more artistically designed and kept than anywhere else'. While happy to have another guest with whom to speak animatedly in German, it was clear that the Prince had taken an Englishman's pride in what they saw.

Sometimes during domestic, but rarely private, evenings, Albert was even diverted from chess to cards, one of his intellectual sacrifices to keep the Queen content; but by 1845, when the new American Minister, Edward Everett, visited, some subtle changes were apparent. Court elegance awed Everett, a Massachusetts politician already renowned at home as an orator, almost into speechlessness. At dinner Victoria chatted over 'a range of topics' with 'no stiffness or reserve', and in the drawing-room over coffee 'several quiet games – not cards – were played ... The Prince and I played a couple of games, also new to me, about halfway between chequers and chess. The Queen gave out ivory letters to put together into words.' Had the Minister encountered an early version of Scrabble, more than a century before it became an American board game? Whatever it was, it was 'not cards', and the Queen's intellectual world, under Albert's tutelage, was widening.

Indulging gentlemen to linger at table for hours over brandy, coffee and cigars, while the women had to leave, ended under the Prince. The tradition emphasized that though the Queen might be sovereign, she was a woman, and as such remained in second-class status to the men. *She* had to leave her own table. Albert abbreviated the routine, leaving the men as a signal to break up, then joining the ladies. Often he sang duets with Victoria, who preferred not to perform before gentlemen. Unless there were family members visiting, or a period of formal mourning intruded, evenings were lost to other pursuits, and Albert, a compulsive reader, had to catch up late into the night or very early in the morning.

At Windsor, where invitees had to come by carriage and by rail, and Buckingham Palace, which was easier of access for guests, it was expected that Victoria and Albert, despite her young family and now frequent pregnancies, would entertain daily, at least at dinner, which began, and ran, late. For privacy there was only Claremont, for another residence that the Queen acquired at her accession remained uninviting. Much as Victoria enjoyed the seaside, the Royal Pavilion at Brighton, so loved by George IV, was uncomfortable and orientally ornate – 'a strange Chinese looking thing, haunted by ghosts best forgotten'. The town had grown around it, leaving little privacy. 'I only see a little morsel of sea from one of my sitting room windows', she objected. When she and the Prince walked along the crowded seafront, they were 'mobbed by all the shopboys in the town, who ran and looked under my bonnet, treating us just as they do the Band, when it goes on parade'. A cat may look at a king, but pawing by mongrels was another matter. Before the year had ended, she and Albert had determined to investigate alternative places by the sea. The 1840s were a boom time for railway entrepreneurs. New trackage had enlarged the range of accessibility for royal travel within England and made it possible to think beyond Brighton. Albert promised to look into it.

Princess Alice Maud Mary was born on 25 April 1843. Parliament had convened two months earlier without the Queen, Dr Locock having forbidden her appearance 'in consequence of her present state'. Her speech from the throne, written by Peel and read for her, referred to the successes of military operations in China and in Afghanistan, the burgeoning of the Empire continuing until there would be places named or renamed after Victoria and Albert in every populated continent. As usual Albert filled the long gap in the Queen's calendar, including that of the lying-in. 'I have endless letters to write, to all parts of the world', he wrote to his brother. He also stood in the next week, in mourning habit he thought ridiculous – a wide-brimmed black hat and long black cloak that required a page to carry his trailing train – for the funeral of their uncle, the Duke of Sussex, whom both Queen and Prince had scorned almost as much as they did their other surviving uncles, Augustus of Cambridge, who played petty games of precedence with Albert, and Ernest of Cumberland, who remained troublesome even from Hanover.

With the death of the Duke of Sussex, the presidency of the Society of Arts fell vacant and brought to an end, an historian of the Society has written, 'a long period of happy-go-lucky Hanoverian buffoonery at its public ceremonies'. There was no requirement in its by-laws for a royal patron, but Albert had been a member since June 1840 and a vice-president since 19 April, a week before the Duke's death. A nomination committee composed of two dukes and a marquess asked him to accept the presidency, which he did on 31 May, presiding over its prize-giving ceremonies for the first time on 19 June. Since the Society's claimed interest was in arts in the broadest sense, including manufactures, it would have special importance for Albert in the later 1840s as it fostered annual shows that would lead to the Great Exhibition of 1851.

Always an activist in the organizations in which he consented to be involved, Albert appears to have promoted Act 6 & 7 Vict. c. 36, the Scientific Societies Act of 1843, which exempted from Rates – local property taxes – 'Land and Buildings occupied by Scientific and Literary Societies' if they were 'supported wholly or in part by annual voluntary contributions'. It became known as 'the Prince Consort's Act'.

Although the couple's uncle Ernest Augustus did not attend his brother's funeral on 6 May, four weeks later he turned up at the christening of Princess Alice, determined to make his visit across the

Channel as unpleasant as possible. Bent and thin, using his deafness to advantage where he could, the King deliberately materialized at the baptismal font, Victoria fumed to Leopold, '*just in time* to be *too late*'. He also made a scene over rights to the late Princess Charlotte's jewels, which Victoria wore although he insisted they belonged to the Crown of Hanover. She was 'loaded with my diamonds', he claimed to a friend.

The wedding in July of 'Fritz Strelitz' to Princess Augusta of Cambridge found the King of Hanover still in England seeking ways to air his rancour. He took his controversial seat in the House of Lords, claiming dual citizenship as Duke of Cumberland. At the wedding, Albert wrote to his brother, 'He insisted on having the place at the altar where we stood. He wanted to drive me away and, against all custom, he wanted to accompany Victoria . . . I was forced to give him a strong push and drive him down a few steps, where the First Master of Ceremonies led him out of the chapel.' After the wedding he pushed his way inside again to prevent Albert from signing the register with the Queen. 'He laid his fist on the book. We manœuvred round the table and Victoria had the book handed to her across the table. After a third trial to force Victoria to do what he commanded . . . he left the party in great wrath . . . and, happily, he fell over some stones in Kew and damaged some ribs.'

In August he was still in England, threatening to remain until the matter of Princess Charlotte's jewels was settled in his favour. Worried about the potential embarrassment, Peel queried Victoria for advice. 'The Queen is desirous that whatever is right should be done', she responded on 13 August, 1843, 'but [she] is strongly of opinion that the King of Hanover's threat (for such as it must be regarded) not to leave this country till the affair is decided upon should in *no way* influence the transaction, as it is quite immaterial whether the King stays here longer or not'. It was clearly a letter in which Albert had no hand.

A commission consisting of Lord Lyndhurst, Lord Langdale and Chief Justice Tindal was appointed to review the dispute. All three died before deciding the award. Only in 1857 was a settlement made, substantially in favour of Hanover. By then Victoria, who had come to the throne with little jewellery of her own, had acquired more than she needed.

In the final days of the King's visit, he proposed, according to Greville, that Albert take a walk with him. The Prince made some excuses that walking in city streets would expose them to inconvenience from the London crowds. 'Oh, never mind that', said Ernest. 'I was more unpopular than you are now, and used to walk about with perfect impunity.' With that story about, he could return to Hanover with some satisfaction.

On 24 August the Queen ceremonially closed the parliamentary session and readied herself for her state visit to King Louis-Philippe of France. It would be the first major test of the royal yacht, which Greville had inspected a few days before and pronounced 'luxuriously fitted up, but everything is sacrificed to the comfort of the Court, the whole ship's company being crammed into wretched dog-holes, officers included'. The Queen and Prince never noticed.

*En route*, the new steam paddle-wheeler docked at Falmouth, lowered the royal barge, and permitted Victoria and Albert to glide through a glassy sea amid a throng of nearly five hundred small boats out in greeting. On their return the mayors of Falmouth and Penryn, so the Quaker Barclay Fox wrote in his diary on 1 September, 'presented addresses from their respective corporations and inhabitants. It was explained... that [Tom Fox] the mayor of Falmouth was a Friend & therefore [his head] remained covered. The unfortunate H[enry] Lamb, mayor of Truro, in the excitement of the moment, lost his balance & tumbled into the water & as there was not time to hang him up to dry, he lost the chance of an introduction.'

For diplomatic reasons, Albert described the voyage across the Channel to France, in a letter to Frederick William IV of Prussia, as incidental to a longer voyage, now curtailed by events: 'Owing to Mr O'Connell's agitation' – the fiery nationalist Daniel O'Connell had been drawing excited crowds – 'we have been obliged to give up an earlier plan of visiting Ireland this autumn, and shall have to limit our cruise to the Channel.' The royal houses of Europe treated Louis-Philippe coldly because he was considered a usurper and because he had initially courted popularity as a bourgeois king, thus becoming a traitor to the class into which he had forced himself. Since the Queen's visit to France early in September 1843 was the first by an English sovereign since that of Henry VIII to a country often considered its hereditary enemy, enthusiastic receptions were worked up for Victoria at Le Tréport, *en route* to the Château d'Eu, and she was not displeased at having conveyed some semblance of respectability to the King. 'The

Emperor of Russia will be very much annoyed,' she wrote in her journal, 'but that is neither here nor there.'

For some reason Peel's ministers also looked upon a stop by the *Victoria and Albert* at Ostend as a matter of delicacy, although it was little more than a visit to a favourite uncle. Peel assured the Cabinet that it was not a matter of state, and 'they will be as reasonable as possible – but it does not do to thwart them. I know how to manage them – the way is to receive the proposals [for foreign travel] without objection and show a willingness to meet their desires. Then as difficulties appear they will grow cool.'

Aberdeen accompanied the royal party only to France, and had his own meetings with Guizot, an old friend, but the wily minister no longer had the confidence of the French Chamber, which could see change approaching. The King was old and failing, and the target of repeated assassination attempts – something with which Victoria and Albert had direct acquaintance. His eldest son and heir, the duc d'Orléans, immensely popular and liberal in his views, had been killed in a carriage accident the year before, prompting Alexandre Dumas to remark, 'God has removed the only obstacle which existed between the monarchy and the republic.' Louis-Philippe was emotionally grateful for the royal visit, but the French still resented the nation they saw personified by Palmerston. The King could make only cosmetic compromises on foreign policy with England that kept the chances of his remaining sons intact.

In an age when marriages among the propertied and the politically influential were often arranged for other reasons than affection, Albert had already seen many such alliances contracted by the ambitious Coburgs, including that with the Queen of Portugal. One of the most contentious issues with France was the desire of Louis-Philippe to bind Spain to France through the marriage of one of his sons, if not two of them, to the very young queen of Spain, Isabella II, then thirteen, and her younger sister, the Infanta. If Isabella – declared of age in 1843 despite her years – produced no heir, France would then have an insurance policy on power through her sister. While Albert was busy promoting the cause of his Coburg cousin Leopold, younger brother of the King Consort of Portugal, he and the Earl of Aberdeen were claiming that the marriages were a matter for the young queen and the Spanish people – a polite way to deflect France.

Neither side would win, because Spain and Portugal, once great colonial powers, were becoming too weak and divisive internally to matter, and a pre-emptive betrothal desired by Louis-Philippe for the duc de Monpensier would lead to nothing. There were also fears that Catholic France was once again intriguing to stir up Catholic Ireland. Intrigues, real and imagined, propelled some foreign affairs, and Albert would write to Peel about the King of France, 'Let us show that we are neither afraid of him nor prepared to be made dupes of.' There would be little reality to the Earl of Aberdeen's hopeful coinage, '*Entente Cordiale*', but Peel would insert a reference in the Queen's Speech from the Throne at the opening of the 1844 Parliament to the 'good understanding happily established'. In reality the two countries were rivals for influence not only on the Continent but as far away as the southern Pacific.

Since October was considered a good travelling month within England, Albert accepted an offer of an honorary LLD from Cambridge University to be awarded as part of a visit under the auspices of Trinity College. (On the return journey, the Queen and Prince were to be guests of Lord Chancellor Hardwicke at Wimpole and Lord De La Warr at Bourne.) Only the journey from Slough to Paddington was made by rail; the royal coach-and-six was met south of Cambridge, in the rain, by three thousand mounted yeomanry, all splashed with mud while accompanying the royal carriage along hedges and ditches for a dozen miles.

At the Cambridge Barrier a master-tailor among the horsemen halted the splattered honour guard with a bright red flag scissored from what Adam Sedgwick, Woodwardian Professor of Geology since 1818, described as 'the nether-garments of a livery-servant'. The October weather was gloomy despite the sunny forecast of the Astronomer Royal at Cambridge, but the pageantry of addresses and parades and inspections went on as scheduled, concluding late the next day.

It was already dark when, by torchlight, Victoria and Albert arrived at the steps of Trinity College Chapel, where, in the rain, a red carpet was unrolled. 'But alas! it was too short to serve its purpose; and while the Master and Seniors were conducting her across the Court, there was, for about half a second, a horrible conviction that the royal footsteps would be brought in most unseemly contact with the dusty pavement. But our undergraduates, who lined both sides of the path,

saved our credit by a Sir Walter Raleigh movement. They simultaneously pulled off their gowns, and spread them two or three deep
under the royal footsteps. We had a splendid Levée in the evening.'

The state bed for the overnight stay, Sedgwick added, had imperial
associations. In lieu of the usual featherbed cover was the former prayer-
rug 'of a great Mandarin, and [which] was snatched from the fingers of
his wife at the storming of Ningpo*... It was of bright scarlet, and
adorned with golden dragons. Their claws were symbolical of power,
and their wings of swiftness. ...'

On the Thursday morning of degree-granting, a sunny day, Victoria
and Albert visited the animal and fossil collections before the ceremonies
in the Senate House. Sedgwick, explaining as he preceded them, 'went
through every kind of backward movement to the admiration of all
beholders, having only once trodden on the hinder part of my cassock,
and never once having fallen on my retrogradations... In short had I
been a King Crab I could not have walked backwards much better.'

After the election-eve awkwardness of the reception at Oxford, the
enthusiasm at the sister university was a relief. Albert, observed Sedgwick,

> was looking well and happy. He has, you know, a noble figure, and
> he seemed well-fitted for his place beside the Queen. Far better than
> all this, it is plain that the royal pair love one another. They went
> together to every place she wished to see, and when she required
> some moments of rest he started on some expedition of his own, so
> that he lost not one moment from his entrance at our gates till the
> hour of his departure. As a proof of this I may tell you, that while the
> Queen was putting on her travelling dress just before she left us, he
> started on foot privately with our Master,† and went on to the top of
> King's College Chapel to have a parting bird's-eye view from its
> battlements. In short, everything went on brightly and gloriously
> from first to last, and the Queen and Prince have carried off all hearts
> with them from the highest to the lowest.

* Ning-po, now Yin-hsien, is south of Shanghai and south-east of Hang-chou.
† William Whewell, a recent royal appointment at the recommendation of Albert
and Peel.

Then, with the excitement over and the travelling carriage off to meet the train, the Woodwardian Professor of Geology returned to his 'ill-arranged papers, sometimes listening to the clock, at other times . . . to the melancholy murmur of my dirty tea-kettle'.

Once Parliament ceased sitting, the Queen and Prince as a sign of royal favour also visited Peel and his wife, Julia, at Drayton Manor, depoliticizing the occasion as part of a round of appearances at other great country houses. Much of the trip north was made by rail, in which travellers now reposed great confidence. While Victoria remained at Drayton, Albert entrained for Birmingham, the burgeoning industrial city and Radical stronghold where the mayor – a hosier – was an outspoken Chartist. The Prime Minister considered it as hazardous a setting for the Queen as Dublin, but Albert was impressed by the cheering throng of nearly a quarter of a million, the mayor assuring him of 'the devoted loyalty of the whole Chartist body'. It would match in memory Albert's experience soon after of the great conservatory at Chatsworth, although no paradox would ripen in the princely mind between the Radicalism of the urban industrial masses and the political conservatism of the bachelor squire of Chatsworth, whose income very likely exceeded that of all the labourers of Birmingham and went into the lavish ornamentation of his land-holdings.

The year before, the Queen and Prince had visited the Horticultural Show at Chiswick and lunched with the Duke of Devonshire, President of the Society, who wrote afterwards to Lady Granville, 'Prince Albert was charming, and may be as popular as he pleases.' A visit to Chatsworth, the ducal estate, was considered, but it took until December 1843 to arrange; however, the immensely wealthy grandee did not worry about winter weather. His gardens were indoors as well as outdoors.

The Duke met Victoria and Albert at Chesterfield station with a coach and six, and eight outriders. As they entered Chatsworth Park, a royal salute (prearranged with local military authorities) thundered from the Hunting Tower. After dinner the royal guests thrilled to outdoors illuminations observed from the drawing-room windows – waterfalls and fountains bursting into blaze from gas jets placed by the Duke's ingenious superintendent of gardens, William Paxton. Paxton's Great Conservatory, hung with thousands of lamps, was an enchanted tropical forest under a crystal roof, heated by seven miles of pipes. It was, Victoria would write to Leopold, 'out and out the finest thing imaginable of its kind. It is one mass of glass, 64 feet high, 300 feet long, and 134 feet wide.' There was also the Great Stove and special glasshouse that Paxton had built to house the Duke's gigantic water lilies, christened loyally the *Victoria regia*. A steam pump sent a hot spray fifty feet high, and twelve thousand gas lamps warmed and lighted the huge space. Albert would be reminded of the visit when, seven years later, his plans for a great exhibition of arts and manufactures in London were in trouble.

At Belvoir Castle, he went fox-hunting with the Duke of Rutland's hounds with relaxed éclat, which for Victoria was the high point of the royal progress. 'One can hardly credit the absurdity of people here [in England],' she wrote to King Leopold, 'but Albert's riding has made such a sensation that it has been written about all over the country, and they make more of it than if he had done some great act! It rather disgusts one, but still it had done, and does, good, for it had put an end to all impertinent sneering about Albert's riding. This journey had done great good, and my beloved Angel in particular has had *the greatest success...*'

'People are very strange,' her uncle responded on December 15, recognizing the pettiness of aspersions upon the Prince's reputed Prussian stiffness in the saddle; 'and their great delight is to find fault with their fellow creatures; what harm could it have done them if Albert had *not* hunted at all? and still I have no doubt that his having hunted well and boldly has given more satisfaction than if he had done Heaven knows what praiseworthy deed...'

Praise for Albert came hard to Englishmen. When the Duke of Wellington took him under his wing and the Prince responded with recommendations for the Army – Albert took everything under study and always emerged with suggestions – even the valuable advice earned no credits. In January 1844 he proposed that, as in Austria, duelling in the military be ended, and that, since 'a man whose honour ... has been insulted must possess some means whereby he can recover the treasure that has been taken from him and reinstate himself in the opinion of the world', such grievances be taken for satisfaction to the law. Wellington would ban duelling, but the public would first see Albert's involvement as interference. Even earlier, thinking in *mitteleuropäisch* fashion, the Prince, who was interested in weapons and uniforms, designed a shako (Hungarian for a stiff military hat with a high crown) for army use. The prototype for the Household Cavalry was conical, but flat on top, and with a brim, and was derided as tasteless in the *Illustrated London News* and lampooned by *Punch*, which described it 'as a decided cross between a muff, a coal-scuttle, and a slop-pail'. In unsigned spoof-German W.M. Thackeray chaffed, 'Ven de hat grow old (or vat you call zeedy), Brinz Albert has arranged so dat it vil make a beawdiful and ornamendal flower-bot for a drawing-room vindow.' The hat was adopted and worn until 1855. Caricaturists loved it.

Albert's father died on 29 January in his sixtieth year, a victim of his dissipations. When the Prince determined to return to Coburg, although not for the funeral, to pay his respects to his brother and stepmother, Princess Lieven carped to Lady Palmerston from Paris, and was very likely not alone in thinking, 'I imagine that Prince Albert is to receive a big inheritance; she' – the Queen – 'would not have allowed him to leave her for any trivial reason.' It was, however for the trivial reason of grief – guilty grief, perhaps, for his affection for his father had not been all that ties of blood required.

Both Victoria and Albert mourned as if Duke Ernest had been a paragon cut off in his prime. 'Here we sit together, poor Mama, Victoria, and myself, and weep', Albert wrote to Stockmar from Windsor, 'with a great cold public around us, insensible as stone.' Victoria was a 'consoling angel', he added, and indeed her desolation was excessive in the manner of the time, which exploited the event to create a *frisson* of woe. More revealingly than she understood, Victoria wrote to Leopold, the dead Duke's younger brother, 'One loves to *cling* to one's grief.' Although she hardly knew her father-in-law, he was 'our dearest Papa', and the Court was commanded into deep mourning. The royal notepaper was heavily bordered in black; courtiers dressed in black; official gloom pervaded royal residences already known for a surfeit of solemnity.

Most appalling of all to Victoria – the reality of what was otherwise a distant and overdramatized death – was that it forced Albert into a return to Coburg. In part it was to pay his respects at his father's grave; more significantly it was to caution the new Duke Ernest, his brother, about his excesses, and to secure insincere pledges of good behaviour. Besides, Albert ached for the sights and smells of what Victoria called his '*dearly beloved Vaterhaus*'.

The thought of the empty bed (although she was again pregnant) filled the Queen with alarm. 'I have *never* been separated from him for even *one night*', she confided to Leopold, 'and the *thought* of *such* separation is quite dreadful.' That she meant it, and more, is evident from her later letter to Vicky, recalling being 'clasped and held tight in the sacred Hours at Night when the world seemed only to be ourselves'.

Even before his Channel crossing had begun, Albert wrote to her from Dover, expressing his hope that although his place at the table would be vacant, his place in her heart would not be. By the time she received his note, he assured her, one of the fourteen days he would be away would already have passed – 'thirteen more, and I am again within your arms'. 'The Queen cried all day long after Albert departed', Lady Granville tattled to the Duke of Devonshire on 29 March, irritated at what she saw as self-indulgent immaturity. 'How rare it is for royalty to have such pleasant sorrows.'

By the time Albert arrived in Gotha – where Ernest II preferred to reside – the new duke had already taken hold. The brothers would differ on everything. Albert, so Ernest would write in later years, 'was by no means inclined to consent to an energetic rule such as I adopted immediately afterwards for the perfection of the constitutional system ... His mild amiability really went hand-in-hand with a critical severity ... The greatest warmth and self-sacrificing love would sometimes change to painful coldness ... ' Ernest II was not about to take advice about his personal life or his political absolutism, and Albert had to console himself with the treasured past before he returned, through snow in northern Germany, to an England that looked better than ever. Yet, while at the Rosenau in Coburg, he wrote, full of nostalgia for a boyhood that memory had enhanced, 'How glad I should be to have my little wife beside me, that I might share my pleasure with her.' Nevertheless, his diary for 11 April 1844, noting his arrival back at Windsor that evening, ended with the two words 'Great joy'. They suggested much more.

Royal travel on state visits, rare before the age of rail and steam, had almost become commonplace as rulers began using such opportunities for political advantages once left to arranged marriages. As Victoria waited out her fourth pregnancy, she expected the sovereigns of Russia, Saxony, France and Prussia. Thoughts of lengthy mourning for Ernest I were pushed aside by frenzies of preparation. Tsar Nicholas I had become concerned about England as a result of the state visit of Victoria and Albert to Russia's historic enemy, France. Both had designs upon the Middle East, hoping to appropriate some of the territories of the crumbling Turkish empire. The Queen was prompted to respond to anxieties emanating from France by writing to Leopold, her informal conduit to Louis Philippe, 'If the French are angry at this visit, let their dear King and their Princes come here.'

When Nicholas arrived on 1 June – the same day as King Frederick Augustus II of Saxony – Victoria was seven months pregnant; yet she went to Ascot with the Tsar and to the opera, held a review of troops for him in Windsor Great Park, gave huge dinners for him every evening in Buckingham Palace's Waterloo Room, and listened to his undiplomatic bellowing, carefully directed toward the Prince and Prime Minister – since she was a woman – on European politics, particularly his loathing of France and his contempt for Turkey. Autocratic and severe at home, at forty-eight he had travelled little and was unversed in the niceties of Court behaviour abroad.

Victoria was charmed by his rugged handsomeness (he was six feet two), his 'melancholy' eyes, his stern honesty, and his claim at Windsor that he needed some straw from the stables on which to sleep. Besides, she wrote to Leopold, the Tsar 'spoke in the highest praise of dearest Albert'.

When the King of France rushed to London afterwards, following a suitable period for Victoria's recovery from the birth of Prince Alfred Ernest Albert on 26 August, he also had words to describe Albert that Victoria relished – that '*le Prince Albert, c'est pour moi le Roi*'. The renewal of amity on the highest level between the traditional rivals suggested one dimension, the value of family links. Louis-Philippe's daughter Marie Louise was Leopold's spouse and Belgium's queen. His son, the duc de Nemours, was married to a Coburger cousin, Victoire. When Victoria and Louis-Philippe had met at Eu, they had kissed as family. When the King paid his return visit via Portsmouth, he was greeted by such an array of boats in informal escort, from great vessels to cutters and skiffs, that the *Gomez* had to slacken speed. There seemed to be national joy at the apparent end to hostility from across the Channel.

Since the King was not going beyond Windsor, the Lord Mayor and a delegation of dignitaries from London came to present a formal address to Louis-Philippe, and in expectation, Guizot recalled, 'I had written [a response for the King] in the morning and had it translated by M. de Jarnac ... The Queen and Prince Albert spent half an hour in the cabinet of the King, reading and correcting the translation. It is like a family intimacy.'

Louis-Philippe's praise of Albert as '*le Roi*' remained far from possible in reality. The MP for Evesham, Peter Borthwick, early in the next year upset any expectations which Victoria might have had for renewing her attempt to secure for Albert an English title. A paragraph had appeared in the *Daily Chronicle* in February rumouring that the Prince would be named King Consort, and Borthwick, in the Commons,

*Setting a hoped-for example, Albert had established a model farm at Windsor. Punch mocks it as a dilettantish operation, but the Prince was serious, and won legitimate livestock prizes at agricultural shows.*

raised the question with Peel. When the Prime Minister correctly denied that any title was being considered, Victoria, embarrassed by the speculation, quickly picked up by provincial papers, wrote to Peel that she was 'positive that something must at once be done to place the Prince's position on a constitutionally recognized footing, and to give him a title adequate to that position'. But Albert's claims to public recognition often took an unexpectedly perverse turn. In December 1844 the press was pleased, as Jane Carlyle wrote to Lady Harriet Baring, that at the annual Smithfield Club Cattle Show of farm animals, 'our poor Prince gained the prize for pigs'. Much was made of Albert's having received *second* prize for his Windsor porker at the show, held at the Horse Bazaar, Portman Square. Albert also exhibited, according to the *Examiner* on 14 December, 'a fine polled ox, of the Scotch breed, which has been highly commended by the judges, although it has not obtained a prize'. That 'fortunate animal', according to the *Examiner*'s 21 December edition, instead of being released to the butcher who had purchased it, was, on the Queen's order, conveyed to Windsor Park, 'where in future it will be kept'. 'Our dear little Queen', Lady Holland gossiped to her son, 'must have imbibed some German sentiment from her two connexions, by sparing the life of the ox, because it licked the hand of Prince Albert at the Cattle Show'. The press made much of Albert's ox.

Emotionally, Victoria had already left such society for private life with her growing family, but the death of Duke Ernest early in the year had diverted Albert from his search for homes remote from Windsor and London. While Parliament sat, Victoria saw need for a retreat that was accessible by rail from Westminster. Some months earlier, Peel had learned of a potential royal seaside residence for sale, in one of Victoria's favourite places, the Isle of Wight. Negotiations faltered when the Prince went to Coburg; they dragged on during the Queen's confinement. The asking price for the two hundred acres at Osborne was £30,000, later reduced to £28,000, including furniture, but that figure was reasonable only if the purchaser planned to use the existing structure. For the royal family the house was far too small, and the furniture of little but temporary use. Whatever was there would have to be replaced.

Peel had warned Victoria and Albert that no Parliamentary grant could be expected, and that there would even be resistance – the times were hard – to the renovation and repair of Buckingham Palace. Expecting no help with Osborne House, they planned to sell the obsolete Pavilion at Brighton, and use the proceeds to compensate the government for any expenditures to improve Buckingham Palace.*

The Privy Purse, in which Albert and Anson had made substantial economies, would pay for Osborne, which became private property, as Victoria put it to Leopold, 'a place of *one's own*, quiet and retired, and free from all Woods and Forests, and other charming Departments who really are the plague of one's life'. Settlement was made on 1 May at £27,814 18*s*. 5*d*. When the Prince decided that more land was required for privacy and guest accommodations, a further £18,000 was spent. It was impossible to imagine a prettier spot, Victoria wrote enthusiastically to Lord Melbourne. It reminded the Prince of the bay at Naples.

Even before settlement, Albert sent for his proposed builder – Victoria was quite willing to leave renovations of the existing property to him. Albert's intention was to enlarge and repair the mansion, which already had sixteen bedrooms, but not nearly enough service area. He consulted not an architect, but an imaginative and successful London builder, Thomas Cubitt, who had made a fortune out of developing the district now called Belgravia. Cubitt, then in his late fifties, had first been called upon at Christmas 1844 to prepare a survey of the house. His report recommended a new structure as 'less expensive in the end than the repair of the present one'. Victoria and Albert had agreed, but wanted to live there as soon as possible, and directed that the old house be repapered and painted for occupation while plans went ahead to design and build a new house. Architects grumbled at the slight to their calling, but the self-taught Cubitt went ahead with the Italianate structure Albert outlined with the expert assistance of Ludwig Gruner. After Easter, Cubitt walked around the property with the couple, explaining his ideas for the new house as well as his plans for immediate

---

* The Queen ordered the stripping of the Pavilion begun in 1846, and by 1848, 143 van-loads of furniture, decorations, porcelain, pictures, clocks, and carpets had been removed to Buckingham Palace, Kensington Palace and Windsor Castle. In 1847 a sale of many of the objects was held; in mid-1848 the remaining items were sold. On 7 June 1848, the doors of the Pavilion were locked and the keys given to the Lord Chamberlain. However, demolition by the government met with opposition from the town councillors of Brighton, who bought it in 1850 (for £60,000 – but not before the fixtures had been removed by the Board of Woods and Forests, which wantonly destroyed much of the interior in the process).

improvements to the existing one. He would become one of Albert's few real friends in England.

The next year, once Victoria and Albert moved into Osborne House, Cubitt was also given the task of rehabilitating Buckingham Palace, most parts of which, the Queen had told Peel in February 1845, 'are in a sad state'. A large sewer had been discovered under the forecourt, which explained why substantial portions of the palace were, in her words, hardly '*decent* for the occupation of the Royal Family or any visitors'. There were also too few rooms for formal or family use. A study commission representing the rival bureaucracies was appointed, and the Commons, on receiving its report, voted to add £150,000 to funds available for what was called the enlargement of the palace; but plans for the project were not unveiled until 1847.

Even then there were some things the managerial Prince could not do. By 1846 gaslight would penetrate the public rooms at Windsor, and then at Buckingham Palace, but in private Victoria would insist upon candlelight all her life. Disliking the smell of coal, she would insist upon beech logs in her fireplaces, and however much Albert complained of the cold, Victoria kept thermometers in ivory obelisks in most rooms to ensure that they remained invigoratingly chill. About him were constant reminders that he was the Queen's husband.

A contemporary ballad by the pseudonymous 'Bon Gaultier'* put Albert in his proper place:

> The Queen she kept high festival in Windsor's lordly hall,
> And round her sat the gartered knights, and ermined nobles all;
> There drank the valiant Wellington, there fed the wary Peel,
> And at the bottom of the board Prince Albert carved the veal.

* William Aytoun and Theodore Martin.

# VIII

# *The Queen's Business*

## *1845–1848*

H UNTING AT BAGSHOT with the Duke of Bedford, Albert spoke openly about problems facing Britain, including 'the long course of misgovernment [in Ireland], and the necessity of doing something'. Peel's administration, faltering yet not falling, had become hopelessly divided by the issues of Ireland and Free Trade. Famine was worsening – the potato blight of 1845 struck at the dietary staple of the chronically impoverished – but Protectionists representing the landed interest were more concerned about cheap grain from abroad than feeding hungry Irishmen. Albert felt helpless to interfere; but despite a sense of futility, he continued, with Victoria, to meet with her ministers, ask questions that pointedly revealed royal attitudes, and listen. Their efforts to remain above party politics limited their freedom to speak out, yet in private the Prince's Peelite sympathies were undisguised.

For Albert, the dilemma was that he had no privacy in which to operate. Little that was said and done at Court remained confidential, he deplored to Bedford. Somehow, he charged, governments on the Continent knew through their agents and informers whatever was discussed and done at the highest levels. Also, indiscretions of any sort found their way quickly into public currency, as when the new Bishop of Oxford, 'Soapy Sam' – for his charm, rather than his theology – Wilberforce wrote to Albert to ask the Prince's views on his position as a bishop in the House of Lords. 'A Bishop', Albert would pontificate on 19 October 1845, 'ought to abstain completely from mixing himself up with politics of the day, and beyond giving a general support to the *Queen's government*, and occasionally voting for it, should take no part in the discussion of State affairs . . . ' The concept of neutrality in an essentially honorific situation was Albertine to the core, but religious practice then was inextricably involved in politics, and Wilberforce could not keep a confidence. The Prince would be embarrassed.

Earlier in the year the Duke of Bedford had shrugged off the royal dilemma about privacy as 'the tax they' – Victoria and Albert – 'paid for their situation; that the world was curious to know and hear about them, and therefore the press would always procure and give the information . . . All conspicuous people were brought into public notice in the same manner.' It was 'the misfortune of princes'. Albert had been referring to matters of policy, but the Duke interpreted the complaint as about the exposure of gossip. In either case the functionaries who came and went at Court and were faceless presences whose eyes and ears might be bought were, indeed, the tax paid to keep the royal residences running. Acquiring Osborne would limit their numbers and their access to a few dozens rather than Brighton's thousands.

Writing to her husband's sister, Sarah, on 20 January 1845, just about the time of Greville's journal entry, Mary Anne Disraeli gossiped of the Royal visit to Stowe, the sprawling seat of the Duke of Buckingham and Chandos. A few grandees had personal railway sidings on their estates, with facilities that were almost regal. For the Queen, the platform 'head woman' told Mrs Disraeli (a palm extended, probably, for a coin), 'a large red curtain' was hung across the staircase 'when her Majesty went to the Cabinet'. On her return 'the Queen asked the woman, *Where the Prince could go* – but there was *no second convenience*'. Despite a lavishness that concealed the Duke's financial straits, there were curious limits to privacy.

In the immensity of Stowe, a great political conclave discussed possible alterations to the Corn Laws, and most Tory leaders were present. Despite the political nature of the event, the Queen and Prince were there ostensibly for its social aspects. With the issue of domestic precedence for Albert having died with the Duke of Sussex, what pleased Victoria was the respect afforded the Prince, a result of his increasing, if informal, authority rather than recognition of her desire. A 'trifling instance', she explained in a letter to Leopold, was 'the Duke of Buckingham, who is immensely proud, bringing the cup of coffee after dinner...to Albert himself'. But, in no public relations boon, *The Times* reported that the Duke's game preserves, in expectation of the visit, had been off limits for other hunting so that sixty beaters could drive enormous numbers of hares before the sportsmen. 'The ground immediately in front of the shooters became strewn with dead and dying; within a semicircle of about 60 yards from his Royal Highness, the havoc was evidently greatest. The gun was no sooner to his shoulder than the animal was dead. In other cases' – the aim of other gentlemen was less than unerring – 'wounded hares vainly endeavoured to limp away, but every provision had been made to avoid the infliction of prolonged torture. Keepers were in readiness to follow up and kill such as were maimed.' With the proliferation of London newspapers, each appealing to different classes and parties, it was to Albert's advantage that few carried the story in as much detail.

While publicly the Prince remained politically neutral, privately he supported the economic liberalism of Peel. As others – including Whigs who actually liked the legislation – attacked the extension of the income tax as inquisitorial and intrusive, Albert wrote realistically to the Prime Minister, 'It is evident that everybody wants you to bear the abuse of it and still have the 5 million in case of getting into office.' Peel found the votes for his taxes and tariffs. He did not have his own right wing with him but he had nearly everyone else.

On 3 April 1845, Thomas Cubitt was authorized by Albert to proceed with a new residence at Osborne while his workmen were still making Lady Isabella Blatchford's 'Old Osborne House' temporarily habitable. Walls were papered – still a rather new extravagance – a new water-closet was added for Victoria's bedroom; new stoves and chimney-pieces were installed. 'It does one's heart good', the Queen wrote in her journal after yet another exploration of their grounds at their springtime best, 'to see how my beloved Albert enjoys it all, and is so full of all the plans and improvements he means to carry out. He is hardly to be kept home a moment'. On 15 May they took a last look before some venerable trees obstructing the builders were cut down, and by 23 June they were able to return to take the children into the newly laid foundations to place a box of coins of the realm, each bearing their mother's profile, along with the names of the participants in the ritual. It was Victoria's ceremony, but the house in almost every way would be Albert's. Within months the Italianate tower would be rising.

Between events on the Isle of Wight was the royal *bal poudré*, again in period, the 'powder' motif to suggest the 1740s. Society was ecstatic. As the royal family withdrew into family pleasures, a Buckingham Palace extravaganza was now rare. The élite hairdressers were rumoured to be asking ten guineas *par tête* and were so busy that women had to be prepared days ahead and hope for the best. The Queen and Prince would come in costumes of the court of George II, and invitees researched the prints of Hogarth for ideas.

To free the fortunate for the event, the Lords did not sit that evening, prompting abuse the day before from Lord Brougham, who grumbled something *sotto voce* and unheard by *Hansard*. Lady Holland claimed it was about 'Albert & his *ugly* wife'. Yet, she added, 'Strange to say, all' – but Brougham – 'were pleased, young & old; & even those who did not go enjoyed the success. The streets were crowded; large groups assembled at the doors of those invited, to catch a glimpse of their costume; & many persons in their strange fashions stopped to shew themselves to the assembled crowd[s] & got cheers for their obliging-ness.'

By then, to mark the move to Osborne, the Privy Council had met there, the first of hundreds of voyages across the Solent that members of the government would have to make over the years. A more important concern for officials accompanying the Queen was the forthcoming journey to Coburg that she and Albert had planned. So that no regency need be declared in the Queen's absence, a Minister of State would join the party. The arrangement was a sign of the revolution in communications. The steamship and the railway had been followed, in the year of her accession, by the first practical electric telegraph. By 1845, telegraphy was operational in America and England, and on much of the Continent. If necessary, an Act of State could now be performed abroad.

Anticipation of the August journey to the cradle of her family excited the Queen. Her first impression, as she crossed into the conglomeration of states east of the Rhine, was of the singularity of hearing 'the *people* speak German'. At Bonn, the seventy-fifth anniversary of the birth of Ludwig van Beethoven was being celebrated on 12 August by the unveiling of a statue and an outdoor concert conducted by Franz Liszt.

The King and Queen of Prussia had promised to attend, and to bring with them Queen Victoria and Prince Albert.

The last day of the festival opened with a memorial concert in the *Festhalle*, featuring Marie Pleyel, Jenny Lind, and Liszt himself. The programme began without the exalted guests. When Liszt approached the rostrum to conduct the cantata he had composed for the occasion, the King's party was still absent. He held his baton until the restlessness of the crowd forced him to begin, and he was at the closing bars of the long, lugubrious work when the royal guests finally arrived. For them, Liszt conducted a second full performance, although the audience evidenced unmistakable signs that one had been enough.

Victoria was less concerned about the King of Prussia's lack of interest in music than about his failure to accord Albert the precedence at official functions 'which common civility required', she recalled in a memorandum in 1856, 'because of the presence of an Archduke, the third son of an uncle of the then reigning Emperor of Austria . . . whom the King would not offend'. But her uncle, the King of Hanover, was delighted, writing to a friend in England that the behaviour of Victoria and Albert was 'childishness'. He pretended to be 'mortified' by the 'complete failure' of the Prussian visit – that Victoria was allegedly 'cold and uncivil', while Albert 'was represented as being full of pretensions, and ignorant of the common usages of the world'. He had appeared at a military parade at Mainz 'in a great frock coat and round white hat, looking more like a tradesman or *garçon de boutique* than a prince'. And he failed to wear his Prussian insignia of the Order of the Black Eagle – an alleged discourtesy to his royal host. It was Victoria who was mortified, blaming Prussian pettiness on Albert's lowly rank. English law 'does not know of him'.

Albert's forebodings about Coburg caused him to question coming at all. Ernest resented his brother's intrusive advice, and Albert had responded, unrepentant, 'The worm that is gnawing at your heart and which often robs you of pleasure in life is *mistrust*. Those who really love you must have the sincere wish to lift this veil from your soul . . . You might think we are coming to govern you or to do you some damage.'

The London press followed the royal couple to Coburg, filing reports that made the Queen's indignation about mere title appear mild. Albert had written to his brother about appropriate entertainment for the

Queen, who wanted nothing arranged on a 'grand' scale, and because of the 'English way of keeping Sunday and the scruples belonging to it', nothing but a family assemblage on the Sabbath. She hoped to see German plays, participate in small folk dances and attend a children's festival. 'You needn't arrange a chase, as Victoria does not like such pleasures, and *I* prefer to stay with her.' Ernest however had managed a way for gentlemen to shoot without leaving their ladies. Albert found himself in a Germanic liquidation of deer.

The Continental *battue* did not merely employ beaters to drive game toward marksmen but herded targets into a broad enclosure which made chase unnecessary. To English newspapermen reporting home on the new telegraph, that was murder rather than sport. Reading press accounts, Greville dismissed the 'clumsy (and false) attempt to persuade people that she' – Victoria – 'was shocked and annoyed. But the truth is, her sensibilities are not acute, and though she is not at all ill-natured, perhaps the reverse, she is hard-hearted, selfish and self-willed.' A Leech cartoon in *Punch*, in two panels, compared bear-baiting in Elizabeth's time with dead and dying stags piled up before the royal tent, and verses by 'Jeams' (Thackeray) scoffed at 'Halbert Usband of the British Crownd' and his 'pore Germing sport' which was nothing less than a 'massyker'.

Rather than one massacre, unfortunately, there were two, the second when Victoria and Albert were guests on an elevated stand in an enclosure where thirty wild boar were released to be speared, or shot. According to her journal the platform for the audience was 'charmingly arranged' – curious words in the aftermath of a butchery. 'After this,' she concluded, without confessing any lacerated feelings, 'we walked away & then got into our carriage & drove home.'

The German entertainment arranged for Albert proved a public relations embarrassment in the English press. 'We understand', went one pseudo-report, '[that] several of the Civic Companies have invited Prince Albert to a day's sport in the City. They have offered to collect in the area of the Stock Exchange all the bulls and bears that are in the habit of prowling about the neighbourhood.'

Hunting would continue to be a public relations cross for Albert to bear. To hobnob with powerful peers on the informal terms necessary to conduct his extra-legal business, he needed to be with them as he was at Bagshot with the Duke of Bedford. That meant the hunt and chase.

SPORT! OR, A BATTUE MADE EASY.

*Another in* Punch's *campaign against bloodthirsty gunnery. Although the Prince was the captive of his hosts on such occasions, attacks like this one in 1845 were unsparing.*

Yet invariably that would lead to abuse from other quarters. 'Didst thou see in any of the papers that account of the battue at Lord Salisbury's,' Radical MP John Bright wrote to Elizabeth Leatham, 'when Prince Albert, the Duke of Wellington, Lord John Russell and others were present? . . . I think the Queen, as patron of the Society for the Prevention of Cruelty to Animals, should counsel her "subject" husband against such barbarous slaughter of defenceless animals for amusement only . . .'\*

* Albert's eldest son would 'hunt' no differently, especially when out of England; and his heir in turn would take shooting as target practice. When in India in 1911, George V would bring down thirty-nine rare tigers and eighteen rhinos beaten, at his request, into his range.

The attacks on Albert in *Punch,* which had especially glorious fun with Albert and hunting, became so vicious in 1847 that a rival comic miscellany, *The Man in the Moon,* published an attack by Shirley Brooks in its November number, misidentifying the chief culprit at *Punch* as Douglas Jerrold, whose hands, too, were not clean:

> We'll clear thy brain. Look westerly [from Fleet
>     Street]. See where yon Palace stands;
> Stains of the mud flung there by thee are on thy dirty
>     hands...

Realizing that the lines were meant for him, Thackeray declared his loyalty to, and admiration of, the Prince, claiming to have composed more chaff than rebuke. Significantly, one line by Brooks – certainly no accident – had referred to honouring 'the King'.

Aside from the public slaughter of deer and boar, in which his brother had literally met Albert's wishes (as he was not separated from the Queen), Ernest unexpectedly proved a genial host. Albert gloried in the *Gemütlichkeit.* Uncle Leopold and Aunt Louise had arrived even earlier for the family reunion, as had Victoria's mother and half-sister, Feodora, and even Albert's stepmother Marie. At the ducal palace on 19 August, Victoria's journal records, 'The staircase was full of cousins.'

In the Rosenau, where Albert had spent his boyhood, the royal couple used three rooms atop winding stairs which overlooked the sparkling Itze and the tree-shaded *Eremitage* in a bend of the stream where the Prince, as a boy, once slipped off with his books. 'I felt', she wrote, 'as if I should always like to live here with my dearest Albert, and if I was not what I am – this would be my real home...It is like a beautiful dream.'

The presence of Lord Aberdeen and Lord Liverpool were reminders of reality, yet the days passed in a fairy-tale atmosphere suggesting that time had bypassed Duke Ernest's mini-state. On a quiet Saturday afternoon she 'sent for Bratwürste which is the national dish of Coburg – from the Markt & ate them & drank some of the excellent Coburg beer – they were so good'.

On August 26, Albert's twenty-sixth birthday was celebrated at his birthplace – '*more than I ever hoped for*', Victoria wrote. Her gift, brought from London in the couple's voluminous baggage, was a painting, with an abundance of warm flesh, by Thomas Uwins, *Cupid and Psyche.* Albert knew Uwins and liked his work. Also among Victoria's gifts were a walking stick and a snuffbox. (At Osborne, reflecting the Queen's distaste for tobacco, the only room not to be monogrammed above the doorway with a 'V & A' was the smoking-room. Only an 'A' identified it – although Albert did not smoke and intended the convenience for male guests.)

'From Mamma,' Victoria added scrupulously in her journal, 'he got trifles, and from Ernest a beautiful chessboard.' Albert's health was drunk at dinner, after which the family adjourned to a concert in the trompe l'oeil *Marmorsaal* (Marble Hall), where two of the pieces performed were compositions by Albert and Ernest.*

'God grant that we may come here again ere long!' she wrote. The next morning, they left in carriages for the long ride to the nearest railway station. Fifteen years later, when finally they were able to return, there were tracks laid all the way. Modernity would creep up even on Coburg.

Although, for Christmas and birthdays, Victoria and Albert often gave each other pictures innocent enough to hang in public view in any Evangelical home – children and angels and domestic scenes – the art in which they delighted and would display in their private chambers, especially at Osborne, revealed their pleasure in the nude, male and female. In all sizes from grand to miniature, these reflected fashion much less than preference. It may have been the Italianate quality of structure and setting of the Albert-designed Osborne House which would replace the original structure which suggested to Victoria and Albert commissioning statues of themselves in Roman dress. One by the German sculptor Emil Wolff shows the barefoot Prince in a warrior's short-skirted tunic, shield at his side, left arm resting on his belted scabbard. A Victoria by John Gibson shows a Roman queen, crowned and sandalled, in bare-shouldered dress and cloak, scroll in one hand, wreath in the other. Both are at Osborne House still, where the Queen and Prince accumulated a long corridor of classical reproductions as well as new works in Roman style.

---

* Albert wrote thirty-seven *Lieder* as well as pieces for organ and piano – 'pleasant music without presumption', according to Yehudi Menuhin. Ernest also dabbled in opera, producing several at his own opera house and even singing in them.

Bought at the Great Exhibition of 1851 and given by Albert to the Queen as a Christmas gift was William Geefs's heroic and half-nude *Paul et Virginie*. John Bell's neo-classical nude and erotically posed *Andromeda*, exhibited by the sculptor ostensibly as an example of modern bronze casting, was purchased by Victoria in 1851 for Albert. Still another was William Theed's neo-classical *Narcissus*, totally nude in the original but fig-leafed in Victoria's copy, perhaps because the exposure of male genitals would have made guests uneasy: Victoria and Albert demonstrated few qualms about flesh in art. The Queen even bought a marble, nearly life-size, *Venus Anadyomene*, an authentic Roman nude found in the baths of Caracalla. It had been in the Duke of Buckingham's collection at Stowe, where it had been admired by Albert. When the Duke, in bankruptcy because of the royal state in which he lived and entertained, had to dispose of his art, Victoria presented the statue to the Prince on his twenty-ninth birthday.

Perhaps the last of the suggestive statuary purchased for Albert was his birthday gift for 1857, when both Queen and Prince were thirty-eight. Designed by Emile Jeannest, it was a gilded silver Lady Godiva, wearing only her hair, and sitting side-saddle on her horse. In art, at least, Victoria offered continuing access to fleshly attractions while her own physical appeal diminished with poundage and pregnancies.

Possibly the most intriguing painting to be hung at Osborne House was one not publicly visible – a startling, sensual, well over life-size *Omphale and Hercules*, by Anton von Gegenbaur that covered much of the wall opposite Albert's bathtub in the couple's private apartments. The canvas, which would be astonishing in the household of a truly prudish pair, confirms that Victoria and Albert were not. But perhaps *Omphale and Hercules* is also an index to Albert's subconscious. The seductive young woman, dandled on the broad thigh of the muscular god and clad only in alabaster flesh and a head scarf, is in Greek myth the Queen of Lydia, who once kept Hercules as her sex slave. Omphale, Greek for the navel, seems to have acquired her name not only from her exposure of it, but because the umbilicus was considered the seat of the passions. Foreshadowing Albert's public role, the Omphale–Hercules relationship also represented a stage in the shift from matriarchy to patriarchy, for as the Queen's consort Hercules often ceremonially deputized for her. Dated Rome, 1830, it was bought by the Prince in

1844, when furnishings were being acquired for Osborne. It hangs there still.

Albert was not unaware of what he was doing, although such pictures contrasted oddly with the early Italian masters he bought for their design values rather than their naïve piety. Out of keeping with Christian piety but reflecting Albert's interest in fresco was a scene he commissioned in 1847 from William Dyce. Is there a message in it? In the panel a nude Neptune, king of the seas, offers his crown to a modestly clothed Britannia. The head of a rearing horse conceals the god's genitals, but the stallion's dark forelock itself strikingly suggests, in the anatomically appropriate place, luxuriant pubic hair. All Neptune's sea-maidens are nude, as are several sinewy males in his ranks.

Paintings remained a private language to Victoria and Albert. The year before Albert had purchased the *Hercules and Omphale*, each had Sir Charles Eastlake do a birthday present for the other, with the artist charged to keep the secret. Daniel Maclise, whose pictures often had an erotic edge, was also kept busy. 'He is in great favour with the Queen', Dickens gossiped to Cornelius Felton, 'and paints secret pictures for her to put on her husband's table on the morning of his birthday, and the like.'

The impression left by some of the Queen's choices is that if suggestive nudity in art stirred the libido, it had rewards beyond purely aesthetic ones. The pastel male nude she secured from William Mulready for the Prince seemed more a reflection of her own taste than that of her husband. Its seated subject, legs stretched out, looked thoughtfully upward, hoping perhaps for release from the pose. Victoria admired Mulready's nudes of both sexes (while Ruskin called them 'degraded and bestial'), yet Albert sought unsuccessfully to have Mulready copy his quite innocuous *Choosing the Wedding Gown* (1846) for the Queen.

Victoria even recruited Franz Xavier Winterhalter, the favourite Court painter of family scenes. As late as 1852, when both the Queen and Prince were thirty-four, she commissioned from the usually decorous Winterhalter a sensuous *Florinda* for Albert's birthday. Ostensibly a scene from literature, the canvas displayed a bevy of bare-breasted young women, the sun dappling their generous flesh. It was hung in Victoria's private sitting-room, where the couple often worked together. An even earlier queenly birthday present to Albert was William Frost's

*L'Allegro* (1848), from John Milton's poem. The grave poet would have been appalled by the treatment – three dancing girls, two of them bare-breasted. Frost also painted, for Albert, a *Disarming of Cupid*, again with warm nudes and semi-nudes. An earlier birthday gift, this time from Victoria to Albert, in 1843, had been Maclise's *A Scene from Undine*. The subject came from a romantic German novel, possibly the reason Victoria chose it, but despite the proper young lovers who are the central images, the painting bursts with unclothed goblins and sensual, nude, water-nymphs.

Albert's chairmanship of the Fine Arts Commission, dedicated to the cultivation of the arts but largely focused upon internal decoration at Westminster, had put him in regular contact with major English artists and demonstrated as well his artistic pragmatism. An exhibition of the prize cartoons – the sketches of the winning pictures – in Westminster Hall in the early summer of 1843, managed by the secretary of the commission, Charles Eastlake, drew large crowds at a shilling a head after Albert brought the Queen and gave her a guided tour. The Prince favoured the fee, and made the exhibition fashionable enough that from the proceeds the Commissioners could award ten additional competition prizes. Although some artists found Albert's tours of inspection distracting and even demeaning, he was putting a useful imprimatur on their work by openly caring about it.

No art scholar, he also added a touch of simple pragmatism when the committee looked at interior niches as suitable for statuary. Summoning a mason, Albert asked him to stand inside a questionable space so that viewers could assess the effect.

Often artists found that a royal purchase or commission resulted from the parliamentary competition, sometimes a work less close to history – and less clothed. For the Palace of Westminster, J.C. Horsley, later derided as 'Clothes Horsley' because he had become so prudish, offered to paint a combination of 'L'Allegro' and 'Il Penseroso', but T.B. Macaulay, one of three historians on the Commission, insisted – as if it were true history – that no topic could illustrate Milton unless it were from *Paradise Lost*. Horsley painted, instead, *Satan Touched by Ithurie's Spear while Whispering Evil Dreams into the Ear of Eve*. Albert, impressed by the artist's semi-nudes, had him do his Milton for Osborne.

Hardly a birthday went by without the Queen's presenting an image of herself, and soon of the family. So many portraits and statues of

Albert were commissioned in so many attitudes and costumes that the press joked it was the primary subsidy for the arts in Britain. Art dealers were also patronized, as Albert had Ludwig Gruner alerted for early Italian pictures. Albert even commissioned a painting in pre-Raphael* style, a *Virgin and Child* by William Dyce (1846). Albert also had Gruner watch for works by the sixteenth-century Saxon painter Lucas Cranach, his favourite among German artists. (One Cranach purchased in 1846, an *Apollo and Diana*, was a double nude.) But for the sculptures of Carlo Marochetti and the paintings of Franz Winterhalter, most royal commissions were from English painters. Masterpieces of their time, J.M.W. Turner's impressionistic waterscapes and landscapes moved neither Victoria nor Albert. Turner's bid for Court recognition failed. Instead, recognizing Albert's admiration of George Eliot's *Adam Bede*, Victoria commissioned two scenes from the novel to be painted by George Henry Corbould.

Birthday pictures had been important to the Queen and Prince from the beginning. When they had been married only eighteen months, Victoria had asked Edwin Landseer, one of the great animal painters of his day, to do a portrait of the infant Princess Royal with Albert's greyhound Eos in time for his birthday on 26 August 1841. A birthday present was no vaguely deadlined commission. When it had not arrived by eleven in the evening on the twenty-fifth the Queen sent a footman from Windsor in a carriage with instructions to return with the painting, 'done or not done'. He awakened Landseer at two in the morning and was back at six with the picture wrapped in a tablecloth.

Twice Albert found himself as purchaser of art collections he had not bargained for and which did not represent his own taste. In April 1847 his brother, short as usual in spending money, attempted to sell family portraits from the castle in Coburg. It evidenced, Albert appealed, a 'want of feeling' which would embarrass 'the whole family'. The publicity 'must damage your reputation in your own country and abroad', he warned. 'I cannot imagine how anyone could think of such a thing.'

---

* But not 'Pre-Raphaelite'. The self-anointed 'PRB' fellowship organized by Dante Gabriel Rossetti, Holman Hunt and John Millais to promote their pre-Renaissance ideals of simplicity, sincerity and fidelity to nature in 1848, first exhibited in 1849, and announced their goals in the short-lived Pre-Raphaelite Brotherhood journal *The Germ* in 1850.

In Gotha, where he now spent most of his time, Ernest was unmoved. Albert bought them.

More complicated and more expensive were the affairs of a remote, and hard-up, relation, Prince Ludwig Kraft Ernst von Oettingen-Wallerstein, who had visited Windsor in November 1843, when he was characterized by Victoria as 'gentleman-like and clever but slightly effeminate'. While in Bavarian government service, he fell into serious debt and asked Albert to co-sign a note with the London Rothschilds for three thousand pounds, then a substantial sum, against which he would deliver as surety to Albert a collection of early Italian, German, and Netherlandish pictures. Lionel de Rothschild came to Buckingham Palace on 13 May 1847 to explain what Albert's risks were, and he hesitated for three further weeks, finally signing a letter to N.M. Rothschild & Sons guaranteeing that if any of the three promissory notes, each for £1,000, were not paid, with five per cent interest, on time, he would, 'immediately after default', make the sums good.

By the first due date a year later it was already clear that his cousin, now fifty-seven, had neither the intention nor the wherewithal to clear his loan, and Albert, hoping to attract a buyer, put the collection of a hundred paintings on display at Kensington Palace.

When no purchasers emerged, Albert tried vainly, through the dealer Henry Mogford, to interest the National Gallery, which, had it the gift of foresight, would have recognized that among the mediocrities were individual works worth the total asking price. When that ploy failed, Albert became the poorer, as well as the possessor of the lot, while the press carped 'that the Prince was forcing the nation to buy the possessions of his German relatives'. Some, then, were what Peel would have called 'curiosities', including a portrait of Cosimo I of Tuscany by Angelo Bronzino, and works by or attributed to Jan van Hemessen, Bernard van Orley, Martin Schongauer, Hans Memling, Gerard David, Jan Provoost, Adriaen Isenbrandt, Quintin Metsys, and Giusto de Menabuoi. In the 1930s, a restorer discovered that the haloes of some of the saintly personages in the fourteenth- and fifteenth- century paintings had been 'improved' by spiky pseudo-Gothic ornament. Albert probably never knew.

Eventually the Queen, in Albert's memory, would present twenty-five Wallerstein paintings to the National Gallery – five German, sixteen Dutch and Flemish, and four Italian. Many now hang in the

Sainsbury Wing of the Gallery; the rejected canvases are at Hampton Court and Buckingham Palace.

Although Albert influenced English art largely by patronizing English artists, the Italianate Osborne House he designed with Gruner had real architectural influence from the moment the royal family moved into it. Not only was it pictured regularly, inside and out, in the illustrated magazines; it could be admired, even when under construction, from ships arriving at or departing from Southampton. Stucco became more fashionable, as did the short towers and the avoidance of exact symmetry. Suburban villas on both sides of the Atlantic echoed aspects of Osborne for decades and, despite its red brick, the Smithsonian Institution in Washington has an Osborne look, as do many American college buildings of mid-century and after.

Among the problems which Peel brought to the royal couple on their return from Coburg was his government's continuing inability to repeal the Corn Laws. Hunger in Ireland was worse than ever, causing wholesale emigration into Liverpool, where tens of thousands who could not afford steerage to America remained in teeming slums. Protectionists in Peel's party, even the revered and godlike Wellington, would deprecate the 'fright' given to Peel over 'rotten potatoes', and vote with the squirearchy. While the royal family was at Osborne in December, Peel announced his intention to resign.

'We were, of course, in great consternation', Albert noted in a memorandum. While he conducted much of the Queen's business, it was often now in both names. His notes of meetings with her ministers almost always employed 'We' rather than 'I', but Peel usually consulted Albert before going to the Queen. As 1845 wound down, it was clear to officialdom, as Greville observed, that Albert had been 'so identified' with the Queen 'that they are one person, and as he likes and she dislikes business, it is obvious that while she has the title, he is really discharging the functions of the Sovereign. He is King to all intents and purposes.' Even had he been the king he would have had no constitutional means but to persuade privately, and Albert wondered in his memorandum why measures similar to those adopted by other European countries affected by the potato blight could not be enacted – opening Irish ports and otherwise taking 'energetic means' to replace the 'usual food' of the 'poorer class'. The poor, however, had few votes in Parliament, and peers who preferred price stability whatever its consequences could block compromise.

All that Victoria and Albert could do, and then only when the founding of the charity made it possible, was to contribute to the British Association for the Relief of the Extreme Distress in the Remote Parishes of Ireland and Scotland, created by Lionel de Rothschild and Abel Smith. Even that was kept low-key. Legend had it that the Queen subscribed a mere five pounds; in fact, in the subscription list preserved in Dublin the first three names are 'HM The Queen, £2,000; Rothschilds' £1,000; Duke of Devonshire, £1,000'. Albert contributed £500 on his own.

It had been easy for Victoria and Albert to believe, confident as they were of Peel's efficiency and integrity, that he would go on for ever. Each reorganization of government further demonstrated the instability of electoral office and the continuity of the sovereign, political realities that Victoria would not allow herself to forget. Less concerned about distress in Ireland than about relations with France if Lord Palmerston, as seemed inevitable, returned as Foreign Minister, Victoria and Albert hoped that Lord John Russell – the heir apparent as Prime Minister – would be unable to form a government. After a fortnight he did indeed fail to patch a Cabinet together from his split party, and Peel was asked to continue. Meeting with Victoria and Albert at Windsor, according to the Prince's minutes, Peel was 'much moved' by their desire to have him return to office. 'There is no sacrifice that I will not make for your Majesty', he assured the Queen, 'except that of my honour.'

Peel's patched-up Cabinet promised only a delay of the inevitable. Attempting to help him, Albert went to the gallery of the Commons on 27 January 1846, to lend silent moral support at a Corn Laws debate. On the floor, Lord George Bentinck deplored the Prince's presence as giving 'the semblance of a personal sanction of her Majesty to a measure which, be it for good or for evil, a great majority, at least of the landed aristocracy of England, of Scotland, and of Ireland, imagine fraught with deep injury, if not ruin, to them'. Albert would never again make the mistake of going to the House.

More and more, as Peel struggled through the tumultuous last months of his Ministry, Albert was king without a crown. Pregnant again, Victoria left nearly everything but a few ceremonial functions to her husband. 'When politics are chaotic,' Lady Palmerston complained to Dorothea de Lieven, 'evening parties become duller. The Queen is in good health, but her pregnancy is the despair of her dressmakers...' Albert's memoranda of conversations with the embattled Prime Minister more often read, 'I saw this day R. Peel' than the more circumspect but misleading 'We'. Victoria's letters suggest more involvement with affairs than was the case, because she routinely commented in writing on matters brought to her; but tangible evidence otherwise appeared in Emily Palmerston's letter to Princess Lieven early that June: 'Prince Albert has just driven past my window with Ibrahim Pasha, on his way back from a review.' The son of Mehmet Ali, Pasha of Egypt, was visiting European powers as his father's agent, and Albert was acting for the Queen. Pregnancy and postpartum confinement had been the Queen's reasons in the first half of 1846, but Victoria no longer needed to furnish excuses for Albert.

A frank memorandum dated from Buckingham Palace that April – Albert seldom threw any document away – shows the Prince in action as he struggled to keep Peel in office. He had called in the Prime Minister and opened by offering him a six-page summary of their conversation five days earlier. Peel scrutinized it, and after a long pause said, uneasily, 'I was not aware when I spoke to your Royal Highness that my words would be taken down, and don't acknowledge that this is a fair representation of my opinion.' Had he known that his remarks would be committed to paper, he confessed he would have spoken with more caution.

'I was anxious', Albert, who seldom discarded a document, minuted, 'that nothing should prevent his speaking without the slightest reserve to me in future as he had done heretofore. I felt that these open discussions were of the greatest use to me in my endeavour to investigate the different political questions of the day and to form a conclusive opinion upon them. As Sir Robert did not say a word to dissuade me, I took it as an affirmative, and threw the memorandum into the fire...'

Only twenty-six, the Prince was dealing with statesmen who were already in office when he was born – in a different country and political culture under a different language.

As with ministers, Albert attempted to speak frankly to sovereigns, assuring them, as he did (2 April 1847) to the authoritarian Frederick William IV of Prussia – whom *Reichsmarschall* Hermann Göring a century later strongly resembled – that confidences would be treated 'by us both with the strictest secrecy, and to be withheld from every one, including our Governments'. Not only would the exchanges be valuable, he argued, but they would be handed down to 'the Prince of Wales, your dear god-son, as the best endowment for his future kingly office'. Although the King might expect 'a certain excess... of purely British feeling', Albert conceded, because 'I am incidentally the Queen of England's husband, I am also one German prince speaking to another.' Albert sought not only Anglo-German understanding, but democratic evolution in Prussia that might lead to a unified Germany under a constitutional monarchy on the British model. Unreserved about bringing up political reform, he felt it necessary to interject, 'I venture to hope that our correspondence may not come to a close with this present letter.' It almost did. Albert's letters were often emotional and idealistic, stressing his Germanness, yet written as the uncrowned king of another nation. Only political necessity kept Frederick William writing – but not on the terms Albert hoped for.

The family spent the early spring at Osborne while Albert oversaw Cubitt's builders. In May the couple returned to Buckingham Palace, where Princess Helena Augusta Victoria was born on the twenty-fifth. Albert's surrogacy by now was seamless. He managed the Queen's business, attempting to prop up Peel, although Peelites – there was no longer one Tory party – were harassed by Protectionists on both Irish legislation and repeal of the Corn Laws. The rejection of Peel's Irish Bill came as Albert and family were back in Osborne, and the Prime Minister took the train to Gosport and a packet to the Isle of Wight to tender his resignation to the Prince. Ironically, Peel had won on the very issue that had split the Tories, but he needed Whig votes. (The parties were gradually realigning, with Peelites, the liberal Tory wing, largely joining the Whigs, now beginning to call themselves Liberals, while the Protectionists among the Tories were becoming known as Conservatives.)

Peel arrived at Osborne on the evening of 28 June, leaving the next morning to confer in London with his Whig successor, Lord John Russell, for whom he was certain Victoria would send. She and Albert were unhappy at losing Peel, but they had expected the event for six months, and his departure had only depended upon which bill would precipitate it – one to diminish the powers of the Church of Ireland, which had long colonialized Anglicanism, or Free Trade and cheaper grain. Victoria had resisted Peel earlier; now she wrote that she would miss 'a kind and true friend' whose loss was England's. Diminutive Lord John Russell arrived the next day, his interview conducted in Victoria's presence by Albert; and in the first days of July the Queen returned to Buckingham Palace to install the new Ministry.

Almost as great a loss was the replacement of the deliberate Earl of Aberdeen at the Foreign Office by the impetuous Viscount Palmerston, whose francophile sympathies were at odds with the Palace on the long-threatened Spanish marriages. Blocked in having one of his sons marry the adolescent Queen of Spain, Isabella, Louis-Philippe arranged to have him marry, instead, her younger sister, the Infanta Louisa, then fourteen, while the Queen, sixteen, would be provided with a Spanish Bourbon cousin, Francisco, the Duke of Cadiz, who was effeminate and believed to be impotent. In that way, Antoine, duc de Montpensier, might inherit the throne, or at worst a son of his marriage with the Infanta would be heir. With the European power structure still visualized in terms of crowns, Victoria and Albert, to prevent the political levelling of the Pyrenees by a dynastic betrothal, suggested for one or the other of the girls – and they were hardly more than that – their cousin Leopold of Saxe-Coburg-Kohary. Beyond Windsor Castle, that appeared to be the usual Coburger aggrandizement.

No marriages had been settled when Palmerston took office, but King Ernest of Hanover spitefully – yet accurately – accused the Prince of meddling. Meddling in the Spanish marriages seemed the foreign policy pastime of the mid-1840s, and Palmerston was no less involved and no more successful. Montpensier would never achieve any sort of power in increasingly anarchic Spain although he wed Louisa on the same day, 10 October 1846, as Isabella II was married to Don Francisco de Asis. The Queen would console herself with officers and men of the royal guard, among others, causing Albert to write, resentfully, of the marriages in April of the next year, 'The [new] King follows the inspirations of a miraculous nun who is paid from Paris, the Queen has her lovers and at present she is kept a prisoner in the castle . . . What will Louis-Philippe have to answer for in heaven!'*

* Isabella's house arrest evaporated quickly. She would bear a son, later Alfonso XII, and four daughters, all of questionable paternity. Louisa and Montpensier would have three sons and three daughters. One son, Antonio (1866–1930), survived childhood, becoming the duca di Galliera, an empty title. A descendant of Isabella,

With the new Ministry functioning, although not as Victoria and Albert would have liked it, the next dissatisfaction came with events in Portugal. Another cousin, Ferdinand of Saxe-Coburg-Kohary, was King Consort, and correspondence flowed between Buckingham Palace and both Ferdinand and Donna Maria that furnished royalist points of view very different from those of Palmerston's typically interfering – and liberal-minded – representatives, who took partisan sides in troubled Portuguese affairs. With still another cousin, Count Alexander Mensdorff, Austrian ambassador in Lisbon (later to become Foreign Minister), the family became involved when a revolution arose against what was a despotic but Coburg-related reign. Albert crossed Palmerston again in 1847 when Austria illegally annexed the rump Polish Duchy of Krakow, claiming that it encouraged rebellion within Austria's Galician and Silesian territories. An outspoken liberal on self-determination of peoples, Palmerston was almost always at odds with Albert's desire for stability, whatever the regime. Even the Prince conceded, however, that Austria was no model government. Perceptively ahead of his time, he observed, later, to Lord John Russell, 'The conduct of Austria can only be explained in one way: that it is one of the convulsions of a dying man. Her system is rotten, and conscious of her own disease and weakness, she struggles in despair.'

The volume and bulk of the letters sent and received by Albert, plus those he drafted for Victoria to rewrite in her own hand, suggest an enormous expenditure of time and energy. Many of Albert's exchanges with Peel and Palmerston run to ten or twelve handwritten pages from each correspondent. It was an age of copyists, a major task for clerks and secretaries, but most letters were laboriously penned first by the signer. It is easy to imagine a sleepless Albert writing and reading by candle-light or gas into the early hours of each new day.

A continuing distraction from external affairs was the rising of Osborne House adjacent to and overwhelming Lady Isabella's original dwelling. Throughout the year Victoria and Albert crossed the Solent to supervise the placement of furniture and the hanging of curtains and

however, a great-grandson of Alfonso XII, became King Juan Carlos when the monarchy was restored after the death of Generalissimo Francisco Franco in 1975. An irony which neither Albert nor Victoria lived to see was that Alphonso XIII, Isabella's grandson of dubious lineage, in 1906 married Victoria and Albert's granddaughter Victoria Eugenie Julia Ena of Battenberg, who became queen of Spain.

pictures in what they called the Pavilion. In a niche on one landing the bare-legged Wolff statue of Albert in Roman garb already looked down on the central staircase around which the rooms were grouped. Finally, on the evening of 14 September 1846, after a lady-in-waiting threw an old shoe into the house for luck, the royal family moved in for their first night in the unfinished structure. Lady Lyttelton, remaining in charge of the royal nursery, oversaw the children scampering about, each attended by a scarlet-clad footman, and Victoria called the occasion 'like a dream to be here now in our own house, of which we laid the first stone only fifteen months ago'.

At their first dinner in Osborne House, everyone rose to drink to the royal couple's health, and Albert responded with a house-warming hymn of Luther's, from the 128th Psalm:

> So shall thy wife be in thy house
> Like vine with clusters plenteous,
> Thy children sit thy table round
> Like olive plants all fresh and sound.

'The windows,' Lady Lyttelton wrote, 'lighted by the brilliant lamps in the rooms, must have been seen far out at sea.'

Cubitt and the Prince had meticulously planned everything down to the height of the furniture, some chairs, desks and tables slightly scaled down to compensate for Victoria's small stature. Despite its formality, even the drawing-room was planned for efficiency, as off to one side was a billiard room separated from it only by open columns so that gentlemen of the Household, technically not in the same room, could sit in the Queen's presence on call. The private suite above the rooms for entertaining guests had splendid views of the sea enhanced by large windows of expensive new plate glass. In the Queen's dressing area her water-closet was disguised as a large wardrobe, and in Albert's bathroom *Hercules and Omphale* already hung. Perhaps the most curious feature of the suite was a mechanism beside their large bed which locked the door to the bedroom without the occupants having to stir from the sheets. For soundproofing and fireproofing Cubitt had insulated the walls with crushed sea shells.

Only a week remained of their scheduled autumn stay when the relocation had taken place, and Lady Lyttelton very likely spoke for the family when she wrote, 'We are miserable at having to leave this

Paradise, with this perfect house, so soon.' For Victoria it was Albert's house, which made it all the more perfect. 'When one is so happy & blessed in one's home life, as I am,' she had written in her journal a few months earlier, 'Politics (provided my Country is safe) must only take a 2nd place.' Home life meant the proximity of Albert rather than the presence of her children, as she confided to Stockmar when, in July 1846, the Prince had gone off on one of his many ceremonial journeys, this time to dedicate the Albert Dock at Liverpool. 'I feel lonely without my dear Master', she wrote, 'and though I know other people are often separated for a few days I feel habit could not make me get accustomed to it. Without him everything loses its interest. It will always be a terrible pang for me to separate from him even for two days; and I pray God never to let me survive him.'

In December, when the family returned,* Cubitt arrived with plans for Household and Main Wings. The old residence continued to be a service structure until the next stages were constructed. (By the time Victoria and Albert were finished building and furnishing Osborne, it had cost them £200,000, all of which they were paying for out of their own income, now efficiently managed.) The plaster walls of the new building were nearly dry, furnaces having been run while the family was away, and more of Victoria's and Albert's personal pictures could be hung. For the dining-room's largest walls, Winterhalter was painting a large group portrait of the royal family, the Queen and Prince seated, the children around them.

Royal differences with the new Whig (Liberal) ministry were not merely with personalities. Albert saw a philosophical chasm. He told Russell that he disagreed 'totally' with the view that the Crown had no activist role. Seeing royal authority in male-pronoun terms although he was ostensibly referring to the Queen, he insisted that the sovereign had 'an immense moral responsibility upon his shoulders with regard to his Government and the duty to watch and *control* it'. Both Albert and Russell understood that leashing Palmerston was close to impossible, but the Albertine doctrine rested on the need for something more than

---

* Albert had written to his aunt Julie (Anna Feodorovna) on 18 December 1846 that leaving Osborne for draughty and poorly heated Windsor would be 'a cold sort of pleasure'.

**CINDERELLA; OR, LORD JOHN TRYING IT ON AGAIN.**

*Lord John Russell was a Prime Minister in waiting, or actually in Downing Street, for more than two decades. Punch satirizes his aspirations, and his diminutive size, in 1846 while openly observing that it was Albert who made the political decisions for the Crown. Victoria is not even in the picture.*

historical precedent behind a royal seal or signature. Acting, rather than standing by, for Victoria required confidence that the royal will counted for something more than ceremony. Yet 1847 was the year that political economist Nassau Senior postulated to his friend Alexis de Tocqueville, 'Our Queen is a phantom, put there not to act, but to fill space, to prevent anyone else from being there.'

The risks of royal activism would touch Albert directly, and soon. The Chancellor of Cambridge University died on 12 February 1847. The proponents of Edward Herbert, second Earl of Powis, a former Tory MP and popular 'old boy' from St John's College, immediately put forward his candidacy, but he was regarded with distaste by the Master of rival Trinity College, Dr Whewell, who owed his place to Albert. The Vice-Chancellor, Dr Henry Philpott, Master of St

Catherine's and the real executive of the university – the Chancellorship was ceremonial and honorary – suggested to Albert, possibly at Whewell's bidding, that it was the unanimous wish of the heads of the colleges that the Prince stand. Since that suggested a solid internal base, Albert invited a deputation which waited upon him at Buckingham Palace on 17 February. He was assured of 'lively satisfaction' within the university, Philpott assuming that Powis would step aside.

With his interest in education, particularly in applied science, already established, Albert might have expected enthusiasm for him beyond the Masters of Colleges. He had even attended the previous annual meeting of the British Association for the Advancement of Science, at Southampton, in September 1846. At the mathematical and physical section he listened, with Sir John Herschell on his left and Sir Roderick Murchison on his right, to a paper on instrumentation to measure wind velocity. At the mechanical section he heard an explanation of the weight capacity of tubular construction for railway bridges, and another on methods of deep boring for wells and mine-shaft ventilation. Albert was earnest about enhancing the academic climate for technological change, yet that was a drawback to the many old boys and ageing dons who preferred tradition to innovation and who saw universities as places to prepare clergymen and gentlemen rather than engineers and chemists. Even William Whewell, whom Albert admired for his interests in geology and astronomy and who would promote the 'moral sciences' and 'natural sciences' Triposes at Cambridge, had published, in 1834, a treatise to be expanded into *Of the Plurality of Worlds* (1853), insisting that man was, by faith and fact, an unique creation and that no other life could exist elsewhere in the universe. With Whewell as with so many, science had to be reconciled with theology, not theology with science.

To Henry Reeve of *The Times*, Greville predicted on 21 February that Powis and his High Tory supporters would not back off – that it would be 'a sharp contest, which will, I take it, rather astonish foreigners. The victory will be quite as mortifying as pleasing to the Court...' Greville assumed that, somehow, the Prince would win, but Powis was well financed, and opened a campaign office in a hotel in Cockspur Street, London. Albert thought of withdrawing, which would look like cowardice, while his aides Anson and Phipps – in a memo by Anson –

warned of 'a disagreeable Encounter, & one which those who support YRH ought not to have subjected you to'.

Consulting Peel, whom he trusted above all other Englishmen, Albert asked on the twenty-second whether he should 'stop the possibility of my name appearing in the Contest'. Even if he should win, he asked, should he refuse a tarnished honour? Peel responded tartly the next day that he was 'strongly in favour of permitting the Election to take its course'. Phipps intercepted an election circular sent from Whewell and warned the Master of Trinity that Albert should have no knowledge of the steps taken on his behalf. At the same time, the Master of Clare Hall publicly called for Albert – who knew nothing about it – to withdraw, and Whewell produced another circular contending that Powis would only be 'a Chancellor of St John's'.

Polling was to begin on 25 February. At the end of the first day Albert was ahead, at only 582 to 572, a crowd of Powis voters having arrived on the train from London. Ineligible to cast ballots, undergraduates crowded the Senate House, raising the excitement. The next day, learning of the tight race, Thomas Carlyle wrote to Scots theologian Thomas Erskine with mock concern, 'Poor Prince Albert, it will be an ugly thing if he is beaten in this Inanity.'

At the close of balloting on the second day Albert had drawn ahead, 875 to 789. It had not been easy to vote that Friday, *The Times* reporting that crowds outside the Senate House campaigning for both sides threw 'missiles of all sorts' at people entering with their voting cards, 'and some refrained from voting at all, after having travelled many miles for the purpose, rather than subject themselves to the fury of the storm ...' The third and last day for voting was Saturday, 27 February. Powis-supporting Cantabrigians struggled in, casting almost as many ballots that day as the Prince's men. The final tally was 953 to 837 – so underwhelming a victory that Albert asked Peel whether the Chancellorship should be accepted.

'The acceptance of the office without reluctance or delay', Peel advised, 'has about it a character of firmness and decision', and he offered the Prince a draft reply in the affirmative. Victoria also advised acceptance, assuring herself in her journal, and, presumably, Albert, that 'all the cleverest men were on my beloved Albert's side'.

Like campaigns for public office, inaugurations of the victors were not unduly delayed in the efficient 1840s. Albert was invested with the

ELECTING A CHANCELLOR AT CAMBRIDGE.

Punch *late in 1847 describing the campaign for Chancellor at Cambridge, and Albert's alleged qualifications.*

seals of the Chancellorship on 25 March 1847, in the Green Drawing-Room at Buckingham Palace in the presence of the Masters of the Cambridge colleges. 'It is my first chance', he wrote to his brother, 'to do something in my own name for my adopted country.' Personally invited by the Prince in a spirit of reconciliation, the Earl of Powis found excuses not to be present. Within a year the Cantabs on both sides found reasons to be grateful for the outcome. In January 1848, while pheasant shooting in Wales on his estates, Powis was accidentally shot and killed by one of his sons. Had he been Chancellor, another election would have been necessary.

Albert would be an activist Chancellor in the best interests of the university. Appealed to by geologist Charles Lyell about Cambridge's forlorn and nearly non-existent coverage of modern science and literature amid its preponderance of classical and theological studies, Albert agreed to look into the problem, and appointed Adam Sedgwick as his on-site Secretary. In preparation for the formal installation, Albert had Charles Phipps write to the aged Poet Laureate, William Wordsworth, to request verses for the occasion, and Wordsworth, a St John's man whose brother Christopher had been Master of Trinity, agreed 'to retouch a harp...which has however for some time been laid aside'. The result was mediocre, describing Albert as 'the chosen lord' of the university. *Punch* parodied it in 'the Laureate's Installation Ode, as (it might have been) originally written', hailing Albert as

> One who, if not a King,
> He can be quite declared to be
> ...the next thing.
> And though thou wearest not a crown,
> (To Majesty alone belongeth that),
> Thou own'st a coronet of high renown,
> Thy memorable Hat.

While pleased with the versatility for satire of Albert's memorable shako, *Punch*'s writers put it aside to suggest other ceremonial offices which he might now fill, from Lord Mayor of London to Ranger of the park at Whetstone and Professor of Hebrew at the University of Houndsditch.

The installation ceremonies, beginning on 5 July, were graced by eminent Continental as well as British academicians, and nobility from Albert's friend Prince Löwenstein to the Duke of Wellington. Upstaging all the recipients of honorary degrees to be awarded by Albert as Chancellor was Sir Harry Smith, who arrived in Cambridge preceded by a regimental band and mounted on the Arabian charger which he had ridden at the Battle of Aliwal in the Punjab the year before. 'Almost covered with diamonds', as Sedgwick described her, the Queen was Sir Harry's chief rival for attention, but as a woman she was ineligible for an honorary degree.

For a couple used to having few private moments in public, the Queen and Prince had to take what opportunities they could, and one evening they walked, an entourage discreetly following, along the Backs – in Victoria's journal, the Cam 'waterside' – Albert covering his formal black-and-gold academic regalia, all but his Chancellor's cap, with a mackintosh, and the Queen a contrast in evening clothes but 'with a veil over my diamond diadem'.

For the Prince, it was the prelude to the real work of reforming the hidebound Oxbridge system and dragging university education in England into the nineteenth century. He began following up Lyell's plea with a request to the Vice-Chancellor for curricular data, intended for comparison to German universities. The British Association for the Advancement of Science had already condemned the university hierarchies as interested in preparing students only for a Church vocation. Albert also asked for suggestions from both Peel and Russell, observing to Peel that Whewell, whom both had admired, felt that no scientific discovery was appropriate for academic instruction until it had been sanctioned for a century. Peel derided the 'absurdity'. To Russell, Albert outlined the antique course of study that omitted history, economics, law, psychology, chemistry, geography, art, astronomy, natural history and modern languages. The Professor of Oriental Languages, he noted, lectured on Sanskrit to one pupil.

Sedgwick would carry proposals to and from Osborne, and in the last days of 1847 Albert at Osborne was working out reforms with Vice-Chancellor Philpott – but not without internal resistance that would last well into 1848.

The winter of 1847 had been too vile for the family to remain at Osborne while work on the new structure continued. With the Irish enduring another year of famine and little government effort at relief beyond inadequate soup kitchens; foreign policy disappointments in Portugal, Spain, France and Austria; and a section of scaffolding collapsing at Osborne on 10 March, killing one of Cubitt's men and injuring several others, Albert had sunk into one of his frequent periods of gloom. 'We betook ourselves here,' he wrote to his stepmother that March from the Isle of Wight, 'in the hope of getting a breath of spring . . . but have found nothing but frost and a parching east wind; the day before yesterday for a change we had a foot of snow.' Finally, April brought real spring; Albert busied himself overseeing construction work, and Victoria received dispatch boxes from London and planned another Scottish trip. Their savings from Privy Purse income and other sources raised the possibilities of leasing or buying property in Scotland, which reminded them of Albert's Thüringia. The Duchies of Lancaster and Cornwall, income from which accrued to the royal family until the Prince of Wales was of age, were now managed by Albert and earned significantly more than the £3,000 a year he brought with him from Coburg and the £30,000 he was allowed by Parliament. Albert also anticipated, despite his experience with Wallerstein, that he could borrow more on the strength of his status and his augmented income.

With the new Osborne House a reality, Albert remained preoccupied beyond state business. He was planning formal gardens to emphasize the Italianate nature of the structure – patios, balustrades, stairways, topiaries, pathways, lawns, parks, external statuary and urns. He was ecstatically busy. And he seemed never still.

The Queen and Prince left Osborne Pier for Scotland in the *Victoria and Albert* once Parliament recessed in August. With them were the Queen's half-brother Prince Charles of Leiningen and the two oldest royal children. The convoy, including four warships and the packet *Fairy*, steamed up the Welsh coast and past the Isle of Man, into the Firth of Clyde. The steam yacht continued on with the accompanying ships to anchor off Strathclyde in the Sound of Jura. Undisturbed by the incessant rain or the Queen's new pregnancy, the family transferred to the smaller royal vessel to visit sparsely populated and wilderness country.

Nosing into the forest-ringed lochs and glens, the *Fairy* disembarked the party at Fort William, just west of 4,406-foot Ben Nevis, from which they jolted in pony carriages up what Victoria described as 'a very wild and lonely road' to Loch Laggan, just below the southern end of the long diagonal of Loch Ness. James Hamilton, Earl of Abercorn, had offered the use of his lakeside home, Ardverikie. Braving sheets of rain, a band of Highlanders in traditional garb emerged to guide them over the floating bridge to the Earl's long, isolated stone house, decorated as a hunting lodge with stags' horns and drawings by Landseer.

Later in the day, the Earl arrived with his family to be presented to the Queen and Prince. With his children, he had moved from

Ardverikie for the ten days of the royal visit to their more spartan inland farmhouse. Despite the mist and rain his two girls were wearing their best dresses; the boys were in kilts. Upon being presented, Lord Frederic Hamilton recalled seventy-two year later,

> My two sisters made their curtsies, and my eldest brother made his best bow. 'And this, your Majesty, is my second boy. Make your bow, dear,' said my mother; but my brother [Claud, who was four], his heart still hot within him at being expelled ... instead of bowing, *stood on his head in his kilt*, and remained like that, an accomplishment of which he was very proud. The Queen was exceedingly angry [especially as nothing was worn beneath kilts], so later in the day, upon my brother expressing deep penitence, he was taken back to make his apologies, when he did precisely the same thing over again ... *

Albert especially welcomed the privacy the floating bridge guaranteed. It 'belongs exclusively to ourselves', he wrote to the Duchess of Kent. Frustrated reporters, he added, called Ardverikie 'an un-come-at-able place', as they were 'quartered on the other side of Loch Laggan'. The party remained at the lodge in near solitude until September 17, Victoria observing in her journal that the hills and woods 'reminded us much of Thüringen'. Albert wrote genially to Stockmar on 2 September, 'Whenever we stir out we come home almost frozen and always wet to the skin ... The grouse are wild, and the deer very hard to get at, despite all of which we are still very happy.'

However isolated, Albert remained busy with domestic and foreign politics, taking off at the close of their Ardverikie stay without Victoria to inspect the engineering feat of the Caledonian Canal, which ran north-east from Fort William along the lochs to Inverness. Despite the terrible weather his reception was enthusiastic, with the people of the northern shires, already proud of the accomplishment, further pleased that Albert was willing to grace it.

Looking towards Europe, he wrote on 5 September to Lord John Russell, a weak Prime Minister dominated by Palmerston, who

---

* Years later, Lord Claud Hamilton was an MP and, from 1887 into 1897, ADC to the Queen.

accepted no advice, that it was not England's mission to '*impose* upon any nation' governmental forms alien to its natural development. He did not need to mention Palmerston. England, Albert insisted, had been fortunate in its head start in 'civilisation, liberty, and prosperity' and needed to be the exemplar rather than intrusive activist, for 'the return for all our zeal is hatred'. Italy and Germany, incomplete still as nations, were progressing 'of their own accord'.

While rain pounded the roof at Ardverikie, he penned a long memorandum defining two reasons for the failure of the German states to unite – 'mutual jealousy' and 'sovereign authority', and the resistance of Austria, 'a State composed less of German than non-German elements, whose policy is governed by other than German interests and views, and whose system of government is so wholly based upon stagnation that it cannot hold out a hand to progress of any kind without shattering its own foundations...' Somehow, he felt, Prussia had to take the lead in both unity and in reform. 'If, on the other hand, she declines to undertake the guidance of a moderate and systematic German development, then the vital forces of the nation driven onwards by the pressure of the times will find some irregular vent for themselves, and produce conclusions of all sorts, the final issue of which no human power can foresee.'

Distant from crowds and affairs, Victoria was content. Albert never abandoned business. The Post Office boat brought, and took, the mail, and between deliveries, when not out in the wet, stalking stag, Albert penned further letters and memoranda. On returning to Windsor in October he was full of plans for reform at Cambridge. Also, he intended to prod the King of Prussia gently toward reforms of a different kind, using the bogeyman of a German federation guided by Prince Metternich, who had been trying to keep Europe in stagnation since the Congress of Vienna in 1815.

While the luxuriantly bewhiskered Sir James Clark was attending the medical needs of the royal family in the west of Scotland, his son John was, on fatherly advice, attempting to soothe his weak lungs near Ballater in the drier air of the salubrious east. Young Clark was guest of Sir Robert and Lady Alicia Gordon in a castle – as spacious Scottish country homes, often with decorative towers and turrets, were sometimes referred to – called Balmoral. (The Gordons were brother and sister of Peel's Foreign Secretary, the Earl of Aberdeen.) Although Clark was only forty-five miles away as the corbie flew, he wrote to his drenched and chilled father of one sunny day after another. Impressed, the Queen and Prince asked Sir James to make inquiries about estates in the area which might be rented. A Deeside artist was commissioned to make sketches – which arrived at Windsor just before the news that Sir Robert Gordon had, on 8 October, died suddenly at his breakfast table.

The demise of the lessee of the owner of Balmoral seemed unconnected with its geography, and Lord Aberdeen, who had been brought into the royal search for a Scottish home, suggested that Victoria and Albert take up the unexpired twenty-seven years of the lease. Busy laying out the elaborate terraces at Osborne, Albert authorized James Giles, the artist who had drawn the earlier sketches, to paint watercolours of the whitewashed granite castle and its grounds and bring them to London. Before the close of 1847 he was back, and Victoria and Albert were impressed enough to have a solicitor initiate negotiations with the owner, the Earl of Fife.

Royal accommodations north and south were the chief Court priority that December. Parliament had voted, reluctantly, to rehabilitate and enlarge Buckingham Palace, with its wings to be extended and joined to create an inner court. Thomas Cubitt, now a friend of Albert, refused, as demeaning to his reputation, to bid for the job, but Edward Blore, the assigned architect, recommended to the Commissioners for the Enlargement of Buckingham Palace that Cubitt be accepted unconditionally. The work in London had already begun when Cubitt's crew at Osborne began stripping and disassembling Lady Isabella's former home. Nearby, Victoria and Albert and their children, at the new Osborne House for Christmas, watched. On the last day of 1847, Albert was away on business in London. The Queen was in her seventh month of her sixth pregnancy and leaving affairs to her husband. Alone on New Year's Eve, she went to her diary to reassess her life. 'When one is as happy as we,' Victoria concluded, 'one feels sad at the quick passing of the years, & I always wish Time could stand still for a while.'

The year 1848 was half an hour old when Albert returned by rail and packet and carriage and wished her a '*Prost Neujahr!*' It would be anything but that.

# IX

## *The Violent Year*

### *1848*

'THINGS ARE GOING badly,' Albert wrote to Stockmar in rare panic on 27 February 1848. 'European war is at our doors, France is ablaze in every quarter, Louis-Philippe is wandering about in disguise, so is the Queen; Nemours and Clementine have found their way to Dover; of . . . the others, all we know is, that the Duchess of Montpensier is at Le Tréport under another name; Guizot is a prisoner, the Republic declared . . . ' Exaggerating local unrest, he claimed that radicals 'refuse to pay the income tax, and attack' – he meant verbally – 'the Ministry'. Further, following a litany of troubles, 'Victoria is on the point of being confined'.

European economic crises in 1846–47 prompting widespread unemployment and misery had been mishandled by reactionary post-Waterloo governments that feared 'the spectre of communism' but not enough to liberalize their societies. Secret revolutionary groups and working-men's radical organizations took their frustrations into the streets. The first uprisings, the 'February Revolution' in France, sparked equally uncoordinated and generally futile revolutions elsewhere on the Continent, the discrepancies in aims between bourgeois and working-class leaders thwarting any chances of permanent change. But while regimes were being threatened, and some unseated, it appeared at first that the instability was not sufficiently contagious to cross the Channel.

*En route* to visit Albert in January, Ernest had stopped first in Berlin and then in Brussels. In Prussia, Frederick William IV assured Ernest that agitation for political reforms could be satisfied by window-dressing changes. In Belgium, Leopold worried that his rather liberal regime might be menaced by the hopeless erosion of the monarchy in France. Paris was particularly explosive. 'My father-in-law', he predicted, 'will soon be driven away, like Charles X. The catastrophe is coming unavoidably over France, and, in consequence, into Germany also.'

Thrones trembled across Europe. As Albert and Palmerston argued over the future of incompetent King Otho, an unpopular Bavarian who had been imposed upon Greece in 1833, other crowns were in even greater jeopardy. As Foreign Minister and most knowledgeable Englishman about external affairs, Palmerston cared nothing for European stability – as did Albert – if the alternative was liberal change. In a long entry on 22 January Greville gossiped in his diary that a Palmerstonian paragraph on the Spanish succession had been taken to the Queen and Prince by Russell with the suggestion that it be expunged. 'It did not become *us*', said the Prime Minister, 'to lay down the constitutional law of Spain.'

The Queen and Prince agreed. 'It was returned (so altered) to Palmerston; but when the despatch was published, it was found that Palmerston had re-inserted the paragraph, and so it stood!' What impressed Greville most was 'that they all *stood* it, as they always will'. The upheavals of 1848 would be responded to by Britain in two voices, the Palace's and Palmerston's, although the domineering Foreign Secretary would close his contrarieties to Albert with 'I have the honour to be Your most obedient Humble Servant'.

As messages flooded in with particulars about risings across Europe, 'Oh!' Victoria recalled to her eldest daughter after Albert's death, 'how much we talked over all those events day by day and hour by hour.' Even at eight, however, Vicky was considered a small adult, her father's protegée, and up to serious talk, while nothing was ever expected of the eldest royal son. As Greville observed, the Princess Royal was already 'very clever' while Victoria considered Bertie at seven 'a stupid boy'. It was 'the hereditary and unfailing antipathy of our Sovereigns to their Heirs Apparent . . . thus early to be taking root'. According to one of the Queen's ladies, Greville added, Bertie confided that during the voyage to Scotland – the episode sounds more like Albert than Victoria – 'he was very nearly thrown overboard'.

Paradoxically, as soon as the *status quo* began to crumble, the King of Hanover blamed both the Prince and Palmerston for the unravelling. It was Albert who was encouraging the King of Prussia to unite Germany under a liberal constitution, yet also tempting his brother to amalgamate the Ernestine statelets into a Kingdom of Thuringia. At the same time Palmerston was encouraging the ethnic fragmentation of authoritarian Austria and the unification, at Austria's cost, of Italy. Even Switzerland was, early in 1848, in the turmoil of further federation. 'What has Palmerston to answer for,' Ernest Augustus wrote to the Tory Lord Strangford on 21 February, 'for his conduct in throwing fire and flame throughout Europe?'

Duke Ernest was with his brother when news arrived from Gotha on 22 February that their step-grandmother, Dowager Duchess Caroline, had died. He rushed back for the obsequies. Albert could not leave the Queen in her ninth month of pregnancy, and was worried, further, about the imminence of trouble, foreign and domestic. Just before five in the afternoon of 25 February the Belgian ambassador to London, Van de Weyer, was in *The Times*'s offices looking for news, as telegraphic and rail communication with Paris had ceased the day before. As he was about to give up, a dispatch clicked in from Brussels with the first reports from travellers of the proclamation of the French Republic. He carried the news himself to Prince Albert, who brought it to Victoria.

On the leap-day of the 29th, Albert wrote to Duchess Marie, his stepmother, that the scattered royal family of France 'have come to us one by one like people shipwrecked'. The portly Louis-Philippe, his whiskers shaved, had managed with the connivance of the British consul at Le Havre to sail from Honfleur. On landing in England he appealed for asylum. Claremont was reopened for the Orléanist refugees. Albert went to see them on 4 March and despite his past hostility toward the Spanish marriages invited them to Buckingham Palace. The King, Queen, and duc de Montpensier came on the seventh, looking, Victoria noted, 'very *abbatu*'. Since they had 'hardly the means of living', she asked Palmerston to arrange for the family's expenses from a secret Intelligence account. (To avoid awkwardness, the ex-king and queen would refer to themselves thereafter as the Comte and Comtesse de Neuilly.)

Other royal refugees arrived. On 6 March, with revolutions in France, Sicily, Austria and, it seemed, additional places daily, Albert wrote with foreboding to Frederick William IV of Prussia that the uprisings of January and February let loose 'the evil spirit of communism, the hereditary foe of all society, and threatens the fall of other states'. Even in conservative Gotha there was unrest, with demands that much of Ernest's property become public – he had a proliferation of palaces and estates – and that citizens be guaranteed constitutional rights. 'My house is like a headquarters,' he reported to Albert on 20 March. ' ...I thank Providence for not having given me any children, for I should tremble for them.'

Unaware yet of outbreaks in Germany, Albert had written again, on 18 March, to the King of Prussia, this time about the birth that morning of Louise Caroline Alberta. He had no idea that Berlin had boiled over and that the King would be forced by fighting in the streets to mourn the revolutionary dead publicly, concede freedom of the press, and call for the assembly of a representative Diet in April. Scurrying under the umbrella of a liberalism in which he did not believe and a pan-Germanism he distrusted, Frederick William even called for the unity of the German states in defiance of faltering Austria, which was losing control of Lombardy and Venetia to Italian nationalists and seemed likely to unravel further. That France supported Italian unification at Austria's expense troubled Albert. An Italy shaped by France, with its radical republican tradition, he would write to Lord John Russell on 17 May, would be in its neighbour's debt, and France 'is sure to bring only developments of destruction into any matter'. Further, he saw the need for a formidable Austria to offset the ambitions of Russia.

Prince William of Prussia added to Albert's cares in England, arriving on 27 March. Although it was an opportune moment for him to be godfather to the new princess at her christening, when the Foreign Office advised against it, Albert asked Palmerston instead to give the Prince the dignity of diplomatic status – he had settled at Baron Bunsen's Prussian embassy – rather than have him identified as a political refugee. 'The poor Prince of Prussia', Albert wrote to Ernest, still safe in his backwater, 'is much to be pitied. He is very unjustly under a cloud.' He had been accused of ordering troops to fire on the barricades but claimed it was a canard.

In a long memo, in German as usual, and dated the next day, Albert thought out an idealistic plan for which events had now created an opportunity. He envisioned a German 'Federative State' with a strong sovereign, chancellor and parliament which would retain the 'States complete in themselves' with their 'dynastic forms' that embodied 'the Individualities of these People'. Thinking well of it, he had copies made and sent to King Frederick William and to Baron Stockmar, to Duke Ernest and to Frederick Augustus II of Saxony (deposed by revolutionaries but restored a week later by Prussian troops), to Ludwig I of Bavaria (driven to abdicate later in the year in favour of Maximilian II, who was forced to institute domestic reforms), and to the weak-minded Emperor Ferdinand of Austria, who would abdicate before the frenzy of 1848 ended and be replaced by his nephew of eighteen.

The young emperor, Franz Joseph, would be immediately fortunate in his Chancellor. As innocent of government as was Albert on arriving in England, the new sovereign learned quickly how an authoritarian state was run from the sophisticated Prince Schwartzenberg, who had been with General Radetzky's headquarters in Italy. By then the Austrians were turning back the Italians, and had tired of Palmerston's efforts to settle the destiny of their lower Alpine provinces. 'We never pressed on him *our* advice', Schwartzenberg wrote wryly to his Under-Secretary for Foreign Affairs (the Prince had also taken the foreign office portfolio), 'concerning the affairs of Ireland'. He would send, Schwartzenberg went on, an Austrian archduke to every European court but England to announce formally Franz Joseph's accession. No emissary would go to London to be exposed to 'the devoted protector of the Emperor's rebellious subjects' – and he identified Palmerston by name.

The British ambassador in Vienna forwarded a copy to his chief, who dismissed the complaint as 'the outpourings of an enraged woman of the town when arrested by a Policeman in the act of picking a Pocket'. Albert's secretary Charles Grey told the Prince years later that Palmerston had ordered Schwartzenberg's letter to be removed from the embassy files and destroyed.

Later Albert assumed that Prince William's two months of gentle exile in England – and education in politics for the likely emperor of Albert's ideal German government – meant that the Prussian heir apparent had become 'wholeheartedly' for reform. He had even praised English democratic institutions, and his wife, Augusta, to whom Victoria warmed, would vainly remind him of such virtues as William slipped back into traditional Junker attitudes.

More than one convert to constitutional monarchy was needed, however, and Albert also urged his reluctant brother, 'if some important

German prince' – there was flattery in the description – 'fails to under-take the task, it will fall into the hands of clubs, societies, professors, theorists, and humbugs; and if the work is not begun soon, the masses will seize the control of it'. Dragged-out attempts to patch together a new German federation would fail, as would the squabbling revolutionaries. At the end of May, it was safe enough for Prince William to return to Berlin.

England expected its own share of instability. Financial panic had cost jobs and savings; speculators caused huge losses in inflated railway stock; wheat prices had plunged to new lows although the hungry Irish could not afford it and would not eat it; unemployment and poverty – even many who worked earned starvation wages – had given new impetus to Chartism; and as a late winter gave way to cold spring, the homeless and the hungry thronged London and other grimy industrial cities. Benjamin Disraeli, the ambitious MP who led the anti-Peel faction among the Tories, privately considered a bounder by Albert, had published a much-discussed novel, *Sybil, or The Two Nations*, in 1845, in which he described England as two nations which had little understanding or even communication with each other – the Rich and the Poor. Their clash seemed inevitable, and Albert, worried about the turmoil, foreign and domestic, asked Peel, whom he trusted more than anyone else in public life, to call at the Palace for a talk on 'the many awful events that are taking place around us'.

Chartist demonstrations in English industrial towns had been grow-ing larger and noisier since the routing of the Orléanists in Paris. To prevent the disaffected from rallying around symbolic martyrs, the government in London shrewdly released radical agitators who had been imprisoned for sedition. Chartist leaders then announced a non-violent mass meeting on Kennington Common, south of the Thames. From there, a procession of tens of thousands of sympathizers would convey a huge petition to the House of Commons, demanding the liberalized enfranchisement spelled out in their charter. Allegedly endorsed by more than a million people, its roll of signers cast some doubt as to the genuineness of the document. The bogus signatures included the Duke of Wellington – seventeen times – and Queen Victoria. Even the reality represented a formidable following of the disaffected. The date set for what could possibly be a peaceable revolu-tion was 10 April.

Alarmed, the Home Office and War Office called up reserve troops to patrol the streets, and across Britain 150,000 special constables were enlisted. 'Every gentleman in London was sworn', Greville wrote. (Among them was an ambitious French exile, Louis Napoleon Bonaparte.) Her child of three weeks with her, Victoria prudently left for Osborne with Albert in the morning of 8 April, Waterloo Station having been cleared by police in advance. Concerned that there would be talk of royal cowardice, Colonel Phipps quietly walked the streets listening for any disparagement of the flight from London, reporting to Albert, 'her reputation for personal courage stands so high, I never heard one person express a belief that her departure was due to personal alarm.'*

In the short run, the Chartists had failed; yet as with many once-radical movements, its aspirations largely became law. Despite the Combination Acts which restricted mass agitation, popular frustration could not be wholly contained, and small demonstrations occurred in parks and squares, all easily put down. 'We have Chartist riots every night', Albert exaggerated to Stockmar from the Palace on 6 May, adding dramatically that they resulted 'in numbers of broken heads'. Another failure was an abortive Irish rising in July, inspired by very different motives. Hunger had led to apathy, and there was no end to the famine.

Most outbreaks on the Continent sought political liberalization or national separatism, and concluded in confusion of leadership and restoration of the absolutism that inspired them. Even in Austria, from which stretched an ethnic hotchpotch of an empire and where Metternich was ousted as the power behind a succession of weak sovereigns who fled to England, the regime survived. Warily, Metternich also returned, but the aged relic of the Congress of Vienna in 1815 would

---

* Nevertheless, the English radical G. Julian Harney would write to Friedrich Engels – Karl Marx's collaborator on *The Communist Manifesto* (1848), who had been living in Manchester since 1842 – that 'we Englishmen have but a very poor opinion of your German *princes*. We have a noted German prince amongst our field-marshals – well when the Chartists were about to hold their meeting on Kennington Common to *petition* for Parliamentary Reform, the said Prince *bolted* (do you understand the expressive English vulgarism?) from London to the Isle of Wight, and there his princeship remained until he was quite sure the naughty Chartists had gone back to their homes. After all the Prince I speak of was more of a hero than the celebrated Orléans princes. *Our* prince ran away *with* his wife, but the precious sons of Louis-Philippe ran away *from* their wives!' (28 March 1849)

never regain office. Nationalism was also behind the succession imbroglio in the Duchies of Schleswig and Holstein, part-Dane, part-German. The death of Christian VIII, who had declared their union with Denmark inseparable, and his succession by Frederick VII, prompted uprisings by the German population on 18 March. Prussian troops came to their support, driving the Danes out. The situation would fester after the Danes fought back and achieved a temporary truce. The dilemma required a Solomon.

Explaining away what seemed a partisan view of the conflict to Lord John Russell on 1 May, Albert wrote painfully, 'The Schleswig-Holstein question causes me much anxiety as I am afraid that we may be dragged by the Danes and Russians, perhaps even by French insinuation and diplomatic efforts, into an open opposition of Germany. I assure you that I try to divest myself of every particle of German feeling.' British opposition, he cautioned, might appear as hostility towards German 'regeneration and consolidation'.

Fourteen years later, the question would involve the Crown again, and with even greater anxiety.

With the threat of internal upheaval diminished, many in power were content to see a return to the *status quo*, but Albert, out inspecting working-class conditions in April, was appalled by the dank, dark slums, widespread malnutrition and unemployment. Poor relief, he learned, went to four and a half million people out of the thirty million in the United Kingdom, yet had almost no impact upon the poverty and misery. 'Surely', he wrote impatiently to Lord John Russell, 'this is not the moment for the taxpayers to economise upon the working classes!' Albert had been nominal president of the Society for Improving the Conditions of the Labouring Classes since 1844, taking the title at the request of Lord Ashley, the philanthropic future seventh Earl of Shaftesbury, but had done little other than lend his name. When Ashley now asked him to take the chair at a public meeting which would air the abominations, Russell's colleagues objected that the Prince might be exploited by noisy demagogues. As evidence, the Prime Minister showed Albert a pamphlet attacking the royal family for its guilt in the plight of the poor, which only reinforced his determination to speak out. The people, he wrote to Russell on 29 April, had as yet no 'tangible proof' of any interest in their plight on his part or that of the Queen. Despite Cabinet objections, he presided at the meeting on 18 May after an inspection of a model house to lodge the labouring classes.

His recommendations were paternalistic yet his reasoning was radical. 'Wealth should lead the way,' he exhorted. 'Wealth is an accident of society', and those happy possessors of it should intervene to ameliorate 'the evils produced by other accidents'. Those who 'enjoy station, wealth, and education' owed it to the disadvantaged to furnish, without being forced to by legislation, the means of self-help through making land, loans and lodgings available so that 'their poorer brethren' would have opportunities to work toward their own improvement. Further, he exhorted, the increasing prosperity of 'that class of our community which has most of the toil, and least of the enjoyments, of this world' would contribute to the happiness of all classes. 'Depend upon it that the interests of often contrasting classes are identical, and it is only ignorance which prevents their uniting to the advantage of each other.'

'At a time when it is much easier for Royal personages to lose popularity than to win confidence', *The Times* commented the next day, loyal subjects should greet the Prince's address with satisfaction. 'It is thoroughly English in feeling, English in language, and English in sense. Among the many speeches it has been our lot to peruse, we have not seen one which for brevity and plainness, for goodness and truth, would be more worth the reading of every man in these islands.' Widely reported, Albert's words encouraged even the illiterate, and would exert moral pressure upon business into acting in its own interest, and, eventually, even government. The Prince had found an unofficial pulpit.

On the housing issue, Albert proved as good as his words, commissioning out of his own pocket the construction of model working-class flats. Henry Roberts, who had designed Fishmonger's Hall in the City, planned the 'cottage flats' with simple but neo-classical façades and with two levels, each with two living areas divided by a central staircase. In 1851 they were exhibited on the edge of Hyde Park, then re-erected for use in Kennington Park in South London.

One of the first to take the Prince seriously was an elderly American expatriate banker. George Peabody had settled in London in the year of Victoria's accession, aged forty-two. He quickly made a fortune in brokerage and returned his wealth in great measure through philanthropic efforts on both sides of the Atlantic. Setting up trusts later worth tens of millions, he had vast tracts of tenements cleared and low-income housing erected that would be models for the future. (Many Peabody Trust buildings still house low-income Londoners.) Victoria would offer him a knighthood but he chose to remain an American citizen, and instead accepted a miniature of her portrait.

Pleas to Albert to lend his name and prestige to, or to speak or act for, myriad causes and committees and conferences filled his mail and sometimes emptied his purse. His personal Household cost half his allotment from Parliament, and he was always working to make royal lands turn more of a profit while paring the managerial costs that came from the royal family's pockets. Sometimes, although not always – as occurred with Irish relief – there was a public relations as well as a philanthropic benefit. When Albert became head of a fund to purchase Shakespeare's cottage in Stratford-on-Avon, and contributed the first £250, even *Punch* praised him, yet hoped, cheekily, 'that, having helped to buy Shakespeare's house, you will also buy his book'.

Albert also had another house in mind. Even more than her husband, who saw Scotland through a Thüringian lens, Victoria was eager to acquire a permanent home there, unconcerned about its inaccessibility for state business. However difficult it might be for her ministers, one of them would have to accompany the royal party, to represent the government. Despite railway lines that would eventually take passengers as close as Ballater, ministers would dread the assignment, while the distance would further attenuate the Crown's influence on events. Telegrams would not have the effectiveness of talk, and the bracing climate would not buoy up politicians who preferred the smoke and fogs of London to the sunny brilliance of the Solent. But at least the rail terminus at Gosport was only two hours from Waterloo Station, as opposed to the night-and-day journey to the north. Although the Prime Minister warned that Parliament would not finance a private royal home – and a second one at that – Albert went ahead, confident that he could support not only a lease but the unpredictable upkeep.

Two bills to recognize the right of Jews to sit in Parliament failed in the Lords in 1848, as they had failed in previous years. Lionel de Rothschild had been elected overwhelmingly and often by the City of London, but continued to be denied his seat. When the first of the bills in 1848 had again passed the Commons in February, largely with Liberal votes, Nathaniel ('Nat') de Rothschild, working since 1840 in the Paris offices of the firm (it would be untouched by events), suggested to his three brothers in London that in order to ease the bill through the Tory-dominated Lords, 'You should work with the Court party. Get your friend Prince Albert to use his influence and then perhaps it will go through.' Suddenly Albert's negotiations for the Balmoral lease (little escaped the Rothschilds) and the Oettingen–Wallerstein loan for which the Prince had been co-signatory intersected in the fertile brain of one of the brothers at St Swithin's Lane.

Albert's sympathies with Jewish aspirations were known to be stronger than those of the Queen. When legislation opened the path for Jews to sit on governing bodies in the City of London, David Salomons became an Alderman in 1847 (he would be Lord Mayor in 1855), allegedly prompting a liberal bishop to observe to the Prince, 'Thank goodness we've got a gentleman in the civic chamber, at last.'

'Yes,' Albert agreed, 'but you had to go beyond the pale of Christianity to find him.'

Working the Court party meant little more than having Albert or his surrogate, possibly Peel, attempt to sway peers closest to the Prince. The carrot suggested by the brothers in response to Nat was, apparently, the waiving of the £3,000 Wallerstein loan through accepting his worthless pictures held by Albert, and the offer of a further loan of £15,000 for a Scottish lease or purchase. But Nat turned bluntly negative. Conditions had become unpredictably chaotic. Further loans to royalty were unsafe. On 10 May, as Albert was close to agreement on Balmoral, Nat responded to 'My dear Brothers' – Lionel, Anthony and Mayer – to put all ideas of a *douceur* aside:

> You ask my advice respecting a loan of £15,000 to P[rince] A[lbert]. I think there is not the slightest occasion to consent to it. You will find yourselves in the same position with regard to him as we are with L[ouis-] P[hilippe]. If I do not mistake, my dear Brothers, he already owes you £3,000 which we paid here to the Bavarian minister. I really do not think you are authorised to advance so large a sum considering the state of things, and you should in my opinion tell him so. There is not the slightest reason to make compliments with him & I am convinced that whether you give the cash or not it will not make

the slightest difference in the fate of the Jews Bill. I can only repeat that I am decidedly against the advance & under the present circumstances I do not think you are authorised in consenting to it.

Nat's reply was more than a veto – it suggested that one of the brothers in London had already made quiet soundings with the Prince. Given the already legendary Rothschild secretiveness, confidences could have been exchanged in such an informal setting as a hunt – a favourite pastime of both Anthony and Mayer. Yet within a fortnight Albert had Balmoral. Sight unseen, and through a solicitor, he arranged to purchase the remaining twenty-seven years of the Gordon lease, including 10,000 acres of forest, for £2,000. On 20 May 1848 in the Tory bastion of the Carlton Club on Pall Mall, Captain Alexander Wharton Duff, acting for the Fife Trustees, signed after adding a clause that exempted them from any claim 'on account of additional buildings' put up by the Prince. Both Osborne and Balmoral would be Albert's properties, unconnected with the Crown.

At the time of his twenty-ninth birthday, he and Victoria were preparing to establish themselves on Deeside. Furniture, pictures and personal belongings had already been shipped and placed according to instructions. In time to mark the Prince's birthday on the 26th, King Leopold had sent greetings, and three days later, from Osborne, Victoria responded to him that the '*dearest* of days' was to her one of 'eternal thankfulness, for a purer, more perfect being than my beloved Albert the Creator could *not* have been sent into this troubled world. I feel that I could *not* exist without him, and that I should sink under the troubles and annoyances and *dégoûts*' – disgust – 'of my *very* difficult position, were it not for *his* assistance, protection, guidance, and comfort. Truly do I thank you for your *great* share in bringing about our marriage.'

Victoria and Albert saw Balmoral for the first time on 8 September, after a voyage north to Aberdeen. The railway from London had not yet extended that far into Scotland. The land around the castle that was part of the lease included bothies in which peasants lived in near-feudal simplicity – two-room hovels of unhewn stones closed up with a mortar of mud and thatched with heather. Light came through small sealed windows and a wide fireplace sometimes gave out enough heat to keep the earthen floor dry. For the occupants, a nearby royal residence meant prosperity of a sort – year-round and part-time jobs for footmen and housemaids (supplementing staff brought from the south), gillies and gardeners, keepers and coachmen. By comparison with even the finest cottages in the area, quickly requisitioned for retinue who could not fit into the castle, the structure called Balmoral was regal, with mullioned windows, gables, turrets and round towers with conical roofs. The Household would dread its chill and loneliness, on both of which the Queen thrived. In the violent year of 1848 her journal entry was especially meaningful: 'All seemed to breathe freedom and peace, and to make one forget the world and its sad turmoils.'

The excitement surrounding the rare residence of a British sovereign in Scotland was such that even on Deeside the Queen and Prince could not shut out the world. In the form of press coverage the world arrived in advance of the royal family, and illustrated papers were rushed drawings as soon as the principals could be penned into them. One in the *Illustrated London News* showed the Queen, Prince and a kilted Bertie rushing across a bridge into beflagged Ballater. Press efforts to bribe backstairs maids and brawny ghillies would become such a nuisance that even the irreverent *Punch* would publish a John Leech cartoon of a reporter-artist at a keyhole – 'Gross Outrage: or, Paul Pry in the Highlands, making a sketch'. Once the stays in Scotland became routine, newspapers lost interest.

As with Osborne, the original structure and outbuildings were insufficient for the Household and such visitors as the Minister-in-Residence, and at first much of the adjacent land could be leased but not purchased. Eventually the royal estate would encompass 24,000 acres, and miles along the Dee. All farmers and cottagers on the estate would be forbidden to let their houses or to receive lodgers – a drastic protection of the Queen's privacy. The funds needed for the acquisition came unexpectedly in 1852. Even by English standards, James Camden Nield of 5 Cheyne Walk, Chelsea, was an eccentric, the uncharitable child of a wealthy amateur sociologist who had visited English and Scottish prisons in fifty-nine counties, gathering material for a book, *The State of Prisons* (1812). His son inherited only the elder Nield's frugality and his fortune in Home Counties properties. When 'Miser Nield' died in a nearly empty, cobwebbed house that might have excited the admiration of Dickens's Miss Havisham, there was little more to tally of his possessions than a bed made of a board, a few shabby sticks of furniture, a tallow candle, and a cat. But Nield also had holdings that would realize more than £250,000, then fifty times the annual salary of the Prime Minister. Having no family, he left it all to the Queen. Nield knew, Victoria observed, that she 'would not waste it'. Leased lands could be purchased, and a grander Balmoral built. Nield's largesse also went into the improvement and expansion of Osborne.* Stockmar wished Nield 'a joyful resurrection'.

Before the expansion of Osborne and the rebuilding of Balmoral, family life for Victoria's brood in both settings was *gemütlich* in the extreme. Limited as the facilities were, especially at Balmoral, Victoria preferred being away, in conditions far from royal, to the gloomy grandeur of Windsor and the city seediness of odoriferous drain-clogged Buckingham Palace. Charles Greville, who visited Balmoral with Lord John Russell, was amazed at the limitations of the Scottish house and the lack of 'any state whatever':

> They live not merely like private gentlefolks, but like very small gentlefolks, small house, small rooms, small establishment. There are no soldiers, and the whole guard of the Sovereign and the whole Royal Family is a single policeman, who walks about the grounds to keep off impertinent intruders or improper characters. Their attendants consisted of Lady Douro and Miss Dawson, Lady and Maid of Honour; George Anson and [John] Gordon; [Henry] Birch, the Prince of Wales's tutor; and Miss Hildyard, the governess of the children. They live with the greatest simplicity and ease. The Prince shoots every morning, returns to luncheon, and then they walk and drive. The Queen is running in and out of the house all day long, and often goes about alone, walks into the cottages, and sits down and chats with the old women . . . We were only nine people, and it was all very easy and really agreeable, the Queen in very good humour and talkative; the Prince still more so, and talking very well; no form, and everybody seemed at their ease. In the evening we withdrew to the only room there is besides the dining-room, which serves for billiards, library (hardly any books in it), and drawing-room. The Queen and Prince and her ladies and Gordon soon went back to the dining-room, where they had a Highland

---

* The Queen and Prince put aside some funds for a window in Nield's memory at his church.

dancing-master, who gave them lessons in reels. We (John Russell and I) were not admitted to this exercise, so we played at billiards. In the process of time they came back, when there was a little talk, and soon after they went to bed...

The Queen and Prince travelled without the burden of the youngest children, who were left at Osborne. Albert loved his brood with real affection and enjoyed playing with them, unlike the remote Victoria, who disliked children, especially small ones, almost as much as she abhorred the pregnancies that produced them. Nevertheless, she left them with morning and evening prayers by which to recall their mother and father. For Alice, the Queen inscribed on her gold-embossed and crested letter paper

*Evening*
O kind and good God, I thank thee for this happy day; pray keep me, and dear Papa & Mama, & my dear Brothers and Sisters & Relations Safe this Night.
*Morning*
O heavenly Father I thank thee for this quiet night; – pray make me a good little child, & keep me, & dear Papa & Mama & my dear Brothers and Sisters & Relations, safe through this day.*

Left at home with her prayers while Alfred, at four a year younger but required to keep Bertie company, went along, Alice was rewarded by a letter from her father, which he penned, in large print, on 16 September from Balmoral. 'You have written me another very nice little letter,' he complimented the precocious Alice. '...We hope soon to be with you again. ...Affie is grown still fatter and wears a cap, "who goes over my eyes" he says. Mama embraces you and I am your affect[ionate] Papa, Albert.'

Three days after the royal party's arrival in Balmoral, Albert wrote to his stepmother in Coburg, Dowager Duchess Marie, 'We have withdrawn for a short time into a complete mountain solitude...where the snow already covers the mountain tops, and the wild deer come creeping stealthily round the house. I, naughty man, have also been creeping

---

* Victoria actually wrote the prayers for Alice's fourth birthday, on 25 April 1847; presumably they were for general use thereafter.

1. Prince Albert and Prince Ernest in 1829 as painted in Coburg by Louise Leopoldine von Meyern, daughter of Baron Ferdinand von Meyern, a Court chamberlain, who was herself only fourteen at the time

2. Duchess Louise, first wife of Ernest I of Coburg, with her children. The future Ernest II is on her left, Prince Albert on her right. Painting in oils by Ludwig Doll, Gotha, 1823–4, Schloss Ehrenburg, Coburg

3. Schloss Rosenau, as it appeared in 1857 to the camera of Francis Bedford

4. Schloss Ehrenburg in Coburg in 1857 as background to the recently erected (1849) statue of Ernest I, Albert's father, by Ludwig Schwanthaler. Photo by Francis Bedford

5. The Royal Marriage, engraving from a painting by George Hayter, 1840

6. Edwin Landseer, *Queen Victoria and Prince Albert at the Bal Costumé of 12 May 1842* attired as Queen Philippa and Edward III

7. The baptism of the Prince of Wales, 25 January 1842. Engraving from a painting by George Hayter

8. Edwin Landseer's *Windsor Castle in Modern Times* shows the young married couple
in the early 1840s with their first-born, the Princess Royal, dressed as an angel.
Albert has just returned from shooting, and the results are spread out to admire. The
Queen seems to be admiring her husband's handsome figure

9. *Omphale and Hercules* (1830), purchased for Osborne House by Albert in 1844. Joseph Anton von Gegenbaur shows Hercules holding weaving implements to emphasize his having been purchased by the Queen as her slave for domestic duties, including, as is obvious from their unclothed state, siring her children

10. Albert's portrait by Alexander de Meville, 1845, Schloss Friedenstein, Gotha

11. Albert presiding at a German-style table-top Christmas tree, in an 1848 lithograph

12. Albert and Victoria sitting in the royal railway carriage with King Louis-Philippe, late in 1844. From a contemporary lithograph

13. *Punch* in 1843 satirizing Albert's design of military paraphernalia, especially the shako hat

**PRINCE ALBERT'S STUDIO**

**A CASE OF REAL DISTRESS**

14. *Punch* in 1846 taking note of the royal family's alleged needs as its numbers burgeon. The waifs in the foreground represent widespread public distress

**PRINCE ALBERT "AT HOME."**
WHEN HE WILL SUSTAIN (NO END) DIFFERENT CHARACTERS

15. *Punch* in 1847 displayed a plethora of Alberts.
The Prince was soldier, statesman, academic
administrator, sportsman, designer of army regalia,
courtier, and whatever else was needed

16. When Albert was admitted to the Guild of
Merchant Tailors in 1845 – many City
guilds so honoured him – *Punch*
put him in his Field-Marshal's
uniform for the investiture,
doubling the satire by
turning the tailor's iron
into the torso of a
rocking-horse

This is the Palace the Prince had built.

17. Opening page of an 1851 children's book in the 'Aunt Busy-Bee's' series (London), showing Joseph Paxton offering his plans to Prince Albert

And this is the Man submitting his plan
To the Prince who approved, and said it was good,
That a Palace of Glass should be built on the grass,
For the great World's Fair, which has since been held there,
And that Palace so famed, is everywhere named,
The fine Crystal Palace the Prince had built.

18. Charles Phipps, F.W. Gibbs, tutor to the Prince of Wales, Bertie, Albert, Baron Stockmar, Dr Ernst Becker, Albert's German librarian, and Stockmar's son, Ernst. Windsor Castle, April 1857. Photograph by L. Caldesi

19. Osborne House in its completed sprawling state

20. Balmoral Castle, with the River Dee in the foreground

21. The Royal Family at Osborne, May 1857. *Left to right* : Princess Alice, Prince Arthur, Prince Albert, the Prince of Wales, Prince Leopold, Princess Louise, Queen Victoria with Princess Beatrice, Prince Alfred, the Princess Royal and Princess Helena

22. The Royal Family assembled for the marriage of the Princess Royal (*right*), 25 January 1858. Engraving from a painting by John Philip. Standing kilted in front of his father (*left*) is the Prince of Wales. Behind Victoria's left shoulder is her mother, the Duchess of Kent

23. Prince Albert, idealized in his uniform as Colonel of the Rifle Brigade, in 1859. Painting by Franz Xavier Winterhalter

24. Queen Victoria and
the Prince Consort,
Osborne, July 1859.
Photograph by Miss Day

25 Victoria and Albert, 1860,
from a *carte-de-visite*

26. Albert in his last years, in a lithograph from a watercolour by Edward Corbould in his sitting-room at Windsor. His need for fireplaces and warmth is obvious, as is his balding, revealed in the mirror

27. An artist's conception of the death of Prince Albert, December 1861. The room is dramatically enlarged, and solicitous personages not actually present are added for effect. The artist may have been Octavius Oakley, but attribution is uncertain

28. The funeral of the Prince Consort in the Chapel Royal of St George's, Windsor, 23 December 1861, *Illustrated London News*

29. Victoria visiting Albert's sarcophagus and effigy at Frogmore, where she would be interred on her instructions at his side. From a contemporary engraving

30. The Albert Memorial. Photograph by Albert Kerstig, 1970, before conservation repair work began

stealthily after the harmless stags, and today I shot two red deer – at least I hope so, for they are not yet found [by the ghillies], but I have brought home a fine roebuck...' The self-reproaches are of great psychological interest. He knew his behaviour was morally dubious, yet compulsive. That recognition would change nothing. Something pent up in him needed violent release, which could emerge from the end of a double-barrelled shotgun.

Although Victoria and Albert received daily messages about the state of the Continent and the condition of Britain, nothing but urgent business would keep them long in London. On 28 September they left for Buckingham Palace, where they stayed overnight, then departed for Osborne. On 9 October they returned – to Windsor.

Even in Scotland, Albert had worked on his reforms for Cambridge, and over the months since his election had Sedgwick and Philpott come to Osborne to discuss the necessary university rules changes. As a dramatic gesture in the direction of modern ideas, he had the most distinguished scholar at Cambridge, Charles Lyell, visit Balmoral. He was knighted there by the Queen. Lyell's 1,600-page *Principles of Geology*, published in 1833 to the dismay of biblical fundamentalists, demonstrated, as Disraeli would write to a friend, 'that the great changes which have taken place in our globe are not the consequence of fast, sudden, and spasmodic changes but the result of that continual change, thro' countless ages, which is now, as it always has been, going on'. Darwin's work in the same spirit would not appear until 1859. Since Albert's boyhood explorations with Florschütz in Saxony, he had been fascinated by geology. Excursions with Lyell to nearby Scottish crags not only tapped that interest but demonstrated that the Prince would not be a merely ceremonial Chancellor.

On 31 October the Senate of the University carried the Albertine reforms although a considerable minority vote evidenced donnish antipathy to change. A new Moral Sciences Tripos included philosophy, political economy, modern history and law; a Natural Sciences Tripos, dear to Albert's heart, included anatomy, physiology, chemistry, botany, and geology. 'Some men will cling to their ignorance with their hands and feet,' Albany Fonblanque wrote in the *Examiner* of the reluctant minority. 'The student of Saxe-Gotha', he went on, had 'weighed Cambridge in the balance', and found what it called

H.R.H. FIELD-MARSHAL CHANCELLOR PRINCE ALBERT TAKING THE PONS ASINORUM.

Punch *in 1848 saluting Albert's victory in modernizing the Cambridge curriculum.*

university education only 'a sham'. *Punch* published a Leech cartoon, 'HRH Field Marshal Chancellor Prince Albert taking the Pons Asinorum' – Bridge of Asses – 'after the manner of Napoleon taking the Bridge of Arcola'. Oxford would be forced by the example into its own reforms.*

Albert legitimately resented the action of Lord John Russell in 1850 in establishing a 'Royal Commission' on universities without consulting the Chancellor of Cambridge. It was still another signal of the reluctance of the English power structure to move quickly and decisively into

---

*\*Punch* – and John Leech – were counting upon their educated audience to recognize an additional inference in *pons asinorum*, which was a satirical allusion to the fifth proposition from the first book of Euclid, representing something difficult for beginners to get over. Tobias Smollett had employed the expression in his still-read novel *Peregrine Pickle* (1751). Albert, *Punch* was suggesting, was a political beginner, but a success at it.

the new world of science and technology. Albert would look for other and more visible means to educate a society that preferred to be left alone.

As the difficult year dragged to a close, Albert even found himself – through his affidavits and attorney – dragged into a court of law. Almost since the first days of their marriage, the Queen and Prince had been enthusiastic etchers of family, friends and domestic scenes. From October 1840 through November 1847 they sent their copper-plates to a Windsor printer, J.B. Brown, who had his journeyman, Middleton, make the impressions, dutifully returning all the paper, perfect and imperfect.

Before he returned the plates to the Castle, however, Middleton quietly ran off copies on card or common paper. When it became known 'in the street' that the copies existed, he was approached by Jasper Tomsett Judge, now arraigned, and the etchings, many signed in the plates, turned up in Paternoster Row in the publishing firm of William Strange, also charged. Strange had produced for sale, to the embarrassment of the Crown, *A Descriptive Catalogue of the Royal Victoria and Albert Gallery of Etchings* for an exhibition of sixty-three of them, ranging from heads of terriers to portraits of Vicky and Bertie. 'Every purchaser of the catalogue', the preface promised, 'would be presented (by permission) with a *facsimile* of the autograph of either Her Majesty or of the Prince Consort, engraved from the original, the selection being left to the purchaser'.

In the Vice-Chancellor's Courts the case was first heard on 6 November, with Albert's attorney, W.M. James, requesting that the defendants be enjoined from exhibiting the works or selling or other-wise distributing the catalogues, and that all impressions be delivered up to the Queen and Prince. In this they were joined by the Attorney General, Serjeant* Thomas Talfourd. The case was taken up on 6 December in the court of Sir J.Knight Bruce in Lincoln's Inn amid a flurry of affidavits from Brown's barristers and the formalities of appointing counsel to represent Jasper Judge, who claimed to be in *forma pauperis.*† A temporary injunction was granted and the case

* A serjeant at law was a member of a superior order of barristers. The term has fallen into disuse.
† 'in the character of a pauper', i.e. granted exception from court fees.

continued. On 13 December a barrister for William Strange claimed that the printer, rather than committing 'wilful misconduct', had offered 'a voluntary tribute of loyalty to Her Majesty, and of respect to her illustrious consort'. Nonetheless, the Prince had 'no right of property in any of the drawings or etchings, or impressions from the same, which have been done or executed by Her Majesty...and no right in this suit to restrain the exhibition or publication of the same'. The Queen chose not to be a party to the action. Further, descriptions of private works did not constitute reproduction of them. 'The plaintiff was bound to show that he had a property some injury to which was now sought to be restrained.'

Serjeant Talfourd responded that he supported the Crown not on grounds of the questionable morality or propriety of the plaintiff's 'adventure' but on the more limited issue of property. Could anyone doubt the profitable return to the adventurers who wished to utilize property in its 'tainted state'? Albert, it was argued, had legal standing as the Queen's husband to act on behalf of his wife because the property involved was marital rather than royal. That the Queen's husband had to go to the courts like any common citizen for a redress of his and Victoria's grievances said much about the independence of the British judiciary.

The end, after many defence postponements, was not reached until 1 June in the next year, when the injunction was made permanent and the catalogues ordered to be destroyed (although their entire contents had already appeared in *The Times* as a matter of court record). In a conciliatory gesture, the Solicitor General observed of the defeated printer that he was 'happy to state that the advisers of Her Majesty and the Prince felt it consistent with their duty to take a decree against him, but without asking any costs against him, because he might have been misled [by the seller]'. The barristers for Strange accepted the decree with gratitude that forgoing costs relieved their client 'from the imputation that had rested on him'. The counsel assigned by the Court to represent Jasper Judge was eager to argue his client's side further, but in effect the case was over at the 1 June hearing. The hapless Judge had already spent some days in Reading Gaol the previous August for contempt, having failed to pay a judgement of £181 1*s.* 8*d.* in costs to Albert, and wrote to the press from confinement, 'I have been compelled to pawn the very blankets off our beds.' It had been an embarrassment to the Crown, but the Royal art was safe from commercial contamination. *His Royal Highness Prince Albert* v. *Strange* was over.

Many who perceived the case only as the harrassment of insignificant men of business rather than the invasion of privacy, considered Albert a troublesome foreigner, meddling, as the Queen's husband, in matters beyond his place. The Prince seemed to intrude at every level. Always reluctant to delegate authority, had he been qualified to plead a case he might even have represented the Crown.

Even from Balmoral, as Victoria began making what would be continuing demands that the arrogant Palmerston be replaced at the Foreign Office, it was clear that whether messages to Russell or to Palmerston were from the Prince under his own signature or from the Queen under her own, they were all drafted by Albert. In communications to other governments, Palmerston was committing the nation to actions in the Queen's name about which she knew little or nothing, as he either omitted to inform her or deliberately altered messages she had seen without asking her. Some of the Queen's letters on the controversy were composed on the *Victoria and Albert* on the voyage to Aberdeen or on the return trip, and others followed in October from Osborne. The Queen in one draft by Albert was 'highly indignant at Lord Palmerston's behaviour', and both would continue to be outraged into 1849 as many of the revolutions on the Continent were flickering out and the Foreign Secretary tried every diplomatic means to keep them going. Radetzky's Austrians had overwhelmed the poorly led and poorly equipped Italians in Lombardy and Venetia, and – taking sides as usual – Palmerston pressed for Austria to make good on concessions offered when it was losing. Palmerston was also at odds with the Crown on Greece, on Schleswig-Holstein, and on France, while the Queen pressed Russell – since she was ignored by Palmerston – 'to keep a watchful eye upon our foreign relations, in order to prevent any other gradual deviation from the line of justice and impartiality which alone befits the dignity of the British Government'.

To rein in Palmerston's independent foreign policy, Albert asked Russell directly to require that all Foreign Office drafts be sent first to the Prime Minister for his reaction and then to the Queen for her approval. When Russell caved in and instructed Palmerston accordingly, the Foreign Secretary gave lip service to the command while establishing his privilege to claim extenuating circumstances – 'that her

Majesty should give every facility to the transaction of business by attending to the drafts as soon as possible after their arrival'. John Henry Temple, 3rd Viscount Palmerston, sixty-four, had his own cause for indignation. He had been in the Cabinet as early as 1809, ten years before the Queen and Prince were born, and he was schooled in a great nation numbering more than a hundred times the population (even excluding Britain's many colonies) of Albert's puny and backward duchy. Consultation with comparative children was not his style.

Albert's foreign policy arguments in the violent year of 1848 carried as little weight with blood relations. At odds with him on Germany was his brother, who preferred as little reform as possible, and also his cousin, Victoria's half-brother (by her mother's first husband), Prince Charles of Leiningen. By virtue of his powerlessness as heir to a mediatized, formerly sovereign, principality, the Prince had been named in August – he did not last long – President of a Reich Ministry set up in Frankfurt as a façade for nominal German unity while the individual states retained all former authority. Attempting to have it both ways, Albert protested that unity without impotence could only come about by strong Prussian leadership, and he protested against Leiningen's radicalism in relinquishing his own estate – his lordly prerogatives – as *Standesherr* for his family. Albert reminded him of the duc d'Orléans in the French Revolution, who 'forswore his estate' and was then sent to the scaffold anyway. But implicit in Albert's argument was his own family standing in Coburg. With Ernest childless, he wanted to reserve ducal sovereignty for one of his own sons. And he wanted to protect his German property and annuity, which the ducal financial administration, hard pressed in difficult times, had just taken away. 'It is my private fortune to which the *Kammer* is not entitled in any way,' he protested to Ernest. 'If it is bankrupt, it has to declare this . . .' He 'could not afford to loan out' his income.

It was a very bad year.

# X

# Master Mason

## 1849–1851

T HE NEW YEAR of 1849 opened with the colour, tradition and serenity which only masked the unsolved problems of 1848. At Windsor there were nightly theatricals with imported London casts. One farce, only the tailpiece to a long-forgotten comedy, *Used Up*, remains memorable – *Box and Cox*, a single-act 'Romance of Real Life' by John Maddison Morton. Once Lord John Russell's clerk, Morton had become one of the most prolific writers of burlesques, many adapted from the French, complete to the *double entendres*. Produced at the Lyceum late in 1847, *Box and Cox*, the story of the complications of John Box, a journeyman printer; James Cox, a journeyman hatter; and Mrs Bouncer, a lodging-house keeper, would become the most often-revived farce of the century (and set to music as *Cox and Box* by Arthur Sullivan). Refreshments were served in the Throne Room and the Castle's private band played.

Two evenings later Twelfth Night was celebrated with a superb, crown-shaped cake thirty-inches in diameter, on top of which were sixteen figures in eighteenth-century costume, dancing alfresco under several edible trees. Even their miniature picnic, designed by the royal *confiseur*, Mr Mawditt, appeared real. Yet the same day, 6 January, reality itself had intruded, Albert imploring Prince William of Prussia to seize the opportunity of the eclipse of revolutionary zeal to return sufficient power 'to the princes and Governments' to enable them 'to undertake the shaping of the future'. And in that tomorrow he still saw Prussia, freed from Austrian backwardness, unifying Germany in a manner that would preserve regional sovereignties. 'I sing you the song of Cassandra,' he appealed, 'to get you to help in preaching energy, unity and patriotism to all whom you are in a position to influence.' A few weeks later Albert would encourage William, who seemed more forceful than his elder brother, the King, not to 'give up German unity'. He wrote similarly to Frederick William IV, but the pleas were futile. The Frankfurt Assembly would decide in March to offer the title 'Emperor of the Germans' – rather than Germany – to the King, a splendid title he declined for its emptiness.

Albert urged exploiting the illusory unity to accomplish larger goals – an empire of *immediate* territories under Prussian rule and *mediate* territories made up of other states in the *Bund*, with all international powers – diplomacy, peace and war, post, customs – under the Emperor. Trying to have it both ways, he was playing the part of a Saxon duke while a royal outsider in England. At the same time he and Victoria were busy attempting, one more futile time, to rein in the personal diplomacy of Palmerston – 'Pilgerstein' to the indignant Queen and Prince – who was representing the British Empire all by himself, especially in encouraging the breaking away of Austria's Italian provinces. Aside from instinctive loyalties toward a monarchical system under threat of nationalist implosion, the Queen and Prince saw detestable Austria as a crucial bulwark against expansionist-minded Russia. Albert explained to King Leopold of the Belgians, 'We . . . have incessantly waged war . . . with Pilgerstein, in which he got many an ugly poke, as it says in the White Cat.'* What he meant is that they constantly badgered the Prime Minister, Lord John Russell, to keep his Foreign Minister from acting independently, calling him to Windsor on 24 January for two hours of exhortation. Albert meticulously recorded the gist of the audience in just over a thousand words, explaining that it was only an extract. The key line was their contention that Palmerston had been 'careful not to place anything in writing before us'.

The Earl of Clarendon, a once and future ambassador close to Palmerston and now Lord Lieutenant of Ireland, was also summoned, and Russell sighed sympathetically, 'Oh, so you've had that, too'. Palmerston, both knew, habitually altered the texts of messages, even

---

* One of the *Fairy Tales* of the Comtesse d'Aulnoy. *Pilger* is the German for palmer, or pilgrim, while *Stein* means stone (ston).

when already approved by the Prime Minister or the Palace. The Foreign Minister, Russell confided to Greville, would have to go – but only after the parliamentary session was over. Until then, Albert wrote to Russell, if the Queen had 'any remark' on foreign affairs, 'she will make it to you'. And, obviously, the Prince would draft it.

Recognizing that the ground was shifting under him, Palmerston became, at least outwardly, more conciliatory toward Albert, responding to one of the Prince's many messages (this on 19 June) that he agreed that Germany 'under one body politic' – at least for foreign affairs – would be desirable. But as far as the various formulas proposed for unity, the government of Britain 'would, I think, be stepping beyond its legitimate or its safe grounds, if it were to become the partisan or the advocate of any particular scheme *or of the views of any particular German Power*'. When he spoke of the dangerous practice of becoming champion of a policy not thoroughly understood, he may have implied irresponsibility on the part of the Prince, but cagily confessed failure to 'comprehend the Plans' himself, or to 'foresee the consequences'. The Prince knew his own objectivity in German matters was at risk.

Although Albert's brother was leading a Thüringian contingent against the Danes in politically unsettled Schleswig-Holstein, Albert saw his own prejudices as unfamilial. Germany represented something unpolitical for Albert, an energetic people who in the most advanced of its states were in the vanguard of modern science – a model in that sense for his adopted country. Tirelessly keeping his hand in domestic affairs, he was determined to coerce what he saw as a reluctant England into the technological and industrial competition certain to dominate the economy of the second half of the century. He was pushing Cambridge University, as his example, into recognizing the need to educate the next generation differently.

Utilizing his various pulpits, such as the presidency of the Society of Arts, Albert was pressing for the increased visibility of British manufacturing. He regularly demonstrated his interest in new industrial techniques by visiting factories, going on 24 February with Lieutenant-Colonel (as he now was) Seymour to Minton & Company in Blackfriars, best known for its porcelain, to examine its new processes for making encaustic pavement tiles. Victoria, with Albert, went only to the Drury Lane Theatre that evening. Science and technology were the province of the Prince.

Carefully choosing his exemplars, Albert had already established friendly relations with Michael Faraday. Described by *Punch*, not noted for its enthusiasm for technology, as the man 'who can freeze water for you in a red-hot crucible', Faraday, then fifty, was at the acme of his reputation. A blacksmith's son once apprenticed to a bookbinder, he had acquired his science as a part-time assistant to Sir Humphry Davy at the Royal Institution, to whose Chair of Chemistry he succeeded in 1832. 'The prince of scientific expositors' (to Thomas Huxley), Faraday, when asked 'How much may a popular lecturer suppose his audience knows?' answered, emphatically, 'Nothing.'

For a country which prized church-going, Albert recognized the appeal of Faraday's devout Christianity, which remained unaffected by his discovery of electromagnetism. His view of the physical world was strongly theistic – that the properties of matter and the state of the physical universe emanated from divine creation – 'established from the beginning'. To bring to the English establishment the sense that supporting science was the highest – even the godliest – of undertakings, Albert asked Faraday to speak to an invited audience at the Royal Society on 26 February, a Monday afternoon. Court sponsorship made it an event. The audience was a non-scientific one, and included women as well as men – one of the ladies was the banking heiress and philanthropist Angela Burdett-Coutts. Electromagnetism, Faraday explained, utilizing what the *Illustrated London News* called 'ingeniously arranged machinery' to demonstrate effects on metals, flame, smoke and gases, was not a theory but a cosmic reality. 'What its great purpose is, seems to be looming in the distance before us . . . and I cannot doubt that a glorious discovery in natural knowledge, and of the wisdom and power of God in the creation, is awaiting our age.' The interest of his Royal Highness, Faraday closed, would be 'an additional incentive' to investigators of forces likely to benefit man.

'On the termination of the address,' the *Illustrated London News* reported, 'his Royal Highness approached the lecturer's table, and himself performed, under the superintendence of Dr Faraday, several of the experiments which had been exhibited. The Prince retired amid the loud applause of all present.'

Like the study of science, the professional study of history lagged behind Germany. Only eight of Oxford's 1,600 students enrolled in modern history – which meant anything beyond medieval studies.

Cambridge offered no lectures in modern history. Albert tried to interest T.B. Macaulay in accepting a chair in history at Cambridge, but when he declined, settled on Sir James Stephen, who had retired from the Colonial Office and now wrote for the distinguished *Edinburgh Review*. It was an unappreciated appointment, as Stephen had made many enemies in both incarnations, but Albert was Chancellor. 'Never have I seen an Englishman with a mind more open and free from prejudice', the Prince explained to Stockmar. 'I understand now why he was unpopular; for he hits hard at the weak points of his countrymen.' Cautiously, Albert had omitted the chief detail. Sir James's public scepticism about the existence of hell-fire had outraged the devout, who charged Albert with encouraging a heretic. Stephen, nevertheless, owes his being remembered at all to having been the grandfather of Virgina Woolf.

Not only *higher* education was on Albert's mind. Bertie, the Prince of Wales and future King of England, was now a few months past seven and, Lady Lyttelton reported, doing lessons out of the same book as his younger sister, Alice. He was handsome and polite, but backward in his studies. His father, who doted on the clever, articulate Vicky, put pressure on Albert Edward to approach her standard. Bertie responded with disobedience and tantrums. On 10 April, Albert wrote to his stepmother, 'Bertie will be given over in a few weeks into the hands of a tutor whom we have found. He is a Mr Henry Birch, a young, good-looking, amiable man, who was a tutor at Eton, and who not only himself took the highest honours at Cambridge, but whose pupils have also won especial distinction. It is an important step...'

No pupil of Birch's would achieve greater distinction, as Bertie would become King Edward VII. But Birch would never again undertake so difficult and distasteful a task, one that he eased by combining Bertie's lessons with those of Prince Alfred, who was even younger than Alice. It enabled Birch to survive into 1852, when he escaped to the Rectory of Prestwich, near Manchester, promised to him earlier by Lord Wilton.* However distasteful to Birch's Puseyite predilections, when at Balmoral

---

* Young Birch would receive a living worth £3,000 a year plus the assistance of four curates – an astounding emolument that would put him immediately into the ranks of the well-to-do. Anthony Trollope would write scathingly of moneyed clergymen who would take their cabinet minister salaries and move to gentlemanly leisure in Italy while poorly paid curates tended the flock.

with the Prince of Wales he had to attend Presbyterian worship at Crathie Church, and at the Queen's further insistence, observe with Bertie such 'innocent amusements' as dancing, theatricals and shooting. Albert Edward would never become the intellectual counterpart of his father, which was not the fault, either, of Birch's successor, Frederick Gibbs, recommended by none other than Albert's Cambridge appointee Sir James Stephen. With Gibbs, the Prince of Wales's lessons would be extended to six days a week, from eight in the morning to six in the evening. The regimen would not improve the heir's ungovernable temper, nor accelerate his learning.

Albert would see to it that the future king's tutoring would not flag as he travelled with his parents to Ireland and Scotland. But before the journey to Ireland, which was anticipated with alarm by Whitehall, Albert had still further gestures to make on behalf of British technology. He had become so ubiquitous at laying foundation-stones that *Punch*, in a piece entitled 'the Prince of Bricklayers', observed that he had even set the first stone of the Ladies' wing to be added to the Licensed Victuallers' Asylum. 'His Royal Highness is now always laying the foundation of some charitable institution or other, and we congratulate him on employing his time...in this praiseworthy occupation of dabbling in bricks and mortar... *Punch*, in order to reward him in kind, hereby spreads the mortar of approbation, with the trowel of sincerity, upon a Prince who really appears to be coming out like a regular brick.' It was a long way from the vicious attacks of only a few years before. *Punch*'s gibes were now good-humoured. The Prince – for the moment, at least – had earned acceptance.

Albert's most newsworthy trowelling required rail passage to Lincolnshire in mid-April to the Great Grimsby Docks at the mouth of the Humber. There, shipments from the Continent could be transferred by rail to the manufacturing districts of Manchester, Sheffield and Birmingham, or to the port of Liverpool for the Atlantic trade. The banquet to celebrate the event, Lord Yarborough observed in introducing the Prince, would be held in a spot once nineteen feet below sea level. Into the eleven-ton 'stone', Albert placed a glass vessel containing the current coins of the realm; then he sealed the opening, using a silver trowel displaying the prow of a ship, a Triton figure, a young man representing dockyard labour, and a shield with the arms of England

*Prince Albert dedicating the new docks at Great Grimsby in April 1849* (Illustrated London News, *21 April 1849*)

quartered with the Saxon emblems of the Prince. He was acquiring perhaps the largest collection of ceremonial trowels ever earned.

Here, the Prince predicted, would be 'a great commercial port. This work, in future ages, when we shall long have quitted this scene, and when, perhaps, even our names shall be forgotten' – here there were shouts of 'No, no, never!' – 'will, I hope, become a new centre of life, with the vast and ever increasing commerce of the world, and a most important link in the connexion of east and west.' After another burst of cheering faded he went on, linking two of his major themes in opposing the revolutionary spirit abroad. 'This work has been under-taken, like almost all great enterprises in this great country, by private enterprise, private capital, and at private risk; and it shares also in that feature so peculiar to the enterprises of Englishmen, that, strongly attached as they are to the institutions of their country, and gratefully acknowledging the protection of the laws under which those enterprises are undertaken and prosper, they love to connect them with the authority of the Crown and the person of the Sovereign.' There were loyal cheers as he went on to note that the Queen reciprocated their feelings. But she was far off at Windsor, where a messenger took a letter to his 'Dear Wife' reporting that he was still alive after a late snowstorm that had blown in from the North Sea, that in the circumstances the new North Pole seemed to be the spire of Lincoln Cathedral, and that he had icicles at the end of his nose.

Recuperating briefly under his own roof, Albert went off again in early May as an informal member of the Guild of Masons, this time to a hamlet south-east of Barnet that has given its name to the language.* At noon, on an elevated plot near the Great Northern Railway, in the presence of the magistracy and leading gentlemen of the country and using a silver trowel with a miniature crown on the handle and a scoop shaped like an oak leaf, Field Marshal His Royal Highness Prince Albert, Her Majesty's Consort, as the foundation stone inscribed him, raised a bricklayer's level vertically and horizontally, declared the stone well placed, and spread the first mortar for the Middlesex New Pauper Lunatic Asylum at Colney Hatch.

From there the Prince, having time only to take coffee from the luncheon spread for the guests by the Messrs Staples of the Albion Tavern, rushed back to Buckingham Palace by carriage. There he and Lt.-Col. Seymour left with the Queen's party for the annual visit by the sovereign to the Royal Academy on the Thursday prior to the opening of its annual Spring Exhibition. With the Queen and Prince at Trafalgar Square were, to the delight of the Academicians, the Prince of Wales, the Princess Royal, and Princess Alice. Greeted by the officers of the Academy, they were shown paintings squeezed frame to frame and reaching nearly to the high clerestory windows. At a quarter to five the royal party left in several carriages, with Albert's only remaining duty the usual formal dinner for distinguished guests. His days were often far more crowded than the bland descriptions in the Court Circular suggested.

Early the next morning he was busy writing to Lord Palmerston to set up a meeting to discuss, once more, the future of Germany. Some states were still chaotic. Baden was, for the moment, a republic as the contagion from France spread. 'If Germany is not yet constitutionally organised, if Prussia has not assumed the leadership of German affairs legally and according to contract', Albert would write to his brother, 'the poor Fatherland will have but poor prospects!'

---

* For institutions for the insane.

Despite Albert, England's priorities remained internal, with Ireland still on the edge of insurrection, and many of its poorest and most hungry flooding across to Liverpool, now the worst slum in the United Kingdom. Yet Victoria remained determined, whatever the security problems, to visit Ireland and demonstrate royal concern, although her government demonstrated little interest. From Dublin, Lord Fitzwilliam warned that a visit in ceremonial splendour, after the failure of another annual potato crop, would be an act of stupidity. 'A great *lie* is going to be acted there . . . I would not have her go *now* unless she went to Killarney workhouse . . . Galway, Connemara and Castlebar. That would have been *my* tour for her.' The Queen and Prince asked the Lord Lieutenant, the Earl of Clarendon, and the Chancellor of the Exchequer, Sir Charles Wood, to work out an unostentatious tour that could be accomplished as the *Victoria and Albert* steamed toward Scotland and their Highland retreat. Referring to the still-endangered vegetable of the Queen's other island, *Punch* quipped that on her austere arrival in Dublin, 'The Queen will . . . proceed to the [Viceroy's] Lodge, where she will be met at the door by the Countess of Clarendon with a dish of buttermilk and potatoes. Upon this the Queen will lunch; and, afterwards, in a thimble-full of regal punch, drink [a toast to the] Prosperity of Ireland.'

Albert, meanwhile, had become involved with the most formidable and frustrating task of his life, a project that had been germinating since the previous year. Science and technology had always fascinated Albert, but as consort to the Queen they became his mission in England's interest. In a speech later in 1849 he linked them to destiny. 'No human pursuits make any material progress', he declared, 'until science is brought to bear upon them.' Some cultures had slumbered for centuries, 'but from the moment that science has touched them with her magic wand, they have sprung forward . . . Look at the transformation which has gone on around us since the laws of gravitation, electricity, magnetism, and the expansive power of heat have become known to us. It has altered our whole state of existence . . . We owe this to science, and science alone; and she has other treasures in store for us, if we will but call her to our assistance.'

Such attitudes were not easy to impose upon the squirearchy, which preferred things as they were, and still dominated the House of Lords. When the renowned German chemist Baron von Liebig had visited from the University of Giessen in 1842, merchants and industrialists were impressed by his concepts of the future, but he left with the unpromising appraisal, 'England is not the land of Science.' Albert was eager to use the impetus of Liebig's visit to found a Sir Humphry Davy College of Practical Chemistry within the Royal Institution. When the school's hierarchy resisted change, in 1845 Albert (with Royal Physician Sir James Clark) was instrumental in the founding of an independent institution, the Royal College of Chemistry, in Hanover Square. Through Liebig's recommendation, the Bonn chemist A.W. Hoffmann was imported as director, contributing to the beginnings of the organic or aniline dye industry, which became crucial to English textile manufacture.

Through the Society of Arts, which Albert had joined in 1842, other means of encouraging technology were explored, and in 1845, the year he assumed the presidency, the Society promoted the idea of annual exhibitions of British manufactures on the model of France and Belgium. Albert asked to be informed when sufficient support made the idea practicable. Although a committee was formed to raise immediate expenses, the attempt, they reported, failed. Even manufacturers were lukewarm, some of the most eminent among them hostile to the idea of competition for prizes. One might not win, and then ... In 1846, some came forward, and the Prince distributed a few prizes, acknowledging that although English manufactures excelled 'in solidity and excellence', they were 'outdone in beauty of design' by other countries. He suggested expanding the series of products to be open for prizes.

The 1847 exhibition, the first of any magnitude, was held in the Society's Adam-designed building – which it still occupies – in the Adelphi. To the astonishment of the manufacturers, twenty thousand people came. Twenty thousand people learning how to separate the good from the bad were a spur to the next competition, in March 1848. Seventy thousand came, crowding the Society's exhibition rooms daily. The success led Albert to propose two new prizes for the 1849 exhibition – for the encouragement of art in the colonies and for 'the improvement of an important Art'. The Queen contributed objects for display, as did the Duke of Richmond, the Duke of Bedford, and even Mr Henry Greville. Exploiting the momentum, the Society in March 1849 asked the Commissioner of Woods and Forests, who also had Windsor Castle and Buckingham Palace in his purview, to furnish a London site for periodical exhibitions of British industry. The Society also asked for the co-operation – which meant financial support – of both houses of Parliament. For the Prince, whose philosophy emphasized the private sector, seeking public funding was a recognition of the scale of the undertaking. Neither House, however, would be willing to spend anything.

On Saturday, 30 June 1849, Henry Cole, Francis Fuller, and John Scott Russell of the Society met at the Prince's invitation in Buckingham Palace at noon to discuss a more ambitious exhibition. Because a hall of large dimensions would have to be erected or acquired, Albert also summoned Thomas Cubitt, who, although a friend, proceeded to scotch the Prince's idea for a permanent building in Leicester Square – or any public square. 'Your Royal Highness proposes to accomplish a great public good by the Exhibition,' Cole quoted Cubitt as explaining, frankly, 'but if you build on a square on which the public had a moral, if not a legal, right, you will do a great wrong, and set a bad example.'

Albert did not see the loss of his easy solution as the end. Putting the site problem aside, he proposed four exhibition divisions – 'Raw Materials', 'Machinery and Mechanical Inventions', 'Manufactures', and 'Sculptures and Plastic Art'. The deputation assumed that he was thinking of encompassing all of Britain, but Albert had grander ideas. 'Whilst it appears an error', he proposed, 'to fix any limitation to the productions of Machinery, Science, and Art, which are of no country, but belong as a whole to the civilised world, particular advantage to British Industry might be derived from placing it in fair competition with that of other nations.'

The Society accordingly undertook an 'Industry of All Nations' exhibition for 1851, and recommended, for oversight, a Royal Commission. With the Prince at the head, financial guarantees might be secured and land made available. They expected the venture to be self-supporting.

The Prince took the enterprise under his personal purview, and asked John Scott Russell to visit at Osborne on 14 July to go over a proposed announcement, and to discuss the composition of a Royal Commission. Albert also proposed sending members of the Society as his deputies across the kingdom (as the credentials prepared put it) 'to collect opinions and evidence with reference to the expediency of forming a great Exhibition of the Industry of all Nations . . .' In effect they were to solicit support. Henry Labouchere, then President of the Board of Trade, was also present, and the three went over a plan of operations, from invitations to other nations and the values of prizes to the means of financing construction. Since the Society had no appreciable funds, its Council employed its solicitors, Tooke, Son, and Hallowes, to work out an arrangement that would give the contractor a substantial share of profits after expenses if the firm guaranteed a prize fund and built the exhibition hall, much of that cost presumably defrayed by sub-scriptions.

During the trip to Ireland and Scotland, the first an unexpected popular success for the Queen in the face of dire predictions, Albert never lost sight of the Exhibition. At Queenstown (now Cobh) on 3 August he arranged for Scott Russell to have princely letters of intro-duction to foreign ministers. At Balmoral on 3 September the signatures of directors of large manufacturing firms willing to support the Exhibi-tion were delivered to him. 'I do not lose patience', he told Stockmar on 10 September. The direct reference was to ill luck in hunting, but in a birthday summing-up on 26 August, as he reached thirty, he had confided to the Baron his contentment 'with everything', wanting only 'more energy and perseverance'. He had much on his mind. With Peel and Clarendon, he was pressing for university education in Ireland that would not (as he put it to Peel) 'degenerate in the South into Roman Catholic Seminaries, and in the North into a Presbyterian School'. He was still promoting better homes for the poor, 'and the boon will tell in improved health, sobriety, and domestic peace'. He was constantly – from whatever distance – attempting to rein in Palmerston on foreign affairs. And he was keeping watch on Exhibition matters, as the con-tractors, worried about the large advance expenditures, wanted their agreement renegotiated.

Much of Albert's business, especially when remote from London, had to be transacted through his secretaries Anson, Phipps and Grey, and it was while the Queen and Prince were travelling from Balmoral to Osborne that they received word of Anson's sudden death. He was only thirty-seven. His wife, whose previous children had died in infancy, was expecting a baby in two months. (It would be a healthy daughter.) Anson had been experiencing severe headaches for more than a year and seemed to have suffered a stroke – possibly an aneurysm. The Queen's journal on 8 October recorded her grief and Albert's woe. 'To see my poor dear Albert's deep distress made me wretched, for he loved and valued Anson who was almost the only intimate friend he had in this country, and he mourns for him as for a brother.' Anson's adroit balancing of the strong personalities of the Prince and the Queen was one of the least-kept secrets at Court. On 13 October 1849 *The Satirist* cautiously ventured that Anson's 'dexterous management often warded off a "blow-up" from his Royal Highness, when *the wind lay in the wrong direction*, in the *highest quarter*.'

Needing someone to lean on in his grief, Albert again turned to Stockmar. 'If you could come to me now', he wrote, 'I should regard it as a great act of friendship.' Because George Anson had been failing in ways no one wanted to notice, some of his work had been quietly taken over by Charles Phipps, who now took the secretaryship, while Charles Grey moved up to Phipps's place. Shaking off his despondency, Albert presided on 30 October over the opening of the New Coal Exchange in the City in place of the Queen, who had caught chicken-pox from one of her children. In state, the Prince travelled from Westminster Pier with his two eldest children in the royal barge, rowed by twenty-seven watermen. Bands played and bells pealed, and the Tower guns shook the air. At the Exchange not only was Albert introduced, but also the Prince of Wales. The Lord Mayor described him as 'the pledge and promise of a long race of kings'. Lady Lyttelton, accompanying the children, wrote to Catherine Gladstone, 'Poor Princey did not seem at all to guess what he meant.'

Albert's major anxieties into the new year of 1850 were the siting and financing of what was already being called, with derision in some cases, the Great Exhibition of 1851. A *Punch* cartoon showed the Prince, hat in hand, as 'The Industrious Boy' seeking donations:

> This empty hat my awkward case bespeaks,
> These blank subscription-lists explain my fear;
> Days follow days, and weeks succeed to weeks,
> But very few contributors appear.

Failure was widely forecast, but under Her Majesty's warrant an Executive Committee was appointed, and a full Royal Commission announced on 3 January 1850, each name preceded by such elaborately formal language as 'Our right trusty and well-beloved...' Bankers, brokers, scientists, engineers, architects, artists, merchants, and Mem-

## THE INDUSTRIOUS BOY.

### "Please to Remember the Exposition."

*Since Albert in 1850 had to raise the money for the Exhibition as well as oversee it,* Punch *shows him as refusing no donation, however small.*

bers of Parliament appeared in the list, along with a few of the socially eminent. Among the Treasurers, for public reassurance, were Arthur Kett Barclay and Lionel de Rothschild. At its first meeting, in the still-unfinished new Houses of Parliament, presided over by Prince Albert on 11 January, the financially risky contract with Messrs Munday was cancelled. At a second meeting on 18 January, a fundraising scheme was developed, and at a third, six days later, subcommittees for each of the exhibition areas were named, the ten members for Machinery and Mechanical inventions including such technological luminaries as mathematician Charles Babbage, inventor of the first calculating machine; Isambard Kingdom Brunel, designer of great ships, docks, railways and bridges; and Robert Stephenson, railroad and bridge engineer and son of the builder of the first locomotives. The meetings continued weekly – and almost always with Albert in the chair.

The day after the third session a public meeting was convened at the Mansion House by the Lord Mayor, Thomas Farncomb, to pass a resolution by City bankers, merchants and manufacturers 'That the proposal of His Royal Highness the Prince Albert to open an Exhibition of the Works of Industry of all nations in the year 1851, in this metropolis, is a measure in harmony with public feeling, and entitled to the general support of the community and is eminently calculated to improve manufactures, and to end in diffusing the principles of universal peace'. It carried unanimously.

A second resolution, moved by Lord John Russell in his private capacity rather than as Prime Minister, and seconded by Lionel de Rothschild – listed in *The Times* as MP from the City of London although still refused his seat because he would not take a Christian oath* – concurred in the cancellation of the Munday contract and declared that 'the large funds requisite for this purpose ought to be provided by the voluntary contributions of individuals, rather than from the public revenue'. It passed unanimously, whereupon the first announcement of subscriptions, in anticipation of the move, was released, beginning with a thousand pounds from the Queen and five hundred from the Prince. Lord John Russell was listed at £100 and his Chancellor of the Exchequer, Sir Charles Wood, also for £100. Bankers Joshua Bates, Thomas Baring, Lionel de Rothschild and Anthony de Rothschild each subscribed £500, as did several other financiers. The Governor of the Bank of England, H.J. Prescott, offered a paltry fifty pounds, while Charles Chubb and Son, the prosperous safe and lock company, managed only £25. Albert's hat would remain extended for many months, his sleep disturbed by funds worries and the increasing controversy over the proposed Hyde Park site.

---

* Rothschild was seated in 1858, after other re-elections, when the Lords gave in and permitted the Commons to prescribe its own oaths.

A *Punch* cartoon, 'London in 1851', predicted mobs from the lowest classes descending upon London for the Great Exhibition. It also forecast the destruction of the south-east corner of Hyde Park, 'the lungs of the metropolis', by massive crowds, the grassy expanse 'pulverised'. Why, *Punch* asked, should the park's turf be wasted? 'As it must inevitably be walked off, why not sell it, and let the proceeds go in aid of the Exhibition, which, we fear, is not supported with the liberality a project so laudable indeed deserves.' One issue cartooned the Queen 'interceding' with Albert, who stood adamant, arms crossed and stern face under his lampooned army shako, before an attendant displaying a rolled-up plan 'for spoiling Hyde Park', while a plaintive Belgravian lady representing socialite inhabitants threatened by the Exhibition site, watched workmen lowering ugly building cranes. Another cartoon showed a 'simple design' suggested for the Exhibition hall – a Brobdingnagian (and Albertine) shako. A verse began, 'Albert! Spare those trees...'

The Hyde Park elms were no joking matter, as Members of Parliament began to demand that no heretofore-ignored tree be felled to create exhibition space. In the Lords, the inevitable Baron Brougham

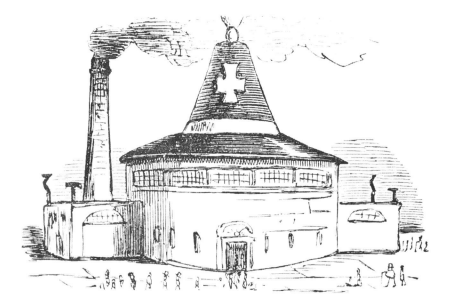

Punch *in July 1850 satirizing designs for the Exhibition building by devising one in the shape of Albert's* shako *hat for the army.*

made a fiery speech condemning the use of any West End park and suggested instead one to the east, as few who counted lived in such benighted locations as Spitalfields. 'The opponents of the Exhibition', Albert wrote, 'work with might and main to throw all the old women here into a panic and to drive myself crazy. The strangers, they give out, are certain to commence a thorough revolution here, to murder Victoria and myself, and to proclaim the Red Republic in England; the plague is certain to ensue from the confluence of such vast multitudes, and to swallow up those for whom the increased price of everything has not already swept away. For all this I am to be responsible, and against all this I have to make efficient provision.'

'An absolute prostration of the understanding takes place even in the minds of the bravest', Brougham asserted in the House of Lords, 'when the word "Prince" is mentioned in this country.' He displayed a petition against the desecration of any part of Hyde Park for exhibition purposes. *The Times* kept up the pressure by publishing a report on 16 March that according to rumour, four secretaries working for the Exhibition commissioners were each being paid £800 a year, then a very large salary, and that such extravagances were harming subscriptions. Not yet done with Albert, *The Times* on 25 June warned that the Exhibition would turn Hyde Park into 'the bivouac of all the vagabonds of London', and that the Exhibition building – predictably an oversized brick warehouse that would cost almost as much to disassemble as to erect – would be a 'vast pile of masonry' that would for ever destroy the character of 'our pleasant Park, nearly the only place where Londoners can get a breath of fresh air'. The Prince blamed the editorial turnabout on the recent purchase by *The Times*'s solicitor of a house near the Park.

Three days earlier – and very likely the reason for the outburst in the press – the *Illustrated London News* had published a drawing by commission member Isambard Kingdom Brunel, who had just constructed Paddington Station, of the building committee's likely design, a hybrid of ideas lifted from some of the entries. A series of connected, barn-like structures, it had at its centre a huge dome unrelated to anything else.

The Exhibition executive committee stubbornly laboured on, its meetings largely chaired, as in earlier months, by Albert. He spoke at one fundraising dinner after another, promoting his vision of the Great Exhibition of All Nations, 'We live in a period of most wonderful transition', he would say, 'which tends toward that end to which all history points – the realisation of the unity of mankind.' He felt confident that the application of new technologies was the key to a better future.

There could be no public sign of turning back. The location was firm, and cancellation or even delay risked national and royal embarrassment. Earlier in the year the Prince had reported that, despite public outcry, the Commissioner of Woods and Forests would lend no other site in London but that east of the cavalry barracks in lower Hyde Park, and extending to Rotten Row, above Knightsbridge. The mandate failed to silence objections, which were made more shrill by attacks on proposed building designs and materials. Yet amid the agitation, the Commissioners went ahead with plans for managing a huge international show without any practical concept of an acceptable structure. Despite Brunel's protest to Albert that prizes were 'mischievous as conferring undue advantages upon a thing well displayed ... The opportunity of exhibition will be quite sufficient to induce all the competition we can desire', rules for exhibiting and standards for prizes were adopted, and communications sent and received for exhibitors and exhibits – even one from Berlin about showing a steamship. The announced opening date of 1 May 1851 somehow had to be met.

Sleep came less and less to Albert as other dilemmas and controversies kept him agitated. With the grand dream in jeopardy, he continued his running warfare with Palmerston, and involved himself – but cautiously, from the outside – in the anti-papal debates in Parliament which had followed the naming by the Vatican of Nicholas Wiseman as Cardinal and Roman Catholic Archbishop of the See of Westminster – the first such appointment in England since the Reformation. Both Church and State had condemned the designations as encroaching upon British sovereignty. The empty and unenforced Ecclesiastical Titles Act would follow. Another prospective appointment both teased and anguished Albert. The aged Duke of Wellington understood that he could no longer function as Commander-in-Chief of the Army. In the ten years he had known Albert, who had arrived for his marriage with an honorific and much derided title of Field Marshal, Wellington had learned to appreciate the Prince's efficiency and ability, and suggested on a visit to Windsor that he was the best man in England to succeed the hero of Waterloo. Despite rumours in the press since early in 1848 that the Queen herself wanted to have Albert in command at the Horse Guards in Whitehall, he had not been approached by the Duke before, and professed to be taken by surprise. Flattered, he agreed to consider the prospect.

It was an even grander dream than the Great Exhibition, which might come once in a lifetime and, if successful, be only the model for another place and time. To sit at Wellington's historic desk and command the army of the burgeoning empire – even the temptation was worth some sleepless nights. Yet Albert knew the impossibility of it all. Candidly, at Wellington's annual Waterloo Dinner at Apsley House in June 1849, Albert had responded to a toast proposed by the Duke that he appreciated the honour of being able to participate in an occasion to which 'no merit of my own could entitle me'. There had already been talk of how 'English' troops would respond to the command of 'the German husband of Her Majesty'. Aside from public reaction to what assuredly would be considered an act of gross nepotism rather than the thoughtful judgment of the exalted Wellington, the post would compromise Albert's already overwhelming duties as consort to the Queen. He had 'anxiously weighed' the question, he responded to the Duke on 6 April, and concluded that he had to be guided by 'whether it would interfere with or assist my position of consort to the Sovereign, and the performance of the duties which this position imposes upon me'.

He recognized his situation as 'peculiar and delicate'. If he were successful in his present duty, the Queen might be in an even stronger position than a male sovereign – 'But this requires that the husband should entirely sink his *own individual* existence in that of his wife – that he should aim at no power by himself or for himself – should shun all contention – assume no separate responsibility before the public, but make his position entirely a part of hers – fill up every gap which, as a woman, she would naturally leave in the exercise of her regal functions.' He listed a litany of functions he had assumed, from 'natural head of her family' to 'her permanent minister'. Wellington's proposal was 'a tempting idea' which he 'must discard'.

In some ways Albert had already violated the ideal. He had become, in a competition, an activist Chancellor of Cambridge University. He was also far and away the visible symbol and guiding force of the Great Exhibition. Even so, these were small matters in contrast to

Wellington's succession. And he had his role as sovereign surrogate much in mind in April 1850 as the Queen was again pregnant. Over-worked as usual, the Prince had more than the usual demands on his energies as her confinement approached.

A year to the day before the planned opening of what appeared to be Albert's folly, 1 May 1850, Victoria was delivered of her third son and seventh child. The date was also the eighty-first birthday of the Duke of Wellington, and the child was named Arthur, after him, with the Duke standing as godfather. The delivery had gone well; the Queen was soon up and able to recuperate at Osborne, where she remained until Prince Arthur's christening. With Victoria largely out of the picture because of her confinement, Albert's supervision of the Household had again become almost total. Although he was willing as a matter of public display to have as elaborate a christening as the Church of England offered, only the month before he had admonished the Prince of Wales's tutor Henry Birch, who was suspected of 'Puseyism', to be less aggressive in his religiosity, and to cease resisting, when in Scotland, the Sundays at the kirk, as the Queen was Defender, as well, of the Scottish, or Presbyterian, Church. Birch offered to resign unless his charge could be taught the proper catechism.

Not needing another Household problem, Albert had relented despite his feelings, which Victoria shared, that all churches were alike but for the ecclesiastical formulas for which neither had much use. Birch finally resigned in January 1852 in favour of his rectorship. The young prince had become attached to him and was unhappy at the loss; his parents were relieved.

Attacks upon Albert's Anglican commitment were unrelenting over the years. His recommendations of knighthoods for scientists put him in bad odour with the clergy, and his and Palmerston's proposal, after *The Origin of Species* was published, that Charles Darwin be knighted was scotched when Samuel Wilberforce, the Bishop of Oxford, advised Victoria not to recommend it. Later, Dean Arthur Wellesley assured Bertie's second tutor, F.W. Gibbs, that it was not the Prince Consort who forbade the Athanasian Creed, with its hell-fire and damnation, to be recited in the chapel at Windsor but George III, 'because I won't allow my subjects to be damned in my own chapel!'

Hardly had the Queen been out in public again after Arthur's birth when, in London for his christening, she was fired at by William

Hamilton, a visiting Irishman, as she drove up Constitution Hill. Although the pistol proved to be loaded only with blanks, the shock was considerable. Eight days later, on 27 June, Robert Pate, an insane ex-officer whose surname was grotesquely appropriate, struck her viciously on the forehead with the brass knob of his cane as she left Cambridge House after visiting her elderly uncle. Fortunately addicted to unflattering bonnets, the badly bruised Queen was less hurt than she might have been. The old Duke of Cambridge died on 8 July, the day before the burial of Sir Robert Peel, whose horse had slipped while trotting up Constitution Hill and fallen on the former Prime Minister. (A broken rib penetrated Peel's lungs, and he had suffered three days of great agony.)

Peel's last speech in the Commons had been on the imbroglio which the reckless Foreign Minister had raised by his gunboat diplomacy against Greece. The Queen and Prince had once more urged Russell to remove Palmerston, but the Prime Minister weakly suggested the alternative of moving him to the leadership of the House of Commons, thus increasing his influence. 'Pilgerstein' had backed the claim of a Gibraltar-born merchant, Don David Pacifico, for alleged damages when his house in Athens was sacked, even insisting on reparations for large unprovable losses. Greece elicited support from France and Russia while Palmerston threatened naval action in a show of brinkmanship. His 'mode of doing business', Albert wrote sharply to Russell, causes Britain, which should be at the height of its influence, to be 'detested, mistrusted, and treated with indignity...'

The Tory leader Lord Stanley (the future 14th Earl of Derby) had offered a censure motion in the Commons on 17 June, and a week of spirited debate followed in both Houses on how foreign policy should be conducted. Gladstone, Disraeli, Cobden, Peel, Roebuck and Cockburn spoke brilliantly, and Palmerston responded with a speech four hours in length, accusing his detractors of abetting foreign conspiracy (in which by implication he included Albert) and 'domestic intrigue'. 'As the Roman in days of old', he defended himself in his peroration, 'held himself free from indignity when he could say *civis Romanus sum*, so also a British subject, in whatever land he may be, shall feel confident that the watchful eye and the strong arm of England will protect him against injustice and wrong.' The motion of censure failed.

Punctuated frequently by cheers, the greatest speech Palmerston ever declaimed 'made all of us proud of the man who had delivered it', confessed Peel, who had been on the other side. Albert wrote tartly to Russell that the Queen 'has no more confidence in Lord P. now than she had before'. He saw no likelihood that Palmerston in his sixty-seventh year would change his nature. The vote would only 'gratify his vanity and self-esteem'. Later in the year, while Palmerston remained above criticism, Greville would observe of the Queen and Prince, 'I find their aversion to Palmerston is rather greater than ever, for to his former misdeeds is now added the part he takes in German affairs, on which Albert is insane; so they hated him before for all that he did that was wrong, and they hate him now for doing what is right. However their love or hate makes no difference to him.' Albert could not resist the compulsion to meddle in what were essentially German domestic affairs, although the states and statelets were each essentially sovereign, and Palmerston, with the increasing arrogance of real power in foreign affairs, found less and less reason to exercise diplomacy toward his own Court.

Mutual animosity led Albert to a rare ethical lapse. He had learned nearly ten years before from Stockmar about Palmerston's attempt to seduce one of the Queen's ladies at Windsor. Mrs Brand was now Lady Dacre, and the potential scandal then had been suppressed in her interest as well as that of the Foreign Minister. Under great anxiety that the Great Exhibition might have to be cancelled, Albert lost his moral compass and tattled to Lord John Russell in hopes of swaying him toward dismissal of Palmerston. The matter simmered into August, Russell informing Palmerston only that the Court was ser-iously unhappy with him. From Osborne, Victoria then sent Russell a memorandum written for her by Albert and Stockmar laying rigid rules for Palmerston's future communications with her.

Realizing that Albert was behind the backstairs intrigue to oust him, the Foreign Minister requested an audience. The meeting on 14 August was a dramatic affair. A master performer, Palmerston had tears in his eyes; his voice trembled as he expressed his pain and regret at the remonstrances he had earned. What remained intolerable, Albert told him coldly, was not their disagreement on issues, but that the Queen, who had the right to be informed, was being treated evasively. They moved cautiously to discussion of cases like Schleswig-Holstein, which Albert worried might lead to further instability in Europe, and adjourned.

Since Palmerston controlled the editorial policies of several London papers, he saw to it that gossip about malign Court influence upon the conduct of foreign affairs surfaced. Again incorrigible in his behaviour, he challenged Russell to prove that his government could survive without 'Pam'. Russell accepted his resignation and replaced him with Earl Granville. Contemptuously, Palmerston refused to go to Windsor to relinquish his seals of office, and that December, Russell, in embarrassment, had to perform the ritual. It would not be the end of Palmerston, as the Queen and Prince hoped, but the beginning of the end for Russell's Ministry.

When a long and anonymous article appeared in the Palmerstonian *Westminster Review* condemning the sovereign's inability to look with 'passive indifference' on foreign affairs because the 'high interests' of the Coburg family prevented objectivity, Albert recognized the authorship and set out his response in a long but private memorandum. In effect it was a debate with himself about the legal and moral responsibilities of the Crown:

> Nowhere does the Constitution demand an indifference on the part of the sovereign to the march of political events, and nowhere would such indifference be more condemned and justly despised than in England. There was no interest of the House of Coburg involved in any of the questions upon which we quarrelled with Lord Palmerston, neither in Greece nor Italy, Sicily, Holstein, Hungary, etc.
>
> Why are Princes alone to be denied the credit of having political opinions based upon an anxiety for the national interests and honour of their country and the welfare of mankind? Are they not more independently placed than any other politician in the State? Are their interests not most intimately bound up with those of their country? Is the sovereign not the natural guardian of the honour of his country; is he not *necessarily* a politician? Has he no duties to perform toward his country?

In the months since the Don Pacifico debates, Albert had been on an emotional roller-coaster not only regarding foreign policy, but about the future of the Exhibition, which had become identified with him personally. Soon after the last of the last of the debates, on the afternoon of 29 June, Peel had left a meeting of the Exhibition Commission, his last official act, for his fatal horseback ride. Setting the accident against that context, the Prince had been plunged into agonies of guilt. A father figure to Albert who had meant much more to him than his unworthy actual parent, Peel was a devastating loss to a still-young man whose position made achieving intimacy with anyone other than his spouse almost impossible. And Peel only followed Anson. Nothing was going right. Even before Peel's fall, deeply depressed because it appeared that the Exhibition might have to be abandoned for want of a structure and the lead-time to build one, Albert had urged the avuncular but now hypochondriacal and doddering Stockmar, 'If you can come' – his usual appeal to the Baron when unhappiness seemed too much to be borne – 'pray do so, as we have need of you.'

Of her own accord, Victoria added her plea to Stockmar: 'It will do you good to be with my *beloved prince*. He *longs* for you.' To Leopold, the Queen wrote that Albert 'felt and feels Sir Robert's loss dreadfully. He feels that he has lost a second father.' Peel dead would have more impact upon the Exhibition's future than Peel (only a former Prime Minister) alive. Many in Parliament knew how much he had wanted the project to succeed, and that he favoured the Hyde Park site. Albert would soon eulogize Peel as 'liberal from feeling but conservative upon principle', and in an indirect Exhibition reference as 'the true type of the English character, which is essentially practical'.

Political opposition began to fade even before Peel's funeral. He had died on the night of 2 July. Two days later the motion in opposition to the Park site was defeated in the Commons by a large majority. It was then withdrawn in the Lords. Yet subscriptions, Albert deplored in his diary, remained 'very backward'. He was forced to recommend raising a guarantee fund, and £200,000 would be collected. Opposition now focused upon the huge masonry edifice everyone assumed would be necessary. Estimates based upon the composite Brunel plan drawn from the 233 designs submitted were that fifteen million bricks would be required. If indeed a structure larger than St Paul's were erected, what were the expectations that it would be torn down after a season's use? On that reasonable suspicion, no specific plan stood a chance of being erected, although 13,937 applications to exhibit had been received and financing was now assured.

A rescuer for the Exhibition, however, stood in the wings. The sideburned, dapperly dressed guiding genius of the Duke of Devonshire's conservatories, Joseph Paxton, had been in London early in June to look over the rebuilt Houses of Parliament, now almost ready for occupancy. The spacious chambers were being tested for sound, with unsatisfactory results. When Paxton commented to his companion John Ellis, the new chairman of the Midland Railway, that he hoped the Exhibition structure would be less of a mistake, Ellis challenged him, although specific plans for estimating contractors' bids had to be ready within a fortnight, to enter the competition. Intrigued, he went with Ellis to Lord Granville at the Board of Trade. Granville introduced them to Henry Cole.

According to Cole, all plans had to meet a basic design on which the Committee insisted in order to house the expanse of exhibits. If it could be done another way, said Paxton, could I submit a proposal? There wasn't much time, said Cole, and the deadline had to be firm, but he would arrange that the Executive Committee would permit review of an alternative design.

'Well, if you will introduce such a clause,' Paxton offered, 'I will go home and in nine days hence will bring you my plans, all complete.'

With nothing to lose, Cole agreed. Before hurrying westward, Paxton took a hansom cab to the Hyde Park site and walked about the twenty-six acres allotted to the Exhibition to get the breadth, length, and tree obstacles in mind. With his weekend already fixed – he had to supervise some work on the Britannia (now Menai) Bridge being built near Bangor in Wales – Paxton could not work on the Exhibition design until the next Tuesday, when he was seated in the boardroom of the Midland Railway for a business meeting. A large sheet of blotting paper lay on the table for each participant, and Paxton used it to pen a plan for Hyde Park based upon the *Victoria regia* greenhouse at Chatsworth. Before he returned to Chatsworth himself, he took his blotting paper to the Midland's chief engineer to ask about calculating the strength of columns and girders. On 21 June he returned to London.

At Derby Station, *en route*, he encountered Robert Stephenson, one of the Royal Commissioners, on his way to a meeting about the Exhibition. Paxton explained what was in his roll of plans, and the engineer scoffed, 'You can't be serious; besides, you're too late – the whole thing is settled and decided.'

By the time the train reached London, Stephenson, having examined the designs, was a convert. The next day Paxton saw Granville again, and afterward brought his plans to a Commission meeting. On the 24th he had a long, private meeting with Prince Albert. When the Commission met again on the 29th, Peel, in the last business meeting of his life, spoke in favour of Paxton's design. Yet the Commissioners, as Stephenson had warned, were largely resigned to the composite, and had already ruled out as unsound a five-domed glass-and-iron model submitted by Dawson Turner, who had designed a palm building for Kew Gardens.

Paxton remained convinced that his 'palace of glass', in effect a long, elegant greenhouse that promised ease in erection and equal dispatch in disassembly, combined vastness with strength. Albert's committee worried, nevertheless, that it could be dangerously flimsy in storm and wind. It might create its own climate indoors and produce rain and fog. With many thousands inside, the air might become intolerably noxious. The best that Albert – and Paxton – could achieve was avoiding a formal negative vote. After the meeting adjourned, Paxton offered his drawings to the *Illustrated London News*, which published a dramatic depiction of a sweepingly elegant building in its issue of 6 July 1850. Editorially, the *News* supported Paxton's design, for it 'has been considered and planned with a view to its fitness for the objects intended, as well as for its permanent occupation or removal to another site for a winter garden'. Further, it would 'form a peculiar novelty in mechanical science' while being much more attractive than the 'official' composite design. Public admiration was instant. The Commissioners' building committee retracted its disapproval to the extent of advising Paxton that if he submitted a detailed tender – a bid for a contract – his design would be reconsidered.

By the time Paxton returned from London he had revised his clean roof line to accommodate rounded transepts creating space for the tops of the big elms. In one section to the rear of the building, an angle from which drawings and photographs were seldom made, trees projected through an opening in the roof – this being the refreshments area. The aesthetic compromises were a practical solution to political necessities.

Confidently, Paxton had already consulted the builders Fox and Henderson, and had secured estimates from suppliers of iron and glass. Now he telegraphed requests for particulars. The following Monday, representatives from manufacturers in Warwickshire and Staffordshire took the train to London to meet with Paxton at the City offices of Fox and Henderson. Within the working week they had detailed drawings and specifications, and a cost estimate for the first building to involve mass production of parts – gutters, sash bars, girders, columns, windows, doors, pipes, flooring – on a large scale. Relieved, the Committee on 15 July accepted Paxton's plan.

With Hyde Park protected and a design which seemed affordable, there was little question that Fox, Henderson and Company of the London Works, Smethwick, would be given the contract for erection. For the Royal Commission, Henry Cole was appointed overseer of the project. The actual overseer proved to be the embattled Prince, as he was concerned with the exhibiting nations, the exhibits themselves, and the exhibit space. Once hostile, the press became an ally. Caught up in the reality of what would become the first World's Fair, even *The Times* was enthusiastic. *Punch*, which earlier had satirized building ideas for the Great Exhibition with its drawing of the 'Albert helmet', christened Paxton's concept a 'Crystal Palace'.

'I dreamt that the Exhibition', went a 'Mrs Mouser' letter to Mr Punch, 'which wasn't in Hyde Park after all, though, being awake, I can't be sworn where – was, as it ought to be, a palace of very crystal, the sky looking through every bit of the roof upon all nations under it'. And Mr Punch himself suggested, in a mock letter to Paxton, that the new Palace of Westminster about to shelter the Houses of Parliament after years of rebuilding, be replaced by a similar glass house. 'Here and there you can insert a pane of magnifying power to make any favourite Minister look a greater man than he is.'

'Crystal Palace' caught on, quickening the excitement of the curious who came to gape at the preparation of the site, the delivery of enormous quantities of parts, and the assembly of the structure, each rising section a small drama. The climax would be the bridging of the great transept late in the year by huge wooden ribs painted black to look metallic and stretching higher than the tallest elms. Before railways, the efficiency of the operation would have been impossible. Iron segments forged in the Fox and Henderson factory west of Birmingham went via the North-Western Railway Company to London and often within eighteen hours after manufacture were fixed in place at Hyde Park.

A secondary enterprise materialized close to the grounds – the sprawling wagons and carts of vendors of every conceivable comestible a gawker might ingest. Each observer was a potential visitor afterwards, and the crowds which thronged Knightsbridge and the Park grew daily;

many attracted by the constant inspections by the Prince, sometimes accompanied by the Queen. More than two thousand workmen laboured at the site, with thousands more fabricating elements of the building elsewhere, and still more thousands engaged in developing and shipping exhibits from as far off as Australia and India. On the site Charles Fox, the managing director of the construction firm, often put in eighteen-hour days and complained that each royal visit cost him pounds in lost work-time.

Exhibitors were encouraged by rules charging them no rent – but they would have to deliver and remove their exhibits as well as maintain them at their own expense. There was plenty of room for them. In scale, nothing like the Crystal Palace had ever been built. The structure was 1,848 feet long* – more than a third of a mile – and 408 feet wide, one of the great engineering achievements of the century.

The ever-malicious uncle of the Queen, the King of Hanover, now becoming senile, warned Frederick William IV that it would be unsafe to attend 'this rubbishy Exhibition' because 'the excommunicated of all lands' were in London and constituted a threat to visiting eminences. According to his informants, 'Ministers will not allow the Queen and the great originator of this folly, Prince Albert, to be in London while the Exhibition is on.' Other forecasts warned that the mammoth structure would collapse in a gale, or cause epidemics because of the masses of people spreading contagion, or, as Albert put it to the worried King of Prussia, 'that his second Tower of Babel would draw upon it the vengeance of an offended God'. But the work went on and the public was awed.

The Crystal Palace, and the preparations for the Great Exhibition, helped alter the face of London. Victoria Street was opened, ploughing a path through Westminster's worst slum. The Marble Arch was moved from the palace grounds to anchor the north-east ('Speaker's') corner of Hyde Park. Trafalgar Square was finally completed, although without Landseer's lions, which were added in 1868. Little-populated areas around new railway junctions underwent building booms, expanding living space, a crucial matter as in 1851 2,362,000 people lived in a far smaller London where open sewers still flowed into the Thames. Kensington, abutting Hyde Park to the west, became citified, and in

---

* Paxton wanted a symbolic 1851 feet, but the dimensions would not work.

Knightsbridge, even closer to the Exhibition grounds, a tea merchant, Charles Harrod, opened a grocery with a large range of merchandise opposite the village green. His trade thrived. To the south-west, Old Brompton lost its fairground, villas and market gardens to urban expansion. Only some of the metamorphosis was related to Crystal Palace expectations, but London was reaching into former suburbs and villages.

Despite the demands of the Exhibition, when Victoria insisted upon her now annual autumn retreat to Balmoral, Albert dutifully accompanied her to Scotland, from which he fired off letters and telegrams to London and foreign parts, and received visitors who undertook the gruelling day-and-night rail journey to Ballater. On Wordsworth's death, he exhorted Russell to name Tennyson for the Poet Laureate's chair. 'There are three or four authors of nearly equal merit,' Russell responded by form to the Queen rather than the Prince, 'such as Henry Taylor, Sheridan Knowles, Professor Wilson, and Mr Tennyson, who are qualified for the office.' Although Alfred Tennyson had become the most respected poet in England with his *Poems* of 1842 and sealed his reputation with the newly published *In Memoriam*, the Prime Minister had hardly heard of him.* Albert had to intervene once more to keep Duke Ernest's debts from causing the confiscation of a castle in Coburg and embarrassment to his brother. Without asking how many women Ernest kept, Albert wrote from Balmoral, 'I must remind you that you are still one of the richest of the small sovereigns in Germany. Besides, you have no family to keep, no brothers or sisters, nor any children.' By 21 October Albert was speaker at a dinner given by the Lord Mayor of York, using every possible occasion to talk up the Exhibition.

In November, as the Crystal Palace was rising spectacularly over Hyde Park, Albert materialized everywhere. Overwork seemed a compulsion. He appeared more aged than his thirty-one years. Thickening sideburns compensated for a thinning pate, and his increasing heaviness of body

---

* John Wilson as 'Christopher North' contributed essays and verse to *Blackwood's* magazine and since 1820 held the Chair of Moral Philosophy at the University of Edinburgh. James Sheridan Knowles, a playwright known for *William Tell* (1825) and *The Hunchback* (1832), had become a Baptist minister in 1845. Henry Taylor, a minor poet and dramatist, wrote the tragedy *Philip van Artefelde* (1834), and the comedy *The Virgin Widow* (1850). On 21 October, six weeks later, Russell conceded that Tennyson was a 'fit person'.

suggested too much desk-work and too many fundraising dinners. Thackeray thought the Prince looked ill, and while impatiently watching William Macready in *Hamlet* at the Haymarket, and wishing himself elsewhere, Thackeray imagined Albert in 'that absurd play'. Not as the Prince of Denmark but as the ghostly dead king. 'Suppose', he mused, 'our beloved monarch were to lose Prince Albert & marry his brother the Duke of Saxe-Coburg? 2 months after Albert's death suppose I saw a company of actors going to Windsor & acting a play full of the grossest allusions to widows marrying, to marriage with a deceased husband's brother & so forth – what a noise there'd be!'

Unable to slow down, Albert spent some early winter weather at Windsor writing memoranda on how a federation under Prussia and without Austria, both of which were threatening war to secure their rights in Germany, might be developed under clauses of the 1815 Treaty of Vienna. Austria, he warned Frederick William IV, was a Jesuit despotism, while Protestant Prussia could prosper as a constitutional monarchy, winning thereby England's support and ensuring (as the fifth and balancing Great Power with England, France, Austria and equally despotic Russia) 'universal peace'. But Albert's concepts were too large for the King, who was busy with more immediate problems. Almost without pause, Albert then wrote to Prince William, the designated successor, pressing him not to permit Prussia's humiliation by Austria. 'I have poured out a flood of considerations', he apologized on 29 December, 'as is bound to happen when one has had to dam the stream for so long...' But he closed with better news. 'The Exhibition is well forward, and its originator still hopes most earnestly it may be possible for you, the Princes, and your son, to be present at the opening. The building was started on November 1st, and will be nearly ready in a few days. It is a real work of art.'

The Crystal Palace was that, and more. The vast building was a technological marvel. None of its iron and glass had been anything but ideas on paper when the contractors accepted the assignment on 26 July 1850. Yet in his enthusiasm Albert exaggerated the frenetic pace of construction. Not a column had been raised until 26 September. Each vertical column was hollow, to act as a pipe to carry away rain and external moisture from the roof. A groove in the topmost gutters was designed to carry condensation from inside the building into the same pipes – part of the thirty-nine miles of piping in the building and foundation – and away from the building. The girders, each seventy-two feet long and intended to support the width of a section of the central aisle, were raised by a hoist powered by a team of six horses. Each girder was first tested on a hydraulic press to support fifteen tons, exceeding any predictable strain.

*Raising the ribs of the transept roof,* Illustrated London News, *14 December, 1850.*

Despite a brief strike – workmen demanded five shillings a day rather than four – they laboured as if they were being paid on a piecework basis. For laying the glass panels from Messrs Chance and Company of Birmingham, Paxton designed trolleys which were propelled backwards on tracks as each pane was placed. In one week in December, eighty men set 18,932 panes in the vast roof, one fixing sixty-eight panes in a single day.

When, two weeks earlier, the sixteen ribs of the transept were lifted into place, Albert had been there to look on, competing for attention with a brewer's dray bringing 250 gallons of beer for the 2,000 men. Both beer and Prince were lustily cheered.

Assembled on site from prefabricated parts and covering eighteen acres of parkland, including the politically precious elms, the glass palace was completed externally (but for painting) on 31 December. The Queen, with Albert, took the children to see it for the first time on 18 February 1851, and described it in her diary as 'one of the wonders of the world, which we English may indeed be proud of'. To Prince William, Albert had scoffed about rumours that the Court would flee London because of all the dire things likely to happen during construction and after. All of them were 'the inventions concocted by the enemies of our artistic and cultural venture and of all progress in civilisation...' In actuality it would prove difficult to keep the Queen and the older children away.

# XI

# *The Palace of Glass*

## *1850–1851*

E VEN AFTER COMPLETION, the Crystal Palace remained a huge problem for Albert. In matters small and large, his responsibilities had hardly begun. The Commissioners were a scattered group, some living very far from London. Until 3 October 1850, Fox and Henderson had not been able to secure an official order from the Commissioners authorizing payment for the work already accomplished and the materials purchased, yet the contractors had already spent more than £50,000 – an enormous sum by nineteenth-century calculation. Even Paxton blundered, intruding with a letter to *The Times* urging the Prime Minister to have the government pay for the construction and open the Exhibition to all-comers free of charge. It was interpreted erroneously as a confession of bankruptcy, which pained the Prince as much as did the concept that private enterprise was not up to the challenge. Once the building was enclosed, it was discovered that sparrows in large numbers nested in the elms under the transept. Worried about what they might do to exhibits and to spectators, the Commissioners brought the difficulty to one of Albert's favourite people, the Duke of Wellington. Hard of hearing and dim of sight, his wits were still sharp at eighty-one. As Ranger of Hyde Park, he allegedly arrived for an audience with the Queen and Prince and advised, 'Try sparrow hawks, Ma'am'. She did not, but somehow the sparrows were ousted.

Albert anguished over larger problems, including the perennial one of money. Additions, alterations, and overtime labour made a subsidiary contract for an additional £27,980 necessary; and then another for

£35,000. Internal costs brought the total higher. The final figure, including fittings – shelving, lighting and decoration – and re-landscaping the site once the construction crews were withdrawn, came to £169,998, many millions by later calculation. Yet income would cover all costs and leave a large surplus.

When public carping continued at each stage in the project, Paxton turned on the detractors and declared, 'It is a grand period in our history when a Prince . . . is engaged in doing all he can to foster the arts of peace, instead of lending his name and the bad example of his influence in fomenting petty distractions, and stirring up passions which tend to perpetuate strife, ill-blood, and the destruction of human life. To foster the arts, to promote the extension of industry and commerce, to knit nation and nation in the bonds of universal brotherhood, was a noble object for Prince Albert to engage in.'

Unconvinced, Colonel Thomas Sibthorp, MP for Lincoln, arose on the first day of the parliamentary session to decry the completion of the Crystal Palace. 'They might call it success,' he insisted of the alleged desecration of Hyde Park, 'but I call it failure. I do not wish to see that building destroyed by any acts of violence, but would to God that some hailstorm, or some visitation of lightning, might descend to defeat the ill-advised project.'

By 12 February – only two weeks after the interior was ruled acceptable for occupancy – goods were arriving. Once cleared by customs officers, objects were escorted to spaces allotted to each country by soldiers of the Royal Sappers and Miners, loaned to Albert by Wellington for the duration of the Exhibition. Given their speciality, they were expected to have some technological know-how. Engineers might have been the better choice, as the press aired public anxieties about the safety of the building when crowded with heavy machinery and subjected to the tread of thousands of visitors. Wellington sent soldiers to march over the wooden footways, and workmen built a test gallery for walking, running and jumping upon, to ensure the sturdiness of every portion of the Palace. The experimentation was deliberately public, satisfying everyone but committed doomsayers.

Almost everything relating to the Exhibition went to Albert for advice or approval. He had to authorize the artists for the *Illustrated London News* to make drawings – 'with the consent of the manufacturers'. He even checked to see that the exhibits were labelled properly.

Meanwhile the business of government became a major distraction. On 22 February Lord John Russell's ministry was defeated on an electoral bill and promptly resigned, forcing the Queen to send for Lord Stanley, whose minority Tories could only govern with external collaboration. Stanley (who succeeded his father on 30 June as 14th Earl of Derby) found, as expected, the Queen and Prince together at Buckingham Palace. 'The Queen said little', Stanley's son Edward reported in his diary, 'but listened with profound attention'. Albert wanted to know whether the Tories had enough talent to form a government, and Lord Stanley emphasized the veteran Herries and the rising Disraeli. One had a 'considerable knowledge of routine [but] was not possessed of distinguished ability'. The other 'had extraordinary talent, but no practice in official duties'. He would have problems, Derby added, in maintaining office, as it would require 'retraction of avowed opinions' – a reference to Tory policy in favour of protectionist tariffs. The Corn Laws had been repealed by Peel's ministry in 1846 at the cost of Conservative unity. Now the Peelite faction was melting into the Liberal (Whig) Party, leaving only the minority Rightists, whose goal to restore some restrictions elicited no sympathy from Albert.

'The Prince seemed inclined to press this subject and enter into argument, but my Father saw that the Queen wished to change it, and hinted that the details...would be better discussed bye-and-bye.' Clearly, Albert saw the year of a world fair keyed upon world manufactures as the wrong time for Tory trade ideology, but it was obvious that Stanley could find no coalition partners anyway. By early March, Lord John Russell, a perennial survivor, was reconfirmed in office after Lord Aberdeen and Sir James Graham had also found no workable combinations and Wellington advised settling once more for Russell. At each session Albert asked most of the questions and afterwards penned memoranda of the exchanges without identifying himself as anything but an observer, noting that with Stanley the Queen had pointedly warned that he would have to be responsible for Disraeli's conduct – neither she nor the Prince trusted the ambitious upstart. With Russell on 3 March she warned that she did not want Palmerston back, a matter she could not finally block, as (in Albert's words) 'Lord John...was in fact the weakness and Lord Palmerston the strength of the Government from his popularity with the Radicals'.

That the public understood how the monarchy was being administered was evident from a clever *Punch* cartoon, 'Cinderella; or Lord John Trying it on Again'. The scene, with a wonderful old crone with a cane – a fairy godmother in disguise – a frowning stepmother, various hangers-on in Court dress of a bygone age, and a diminutive Russell in a chair trying on the slipper of state once more, has at its centre to oversee the proceedings a cautious Prince Albert. Victoria is not even in the picture.

Two days later, while the Exhibition Commissioners met, Albert called Lord Stanley aside for a conversation on politics. Edward Stanley noted after talking with his father 'that the Prince's mind appeared to have been formed by Sir R. Peel, whose sayings and acts he continually quoted'. But Albert's mind was moulded more by the men he had encountered in working on the Great Exhibition, for 'He talked much of the necessity of a Conservative policy, expressed alarm at the [Radical] policy of Manchester, but said "What is to be done? Here are your rising men, sons of the aristocracy, educated in the best schools and universities, and among them there is not one that can compete with the self-taught middle-class manufacturers." Unluckily, this is true . . .'

Albert's concerns about the Exhibition were focused, by April, upon internal arrangements and the arrival and placement of the exhibits themselves. Could London's streets handle the traffic, and its police cope with security and crowd discipline? A *Punch* cartoon showed Albert bursting into the Crystal Palace, coat and shirt awry in his haste, confronting Britannia still trimming candlewicks. 'Here's a to-do!' he shouts. 'Here's all the Company come, and the Street's full of Carriages and Brooms – and there's such a Row! – and the Candles arn't Lighted, nor the Supper Ready, nor the Man dressed who's to Wait, nor the Music – nor Nothing.'

As opening day neared, Lieutenant Henry Tyler, an engineer and much later (as Sir Henry) Chairman of the Grand Trunk Railway Company of Canada, made a very likely modest estimate for Albert of the value of the objects in the Exhibition, excluding Victoria's acquisition from Kashmir, the Koh-i-noor ('mountain of light') Diamond, expected to magnetize visitors. Those of the United Kingdom were valued at £1,031,607 4s. 9d; of the Colonies – largely raw materials rather than manufactures and equipment – at £79,901 15s. Foreign countries had

**BRITANNIA'S GREAT PARTY.**

*Early in 1851,* Punch *observes Albert's concern that the exhibitions in the Crystal Palace may not be in place for the opening on 1 May.*

brought in objects estimated at £670,420 11*s.* 7*d.* How to protect the property at night engaged the minds of the Prince, the Commissioners, and the Police. Colonel Reid of the Metropolitan Police suggested a barbed-wire entanglement with upright iron railings eight feet high, a prison-like vision which Albert reduced to an ornamental iron railing, and a force of four inspectors, twenty-five sergeants and 334 constables. The fire watch would consist of two hundred Royal Sappers, twenty-four of whom would begin night duty at eight each evening.

There would be no disorder, even when, on 7 October, there were 109,000 visitors in the building – a daily record. The only fire was a small blaze of cotton waste, easily extinguished. The myriad of detail left the Prince, he wrote to his stepmother in Coburg, 'more dead than alive from Overwork'.

'My poor Albert', Victoria wrote in her journal the day before the opening, when she visited the site for a preview, 'is terribly fagged. *All* day some question or other, or some difficulty, all of which my beloved one takes with the greatest quiet & good temper.' Even the Exhibition's motto, at the head of the catalogue, was chosen by the Prince – '*The earth is the Lord's and all that therein is.*' That too would inspire controversy, as the president of the Bible Society complained that Albert had used the Prayer Book version of the line rather than that of the King James Bible. There could also be too much religion. Augustus Pugin, an ardent Catholic, had designed a Medieval Court that would become one of the most popular exhibits, but he was required to remove the large crucifix overlooking his medieval fantasies. On the eve of the opening Albert wrote in his journal, '*Entsetzliche Unruhe durch die Arrangements für die Eröffnung*' – irresistible anxiety during the arrangements for the opening. Yet Victoria would have had good reason, as she entered, to recall what she had written in her journal more than a year earlier: 'I *do* feel proud at the thought of what my beloved Albert's great mind has conceived.'

Nothing went awry – except that a Chinese trespasser in traditional robes, actually the proprietor of a junk moored in the Thames, was mistaken for be an emissary from the Celestial Kingdom and placed in the procession between the Archbishop of Canterbury and the Duke of Wellington. Ecstatically, the Queen recorded in her journal one of its longest and most vivid entries. The bustle, the crowds, the excitement – even her own dread – reminded her of her coronation day. With Vicky and Bertie and the Prince in her carriage – one of nine state coaches – they arrived in 'Queen's weather', the light rain that fell as they left having stopped. 'The sun shone & gleamed upon the gigantic edifice, upon which the flags of every nation were flying...The glimpse through the iron gates of the Transept, the moving palms & flowers, the myriads of people filling their galleries & the seats around, together with the flourish of trumpets, as we entered the building, gave a sensation I shall never forget, & I felt much moved.'

The spectacle was 'magic and impressive' as light danced about the dazzling interior, sunlight streaming through its 293,655 panes of glass and reflecting off the facets of a twenty-seven-foot crystal fountain that was the structure's centrepiece. The four faces of the clocks on the building were about to record noon when Albert escorted Victoria in, Vicky at his right hand, Bertie (in Highland dress) holding his mother's hand. 'The tremendous cheering, the joy expressed in every face, the

*The Queen, Prince and their older children visiting the Machinery Department of the Great Exhibition in May 1851. From the* Illustrated London News, *which advertises itself on the signboard, centre left.*

vastness of the building, with all its decorations & exhibits, the sound of the organ (with 200 instruments & 600 voices), & my beloved Husband the creator of this great "Peace Festival", uniting the industry & art of *all* nations of the earth, *all* this, was indeed moving, & a day to live forever. God bless my dearest Albert, & my dear Country which has shown itself so great today ... '

To Leopold, Victoria called the Crystal Palace 'astonishing, a fairy scene. Many cried, and all felt touched and impressed with devotional feelings.' It was a reaction that united onlookers. The historian and politician Thomas Macaulay, cautious with his words, in his diary called the interior 'a most gorgeous sight; vast; graceful; beyond the dreams of the Arabian romances'. Greville marvelled at 'no soldiers, hardly any policemen to be seen, and yet all so orderly and good humoured' – and although 6,063,986 visitors, equal to a third of the kingdom, poured through the Crystal Palace over 140 days (no Sundays), there would be no damage and no violence. 'The *frondeurs* are all come round', Greville wrote on 10 May, 'and those who abused it most vehemently now praise it as much.'

A rare complaint about the opening was John Bright's dismissal of Court dress as 'absurd', but for the tens of thousands at the opening such colour added to the spectacle. The vista had been everyone's realization of fairyland. 'Such a beautiful scene', Harriet, Countess Granville, wrote, 'never was seen in the world before, for there was never a place to show it. The bright, fairy-like decorations of the place altogether, visible in its whole length and breadth, filled below and lined above with thousands of well-dressed people, was the prettiest and most imposing sight I ever saw; and when one saw that it was formed of a combination of all nations, all classes, and almost of all times, from the last inventions of the present day to the old Beefeaters of the thirteenth century, it caused one's pleasure to consist of a mixture of feelings and sensations almost impossible to define to oneself.'

Lady Charlotte Guest, wife of a Welsh iron-and-steel baron and a writer and translator, watched the Queen and Prince arrive with their children to stand on the broad, raised dais, their Court surrounding them, and watched by thousands of renowned and the loyal subjects, and recognized that 'all this pomp and panoply were called together to do honour to the industry of millions, whose toils, erst scorned upon, seemed suddenly ennobled.' It was an enterprise unlike anything any-one had ever known. 'I am lost in thronging thoughts, I cannot fitly express what I would say. But as the wife of the largest manufacturer in the world I could not but feel this to be a most impressive sight. Parts of the ceremony were to me most touching, and many times I found the tears starting from my eyes. I need not describe what any newspaper of the day will tell more accurately. I only know it was the most dazzling sight I ever beheld . . . '

Charlotte Brontë, visiting London for the Exhibition, would go five times, writing to her father, gloomily living that June in her house in Yorkshire, that its grandeur did not consist in one thing, 'but in the unique assemblage of *all* things. Whatever human industry has created, you find there, from the great compartments filled with railway engines and boilers, with mill-machinery in full work, with splendid carriages of all kinds, with harness of every description – to the glass-covered and velvet-spread stands loaded with the most gorgeous work of the gold-smith and silversmith, and the carefully guarded caskets full of real diamonds and pearls worth hundreds of thousands of pounds.' To the author of *Jane Eyre*, the awed multitude thronging the long aisles was subdued beyond ordinary explanation. 'Amongst the thirty thousand souls that peopled it the day I was there, not one loud noise was to be heard, not one irregular movement seen – the living tide rolls on quietly, with a deep hum like the sea heard from a distance.' On 13 June she was rewarded by the sight of the ex-royal family of France venturing down the transept – the former queen and her daughter-in-law the duchesse d'Orléans with her two sons.

Also there, fictionally, were the Sponges of Robert Surtees's *Mr Sponge's Sporting Tour*, the last instalment of which appeared in the *New Monthly Magazine* only a few weeks before the Great Exhibition opened. Miss Howard wonders about 'the sliding-scale of children' she sees thronging outside a shop window, and Miss Glitters explains, 'They must be on their way to the Great Exhibition of National Industry to show' – compete – 'against the Prince's little people'.

'There you go again, Miss G', exclaims the mortified Captain Cutifat while the lady, 'looking quite innocent' about her jest, claims, 'I said nothing'.

Victoria and Albert had already produced seven children since 1840, and the *double entendre* about Prince Albert's industry was so easily apprehended that when Surtees's one-volume edition appeared in 1853 the witticism was withdrawn. Although Albert's productivity as a stud was in the tradition of George III and at least two of his sons (whose children were almost all illegitimate), Prince Albert's brood with Victoria may have also recalled the last reigning queen, although of Anne's eighteen pregnancies most miscarried. In boisterous circles, jokes were not uncommon about Prince Albert's parenting efficiency, the Queen usually unmentioned out of respect for the Crown. At much the same time as the Surtees story, T.W. Booker, MP, later Booker Blakemore, spoke to the Herefordshire Agricultural Society (reported in *The Times*, 20 October) in praise of the fecundity demonstrated in their county. 'It would be a libel on the buxom, rosy-cheeked women of Herefordshire', he smirked, 'to say that at least they were not as good breeders as their own cows, or that their qualifications were not superior to those of the half-starved creatures in the overcrowded alleys of the towns, called women, but who had none of the "points" of a woman, either before or behind; and it would be a libel, too, on the broad-shouldered men of Herefordshire to say that they were not as sure foal-getters as the men of any other county, or even as Prince Albert himself.' There were exclamations of 'Oh! Oh!' heard from the audience, and the next day *The Times* printed a letter to the editor deploring 'the most indecent manner' in which the Prince's name had been used.

*The Times* on 2 May 1851 published an unprecedented three pages and thirteen columns of description of the opening events, plus a plan of the building and catalogue of exhibits, country by country, with a last line, 'To be continued'. The contents of the Crystal Palace had overwhelmed even the newspaper of record. 'Certain it is', *The Times* began, 'that people who had never before seen the sun rise, except through a ballroom window, were in full activity soon after dawn, impelled by the impulse which seemed to lend life and energy to the whole substance of the great and somewhat lethargic metropolis.' In grand hyperbole, *The Times* went on, 'Never before was such a vast multitude collected together within the memory of man. The struggles of great nations in battle, the levies of whole races, never called forth such an array as thronged the streets of London on the 1st of May; ... but here was an occasion which might be celebrated by the whole human race without one pang of regret, envy, or national hate.'

Perhaps the greatest tribute came from Thackeray, in the person of Mr Punch himself, who was shocked into sentimental awe, an unusual if not unprecedented condition:

> I remarked that the scene I witnessed was the grandest and most cheerful, the brightest and most splendid show that eyes had ever looked on since the creation of the world; – but as everybody remarked the same thing, this remark is not of much value. I remarked, and with a feeling of shame, that I had long hesitated about paying three guineas – pooh-poohed – said I had seen the Queen and Prince before, and so forth, and felt now that to behold this spectacle, three guineas, or five guineas, or any sum of money (for I am a man of enormous wealth) would have been cheap; and I remarked how few of us know really what is good for us – have the courage of our stations, and what a number of chances in life we throw away. I would not part with the mere recollection of this scene for a small annuity; and calculate that

after paying my three guineas, I have the Exhibition before me, besides being largely and actually in pocket.

I remarked that a heavy packet of sandwiches which Jones begged me to carry, and which I pocketed in rather a supercilious and grumbling manner, became most pleasant friends and useful companions after we had been in our places two or three hours; and I thought to myself, that if I were a lyric poet with a moral turn, I would remark how often in the hour of our need our humble friends are welcome and useful to us, like those dear sandwiches, which we pooh-poohed when we did not need them.

I remarked that when the Queen bowed and courtesied, all the women about began to cry.

I remarked how eagerly the young Prince talked with his sister – how charmed everybody was to see those pretty young persons walking hand in hand with their father and mother, and how, in the midst of any magnificence you will, what touches us most is nature and human kindness, and what we love to witness most is love.

The opening of the Great Exhibition in the Crystal Palace was indeed a love feast.

Season tickets were three guineas for men and two for women. (Albert held Season Ticket No. 1, his signature at the bottom as 'Proprietor'.) After the first two days at £1, admission until 24 May was five shillings. After 26 May, admission Monday through Thursday was one shilling and on Friday and Saturday two-and-sixpence. Cheap tickets enabled the working classes to visit the Exhibition, and employers released labourers to attend with their families. On one excursion day the Great Western Railway ran a train with 151 coaches carrying five thousand ticket-holders. (People paid a few pence weekly to a savings fund for the trip.) No alcohol was sold in Exhibition restaurants, and while the press complained about the public necessity to drink ginger beer, sobriety was a crucial element in an orderly flow of visitors. The cuisine was deliberately limited: 1,092,337 bottles of soft drinks were sold, 934,691 fluffy, currant-filled Bath buns and 870,027 ordinary sweet buns. In a pre-deodorant society, the Commissioners arranged to distribute 270 gallons of eau-de-Cologne and other scents through the building.

As befitted a design extrapolated from a greenhouse, the interior was colourful in objects and people and decoration. Paintwork in red, blue, yellow and white, with crimson banners identifying the exhibit areas, accentuated by light streaming from the glass walls and roof. Crowds grew daily but exhibited Sunday decorum, belying Colonel Sibthorp's cranky prediction of mass criminality and sexual licence. The forecast of the Astronomer Royal, George Airy, that the building would collapse under the strain of wind and storm, equally proved false, as did the dire prognostications by King Ernest Augustus of Hanover. For many, the Exhibition was an opportunity for a first railway experience, as excursion trains brought hundreds of thousands of sightseers (the word dates only from 1847) to London, while tens of thousands more came by boat from the Continent and from America. For exhibition-goers, the odds were good that they would see the Queen and Prince. Albert was there almost daily when he was in town. Victoria herself visited often until

THE SHIPWRECKED MINISTERS SAVED BY THE GREAT EXHIBITION STEAMER.

*The government is rescued from public wrath about its legislative failures by the distractions of the Great Exhibition. In the background,* Punch *shows the Crystal Palace with a steamer's funnel.*

the formal closing in mid-October, inquisitive about everything and unconcerned about security.

In June, *Punch* would print a cartoon of a shipwrecked Lord John Russell government saved by a steamer labelled *Exhibition*, which was substantially true, in that the marvels of the Crystal Palace were a distraction for both Parliament and the press. 'It was such a time', Victoria wrote in her journal (18 July 1851), 'of pleasure, of pride, of satisfaction & of deep thankfulness; it is the triumph of peace & good will towards all, – of art, of commerce, – of my beloved Husband – & of triumph for my country.' For many who came, it was their first glimpse of the new realities of mechanical invention and accomplishments in arts and crafts, a revelation of the technological future and of an English pre-eminence in mass-produced industrial goods that, ironically, the spread of know-how afforded by the Exhibition would soon threaten.

Victoria was not the only ticketholder who would come again and again. 'A very fine thing,' said Gustave Flaubert, 'despite being admired by everyone.'

With rare exceptions, enthusiasm for the Exhibition ran high and across the classes. Cantankerous Thomas Carlyle had 'no patience' with the Prince and 'that Cole', who had contrived to bring so many out-siders to London. He told *Westminster Review* publisher John Chapman that he had been 'worn to death with bores all summer, who present themselves by twos and threes in his study, saying "Here we are".' A few were as surly as Carlyle. Herman Melville dismissed it as a 'vast toy, . . . overdone', but his pastor at All Souls' in Manhattan, Henry Whitney Bellows, perceived 'a noble & unmistakable tendency to unite man with God', and described the Crystal Palace as 'the digest of the universe'.

Charles Dickens complained that the Exhibition complicated his life, and visited only twice, but he had already received a private tour of the frigid, nearly empty, building from Joseph Paxton himself in February, and since April had been busy managing and performing in amateur theatricals to raise funds for creative fellowships for artists and writers. The Queen and Prince had even agreed to attend the première perform-ance of the first benefit production, Sir Edward Bulwer-Lytton's costume piece set in the reign of George II, *Not So Bad as We Seem.* Paxton's patron, the Duke of Devonshire, had offered use of the picture gallery in his mansion, Devonshire House, and the price had been set steeply at five guineas. At Victoria's suggestion, the date fixed was 30 April, the eve of the opening of the Crystal Palace, to capture the aristocratic élite in London for the Exhibition, but the sudden death of eight-month-old Dora Annie Dickens on 14 April postponed the play. 'Queen's Night' – Albert did not reign and did not count – became 16 May. Special care was taken to have a character smoking a clay pipe only feign the act, with the smoke merely whorls of cotton on fine wires. 'The Queen can't bear tobacco', Dickens had warned.

When the Queen and Prince attended a ball at the Guildhall on 9 July, 1851 to celebrate the success of the Exhibition, excitement about it seemed to have been reached flood stage. The royal party left Buckingham Palace at nine, travelling through the city in state carriages to swelling acclaim from Londoners lining the streets. Rather than dispersing, the crowds continued to grow, awaiting the return of the Queen's carriage. Since the ball was a brilliant extravaganza, the Queen stayed late; but so did the waiting crowds. As Albert wrote to Stockmar, 'A million of people remained till three in the morning in the streets, and were full of enthusiasm towards us.' It was an occasion without precedent.

More than ever, Albert seemed wanted everywhere to make an occasion memorable, but he was wearing down. Before the Guildhall event he had presided at the close of the academic year at Harrow, and his appointment calendar was full. At the annual Royal Academy dinner he spoke of the rapport that the artist must seek with some audience, for no creation truly existed without welcome response. 'Gentlemen,' he put it, 'the production of all works in art or poetry requires, in the conception or execution, not only an exercise of the intellect, skill and patience, but particularly a concurrent warmth of feelings, and a free flow of imagination.' In the increasing gulf between creator and critic he saw potential problems for artists even as the consumers of art were increasing. There was now 'as judge, a great public, for the greater part uneducated in art; and thus led by professional writers, who often strive to impress the public with a great idea of their own artistic knowledge, by the merciless manner in which they treat works which cost those who produced them the highest efforts of mind and feeling'.

Painter Thomas Uwins was ecstatic at Albert's perspective. 'The speech of this accomplished prince', he wrote to his friend John Townshend, 'beat all the dukes, and lords, and ministers of state. The whole was much beyond anything of the kind I ever witnessed.' Every critic, *Art Journal* advised, should take the Prince's words to heart, but Thackeray called his appraisal 'mistaken benevolence': 'Art, like a foot-ball, bounds the higher the more you kick it.' Pleasing a public would turn art 'effeminate'. He preferred critical tension. 'No, no; let us still dab mud on the pallette of the painter; let us still mix dirt in the ink of the writer.'

Albert's plate was varied. At a cattle show in July, he wrote to his brother, 'I had a dinner . . . with two thousand farmers, and I had to give a long address. The dinner lasted five hours.' Later in the month the family left Windsor for Osborne, 'the haven of peace and rest', from whence Albert deluged Whitehall and other London venues with business mail; and when they retreated further to Balmoral for six weeks, he was preoccupied at a distance with winding down the Exhibition and with foreign affairs, which meant the continuing exasperation of dealing with Palmerston. Feeling among Liberals was still heated about Austrian suppression of independence movements in northern Italy and in Hungary. Among the foreigners attracted to London at Exhibition time was Baron Julius von Haynau, the general who had put down the rebels with what most English considered savagery. When 'General Hyaena' arrived and was recognized by his trademark moustachios, he was roughed up by a crowd and Victoria wrote to ask Palmerston to apologize on behalf of the nation 'at the brutal outrage on one of the Emperor's distinguished generals'. Palmerston duly penned his regrets, but tactlessly added that someone of Haynau's notoriety risked such a reception. The imbroglio continued into the Balmoral weeks and after, souring the good feeling about the Great Exhibition.

Good feeling, in any case, Dickens forecast, sceptically, would be the inevitable outcome, rather than enlightenment. The public was bewildered by the profusion of the unfamiliar, he explained to W.H. Wills. 'My apprehension – and prediction – is, that they will come out of it at last, with that feeling of boredom and lassitude (to say nothing of having spent their money) that the reaction will not be as wholesome and vigorous and quick, as folks expect.' Yet Albert's perennial adversary, Lord Brougham, spoke in the Lords in favour of Paxton's petition against dismantling the Crystal Palace – Albert stood by his guarantee to take it down – by declaring it 'not only a work of great national utility, but of European usefulness'.

At her final visit to the Crystal Palace on 14 October, arriving with Albert, Victoria found the building, still filled with eager visitors, in the process of being dismantled. A huge brass organ, labelled a Sommerophone, was playing, and the booming notes, she wrote, 'nearly upset me'. The glass fountain was already removed, and exhibits being taken down. 'The canvas is very dirty, the red curtains are faded, and many things are very much soiled, still the effect is fresh and new as ever, and most beautiful.' So much remained beautiful, she noted, 'I could not believe it was the last time I was to see it ... It made us all very melancholy.' There at the close, in the crowd, was an old Cornishwoman, Mary Kerlynack, 'who had walked hundreds of miles to see the Exhibition'. A 'most hale old woman', she was 'at the door to see me', and was 'near crying at my looking at her'.

The next day saw the official closing, and the Queen regretted not being there. (It was 'not to be in state'.) Albert left at ten for the ceremonies, where an estimated fifty thousand people crowded inside, despite dripping skies, for a last look. The only formalities were Albert's address to the prize juries, and their reports. The high dignity of the opening was impossible in the already disassembled state of the interior.

'Albert was right', Victoria confided to her diary. '...I could hardly have been there as a spectator ... How sad and strange to think that this great and bright time has passed away like a dream ... I feel as if it were doing my dearest Albert an injury that it should be gone by ...'

Some of the ideas, devices and products exhibited would lead to real change, as Albert had hoped, and the traffic was not all *from* Britain to overseas markets. For example, John Sutton Nettlefold, a Birmingham manufacturer of wood screws (and uncle of Joseph Chamberlain, the future apostle of British imperialism), came upon an American-patented machine which fully mechanized the screw-making process. Birmingham screws were made laboriously by hand, a costly method that also prevented uniform quality. Thomas J. Sloan's machinery had afforded small metal goods from America technological superiority and competitiveness in cost, and Nettlefold adopted the process, boosting Birmingham's economy.

To avoid chaos, exhibitors displayed, rather than sold, their wares at the Palace, but were permitted to dispense leaflets and other hand-outs –

the chief means of creating markets for them. Souvenirs were plentiful, ranging from models of the building and peepshows (with an eyepiece) of the interior, to coloured lithographs ('from the originals painted... for HRH Prince Albert'), of which fifty-five scenes were printed. Among the handbills sold were songs and ballads related to the Exhibition, one of them, 'How's Your Poor Feet?' – its subject a tourist who came by train – typical of what visitors took home with their sore feet.

> I, the Exhibition came to see,
> and gaze at London town;
> I really was amazed...

There was even a children's illustrated book, beginning,

> And this is the man submitting his plan
> To the Prince who approved, and said it was good,
> That a Palace of Glass should be built on the grass,
> For the great World's Fair, ...
> The fine Crystal Palace the Prince had built.

A silent success of the Exhibition was the operation of 'Public Waiting Rooms', as reported afterward to the Society of Arts. For tuppence admission, a person secured lavatory privileges, and for fourpence also a clean towel. Two 'sets of rooms' were set up 'by way of experiment', one for ladies at 51 Bedford Street, near Coutts's Bank, and one for gentlemen at 95 Fleet Street. They were a long walk from the Crystal Palace, and the accommodation was 'of so novel and delicate a character' as to be difficult to make widely known, but the facilities turned a large profit. On expenses of £680 during the five months of the Exhibition the 'Waiting Rooms' earned £2,470. Of all the innovations of the Great Exhibition, clean public lavatories at nominal cost may have been the most civilized.

Among Albert's aggravations were the choices of medals, which became a diplomatic nightmare, especially as the French jurors, to the dismay of Stafford Northcote, claimed that most major prizes should go the French exhibits, putting forward a list of twenty-five claimants. To allay trouble, five had to be awarded to France. In general the policy of the Commissioners was to award medals to international exhibitors. As much as national rivalries permitted, it was to be a fair of good feeling.

For Albert, who was barely thirty-two at the close of the Great Exhibition, and still held no British rank or title, the most immediate result was a prestige he had never known and which would never be higher in his lifetime. Many of his collaborators would earn royal honours. Paxton would even be awarded a bursary of £5,000 by the grateful Commissioners once they recognized that even with shilling admissions the fair had accumulated a sizeable profit. Matthew Digby Wyatt, architect and art critic, and secretary to the Exhibition Committee, received a special gold medal from Albert for his services, after which the Prince promoted him for government posts as 'industrious, upright & amiable'. Cole and Northcote each became Companions to the Order of the Bath, with knighthoods going to Fox, Cubitt, Paxton and the Exhibition Commissioners – except for the reluctant Cobden. He wrote to a friend that the Exhibition was 'truly a spectacle that will make your heart expand . . . Description is powerless, and the imagination fails to picture the beauty and variety of the glass palace'. Yet the strict Radical principles that kept him from appearing at the opening in Court dress also kept him from accepting any royal honours.

The summit of Albert's public career came at a cost. He had regularly complained of a 'weak stomach', and was increasingly subject to severe stomach cramps which he blamed on the tension of his crush of activities and which were assumed afterwards to be the price of his conscientiousness about detail. On 10 October, when he was involved in planning the elaborate closing ceremonies at the Crystal Palace, he was ill through the night that followed with what Victoria described as another stomach 'attack'. Now balding and paunchy, he looked prematurely old. But not to George Eliot who, at Covent Garden to hear *La Juive*, claimed to have fallen in love with the Prince, 'who was unusually animated and prominent. He had a noble, genial, intelligent expression and is altogether a man to be proud of. As for the Queen, she is deplorable – worse and worse the more one looks at her – so utterly mean in contour and expression.'

As it became accepted that the Crystal Palace would indeed have to be removed from Hyde Park as promised, press speculation burgeoned as to what would happen to it and to what uses it would be put. The formal vote for its removal did not come until 30 April, 1852, after which a Crystal Palace Company for its dismantling and reassembly was formed by Samuel Laing, Chairman of the Brighton and South Coast

Railway; John Scott Russell, a Millwall shipbuilder and a power in the Society of Arts; Charles Geach, an ironworks owner and Chairman of Midland Bank, and several others who had been associated with the Great Exhibition. It would cost nearly £200,000 for its purchase and reconstruction at Penge Park on Sydenham Hill in the Kent countryside.

The reopening would attract vast crowds. The new art and science of photography, which fascinated Albert, an early *aficionado*, recorded the dismantling and the reconstruction with a new roof line; and the opening ceremonies at which Victoria and her family participated amid choruses, orchestras, and audiences of thousands provided history's most populous daguerreotype. Shortened and slightly heightened by a barrel-like roof, the new Crystal Palace prospered as a concert and exhibition centre until it was destroyed by fire in 1936.

Sale of the building in 1852 added to the Commissioners' parallel problem by supplementing a surplus that had already reached £200,000. Disposing of the largesse was a politically sensitive matter. The Prince's scheme was to purchase eighty-seven acres in South Kensington to continue the goals of the Great Exhibition. With the help of Disraeli, then Chancellor of the Exchequer, the Commission paid £342,000 for the site, nearly half of which (£165,000) came from Crystal Palace earnings. Sceptics would label the idea 'Albertopolis', but the educational, cultural, and scientific institutions initiated by Albert's energy and foresight would materialize into a great South Kensington complex of museums, colleges, and concert halls, keeping Victoria busy at dedications for decades. Overlooking them from the southern edge of Hyde Park, within the neo-Gothic Albert Memorial, the Prince, in John Foley's bronze statue, holds on his right knee one of the volumes of the Great Exhibition catalogue, his forefinger slipped into its pages as if he is anxious not to lose his place, and looks over his legacy.*

---

* The Royal Commission for the Exhibition of 1851 operates still, now under the presidency of another queen's husband, Prince Philip, Duke of Edinburgh. The interest from the unexpended surplus remaining after the establishment of the educational and cultural estate in South Kensington amounted annually by the 1990s to more than £900,000. Much of this income has been used for fellowships and other grants for advanced study and research in science, engineering and the

In the aftermath of the Exhibition, with its effervescence evaporated, Albert returned to the routine tasks of the Court only to find that Palmerston's handling of the Foreign Office had become even more irksome while royal attention was elsewhere. Haynau's visit had been followed by his opposite number, Lajos Kossuth. The Hungarian revolutionary, although ousted at home, was the darling of Radicals and Liberals alike. As the Queen's government maintained friendly relations with imperial Austria, any official acceptance of Kossuth would be awkward, and Victoria wrote a cautionary letter to Palmerston, who had declared his enthusiasm for the resistance hero. Also in December the 'Prince-President' of France engineered a *coup d'etat* and named himself Emperor Napoleon III. The Queen and Prince were outraged, but Palmerston was an admirer of Louis Napoleon and embarrassed the Court by avowing it. Victoria and Albert appealed to Lord John Russell to keep Palmerston in bounds, both of their letters very likely drafted by Albert, as was the royal manner. Kossuth was not to be received by Palmerston publicly or privately, as his position made any gesture public.

Intemperately, Palmerston replied to his Prime Minister, 'I have just received your letter...I am told, your messenger waits for an answer. My reply then is immediate and is: That there are limits to all things, that I do not choose to be dictated to as to whom I may or may not receive in my own house and that I shall use my own discretion on that matter. You of course will use yours as to the disposition of your government. – I have not detained your messenger five minutes.'

The contretemps kept Victoria and Albert at Windsor, rather than Osborne, during Christmas, and at a Privy Council meeting the next day Palmerston failed to arrive to deliver up his seals of office, writing to Lord John instead of his 'just indignation'. In due course the seals went to his former deputy, Lord Granville. The Queen and Prince considered ousting 'Pam' a victory, and saw the old year out happily. 'And now the year is ending', Albert wrote to his brother, 'with the

arts. Among Exhibition Awardees have been eleven future Nobel Prize winners, six future holders of the Order of Merit, and three Presidents of the Royal Society. Such opportunities had been foreseen in the Commissioners' Second Report (1852), under the leadership of the Prince Consort, which recognized the inadequacy of both public and private support of science and art, and suggested judicious investment and application of Exhibition funds.

lucky circumstance for us that the man who has been embittering our whole lives by setting us the shameful alternative of endorsing his misdeeds throughout Europe, or of raising the Radical Party here to power under his leadership ... – that man has cut his own throat'. Yet Albert realized in his rush to gloat that 'Pam' was far from dead, and that his incised gullet would mend. 'We shall have plenty of trouble with Palmerston, who is raging', he predicted. Palmerston would become the most courted politician in Britain, the sought-after saviour of every party, while John Russell's government, bereft of its strongest member, was destined to drift into dissolution.

Among other misdeeds, Palmerston had become, Albert wrote to Prince William of Prussia early in 1852, 'Louis Napoleon's accomplice ... There is no doubt that now he is thinking solely of revenge, but I think him less dangerous in opposition than he would be in power, for there are not at his disposal those vast possibilities of doing harm, which the Foreign Office gave him.'

Albert had already made his feelings known as to where to apply the surplus left by the Great Exhibition and the prospective sale of the building, yet early in the new year he was still receiving proposals. One, from Lord Seymour of the Office of Works, had behind it the desire to move the Royal Society out of its rooms in Somerset House, needed for other government uses. The Society had once been a progressive scientific body, but the Prince viewed it now as an anachronism. 'To give the surplus away however,' he responded testily, 'in order to provide with better accommodation a Society, which as at present constituted has forfeited the sympathy of the generality of the Public, by its lethargic state & exclusive principles, could not, I am sure, be thought of for a moment.'

Seeing for himself 'hardly ... any time for peace' in the aftermath of the Exhibition, and the political instability occasioned by Palmerston's exit, Albert, and Victoria as well, worried that Napoleon III might look for a war to deflect any opposition to his seizure of power. Early in February, as the Queen waited to drive off to the Lords to reopen Parliament – the moment was only two hours off – she used the pause in schedule to write to her uncle Leopold, who was anxious about possible French designs on his small and weak country. 'With such an extraordinary man as Louis Napoleon,' she conceded, 'one can never be for one instant safe. It makes me very melancholy; I love peace and quiet – in fact I *hate* politics and turmoil ...' Fortunately, she thought,

Albert loved both. 'Albert grows daily fonder and fonder of politics and business, and is so wonderfully *fit* for both – such perspicacity and such *courage* – and I grow daily to dislike them both more and more. We women are not *made* for governing – and if we are good women, we must *dislike* these masculine occupations; but there are times which force one to take *interest* in them *mal gré bon gré*, and I do, of course, *intensely*.'

So she concluded, as it was time to dress and go off with Albert to Parliament.

# XII

# From Glory to Gloom

## *1852–1853*

S AILING IN THE arctic north-west of Canada, Captain Edward Augustus Inglefield indulged in the contemporary practice of christening geographical features he encountered, whatever natives may have already named them, to satisfy his own whim. Thus Victoria Island had its Prince Albert Peninsula and Prince Albert Sound, while to the east was the smaller Prince of Wales Island. On the east side of Smith Sound, 'some extraordinary table-topped cliffs attracted our notice', he wrote, 'and so perfectly even and marked into galleries did they appear, that my mind associating them with the glassy sides of the Great Exhibition, I named them the Crystal Palace Cliffs.'

In his years with Victoria, Albert travelled to no setting more exotic than Coburg – and Inglefield duly named an expanse south-east of Ellesmere Island in the Prince's honour (although spelled in un-German fashion) Cobourg Island – but in June 1852 Albert ventured vicariously, without leaving London, into Continental mountain climbing. Another Albert, surnamed Smith and a proprietor of dioramas, had opened an 'Ascent of Mont Blanc' exhibition at the Egyptian Hall in Piccadilly. At a command performance, Prince Albert brought his sons Bertie and Alfred. Other than escaping to the royal retreats at Osborne and Balmoral, Albert was too busy for holidays.

Among his reasons to be close to home was the liability of Lord John Russell's lame ministry, which failed within weeks of Palmerston's exit. Back came the Earl of Derby, who had failed to cobble a Tory ministry a year earlier. This time he succeeded, with Disraeli as Chancellor of the

Exchequer and Leader of the House of Commons, although he could never balance his cheque-book at home. With few experienced hands, Derby promised the Queen and Prince little more than to weather out the parliamentary session and ask the Crown for Dissolution and a General Election before the year was out. As usual, Albert sat in on meetings with the Queen's ministers, asked probing questions, and kept memoranda which deliberately suggested that he did little more than secretarial duties.

Palmerston's former post went to James Howard Harris, 3rd Earl of Malmesbury and Tory whip in the Lords, who was forty-five. His most persuasive claim to the job was that his grandfather and father had both been diplomats and that he had edited, despite a reputation for execrable grammar, his grandfather's *Diplomatic Journal and Correspondence*, which taught him 'all the verbiage of the profession'. His interest in foreign affairs also extended to his having married a Frenchwoman with social cachet, but that was hardly enough, and he was handicapped by Derby's appointment of his son Edward Stanley as Under-Secretary for he was, Malmesbury recalled, far off 'in India for his pleasure'. Fortunately there was a Permanent Under-Secretary who had been Minister in Washington, and there were 'the Queen and Prince, who, in the kindest and most gracious manner, gave me a great deal of private information of which I could know nothing as to foreign, especially German, Courts'. Although Malmesbury basically endorsed Palmerstonian policies, they were both grateful not to have Palmerston at the Foreign Office.

Among other moves his larger-than-life predecessor would have taken, Malmesbury accepted the reality of an another imperial Bonaparte, first satisfying himself that Napoleon III was the correct numeral. Louis Napoleon had bypassed the 'II' which the unlucky young son of the first Bonaparte would have had. It was not long before Victoria began addressing the new emperor formally as 'brother'. 'With us he has become *mon frère*,' Albert remarked, 'but he must not become *frère* Cain.'

Less well received at Court were Derby and Disraeli, both regarded with distrust. Derby seemed too cautious, his lieutenant too much the reverse. Yet Disraeli's memoranda on Cabinet and Commons matters, witty and colourful in characterization as befitted the successful novelist, won over the Queen and softened the suspicions of the Prince. 'Disraeli appears to have a certain degree of influence over Prince Albert's mind', Edward Stanley noted in his diary, very likely from Disraeli's boastful confidences that spring. 'Disraeli describes him as one of the best educated men he knows, indeed over-educated, something of a pedant and theorist, but a man of talent nevertheless.' One reason for the change in Albert toward Disraeli, however inefficient the minority ministry seemed, was that the Tories had all but abandoned protective tariffs as principle, while the opposition appeared to employ religion for the votes it might draw. Anti-Catholic agitation was running high as a result of the Vatican's efforts to reorganize the Church in England, its adherents having grown in numbers with the exodus of the hungry from Ireland into the industrial Midlands and London. 'Mr Gladstone', Albert had written to his brother that March, 'pursues bigotry'.

'We are at the point of breaking up Parliament', he added to Ernest in June. '... Then we shall have General Elections. In October the new Parliament will assemble and then we shall see how the parties will be formed. I will not try to prophesy more than that there will be an end to Protection. The Protectionists are already going to the elections as Free Traders.' Albert hoped to be able to stay remote from the campaign while in Osborne, then to entrain for Balmoral in August before the new Parliament sat.

Much as Albert loved Osborne once it was built, landscaped and occupied, it lacked the useful distractions of Balmoral. No hunting, no climbing, no activities that distanced him from the burdens and anxieties of his position. And so he worked, which often meant dictation to his secretariat, convening consultants summoned to Osborne. One who came in July was Adam Sedgwick of Cambridge, to discuss the Oxford Commission recommendations on university reform. Albert wanted to experiment with a combination of Continental and English systems, and was disappointed when Sedgwick felt that the two could not mix. As for the Oxford report, he said, 'We have not half so much to reform as they have.' Albert, he discovered, had studied the report 'from end to end ... [although] I read it the way Jack Horner ate pie'. The Prince was less smug. Further changes would be mandated at Cambridge, with Sedgwick doing much of Albert's on-the-scene work. At Osborne, however, he remained far more interested in how little ostentation there was in day-to-day life. The Queen and Prince cantered out most mornings, 'followed only by one lad on horseback to open gates

... There is a policeman at the gate of the Park, and at the landing-place; with this exception there is nothing here that much differs from a private gentleman's house.'

The Prince was still at Osborne for his thirty-third birthday, which Victoria made an occasion for the servants, soldiers and sailors on duty in the vicinity. To the strains of a band playing 'The Roast Beef of Old England', several dozen sailors and marines carried kegs of beer and bowls of plum pudding to tables set on the Osborne green, and the royals walked among them greeting their guests, then sat under their marquee to watch young ladies in their beribboned Sunday best, with white stockings, dance with the blue- and scarlet-coated men. When at seven, the band struck up 'God Save the Queen', Victoria and Albert rose and withdrew indoors.

On 16 September 1852, the royal family learned by telegram at Balmoral that the Duke of Wellington, eighty-three, had died two days earlier. 'A gloom cast on everything!' the Queen wrote in her diary. 'Albert dreadfully sad at the news.'

Rushing back to London seemed unnecessary. The nation clearly expected a grand funeral for the greatest Englishman of their time, and such planning necessitated refrigerating the Duke's cadaver as effectively as circumstances permitted. While Albert contributed ideas for the occasion, which would become a funereal orgy for a generation that indulged itself in death, he could continue, with Lord Malmesbury, the Minister in Residence, to pursue stags, and to plan the rebuilding of Balmoral, no longer a rented estate but the property of the Queen and Prince.

At first, Malmesbury's education in foreign affairs had been conducted by the Queen and Prince, but in ensuing months he and Derby began to complain to each other about Albert's 'interference ... in matters of foreign policy', largely through bypassing the minister to consult directly with an envoy abroad. His exchanges with family and assumed friends in high foreign places would amount to a *Papierberg* – a paper mountain. While he had every right to personal communication with his brother, his uncles and his cousins, and rulers called *cousin* by royal courtesy, Albert seldom composed an unbusinesslike sentence. Ministers had little idea of the extent of his network, and for how long his and the Queen's private correspondence had been going on, for their most confidential letters were carried by couriers for N.M. Rothschild and Sons. A thank-you note from Albert's secretary George Anson for such services dated 4 January 1845 still exists in the Rothschild Archive, and other documents indicate that the couriers were busy into 1861.

An indignity which went on before ministerial eyes, according to Edward Stanley, was that Albert was 'constantly in the habit of expressing to Lord Derby and his colleagues what he states to be the Queen's wishes on this and that point'. While they took that as high-handed and dictatorial, soon they accepted that the Queen wanted it that way, and reinterpreted Albert's style as 'friendly and confidential'.

By the time that Malmesbury paid his first ministerial visit to Balmoral he had become used to consulting with Albert in Victoria's presence, but he could not get used to what they called a 'castle'. It was, he noted in his journal, 'in bad repair, and totally unfit for royal personages'. Also for lesser ranks, he thought. 'The rooms are so small that I was obliged to write my despatches on my bed and to keep the window constantly open to admit the necessary quantity of air.' His private secretary, for whom there was no room, had to lodge three miles away. 'We played at billiards every evening, the Queen and [her mother] the Duchess being constantly obliged to get up from their chairs to be out of the way of the cues.' Still, 'Nothing could be more cheerful and evidently perfectly happy than the Queen and Prince, or more kind to everybody around them. I never met any man so remarkable for the variety of information on all subjects as the latter, with a great fund of humour *quand il se déboutonne*.' It would have surprised many to have unbuttoned humour ascribed to Albert, who remained Germanically stiff in public appearances.

To mark Balmoral's possession, the Queen noted in her diary for 11 October 1852, most of the Household set off mid-morning to climb to the top of Craig Gowan to build the traditional cairn establishing claim to the site, the former pile having been pulled down by the servants. 'I then placed the first stone, after which Albert laid one, then the children according to their ages.' Then, in turn, the ladies, gentlemen, servants, and tenants, including spouses and children, each placed stones on the cairn, while a piper played and whisky was 'given to all', and 'some merry reels were danced'.

When the cairn reached its final height – about eight feet, Victoria guessed – 'Albert climbed to the top of it, and placed the last stone, after which three cheers were given.' She was touched by the event and the setting, and 'felt almost inclined to cry. The View was so beautiful over the dear hills; the day so fine; the whole so *gemütlich*. May God bless this place, and allow us yet to see it and enjoy it many a long year.'

Reluctantly they left for London. Once, Victoria had wanted to exclude the Duke of Wellington from her wedding. Now he was, she announced, 'Britain's pride, her glory, her hero'. The mourning period had already reached royal dimensions, and the lying-in-state had become one of legendary length, 65,073 persons filing by the sable catafalque surrounded by rows of colossal candelabras.

For the final procession on 18 November, the Prince designed a huge funeral car so awkward and heavy as to give the horses and men dragging it extraordinary difficulty. Prevented by protocol, the Queen was not present at the final ceremonies at St Paul's where 'the Car', as Greville sneered, 'tawdry, cumbrous and vulgar . . . contrived by a German artist attached to the School of Design, and under Prince Albert's direction', was met by the Prince at the cathedral steps. The ceremonies within were tedious and exhausting. Even reading newspaper accounts, overwhelming in their detail, was exhausting. Victoria remained at Buckingham Palace. She was again pregnant.

The Duke had worked until close to the end, reporting regularly to Albert, whom he regarded as his moral if not his actual successor,* and the Prince took the old soldier's pride in his troops to be an index to their readiness for a modern war. 'It is stated', the Duke deplored, 'that the British Infantry cannot march, that the Cavalry cannot ride, that the Officers are ignorant, that the Soldiers do not know the use of and cannot use their Arms!' He did not want Albert to believe that, and the Prince's veneration of Wellington ensured that the armed services, beset by parliamentary parsimony and purchase of commissions, would go into the unstable 1850s able to defeat bands of alleged savages in petty colonial skirmishes, but little more.

Although Albert was not blind to shortcomings in the services, Wellington had been untouchable and unapproachable. Now, the day after the Prince learned about the Duke's death, he penned a memorandum to himself, based upon his immediate exchanges with

---

* Wellington's actual successor as army chief would be Viscount Hardinge. General Henry Hardinge, already sixty-seven, was a hero of the Napoleonic wars, a veteran of parliamentary life and a governor-general of India.

the Prime Minister, Lord Derby, observing that the loss had been one of '*authority*' rather than '*efficiency*'. When Derby had proposed Victoria's cousin George, the Duke of Cambridge, prematurely at thirty-three a major-general, as the new commander-in-chief, Albert brushed the suggestion aside. 'He would have carried no weight with the public, and we must not conceal from ourselves that many attacks on the Army which have been sleeping on account of the Duke will now be forthcoming.' But Albert had a list of titles and duties belonging to Wellington to be parcelled out to successors, from Constable of the Tower of London to Chief of Ordnance, effectively the second most important job. For that he proposed a popular general, Fitzroy Somerset, with a step up in the peerage, and when Somerset, younger son of a duke, claimed that he could not afford the expense of an elevated title, Albert told Derby in confidence on 22 September that the Queen would pay the fees, and – to spare the general's feelings – 'you could easily manage it so that he need never know from what source the £500 came.' At sixty-four a desk officer who had been Military Secretary of the Horse Guards for twenty-five years, and close to Wellington for forty, Somerset had lost his right arm at Waterloo, which gave him a special cachet. He became Lord Raglan.

Greville privately carped that the Prince had 'shown little judgement' in the new military appointments, and had effectively made 'himself the Heir', which was 'ridiculous as well as odious', but he had no knowledge of Albert's actual refusal, in Wellington's lifetime, to become his chosen successor, nor that Somerset – Greville's favourite – had nearly, but for Albert's intervention, declined his own promotion. However the Prince did set himself up for trouble by reserving one of the relinquished appointments for himself. He informed Derby that he would take the colonelcy of the Grenadier Guards, with which came an annual emolument of £3,000, exchanging that for the Coldstreams, and £2,000, which would go to cousin George. When that became publicly noticed through debate on the Army estimates on 28 February 1853, press reaction was unkind, and it triggered what would be a year of indignities for Albert just as new causes for rearmament were emerging.

Although Albert's lifelong need for a father figure caused him repeatedly to summon Stockmar, who now largely kept to Coburg and when in England was regarded with suspicion, the ageing Baron was more out of touch with England than ever, and his advice often ranged from bad to dangerous. After Wellington's death he wrote to advise Albert to use the opportunity of the vacuum left by the Duke to become 'the idol of the people'. The Prince's popular success with the Great Exhibition may have prompted the suggestion, but the Prince understood that he could not and should not attempt anything of the sort. When he had responded to Wellington's offer of succession in the army that his primary responsibility was to submerge himself in his wife's position, he had recognized a role that was as crucial as it was difficult to perform. Irresistible temptations were always surfacing, as with the Grenadier Guards, or acting politically on his own. But he told Stockmar that much as his role as 'merely the wife's husband' was a presupposition of 'inferiority', he would keep to it. 'Now silent influence is precisely that which operates for the greatest and widest good, and therefore much time must elapse before the value of that influence is recognised by those who can take cognisance of it, while by the mass of mankind it can scarcely be understood at all. I must content myself with the fact that constitutional monarchy marches unassailably on its beneficent course, and that the country prospers and makes progress.' Yet it was hard to be silent or to appear nearly invisible.

Among the myriad of vacancies created by the death of the Duke was the Mastership of Trinity House, a charitable corporation under the sponsorship of the [Harbour] Pilots Guild which maintained good works from almshouses to lighthouses. Albert had been an Elder Brother, an honour open only to leading members of the establishment, and on his moving upward he arranged for the Prime Minister, the Earl of Derby, to become an Elder Brother to fill the emptied office. As with everything the Prince undertook, he carefully studied the rules and goals of the corporation and recommended reforms to rectify the failing Wellington's lack of oversight, such changes requiring parliamentary action. The annual banquets of the Trinity Brotherhood at its grand building just north of the Tower of London were events, and Albert would use his first as Master (4 June 1853) to press for an end to the penury which hobbled the armed services. Proposing a toast to the Army and Navy, he hoped that Britain was not 'so enervated by the enjoyment of riches and luxury, or so sunk in the decrepitude of age, that, from a miserable eagerness to cling to our mere wealth and comfort, we should be deaf to the calls of honour and duty'.

The coded message was easy to interpret. The riches and luxury had been secured at someone's cost. India was a collection of fiefdoms which benefited few Indians. The Opium Wars that opened China to commerce had an incalculable moral cost. The colonization of more and more of Africa had made the continent more accessible to missionaries – and slavers. Few Africans were the better for it. The armed services which had planted the Union Jack worldwide and could win an occasional colonial war were in no condition to defend Britain itself.

Albert's applause was less enthusiastic than polite. Ornaments of the class whose interests they thought he represented felt badly served by such badgering, and had he not already explained to Baron Stockmar that such populist declarations were not made in purely Albertine interest, the Baron would have assumed that his mentoring was being heeded.

With Louis Napoleon about to formalize his Second Empire with a pompous coronation, sabre-rattling from France increased as a symbol of new imperial assertiveness, and renewed fears of invasion obsessed the English. Malmesbury even learned from the excitable Lord Raglan on 30 October of alleged plans not only to invade England but to 'carry off the Queen from Osborne by a *coup de main*'. Lord Hardinge claimed to be anxious about the obsolescence of his artillery, which used gun carriages manufactured before Waterloo, and Albert suggested a huge rise in expenditure for the Army and Navy, including two thousand additional artillerymen, a thousand horses and five thousand seamen, which alone would add £230,000 to Disraeli's straitened budget.

'We are cleaning our rusty cannons and building fortifications,' Albert wrote to Ernest on 2 November. 'We have 80,000 men ready and we are improving our weapons.' For that he asked his brother to procure a 'Prussian needle gun' which the English might copy. '*We are quite unprepared*', he emphasized to Hardinge on 8 November, underlining his words. Comparing slow Wellington-era muzzle-loaders to the breech-loading, rapid-fire gun when it arrived from Gotha, Hardinge worried to Albert about 'expense', but the Prince insisted it was worth a trial. Only invasion scares from France, however unfounded, prompted any efforts to bring the army closer to Continental standards.

Whatever the resistance from within the armed services and from supporters of the *status quo* in the press and in Parliament, the Prince was one of the few possessors of influence to press for continuing modernization. In later years he would badger the Cabinet to equip the army with breech-loading arms while the generals insisted, still, on obsolete muzzle-loading guns abandoned by European armies. *Punch* would make fun of his shako, but thirty years after Wellington's obsequies, General Sir Garnet Wolseley, whom Disraeli would call 'our only soldier', wrote to the Queen's private secretary 'that we have never had any substantial reforms in the Army since the Prince Consort died, and that were he living now, Army Reform would be in a very different position ... Prince Albert was a very sensible man.'

The new Parliament had opened on 11 November, a week before Wellington's state funeral, and limped into December 1852 still under Tory leadership; but a budget bill in December, attacked passionately by Gladstone, was defeated by 305 to 286, and Derby, the next day, took the train to Portsmouth and the ferry across the Solent to the Isle of Wight. Victoria and Albert were spending their Christmas at Osborne, and the Earl's duty was to resign in person. On returning Derby described the meeting to his son, and Edward entered the details in his diary:

> The Queen received him cordially: she seemed grave and anxious: the Prince entered into confidential discussions on many subjects, appearing desirous to take upon them the last opinion that he could receive from his ex-minister. He spoke often of Disraeli, extolled his talent, his energy, but expressed a fear that he was not in his heart favourable to the existing order of things. My Father defended his colleague: said he had been unnaturally kept down for several years, and then suddenly raised to the highest position. 'He has better reason than anyone to be attached to our constitutional system since he has experienced how easily under it a man may rise.' The Prince was glad to hear it, but still thought Disraeli had democratic tendencies 'and if that is the case, he may become one of the most dangerous men in Europe'.
>
> My Father, with his accustomed frankness, related the substance of this conversation to Disraeli.

The Prince feared, Derby added, that Disraeli's example might 'raise up a host of inferior imitations'. Albert may very well have dreaded a potential Louis Napoleon arising on English soil, and noted, when the outgoing ministers returned their seals at Windsor Castle on 28 December, 'Mr Disraeli seemed to feel most the loss of office.' Yet a curious metamorphosis in his relationship with the Court was already in progress, with Disraeli returning to Albert a state paper late in December with the awkward if fulsome parting words, 'I may, perhaps, be permitted to say that the views which your Royal Highness has developed to me in confidential conversation have not fallen on un-grateful soil. I shall ever remember with interest and admiration the princely mind in the princely person, and shall at all times be prepared to prove to your Royal Highness my devotion.' And at Windsor, as the opposing sides gathered for the transfer of seals, Disraeli, according to a later Cabinet member, John Morley, 'with infinite polish and grace asked pardon for the flying words of debate, and drew easy forgiveness'. Prince Albert's minute remarked, 'We owned that we had been astonished to find them all so *well bred.*'

The Tory ministry had been brought down by a combination of Whigs, Peelites, Radicals and Irish who had no common interest but to drive Derby and Disraeli from Downing Street, and for the Queen and Prince the dilemma was to find a Prime Minister from among them acceptable to the Crown. Without being asked for advice, Derby recommended Lord Lansdowne, and was dressed down for his intervention. The 3rd Marquis of Lansdowne, seventy-two, was a cautious Liberal and a veteran of Cabinets since 1806: too old, they felt, for the job. He was invited to Osborne with the safe and unremarkable 4th Earl of Aberdeen, only four years younger, but a Peelite. But Lansdowne fell ill. Aberdeen came alone, and was offered the Ministry, less on his own long experience, largely in foreign affairs, but because he was neither Russell nor Palmerston. And Albert handed the Earl a list of persons whom the Crown preferred to see named to his government. Politely, Aberdeen thanked him for 'these valuable suggestions', but the Cabinet remained his to propose and the Queen to review, and he departed inconclusively.

To settle the transition, the Queen and Prince interrupted their usual Christmas at Osborne, leaving by packet and rail early on December 28 to meet Aberdeen that afternoon in Windsor. The Earl was in difficulties, Albert recorded in one of his many memoranda, which by now filled dozens of volumes. No one expected the government to survive unless a place could be made in it for Palmerston, to whom Aberdeen, a friend of sixty years' standing, since they were boys at Harrow, had offered any post but the Foreign Office. To emphasize how indispensable he was, Palmerston was biding his time. To keep him out, Victoria and Albert were even willing to accept Lord John Russell, who was not interested and kept the Foreign Ministry only briefly, turning it over early in 1853 to the Earl of Clarendon. With the only portfolio to which Palmerston aspired (other than that of Prime Minister) foreclosed, to keep his hand in he accepted the powerful but ponderous Home Office. Albert was pleased, he told the new Prime Minister. Since the Home Office 'is a department where he has to work like a horse, he cannot do any mischief'. Meeting Palmerston two days later, Albert was even more satisfied, observing, hopefully, 'He looked excessively ill, and had to walk with two sticks, on account of his gout.' That augured to the Prince the end of Palmerston's ambitions, but at sixty-nine the wily 'Pam' was far from finished.

On the final day of the former Ministry, Lord Malmesbury had been at Windsor with all his colleagues but Derby (who had taken his leave earlier), to give up their seals. During a private half-hour the Prince, who respected Malmesbury's inside knowledge of France, read a surprising letter from the distrusted usurper who was now calling himself Napoleon III to Prince Hohenlohe, the husband of Victoria's half-sister, Feodora. Seeking to found a dynasty and in need of an appropriate bride, he was interested in Her Serene Highness Princess Adelaide of Hohenlohe, aged seventeen. Her father raised objections about religion and morals, and 'was not sure of the [financial] settlement being satisfactory'. He was a pragmatic German who was short in ready money, and just as Albert regularly and usually covertly paid Ernest's debts, so had Victoria regularly rescued the Hohenlohes.

'The Queen and Prince', Malmesbury wrote, 'talked of the marriage reasonably, and weighted the pros and cons.' There were more of the latter, but they were 'afraid the Princess should be dazzled if she heard of the offer'. It could not be concealed from her, and Napoleon's envoy to London, Alexandre Florian Walewski, was prepared to convey the Emperor's bid in person. Ironically, Count Walewski, an illegitimate son of the first Napoleon, was the complaisant husband of one of the Emperor's mistresses, Maria, Countess Walewska. The élite of the Second Empire never confused marriage with sex, or politics with passion. By 1855 the Polish-born Walewski would be Foreign Minister.

To many Englishmen, Charles Louis Napoleon, forty-four, was a charismatic figure. He was not only the nephew of a legendary hero but a man who had survived by his wits and accomplished the impossible. He had lived in conspiratorial exile in England, had English friends in high places, and even a wealthy English mistress, Elizabeth Howard, whom he was now prepared to discard. Both Victoria and Albert despised him as a vulgarian and immoralist, but neither disability ruled him out any more than his politically necessary Roman Catholicism, as husband for their niece less than half his age, if he were the means of making 'Ada' an empress and creating yet another rapprochement with historically inimical France.

That the sleazy bargain was taken seriously by the rigidly moral Queen and Prince suggests the power of pragmatism, for it was easy for Victoria to recall the disgust of her own mother at the possibility that Feodora – Adelaide's mother – might have been taken as wife by the wicked and gross – and aged – George IV. Paradoxically, however physically unhandsome Louis Napoleon was, in the popular mind in England he was more dashing and attractive than the cramped foreign intellectual who was the Queen's consort. Feodora might have looked on the match as a way out of the difficulties that had dogged her since 1848. Although her husband had rescued his principality when revolutionary fervour receded, they had been living 'a new existence of privations' (as she wrote to Victoria) that was alleviated largely by 'loans' from her sister and mother, and frequent residence for her daughters in England. 'Ada' was even with Victoria when the marriage offer was transmitted. Indirectly through her ministers, Victoria replied that the proposal was a matter for the girl and her parents. Feodora considered the bargain 'disagreeable', not because of the religious *mésalliance*, but because of her daughter's immaturity and the Emperor's morals. Yet she thought that Ada would 'rather like' the dazzling marriage, a misunderstanding of her daughter, who rejected 'a position as elevated as it is perilous'.

By the time Princess Adelaide of Hohenlohe had written her refusal, the question was moot. Expecting otherwise, the Queen had said frankly to Lord Derby, 'You know *our* family [the Coburgs] have always been accused of being too ready to pick up any crown that had tumbled in the dirt.' Anticipating a rebuff, however, the Emperor remained susceptible to signals from other marriageable women, even those only on the fringes of acceptability. On 31 December 1852, Count Walewski arrived from London to report on the likely failure of his mission, and was greeted to his surprise with '*Mon cher, je suis pris!*' Louis Napoleon had met and been captivated by the beautiful, ambitious Eugénie di Montijo, who was appropriately Catholic, a mature twenty-seven, and ostensibly the daughter of a Spanish count. The ambassador reminded him that his engagement announcement was premature; he could not jilt Queen Victoria's niece. He would not have to. Ada's letter would arrive the next day.

The sordid business of government, from political marriages to cynical foreign-policy machinations, left Victoria feeling very different from the way she had when she stood on the dais in the Crystal Palace and felt at one with what she visualized as the aspirations of humankind. Napoleon III had only personal aspirations, identifying them with France. His reign needed the sense of continuity only a legitimate heir could create, and it needed continuing instability elsewhere on the Continent because such distractions further coalesced support for his throne. In that he was inadvertently assisted by Austria's heavyhandedness in Italy, where new insurrections flared, and France declared its sympathies with Italian aspirations. Another opportunity arose from Russia's territorial greed in eastern Europe, Tsar Nicholas I seeing gains to be made at the expense of mismanaged Turkey, a sick octopus losing its tentacles to ethnic risings and opportunism. Even there Napoleon found a cause – the protection of Roman Catholics in the Turkish-held Holy Lands. In every foreign crisis area Prince Albert was seen as interfering. The exposure of his Grenadiers sinecure, and two caustic leading articles that followed in *The Times* on 1 and 2 March, raised his ire and that of the public. Incautiously his private secretary Charles Grey told Greville that 'he never saw the Prince so riled at anything'.

Although the pinnacle of esteem that was the Crystal Palace could not have been permanent, Albert was seeing his reputation begin to unravel often for no fault of his own. The *Spectator*, in Palmerstonian terms, even viewed his German origins as dangerous for the times. 'It is evident', it wrote, 'that a serious disturbance in Europe might be very inconvenient to the minor German Powers; and that fact has perhaps suggested that rough guess that a Prince bound up with German interests by family relations, has used his position near the British

Sovereign...' The implication of 'officious meddling with affairs which are not his' would appear in the press often through the year, sometimes by raising the charge and then piously but weakly denying its truth. Even Lord Aberdeen's keeping England aloof from Continental quarrels was interpreted as a policy of permissiveness.

With Palmerston as a very activist Home Secretary, Albert could not evade further involvement with the man he disliked more than anyone else in England, for 'Pam' had responsibility for the militia. Late in March the Prince was writing to the Home Office about professionalizing amateurish militia leadership. Albert also promoted the purchase of a permanent training site at Chobham in Surrey, an idea he had unsuccessfully offered to Wellington, based upon his youthful visits to King Leopold's manœuvre area at Beverlo. Like the 'Albert hat', such innovations were derided in the press as his 'army mania'.

Fuelled by popular francophobia, the Chobham Heath 'camp of instruction' was established, with troops quartered in a vast tent city.

*In a mock medallion,* Punch *shows the Queen and Prince at the Chobham military exercises.*

(The experience would lead to the establishment of Aldershot.) An elaborate review was planned for 21 June 1853, with the Queen present on horseback to take salutes. Regiments of the home garrisons were under Lieutenant-General Lord Seaton. John Colborne had served under Wellington at Waterloo and Hardinge at Quatre-Bras. The Earl of Cardigan was there with his smart 11th Hussars, and Albert was present as colonel of his own Grenadier Guards.

Large crowds of the curious, the colourful uniforms of élite units, and the presence of foreign observers from the King of Hanover to Prince Lucien Bonaparte, created a holiday atmosphere akin to Derby Day. The cavalry charges, with ten thousand horsemen brandishing swords over the heath, and the infantry sweeps, with foot soldiers holding their weapons at the ready, were dramatic. From the adjoining height where Victoria watched, Duke Ernest and his German party scoffed privately at the 'few tactical evolutions, which appeared to be rather childish'.

Favoured guests, including ladies, then retired to tents for a six-course luncheon, with sherry and champagne, until a storm materialized. When the rain and wind lifted the canvas, officers and guests had to flee to the cavalry stables before breaking camp. But the press had covered the event, and military attachés were present, so that potential foreign adversaries might be impressed by the state of English preparedness, which in actuality was poor for anything but a very small war.

Three days later, Albert returned for another look. Rain had becalmed the camp. Tents were blown awry by the wind, and mud was everywhere. Food for the ranks was bad and facilities at best were inadequate. In the afternoon his own brigade had polished itself up for his inspection, but he knew that beneath the spit-and-polish they were as unready for warfare as were their Waterloo-era guns.

While preparations had been underway for the Chobham Heath review, which Albert left feeling ill – two days later he was in a sickbed – he had problems close to home as well. In Victoria's last month of her eighth pregnancy there was a serious fire at Windsor Castle. She was, Albert wrote to his stepmother on 23 March 1853, 'quite well, and has suffered absolutely nothing from the agitation into which we were naturally all thrown by the danger. We had to battle with the flames from ten at night till four in the morning before we got them completely under [control]; nevertheless the injury was confined to one tower of the Castle, which has been gutted by the flames through four stories.' The chief loss had been 'the beautiful dining-room'.

Two weeks later, on 7 April, the Queen gave birth to her fourth son, Leopold, with the assistance, for the first time, of 'blessed chloroform'. Two weeks later, in her journal, she recalled its effect as 'soothing, quieting and delightful beyond measure'. Yet she had not been quieted long, for there were problems with the new baby. Victoria was suffering again from postpartum hysterical crises, which went on to become intermittent bouts of depression and recrimination, embittering her relationship with Albert.

It was a matter of class and rank as well as of sheer lack of interest that the Queen and Prince quickly turned over to their attendants all parental involvement with their infants, short of formal social occasions. They had often seen Vicky and Bertie bathed and put to bed. Now that they had less time for that, the Queen confessed, she saw the 'younger ones' on such occasions 'once in three months perhaps'. But she was able to tell her uncle, after whom Leopold was named, that he seemed 'a jolly fat little fellow', belying his diagnosis as a haemophiliac, which added to Victoria's anxieties. She sent vicious, accusing notes to Albert, usually about alleged affronts too trivial to suggest anything but emotional breakdown, and her surviving official correspondence of the period is so slight as to suggest unusual inattention on her part.

Albert would respond in notes addressed to 'Dear Child', once calling attention to a 'distressing scene' caused by a 'miserable trifle', yet realizing that he only increased her distress by referring to the 'groundlessness and injustice of the accusations'. Pregnancy always increased her hostility to her husband because she brooded over the injustice of woman's lot in suffering disfigurement and discomfort. The baby's poor health – Albert blamed the difficulties on her insistence upon a wet nurse from the Scottish Highlands whose milk seemed to disagree with the child – aggravated her feelings about the futility of repeated pregnancies. The Queen's testiness – a recurring agony to Albert – would continue off and on for years, into and beyond her ninth and last pregnancy in 1857. When she told her eldest daughter in 1859 that too many pregnancies too soon had made life 'wretched' for years – 'one becomes so worn out and one's nerves so miserable' – the lesson was from still fresh and painful experience.

Few husbands in history can have tried as hard as Albert to maintain the emotional equilibrium as well as the professional effectiveness of a wife. His love survived the trials of his inferior position and his continued unacceptability as an alien, and it survived the pendulum swings of Victoria's almost helpless doting upon him and her using him to vent frustrations of which he was victim rather than cause. He thought constantly of her emotional and physical needs, writing from Chobham that he was happy that she had got through her day without needing him, and signing off with the familiar German love song,

*Du, Du liegst mir in Herzen,*
*Du, Du liegst mir im Sinn,*
*Du, Du machst mir viel Schmerzen,*
*Weisst nicht wie gut ich Dir bin.** 

One matter that continued to mar their domestic happiness, and remained a matter for mutual accusation, was the apparent backwardness of the Prince of Wales. While Vicky was rapidly growing into a miniature of Albert, all that Bertie seemed to have in common with Vicky was Hanoverian obstinacy. No study regimen, however meticulously devised by Albert, made any impression upon the Prince of Wales. Whether he would have been a better scholar had the pressure upon him been less intense is idle speculation. Victoria sensed that Albert was requiring too much of the child and asked Lady Lyttelton to see that Bertie was not 'overworked'. But Bertie remained overworked for his capacities. He would take out his frustrations in Hanoverian blind rages at his tutors, and occasionally at his parents, who perceived nothing of the potentially effective ceremonial sovereign in the amiable young man already at social ease with adults. With their hopes for the future of the monarchy invested in him, they saw only a vacuous future king. The other children were unimportant. The girls would have to be found appropriately arranged marriages, perhaps with a diplomatic intent; the other sons were only insurance.

---

* You, you are in my heart,
You, you are in my thoughts,
You, you give me heartache,
Don't you know that I love you?
Popular English adaptations of the folk song appeared in the 1940s and 1950s as 'You, you, you are the One'.

*'The Queen and Prince Albert at Home' – a contemporary lithograph, dated possibly (from the existence of only three royal children) as late in 1843.*

Such attitudes suggest an insensitivity to their children that contradicts the *gemütlich* image that has come down to us of family picnics and outings, Albert on a sledge in the snow with a child, or crawling about on the hearth rug at Osborne playing children's games, Victoria sketching outdoors with the girls. At Osborne and Balmoral there was more togetherness, but the royal parents were like other rich parents of their time except that they had a far busier social and official life. The doting, devoted, and cosy family of the illustrated papers and the gossipy articles was largely mythical, yet the illusion of domesticity seemed to democratize the crown. When the royal children were small, they seldom appeared at the table, or anywhere else where their parents happened to be in the servant-saturated households. Except on holiday or ceremonial occasions, they were overseen rather than seen.

But for Prince Leopold's christening, the Chobham appearance had been Victoria's re-introduction to public life, but her activities were cut short the next month by measles, which had been running through the family. Bertie was first to be sick, and recovered quickly. The others were treated – incompetently, as usual – wherever they happened to become ill, Helena and Louise at Windsor, Vicky and Alice at Buckingham Palace, Victoria and Albert at Osborne. Even Albert's valet, Löhlein, kept to his bed, and Cart oversaw both him and the Prince, who, run down from overwork and lack of sleep, had the worst case – a high fever that left him delirious, and with temporary weakness that required him to walk with a cane. Sir James Clark, his physician, saw no cause for alarm. But only in August was he up again, prompted largely by preparations for the great naval review at Spithead, the area of the eastern Solent between Portsmouth and Ryde.

Spithead was to be a nautical Chobham. Among foreign invitees were Prince Adalbert and a Prussian naval contingent, part of Albert's continuing effort to establish a special relationship with Prussia – to influence its foreign policy and to have an indirect role in inevitable German unification. (He would be frustrated in both.) Spithead was a showplace to demonstrate to Europe the screw-propelled, 131-gun, three-decker *Duke of Wellington*, new pride of the Royal Navy. On 16 August, in a letter to Stockmar, Albert boasted that the fleet now had sixteen steamships, with ten more under construction, and that at Spithead '300 ships and 100,000 men must have been assembled in one spot', with the Navy itself carrying '1,100 guns and 10,000 men'. In his enthusiasm for the apparent efficiency of the fleet, Albert shut his eyes to the fact that even the new *Wellington* had been designed and launched, decades after steam propulsion, as a sailing ship, and only fitted afterwards with retractable funnels and screw. The Royal Navy was far behind France in modernization – and imagination. It was still considered unseamanlike to use steam except in a flat calm, and a mixed fleet of screw-propelled, paddle-wheeled and sailing frigates was considered appropriate. Most ships were obsolete hulks unfit for battle or for ferrying troops, and in the highest Admiralty positions were dodderers who dated back to Trafalgar.

A major problem in modernizing the services remained money, and Gladstone, as Aberdeen's Chancellor of the Exchequer, reluctant over a long lifetime to furnish funds to the military, did push through for the first time an inheritance tax on property while extending income tax for two further years. Knowing what uses the funds might have, Albert wrote, to Gladstone's surprise, a congratulatory letter. It was probably improper for Albert to do it, out of keeping with ostensible party neutrality, but the Prince found it difficult to be uninvolved.

Through the spring and summer, as Victoria and Albert moved to Osborne and then to Balmoral on what had become the Queen's annual cycle, Albert was unable to remain because of military preparations, yet he managed to oversee the rising of a new Balmoral Castle, which by early September was 'up one story' and faced with granite. But, he wrote to Stockmar on 12 September, 'the workmen, who have to be brought here from a distance and to camp in wooden hutments, have already struck several times, which is now quite the fashion all over the country'. He attributed that not to the 'terribly hard' work and the terrible living conditions, but to the shortages of labour caused by emigration.

Even before Spithead, it was clear that Europe would soon be at war. It was merely uncertain who the opposing nations would be, and who could safely remain neutral. Briefly Foreign Minister before transferring the seals to Clarendon, Russell, who was anti-Napoleon, sought accommodation with Tsar Nicholas by conceding Tsarist claims to be the protecting power on behalf of adherents to the Orthodox Church in the Eastern Holy Places. Albert warmed to the idea as a reasonable parallel to powers granted to the French. Tsarist ambitions, however, were more than spiritual, and the privileges claimed by Napoleon III, whose forces were distant, were looked upon at Constantinople far more favourably than those of adjacent and overwhelming Russia. When it became obvious that the hardly covert aim of St Petersburg was to establish a protectorate over millions of the Sultan's Orthodox subjects wherever they were, Victoria – in a memorandum written by Albert – declared to Lord Aberdeen that the claims of Nicholas I were inadmissible. 'We must take care not to become the dupes of Russian policy,' Victoria wrote on 4 May.

With the Palmerston wing of the government for a hard line against Russia and the Russell–Clarendon wing less than eager to drift into war on Turkey's behalf, Aberdeen, agreeing to station warships in the Black Sea area for their symbolic value – and to keep his Cabinet from collapse – dithered. Russia exploited the time to move up troops to the Turkish borders, then invaded the Danubian provinces. Turkey then recognized a state of war with Russia on 4 October 1853, and the news of both events spread quickly in the new age of telegraphic transmission. Stratford Canning, recently elevated as Viscount Stratford de Redcliffe, had, as ambassador, encouraged Turkish resistance, putting his country on a side opposite from the one Russell had taken in January, and Albert wrote wryly, although alarmed, 'Lord Stratford fulfills his instructions to the letter, but he so contrives that we are getting deeper and deeper into a war policy.' Weak within his own Cabinet, the Earl of Aberdeen could do little more than deplore. What were the limits of Russian expansion which England and its empire could safely countenance? Without outside help, the Turks would lose, and Russia would emerge into the Mediterranean.

Aberdeen's ministers were divided. For imperial reasons, and to keep Russia from dominating Europe, the Tsar's imperial ambitions had to be curbed, and Turkey propped up, however much the Sultan might have to relinquish in Europe to ethnic aspirations and Russian greed. The Cabinet ranged from Gladstone's pacifism at almost any cost to Palmerston's bellicosity.

With a sense of despair Aberdeen wrote to the Queen on 6 October, 'No doubt it may be very agreeable to humiliate the Emperor of Russia; but Lord Aberdeen thinks that it is paying a little too dear for this pleasure, to check the progress and prosperity of this happy country, and to cover Europe with confusion, misery, and blood.' The Queen and Prince would have preferred to see truculently Palmerstonian Stratford de Redcliffe replaced at Constantinople, and ethnically un-Turkish Wallachia and Moldavia fly whatever colours emerged from the confusion. The fraying Ottoman Empire was too weak to maintain them anyway. Yet squadrons flying the British White Ensign were already at the Dardanelles, a commitment to check Russia somewhere.

That the Tsar was willing to acquire segments of European Turkey one at a time had already been clear from his acceptance of a diplomatic 'Note' from England, France, Austria and even Prussia that implicitly only slowed Russian expansionism, for the message had been rejected by Turkey, which had everything to lose from appeasement of Russia. Turkey, then, held moral hostage the English and French flotillas in its waters, which had not cowed Russia, and on 8 October 1853, Aberdeen wrote to Sir James Graham, sending a copy to the Queen, that he preferred, if possible, a 'defensive war' on behalf of Turkey with 'a French army, and perhaps English money'. To Nicholas I, England and its accidental ally, France, seemed too remote to matter militarily, and Austria and Prussia saw something to gain at virtually no expense in the further dismemberment of European Turkey. 'The Queen', Albert wrote helplessly in a memorandum at Balmoral on 10 October, 'might now be involved in war, of which the consequences could not be calculated, chiefly by the desire of Lord Aberdeen to keep his Cabinet together; this might then break down, and the Queen would be left without an efficient Government, and a war on her hands.' And Albert knew from the experience of Chobham and Spithead, whatever his apparent boastfulness, that England was unready.

From Balmoral, the wrong place at the wrong time because the Court had little influence on events from there – yet Victoria stubbornly stuck to her Balmoral cycle – Albert admitted in a memorandum of 16 October that to prevent Constantinople and the Dardanelles from falling into Russian hands it might even be 'right and wise' to go to war. However, the peace that inevitably would follow had to include 'arrangements more consonant with the well-understood interests of Europe, of Christianity, liberty and civilisation, than the reimposition of the ignorant barbarian and despotic yoke of the Mussulman over the most fertile and favoured portion of Europe'.

Albert was hoping to have it both ways, but there was little to choose between Tsarist oppression and Ottoman oppression, and meetings at Balmoral and then Windsor, each carefully recorded by Albert, complete with snatches of memorable dialogue, evidence of how much the decisions on behalf of the nation about war or peace were subject to the rivalries of Liberals, Radicals, and Peelites, and to individual ministerial aspirations. Even parliamentary reform (which Palmerston opposed under any conditions) was hostage to war, and Lord John Russell claimed that he had a bill ready but under the 'present circumstances' it had no future. 'You mean unless you sit in the chair which I now occupy?' asked Aberdeen. Russell laughed.

Several Ministers hoped to exploit Aberdeen's weakness into a turn at Downing Street, and the 'Eastern Question' offered an opportunity. Graham, Palmerston, Russell and even Gladstone made little secret of ambitions for higher office. Gladstone's pacifism was the closest to a pro-Russian stance of any minister, but based upon his desire (not uncommon since the days of Peel) to spend as little as possible on the military budget, and on his Christian fervour, which accepted Russian domination in the east as preferable to Islamic rule, however benign.

Recognizing that sooner rather than later, they might have to accommodate themselves to Palmerston, the Queen and Prince even agreed to have the Home Secretary take a one-week tour of duty as Minister-in-Residence in the close confines of Balmoral. It was not a success. He would discuss no business, and seemed interested only in playing billiards with Albert, who was drawn away from overseeing the start of new construction. As he had helped to design Osborne with a builder, Thomas Cubitt, at his side, Albert worked in Scotland with William Smith to reshape the land as well as to give the structure character. Two terraces were to descend from the ground floor to the bank of the Dee, and pepper-box turrets and a nearly detached tower were to suggest a larger castle. The granite from a quarry in Kemnay was to be crystalline and almost white. Victoria's diary contains an account of Albert's modelling for Smith's men a sand-castle and terraces to realize his vision.

Not only was a new and larger residence going up, but also new living quarters for the workmen. A fire had gutted the row of huts, which had to be rebuilt. Albert paid out £318 11s. 7½ d. for workmen's belongings also destroyed.

The losses in Aberdeenshire were only inconvenient; in the East there were debits about which he could do nothing, but for which Albert would have to pay. Late in November, with the Eastern Question having turned from threats to war, the unprepared Turks suffered a Black Sea disaster at Sinope (modern Sinop), on their central coast, which turned the newspaper-reading public in Britain furiously Russophobic. While the Turks were resisting incursions on their Danubian fronts, a Russian fleet had surprised Turkish ships under anchor and burned them to the waterline, with four thousand dead. Although a victory of Russian enterprise over Ottoman somnolence, the London press declared the catastrophe 'a crime', and called for revenge. While

Aberdeen's government vacillated about a response, Albert was targeted as the pro-Russian, power-hungry villain emboldening the Tsar.

A series of blunders, some Albert's own, had focused public attention on him anew. Reports surfaced that his admirers were lobbying for a statue of the Prince in Hyde Park on the former site of the Crystal Palace. Rumour had it that statues of George III and George IV, and a pillar memorializing the little-lamented Duke of York, Victoria's insolvent uncle, would be melted down for their bronze. The basis for the allegations was that Thomas Challis, a hide-and-skin merchant and Lord Mayor of London, late in 1853 had also proposed that it was time for a statue of Prince Albert to be erected in the City. *Punch* made fun of the idea with a column, 'The Albert Statue Movement', accompanied by a cartoon, in which 'the principal metropolitan Statues' reportedly met to consider adding to their number one of the Prince, to watch over Temple Bar at the Strand entrance to the City rather than at Hyde Park Corner, 'to conciliate the protection of Royalty for the City'. Rising together, 'Gog and Magog . . . loudly expressed their approbation of this view; the adoption of which would tend to secure themselves in their own places, which they wished to retain as long as they were able, like all others holding comfortable situations in Guildhall.'

Embarrassed by the proposal, and even more embarrassed by its reception, the Queen and Prince quashed such ideas. Writing to Earl Granville on 3 November, Albert attempted to deride the idea of a statue in Hyde Park with humour. 'I can say, with perfect absence of humbug,' he claimed, 'that I would much rather not be made the prominent feature of such a monument, as it would both disturb my quiet rides in Rotten Row to see my own face staring at me, and if (as is very likely) it became an artistic monstrosity, like most of our monuments, it would upset my equanimity to be permanently ridiculed and laughed at in effigy.'

Seeking causes for governmental unwillingness to confront the Eastern Question, which had implications for British pride, British trade, and British imperial security, the press found an explanation in Albert's alleged aggrandizement of power, symbolized now by the statue imbroglio. He was known to intrude into foreign affairs, but rumour reversed his position. When Prince William of Prussia was in London for the christening of Leopold, Albert had encouraged him to have his brother, King Frederick William IV, join other Western nations in urging restraint upon Russia. The King, however, refused to intervene with his brother-in-law, the Tsar, or expose, he claimed, his country's eastern frontiers to instability. Albert fumed about Prussia's 'wicked policy' – which seemed to him 'fish[ing] in troubled waters'. Yet, trying to have it both ways later, he had written to Stockmar on 7 November, 1853 that Prussia's position – it had agreed to be a party to the innocuous Vienna 'Note' accepted by Russia – had become 'very useful for the maintenance of peace' because Berlin's neutrality meant that Nicholas could not count upon Frederick William as ally.

To Aberdeen, who sent Albert's memorandum to Palmerston for comment, the Prince proposed keeping Russia out of the Balkans by creating an imperial Greece at Turkey's expense – a Greek Orthodox state in Europe that would protect all Christian denominations and holy places in the Ottoman provinces. Scoffing at the idea, Palmerston wondered, then, why Albert failed to support Russia against Turkey, as the result would be the same. To Palmerston, Britain's goals were, simply, 'the Relinquishment by Russia of inadmissible Pretensions and her Retirement from Turkish Territory'.

Aberdeen showed Palmerston's objections to the Queen, and Albert urged the Prime Minister to use Palmerston's bellicose tendencies to get rid of him, but to fashion a Home Office excuse – perhaps differences over Reform.* But while the Eastern Question simmered at home, news arrived in London on 11 December of Russian 'treachery' at Sinope. The press wrote of England's 'shame' – and blamed timidity in Whitehall about sending the Royal Navy into the Black Sea. Palmerston, popular feeling went, would not have permitted the massacre to happen.

Adopting Albert's strategy, Aberdeen wrote at length to Palmerston on 14 December to disagree about a Reform bill and to suggest that as the ostensible reason for him to leave the Cabinet. The Home Secretary had no doubts as to the source of the suggestion and responded curtly, 'My dear Aberdeen, I have received your note of this Morning and in Consequence I have to request you to lay before Her Majesty the Resignation of my Office. I shall be ready to give up the Seals at any Time that may best Suit your Convenience. Yours sincerely, Palmerston.'

---

* Palmerston had no Cabinet role in foreign affairs but his stewardship of the Home Office gave him a voice in internal reforms.

Newspapers the next day published the text, which Palmerston was quick to supply. The *Morning Post* added the observation, almost certainly also from Palmerston, that although disagreement over Reform was the supposed grounds for the resignation, the actual reason was his disgust with the Ministry's craven behaviour toward Russia, which had led to the disgrace in the Black Sea. Word got about quickly as to who appeared responsible for driving him out of the government. If foreign intrigue was involved – someone with a key to diplomatic red boxes – who was the only foreigner in the highest circles? Hadn't that ambitious eminence also driven Palmerston out of the Cabinet only two years earlier? 'The public had graciously selected me as its scapegoat', Albert would write more dismissively than he should have to his brother, 'to answer for its not yet having come to war, and says "logically" that the interest of the Coburg family, which is Russian, Belgian, Orleanistic, Fusionistic, is preferred to the alliance with Louis Napoleon. The Emperor of Russia now governs England. He telegraphs to Gotha, to you in Brussels, Uncle Leopold to me, I whisper in Victoria's ear, she gets round old Aberdeen, and the voice of the only *English* Minister, Palmerston, is not listened to – ay, he is always intrigued against, at the Court, and by the Court.' Reflecting insider understanding, Edward Stanley observed in his diary on Christmas Day 1853, 'The more probable version [of events] is, that Lord Aberdeen and Albert jointly have contrived the affair, the latter being the prime mover, the former only his tool. This . . . is certainly the idea commonly received out of doors: and has led to loud and growing complaints of the secret influence exerted by the Prince Consort.'

Newspapers in Palmerston's web led denunciations of the Prince as the agent of Russian interests who operated through German connections related to the Tsar. A conglomerate of little-related suspicions and antipathies had finally converged. Albert was in trouble.

# XIII

# Impeaching the Prince

## 1853–1855

O N CHRISTMAS DAY 1853 Palmerston was back. At Windsor the day before, in audience with the Queen and Prince, Aberdeen reported that not only had his Cabinet been eager to have Palmerston return, but that he had been under pressure from Emily, his wife, 'to have his resignation', as Albert reported it, 'considered as not having taken place'. Emily Palmerston, the late Viscount Melbourne's sister, was too politically astute to let her husband burn his bridges to Downing Street. He was the only alternative to Aberdeen's motley Ministry. Thus the day after Christmas the Prime Minister disclosed Palmerston's letter avowing that he had misunderstood the details of the 'intended Reform Bill' and was withdrawing his resignation. The entire affair had been dishonest, and everyone in politics could decrypt the language.

The failure of Albert's scheme, however, only sank him deeper into trouble. No amount of exposure to English ways seemed to make Albert more acceptable; if anything, the Queen was becoming more German. Blindness to the symbolism of small things did not help. Albert, for example, had brought small green German table lamps with him when he first arrived in England, and he still used their successors in his study, whether from nostalgia or a feeling that they were more efficient than domestic counterparts. He often wore, for hunting or stalking, thigh-high leather boots from Germany and an open-necked shirt, which to one gossip made him look like a *Heldentenor*. He not only spoke English slowly, but was not 'fast' in accepted upper-class recreations like betting, swearing and wenching. 'They call him slow', a letter to

*The Times* defending him went, 'because he does not gamble, does not use offensive language, and does not keep an opera dancer.'

Whatever he did seemed to call attention to his origins. He kept his diary in German. He spoke German within the family – when he would wake Victoria at eight, it would be with '*Es ist Zeit, steh' auf!*' ('It is time, get up!') – and he would always feel insecure with his English correspondence, giving much of his mail to Victoria or his secretaries to read, to reassure himself about his understanding. To Anson, earlier, Victoria had explained, 'The Prince and Queen speak English ... quite as much as we speak German.' That was hardly enough.

The strain affected both Queen and Prince, who felt that they had no one on English soil with whom to share their misery. 'If our courage and cheerfulness have not suffered,' Albert confided to Stockmar in Coburg, 'our stomachs and digestions have, as they commonly do when feelings are kept long on the stretch.' On 27 December he was less restrained in reporting what appeared to be a newspaper campaign to drive him out. 'The stupidest trash is babbled to the public, so stupid that (as they say in Coburg) you would not give it to the pigs to litter in.' Had Albert waited two more days he could have included an issue of the *Morning Herald*, in which a letter under the initials 'M.P.' – actually young Edward Stanley – reported without attribution his gossip from Malmesbury and from the pro-Russian diplomat Lord Howden (he had married a great-niece of Prince Potemkin) about Albert's allegedly unconstitutional role in ousting Palmerston. 'It was too bad', the diatribe charged, 'that one man, and he not an Englishman by birth, should be at once Foreign Secretary, Commander-in-Chief and Prime Minister under all administrations.' In his diary for 3 January 1854, Stanley 'expressly decline[d] vouching for' the 'rumour', but it did Albert further harm when provincial papers reprinted the charge.

The new year had begun very badly, contributed to by Victoria, who wrote heatedly to Aberdeen on 4 January that she intended, on her own authority, to legitimize 'Prince Consort' as her husband's title, as he was known by it anyway. If that gesture were to cause further attacks on Albert and convince her that these represented the popular will, 'she would LEAVE a position which nothing but her domestic happiness could make her endure, and retire to private life – leaving the country to choose another ruler after their own HEART'S CONTENT'. Although she did not 'think so ill of her country' to believe that her subjects would prompt her to abdicate, she claimed '*very bitter* feelings in her breast, which time alone can eradicate'.

Although she did not test public sentiment with a title for Albert, the attacks continued for other reasons. By extrapolation, German connections meant Russian ones, and on 7 January the *Daily News* charged, absurdly, 'Above all, the nation distrusts the politics, however they may admire the taste, of a Prince who has breathed from childhood the air of courts tainted by the imaginative servility of Goethe.' One cause for hostility, Albert felt, was popular frustration that war fever against Russia had not yet exploded into actual war. Allegedly, he had blocked all efforts to curtail Russian ambitions in Europe and Asia. Another adversary he identified in a letter to Stockmar was the army faction under Lord Raglan – 'the Senior United Services Club, with all its grumblers'. Raglan loyalists felt that the former Fitzroy Somerset's military secretaryship to Wellington over thirty years should have earned him succession to the Duke over the more senior Lord Hardinge, who had the advantage of 'confidential intercourse... with myself in all military matters'.

As attempts to embarrass the Prince multiplied, Edward Stanley noted in his diary, evasively, 'I did not follow up the attack [on Albert] farther than by a single letter under a different signature, and that rather in defence of M.P.' – himself – 'than with any intention of rousing further passion'. And via the *Daily News* of 11 January, the Radical MP John Arthur Roebuck announced that he would demand explanations in the Commons from ministers about the improper interference of the Prince in government business. *Punch*'s most striking cartoon as 1854 opened had no humour in it. Long familiar to the public as an ice skater, Albert appeared, to the horror of watchers, skimming into an area marked off as thin ice and posted with a warning, 'FOREIGN AFFAIRS. VERY DANGEROUS'.

In London on 12 January a curious letter in Albert's defence appeared as news in the *Morning Chronicle*, which had taken it from the Dublin press. Newspapers in both British isles were evidencing how much the Prince's alleged intervention in political affairs had become a matter for public debate, and he knew it as well from his own mail, as writers would often rush off to a local newspaper a copy of a letter to Windsor Castle. Thomas Mulock 'of Killiney, near Dublin', had waited until he received a courteous but innocuous note from Charles Grey acknowledging the 'kind consideration' before sending both letters to the *Free-man's Journal*. Despite evidence to the contrary, the *Chronicle* described the correspondence as looking 'very like a hoax'. Mulock, however, was authentic, listed in *Thom's Directory* of Dublin as 'Esq.' – and therefore a gentleman.

When a writer impugned the genuineness of the reply from Albert's secretary the next day, Mulock responded in print that he had 'exhib-ited...the respective autographs' to the editor prior to publication; however the London story carried only the negative bias. Nevertheless there were many who felt, with Mulock, 'pain and indignation' at the 'unjust and anti-Christian accusations' that there was something wrong in a husband's offering advice to his wife even when she was the Queen, or that 'your Royal Highness is invariably present when her Majesty grants audiences to her Ministers'. Although the Prince, Mulock con-tended, 'cannot act as the political head of the State,...when the Queen voluntarily selected your Royal Highness to be her consort, you became her head by sacred rite of marriage. What object can your Royal Highness have in view but that the best interests of the British Crown may descend to your royal posterity?'

It was difficult to see how Mulock's argument could assist Albert, and his second point may have been even less helpful. 'The peculiar position of a female Sovereign', he argued, 'renders it highly decorous and eligible that, in all interviews with her Ministers, the Queen should enjoy the protective presence of your Royal Highness...as an effectual safeguard against even the surmised exercise of sinister influences'. That the ministers of the Crown could be malign was a suggestion unlikely to bolster the Prince's credit.

Since charges often convert themselves in the public consciousness into proven guilt, rumours raced across London in mid-January that Albert, having acted as the Queen's ventriloquist and run the Empire in her name, had been arrested for treason. 'It was like the man in *Martin Chuzzlewit*', Julian Osgood Field later wrote, 'who absolutely refused to believe that Queen Victoria did not live in the Tower of London, since he felt sure she ought to live there and therefore did live there.'

'One word more about the credulity of the public', Albert wrote to Stockmar on 24 January. 'You will scarcely credit that my being committed to the Tower was believed all over the country – nay, even "that the Queen has been arrested!" People surrounded the Tower in the thousands to see us brought to it!' Laurence Housman dramatized the episode in *Victoria Regina* by having the Prince read to the Queen from one of the more circumspect newspapers:

'We learned on what we believe to be good authority, that at a late hour last night two Personages of the highest rank' – ('Personages of the highest rank' can only be you and me, Vicky) – 'were secretly conveyed to the Tower, under a military guard, by order of the Government, and have there been lodged in safe custody to await their trial on a charge of high treason for conspiring against the safety of the Realm.' There, Vicky, what do you think of that? 'This news, which it was not intended should at present be made public, will be received with the greatest satisfaction by all who have been aware of the danger to which our Country has lately and increasingly been exposed by the machinations of a certain powerful foreign influence behind the Throne.' (That means me, Vicky.)

The suggestion that Albert was a Russian agent seemed logical enough to Englishmen of anti-German persuasion, and that he had somehow given cause to be marched off through the Traitor's Gate into the Tower, seemed to some appropriate justice. The inevitable ballads giving spice to the rumour were sung in London streets, 'Lovely Albert' suggesting that the impatient Queen had ceased to tolerate the Prince's obstruction of the laws, his 'mingling' in politics, and his outright treason. 'Little Al, the royal pal, They say has turned a Russian', the ballad went, and the chorus included the line, 'We'll send him home & make him groan'. When he had come to England

> He brought with him no riches,
> He had scarce a rag upon his back,
>     And great holes in his breeches;
> Oh, England on him pity took,
>     And changed his sad condition,
> And soon he planned you understand,
>     The National Exhibition.

But he had gone 'a begging for the Russian bear', which he had led 'to [a] massacre [of] the innocent Turks', an outcome exasperating

Victoria, who tumbled him out of bed 'and wopped him with her night-cap'.

> There with the bolster round the room,
> Vic gave him dreadful lashes,
> She scratched his face and broke his nose,
> And pulled out his mustachios;
> You German dog, you shall be flogged,
> She hallo'd like a Prussian,
> How could you dare to interfere,
> And turn a cursed Russian?

The verses interrupted the vilification of the royals with an anti-Tsarist exhortation,

> You jolly Turks now go to work
> And show the Bear your power,
> It is rumoured over Britain's isle,
> That A–– is in the Tower...

Once the vilification reached inane proportions, reason began to surface. An article in the *Morning Chronicle* on 16 January took 'quite the *right line* upon the infamous and *now* almost ridiculous attacks', Victoria wrote to the Prime Minister. 'Has Lord Aberdeen any idea who could have written it?'

The author, he responded, was W.E. Gladstone, 'although he would not wish it to be known'. There were further loyal rejoinders, he observed, suggesting a disposition on the part of some of the 'scurrilous' papers to change course before the opening of Parliament, when airing of the matter might quiet the hysteria.

Albert could hardly wait for Parliament to sit. 'All the gossip and idle talk of the last fourteen years', he wrote to Stockmar, 'have been brought to light by what has occurred. Everyone who has been able to express or surmise any ill of me has conscientiously contributed his faggot to burn the heretic... It was anything but pleasant to me amidst it all, that so many people could look upon me "as a rogue and traitor", and I shall not be at ease until I see the debate in Parliament well over; for it is not enough, that these rumours should be dispelled for the time; they must be knocked on the head, and the disease radically cured.' Another portent followed Palmerston's letter of 25 January to Peter

Borthwick, since 1850 editor of the *Morning Post*, instructing him, 'I think it would be useful if you were to put into the Post the following paragraph: We have observed that some of our contemporaries have endeavoured to connect the resignation of the Home Secretary with some proceedings on the part of the Court. Now we believe we may confidently affirm, without the slightest fear of contradiction, that the resignation of the noble Lord was the result of some misunderstanding between himself and some of his colleagues, and had not the remotest connection with anything on the part of the Court.'

Palmerston's instructions to Borthwick signalled that an end to the crisis was coming. His move had followed publication in the *Morning Advertiser* on 20 January of a letter by William Coningham, a failed candidate for Westminster in 1852, describing a pamphlet demonstrating the Court's interference which he had helped produce after Palmerston was dismissed in 1851. It had been based, Coningham alleged, on documentary evidence involving the Court, but was suppressed when the author was bought off. Greville 'fancied it was all moonshine', but queried the editor of *The Times*, John Delane, who knew almost everything unfit to print. He knew all about it, Delane confided. Palmerston at the time had sought revenge and had procured a journalist who had written leaders for the *Morning Herald*, Samuel Phillips, whom Tory leader Lord George Bentinck called 'that circumcised renegade' (Phillips was a converted Jew), and offered him £100 for the job. Phillips 'went down to Broadlands, where he was instructed by P[almerston] (who Delane said, gave him heaps of papers to read, though there is no proof of this), and he composed the pamphlet and had it printed. Before it was published P[almerston] thought the better of it ... The copies were all bought up and destroyed, but a few remained behind, and one of these Phillips gave Delane.'

On the evening following the publication of Coningham's letter, Delane showed the pamphlet to Greville and Earl Granville, 'and we found it a very harmless production. It would not harm the Prince if it should appear; but ... would be immensely damaging to Palmerston.' A deal was arranged with Delane, and Greville dashed off a letter, signed 'Juvenal', which *The Times* published the next morning, describing the *Advertiser* as unworthy of credit. And on 24 January, *The Times* published large extracts from 'Letters by William Coningham', which alleged that the turning out of Palmerston in 1851 was 'a *coup d'état*' arranged by Albert through Lord John Russell. Further, it claimed, Blackstone's *Commentaries* did have something appropriate to say about a Prince Consort: 'The husband of a Queen Regnant, as Prince George of Denmark was to Queen Anne, is her subject, and may be guilty of high treason against her.' The intemperate allusion to another consort of a Queen Regnant was a potential embarrassment to Palmerston, who had been identified as the pamphlet's sponsor.

The day before the reassembly of Parliament, gullible crowds gathered on Tower Hill to see Prince Albert and the Prime Minister committed to the Tower. Both were burned in effigy. It was obvious that the shift in attitude by the more respectable press had not yet made a difference. 'It was actually hinted to the Queen', Baron Vitzthum von Eckstaedt, Saxon Minister to England, recalled, 'that she would do well to open Parliament alone, as the presence of the Prince might expose her to the insults of the mob. The Prince behaved admirably . . . He refused to be intimidated, and on the morning of the day when Parliament was opened, 30 January, rode, accompanied only by a groom, through the most restless quarters of London, as if to say to the masses, "I am not afraid; here I am, if you have anything against me, speak out." '

The bold morning ride through the Strand and Fleet Street, beyond St Paul's into the teeming East End, either created the changed climate or confirmed it. When, that afternoon, seated beside the Queen in the State carriage drawn by eight cream-coloured horses, Albert drove to Westminster, 'an immense concourse of people', Victoria wrote to Stockmar, was 'very friendly'.* Yet the crowds reserved their greatest enthusiasm for the Turkish Minister, foreshadowing the war to come.

In the Lords, Aberdeen scoffed that unseemly allegations had led thousands of Londoners 'to attend at the doors of the Tower to see His Royal Highness go in'. Further, many expected to see the Queen imprisoned as well, as they had heard that she had 'announced her intentions to go with him'. The Prince's 'unimpeachable loyalty to the Crown and to the Country' should put to rest such calumnies 'at once and for ever'.

In the Commons, Lord John Russell ridiculed 'these delusions, blind as they have been', which, now exposed, 'will . . . attach the Crown still

---

* Lady Charlotte Guest, nevertheless, reported hearing Albert 'hissed'.

more strongly to the realm'. The 'abomination', Greville concluded, 'may be considered to be destroyed altogether, and we shall probably hear no more of it'.

Despite the publication of the 'Suppressed Pamphlet', with additional material by William Coningham, early in February by the printer Effingham Wilson at the Royal Exchange, talk of impeachment of the Prince faded into anti-Russian sentiment as the Queen and Albert returned to Windsor to celebrate the fourteenth anniversary of their marriage. Among the guests, on the afternoon of 13 February when the royal children put on an entertainment based upon recitations of James Thomson's once-popular *The Seasons*, were the Prussian ambassador, Baron Bunsen, and his wife. 'A red curtain was let down', the Baroness wrote to her granddaughter Lilla, 'and we all sat in the dark, till the curtain was drawn aside, and the Princess Alice, who had been dressed to represent Spring, recited some verses... enumerating the flowers which the Spring scatters around'. And she did it, the Baroness added, in 'a tone of voice like that of the Queen'.

Once the curtain was drawn and reopened, Princess Vicky appeared as Summer, with Prince Arthur, not yet four, 'lying upon some sheaves, as if tired with the heat and harvest...' After the Princess Royal's verses there was another change of scene, and Prince Alfred, nine, 'with a crown of vine-leaves and a panther's skin, represented Autumn, and also recited verses'. Lastly, the scene represented snow, and the Prince of Wales appeared as Winter, 'with a white beard and a cloak with icicles or snow-flakes (or what looked like such), and the Princess Louise warmly clothed, who seemed watching the fire: and the Prince also recited well...' Again the curtain closed and reopened to disclose all the participants, 'and far behind, on high, appeared the Princess Helena, with a long veil hanging on each side down to her feet, and a long cross in her hand, pronouncing a blessing upon the Queen and Prince, in the name of all the Seasons'.

Although that was the formal close, Victoria asked that the curtain be reopened, 'and the Baby Prince Leopold was brought in by his nurse, and looked at us all with big eyes, and wanted to go to his papa, Prince Albert'.

The family festival was the last in peacetime. War had not yet been declared but the Russian ambassador had left London on 7 February. The British envoy in St Petersburg departed the next day. In the new age of telegraphy it was possible – where wires were strung – to communicate more quickly, but not to prepare for war or to prosecute it at long distance. There was no direct wire link to Constantinople.

If the national blood was indeed up, it was not because Victoria and Albert had encouraged a diversion from their own problems. At the Sublime Porte, Stratford de Redcliffe had taken advantage of the semi-primitive communications with Turkey by conducting personal diplomacy, which meant reading the worst intentions into any Russian communication – an easy enough task – and frowning at his own instructions. If there were opportunities for compromise, he ignored them.

It would take weeks to learn that in London, and to send him fresh dispatches. The Cabinet was divided. To her Foreign Secretary, the Queen (almost certainly in conjunction with Albert) had written a candid warning that Stratford's actions in Constantinople 'exhibit clearly a *desire* for war, and to drag us into it', and she wondered how long he should be permitted 'to remain in a situation which gives him the means of frustrating all our efforts for peace'. Had her Government wanted the ambassador to do otherwise, Stratford long before would have been ordered home.

As with most wars, popular expectation was for a short and victorious affair. It was easy to ignore the reality that Britain had fought no war for forty years and was not ready to fight one now.

On 21 February Albert inspected his battalion of Guards. Cousin George, Victoria wrote to her uncle, the King of the Belgians, about the Duke of Cambridge, 'is quite delighted to have a division'. Five days later the government drafted an ultimatum to be sent by Lord Clarendon, the Foreign Minister, to his counterpart in St Petersburg, Count Nesselrode, demanding that Russia evacuate the Danubian principalities. A similar message was to be sent by France. The bearer would be directed to wait six days for an answer. Refusal, or silence, was to be considered as equivalent to a declaration of war.

The official courier delivered the message to Nicholas I on 14 March. The Tsar's decision that it was not fitting to reply became known in London only on 24 March, however early in the month of limbo between peace and war – on 23 February – an initial force of 12,000 men with 30 cannon left for the war zone via Malta. '*Until now*', Albert wrote to his brother, exasperated with the inaction of Prussia and other German states, 'Napoleon has behaved loyally, peacefully, justly and reasonably on all points. Our alliance will, we hope, keep him so. How Russia can accept a war in these circumstances, the Gods only know. The Czar must be mad if he does it. But whether he does it or not, the wand with which he ruled Central Europe is broken. We can only pity the poor German Kings who considered it an honour to clean his shoes.'

Despite Albert's words about Louis Napoleon, the Queen and Prince were still so markedly concerned about how much trust to put in him that Duke Ernest, on a visit to Paris, was entreated by the Emperor to help thaw relations. Pre-Waterloo animosities persisted on the military level as well, making co-operation awkward and ineffective. Lord Hardinge was sixty-nine, and his deputy, the one-armed Lord Raglan, whom he appointed commander of the expeditionary force to the East, was sixty-five. Most senior generals and admirals were veterans of the wars against the first Napoleon, and physically unfit for the rigours of

### GRAND MILITARY SPECTACLE.
#### The Heroes of the Crimea Inspecting the Field-Marshals.

*At the beginning of the Crimean War, Albert was the only non-doddering Field Marshal. At the close, he was the only Field Marshal.*

combat service. Recognizing that, *The Times* had already quoted Lord Chatham's wry remark about the senior officers ordered off to put down the American revolution, 'I do not know what effect these names have on the enemy, but I confess they make *me* tremble.'

A case in point was the admiral of the battle fleet assembled at Spithead, which the Queen and Prince reviewed on 10 March. Sir Charles Napier, sixty-eight, had captained the *Thames* in battle against the French in the Mediterranean in 1811, and led ships up the Potomac against the young United States in 1814, landing near Baltimore. He was to command a fleet to move into the Baltic against Russia.

Few in Britain worried. War fever had seized the nation. All generals and admirals associated with past victories, however remote in time, were again heroes. Crowds cheered troops marching off, equipped for the last war, and no one felt more helpless than the Prime Minister, Lord Aberdeen, who could carry few of his Cabinet with him when he expressed grave doubts about the outcome. As Albert explained to King Leopold, the masses *felt* even when they failed to think. 'In the present instance their feeling is something of this sort: "The Tsar of Russia is a tyrant, and the enemy of all liberty on the Continent . . . He wanted to coerce the poor Turk. The Turk is a fine fellow; he has braved the rascal. Let us rush to his assistance."'

With the ultimatum to Russia about to expire, most newspapers fanned the excitement, and Albert, at least in his messages to his brother, intended indirectly for Prussia, appeared enthusiastic about reducing the 'Russian Colossus'. The Baltic fleet, he predicted, 'will be magnificent, unless it be too heavy for that shallow sea. The 25,000 men for Constantinople are organized; 10,000 of them have already arrived in Malta; the artillery has left; and the calvary will go by way of France, and march through Paris, at the Emperor's desire! Who could have imagined such a thing a year ago?'

Much had gone beyond Albert's own imagining since his idealistic words opening the Crystal Palace only a few years earlier. The Utopian vision of unity and progress and peace had become Prospero's 'insubstantial pageant faded'. Greed, hate and violence were proving the more natural condition of humanity. If, too, his unremitting industry, subsuming all personal ambition into others who represented the present and future for his adopted country, led only to popular eagerness to see him committed to the Tower, where was the democratization of monarchies leading? Albert was hard put to fend off dismay and depression, which he tried to do by longer hours and harder work.

On 27 March the Queen's war message was read in the Commons, and war was declared the next day. The paradoxes of power politics set the Christian British and French on the side of an Islamic empire against other Christians, leading to Disraeli's wry summing-up that his nation was going to war in order to prevent the Tsar from protecting the Christian subjects of the Sultan. And by 6 April, with the Queen's forces landing in Turkish areas bordering the Black Sea baffled and helpless in the local squalor, heat, and disorganization, questions began to be asked in the Lords about conditions in which Her Majesty's troops would operate. Heartsick about the war, which seemed to him stupid and unnecessary, if inevitable, the Earl of Aberdeen watched his second son, Alexander, leave the same day to join his regiment, taking with him a fine horse that was a parting gift from Prince Albert.

The western allies planned to take the war to Russia by landing in the Crimea, and the Duke of Cambridge, his infantry division designated for the mission, went via Vienna by rail. While hastily assembled troops crowded on to obsolete ships bound for Black Sea ports, the war at home was a skirling of pipes and a flashing of uniforms on parade grounds, bellicose editorials in the press, and confusion and disunity in the Cabinet. 'The Ministry causes us much trouble', Albert confided to Ernest. 'Aberdeen is still in 1814, Palmerston in 1848, and Lord John [Russell] in 1830. Parliament and the Press are, one and all, suddenly born generals...' Cholera and dysentery would soon begin to travel with the army to the war-zone even when modern ammunition and guns did not. Mismanagement of sanitation, supplies and soldiers by both the British and the French was easy to perceive in the collection areas on the Bulgarian coast, but disconcerting disclosures were filtered home through a haze of slow and inadequate communications and deliberate obfuscation.

For the public, few events could distract attention from the war. One, briefly, was the reopening of the Crystal Palace on a brilliantly sunny 10 June 1854 on a hill south of London in Sydenham. Unlike its original, it had taken two years and the lives of twelve workmen – and the promised railway to the site was unfinished, like the huge structure itself. But Victoria and Albert came; 1,500 singers featuring soprano Clara Novello and under the direction of Michael Costa sang the

'Hallelujah Chorus', and an orchestra augmented by two hundred brass instruments failed to shatter the glass.

The Queen also went to Woolwich Dockyard to launch the new warship *Prince Albert*, one of the enormous new military expenditures which required politically painful new taxes, few of which Parliament cared to extract from landed wealth. Suddenly the war took a new turn when the denizens of drinking establishments had to pay for it, and *Punch* quipped, 'Owing to the imposition of the malt tax, the Marquis of Westminster and Baron Rothschild are the only persons in the country besides the Queen and Prince Albert who can afford beer: and consequently all the cab-drivers and coalwhippers are in a state bordering on revolt.'

In France, Napoleon III was in a spendthrift frenzy that had few connections to the war but many to his sense of power and status. His subjects would be burdened by debts they hardly knew then existed as they basked in the splendour of his state. He intended, with Baron von Hausmann's planning, to transform Paris into Europe's most awesome capital, and to live palatially wherever he and his empress pleased. In the summer of 1854 he was also having the sumptuous Villa Eugénie built as a holiday estate in Biarritz, leaving there on 27 August to observe manœuvres of 70,000 troops near Boulogne. Both King Leopold and Prince Albert had been invited, *Punch* marvelling at the ironies of history,

I wonder what his thoughts were – that sad-eyed, silent man,
As alongside Boulogne's jetty England's royal steamer ran;
While with a King beside him, that adventurer was seen
Greeting, as Emperor of France, the Consort of our Queen?

As Albert was not Head of State, but only the husband of one, he fulfilled his diplomatic obligation once he entered Napoleon III's carriage by handing the Emperor a letter from Victoria. It prompted *Punch*, on another page, to remark that he thereby 'infringed the rules of the French Post Office, and subjected himself to a rather heavy penalty. It is against the law to carry a sealed letter from England to France, though it may perhaps be urged on behalf of the Prince, that the letter was in fact stamped, for the Queen had given her head to it.'

The Anglo-French alliance seemed a reality during the four days of the Prince's visit, more carnival on the surface than military conference.

## THE ENTENTE CORDIALE.

*Albert, according to* Punch *in 1854, acting as actual sovereign in his meetings with Emperor Napoleon III.*

Cheap excursion trains from Paris brought thousands of sightseers, and the streets were beflagged by day and illuminated at night. The letters *V.N.A.* were inscribed everywhere, for Victoria, Napoleon and Albert. (Some said they also stood for *Vive notre amitié.*) Despite the unbusinesslike air, the Emperor and Prince arose each day at six for the military exercises, and conferred at length over breakfasts and lunches, sometimes with military and diplomatic advisers, the uncrowned king an equal with the self-appointed emperor.

On a holiday from editing *Household Words* and yet to begin *Little Dorrit*, Charles Dickens was also in Boulogne, indulging in escapist reading and dozing against a haystack in the sun, and seldom going into the town, 'which looks like one immense flag', he wrote to John Forster. On the day of the culminating review Dickens went off on his daily country walk along the Calais road, only to be showered with dust as Napoleon and Albert cantered toward him, accompanied by mounted guardsmen and grooms. Dickens loyally removed his hat, and the

Emperor and Prince, both of whom recognized him, raised their cocked hats. Louis Napoleon had been a Gore House crony* in his conspiratorial London days, and Albert was devoted to Dickens's novels and theatrical ventures. Determined that evening to join in the festive illuminations of Boulogne, Dickens set up a hundred and twenty wax candles in the windows of his rented cottage.

To the Queen the rare absence of her husband was trying, and she did not conceal that, prompting Greville to write that 'H.M. thinks nothing' of absenting her Ladies from their husbands during her holidays to Osborne or Balmoral – or ordering their husbands to Baltic or Black Sea regions from which their absences could become permanent. From Boulogne, Albert wrote to Victoria several times daily during pauses in military business, addressing her as 'Dear little Wife' and 'Dear Child'.

The French command made no secret of its dissatisfaction with gerontological British leadership in the Crimea, to which Albert had explained that 'to carry public opinion with us is the main point'. Popular generals and admirals had to remain until they were less so, or confirmed popular, if unrealistic, expectations.

On 5 September he wrote to Victoria before retiring for the night, 'The Emperor thaws more and more. This evening after dinner I withdrew with him to his sitting-room for half an hour ... in order that he might smoke his cigarette, in which occupation, to his amazement, I could not keep him company.' Nevertheless, newspapers reported as a favourable omen that Louis Napoleon and Albert 'are said to have smoked cigars together'.

An even more unusual tête-à-tête for Albert occurred in November when on the 8th, on returning from business in London, he was told that Thomas Carlyle, then working on a life of Frederick the Great, was in one of the Windsor galleries examining prints and engravings of the King. It was four on a darkening afternoon when the Prince entered to chat with Carlyle, who may have felt awkward about his appearance as, at fifty-nine, he had just begun to grown a beard the month before. Albert put him at ease – 'civility itself', Carlyle wrote to his sister, Jean Aitken, two days later. He was impressed by the 'strong steady eyes', and

---

* Marguerite, countess of Blessington, and her lover, Count Alfred D'Orsay, hosted high Bohemian soirées at Gore House until their debts – and illnesses – forced them into French exile.

Albert's 'briskness'. They 'talked first of Frederick's portraits; then went, by a step or two, into the Saxon genealogy line', especially Albert's ancestors, with 'abundant scope of talk'. A hour passed before a servant came to inform the Prince that the Queen was on the Terrace, and he bowed himself out with a reference to his pleasure with 'your Works'. The usually morose Scot was charmed.

Carlyle lost no time, once back in Chelsea, in preparing, with many semi-colons, 'The *Prinzenraub*', about Albert's line, focusing upon the story of the young Saxon princes Ernest and Albert, abducted from Altenberg on 7 July 1455 by Kunz von Kaufungen. Describing the article as 'pearls of memory', he sent it off to the *Westminster Review*, which published it that January, when he explained the title to Mrs Aitken as ' "Prince *rob*", or the stealing of Princes'.

The war in the Crimea heated up further in October and November. Accounts arrived of severe losses accompanying glorious victories which were only victories in that the allies kept a foothold in Russia that was equally exhausting to the enemy. To Colonel Francis Grosvenor Hood of the 1st Grenadier Guards the Prince wrote, on 17 October 1854, of his 'admiration of the manner in which the battalion of my regiment under your command bore itself in that desperate fight at the Alma, and my pleasure and satisfaction at the fact, that upon the whole it suffered less in action than the other battalions of our noble Brigade of Guards'. It was an index to the realities not only that Albert wrote in relief that his troops experienced fewer casualties – rather than rewarding triumphs – but that before his letter arrived, Colonel Hood was killed in the trenches near Sevastopol.

Not long after, the Member from Lambeth complained in the Commons that the Prince was collecting £3,000 for the colonelcy of a battalion he was not leading into battle while others of similar rank were risking their lives for half his stipend. Another MP, Lieutenant-Colonel Brownlow William Knox, responded, 'If the honourable gentleman would look at the number of battalions commanded by his Royal Highness, he would find that the increase was a perfectly just one ...' Although the implication was that Albert had a major role in the prosecution of the war, *Punch* felt that the defence rested upon the wrong grounds. Would it not be better, it asked, to recognize him for 'what he does, than for what he cannot do; for value received rather than value irreceivable? His Royal Highness cannot discharge the functions of a Colonel . . . You will not permit him to go to the wars, very properly. Of course it would never do to have the husband of our Queen returning from the field of glory [preserved] in a cask of rum, or curtailed by the loss of an arm or a leg, or of his fair proportions. He, doubtless, would be too glad to go, and be instrumental in scattering the enemies of his August Lady. But you won't let him . . . '

Whatever Albert's efforts, which included liaison with the Emperor of France, the 27,000 men shipped from England to the Black Sea in 1854 had almost no reserves behind them, and carried weapons that Wellington's soldiers had used decades before. There was almost no system for the care of sick and wounded, and it took a letter to *The Times* from Sir Robert Peel, the late Prime Minister's son, to raise £25,462 for medicines by popular subscription. As there was no provision for widows and orphans of war dead, Albert arranged to be head of a royal commission, soon known as the Patriotic Fund, for such war relief. It would raise more than a million pounds. Parliament had voted little support for military chaplains – who were often little more than nurses, and then undertakers. Soon another subscription drive was begun to send more men of the cloth to the Crimea. Finally, a lady with a bent for hospital work and a genius for organization, Florence Nightingale, recruited thirty-seven lady nurses for service, and, with several chaperons of appropriate dignity, embarked for Scutari (on the Asiatic side of the Bosphorus), reaching there on 5 November, in time to succour the surviving wounded from the battle at Balaclava.

Governmental stinginess, inflexibility, and absence of compassion were not partisan matters. Whigs and Tories had been of similar penurious mind for decades, happily accepting a military policy that made generals of gentlemen from good families who liked colourful parades, dashing uniforms, champagne with lunch, and remoteness from action. Undrinkable green coffee was the least of the hardships of hastily trained soldiers who had no fires in winter, huddled in wet blankets when they had any at all, died of pneumonia and dysentery by the thousands, had no ammunition for their obsolete weapons, and, if able-bodied, were thrown into combat in textbook drill formations that were little short of suicidal. Only the enemy's equal incompetence kept the war at stalemate.

As the bad news continued, and was received at home with indignation, especially the disaster of Lord Cardigan's Light Brigade, committees of inquiry were called for in the Commons, and there were private investigations by the Queen and Prince.

Matters would get even worse in November. Of the men who came to the Crimea, six thousand, including three generals, were killed in action in October and November, and a further eight thousand were wounded or desperately ill with cholera. Half the original English force was gone, and Louis Napoleon offered twenty thousand more Frenchmen if London could send ships to convey them. But there were no ships available, as every Navy bottom that was seaworthy – even obsolete sailing ships were resorted to – was being used to send supplies, including winter clothing, to the Black Sea.

Exasperated, Albert fired a long memorandum to Aberdeen on 11 November that failed to include the friendly language that had long been exchanged between them. 'The Government will never be forgiven, and ought never to be forgiven', he warned, 'if it did not strain every nerve to avert the calamity of seeing Lord Raglan succumb from lack of means.' Prosecuting the war in any case was beyond the general's abilities, but troops were badly served in every way. A battle at Inkerman had been fought on 5 November, and it took ten days for news to reach England of an expensive victory that settled nothing but that Sevastopol would eventually fall, and with it, probably, the Russian government. Yet the siege would outlast Aberdeen's faltering Ministry, and the Prime Minister, a compromiser rather than a leader, was distracted with anxiety about his son Alex, and only able to find out about him when a list of dead and wounded was telegraphed to London on the evening of 22 November. Alex's name was not on it.

Later, Colonel Gordon's letters from the front arrived. His troops had been successful 'but with a loss which we can ill afford'. Also, the charger given to him by Albert had been shot from under him, while most other horses 'are fast dying of starvation and cold'.

Aberdeen called for a special session of Parliament early in December to vote funds for reinforcements. With the mood in England turned ugly, enlistments were not filling the army's needs, and Albert suggested hiring mercenaries from Switzerland and the German and Italian states. Palmerston liked the idea, especially as it would promote his idea of a unified Italy, and Victor Emmanuel, King of Sardinia and ambitious to be more than that, offered 15,000 Piedmontese troops if British ships could transport them. Napoleon, who preferred the glory of using Frenchmen, recognized reality, and approved.

Parliament was to meet on 12 December 1854, to pass a Foreign Enlistment Bill, authorizing the financing of 15,000 recruits to be trained in England. In a meeting at Windsor, Lord Aberdeen went over the legislation and confided the turmoil in his Cabinet over the domestic sacrifices being made to pursue the war. Offering to resign, he pointed out to Victoria and Albert that no new Cabinet could be formed under the ubiquitous but divisive Lord John Russell. It would have to be Palmerston, and early in the new year the unspeakable would happen.

A watered-down version of the Foreign Legion Bill would survive, but not before an unlikely opposition of Tories and Radicals raked over old allegations against Albert. Popular feeling, he wrote Ernest, was that mercenaries represented 'ingratitude against the brave army in the Krim [Crimea]. They say it is a foreign idea and that it must have come from me.'

Three German battalions and a Swiss battalion would be formed, and a Sardinian division would actually exchange fire with the Russians, but the discomfort of needing foreigners to fight British battles was repugnant enough to hasten the demise of Aberdeen's government. The influential *Times*, bolstered by W.H. Russell's dispatches, raged on the day that Parliament again rose, just before Christmas, that 'the noblest Army England ever sent from these shores has been sacrificed to the grossest mismanagement. Incompetence, lethargy, aristocratic hauteur, official indifference, favour, routine, perverseness and stupidity reign, revel and riot in the camp before Sevastopol, in the harbour at Balaklava, in the hospitals at Scutari, and how much nearer to home we do not venture to say.' The day after Christmas *The Times* added that it was 'disgraceful that England, so wealthy, so mechanical, and with such an infinity of resources', should waste its soldiers 'wholesale' out of a lack of 'military science, not to say common sense'. In an image out of the Crusades, Albert's brother deplored British tactics as 'quite as imprudent as those of Louis the Holy against the Mamelukes'.

Aberdeen's coalition fell on 29 January 1855, after a vote of censure carried by a large majority, and the wily Palmerston became Prime Minister for the first time. With both reluctance and relief, Albert closed the hostile files on Palmerston which he had been keeping in mistrust of his machinations since 1848.

In Paris, Louis Napoleon could evade the parliamentary fate of Aberdeen, but seemed left with only one public defender of his conduct of the war, the Turkish ambassador, Vely Pasha. Yet fortune soon rescued both Palmerston and the Emperor. Early in March, Nicholas I died unexpectedly. His son and successor, Alexander II, only a year older than Victoria and Albert and once thought of as a possible husband for her, was eager to end the war, but no one expected a resolution very soon, as he would have to extricate Russia with some perceived dignity.

As the Tsar already realized, Russia's defeat would mean a gain for someone else, and an Anglo-French bargain had already been struck with the Victor Emmanuel II of Sardinia. In exchange for a loan of a million pounds from England and a joint guarantee of his borders, the King's Piedmontese troops would fight in the Crimea. To furnish shipping for that and other war needs, the government hired Samuel Cunard's passenger steamers, embarrassing the already abashed Admiralty.

The Queen's ire about the press would continue through the war, and into the new Ministry, a draft from Balmoral to the Prime Minister, in the Prince's hand, declaring that the Queen was 'much disgusted with the late atrocious articles in *The Times* on the Army in the Crimea...' The Prince's opinion was that 'soon there will not be room enough in the same country for both the Monarchy and *The Times*'. The Queen's feeling was that 'repressive laws' against the press would only 'aggravate the evil', but she wondered to Palmerston 'whether it is right that the Editor, the Proprietor and the Writers of such execrable publications ought to be the honoured and constant guests of the Ministers of the Crown'.

Delane of *The Times* paid no attention to threats and social disapproval. 'Continue as you have done, to tell the truth', he wrote to William Russell, 'and leave such comment as may be dangerous to us, who are out of danger.'

Russell did exactly that, although Albert was unrepentant about condemning what he described to Clarendon as 'mischief which the gaining of three pitched battles could not repair'. With Parliament following the press in criticism, J.A. Roebuck, MP, was busily seeking goats and scapegoats via an investigating committee on conduct of the war. In March 1855 he asked the former Secretary for War, the 5th Duke of Newcastle, whom Palmerston had not kept on, whether he objected to being examined, for the key to the Crimean 'mysteries' could only be found in high quarters. 'Now I must be careful how I talk further with you', said the Duke. 'I see you are laying the ground for an impeachment, as you can only mean me by a *high quarter.*'

'Oh, no!' said Roebuck, 'I mean a much higher personage than you; I mean Prince Albert.'

# XIV

# Albert's War

## 1855–1856

A S ALBERT WAS drawn more and more into the prosecution of
the Crimean War, he had to consider his every public move. The
accusations of unconstitutional interference might revive. Because Prussia and the lesser German states could not be drawn in on the Western
side, and he remained, in English perception, a German, his reluctance
on purely military grounds had appeared to some as pro-Russian.
Russia, however, was not only distant and difficult of access, but
possessed what seemed to be infinite manpower and infinite space. Yet,
because Napoleon III often interfered with his generals, a royal dimension to British involvement became necessary. English generals could
negotiate on even terms with their French counterparts, but the intrusion of Napoleon III, who fancied himself to be above mere military
rank, made the presence of the Prince essential. Ceremonially, the
Queen represented the Crown. Where war strategy was hammered out,
she remained only a woman.

With an entourage of ministers and military men, Albert had thus
gone to the Boulogne encampment the previous summer. There he
achieved a wary rapport which the Emperor, possessed of a throne that
as yet lacked external dignity, attempted to build upon. Eager for a
State visit to England to add cachet to his position, he had poured on
the compliments about the Prince to '*Madame et bonne Soeur*' and, at
greater length, to the Earl of Clarendon (via Count Walewski) for
transmission to the Queen. 'In all his experience', the Count quoted
his master as gushing, 'he had never met with a person possessing such

various and profound knowledge, or who communicated it with the same frankness ... He had never learned so much in a short time, and was grateful.'

Clarendon and Granville, accompanying Albert, had suggested that following the hard Crimean winter and an expected stalemate in early 1855, the Emperor pay a visit to Windsor, which would add a Royal imprimatur to his reign, and during which the war situation could be reassessed. Albert proposed that Napoleon visit with his Empress in the early spring. Delighted, the Emperor suggested a reciprocal visit to Paris, and the meetings ended warmly although no quick military results were expected. In fact, there were further disappointments, and to reverse them as well as retrieve some military lustre for the Bonaparte name, Louis Napoleon proposed going to the Crimea himself. That was a more impelling reason for a person-to-person meeting, this time in England, a better venue in which to dissuade him. To Prince William of Prussia, Albert joked, 'I shall have to have precautions taken in the Crypt of St George's Chapel, to see to it that George III does not turn in his grave!'

The Emperor had every reason to go to the Crimea except one. He might have no crown when he returned, if he could return at all. Further setbacks might endanger his regime, and he was no Napoleon I. Yet he recognized that British generalship and disorganization in the Crimea were contributing to his problems. Whatever his censorship at home, the freer press in London was reporting every embarrassment, and bad news crossed the Channel. Albert had tried his best to establish some efficiency at the Horse Guards and beyond, but each intrusion risked his regained reputation as above politics. On the last day of the old year of 1854 he had warned the obviously outgoing Minister for War, the Duke of Newcastle, of 'the want of system and order in our army before Sebastopol', which caused confusion and suffering to the troops, and 'painful uncertainty' at home. Both to him and the succeeding Minister, Fox Maule, 2nd Lord Panmure, Albert pressed the urgency for regular and honest reports from the field on the conditions troops faced – the state of rations, forage, clothing, sanitation, fuel, quarters, ordnance. The language of Panmure's orders to Lord Raglan followed closely Albert's memoranda, complete to the complaint that Panmure was 'at present compelled to rely on reports of unofficial individuals' – a euphemism for the press.

The bungling and blundering revealed by the war had exposed the cumbrousness of military administration. The problem for would-be reformers before 1852 had been the continued immunity of Wellington from criticism. He had seen little reason to alter the system that won at Waterloo and Trafalgar. No authority remotely so overwhelming, civilian or military, had succeeded him. When an Army Board had finally been set up in Newcastle's last days to co-ordinate fiefdoms, Albert drafted a request for the Queen that she be sent minutes of its weekly meetings. It was another way he could keep his hand in events. A further opening came when Panmure, on the eve of taking office, alleged to Albert, 'The lamentable results which have attended to our present expedition . . . are solely to be attributed to the want of proper control by a single Minister of every department of the Army.' Albert had, then, his opportunity to prepare a 'Paper on the organisation of the Army' for Panmure, and would not only offer military advice throughout the war to Panmure and Palmerston but be asked for it.

Publicly, the Queen supported the incompetent Lord Raglan, whose position Roebuck attributed to Albert. Yet she and the Prince knew the disconcerting truth about command failures in the Crimea. So did the outgoing Prime Minister, the Earl of Aberdeen, whose son, Colonel Alexander Gordon, wrote to Albert's secretary, clearly for the Prince's eyes, that toward the end of January, in the mud and cold before Balaclava 'our effectives today are only 10,362!' The Palmerston government that replaced Aberdeen had almost the same personnel but promised more vigorous prosecution of the war, which was likely as winter left the Black Sea and further reinforcements arrived. The new Ministry was also goaded by the Roebuck investigatory committee and the forthcoming Imperial visit. If matters did not improve, the government faced the additional shame of having Napoleon III, only seven years earlier a penniless exile in London living on the purse of an English mistress, and a volunteer special constable on the day of the failed Chartist demonstration, go out to command the Allied armies against Russia.

As preparations were hurried for the arrival, Albert also managed time for other matters. On 28 February, at the end of the first month of Palmerston's Ministry, he again presided over the Exhibition Commission, which met regularly to disburse its funds, and drew up a proposal to purchase, for £50,000, a major portion of the Bernal Collection – as the government would not participate in buying it outright. Ralph Bernal, the father of MP and wit Bernal Osborne, had died the year before, leaving a vast collection of glass, plate and miniatures. Of Sephardic origins and with lucrative inherited West Indian properties, he had abjured his faith to matriculate at Cambridge and, as was then possible, buy a parliamentary seat. Albert's purchase was the foundation of what would be the South Kensington Museum of Art and Manu-factures, later the Victoria and Albert Museum.

A few days later, Albert's secretary wrote to John Scott Russell of the Eastern Steam Navigation Company asking whether the Prince could visit the 'Great Ship' under construction while he was there inspecting a floating siege gun being built for the Crimea. The shipyard on the Isle of Dogs in a loop of the Thames was building a colossal iron vessel 693-feet long, 'the Crystal Palace of the sea'. Designed by Isambard King-dom Brunel, it would be christened *Leviathan* (then altered to *Great Eastern*). Beneath its five funnels it would displace 22,500 tons – five times the size of anything afloat – and for insurance it would carry masts and 6,500 yards of sail. Its proposed engines for paddlewheels could power all the cotton mills in Manchester, and battalions of recruits could be drilled on its 120-foot-wide deck while steaming to war. Noah's Ark, it was estimated, had been only two-thirds the size of the new behemoth. The ship, which would have a chequered history after its launch in 1858, was considered the 'child of the Mechanical Section of the British Society for the Advancement of Science'.

Albert's siege gun was another such child. He had envisioned proto-type 'floating cupolas' – partly submerged floating gun turrets – for bombarding shore fortifications, hoping to have one ready for use against the Russians. Albert was always designing something. But the Scott Russell cupola would be gutted by fire in May, on the night before it was to be launched. The £45,000 investment was only partly covered by insurance but rumour had it that the fire retrieved what was possible of an investment expected to fail. The war would have to be won some other way.*

---

* Another abortive victory weapon was Robert Mallet's 42-ton monster mortar, intended also to break the siege. With its thirty-six-calibre bore, it was designed to launch a 2,395-pound projectile 1.56 miles. The first of two was not ready until the war was over. When it was tested and proved to cost £675 per shot, the War Office rejected both guns.

By then Napoleon III had come and gone, and the matter of his leading troops in the Crimea had been solved. His ship delayed and his waterside greeting muted by heavy fog, the Emperor, with Eugénie, arrived at Dover at noon and was met by Albert, who conveyed them by rail and then by procession through Lambeth and London to Paddington for the special train to Windsor. In passing from Pall Mall to Piccadilly, as they went up St James's Street, Louis Napoleon pointed out King Street, to show Eugénie where he had lived in less grand days.

At Dover a telegram had awaited the Emperor – that allied batteries, four hundred guns in all, had opened fire on Sevastopol on 10 April, the very anniversary of his constable duty as exile in 1848. He gave the bulletin to Albert, who kept it among his prized papers.

Since conferences that had gone on in Vienna for a month to discuss a settlement had been going nowhere, the English visit was one of military conferences sandwiched between concerts, operas, parades and presentations. To allay sensitivities, the Waterloo Room at Windsor was renamed the Picture Gallery for the duration of the visit. In it the Queen danced a quadrille with the rather short, swarthy, moustachioed Emperor, whom she found magnetic and charming – 'as if he had been born a king's son'. When they left for London on the nineteenth, Napoleon voiced regret at leaving. She had heard, Victoria noted in her diary, 'that the Empress was equally sad at going away from Windsor . . . Altogether I am delighted to see how much Albert likes and admires her, as it is so seldom I see him do so with any woman.' It may have assuaged the Queen's sense of having been charmed too easily by Louis Napoleon to feel that Albert had been smitten with the beautiful Eugénie.

Planning to emulate Albert's Great Exhibition with a Parisian one, the Emperor was eager to inspect the Crystal Palace in Sydenham, which they visited on 10 April, Napoleon's forty-seventh birthday. The next day, after further meetings in Buckingham Palace, the French party left. It had all been, Victoria confided to her journal, like 'a dream, a brilliant, successful, pleasant dream'. The success had come not only in the '*amitié*' which the Emperor had signed into the Queen's visitors' album, but in the military decisions reached. Rarely had Victoria sat in with Albert on military discussions, but now she did, claiming 'stirring times'. Further, at meetings of the monarchs and their entourages, including Maréchal Jean-Baptiste Vaillant, Ministre de la

Guerre, Napoleon had been persuaded – although he had not yet confessed as much – to leave the prosecution of the war to the generals. His eagerness to lead troops into battle had been blunted by reports reaching London that the Russian artillery answering Allied fire was numerous and effective, with every sign of developing into a long and indecisive siege. Further, as Albert pointed out diplomatically, there was great danger to France in the Emperor's absence. Confirmation came in a letter to the Queen dated 25 April 1855, in which Napoleon reluctantly conceded that he could not leave France, and which closed with appreciation for Royal hospitality. '*Le Prince votre époux a été bien net*' – 'The Prince your husband has been very definite', Vaillant, intimating the outcome, had told Victoria on parting.

Speeches for and against continuing the war stretched into the summer as Roebuck's revelations in the Commons of gross military incompetence were corroborated by the newspapers. Early in June the Prince, in presiding over the annual Trinity House dinner, used his forum to charge the press with irresponsibility in sowing despondency and in revealing information to the enemy of a nature which the Allies could only glean from spies and deserters. Britain had to contend with a less-than-civilized adversary operating under despotic conditions, Albert maintained, 'whilst we have to meet him under a state of things intended for peace and the promotion of that very civilisation – a civilisation [which is] the offspring of public discussion, the friction of parties, and popular control over the government of the State'. Constitutional government, he insisted, was under its heaviest trials in wartime, and it required some voluntary sacrifices of the right to know so that operations – and negotiations – could proceed with secrecy and surprise. Undisciplined liberties could incapacitate governments.

A military strike planned by the Prince (according to Baron Vitzthum, the Saxon ambassador) gave him further cause for leaving the press in the dark. While envoys in Vienna haggled over how to keep the Russian fleet in the Black Sea from becoming a continuing post-war threat to Turkey, requiring the permanent presence of Western navies, Albert devised a surprise attack on the supply base at Kerch, on the eastern tip of the Crimea, where a strait links the Black Sea with the lake-sized Sea of Azov, to the north. On 24 May the expedition, commanded by Captain (later Admiral Sir) Edmund Lyons, struck, landing troops who destroyed installations, beached and burned four warships, and captured Russian stores of grain intended for Sevastopol. No newspapermen knew it had happened until it was over, and no one knew Albert had a hand in it. The vast loss in rations destined for the defenders of Sevastopol would have an impact on the siege.

Lord Raglan, who blamed the French for dragging their feet in the Crimea – for insisting upon delays in joint operations when he was allegedly ready and they were not – died of dysentery at his head-quarters on 29 June. Eleven days earlier the French had suffered another defeat, and the outnumbered British, coming to their aid, had been driven off with heavy losses. Since only ten percent of the 188,000 Allied effectives were British, while half were French (and the rest Turks and Sardinians), Raglan had seen his authority erode with the numbers, and his last days were embittered. Entirely a desk general, he had been the wrong man in the wrong place, but the Crimea may have been the wrong place for any soldier. Lieutenant-General James Simpson, another relic of Wellington's army, replaced Raglan.

The royal return visit to Paris was far more necessary to Napoleon III than to Victoria and Albert. In the aftermath of reverses in the Crimea which could lead to instability at home, the Emperor needed internal spectacles to distract his subjects from external anxieties. Coincidentally, on 16 August 1855, just as the Queen and Prince were due to arrive, a force of largely French troops were victorious at the river Chernaya, beating back an estimated sixty thousand Russians struggling to relieve Sevastopol. It was a good time for Victoria and Albert to appear with the Emperor and Empress at the Grand Opéra to see an overlong ballet which included a scene with a view of Windsor. 'God Save the Queen' was sung, and enthusiastically cheered. After the performance the monarchs returned to the palace at St Cloud, where Louis Napoleon – once a student in Augsburg – and the Prince sang (according to Victoria's journal) 'all sorts of old German songs'.

The needs of the times had overturned centuries of cross-Channel enmity. As late as May 1854, however, the Cabinet had boggled at the expenditure of £50,000 for a major British presence at the *Exposition Universelle*, from arts to manufactures. Intervening, Albert hoped that 'as we were spending so much in destruction (in the Crimea), we ought to spend some in construction'. The government was shamed into supporting British participation, and Albert supported the exhibition further by going to a preview of the paintings to be shown at the new

Palais des Beaux-Arts and seeing to it that a 'sold' notice was put on one. 'Albert was so enchanted with it – so much so', Victoria recorded in her diary about Frederick Leighton's *Cimabue's Madonna Carried in Procession through the Streets of Florence* – it was the artist's first appearance at the Royal Academy – 'that he made me buy it'. Albert had not been in Florence since his student days, but retained an affection for it, and for the early Italian painters Cimabue represented. Stopping to greet W.P. Frith, whose populous *Ramsgate Sands* Victoria and Albert had bought out of her affectionate childhood remembrance of seaside holidays there, the Prince congratulated him on his 'marvellously light and elegant', and equally crowded, canvas, *At the Opera*, which seemed appropriate for Paris. At the Exposition itself, Albert would tour the Palais de l'Industrie and make purchases he thought would be useful for England.

In Paris, Victoria and Albert were greeted everywhere with frenzied acclaim, and were awed by the profound yet rapid alterations in the face of the capital, which Albert remembered as a city of seedy, narrow streets. Broad, tree-lined avenues beautified areas where slums had been cleared, and the Bois de Boulogne, Albert wrote to King Leopold, vied 'with the finest English parks. How all this could have been done in so short a time no one comprehends.' Further, as an electrical storm crackled outside, the Emperor had escorted Victoria and Albert by torchlight into the still-unfinished tomb of the first Napoleon, whose ashes had been returned from St Helena in 1840, 'while the organ of the Church of the Invalides played "God Save the Queen". So numerous were the strange impressions wrought by the contrast of past with present, that one could often only wonder.'

At the coffin, covered with black velvet in a side chapel, the Queen, according to Marshal François Canrobert, broke the silence by turning to the awed Prince of Wales, not yet fourteen, and directing him, 'Kneel down before the tomb of the great Napoleon.' Peals of thunder were shaking the windows, and the event could not have been better staged by his imperial nephew.

As Prussian minister to the *Bundestag* in Frankfurt, the most influential post in the kingdom's diplomatic service, Otto von Bismarck was in Paris at Eugénie's ball for Victoria and Albert, to reconnoitre the couple who had been pressing Frederick William IV to intervene in the war on the side of the West. (Bismarck would be the ambassador to

St Petersburg from 1859 into 1862.) 'The Prince', he wrote much later with undiminished hostility, 'handsome and cool in his black uniform, conversed with me courteously, but in his manner there was a kind of malevolent curiosity from which I concluded that my anti-occidental influence upon the King was not unknown to him...In the eyes of the Prince...I was a reactionary party man who took up sides for Russia in order to further an Absolutist and "Junker" policy. It was not to be wondered at that this view...descended to the Prince's daughter...'

Vicky and Bertie, both with their parents in Paris, were charmed by the exotic Emperor and his beautiful consort. 'You have a nice country', the Prince of Wales told the Emperor after Napoleon had taken the carriage reins himself, followed agitatedly but discreetly by security men, to show Paris to the children. 'I would like to be your son.' Later he asked Eugénie whether she could intercede with his parents so that he and Vicky could stay a little longer. Diplomatically she explained that the Queen and Prince could not do without them. 'Not do without us!' Bertie exploded; 'don't fancy that, for there are six more of us at home and they don't want us.'

Sevastopol seemed about to fall. An indecisive conflict would follow until peace terms could be settled. In the Crimea, Albert's friend since his Italian winter of 1839, now General Sir Francis Seymour, had been wounded for the second time, a grenade fragment grazing the back of his head. There were now 35,000 English troops on the peninsula, along with 110,000 French, 54,000 Turks and 12,000 Sardinians, most finally equipped with viable weaponry. Artillery fire was demoralizing the supply-short Russians, especially the cannonading of heavy mortars, and finally, on 10 September, when Victoria and Albert were back from France and at Balmoral, news came that the siege had been broken.

'Albert said', Victoria wrote, 'that they should go at once and light the bonfire which had been prepared when the false report of the fall of the town arrived last year...In a few minutes, Albert and all the gentlemen, in every species of attire, sallied forth, followed by all the servants, and gradually by all the population of the village – keepers, ghillies, workmen – up to the top of the cairn.' The young princes were awakened to watch the blaze, which flared as the Queen's piper played. Ghillies fired their guns in the air. Prudently, Victoria remained distant, but 'about three-quarters of an hour after, Albert came down, and said that the scene had been wild and exciting beyond everything. The people had been drinking healths in whisky, and were in great ecstasy'.

The Queen ventured out to watch, remaining until close to midnight, 'and just as I was undressing, all the people came down under the windows, the pipers playing, the people singing, firing off guns, and cheering – first for me, then for Albert, the Emperor of the French, and the "downfall of Sevastopol".' Noting that whisky was drunk round the Balmoral bonfire – such news travelled fast – *Punch* warned wryly that the 'sad example' of the Prince's participation would cause outrage in the 'Sackcloth Sunday Society'.

The Victoria Cross would emerge from the war. The Queen wanted a medal for extraordinary bravery in battle that could be awarded regardless of rank. The methodical Albert designed it and composed the language of the Royal Warrant, which referred to 'officers or men who have served Us in the presence of the enemy and then shall have performed some signal act of valour or devotion to their country'. *The Times* fussed, 'Never did we see such a dull, heavy, tasteless affair... There is a cross, and a lion, and a scroll worked up into the most shapeless mass that size admits of.' Valour, it concluded, would have to be its own reward; had the medals been on sale at a penny, 'hardly a dozen would be sold in a twelve-month'. The Queen liked it, but objected to the initials 'V.C.' to appear after the recipient's name, preferring 'B.V.C.' – the initial letter for 'Bearer'. After Albert's role at Cambridge she thought of 'V.C.' only as Vice-Chancellor. The abbreviation had to parallel other awards, however, and it was a battle she could not win.

The Crimean War, in which all the major combatant parties lost more than was gained, would not be the last Victorian small war, but it would be the last in which Albert had a principal hand. Only indirectly did it promote one of his greatest desires, the unification of Germany. By breaking the long ties of mutual interest between Austria and Russia it exposed, as never before, the rivalries for control of the buffer principalities between them, and left Austria without a military ally looming over Prussia. That was not the Prince's intention. He had a more peaceful strategy in mind, one that would foreshadow a liberal, rather than a militaristic, united Germany, Albertine at the top. Although dynastic marriages were fading out as grand gestures of international amity, he hoped to bring off the last and greatest of them.

He would marry his most beloved daughter, Vicky, to the future emperor of a future Germany.

The idea had surfaced when Prince William of Prussia had come with his family to the Great Exhibition in 1851. His eldest son, Frederick William, already nineteen, was tall and fair. Princess Victoria, only ten, was pretty and intellectually advanced beyond her years. While Vicky's German was faultless – it was spoken within the privacy of the family – the Prince's English was awkward, and he had no experience of travel beyond the university at Bonn. Privately, Albert explained how inadequately 'Fritz' was being prepared for kingship in the claustrophobic atmosphere of the Prussian court, and Frederick William asked Albert to help him with reading suggestions, and with occasional letters and memoranda. When he left for home, the young prince asked Albert to sign his autograph book, and Albert, never slow to proffer advice, prefaced his signature with 'May Prussia be merged in Germany, and not Germany in Prussia'.

Little correspondence between the Queen and Fritz's mother, Princess Augusta, was exchanged during the Crimean War, and Albert's to her husband, Prince William, was businesslike but unsympathetic. As the war, after Sevastopol, muddled toward peace, both the Prussian and English courts quietly broached the possibility of an eventual marriage although Vicky was not yet fifteen. On 29 August 1855, on the family's return from Paris, Albert sent a note to his mother-in-law, the Duchess of Kent, 'We shall probably have Fritz of Prussia visiting us... for a few days. He has been taking the baths at Ostend, and will come to England. He wishes to see Scotland.' Another and less understated letter went to Baron Stockmar, who had been consulted earlier.

From Balmoral on 20 September Albert wrote to Stockmar, 'The event you are interested in reached an active stage this morning after breakfast. The young man laid his proposal before us with the permission of his parents, and of the King [of Prussia]; we accepted it for ourselves, but requested him to hold it in suspense as regards the other party till after her Confirmation. Till then all the simple unconstraint of girlhood is to continue undisturbed. In the Spring the young man wishes to make his offer to herself...' The marriage, Albert added, would not take place before Vicky was seventeen.

In the relative seclusion of Balmoral, the romance, even under ostensible chaperonage, prospered. In a further bulletin on 29 September, Stockmar was informed, 'The Prince is really in love and the little lady does her best to please him.' In her journal that day the Queen put it more explicitly. Vicky was 'engaged'. She and Albert had been 'uncertain, on account of her extreme youth, whether he should speak to her himself, or wait till he came back again'. However, during a ride they took to Craig-na-Ban, Fritz picked a sprig of white heather, a Scots symbol for good luck, and gave it to Vicky, enabling him 'to make an allusion to his hopes'. Since it had been clear a week earlier that the betrothal would happen, Albert had already informed the Earl of Clarendon, the Foreign Minister, so that official confirmation could go to the Prince of Prussia, Fritz's father, and to Viscount Palmerston.

The departure of Frederick William on 1 October enabled Albert to return to the pressing problems of the Russian war. Although what was diagnosed as rheumatic pains in his right shoulder and arm had left his nights nearly sleepless for a fortnight, and kept him from holding a pen for long, his correspondence went on. Unwisely he informed his brother Ernest of the engagement, which ensured leakage of the news. Whatever the source, *The Times* was out with the story on 3 October. With Prussia's leaning toward the Tsar's interest during the war still embittering the papers' editorial tone, Fritz's family was called a 'wretched German dynasty' which 'would not survive the collapse of Russia's influence'. While the war continued with Frederick William IV's passive support of his brother-in-law, the exasperation of the press was as inevitable as Albert's anguish.

Albert had engineered a marital *coup* planned to bind Britain to the Continental power of the future, but he had not anticipated the continuing undercurrent of anti-German feeling that had been a personal misery to him since his own betrothal to Victoria, and would outlast them both. Theodor Fontane, the Berlin novelist born in the same year as the Queen and Prince, and then visiting England, noted in his diary a scrap of street ballad invective that demonstrated the persistence of that paranoia:

> Bad luck they say both night and day
> To the Cobugs and the humbugs,
> The Wirtembugs, the Scarembugs,
> And all the German horse-rugs...

The elation and the anxieties of the matchmaking could not shut out the reality of the war. In the Crimea itself, Raglan's timid replacement, General Simpson, was not a success, and nearly invisible. For internal political reasons, Louis Napoleon was planning to return home a hundred thousand of his troops, who were bogged down anyway beyond Sevastopol. Russian inefficiency contributed to the favourable Allied position, as there was no rail link to the Crimea, and reinforcements and supplies had to move the final 230 miles by animal and human transport. 'At Sebastopol', Albert wrote tartly to Stockmar, 'our Generals appear to be suffering from a remarkable lack of brains.' By 29 October he had worked out, due to lack of initiative at Whitehall, a reorganization of the army in the Crimea 'into two *Corps-d'armée*', under one chief, which has been adopted by the [War] Ministry... Sir W[illiam] Codrington becomes Commander-in-Chief, Sir Colin Campbell and Sir W[illiam] Eyre take the Divisions, General [C.A.] Windham becomes Chief of the General Staff...' Among those to return was the relieved commander, General Simpson. Both he and Raglan, Albert told Stockmar irritably, 'declared their inability to trouble themselves much about plans of campaign, while their whole time was taken up with writing and correspondence'.

'I and all the other members of the Cabinet', Albert's former *bête noir*, Lord Palmerston, wrote to him, 'feel greatly obliged to your Royal Highness for having suggested an arrangement which had not occurred to any of us, but which when proposed and explained at once obtained the assent of all those whose duty it was to take it into consideration.' The Prince by his own decision had declined to replace Wellington, but informally he found himself overseeing the winding down of the war. Ironically, at the time, despite years of jokes at his expense about his exalted military rank, he was, through attrition, the only Field Marshal in the army. Since that seemed to Victoria and Albert impolitic, three active generals were promoted, including Lord Hardinge.

Albert now carried on a regular exchange with Palmerston on the war, planning to resume naval operations in the Baltic in the spring of 1856 if necessary, to pressure the Russians further into signing a peace treaty. 'We might have struck home at Cronstadt and St Petersburg in the first year of the war', he confided to Baron Vitzthum, 'had our fleet been managed by a more resolute man than Sir Charles Napier.'

Methodically looking farther ahead, the Prince worked out an agenda, once peace came, for transferring equipment and stores stockpiled in the Black Sea region to Malta and Gibraltar.

While the war remained Albert's chief concern, its political, economic and social dislocations far out of proportion to the manpower committed to the Crimea, he put in many more hours on the future. He was preparing an address, he explained to Stockmar, on 'the influence of Science and Art on our Manufactures', for delivery on laying the foundation stone of the Birmingham and Midland Counties Institute. He was working on reform of the examinations for aspiring diplomats, and was still working, as Chancellor, on further academic reforms at Cambridge. And while he managed to see his other children only briefly, and to consult with Henry Birch about Albert Edward's lack of progress and developing stammer, he set aside an hour every evening to tutor Vicky on German history, on politics and law, and on other matters which he felt might prepare a future queen. To Fritz, she wrote, 'from dear papa I learn more than from anyone else in the world'. A demanding tutor, he gave her, nearly a year later as their lessons continued, a pamphlet to translate, *Karl August und die Deutsche Politik*, by Johann Gustavus Droysen. Since it dealt with Fritz's grandfather it was doubly useful as preparation for her new position. Pleased with the result, Albert sent her manuscript to Lord Clarendon to examine. Praising father and daughter simultaneously, the Foreign Minister described the translation as 'the reflection of a highly cultivated intellect'. It was no exaggeration. The Princess Royal was very likely the brainiest royal offspring to be born in Britain, and Albert described her to her future bridegroom as having 'a man's head and a child's heart'.

The Queen had far less interest in her firstborn. To Victoria, only the hours with Albert were crucial; hours with the children were dispensable. 'When Albert is often away all day long', she confided to the Queen of Prussia, Fritz's aunt, 'I find no especial pleasure or compensation in the company of the elder children.' She was only '*à mon aise*' when Albert was with her, for she had grown up without the company of other children and always knew adult society. 'Lastly I cannot get used to the fact that Vicky is almost grown up. To me she still seems the same child, who had to be kept in order and therefore must not become too intimate.'

Albert may have expected too much of his children. The eldest ones represented to him the future of England and Germany. Even Alfred was expected to succeed his childless uncle as Duke of Coburg – if Coburg survived. All the children but Vicky, whom he adored, were afraid of him as master of the family, but except for Bertie they could penetrate his Germanic reserve and enjoy his company. Victoria merely summoned them on occasion, Albert once writing to her (1 October, 1856), preferring to offer bad news in notes rather than quarrel in person, 'It is indeed a pity that you find no consolation in the company of your children. The root of the trouble lies in the mistaken notion that the function of a mother is to be always correcting, scolding, ordering them about and organising their activities. It is not possible to be on happy friendly terms with people you have just been scolding.'

Vicky's husband-to-be, Albert dreamed, would be another child to be moulded, like his eldest daughter – a son more than son-in-law. In that he failed to reckon with the conservative Prussian milieu in which Fritz's future rested. Still, among the additions to Albert's *Papierberg* of correspondents was Prince Fritz, who was showing, happily, clear indications of political liberalism. What was Fritz to do in response to reactionaries who were pushing the monarchy, despite the lessons of 1848, back toward the past? Albert considered his future son-in-law's sensitive position and suggested that he defend individual rights – 'those of my country and my people' – but in order 'that my conduct might be divested of every semblance of being dictated by a spirit of opposition or desire for popularity – and in order, it may be, to make the step itself unnecessary – I should in all confidence make those who are contemplating the wrong aware, that if it were persisted in, I should feel myself compelled to adopt this course'. Stepping even more gingerly, Albert added, 'this done, I should certainly entertain no animosity towards my friends, but, on the contrary, should live upon terms of peace with the reigning powers'. Some guarded measure of activism, he felt, was necessary 'to keep the nation from losing all hope, and there is no such solid basis for patience as hope'.

It was clear that Albert saw Prussia as slipping backward into traditional authoritarianism, and that the hope he had borne for a liberalized monarchy under Fritz's father was no longer to be counted upon. 'The German', he explained to his future son-in-law, 'stands in the centre between England and Russia; his high culture and his philosophic love of truth drive him towards the English conception, his military discipline, his admiration of the Asiatic greatness...which is achieved by the merging of the individual into the whole, drives him in the other direction.'

Vicky, he told Fritz, 'comes to me every evening from six to seven, when I put her through a kind of general catechizing, and in order to give precision to her ideas, I make her work out certain subjects by herself, and bring me the results...Thus she is now engaged in writing a short Compendium of Roman History.' Like her father, she promised to be an activist consort, one to be dreaded by Prussian rightists who might have already arranged to have Fritz's mail secretly opened and read. When Otto von Bismarck came to power as Minister-President of Prussia in 1862, such spying became routine.

The pressure within France to end the war was straining the still fragile relations between England and its unlikely ally. The Emperor had borrowed as well as cadged money for both grandeur at home and glory abroad, and was riskily close to financial embarrassment. Bringing home most of the French troops and releasing them into the work force was of less anxiety to Albert than Napoleon's willingness, for a quick accord, to readjust the map of eastern Europe and win the peace, if not the war, for Russia. Palmerston conceded, despite his long francophile sympathies, that Louis Napoleon's problems, which were not unknown to the Tsar's informants in Paris, weakened the English bargaining position. To bolster it by a dose of John Bullish stubbornness, Albert drafted a blunt letter to the Emperor, for Victoria's signature, pointing out that Napoleon could do what he wanted as absolute monarch, but for the Queen, 'the peace must be supported by Parliament and acceptable to the nation'. The Emperor was 'answerable to nobody'. She was bound by 'the advice of a Council of Ministers'.

A sticking point in negotiations was the openness and the neutrality of the Black Sea. Another was the disposition of disputed territories. Little was said about the pretexts responsible for the war. To England the issues were the viability of Turkey, the 'Sublime Porte' now only in name, as a buffer to Russian expansion, and the fencing of Russia away from the Mediterranean. Despite the Roebuck investigation into the war, England, as a free and dynamic society, was emerging from the conflict stronger than any of the other belligerents – with the rather small exception of Sardinia, whose bluff king paid a call upon Victoria and Albert toward the end of 1855 and aspired to be monarch of a future united Italy, largely at the expense of Austria, which no longer had a staunch friend at Windsor Castle.

The allies had no idea how desperately Alexander II needed peace for exhausted Russia until the Queen received the professedly secret news on the night of 16 January 1856, in a telegram, puzzlingly sent *en clair*, by the secretive and unstable King of Prussia. Although the message that Russia was ready to discuss peace came by commercial telegraphy, uncoded, the excited Frederick William IV begged that his name be concealed. Albert forwarded the 'telegraphic curiosity' to Lord Clarendon, noting that the Queen wanted him to be aware of the sender as well as the message, since 'the whole line of the telegraph' already knew.

Because of Louis Napoleon's internal needs, the peace conference, preparations for which had long simmered in Vienna, was held in Paris. The Prussian king asked to be seated at it, but Paris and London turned him down, even after King Leopold of the Belgians interceded with Albert. To his uncle, the Prince replied that England's position at the table would be difficult enough with Emperor Napoleon on its side, as anti-German feeling was strong in France, and that went for Austria as well, which was 'as selfish and as little to be relied upon as ever'. To have Prussia in the conference would only bolster the Tsar, Albert contended. 'Russia will not yield one hair's breadth more than she is *forced* to yield.' It was, he felt, 'a perilous precedent for the future to admit the principle, that a Power may take a part in the great game of politics, without having laid down their stake'. Even Vicky's future father-in-law, Prince William of Prussia, failed to budge Albert, but in the interests of giving a settlement broader acceptability, plenipotentiaries from Berlin were seated on 18 March. On 10 March, the English delegates had already yielded to French desires to be easy on the Russians. All the Prussian delegate had to do was sign.

Recognizing gloomily that the results of the war would not be worth the sacrifices, Albert had already agreed to an audience with Baron Vitzthum to vent his exasperations to the Saxon envoy in the hope they would travel farther. He wanted, he insisted, a 'sound peace' or the further prosecution of the war – which he knew would not happen. But, suggesting that alternative, he warned, 'English indolence has taken several years to get [us] ready. Our preparations are now complete, and we can show that England is not made up only of cotton spinners and shopkeepers, as we are told.'

The Treaty of Paris was signed on 30 March 1856. By it, Russia rescued much of the Black Sea territory it expected to be forced to cede, but did return some seized Turkish lands on the eastern shore. The delta of the Danube remained Turkish territory but the Danubian provinces of Wallachia and Moldavia, core of a future Romania, would remain only nominally under Turkish sovereignty. Free navigation of the Danube was mandated, as was the neutralization of the Black Sea. The religious issues that had precipitated the conflict were shelved for Turkish promises to protect Christians.

Albert, who had no role in Paris, was dissatisfied with the terms, which left the 'Eastern Question' unsolved and further partition of European Turkey inevitable. His personality dominating the delegates, Napoleon III got his way on most issues, the unspoken one his desire to make an ally of Russia as his counterweight to the Germanic powers in the European centre. The Prince had hoped that Lord Clarendon and Count Buol* would be able to deal with 'the finessing of the Russians', but biology intervened on 16 March, when the Empress Eugénie, after a difficult pregnancy, gave birth to Prince Eugène Louis Jean Joseph, the future Prince Imperial. A salute of 101 guns shook Paris, and Lord Clarendon observed, 'The Emperor is enchanted with his son... [and] does not care sixpence for the terms.' He had founded, he thought, a new Napoleonic dynasty, and events could thereafter be managed from the perception of imperial continuity.

The treaty left England largely isolated. Russia was, and would be, hostile for decades, and Austria and Prussia had not, as Albert put it, laid down their stake. Further, England's sole major-power ally, excepting disintegrating Turkey, was an unstable France only as reliable as its unreliable Emperor.

For the Queen and Prince the Treaty of Paris did not end the Crimean agony. There would be another year of visits to the grievously wounded, the laying of foundation stones for military hospitals, the reviews of returning troops, the awards of the first Victoria Crosses, the

---

* Count Karl Ferdinand von Buol-Schauenstein was the Austrian Foreign Minister who had chaired the preliminary Vienna conference, and saw gains for Austria in a weakened Russia.

*The royal family, with Albert in top hat, Victoria wearing a bonnet, and Vicky and Bertie at their sides, visiting Crimean War wounded at a London hospital. (From a contemporary lithograph)*

audiences with Crimean heroes – and heroines. One would be Florence Nightingale, who met twice with the Queen and Prince in Scotland, and conversed privately with Albert on metaphysics and religion. The emotional end came on 8 July 1856 when, at Aldershot for a review, the Queen received from Field-Marshal Lord Hardinge the report of the Military Commission on the Crimea, a watered-down rebuke to the military. As he began explaining its findings, he toppled against the table at which he had been standing, felled by a paralytic stroke. Albert assisted him to a sofa, where (the Prince wrote to Stockmar) Hardinge 'at once resumed what he was saying with the greatest clearness and calmness, merely apologizing "that he had made such a disturbance".' Yet his right leg and arm were useless, and he had to be lifted into his carriage. Albert realized, he told Stockmar, that Hardinge, however 'courageous and composed', would have to be replaced. Two days later came Hardinge's resignation. He died on 24 September, a belated casualty of the Crimea.

Victoria preferred to have Albert remember the war through a darkly lit anecdotal canvas they had admired at the Royal Academy show the year before. Joseph Noël Paton's *Home* depicted with Pre-Raphaelite attention to domestic detail the return from the war of a bearded Scots corporal in the Fusilier Guards. A bandage covers a head wound, and his left sleeve is empty. The Crimean Medal, awarded by the Queen to all who fought in the war, is conspicuous on his uniform, and on the floor next to his chair before the fireplace is a trophy – a Russian helmet. Leaning over his shoulder, his bonneted mother weeps; at his knees he is embraced by his anguished young wife. In the background a child sleeps. On a small table in the foreground is an open Bible. In the picture, the glory (the medal, the trophy) is vastly overshadowed by the price. The canvas had a profound impact upon a public disenchanted by the Crimean experience. The Queen commissioned from Paton a reduced-size replica as a Christmas gift for Albert.

XV

# *Managing Destiny*

## *1856–1858*

T HE TREATY OF Paris ending the Crimean War was received in
London, Albert wrote, 'with moderate satisfaction: in Paris with
exultation'. Ten days earlier Vicky's confirmation, the essential preliminary to her marriage, should have been an occasion for parental
exultation but generated only moderate satisfaction. Rigid Prussian
court protocol required official publication of the forthcoming nuptials,
which Victoria and Albert considered premature. Also, the acrimony
between the ruling houses about permitting a traditional German
ceremony of betrothal was threatening to blight the engagement. 'At
present', Victoria wrote to the Prime Minister, 'not even our other
children are acquainted with it, which puts the Princess to great trials.'
Albert, she added, would write to Fritz's father 'and ask him to consider
the German part of the question, whilst the Queen asks Lord Palmerston to consider our own'.

Victoria had hoped that with peace, and the dynastic *coup*, the time
had finally come to grant Albert the title of Prince Consort. It was
already informally in use. Yet any parliamentary action was hostage to
the failure of anti-German feeling to abate. Anything that could remotely be complained of as a German evil remained attributed to Albert.
In the first season of victory, Sir Benjamin Hall, the Commissioner of
Works, whose purview included public parks, thought that it would
promote a festive atmosphere among the masses if military bands were
to play on Sunday afternoons. Both the Cabinet and the Court
approved, and the concerts drew large crowds when they began in May.

Leaders of the movement for strict Sabbath observance were outraged that the working classes might be drawn away from prayer, and promoters of penitential Sundays also objected to the bands as a German sacrilege introduced by Prince Albert.

Few circumstances earned him credit. Among his plans for a cultural and scientific district in South Kensington with seed money from Great Exhibition earnings was the transfer of pictures from the National Gallery in Trafalgar Square to the less polluted atmosphere of Kensington, where an efficient new edifice was to rise. Again there was an outcry. The Prince was tampering with the national heritage, and *Punch* depicted Albert trying to slip out of the Gallery with a framed canvas under each arm, while a policeman confronts him with the charge, 'Only moving the pictures to Kensington Gore! Suppose you leave them where they are, eh?'

He had no business lamenting his ill fortune, *Punch* cautioned:

> Never mind, noble Prince, we our crosses have all,
> Your great matters if I may compare with our small;
> But when you complain of your bad luck, you should,
> I would humbly suggest, also think of your good.

At about the same time, the successor to Hardinge at the Horse Guards was appointed, Victoria insisting upon her cousin George, Duke of Cambridge. An undistinguished general in the Crimea, he had arrived, splendidly accoutred, and pleaded illness when conditions at the front were not up to those at his clubs. No exhortations from Victoria could induce him to return. Still, nepotism remained the first rule of the army, and the Queen had the right of appointment. Again, Albert was blamed, and a *Punch* cartoon that July showed the Duke hurrying to the Horse Guards on Albert's bowed back.

In that inauspicious climate the Queen wrote confidentially to the Earl of Aberdeen, no longer at Downing Street but still a royal favourite, and then to Viscount Palmerston, to broach the matter of an English title for her husband. 'Oh! if I only could make him King!' she had written in her diary in 1845. Victoria had long since reduced her expectations, explaining now to Palmerston (5 June 1856), 'It is a strange omission in our Constitution that while the *wife* of a *King* has the highest rank and dignity in the realm after her husband assigned to her by law, the *husband* of a *Queen regnant* is entirely ignored by the law.'

THE NEW COMMANDER-IN-CHIEF.

*Although Albert was blamed for the nepotism involved in the appointment of the incompetent Duke of Cambridge as commander-in-chief of the Army, it was actually Victoria's favouritism that sent him to the Horse Guards in 1856. Here the Duke rides on Albert's back to get there. (Punch)*

She wanted 'to put this question beyond all doubt... for *all future Consorts of Queens*'. It made her position as well as that of her husband 'humiliating' to have him recognized in English law only as 'her foreign husband'.

Palmerston's political advice was to postpone the matter further. Aberdeen fussed that a title might grant Albert the right to sit in the House of Lords and the Privy Council, giving the Crown legislative powers. Derby worried that by the time the matter was considered by

Parliament, enough months would have elapsed for opponents to mount a negative press campaign. Dragging its feet in hopes that the Queen would withdraw her request, the Cabinet would not consider a Prince Consort Bill until March 1857, when, via the Lord Chancellor, a further complication was raised. In English usage a wife received her husband's rank, suggesting that the spouse of a Queen Regnant would become King Consort, which would not sit well with the people. Further, if the King Consort then survived his wife and remarried, could he communicate his rank to his wife, making her in style, at least, a queen? Nit-picking further, the Cabinet saw a new legal rank as interposing someone not in the line of succession between the sovereign and the Prince of Wales.

The Queen had to coax a response from Palmerston, and when she received it she huffed that he 'will not be astonished when she tells him that the perusal of this document has caused her much surprise...' Having had no success since 1840 in legalizing even the modest dignity afforded Queen Anne's mediocrity of a husband, Victoria determined to do 'merely as much as her Prerogative will enable her'. By Letters Patent she would give Albert the title of Prince Consort, which the Privy Council approved, finally, on 25 June 1857. Long public usage was ratified.

Despite the Sabbatarian frowning at bands on Sundays, the popular relief, and even joy, that troops were coming home made the spring and summer of 1856 a happy one, and a propitious time for balls and banquets to celebrate the Princess Royal's still-informal engagement. Since she was only fifteen, the wedding remained nearly two years away, but her coming-out inaugurated the new concert gallery and ballroom at Buckingham Palace, designed, inevitably, by the Prince Consort. The prospects were not nearly so pleasing to conservatives in the bridegroom's country, where Bismarck, Prussia's representative to the Bundestag at Frankfurt, carped to a colleague about the future 'English marriage' that the 'English' in it failed to please him but 'If the Princess can leave the Englishwoman at home and become a Prussian, then she may be a blessing to the country'. Under Albert's tutelage she was learning how to be a German rather than a Prussian.

With Vicky's grand marriage pending, the Consort Bill in the hands of the Prime Minister, England (with the Prince a primary if mostly silent factor) successful in the now-concluded war, the redesign of Buckingham Palace completed, Osborne finished, and the new Balmoral Castle now occupied, all the portents seemed favourable for Albert. While at Osborne in May 1856, leaving his reputed stuffiness behind, he even visited, informally, Alfred Tennyson, the Poet Laureate, who had just moved to nearby Freshwater. 'Prince Albert called on me the other day here', Tennyson wrote in surprise to Elizabeth Russell, his favourite aunt, 'and was very kind in manner shaking hands in quite a friendly way. We were in the midst of a packing bustle, things tumbled about here and there...he stood by the drawing-room window admiring the view which was not looking its best, and on going away said..."I shall certainly bring the Queen – it's such a pretty place."' Yet, still another of a proliferation of pamphlets about his failure to find a welcome in England had just appeared, *Prince Albert. Why is he Unpopular?*

A political rarity, the tract took his side. Although his unpopularity seemed 'a feeling shared by almost anyone', it observed, 'no one can give a rational cause for its existence'. Inexplicably, 'the consort...of the most amiable and beloved Sovereign that has ever sat on the throne of these seagirt isles, is the most unpopular man in them'.

One of the most admired, returned from the charge in which so many of his cavalrymen were slaughtered, was Lord Cardigan (of Balaclava fame), whose surviving troops were reviewed in Hyde Park on 9 July by Victoria and Albert. A 'halo of heroism' (said a sarcastic newspaperman) hung about him. Among the curious residual problems of the war, relating to officers who did not return, was that some had been gazetted Knights Commander of the Bath but had died before being invested with the title. Panmure and Palmerston brought the matter to Albert. It might be prudent, they suggested, 'to ascertain which of [their widows] are desirous of having the title of Lady, which they would have had if their husbands had lived; it is possible that to some of them the title might with reference to their pecuniary means be an inconvenience'. The honour was monetarily empty. The Prince agreed that they should be offered titles rather than awarded them.

In September and October the Queen and Prince escaped to the 'bracing' climate of Balmoral, where Victoria claimed 'half her heart' was in the 'great loneliness'. Despite her learning to her surprise there that she was again, at thirty-seven, pregnant, she escaped the depression that often followed such tidings. It was the risk run for the pleasure she would not deny herself. Albert's alternative amusements were unavailable to her. While in the Highlands she reported to Fritz's mother, Augusta, in Berlin, the Prince had shot 'twenty-nine very fine stags', delayed compensation, perhaps, for the frustrating Peace of Paris.

Again Albert had taken over all but epistolary functions for Victoria as her pregnancy advanced. Always in charge of the family, he confronted a new problem. The childless Duke Ernest had complained about the seafaring education of Prince Alfred, the nephew already designated to succeed him. 'Affie' might find his enthusiasm for a naval career at odds with residence in a small, landlocked German duchy. Reminding his brother that Alfred was also succession insurance in England, Albert noted that there were 'only two eyes' – those of the Prince of Wales – between Affie and the throne.

Although the Prince promised that Alfred would visit his likely inheritance, and he did travel to Coburg and Gotha in the spring, he was given no special German education for his future, as Vicky was receiving. 'If we make a German of him', Albert explained, 'it might be very difficult for him and for our country.'

Following the journey, the Prince wrote to thank his brother for the two weeks of hospitality for Alfred, and to regret that he could not share, with his son, 'our beloved quiet Rosenau' – 'the paradise of our childhood'. His spirit had been 'lost in the dear memories', but 'the plagues and serious business of which every day brings me plenty' returned him to reality. The confession, he admitted, was an uncommon lapse into nostalgia. 'Sentimentality is a plant which cannot grow in England, and an Englishman, when he finds he is being sentimental, becomes frightened at the idea, as of having a dangerous illness, and he shoots himself.'

As Albert wrote of the loss, some day, of his second son to a German destiny, the Queen was having the birth of their ninth and last child made tolerable by the intervention of chloroform. Princess Beatrice – 'Baby' for much of her life with Victoria – was born on 14 April 1857. While she was still recuperating at Osborne, Albert, on 23 April, asked for a meeting with Palmerston and his Chancellor of the Exchequer to arrange for a request to the Commons for funds for their firstborn, who required the customary dowry. Surfeited with the discomforts and distractions of pregnancy and babies, the Queen was aware that as each child reached maturity there would be more money-grubbing from Parliament and matchmaking on her part (an activity that would consume her later years). She and Albert, Victoria told Vicky twenty years later, considered 'many Princes a great misfortune – for they are in one another's and almost everybody's way . . . Papa felt this so much that he was always talking of establishing if possible one or two of your brothers and eventual grandchildren . . . in the colonies'. Nearly thirty-eight when Beatrice was born, and possibly embarrassed by the prospects of further motherhood – she had called even more fecund women 'rabbits' – Victoria raised the issue delicately with her *accoucheur*. Even more discreetly, he apparently suggested that the only legal and moral solution was abstinence. 'Oh, doctor,' she is reputed to have exclaimed, 'can I have no more fun in bed?' The remark seems too unqueenly to be literally Victorian, but in substance may have represented something of her sexual innocence, even after seventeen years of marriage. Still, recognizing that the Queen feared further pregnancies, and was prone to severe postpartum depression, Dr Clark warned Albert that a tenth pregnancy might threaten Victoria's mental stability.

Many Royal functions had become Albert's because the Queen was either unavailable or uninterested. They also seemed his province because of authentic interest or the realization that something had to be done, and no progress could come without a proposer or initiator. In every case he did his homework, not only to appear prepared, but to *be* knowledgeable. His original need for one secretary-assistant had expanded to three as responsibilities burgeoned – Sir Charles Phipps, General Charles Grey and Sir Thomas Biddulph. It was Phipps who recalled 'a great glass manufacturer' who, once the Prince had left the room, told Sir Charles enthusiastically, 'That is wonderful! He knows more about glass than I do!'

Clearly the Prince did not, but he had readied himself for the audience, and was also a good listener. And just as he learned the rudiments of experimental science from men as accomplished as Faraday and Lyell, he learned about the arts not to exhibit his results or parade his expertise, but to understand their values. Once, at a dinner at Windsor Castle, he explained to Lady Bloomfield – her husband was Minister to Berlin – that he realized 'that persons in our position of life can never be distinguished artists'. Those in his situation had 'too many other duties'. Their business was 'to learn to appreciate and understand the works of others, and we can never do this till we have realised the difficulties to be overcome. Acting on this principle myself, I have always tried to learn the rudiments of art as much as possible. For instance, I learned oil-painting, water-colours, etching, [and] lithography... and in music I learnt thorough bass, the pianoforte, organ, and singing.' He also learned composition – but always 'to enable me to judge and appreciate the work of others'.

For Albert, too, a cultural event had to be purposeful. Dickens's theatricals, while exploiting the snobbery of wealth and position, had a social and charitable function beyond their values as entertainment. Similarly, the Manchester Art Treasures Exhibition which opened on 5 May 1857 was able to borrow from royal art as an example to more reluctant possessors because Albert emphasized its potential for art education, which hardly existed in England. An illustrated catalogue could reach many unable to entrain to Manchester. To give the opening further cachet, he invited all envoys accredited to the Court – 'summoned', the American Minister, George M. Dallas, explained to his Secretary of State, Lewis Cass. And on the appointed day, Albert made the rail journey to Manchester, although already 'half-dead' with a bad cold, and delivered, in a 'quite cracked' voice (so he wrote to Victoria, then lying-in), the main address and officiated at a procession in which Sir Harry Smith again rode his Arab charger to great cheers. After an elaborate dinner at neo-Gothic Abney Hall, he managed to get to bed.

At eight the next morning he was on his way to Peel Park at Salford to visit the Museum and Public Library, and reply to an address. Then there was an exhibition by Manchester local artists, and the unveiling of a statue of the Queen – there would be thousands in the United Kingdom and the colonies – subscribed to by eighty thousand Sunday School teachers and their students. He had almost lost his voice by then, yet struggled to say something fitting for his audience. Art and Manufactures were indivisible, he claimed. All forms of beauty and utility were governed by the same laws of order that govern the universe and give delight to its inhabitants. The feeling and the thought that should go into all kinds of creativity need not be cheap and superficial.

As for the statue of Victoria, the figure was not merely a person: the Queen was 'the representative of the institutions of the country'.

Off, then, he went, to the railway station at Birmingham for the return to Paddington, and then Windsor, and Victoria's retreat the next day, with their expanded family, to Osborne. There, between visits by grand dukes and archdukes, princes (his future son-in-law) and kings (his uncle, Leopold), Albert would find time to plan a European tour for Bertie to help him grow up, to organize the first Handel Festival at the new Crystal Palace, where 2,500 singers and instrumentalists would perform *Judas Maccabeus* (in his diary he would call the event '*ganz vortrefflich*' [quite splendid]), and to prepare for still further occasions. He was particularly worried, he confided to Stockmar, about presiding and speaking at the annual Educational Conference. Given 'all our political and theological antagonisms', he explained, the challenge was 'an extremely ticklish one, and my address, I regret to say, will be very long. One's nervous system, therefore, has something to endure.'

On 16 May, the Princess Royal's engagement was formalized in the Prussian *Official Gazette*. Three days later, on 19 May, the Queen sent a request to Parliament for a dowry for Vicky, with Albert hoping that some precedent for provision for all the royal children might result, to avoid degrading appeals for each of their progeny. The Commons would only take up the issue at hand, but voted 328 to 14 to settle £40,000 on Vicky, with a further annuity of £8,000. Attitudes had changed since the debate on Albert's annuity. Since the annual stipend itself was far more than the salary of the Prime Minister, Albert saw it as a gesture 'of respect for the Queen'. The Princess Royal's allowance was 'not large, but it makes her independent, which is most important for her'. Whatever the considerable sum, the idea that Vicky as a Prussian wife could have any independence save as the daughter of a prestigious monarch with whom Prussia needed to remain on good terms was Albert's wishful self-delusion.

Since Fritz was a future sovereign, there was talk in Prussia of a grand marriage in Berlin rather than, as customary, at the bride's venue. Victoria instructed Clarendon to caution his ambassador 'not to *entertain* the *possibility*'. It was 'too *absurd*, to say the least'. With none of Albert's diplomacy she added, 'Whatever may be the usual practice of Prussian Princes, it is not *every* day that one marries the eldest daughter of the Queen of England. The Question therefore must be considered as settled and closed . . .'

The other question settled and closed was Albert's royal style. As Clerk of the Privy Council, Greville could not 'see the use of it', as the Queen's order conferred on the Prince Consort 'neither title, dignity, nor privileges' and would give him 'no higher rank abroad, where our acts have no validity'. When Albert expressed relief to his brother about being able to write in the new guise, Ernest remarked, 'Of course it should have been done long ago'. *The Times* agreed, observing that in practice the title had been adopted many years before. Even Greville conceded, after Albert attended a royal wedding in Belgium, that the 'Consort' title did have some effect, as the Prince 'signed the marriage contract immediately after Queen Marie Amélie, and before an Austrian Archduke who was present'. In John Bullish fashion *Punch* dismissed the episode. 'We should have supposed it better to be "Serene" in England, than "Royal" on the Continent – as Continental Royalties go.'

Issues of precedence and protocol still mattered a great deal in mid-century. Grand Duke Constantine, uncle of the Tsar, was an example. With French rapprochement in progress, and a mission to woo Western funding for railway construction in the Russian hinterland, Constantine invited himself to Osborne House. The Queen and Prince felt obliged to send their yacht to Cherbourg to fetch him, and were not pleased that ceremony required it to fly the former enemy flag when it returned to English waters on 30 May. Although the visit was supposedly informal, Palmerston rushed to greet Constantine, a guard of honour materialized on the lawn, and the Grand Duke debarked in full military uniform, a preface to his arrogant and absolutist remarks at dinner (not 'well-bred', the Queen concluded), where he also tried to conduct business with ministers.

The next day, again flying the Russian flag, they sailed out briefly in the new *Victoria and Albert* to show Constantine the fleet at Spithead, and naval guns saluted the Grand Duke's welcome departure.

On 26 June 1857, with levées and drawing-rooms in the wake of Ascot week over, and her Order in Council the previous day about Albert's title creating little stir, the Queen decorated Crimea veterans with the first Victoria Crosses at a review in Hyde Park. Even at ten that morning the summer heat had the oppressive feel of India. Gentlemen in the seats reserved for the élite put dignity aside to fan themselves with the tails of their coats; their ladies improvised fans from newspapers and flapped handkerchiefs. Beneath the drooping Royal Standard at the

Queen's dais, Victoria, bonneted and implacable under the broiling sun, pinned sixty-two medals upon the men on parade, one now in the uniform of a police constable and another in the dress of a park keeper, all heroes of Inkerman and Redan.

Returning from the ceremony, Victoria and Albert learned of the 'Sepoy Mutiny' near Calcutta. The news, followed by the 'cruel suspense' (as she put it) of weeks of delay in the convoluted sea-and-land communications from India, came in the aftermath of post-Crimea military retrenchments. Suddenly, Cabinet penny-pinching was abandoned. The Commander-in-Chief of forces in India, General George Anson, was reported dead. Palmerston rushed a replacement, Sir Colin Campbell, who left the next day on the long voyage around the Cape to a situation which was bound to be very different when he arrived from anything he knew as he embarked.*

To the long history of mismanagement, incompetence, penuriousness, confused responsibility and indifference, already the source of embarrassment in the Crimea, were added, in India, guilt on the scale of the subcontinent. Ever since the reign of Elizabeth I, under the transparent cloak of a merchant company, Britain had exploited teeming subject races occupying vast tracts of southern Asia. The East India Company, prospering under a feudal royal charter and gradually relinquishing its political powers to the Crown, was still landlord and tax collector, and paid the bills for the British-officered army that maintained order. By the 1850s a Cabinet minister in London was overseeing the directors of the Company. The Governor General, ostensibly its appointee, was in fact designated by the government.

Beneath the unrelenting sun, Indians toiled for a few farthings a day, under Company and civil-servant employers for whom India was largely the safety valve for British excess population, from younger sons to superfluous daughters. Sepoys – Indian infantrymen serving under British officers in regiments supported by Company funds – represented five-sixths of the quarter of a million troops in India. The rest were in Queen's regiments, British in origin but in effect hired out to serve an Indian tour of duty.

---

* Although Albert's involvement in the suppression of the mutiny would always be indirect, Campbell had proved himself in the Crimea after the Prince had recommended him for the assignment.

Early in 1857 a rumour had raced among sepoy troops that the new rifles, lighter-weight Enfields, required greased cartridges, for which the manufacturer had used beef fat or – even worse – pork fat. Contact with either meant defilement for Moslems as well as Hindus – even rejection from the marital bed. (A related rumour – one that surfaced in Calcutta – was that at Queen Victoria's command, all sepoys would be baptized.) The concern about pollution with unclean grease was real; to save a few pennies, some British weapons manufacturers had substituted for the prescribed mutton fat (acceptable to Indians of any religion or caste but the strictest vegetarians) bullock's or hog's fat.

When, in April, some troops began to reject the defiled cartridges, eighty-five sepoys at the Meerut encampment near Calcutta were court-martialed for insubordination. Their sentences were ten years' hard labour – in chains – on roadbuilding crews. In the heat and dust of India it was, in effect, a death sentence, but there was never any doubt that General George Anson, commander-in-chief of the Indian Army, would confirm the verdicts. Yet Anson had already written to Charles Greville of his forebodings – that, according to Greville's diary, 'there is a strange feeling of discontent pervading the Indian Army from religious causes, and a suspicion that we are going to employ our irresistible power in forcing Christianity upon them. It is not true, but the natives will never be quite convinced that it is not, as long as Exeter Hall and the missionaries are permitted to have *carte blanche* and work their will as they please in those regions.' Exeter Hall was the London meeting place of Bible, religious tract, and missionary societies. The Liberals owed their majority to the evangelical vote.

How much of Anson's concerns were known in Whitehall made little difference until it became too late. And once Anson sanctioned the sentences, and the men were publicly fettered to warn off further dissidents, mutiny flared up – first as an attempt to free the prisoners. Violence spread across India.

In what seemed poetic justice, from the Indian standpoint, one of the first deaths – albeit from cholera – was that of General Anson. Epidemics and massacres would take more lives on both sides than conventional skirmishes, but at the start the British were losing the shooting war as well as the silent one. Through the early months of the uprising, as all the belated news from India remained bad, and as

Victoria feared for the lives of her subjects (Palmerston had once preached that the harming of a single British subject was *causus belli*), she vented her fury on her Prime Minister. 'The Queen must say', she wrote to him in exasperation on 25 August 1857, 'that the Government incur a fearful responsibility towards their country by their apparent indifference. God grant that no unforeseen European complication fall upon this country – but we are really tempting Providence.' To Leopold she confided that the affair was 'so much more distressing than the Crimea – where there was *glory* and honourable warfare, and where the poor women and children were safe... There is not a family hardly who is not in sorrow and anxiety about their children, and in all [social] ranks – India being *the* place where everyone was anxious to place a son!'

Ironically, Albert's promotion of a German Legion for Crimean deployment now proved useful. The East India Company had wanted four of its regiments, but negotiations faltered and the men not eager to return home with the promised £20 in discharge pay were shipped to South Africa. Thanks to the Legion's presence in Cape Colony, it became possible to rush British troops there, five thousand strong, to India.

The Queen considered herself 'a soldier's daughter', and from Osborne fired off to Palmerston memorandum after memorandum deploring the relapse in readiness which required sending troops just returned from 'most trying climates' back into action and urging the raising of additional battalions in England. The detailed messages revealed Albert's organizing hand. In his diary for 22 July he recorded, 'The Cabinet has at last adopted our suggestions for an increase in the army.' His first-person plural is revealing. As Albert wrote to Prince William of Prussia, the English public remained too smug about what was happening, largely because they knew too little, and 'the Ministry [was] *too* calm for my notions, and therefore we are constantly digging our spurs into their sides'. Not only did Albert want the desperate situation in India reversed; he wanted no perception of weakness to be exploited by governments on the Continent. The 'European complication' alluded to in Victoria's memorandum to Palmerston implied, in particular, the regime of her unreliable Crimean ally, Louis Napoleon.

India was more of a calamity than most outside India realized. As the carnage escalated – the British civilian population of East India

Company and Indian Army dependents were at risk – a visit by Napoleon III to Osborne was imminent. The Isle of Wight seemed a safe spot to rendezvous for a monarch who felt under constant threat of assassination, and he had requested the locale. Since Albert as a matter of policy kept state visits away from Osborne, he arranged an informal greeting at the dock with only the Queen and Prince and their children. As American Minister Dallas reported to Washington, 'prodigious pains' were taken to secure the 'personal safety' of Napoleon and Eugénie. 'Nothing was allowed, on the water, to approach within two miles of them. A body of Parisian detectives formed a cordon round them at a distance. And yet the eagerness of his Majesty to greet Prince Albert, when near the landing, led to his stumbling ...and falling heavily on the deck [of the *Reine Hortense*], thereby, as it is said, "grazing his face and shaking himself considerably".' Officially he had a bad fall 'on board' and was 'rather lame' on disembarking on 6 August.

For most of the 'private' visit Lord Clarendon was present for discussions, but before the Emperor returned on the tenth he had a private exchange with Albert. The Prince recorded its substance in a long memorandum which he sent to Stockmar, still his chief confidant, dictated to Princess Vicky 'as a lesson', his authorized biographer, Theodore Martin, later put it, 'in the political studies in which he had for some time been educating her'. The Emperor's unburdenings had disturbed Albert. From Napoleon's conspiratorial standpoint, all other Continental powers were duplicitous toward France, and he was worried most, he claimed, by hostile combinations seeking advantages. He wanted territorial revisions which would satisfy national appetites short of further war.

'If everybody were to get great advantages, where were they to come from?' Albert asked. 'Certainly not from within Europe.'

'That is why I always thought better means "*pour rendre de grands bienfaits au monde*" could be found out of Europe than within.' The Emperor would make '*un lac Européen*' by awarding countries segments of Africa and Asia fronting the Mediterranean made 'useless to humanity and civilization by their abominable governments. France herself wanted an outlet for her turbulent spirits.'

Diplomatically, Albert agreed that was 'a great improvement' over interfering with '*le vieux monde et la vieille société*', but he was disturbed by the inevitable impact of such ambitions on the Old World.

Napoleon III, he realized, could remain in power only by pandering to what the Emperor called the '*esprit de la nation*'. He claimed to prefer the more placid internal state of England, 'but it could not be imitated in France'. And he offered as a guarantee (Albert later told Baron Vitzthum) an offensive and defensive alliance which England's need for freedom of action would not allow. Albert was playing on a large stage, and knew he should not. Accordingly, he informed Palmerston of all the details, having committed England to nothing. Pleased, the Prime Minister conceded to Victoria, 'The Prince can say many things that we cannot.'

Departing, the Emperor bestowed gifts on servants, officials, and the royal children. Vicky and Alice received rings and bracelets, and the younger children were given lockets with wisps of Eugénie's carefully coiffed hair – a nineteenth-century practice now long lapsed. Tears flowed as a band played '*Partant pour la Syrie*' and the imperial guests – much like family, the Queen thought – were ferried back to the *Reine Hortense* in the early afternoon of 10 August 1857. Napoleon's guards and secret police quietly melted away.

They would be needed in Paris. Early the next year came an attempt on the Emperor by four Italian radicals who employed three bombs found to have been made in Birmingham. Ten bystanders were killed, 156 wounded. Napoleon and Eugénie were only slightly injured but two of their carriage horses died. The assailants had been exiles in England on friendly terms with such Liberal leaders as Gladstone. Although Palmerston cautiously did not reply to a French request to expel political fugitives, he prepared a bill to strengthen the conspiracy laws. Anti-British outrage orchestrated in the Parisian press, however, stiffened resistance in the Commons, and on a second reading the bill failed. To the unhappiness of Victoria and Albert, Palmerston would resign in February 1858, and a minority Ministry led by the diffident Derby and the distrusted Disraeli came in.

Early autumn in the Mutiny year of 1857 was a period of continuing calamities in India, of battalions sent too late to save Cawnpore and Lucknow, and of the spread of the uprisings. The Queen and Prince received the doleful tidings in the fastness of Balmoral because Victoria would not alter the calendar of her rounds. 'We are tortured by the events in India', Albert confided to Stockmar. '...The distance and the double government of Crown and Company make all remedial measures extremely difficult and slow. Our first considerable reinforcements will not arrive in India before the middle of October; our latest intelligence is dated August. What may not have happened in the interval!'* Friendly relations with France, however, speeded the task, as troops were permitted to debark in French-controlled Egypt and re-ship on the Red Sea side to continue into the Indian Ocean. Construction of the Suez Canal would only begin in 1859.

Realizing, as did Victoria and Albert, that overwhelming firepower would inevitably prevail, the Governor-General, Lord Canning, was already attempting to ensure tranquillity in reoccupied areas by conciliatory administration, although pilloried by newspapers at home as 'Clemency Canning'. The public wanted retribution for barbarism. The Queen and Prince preferred an end to the East India Company, and an efficiently organized new government, while Palmerston was unready to cross business interests, at least until the violence had subsided. But he was, Greville claimed on 8 October, having listened to Cabinet confidences from Earl Granville, Lord President of the [Privy] Council, 'on good terms with the Court, and behaves very well to the Queen, even with extraordinary deference, and she likes him well enough. The Queen is not clever, and everything is done by the Prince, who is to all intents and purposes King. She acts in everything by his inspiration and never writes a letter that he does not dictate every word of.'

Greville's litany of prejudices, fed from his listening posts at Court, both underrated the Queen's shrewdness and overestimated Albert's overtaxed capacities, which could not have been as prodigious as he and Lord Granville admiringly imagined them. The Prince remained human. Yet, Greville wrote, 'His knowledge and information are astonishing, and there is not a department of the Government regarding all the details and management of which he is not much better informed and more capable than the Minister at the head of it.'

---

* Greville noted on 2 November 1857, when the recapture of Delhi was telegraphed, 'All the advantages of the electric telegraphy are dearly paid for by the agonies of suspense which are caused by the long intervals between the arrival of general facts and of their particular details.'

Lord Clarendon, Greville noted on 19 October, was of much the same opinion. According to the Foreign Minister,

> the manner in which the Queen in her own name, but under the inspiration of the Prince, exercised her functions, was exceedingly good, and well became her position and was exceedingly useful. She held each Minister to the discharge of his duty and his responsibility to her, and constantly desired to be furnished with accurate and detailed information about all important matters, keeping a record of all the reports that were made to her, and constantly referring to them, e.g. she would desire to know what the state of the Navy was, and what ships were in readiness for active service, and generally the state of each, ordering returns to be submitted to her from all the arsenals and dockyards, and again weeks or months afterwards referring to these returns, and desiring to have everything relating to them explained and accounted for, and so throughout every department. In this practice Clarendon told me he had encouraged her strenuously. This is what none of her Predecessors ever did, and it is in fact the act of Albert, who is to all intents and purposes King, only acting entirely in her name. All his views and notions are those of a constitutional Sovereign, and he fulfils the duties of one, and at the same time makes the Crown an entity, and discharges the functions which properly belong to the Sovereign. I told C. that G[ranville] had told me the Prince had upon many occasions rendered the most important services to the Government, and had repeatedly prevented their getting into scrapes of various sorts. He said it was perfectly true, and that he had written some of the ablest papers he had ever read.

The insurrection in India was not yet put down when a financial panic erupted from the contagion of bank failures in the United States. Yet despite the proliferation of bankruptcies and bank closings across Britain, the panoply of the emergency recall of Parliament was as lavish as usual. On 3 December, wearing her crown and a velvet cloak trimmed in ermine, the Queen was escorted to the Lords by the Prince Consort, who then occupied a secondary throne to her left while Victoria read an address prepared by Palmerston's Ministers. On the twelfth, having enacted some stopgap measures, Parliament set itself free without having done anything about reordering the affairs of India, also mentioned in the Queen's Speech, and discussed at length earlier, at Windsor, with Victoria and Albert. By the time that Palmerston sent his draft for a future government of India to them, the Court had adjourned to Osborne for the Christmas season.

At Osborne, too, Albert worked further, no longer with his former enthusiasm, on the preparations for the royal wedding. Aware that Princess Vicky wept often about leaving home, he did not know that the doleful fact was known beyond the Court. Inwardly he wept himself, but he was outwardly optimistic about her brilliant expectations. Early in 1858 he wrote to his stepmother, the Dowager Duchess of Coburg, 'the last year has again brought so much trouble with it that one is glad to leave it behind. The new year begins for us with the separation from a beloved daughter, which will be especially painful to me. I do not, however, let any hint of this be seen, and I rejoice for her in the prospect of a happy future.'

Nearly a year after the marriage the Queen recalled, in a letter of 20 April 1859 to Vicky, 'that last night when we took you to your room, and you cried so much, I said to Papa as we came back "after all, it is like taking a poor lamb to be sacrificed" . . . I know that God has willed it so and that these are the trials which we poor women must go through; no father, no man can feel this! Papa never would enter into it all! As in fact he seldom can in my very violent feelings.'

After a festive fortnight of balls and levées, concerts and dinners, the wedding took place at St James's Palace on 25 January 1858. In the first carriage to leave Buckingham Palace were Prince Albert and King Leopold, both in the uniforms of English field marshals, with Princes Bertie and Alfred. The bride would walk in procession between Albert and Leopold as Fritz waited at the altar. After the ceremony, Prince and Princess Frederick – as they now were in Prussian style – proceeded from the chapel, arms linked, while Mendelssohn's Wedding March was played for the first time at an actual marriage.

Following a honeymoon of only two days – even more abbreviated than that of Victoria and Albert – the Court gathered at Windsor, where Frederick William was invested with the Garter. On 1 February, a snowy day, the Prince Consort and his two eldest sons accompanied Vicky, barely seventeen, and her husband to Gravesend, on the south bank of the Thames, from which they were to sail for Germany. Only an hour after they left, the Queen wrote the first of what would be 3,777 letters to her daughter, confessing how 'trying' it was to 'give up' a beloved child. The letters would be full of the trivia of everyday life, and Court gossip; and the Queen also warned her of the 'yoke of a married woman' – the 'sufferings and miseries and plagues – which you must struggle against – and enjoyments etc to give up – constant precautions to take . . .' But 'with a husband one worships' the married state was a 'foretaste of heaven'. The price, nevertheless, was that she had '9 times for 8 months to bear with those above-named enemies . . . and I own it tried me sorely . . . I think our sex a most unenviable one'. Cautionary words, however, had little impact in Vicky's bedroom, and she was soon pregnant. 'I hope Fritz would not bear for a minute what we poor slaves have to endure', the Queen would write unhappily.

From Albert, who always made an effort to conceal his feelings, would come an agonized letter to Vicky about their farewells at Gravesend. 'My heart', he confessed, 'was very full when yesterday you leaned your forehead on my breast to give free vent to your tears. I am not of a demonstrative nature, and therefore you can hardly know how dear you have always been to me, and what a void you have left behind in my heart: yet not in my heart, for there assuredly you will abide henceforth, as til now you have done, but in my daily life, which is evermore reminding my heart of your absence.'

From the royal yacht, already in Continental waters, the Princess confided to her father, whom she idolized,

My beloved Papa,
The pain of parting from you yesterday was greater than I can describe; I thought my heart was going to break when you shut the cabin door and were gone – that cruel moment which I had been dreading even to think of for two years and a half was past – it was more painful than I had ever pictured it to myself.

Yesterday evening I felt weighed down by grief, today though very melancholy I am able to think with more composure of all that has passed – and of all that is to come.

I miss you so dreadfully dear Papa, more than I can say; your dear picture stood near me all night, it was a comfort to me to think that I had even that near me. I meant to have said so much yesterday, but my heart was too full for words. I should have liked to have thanked you for all that you have done for me, for all your kindness. All your love etc. I shall most earnestly endeavour to deserve. To you, dear Papa, I owe most in this world. I shall never forget the advice it has been my privilege to hear from you at different times, I treasure your words up in my heart, they will have with God's help an influence on the whole of my life. You know dear Papa, how entirely you possess the deep confidence, reverence and affection of your child, who is proud to call herself such; and I may say of my husband too; and we feel secure and happy in the thought that you will never refuse us your precious advice, in anxious moments.

I feel that writing to you does me good, dear Papa, I feel that I am speaking to you, and though the feeling that I cannot see you or hear your dear voice in return makes the tears rise to my eyes, yet I am thankful that this is left to me. Goodbye, dearest Papa – I must end. Your most dutiful and affectionate daughter, Victoria

Duke Ernest would write coldly that 'with the Princess [gone] . . . my brother lost also a pedagogic occupation which had become dear to him, and which had exercised an extremely refreshing influence on his mind'. Ernest was without any perspective to measure the deprivation, which to Albert, who had managed his daughter's destiny, was a bereavement. For that, and other reasons farther into the year, the Prince began to feel that his life was over.

## XVI

# Royal Enterprises, Ltd

### *1858–1860*

I N THE EARLY weeks of 1858, at the time of the royal wedding, the Prince Consort's status under the Crown had stabilized at a very high level. The monarchy had become the corporate personality of Victoria and Albert, and with rare, and increasingly fewer, exceptions, maintained itself above politics. Although common law granted a wife the style and status of the husband, and the Queen had long battled for the gender equivalent for a husband in the Prince's case, both had settled for the 'Consort' title, and found it easily accepted. Albert recognized that whatever titular glory he lacked was more than balanced by his actual power. The xenophobia that had reared up as recently as the Crimean War was gone, and the succession nightmares of past reigns were, to the subjects of the sovereign, non-existent through the insurance of four princes of the blood royal. George Mifflin Dallas, the American Minister, would write to Washington that the Queen was preparing a bill to make Albert King Consort, but that rumour lacked credibility. He had a far more substantial role, and influence, and title, than the husband of a later queen and great-great-grandson of Victoria, would ever have.

That the one authentically Albertine royal sibling in the next generation could never reign in Britain was hardly realized outside the Royal Household. In the first month of the new year she was gone. Hardly had Princess Vicky left for Berlin before both Victoria and Albert recognized that her marriage would be to both a self-inflicted wound. A letter from the Queen to go to Vicky by messenger on 17

February 1858 noted at the start that it would contain matter 'which I do not wish to confide to the post'. Victoria had already been scolded by Albert for quoting him about the Prussian royal family in a letter which had gone by ordinary mail – 'an imprudent remark to go by the post', he warned, opening up vistas of spies and informers that were the natural condition of life in the militarist state to which they had consigned their daughter for her lifetime.

More self-inflicted pain followed on the heels of Vicky's departure. Arrangements were under way for Prince Alfred to go to sea on the *Euryalus*, to learn a midshipman's life. Born on 6 August 1844, he was well short of fourteen, but would not be needed unless something happened to his uncle in Coburg or to his elder brother. Prince Albert Edward, sixteen, desperately wanted to evade the navy, and requested learning the rudiments of officerdom in the army, although he knew he could not actively serve. He was promised some military experience, but Coburg-style education had to come first – and his confirmation.

Victoria had already urged upon Bertie the necessity of his becoming the first Albertine king. 'You may well join us', she wrote to him on his father's previous birthday, 'in thanking God for joining to us all your dearest, perfect Father... *None* of you [his offspring] can *ever* be proud enough of being the *child* of SUCH a Father who has not his *equal* in this world – so great, so good, so faultless. Try, all of you, to follow in his footsteps and don't be discouraged, for to be *really* in everything like him *none* of you, I am sure, will ever be. Try, therefore, to be like him in *some* points, and you will have *acquired a great deal.*'

It would not have been easy for any son to bestow affection and obedience on a father so beatified, and the fault here was Victoria's own, although Albert contributed by raising expectations that were beyond Bertie's capabilities. Even at Osborne and Balmoral, his lessons continued unslackened, and when his father entertained learned eminences, Bertie was brought forward to acquire, if only by osmosis, something from their conversation. And as Vicky was receding from life in the family orbit, Bertie was being prepared not only for confirmation but life apart – with tutors and managers – in White Lodge, Richmond Park, refurbished for him now that its occupant, George III's last surviving child, the Duchess of Gloucester, had died. Vicky had gone her own way after confirmation; it was now Bertie's destiny.

While he recoiled from Albert's carefully planned grooming, Victoria and Vicky were congratulating each other on the good fortune of having the Prince Consort for husband and father. But Vicky was almost a clone of her father – an unfortunate piece of ill-luck for a married woman in Prussia. 'You know, my dearest,' the Queen would write to her, 'that I can never admit any other wife can be as happy as I am – so I can admit no comparison for I maintain that Papa is unlike anyone who lives or ever lived and will live.' And Vicky would respond, 'I do not like to write all the foolish, mischievous things that are said and done [in Berlin]. I wish Papa could just be here for a little, he would see the whole thing in a moment.' To her father she expressed hope that she might surround Fritz and herself 'with good and useful people', for 'scales have fallen from my eyes on so many subjects'. She longed for a visit from him, to talk over 'a store of things'. She trembled to 'think of the awful scrapes I might get not only myself but my husband and mother-in-law into, if I had not your advice, dearest Papa . . .'

From Osborne on 4 March, while Victoria, who was seldom cold, shivered as a late winter wind off the Channel battered the windows and kept temperatures indoors to fifty, Albert posted Vicky's translation of the Prussian political monograph to Palmerston, who had just relinquished Downing Street to Derby's minority ministry. Now that he had 'a moment's leisure', the Prince wrote, there might be opportunity to read the 'peculiarly interesting' work. When it came to Vicky, Albert was a very proud Papa.

At Osborne and then Windsor, Bertie lacked no advice as the confirmation date approached. Examined by the Dean of Windsor in St George's Chapel on 31 March, the day before, he stolidly responded, and Albert was pleased, so he wrote to Stockmar, that the Dean 'prolonged' the questioning for 'a full hour'. Other than for its public demonstration of fidelity to the official faith, the ceremony remained meaningless for Albert. 'Love' for the God of clerical sermons, he told Victoria, who later (7 February 1862) told Vicky, was 'most preposterous'. For him 'the love for God was quite of a different kind – it was the trust and confidence in and adoration of a great, incomprehensible spirit'.

Following the post-confirmation reward of a fortnight's holiday with his tutor in Ireland, the Prince of Wales was established at White Lodge with three companions in their twenties, all 'distinguished' and 'moral' and 'accomplished'. Two had won Victoria Crosses in the Crimea. They would rotate monthly residence with Bertie, based upon a confidential memorandum from Albert about instructing his son in 'Appearance, Deportment and Dress', 'Manners and Conduct towards Others', and 'The Power to Acquit Himself Creditably in Conversation, or whatever May Be the Occupation of Society'. Bertie was to eschew gossip, cards and billiards, and devote some of his leisure time to music and the fine arts. In dress he was to avoid 'the frivolity and foolish vanity of dandyism'. In manners the primary attribute would be 'the absence of selfishness'. And he was to be 'scrupulously courteous, attentive, punctual...'

Albert was a model of efficiency. If high-minded rules and clockwork organization could transform the Prince of Wales into what a king should be, the result would have pleased Plato. And Albert, despite the slings and arrows of nearly two decades in public life, remained high-minded. When his brother offered to send him some writings by Machiavelli, Albert replied (10 July 1858) that he would read them but expected to dislike them. 'He who attacks the eternal laws of morality or who divides them, some for the subject, some for the state, and some for personal use, is the enemy of God and mankind and I should like to kill him.'

In Vienna, Prince Metternich, a disciple of Machiavelli now in enforced retirement, was discussing Albertine politics with Baron Vitzthum of Saxony, the ambassador observing that Albert had questioned whether Napoleon III could 'owe his crown at once to hereditary succession and universal suffrage. This contradiction is bound to be the ruin, I don't say of himself personally – perhaps he is destined to die an Emperor in his bed – but of his system, his dynasty. He has built nothing lasting; he is only a meteor – no fixed star.' Albert, said Metternich, had learned how to exploit for the monarchy the English system of an unwritten constitution, which he compared to a game of whist. 'The Crown's hand', he conceded, 'has not been played so well for a long time as it has been of late years.'

Vitzthum would visit Albert on a confidential matter and see his political pragmatism in action. The Saxon envoy had received a telegram from his sovereign asking whether the Queen could receive a visit from Prince George. 'Tell me honestly', Albert asked, 'what brings

Prince George here? Does he wish to see us or London?' Vitzthum attempted ambiguity, but Albert lacked little information, and rang for a calendar. He understood, and the Minister confirmed, that the Prince wanted private background information about the Portuguese Infanta before he agreed to an arranged marriage. (There was a Coburg connection. The Princess's father was Albert's cousin.)

'Then he will be in Paris at the end of March? On the 2nd of April is the confirmation of the Prince of Wales.* It is no use inviting a Roman Catholic Prince to that. On the 9th, you say, the Brazil steamer goes to Lisbon. That suits admirably. Please telegraph that we should be glad to welcome the Prince at Windsor from the 5th to the 9th of April...'

'All was, therefore, practically settled in three minutes. The way and manner of doing it was characteristic of the Queen's husband. He was completely master of the house, however much he concealed it from the public.'

At the Queen's dinner table nothing would be said to embarrass Prince George. Instead, Victoria and Albert offered the information desired – largely about any possible hereditary problems – to Vitzthum, and the Minister spoke privately to the Prince. 'We like the Prince extremely', said the Queen, an opinion that no doubt was transmitted to Portugal, 'and his noble bearing will certainly not fail to create an equally good impression in Lisbon'.

On the fourth morning after the departure of the Baron and Prince from Southampton on 9 April 1858, the steamer *en route* to Brazil docked in Lisbon harbour. The betrothal followed on the 17th.

Albert's efficiency, intellectuality and conscientiousness had fixed English attitudes toward him at the level of grudging respect. He had also earned esteem, but having never embraced the values of the English gentleman, that seemed denied him. The Royal Literary Fund dinner in the month of Prince George's visit was a case in point. Albert had chaired the event in the past, and was now a distinguished guest. The cause – to grant assistance to needy authors – was one he appreciated, and he looked forward to such literary occasions. Another place was set for a distinguished visiting author, Ivan Turgenev, who described the event in a St Petersburg paper.

---

* The Baron's memory was off by a day.

The once and future Prime Minister, Viscount Palmerston, presided in dignified fashion, proposing, at the start, the Queen's health, which was greeted by literally thumping cheers, as the attendees enthusiastically banged their plates and cutlery. Palmerston's address paid the expected tribute to literature, and noted that Victoria enjoyed reading books – a remark greeted by further cheers from an audience that, except for Albert, did not know that she seldom read a book, but had Albert or one of her ladies-in-waiting read to her. When Palmerston then referred to the Prince Consort, observing that no one could converse with him without having his mind improved as a result, the statement, meant in genuine regard, was received in utter silence. The Russian novelist took that as a sign of Albert's unpopularity, but it was more an indication of unease with his alien sensibility.

Despite Albert's foreign profile at home, he was seldom seen across the Channel except for rare family visits to Germany and the series of diplomatic journeys to France that would culminate with yet another, to Cherbourg, in August. When the Prince had last met with Napoleon III, General Aimable Jean Jacques Pelessier, who had stormed the fortress of the Malakoff at Sevastopol, was still in the Crimea. Since a role recognizing his reputation had to be found for him in peace, the Emperor had decided to impress London by making him ambassador there. The week after the Saxon ambassador left England for Portugal with his princely charge, Lord Malmesbury, again Foreign Minister under the Earl of Derby, escorted the short, plump Pelessier, who lacked all the social graces but was now ennobled as the duc de Malakoff, for an introductory audience with the Queen. 'He had never seen Prince Albert', Malmesbury noted in his diary for 16 April, 'and, as the Queen did not present him, he evidently took him for some lord-in-waiting, for he turned his back upon him whilst talking to the Queen. Suddenly it seemed to occur to him who the Prince was, for he turned towards him and exclaimed' "*Comment! c'est vous!*" and made a low bow. The Queen and Prince were much amused.'

Albert left for Coburg and Berlin immediately after Victoria's birthday in late May. He was inured to long rail journeys – to inspect factories and bases, or to open exhibitions or lay foundation stones – but May 1858 saw his first rail travel almost to the city of Coburg itself, as he changed trains at Bamberg for a special carriage to Lichtenfels, bringing with him a larger retinue than accompanied his day-trips in

England. Colonel Ponsonby and Dr Becker – his English and German secretaries, a courier, a valet, and three servants made the trip, which Albert promised to repeat with Victoria as soon as possible.

In Berlin he found that Vicky, who knew no more than her mother did on her marriage about postponing motherhood, was pregnant. No paragon of bedroom caution herself, the Queen was nevertheless appalled, writing to Vicky from London that it was 'horrid news', but to Vicky's mother-in-law, Crown Princess Augusta, Victoria lied that she was 'very happy'. Chastising Vicky for her professed pride in giving life to an immortal soul, the Queen, in a letter of 15 June which Albert did not see, described 'such moments' as 'our being like a cow or a dog'.

To be in London then, as was necessary for the parliamentary sessions, was to be immersed on the edge of a vast cesspool, which stank even more in sultry summer heat. The Household's month-long stay on the Isle of Wight in July was almost a flight. 'London', she explained to Augusta, 'is very unhealthy on account of the dreadful state of the Thames which smells so frightful that hardly anyone can live nearby.' The day before, the Queen and Prince, with Bertie, had braved the river at Deptford, an open drain now additionally malodorous, to inspect Brunel's still-unfinished *Leviathan,* the world's largest ship. She was 'longing for a rest' from public affairs, she told Augusta. Were it not her duty, she 'should like to retire to the country with my husband and children'. Confessedly, 'everyone has their duty and this of mine is not the hardest!' Albert, she did not add, performed many of the ceremonial aspects of the Crown for her.

Before departing for Cherbourg, Victoria had sent her daughter, who was attached to her Church of England faith, which she found less grim than Prussian Lutheranism, a book by George Combe, a non-believing phrenologist who had died the year before. That Combe had given lectures at Heidelberg only confirmed to Albert that analysis of the contours of the skull to determine a person's dispositions and talents was indeed a science. Albert was open to all advances in science.

Despite his passion for organization and control, in the summer of 1858 matters seemed to be flying apart. He had always experienced difficulty in delegating responsibilities, and now had too many of them. Nothing was done at Court without him, and the weak Derby government consulted him even more than did the fractious Palmerston ministry it succeeded. His red dispatch box went along with him everywhere, and a staff of secretaries and servants. Victoria's demands increased with his absences. She could not finish *Jane Eyre*. He had to read it to her. She attempted in turn to read *Barchester Towers* to Albert but found insufficient romantic interest, she explained to Vicky, to keep going, and disliked the emphasis on clerical characters.

Neither the Queen nor the Prince saw anything positive likely to emerge from the long-scheduled reciprocal visit to the self-aggrandizing Emperor of the French, yet to call it off would further fan anti-English feeling. 'But we are pressed by the Emperor and our Ministers', Albert explained to Ernest on 10 July, 'to go to Cherbourg. As the festivities there, in reality, include a glorification of the army and navy against England, we do not intend to take part in them. We shall leave before they begin and only pay a personal visit.'

The visit became more than that because the government could not be seen as alarmed at a time when Napoleon III was plotting with Prime Minister Cavour of Sardinia to liberate northern Italy from Austrian domination, while sabre-rattling to keep England and Prussia timid and neutral. Ostensibly the French festivities were to open the new rail link between Paris and Cherbourg, the potential military significance of which was obvious. The Emperor was also to unveil a statue to the first Napoleon. Representing their government, Malmesbury and Disraeli were present, Derby being again ill with gout. The Duke of Cambridge and Admiral Lord Lyons represented the military, and thirty MPs the people. To promote Anglo-French friendship, 140 private English yachts crowded Cherbourg harbour as Victoria and Albert steamed across the Channel on 19 August, the Prince reading *Jane Eyre* to the Queen below decks until the low clouds lifted. Toward sunset the skies cleared and turned golden, illuminating the naval fortifications, some still under construction, which gave the scene a more unpleasant look than the Isle of Wight. In the spirit of Osborne, the royal family had brought their eldest children, who did, indeed, sightsee picturesque farmhouses and châteaux, but Napoleon was eager to show off battle-ships and fortresses, and Eugénie contributed a complaint about the hostility of English newspapers. Albert tactfully explained the lack of constraints upon a free Press, which was a bulwark of English liberties.

Despite discussions of furthering the *bonne entente*, Albert noted in his diary, 'I am conscious of a change in the Emperor'. The attempted assassination – by Italians – had reinforced Napoleon's conviction that

Italy had to be united if only to defuse one source of anti-Bonaparte hostility. If that undermined Austria, which clung to its Italian provinces, both Prussia and Russia would be pleased. Albert recognized that England, as a naval power, faced problems with an expansionist Italy. Malta lay within the likely ambitions of Victor Emmanuel and, like Gibraltar, was a non-negotiable base for the Royal Navy in the Mediterranean.

Warm toasts of friendship were exchanged with Napoleon aboard and on shore, and the parting would again be friendly, but now only ostensibly so, with the Emperor assuring France's 'unalterable devotion to the English alliance'. If so, Albert wondered, what was the reason for such formidable and unpacific investment along a coast opposite which was only England? Writing to Stockmar on 21 August 1858, he described Cherbourg as 'a gigantic [military] work that gives one grave reflection'. The visit dramatized disturbing inadequacies at home almost inevitable in a liberal state that armed only in emergencies, and refused to tax itself in order to maintain a constant state of preparedness, or to reform its outmoded administration of the army and navy. England considered itself a first-rate military power, as Cecil Woodham-Smith would put it, 'on the memory of Trafalgar and Waterloo'.

The Queen and Prince returned to Osborne only to prepare to leave again to visit Vicky in a Berlin changing as a result of the mental breakdown of the Prussian king, and his effective replacement in the business of government by Fritz's father, Prince William. Reflecting more and more the conservatism of the Prussian ethos, he no longer seemed an improvement, while Frederick William IV, Albert wrote to Ernest, was a 'ruin' although 'he behaves as a King'. Berlin was, to the Queen, 'sickeningly' hot every day, but there was no allowance for that in the proliferation of parades and reviews in stiff military dress, ostensibly in their honour.

The 26th August, the Prince Consort's thirty-ninth birthday, was celebrated in Potsdam. Victoria gave Albert all the children's birthday letters prepared before they had left Osborne. 'Blessed day!' the Queen wrote in her journal. Both Ernest and Stockmar arrived for the event, and Vicky brought a cake with as many candles on it as years, as was the Prussian custom. The Glienecke Bridge was illuminated, salutes fired, and healths drunk.

'*Der Abscheid sehr schmerzlich*,' Albert noted the next day in his diary – 'the parting [was] very painful'. He kept to himself his anxieties that he might never see Vicky again. The prospect of childbirth was disquieting – she was small and still seventeen – and he was sensing signs of mortality in himself, these apparent to no one but Stockmar, who was not only a father figure but a former physician. His unease predated Cherbourg and Potsdam but it was in Cherbourg, on 12 August, Victoria wrote, that 'While I was dressing, Albert came in, quite pale, with a telegram [from London], saying "My poor Cart is dead, having died quite suddenly." ... I turn quite sick now writing about it ... I burst into tears. All day long the tears would rush every moment to my eyes.' Isaac Cart, long devoted to Albert's service, 'was the only link my loved one had about him which connected him with his childhood ... I cannot think of my dear husband without Cart ... We had to choke down our grief all the day.'

Albert's disappointments in the failure of his eldest son to be Albertine were more than balanced by the frustrations of Albert Edward in failing, even, to want to live up to expectations. He had no intellectual interests, and would have preferred the military career his new brother-in-law in Prussia had managed. That the cultures were different was never explained to Bertie, although his father understood, writing to Ernest (22 April 1858) that it was 'to be regretted' that Fritz had 'taken up the game of soldiering'. It was 'not astonishing in a member of his family and a subject of his country. A good feeling lies at the bottom of this inclination, that of a longing for a manly occupation, duty and self-sacrifice, in the service of the state.' Otherwise the Prince had 'absolutely nothing to do and as affairs are at present, I do not know what [else] he should do'.

Prince Frederick William, however, was as old as the combat-tested officers seconded to Bertie, ambitious young men whose careers were being interrupted at Albert's order. Bertie was still half a child, and Albert sought for signs of maturation that would renew hope for the monarchy. Lessons and lectures, concerts and exhibitions bored him, however, as much as they did his escorts, but since his sister was married when hardly past seventeen, he looked forward to his birthday on 9 November, when he expected some further allocation of freedom, and to a promised visit later in the month to Vicky in Berlin. In London, vast Marlborough House was being refurbished to become his London home. Ironically, it had been a private picture gallery.

On 9 November he received a birthday letter from his parents, written by Albert, which ostensibly emancipated him from their authority. He was to have an annual income, to start, of five hundred pounds beyond all necessary household expenses. It further explained that however severe he thought his education had been, its only object had been his growth into a proper heir apparent. His tutor, Frederick Gibbs, was to be replaced by a governor, Colonel – soon General – Robert Bruce. ('Poor Mr. Gibbs', the Queen wrote to Vicky, 'leaves tomorrow. He has failed completely the last year and a half with Bertie.')

Bertie's military aspirations were to be fulfilled by gazetting him a lieutenant-colonel (unattached) without duties. On ceremonial occasions he could wear a uniform. It was an unearned push that he would resent, but the Queen had a morbid fear of mortality, and would confide in Vicky early the next year, 'Oh dear, what would happen if I were to die next winter! One trembles to think of it. It is too awful a contemplation.' The problem as she saw it was Bertie's 'laziness'. Even 'the greatest improvement, I fear, will never make him fit for his position. His only safety – and the country's – is his implicit reliance in everything on dearest Papa, that perfection of human beings!'

Yet Albert Edward resisted any reliance on his father, whose freedom document enjoined the Prince to liberate himself 'from the thralldom of abject dependence' upon servants, and to become 'a good man and a thorough gentleman', goals which he would find at odds with each other. He was 'to do unto men as you would they should do unto you'. And it concluded in true Albertine fashion, 'Life is composed of duties', which were to be performed in a 'punctual and cheerful manner'.

Bertie took the letter to Gerald Wellesley, the Dean of Windsor, thrust it at him, and burst into tears.

On 17 November, three days before the Prince of Wales was to leave with Colonel Bruce and Major Teesdale for Prussia, Albert wrote to Vicky, 'Do not miss any opportunity of urging him to hard work . . . Unfortunately, he takes no interest in anything but clothes, and again clothes . . . I am particularly anxious that he should have some mental occupation in Berlin. Perhaps you could let him share in some of yours, lectures, etc . . . ' However, he returned three weeks later recalling happily only a round of parties and balls, an atmosphere in which he thrived. 'Bertie has a remarkable social talent', Albert conceded to Vicky while her brother was still visiting. 'He is lively, quick and sharp when his mind is set on anything, which is seldom ... But usually his intellect is of no more use than a pistol packed in the bottom of a trunk if one were attacked in the robber-infested Apennines.'

The Apennines were on the Prince Consort's mind as he intended to send Bertie to Italy on his return to study art, archaeology, and the affairs of troubled parts of Europe. He was to keep a journal for Albert's perusal, and it was predictable that both his parents would find it uninspired and error-ridden. 'I am very sorry that you were not pleased with my Journal', Bertie apologized to his father, 'as I took great pains with it, but I see the justice of your remarks and will try to profit by them.' Albert was left with nothing further to admonish, and Bertie would go on into north Italy in 1859 only to encounter war between misnamed Sardinia and Austria, and the expected intervention of France on the side of King Victor Emmanuel, who reigned over Piedmont from Turin. The British warship *Scourge*, sailing from Malta, would evacuate Bertie and his party to Gibraltar, where he confessed – but not to his father – 'plenty of larking', and then to Lisbon, where the king, Pedro V, was a young cousin.

Not ready yet to give up on moulding Bertie into a proper heir apparent, Albert had further plans for him – a summer (1859) stay at the University of Edinburgh to cram for Oxford in the autumn, where he would enter in the undemanding category of 'nobleman'. Only one thing was certain, Albert told his brother on 18 November 1858 – that the Prince of Wales 'is not to be in London during the [social] Season, as long as he is neither fish nor flesh, as the old saying is. It would not be good for him.'

With mortality on his mind, Albert became more searching about religion, reading, in November 1858, Charles Kingsley's *Two Years Ago*, and praising to Vicky its 'insight into the relations between man, his actions, his destiny and God'. The next year he had the Queen appoint Kingsley as one of her chaplains, and arranged to have him tutor Bertie on history. Albert also read *On the Mind*, by Richard Whately, Anglican Archbishop of Dublin, a near-agnostic who minimized theology and emphasized morals; and he was drawn to the religious questioning in Anthony Trollope's *Barchester Towers* and George Eliot's *Adam Bede*. He awaited with some dread the accouchement of Vicky in January, for she had caught her foot in a chair in September in the old Schloss in

Berlin, and fallen hard to the parquet floor. She would not tell 'dearest kindest Mamma' but she did inform her father.

Confiding in her mother was a risky matter in any event, and Stockmar delicately raised the matter of the Queen's attempting to dictate to a married daughter who was in a delicate condition and sensitive position. Albert cautiously raised the issue with Victoria, and it emerged that Stockmar had intervened with the Prince. The Queen was furious, and Albert left the room to avoid a scene certain to be overheard, and to write his response:

> You have again lost your self-control quite unnecessarily. I did not say a word which could wound you, and I did not begin the conversation, but you have followed me about and continued it from room to room. There is no need for me to promise to *trust* you, for it was not a question of trust, but of your fidgety nature, which makes you insist on entering, with feverish eagerness, into details about orders and wishes which, in the case of a Queen, are commands, to whomever they may be given. This is your nature; it is not against Vicky, but it is the same with everyone and has been the cause of much unpleasantness for you. It is the dearest wish of my heart to save you from these and worse consequences, but the only result of my efforts is that I am accused of want of feeling, hard heartedness, injustice, hatred, jealousy, distrust, etc. etc. I do my duty towards you even though it means that life is embittered by 'scenes' when it should be governed by love and harmony. I look upon this with patience as a test which has to be undergone, but you hurt me desperately and at the same time do not help yourself.

Victoria had little idea why, at thirty-nine, Albert looked like a man of sixty. At Balmoral that autumn he seemed paunchy and overweight. His hair had receded, and his sidewhiskers had grown heavier, and he took to wearing a wig on chilly mornings. Her zealous policing of fireplaces added to his miseries, and he confessed to his daughter early on one cold morning, 'Mama will be much hurt when she gets up and finds I have a fire lit.' Yet he loved his work, and knew he was doing his job well, the job he had created for himself. '*Lese recht aufmerksam, und sage wenn irgend ein Fehler da ist!*' he would instruct the Queen about draft memoranda – 'Read carefully, and tell me if there is any fault in this!'

Or '*Ich hab' Dir hier ein Draft gemacht, lese es mal! Ich dachte es wäre recht so*' – 'Here is a draft for you; read it. I should think this will do.'

Her 'beloved and perfect Albert', the Queen wrote to Leopold, forgetting her occasional rages at her husband, 'had raised monarchy to the *highest* pinnacle of respect, and rendered it popular beyond what it *ever* was in this country'. More wishful thinking than reality, it was nevertheless a reflection of the upward swing of the pendulum of popular appeal to which a foreign war, a colonial insurrection and a dynastic marriage had contributed.

The early winter was a time of waiting for news from Berlin, which came on the morning of 27 January 1859, when a telegram arrived that the Princess Royal 'had been for some time indisposed'. That afternoon came the news that 'the young Prince' had been born, and toasts were drunk across England as well as Prussia.

No one in England sensed a catastrophe. Vicky's pregnancy had been difficult, and in her final months, when, barely eighteen and away from home, the Princess was sunk in gloom, the Queen sent her own mid-wife, Mrs Innocent, to restore some confidence and to be available if labour came unexpectedly early. It did, but the doctors in attendance failed to get an urgent message to Professor Eduard Martin in Berlin, who was on call, about the prolonged, exhausting labour that began in the first hours of 26 January and did not end until the next day. By the time that Martin arrived, mother and child appeared to be dying.

It was a breech birth; Vicky was in great agony. To the distress of the Court physicians, Martin applied chloroform. Both mother and infant came through the ordeal, but only the next day did Mrs Innocent notice the state of the baby's left arm, which had been torn loose from its socket during the bungled delivery. Although the doctors assured Vicky that the damage was temporary, Prince Frederick William Albert Victor (in 1888 he would become Wilhelm II) would have a withered arm, a defect that would warp his personality. Since he was immediately known as William, and inevitably Willy, to avoid confusion with his father and with the King, Albert speculated to Fritz about what poster-ity 'will attach to his name'. He hoped for 'the Great' – as 'there is none with this designation'.

Victoria and Albert could not attend the christening. Parliament was to open with the Queen's Speech on 3 February 1859. Reports from France suggested an imminent war with Austria to assist Italian unification, and, if Prussia came to Austria's aid, an attempt to occupy its Rhenish provinces. The Speech appealed for 'preservation of the general peace', but included the Cabinet's request for large expenditures to put the navy entirely under steam. Albert noted his apprehensions in his diary; Victoria, writing to Leopold in Brussels, predicted that a Prussian war would cost Napoleon his crown.

On 9 February, Albert visited the new public school named for the late Duke, Wellington College, to present the school with a gift of books for its library. Although its charter permitted admission of boys from all walks of life, it was intended particularly for needy sons of army officers who had died in the line of duty. Albert was chairman of the governing board and had, characteristically, designed the school uniform, which E.F. Benson, son of the young first headmaster, E.W. Benson, claimed, 'remarkably resembled that of the porters and ticket-collectors of the Southern Railway – then the Reading–Reigate line – on which Wellington College was situated. It gave rise to little confusions.' (The Earl of Derby once gave the outward half of his return ticket to a student.)

The fervidly High Church headmaster believed in three Chapel services a day to improve his boys, as well as a daily Bible-study class, and permitted only devotional books to be borrowed from the library on Sundays, prompting the Prince to ask Benson 'whether there may not be excessive employment in Religious Exercise in the present system of the College'. Benson replied that he thought not.

Libraries, although not of the Bensonian variety, meant much to Albert, who had just built out of his personal funds a library at Aldershot for the use of young officers, with its emphasis upon military history and technology. Readiness had become an obsession. He worried that Prussia, and possibly Coburg and Gotha, would be drawn in. 'The Emperor Napoleon', Albert wrote to his brother the next day, 'appears bent on producing the storm, and much blood will flow, amongst which a great deal of noble German blood. When, and how, we here are to be drawn into the vortex, I am unable to calculate. But, that we shall not be able to escape it in the long run, this I consider certain.'

The German states, Albert advised Ernest early in March, when Austria was proposing some withdrawals from Italy in the interest of peace, should do nothing warlike unless the Emperor attacked the Rhine. In the end it was not Napoleon, despite his seeking war, who was the aggressor, nor even ambitious Sardinia. Determined to rescue its position through a pre-emptive strike, Austria made the first move. Predicting it in his weekly letter to King Leopold on 19 April, Albert wrote, 'The Austrians seem bent on beginning the war, no doubt hoping to strike a decisive blow before the French can appear upon the field – a very hazardous venture, and one the issue of which is scarcely to be brought within the rules of probability. Here it will turn public opinion at a stroke against Austria and in favour of Sardinia.'

A foreshadowing of the imperial tragedy of 1914, Austria issued an ultimatum to King Victor Emmanuel at Turin demanding the disarmament of his troops. An impossible condition, and intended to be so, it was rejected, and the Piedmont was invaded. As expected, France mobilized against Austria, and Prussia mobilized against France, but only France entered the war. Prince William of Prussia, as Regent, used the emergency as an excuse to extend conscription; to increase the regular army, reducing the influence of the *Landwehr* (citizen army – an equivalent to the British Territorials); and to militarize every possible aspect of government. Albert's dreams of a constitutional Prussia were ending hardly a year after Vicky's marriage.

Although the Prince's first thoughts were of his daughter, he was overwhelmed by other concerns. 'My greatest of all anxieties', the Queen wrote to Vicky, 'is that dearest Papa works too hard, wears himself out by all he does. It makes me often miserable. If it were not for Osborne and Balmoral and then again at Windsor at Easter – I don't know what we would do...' She had become more activist as a result of the Crimea and the Mutiny, and – internally – the Cabinet instability that seemed now chronic. Yet regardless of where the Court relocated, Albert brought worries with him that went beyond the red dispatch boxes. Not only overwork was taxing his health.

There was a single bright day that spring in which the ego he was forced by his role to submerge was permitted a brief and rewarding exposure. Having opened in the Queen's name hundreds of events and edifices, on 2 May, at the broad estuary of the Tamar which separates Devon from Cornwall, the Prince formally opened the Royal Albert Bridge, a long arc that was centrepiece of the new Cornwall Railway, which required in its sixty-mile stretch seven tunnels and forty-three viaducts. Suspension cables from a mid-river pier supported on either side spans of 455 feet that represented nearly half of the bridge's 2240-foot length. Fifteen minutes after noon, booming cannon announced

*Albert being greeted as he opens the Cornwall Railway's Albert Viaduct, 2 May, 1859.*
(Illustrated London News)

the arrival of the royal train on the Plymouth side of the approaches. A
battery on the Saltash shore fired a second salute as the train proceeded
westward into Cornwall. There his Royal Highness alighted and, as was
his practice, minutely inspected the bridge while crowds on both sides
cheered.

The builder, Isambard Kingdom Brunel, his friend of Crystal Palace
days, only fifty-three, was dying of kidney failure, and unable to share
the acclaim. A few days later, lying in a couch placed on a carriage
truck, he crossed his last bridge. He died of a stroke on 15 September
1859, ten days after he staggered away from a final look at his *Great
Eastern* – the renamed *Leviathan* – which was about to sail on its
maiden voyage, to Holyhead on the Welsh shore of the Irish Sea. No
one had better epitomized Victorian-era engineering genius.

There would be other Albert Bridges, the one most associated with
the Prince's name the neo-Gothic span of 1874 opened by the Queen.
Inspired, perhaps, by ships' masts in the Thames, it would link Chelsea
and Battersea in the western reaches of London.

Victoria would write to the Princess Royal that 'poor dear Papa' was
'very much fagged' yet would have to make the early morning journey

and return 'the same night at one'. She did not accompany him. On 2 May as Albert clattered westward to Cornwall, the Queen wrote a long response to the eighty-fourth letter written to her by the unhappy and lonely Vicky. It did not help that Victoria assured her daughter that Papa could not 'enter into Fritz's ecstasy' about the infant Willy. Albert only felt warmly toward infants, she claimed, 'after a certain age if they are nice'. The Queen's own distaste (she considered babies little more than frogs and 'frightful when undressed') seemed deflected on to the warmer parent.

The reported death of the universal German genius Alexander von Humboldt, Victoria added, 'has deeply, deeply grieved us' – but very soon after, Humboldt's letters to writer and diplomat Karl Varnhagen von Ense (who had died the year before) were published, including one of 27 February 1847 in which he quoted Albert as telling him, on their meeting at Stolzenfels, 'I know you feel great compassion for the Poles under the Russian sceptre; but I am sorry to say, the Poles are as little deserving of our sympathy as the Irish.' He was, Humboldt explained to Varnhagen, 'severe only to the mighty ones of the earth, and this man impressed me very uncomfortably...' Among other lapses, Albert had read, in Humboldt's *Kosmos,* the metaphorical 'star-carpet' as 'star-terraces'. With Prussian snobbery, Varnhagen was told that it was 'a Coburg variation from my text, and *quite English* from Windsor, where there are nothing but Terraces'. To Humboldt, whose scientific writings the Prince (a former provincial) had praised, perhaps overly much, he was only 'the handsome husband of the Queen'. When the letters appeared in an English translation in 1860, Albert was briefly embarrassed. Offhand confidences had returned to haunt him before. Still, he dismissed the matter to Vicky as of no consequence, 'for what does one not write or say to his intimate friends under the impulse of the moment?'

In subsequent letters to her daughter, Victoria distracted the Princess Royal from self-pity by employing her to shop among eligible Protestant princesses for a bride for Bertie, as the Queen herself was exploring possible husbands for Alice, for a betrothal following her confirmation. Unable to bring the infant Prince Willy to visit – Prussian doctors ruled against it – Vicky, as soon as permitted, paid an emotional visit to Osborne late in May. Because of the troubled European situation, Victoria and Albert had to put off a return visit to see their first grandchild until the next year. The day before Vicky's arrival, 20 May 1859, the Austrians began paying for their arrogance with a defeat at Montebello. Further disasters followed at Magenta on 4 June and Solferino on 24 June. A revolt in Florence created what would become a predictable Italian solution – its puppet duke changed sides. 'All Italy is now up', Lord Malmesbury wrote from the Foreign Office. Seeing that, the unpredictable Napoleon III concluded a separate peace with Austria at Villafranca on July 8, having extracted what he wanted from the war.

Albert's cousin Alexander Mensdorff-Pouilly, an Austrian cavalry general on the scorching plains of Solferino, wrote to Ernest bitterly of the administrative incompetence of his side, which had snatched defeat from the jaws of victory. 'May the manes of the many fallen', he fulminated, 'sometimes appear in the dreams, and disturb the night's rest, of those who are meanwhile sitting comfortably at their writing desks, and laying political addle[d] eggs'.

In both peace and war the Emperor had deceived Albert, who broke off all attempts at friendly relations. Early that summer, however, the minority Derby ministry collapsed and the francophile Palmerston was back, his dream of a unified Italy apparently realized. Yet to the Prime Minister's disappointment, the Villafranca terms excluded Venetia and reinstalled Austrian puppet regimes in Modena and Tuscany. Despite the expanse of Austria's sprawling and multilingual European domains, the internally weak empire, like Ottoman Turkey, had to be propped up as a bulwark to Russian expansion, Prussian ambitions, and French designs. 'Germany ought to be heartily glad of it', Albert wrote acidly to his brother, 'and would be so, if she herself had contributed something toward this result'. What was saved for Austria, the Prince implied, was some role in the balance of Continental power. England's interest, at least, was to prevent any nation from dominating Europe. 'Prussia's situation', he continued, 'is excessively disagreeable and dishonourable. Palmerston is furious that his victim has escaped him, and his bosom friend has led him by the nose.'

To Palmerston, Albert drafted an ironic note for Victoria to copy in her own hand – that 'She is glad to be relieved by the happy news of the concluded Peace'. Feeling deceived by Napoleon, Palmerston protested to the French, sending a copy to the Queen, and again Albert drafted a tart message to the Prime Minister for Victoria's signature:

The Queen returns to Lord Palmerston the copy of his letter ... The effect of placing Austria in an Italian confederation will certainly be to legalise that influence for the future, the supposed illegal exercise of which was put forward as one of the conditions of peace bought by much blood and the loss of a rich province by Austria. We did not protest against the war and Lord Palmerston personally wished France success in it; we can hardly now protest against the peace, and Lord Palmerston will, the Queen is sure, see the disadvantage which would accrue to this country should he make it appear as if to persecute Austria was a personal object with the first minister of the Crown.

The Queen is less disappointed with the peace than Lord Palmerston appears to be, as she never could share his sanguine hopes that the '*coup d'état*' and the 'Empire' could be made subservient to the establishment of independent nationalities and the diffusion of liberty and constitutional government on the Continent. The Emperor follows the dictates of his personal interests and is ready to play the highest stakes for them, himself entirely uncontrolled in his actions; we are cautious, bound by considerations of constitutional responsibility, morality, legality, etc. – our attempts therefore to use him for our views must prove a failure (as the Russian peace has shown before) and exposes us rather to be made his dupes ...

Although royal impatience with Palmerston had returned, both Prince and Prime Minister would again mellow – but not before the affair of the new Foreign Office building. During the Derby interregnum, Sir Gilbert Scott, Albert's choice as architect, had been commissioned to design the edifice, and did so in the neo-Gothic style admired by the Prince. Despite Albert's patronage, and the advanced state of the plans, Palmerston vetoed them in favour of Regency neo-classicism, the style fashionable when he first came into the government. In the Commons, without mentioning Albert, he railed against the 'hideous Gothic structure' likely to be confused with a European cathedral. Forced to give way, but not give up on his concept, Scott took his design to the directors of the Midland Railway, friends of Albert's since Crystal Palace days, who adapted it for the St Pancras Railway Station, now considered a jewel of mid-Victorian architecture.

Despite the Queen's many messages to Palmerston and to ministers, all in what was clearly her own voice as they had heard it in many audiences, they knew that Albert was a superb mimic and her signature was often a convenient fiction. In return they often wrote directly to Albert, implying that their confidential letters to him were in effect to her informal private secretary. Reports of Cabinet meetings usually went directly to Albert rather than to the Queen. The increase in military readiness was also seen as accomplished under pressure from Albert. Although Panmure was supportive as Minister for War, Gladstone as Chancellor of the Exchequer was reluctant to part with an extra penny. Under Albert's pressure, a Volunteer Defence Force, first proposed by the Prince during the Crimean crisis, was funded by Parliament, and Victoria, now wary of her former friend across the Channel, was delighted. 'Fritz would have been surprised', she wrote to Vicky, 'to see 18,000 volunteers marching at Aldershot like the finest troops, many of the best-educated people, peers, gentry, [and] artists in the ranks.'

For Albert there was, now, almost always a physical price. After the heat of manœuvres, the Queen wrote to Vicky from Osborne, on 24 August 1859, 'Monday and yesterday at Aldershot and here were really fearful. Poor dear Papa had one of his stomach attacks on Monday, which made him look fearfully ill, but he remained in the field in that broiling sun the whole time and said he was all the better for it. He is however not quite right yet. He is so fagged and worked...' She blamed, without identification, since Vicky would understand the sly references to Palmerston and Russell, 'our 2 Italian Masters'. But Albert's recurrent 'stomach attacks' had nothing to do with European politics. For several days at Osborne he could keep down only milk and water, and fainted while attempting to dress. Rudolph Löhlein was alarmed; Albert attributed his weakness and subsequent 'malaise' – his description to Vicky – to 'worry about political affairs'.

On the evening of 29 August, three days after Albert's fortieth birthday, the Court left for Balmoral. From there he was to go on the fourteenth to the annual meeting of the British Association for the Advancement of Science at Aberdeen. A day and night *en route* were to be spent in Edinburgh, largely to consult with the Prince of Wales's frustrated tutors. (They spoke highly of him, of course.) Albert had been preparing his address to the Association for weeks, intending to make a major statement. At the close of the conference on 22 September many delegates were to be the Queen's guests at a Highland fête.

The royal railway journey to Edinburgh was his first by sleeping-car, an advance in travel technology. Albert had a specially designed carriage built at his and Victoria's expense. By 1859 their journey to Scotland was a precise operation. The line and stations were kept clear of other trains half an hour before the royal special was due, and all traffic in its vicinity stopped until the pilot locomotive following the train had passed. At stations where it was scheduled to stop, the public – according to a regulation meant largely for daylight hours – had to remain behind barriers, to prevent crowds from thronging near the halted carriages. At Edinburgh the train was shunted to a secondary line that would take the party to Braemar, where coaches waited to transport the royal family and suite to Balmoral. For the others the trip remained as exhausting as ever. There was only one sleeping car.

'I read thick volumes, write, perspire and tear what I have written into shreds', Albert claimed to Vicky before leaving for Scotland. *Punch* had already published a facetious 'Sights worth seeing in the metropolis' column which included 'Albert's night light. It could be seen without charge, when his Royal Highness is going to bed, by looking at Buckingham Palace...any night between the hours of eleven and six the next morning'. Looking from St James's Park it was 'on the third story, in the thirteenth and fourteenth windows, counting from the tail of the Duke of Wellington's statue'. The Prince's light, however, was often a reading lamp, which he used late at night and in the early post-dawn bleakness. He was making up for the hours snatched by ceremony.

Albert would be away from the Queen in Edinburgh only two days, which Victoria occupied in his absence, in crisp, sunny weather, with ghillies and her ladies in ascending Morven, and then Lochnagar, but to her uncle Leopold she bemoaned, in a letter, feeling 'so lost without him'.

As the Association's president for the year, Albert spoke to an audience of 2,500 for nearly an hour, accepting the honour because 'I felt that I could, from the peculiar position in which Providence has placed me in this country, appear as the representative of that large public, which profits by and admires your exertions, but is unable actively to join them.' Whatever the meanness of spirit he had encountered so recently and posthumously from Alexander von Humboldt, he introduced his name as the example of the need for science and government to work together, and for governments to heed the counsel of scientists. Humboldt's 'personal influence with the Courts and Government of most countries in Europe', Albert observed, 'enabled him to plead the cause of Science in a manner which made it more difficult for them to refuse than grant what he requested'.

The Prince sought more statesmen of Science, and also praised the Association for its encouragement of scientific interdisciplinarity by making it possible for investigators in any area to take part in discussions, learn of relevant ideas and problems, and meet their 'brethren'. Science, he hoped, would be less a province of pedants 'jealously guarding the mysteries of their profession'.

Albert was not only addressing a cause, and an audience, in which he had a genuine interest: he was shaping the modern monarchy. In letters to Ernest, who was more a sounding board than a sincere listener, and believed that people needed, for their own good, a proper dose of authoritarianism, Albert prophesied that European monarchies would either mesh into democratic systems, or disappear. As he watched the political and constitutional powers of the monarchy irreversibly wane, he redesigned its role on the traditional concern of the Crown for the well-being of the people. Without that commitment, the monarchy's relevance as national symbol would vanish. It was not enough, he saw, to cut ribbons and lay foundation stones and be titular patron of charities. Relevance meant responsibility, and he was wearing himself out at making the democratic monarchy meaningful.

On the twenty-second, two hundred scientists came to Balmoral for the afternoon to watch Highland games, unfortunately amid showers alternating with sunshine. After their departure the family had two more weeks in Scotland, disturbed by news of colonial setbacks in China that sent the Minister in Residence, Lord Elgin, twice back to London for Cabinet meetings. The third of the 'opium wars', it was ostensibly to defend the opening of trade, and there were neither scientists nor philosophers to excoriate opium's immoralities. To Britain, which had to fight off the angry Chinese with heavy French assistance, Victoria expressed the prevailing mood when she worried that 'in Eastern Asia[, France] will be looked on as the stronger Power'.

By mid-October the royal family was back at Windsor, where Albert, unable to conceal what he described as a severe chill (and there had been early frost), took to his bed. 'I hope by tomorrow or the next day', the Queen wrote to Vicky, 'he will be nearly his dear self again. Though of no real consequence whatever, it was the severest and most obstinate attack I ever saw him have, the more annoying as it was accompanied by violent spasms of pain; which he had both on Saturday and yesterday for two hours; he had to go to bed at three on Saturday, remained in bed all day yesterday till ten o'clock when he got up for an hour and a half and thank God today (*unberufen, unberufen**) – there has been no return of pain... But it has been such an unusual thing to see him in bed (never except for the measles) and naturally cast such a gloom over us all, but it seems as if everything were turned upside down when dear Papa is not able to go about.'

Stockmar knew of Albert's stomach pains; on a visit to Coburg the year before, the Prince had what he described in a letter to Victoria as 'headache and general *malaise*', and his usual cramps. 'I have eaten nothing all the day', he added, attempting to make light of the problem, 'to rob my stomach of the shadow of a pretext for behaving ill'. To the Baron he wrote, on 3 November 1859, claiming as his reason the need to damp down any exaggerated reports, that he was 'rallying from a gastric attack, under which I have been suffering for the last fourteen days, and which kept me two days in bed... The only new symptom I had was a violent cramp at the pit of the stomach, which lasted very sharply for two hours at noon, several days running... I am able today to move about the house.'

The Queen had characterized the return of Albert's ailment to Vicky as 'his old enemy'. An erstwhile physician himself, Stockmar did not dismiss the 'old enemy' that easily – and Victoria may have revealed less than she feared so as not to alarm the Princess Royal. Shaking off the apathy about responding to letters that had been exasperating Victoria for years, the elderly, rheumatic Stockmar wrote to Albert that the description of his illness 'has disquieted me, and made me very sad'. Among its causes, he suggested, apparently hoping that nothing worse than an ulcer was involved, were the physical and mental pressures upon the Prince, but he saw little way that Albert could avoid 'all disturbing agencies, and in everything he does be governed by prophylactic rules: for under certain circumstances it is possible for the physician to *prevent*, but under all it is difficult to *cure*'.

* Touch wood! Touch wood!

On 8 December, answering Stockmar, Albert wrote from Osborne of the irony of English suspicions of France. 'Throughout the country people think of nothing but measures of protection against our Ally; Volunteer Corps are being formed in all the towns. The lawyers of the Temple go through regular drill. Lords Spencer, Abercorn, Elcho, &c., are put through their paces in Westminster Hall by gaslight in the same rank and file with shopkeepers.' He also added that his stomach was 'decidedly *not* better'.

Osborne was choked with snow in December, but it was there that the family – without Prince Alfred, whose ship was at Corfu – celebrated Christmas. On the last day of the old year Albert penned another memorandum to himself for the record, venting more anger at Palmerston for failing to keep English interests at the top of his priorities. 'All his old tricks of 1848 and the previous period are revived again', he wrote. Having Lord John Russell in the Foreign Office only made matters worse, as his 'inefficiency...love for Italy and fear of Lord Palmerston makes him a ready tool and convenient ally; he tries to carry on a policy of revenge against Austria and to bind us to the Emperor Napoleon more than ever, regardless of all the interests of England or Europe, and if impeded by the Cabinet or Queen he is violent and overbearing, and if this be of no avail, [Palmerston] cheats and tricks'. He had even returned to having 'pamphlets written against me and the 'Coburg Influence' in order to bear down all opposition...'

It would be Louis Napoleon himself who would bring the Crown and the Cabinet together by coercing King Victor Emmanuel to cede to France, in return for past and future military assistance against Austria and the Papal States, the provinces of Nice and Savoy. The Emperor's appetite clearly remained unsatisfied, and ministerial passivity would not sit well with Parliament or the public.

Among Albert's New Year letters was one to Stockmar, reporting on the completion of a rail link from Cologne to Mayence (now Mainz), which would make it possible to travel from London to Coburg in thirty-one hours. The Prince hoped that meant he could see Stockmar again. 'We are all quite well,' he added, 'all except my stomach, which is in a state truly pitiable, and is responsible for my waking early in the morning, and being unable to sleep again – "a shocking bore", as the popular phrase here says.' But to Victoria he would minimize his sleeplessness and pain; and he would drive himself harder.

# XVII

## The Treadmill Donkey

### 1860–1861

TWO WEEKS INTO the new year, craving someone to talk to about European politics, and more at ease in German, Albert invited Baron Vitzthum to Windsor. On departing, the Baron penned a long entry in his diary for 14 January 1860. The Prince, he summed up, 'is still living in the Liberal circle of ideas which prevailed in our learned world between 1830 and 1840'. His 'high view of things' had not been crushed by the experience of 1848 and the relapse from it in Europe. He saw 'insoluble contradictions' besetting all the major powers, among which would soon be Italy. Napoleon III would need 'the halo of a campaign on the Rhine', but it would do him in. Prussia would soon dominate Germany, but the maintenance of 'Particularism' – the independence of the minor states but for foreign and military affairs – was essential as a balance to the 'overbearing temper' of Berlin. The Prince predicted that Napoleon would seize Belgium once the ageing King Leopold was gone. Albert worried, too, that the Emperor would ally himself to Denmark so that Prussia would find itself preoccupied with Holstein just long enough for France to attack the Rhineland. And he expected an Italian attempt to take Venetia from Austria, reopening that war. On he went with his concerns, many of which would become realities, although not as quickly as Albert anticipated in the anxieties of early 1860. 'Of politics I don't speak', the Queen wrote cautiously to her daughter four days later, 'as I hear only far too much of them as it is, and Papa is quite *absorbé* by them'.

With eight children still to marry off over the years, Victoria was absorbed in that process. No longer eager for dynastic coups, but keen to marry off her elder children early, she accepted a visit from a Dutch prince whom Lord Clarendon called 'the Orange Boy' and who lacked what seemed then the essential qualification of being German. Albert had little to do with it, and soon found the bland heir presumptive to the Grand Duchy of Hesse, Prince Ludwig, also paying a call. Victoria's political and diplomatic correspondence remained voluminous, however, with Albert drafting most of the missives and the Queen occasionally crossing out a paragraph that seemed not resounding enough. There were also other than marital plans for the children, more in the Albertine vein of establishing meaningful roles for the monarchy. The Prince of Wales was to go to Canada (soon the United States would be added) and Prince Alfred to South Africa. Bertie's progress was planned to take place before his next Oxford term, and Affie's between naval assignments. The Prince of Wales, Albert explained to his brother, 'is to represent England[,] and the Canadians wish to show the Americans how happy, free and yet monarchical it is possible to be'.

To Stockmar he elaborated upon his concept on 27 April, describing initiatives that went well beyond opening charity bazaars and gracing theatrical benefits. 'Almost in the same week in which the elder brother is to open the great bridge across the St Lawrence in Canada,* the younger will lay the foundation stone for the breakwater for the harbour of Cape Town, at the other end of the world.' The events would demonstrate not only British progress, but 'the useful co-operation of the Royal Family in the civilisation which England has developed and advanced'. And he expected that in 'both young colonies' the royal children would be accepted with 'conscious national pride'. Elaborating on his motives at a Trinity House dinner in May, Albert described the 'present greatness', 'past history' and 'future hopes' that his sons embodied, and 'how important and beneficent is the part given to the Royal Family of England to act in the development of these distant and rising countries, who recognise in the British Crown, and their allegiance to it, their supreme bond of union with the mother country and with each other'.

* The Victoria railway bridge at Montreal, on 25 September 1860.

Albert's responsibilities, all of them self-made over twenty years, ranged from urging his views about European affairs on the Foreign Office to pressing the Prime Minister to fill a vacant professorship at Cambridge. 'The Consort paid me an immense long visit', Lord Clarendon wrote to his most intimate correspondent, the Duchess of Manchester, on 2 May, '. . . & was by no means as violent about men & things foreign & domestic as I had heard – on the contrary he discussed them all in a very practical spirit but he totally forgot the sacred hour of 2 & Eliza' – Clarendon's code for the Queen; the Prince was often *Joseph* – 'will have waited or not waited ¾ of an hour for him.' (The royal couple usually lunched at two.)

After a hard winter and late-arriving spring, the royal family escaped to Osborne, where they attempted each year to mark Victoria's birthday on 24 May. For Albert, who was preparing for the speechmaking season in June and July, it was a welcome respite from conferences and audiences, and an opportunity to pore over books that were not essential to business. A new one (published in 1859) was Tennyson's *Idylls of the King*. The Prince wanted the poet's autograph. 'You would thus add', he wrote, sending his copy to his Isle of Wight neighbour, 'a peculiar value to the book, containing those beautiful songs, from the perusal of which I derived the greatest enjoyment. They quite rekindle the feelings with which the legends of King Arthur must have inspired the chivalry of old, whilst the graceful form in which they are presented blends those feelings with the softer tone of our present age.' Tennyson signed Albert's book, which contained the first four idylls. A later and fuller edition would bear a dedication beginning,

> These to His Memory –
> Since he held them dear,
> Perchance as finding there unconsciously
> Some image of himself.

'We spent the 24th in more than usual gaiety and good spirits', Victoria wrote to Fritz's mother, Augusta, on 26 May. 'Where could I point to another woman who after 20 years of such marital felicity still possesses it? My dearly beloved Albert shows me not only as much affection and kindness as ever, but as much love and tenderness as on the first day of marriage. How can I ever repay him for it? How can I be sufficiently thankful for his goodness?' They had music on the terrace; the weather was kind, and they danced.

Returning to take in the London social season, which went on luxuriously despite unabated war anxieties, the Queen and Prince went to an evening concert at the second Duke of Wellington's Apsley House, visited other great London mansions, and held their own State Ball at Buckingham Palace on 23 June. As guests filed into the dining-room, the American envoy, George Mifflin Dallas, noted in his diary, 'a tremendous crash, sounding like the fall of a chandelier, alarmed us all'. It proved only to be 'one of the golden ornaments, a superb vase, placed against a wall behind the fountain . . .'

Although the leisured élite who had nothing else to do but dress for the next evening's ball could ignore the alarms from across the Channel, Victoria and Albert could not. Shortly after their ball, they left for the encampment at Aldershot, where eighteen thousand volunteers took to the field. King Leopold and Duke Ernest arrived in time to watch manœuvres executed, Ernest wrote, 'by 23,000 men with 56 cannons'. Since most of the troops were civilian reservists, newspaper coverage stressed the faultlessness of the review. Observing their movements as an officer trained in Prussia and Saxony, Ernest carped that their 'dispositions . . . were of so extremely innocent a nature, that I thought I ought not to conceal from the English statesmen, how very little was to be expected from these performances, in the event of an actual war'. If the French emperor 'had not abstained from the much-apprehended invasion from other reasons', he claimed, 'the volunteer battalions assuredly would not have prevented him'. The importance of their being at Aldershot, however, was their very existence. They had made a difference in English attitudes toward France, and acted as a brake upon Palmerston.

Readiness, from Albert's standpoint, was a public relations matter as well as a military one. As a result there were 21,000 volunteers who, for two hours, paraded before the Queen in Hyde Park, six thousand of them paying their own way from places like Manchester, Leeds and Nottingham to demonstrate what they were able to do with only limited leisure for practice. The Prince rode at the side of the Queen's carriage.

It was already early Saturday evening when the militia dispersed. Albert rushed back to Buckingham Palace, dressed anew for the annual

*Prince Albert watching as the Queen fires the first shot from a fixed rifle at the*
*National Rifle Association meeting on Wimbledon Common, 2 July, 1860.*
(Illustrated London News)

Trinity House dinner, at which he presided, and in proposing a toast to
the Army and Navy, made the point that unlike other European
powers, the British armed services in times of danger were drawn largely
from non-professional volunteers. He hoped that the 'noble and
patriotic spirit' which actuated such sacrifices would remain 'ever
unimpaired'.

A week later came the much-publicized rifle-shooting competition
on Wimbledon Common. First prize went to a candidate using Joseph
Whitworth's new steel rifle with a spiral polygonal bore. A machine-
tool manufacturer from Manchester who had exhibited at the Crystal
Palace, Whitworth had been encouraged to upgrade weapons engineering by Albert. To make his point, it was arranged that the Queen open
the National Rifle Association event on 2 July, a Monday, by firing
a shot from a Whitworth weapon fixed in a stationary rest at four
hundred yards. She hit the bull's-eye at one-and-a-half inches above the

centre. Nevertheless the hidebound War Office rejected Whitworth's rifle as having too small a bore for military effectiveness. (Later rifles adopted would have even smaller bores.) Stealing a march on Whitehall and the Horse Guards, the French adopted the weapon – a paradox not lost on Albert.

In London in early July, the Prince Consort worked to secure funding for the South Kensington Museum, accompanied Bertie as far as Plymouth, where he was to sail for Canada, and returned to prepare the opening address for the fourth International Statistical Congress, the first to be held in England. It was an event that Albert was delighted to chair, for its founder had been Professor Lambert Adolphe Jacques Quételet, now sixty-four, the Brussels mathematician and probability theorist who had been one of his tutors when he had prepared for the university at Bonn. Only Russia among reasonably civilized nations failed to send delegates.

While the social season seemed fixed for the best spring weather, Albert's ceremonial obligations made him a man for all seasons. On 27 March he had opened the new hall of the Clothworkers' Company, described in his graceful address as one of 'these little independent republics of the City of London' which linked the generations, and to which he was admitted as a 'Liveryman'. The 'four-hours' dinner, toasts, and songs, [just] under 90° of heat', his having 'to take an oath, and make two speeches after dinner', and to drink to the Princess Royal's health, 'upstanding, three times three', he wrote to Vicky, was not 'the best specific' for his stubborn late-winter cough.

In May the demands were still accumulating. He recalled to Vicky, as always in German, his image of himself and his 'never-ending business' as the treadmill donkey on the Isle of Wight, 'my true counterpart. He too, would rather munch thistles in the Castle Moat, than turn round in the wheel at the Castle Well; and small thanks he gets for his labour.' Two public dinners were imminent, in which again he would be in the chair. 'The one gives me seven, the other ten toasts and speeches, appropriate to the occasion, and distracting to myself. Then I have to resign at Oxford the [year's] Presidency of the British Association [for the Advancement of Science], and later in the season to open the Statistical Congress ... Between these come the laying of the foundation stone of the Dramatic College, the distribution of Prizes at Wellington College, &c. &c.; and this, with the sittings of my different Commissions, and Ascot races...and the Balls and Concerts crowded into the month of June, over and above the customary business, which a distracted state of affairs in Europe, and a stormy Parliament...make still more burdensome and disagreeable than usual.' However allegedly distasteful, he loved his work, and he realized that the Queen, as a woman barred from much of it, could not do what only he could.

To assist him with the Statistical Congress address, Albert called in William Farr, a pioneer in the application of 'vital statistics', and declared, 'now, Dr Farr, I wish to suck your brains!' Farr looked up a paper that he thought would update the Prince, and forwarded it, observing later that Albert had studied far more than the single government report he was sent, and that his address was 'entirely his own'. 'Statistical science', as Albert described it, had been condemned by clergymen as a pernicious scholarly conspiracy aimed at the destruction of religion by making the Almighty's world 'a mere machine working according to a general prearranged scheme, the parts of which are capable of mathematical measurement'. Statistics, the ultra-pious charged, 'deprives man of his dignity'.

'Is the power of God', the Prince asked, opening the sessions on 16 July, 'destroyed or diminished by...the fact that the earth required three hundred and sixty-five revolutions upon its own axis to every revolution round the sun, giving us so many days to our year, and that the moon changes thirteen times during that period; that the tide changes every six hours; that water boils at a temperature of 212° according to Fahrenheit...?' On the other hand, he observed, probability theory had established 'that in the natural world there exist no certainties at all, but only probabilities', based upon calculations valid 'as long as the same causes are operating'. It was the essence of statistical science 'that it makes only apparent general laws, but that these laws are inapplicable to any special case; that, therefore, what is proved to be law in general is uncertain in particular...Thus is the power, wisdom, and goodness of the Creator manifested, showing how the Almighty has established the physical and moral world on unchangeable laws, conformable to His eternal nature, while He has allowed to the individual the freest and fullest use of his faculties, vindicating at the same time the majesty of His laws by their remaining unaffected by individual self-determination.'

The address was a graceful upholding of science in an era dominated by religious dogma, and was intended to be heard well beyond the Congress. In opening, the Prince apologized to his immediate audience of experts for being so 'inadequate an exponent', however much he owed to the 'privilege' of early instruction by Quételet. He hoped that their 'common method' would lead to the 'common end' of utilizing mathematical tools to improve the human condition.

As the applause swelled, then faded, crotchety old Lord Brougham, ever the troublemaker, saw George Mifflin Dallas in the *corps diplomatique* section, and shouted at him, aware that the slavery issue in the United States had reached a high tide of dissension, that there was 'a negro in the assemblage'. It was, the American Minister realized, an attempt to provoke him into some unseemly response, and he remained 'silent and composed'. However, Dallas noted in his diary, 'The gentleman of colour . . . rose, and requested permission of the Prince Consort, as chairman, to thank Lord Brougham for his notice, with an emphatic conclusion, "I am a man!" '

For Albert it had to be a relief that the dignity of the speaker defused the excitement in the hall, and he brought the meeting back to order. Two days later, when a delegate from Massachusetts called upon Dallas on Brougham's behalf to say that the abolitionist-minded peer had meant no personal disrespect, the Minister insisted that if he had an apology to make for the insult to the United States, 'he must do this in the very body where he had made the attack'. On the twentieth, Brougham called upon Dallas but found only his secretary, as the Minister was at the South Kensington Museum. 'You know,' Brougham claimed, 'you don't treat your negroes as well as they are treated in the Brazils!'* Slavery would not come up again in the Congress, but as a foreign policy matter it would continue to beset the Prince.

The Queen and Prince remained at Buckingham Palace through much of the parliamentary sitting, watchful over defence expenditures. Gladstone, the Chancellor of the Exchequer, guarded the national purse as if his own. 'Our Fortifications Bill is at last in the House of Commons', Albert reported to Stockmar from Osborne late in July. 'Gladstone continues in the Ministry but on the condition that he be

---

* Slavery was not abolished in Brazil until 1888.

free next year to attack and denounce the fortifications, to the construction of which he this year gives his assent, and the money. Palmerston laughingly yielded this condition to him.' The Prince would follow up his victory of readiness over penuriousness by urging Palmerston to raise a Naval Reserve, pointing out that such trainees would be doubly valuable through applying their skills in the merchant fleet.

It was at Osborne that Victoria and Albert learned of the birth of Vicky's second child, a girl, on 24 July. She would be named Victoria, although called by the last of her four names, Charlotte. For Albert it furnished the occasion to explain the facts of conception and birth to Alice, who was already on the verge of betrothal. 'Papa told her all', the Queen wrote to her eldest daughter the next day, having been reluctant to explain such intimate matters herself.

On 5 August, the day before the Court moved to Balmoral, an overnight expedition of a trainload of people and baggage, Albert wrote to the Prince Regent of Prussia to congratulate him on the birth of their granddaughter. It was an opportunity to raise such European matters as the likely unification of Italy (the Neapolitan regime was despised, and tottering), and his expectations for political reforms in Austria – a veiled encouragement for liberalization in Prussia. 'May the Emperor Francis Joseph go on with his reforms', Albert hoped, 'and cause justice to be done to Protestants, Hungarians, and Jews... It is high time. It seems to me that one of his chief difficulties consists in fundamental differences between his and his people's way of looking at things. He proposes to make concessions as acts of grace; they, on the other hand, ask to have a legal status, and institutions not dependent on the good or ill will of the Sovereign.'

The terminus of the royal train at Edinburgh offered the occasion to schedule yet another three hours' review of volunteers, again with the Queen in an open carriage and Albert on horseback. As political a gesture as it was an act of preparedness, the gathering emphasized unity of will across Britain. Twenty-two thousand troops paraded, and 200,000 spectators cheered them on, Albert reported to Stockmar. 'The French are as much out of humour at this demonstration', he wrote on 21 August, 'as Messrs Cobden and Bright'. The Radical leaders were long-time pacifists, William Cobden remarking to an American – while both were then in Paris – that 'Prince Albert's rifle mania' was 'mere Germanism in the disguise of British patriotism'. 'The American despatched the whole conversation forthwith to the *New York Herald'*, the Prince explained, 'from which it was come back to our papers!'

The Scots stay was to be abbreviated because of a planned trip to Germany, and Albert's rifle mania, at least when it came to hunting, was no longer what it had been, although he did bring down one stag. While in the Highlands early that September the Queen and Prince went off on a lengthy incognito journey, meant as psychological therapy for Victoria, whose recurrent depressive moods remained a quandary for Albert. In deliberately unsplendid carriages the small royal party travelled along the river Geldie to Loch Inch, crossed the Spey in a ferry, and bounced in 'very rough vehicles' to Grantown, over sixty miles from Balmoral. '*No* one knew us', she bubbled to Leopold – 'anywhere or at the little inn. We went under the names of Lord and Lady Churchill, and Lady Churchill and General Grey who went with us, under the names of Miss Spencer and Dr Grey! Two maids *only* went with us (whom we had sent round with our things), and *no* servants but our two excellent Highlanders, viz. Albert's first stalker or head keeper, and *my own Highland servant* and factotum – *both* excellent, intelligent, devoted people. *Only* when we had *left* was it found out.' Her Highland servant was John Brown, then thirty-four. On the journey he nearly gave the game away be calling Victoria 'Your Majesty' as she was getting into a carriage, and John Grant, head keeper at Balmoral, who was acting as Albert's servant, once called him 'Your Royal Highness'. The slips set the others tittering, and increased the deliciousness of the masquerade.

The secret had been imperfectly kept, as the dogcart in which they had begun the journey carried the Balmoral crest, and someone in the street recognized Albert. 'The lady must be terrible rich', one woman observed. Victoria's fingers were covered with rings. The Queen retorted that the other lady wore even more rings. The sense of freedom in Scotland to play at not being Queen enraptured Victoria. At the inn, Grant and Brown were to have waited on them, not an unusual procedure when a wealthy couple travelled with their own servants, but as Victoria and Albert tidied up in their room, the Highlanders made themselves 'wishful' (the Queen's word in her journal – Scots for *drunk*). A ringletted local woman waited on the royal couple and served them their bottle of wine, brought from Balmoral. The next day, permissive as usual about the tippling of her Highlanders, the Queen was up and ready early to complete the expedition without a word of reproof. 'To my dear Albert', she noted, they owed the lark, 'for he always thought it would be delightful'.

The much talked-of yet much delayed visit to Germany began from Buckingham Palace after their early return from Balmoral, but was in jeopardy almost until the day they departed because of Albert's recurrent stomach cramps. Sir James Clark, called in to review the symptoms, which included chills and aches, diagnosed exhaustion and recommended rest. Albert insisted that they meet their schedule.

To avoid any semblance of a state visit, Prussia was excluded from the itinerary. Instead, Vicky and her family would travel from Berlin to Coburg, which the wizened Stockmar, now seventy and more shrunken than ever, seldom left, and where Albert's stepmother, Dowager Duchess Marie, was in failing health. Lord John Russell accompanied the party to represent the government, as any political matters that were likely to come up were expected to be in his province as Foreign Secretary.

Late in the afternoon of 22 September 1860, they embarked at Gravesend on the *Victoria and Albert*. Princess Alice and a suite of attendants, including William Baly, the young physician who had just joined the Court medical staff, accompanied them. At Antwerp, they were met by King Leopold and his sons, who joined them by rail as far as the station at Verviers. With the Belgians was a telegram from Ernest in Coburg: 'Mama' Marie was dying. The journey should be put off for a day. Albert telegraphed back that it was impossible, and that he hoped for the best. At Frankfurt a further telegram awaited them. Duchess Marie had died.

'To our regret', Victoria wrote in her journal, 'we were received by a guard of honour and a band.' Only just in possession of the sad news, they were already in technical mourning. The next day, after staying overnight at the Hotel d'Angleterre, as they had done fifteen years earlier, they continued along the valley of the Main to Lichtenfels, where they transferred to the Thüringian railway to Coburg, arriving at five in the evening. The quiet welcome, as befitted bereavement, left Albert and Victoria even more agitated than any traditional greeting, in the brightest gala style, would have done. With Alexandrine, the Duchess of Coburg, at the Palace, was Vicky, 'in the deepest German mourning, long black veils . . .', the Queen wrote. 'A tender embrace, and then we walked up the staircase...Could hardly speak, I felt so moved, and quite trembled.'

Stockmar, whom they had not seen since his farewell visit to England in 1856, was there, looking 'a little weak', and also little Willy, 'a fine fat child' with 'very fair curly hair'.

Two days later was the Duchess's funeral, which left Albert shaken, but not nearly as much as he would be four days later, following quiet, nostalgic visits to familiar places. The Queen's journal for 1 October opens, 'Before proceeding, I must thank God for having preserved my adored one! I tremble now on thinking of it...The escape is very wonderful, *most merciful!*' Albert had been riding alone in a carriage drawn by four horses, which suddenly took flight. Two miles ahead lay a railway crossing with a bar across the road, and as Albert attempted to control his team he saw a wagon waiting. With a collision inevitable, he jumped for his life. Cut and bruised, but conscious, he rushed to the aid of the coachman into whose wagon his carriage had crashed. Of Albert's four horses, one was dead; the others raced on the remaining mile to Coburg.

In the town the runaway horses were recognized, and Colonel Ponsonby, the Prince's equerry, rushed to the scene of the accident with the party's young doctor, William Baly, and Carl Florschütz, the Duke's physician. Ponsonby then went on to summon the Queen, who found Albert lying on the bed of his valet, Löhlein, with lint compresses on his nose, mouth and chin. Victoria veered between horror and gratitude. 'I sent off many telegrams to England, &c., fearing wrong messages.' She would not know of Albert's curious confession to Vicky that when he realized his team had bolted, he sensed that his time had come ('*mein letzes Stündlein gekommen wäre*\*), and that he found himself welcoming oblivion.

At dinner that evening he chattered away in the nervous manner of someone pretending to be other than he was. The next day the Prince kept to his room, but claimed he was feeling better. 'Good Stockmar [was] there', Victoria wrote. 'He had been half distracted all night, thinking of what might have happened...Many dispatches and letters; Emperor and Empress of the French inquiring after dear Albert...My heart very full, but would not give way.'

---

\* 'My last hour had come.'

Dispatches to England about Albert's brush with death offered an enterprising *Punch* editor the opportunity to pun, 'It is an extraordinary thing that any sort of vehicular indiscretion should have been manifested in the case of a Prince who has always been so remarkably Prudent in his Carriage.'

Among the letters forwarded from London, unrelated to the accident, was one from the Prince of Wales. On a tour of Canada and the United States – a highly successful venture that proved that whatever his failings with books, he had the social graces – Bertie had reached Niagara Falls.

On 4 October, the Queen drove with Princess Alice to Baron Stockmar's house in the Weber-Gasse, and met his '*zuvorkommende Frau*' (affable wife) for the first time. In none of his stays in England, the months adding up to many years, had she ever travelled with him.

Although Victoria and Albert would not leave until the tenth, every day for the Prince became a farewell, as he absorbed sights and sounds and smells he sensed he might never experience again. The weather, which had been gloriously autumnal, turned cold and wet, and made the process of drawing away somewhat easier. 'Had a last visit', Victoria wrote, 'from dear Stockmar, and talked over many things with him. Towards the end of his stay, dear little William came in and played about the room, and we got over the leave-taking without its upsetting Stockmar too much.'

In the last days, happily for Albert's peace of mind, came foreign affairs distractions from London – 'constant dispatches from Italy and about Italy', Victoria's journal notes. 'Matters become more and more complicated. The Emperor [of France] declares he shall protect the Pope in Rome . . . Albert too busy to go out.' The next morning he was also busy with diplomatic papers, but on Albert's last afternoon in Coburg, Ernest took his brother for a walk. Afterwards he remembered Stockmar's words. Having perceived Albert's despondency and melancholy – unrelated to the accident, Stockmar knew, as he had been in constant correspondence with Albert – he confided to Ernest, 'God have mercy on us! If anything serious should ever happen to him, he will die.'

Very likely something serious had already happened, and both Stockmar and Albert knew it. The Prince, at least, thought that he was slowly but surely dying. 'At one of the most beautiful spots', Ernest recalled, 'Albert stood still, and suddenly felt for his pocket handkerchief.' The

Duke assumed that Albert's facial abrasions had begun to bleed afresh, and went to help, but discovered instead 'that tears were trickling down his cheeks... [and] he persisted in declaring that he was well aware that he had been here for the last time in his life'. The brothers turned back to the Rosenau in silence.

The slow return journey to London, in persistent cold rain, was a prolonged misery alleviated only by the continued presence of Vicky, who – though married to a German prince – had never travelled the Rhine. Victoria had a heavy cold, with a sore throat and fever. Albert, more ill than she knew, attempted to conceal his continuing headaches and stomach discomfort, his cramps and chills, until he was on home soil again, and in royal privacy.

At the railway station in Koblenz, Vicky's mother-in-law and Prince Frederick of Baden joined the party, planning to have the Queen and Prince sightsee along the Rhine and Moselle. In rain and hail, wobbly on their feet, they did what was expected of them, and remained overnight. On 13 October, after two days in Koblenz, they left for Cologne, where the Prussian party was joined by the Prince Regent, Vicky's father-in-law, who talked in the train with Victoria and Albert until Aix-la-Chapelle (Aachen), where the Prussians, 'little William' included, took their final leaves.

Leopold met the train at Verviers, shocked at the appearance of the royal couple. 'I could hardly walk when we got out', Victoria confessed in her journal, 'and with difficulty got up stairs... Dr Baly found my throat very bad, that I had much fever; so I was ordered to remain lying down in my room and to see no one.' The dinner in Brussels that Leopold had scheduled in her honour was held without the Queen.

Even the final farewells in Belgium were delayed by weather. Before the yacht proceeded very far from Antwerp, the sky turned black and a deluge of rain forced the ship to drop anchor. Finally, at six in the evening on 17 October, a week after leaving Coburg, they reached Gravesend.

Shaken by her illness, and grateful for what she considered Albert's deliverance at Coburg, Victoria wrote to Sir Charles Phipps, the administrator of Her Majesty's Privy Purse, to explore the possibility of endowing a permanent charity at Coburg, to be distributed every 1 October – the anniversary of Albert's escape. A modest trust, the *Victoria-Stift* (Victoria Foundation) was established for little over

£1,000. The interest was to enable men and women 'of exemplary character belonging to the humbler ranks of life' to receive small sums for apprenticeships, for purchasing tools and equipment needed for work, or, in the case of women, to secure a small marriage dowry. It would become, in effect, the first Albert Memorial.

The Queen recovered more quickly than Albert. 'My attack', he claimed to Vicky on 11 December, once he was able to work again 'was the real English cholera'. 'English cholera', also called 'summer cholera', is a diarrhoeal disease usually lasting two to seven days, and accompanied by severe stomach cramps. Albert had such symptoms, but had been ill for two months. Now he had to act as if he were fit, for Empress Eugénie, staying in London at Claridge's without her philandering husband, was expected on a private visit ('there was not the slightest allusion to politics'); and in residence at Windsor was Alice's future husband, the amiable but empty Prince Ludwig of Hesse, soon to be 'Louis', for whose bad teeth the Queen found a dentist. Albert gave him some informal lessons on his own German history.

Christmas 1860 was celebrated at Windsor, with both the Prince of Wales and Prince Alfred at home. George Byng, seventh Viscount Torrington, 'in waiting' at the time, sent J.T. Delane of *The Times* an intimate account of what was to be the last family Christmas with the Prince Consort. Something of a sceptic and a wit, Torrington (signing his letter 'Your Windsor Special') was 'agreeably surprised and pleased' by the royal Christmas Eve:

> The Queen's private sitting-rooms, three in number, were lighted up with Christmas trees hung from the ceiling, the chandeliers being taken down. These trees, of immense size, besides others on the tables, were covered with bonbons and coloured wax lights. Some of the trees were made to appear as if partially covered with snow. These rooms contained all the presents for the royal family the one to the other. Each member gave a present to one another, so that, including the Prince of Hesse and the Duchess of Kent, every person had to receive or give thirteen presents . . .
>
> I have never seen a much more agreeable sight. It was royalty putting aside its state and becoming in words, acts, and deeds one of ourselves – no forms and not a vestige of ceremony. Even as in a public

bazaar, where people jostle one another, so lords, grooms, Queen, and princes laughed and talked, forgot to bow, and freely turned their backs on one another. Little princesses, who on ordinary occasions dare hardly to look at a gentleman-in-waiting, in the happiest manner showed each person they could lay hands on the treasures they had received ... Prince Arthur (the flower of the flock) speedily got into a volunteer uniform, which, with endless other things, including a little rifle, fell to his lot, took a pot-shot at his papa, and then presented arms.

Some of the presents were beautiful in taste and suited to the receiver, and even the presents of children to their parents were selected so that even the Queen might find use for them ... I received a supply of studs, sleeve buttons, and waistcoat ditto – handsome, plain gold; a pocket-book, and every one of us a large cake of Nuremberg gingerbread. Whether the Prince Consort had a quiet joke in his mind when he selected certain presents for Phipps, Biddulph, Grey, and Bruce,* I don't know, but Phipps had salt cellars resting on little fish with the *mouths open*, Biddulph a *bread* basket, Grey a sugar basket, and Bruce a claret jug ...

I never saw more real happiness than the scene of the mother and all her children; the Prince Consort lost his stiffness, and your *Windsor Special* had much cheerful and friendly conversation with them both. Altogether, it was a sight I should have liked you to have seen ...

On Christmas Day the windows at Windsor were clouded by frost, although a cold sun shone. The Duchess of Kent came to luncheon, and Leopold and Beatrice ('Baby') were permitted to join the family for dessert. Albert swung Baby in a large dinner napkin.

Christmas dinner was for adults only. Lord Torrington went to the kitchen to watch the roasting of turkeys, geese, and beef – 'a mighty sight: at least fifty turkeys before one fire'. By custom, he reported, the Lord Lieutenant of Ireland sent the sovereign at Christmas a large woodcock pie. Victoria's had one hundred birds in it – 'a worthy dish to set before a Queen'.

---

* Sir Charles Phipps, Private Secretary to the Prince Consort and Keeper of Her Majesty's Privy Purse; Colonel Thomas Biddulph, Master of the Queen's Household; General Charles Grey, Private Secretary to the Prince Consort and later to the Queen; General Robert Bruce, Governor to the Prince of Wales.

The dinner 'was really wonderful. How I live to tell the tale I don't know. I took some of the baron of beef, the boar's head, and the Lord Lieutenant's pie. Fortunately, I did not go to bed till near three o'clock, as we finished the evening with some pool and billiards, and Captain Du Plat and self cleared the remainder out of every silver coin they possessed. Altogether a jolly Christmas Day...'

As the Queen, with Albert, watched the final minutes of 1860 tick away, she worried aloud about war on the Continent and was anxious for England. 'My precious husband', she wrote in her journal, 'cheered me & held me in his dear arms saying "We must have trust, & we have trust that God will protect us." ' 10 February, however, was the real beginning of the year for her – that date in 1861 was the twenty-first anniversary of her wedding to 'that most perfect of human beings my adored Husband!' It was also her opportunity to record her guilt about her 'foolish sensitivity & irritability', which continued to mar relations with Albert. A woman whose instincts were so queenly that she never looked behind her when she sat down could not separate her husband from her other subjects when the royal temper was aroused. She resolved again to be calmer.

The new year was a difficult one in which to remain calm, punctuated as it was from the beginning by serious anxieties. Albert expected little good from it. Napoleon, Albert wrote to his brother, would brew trouble with both Austria and Prussia; Cavour's nucleus of a new Italy was already arming rebels in the sub-alpine Austrian principalities; and Prussia would be taking 'steps' against Denmark in Holstein.

On 2 January, just as the Court was about to leave Windsor for a brief stay at Osborne House, a telegram arrived reporting the death of Frederick William IV. His mind had failed years earlier. To Victoria and Albert the accession of Fritz's father, long the actual ruler of Prussia, seemed an event to celebrate quietly despite the official mourning. Vicky's husband was now the Crown Prince, and the new King, they hoped, would be liberal in outlook – although he would quickly succumb to his bellicose 'Iron Chancellor' Otto von Bismarck, whom he named Prime Minister the next year. In the first dawn of the elderly King William's regime, the dream of Victoria and Albert that their daughter might soon be queen of a progressive, unified Germany seemed to be approaching fulfilment.

Despite such prospects, letters from Vicky were filled with deathbeds and mourning, and the mail she received from England was in a similar vein. At just the time when enlightened medical help was needed in Victoria's household, William Baly, the Queen's new Physician-in-Ordinary, was the victim of a gruesome railway accident. He had arrived at Wimbledon Station, *en route* to Osborne, only to see the train steaming away. When he explained to the station-master that he was the Queen's doctor, the train was stopped and Baly climbed aboard. Soon afterward, the floor of his carriage collapsed, and he fell to his death on the tracks. He was the only passenger killed. '*Sehr traurig*'– very sad – Albert wrote in his diary.

For the Prince, Baly's death was especially sad, as the doctor had been treating him for continuing woes, including gum inflammations that had persisted for two years, and had become worse. 'Papa never allows he is any better or will try to get over it', the Queen wrote lightly to Vicky, 'but makes such a miserable face that people always think he's very ill. It is quite the contrary with me always; I . . . never show it, so people never believe I am ill or ever suffer. His nervous system is easily excited and irritated, and he's so completely overpowered by everything.' Albert indeed felt wretched, although he persisted in his schedule, which expanded with the new parliamentary session.

With the less-than-competent Sir James Clark now semi-retired, a new physician was appointed, William Jenner – 'a great friend of our poor Dr Baly', the Queen wrote to Vicky. 'He is extremely clever, and has a pleasing clever manner.'

As the King of Prussia lay in state earlier in January, Victoria had confided to her daughter, about to confront a grim new experience, 'I have never even yet witnessed a death bed'. That would soon change. Dr Jenner had hardly assumed his duties when the Duchess of Kent began to fail. The Queen's priorities altered. She had been concerned with Albert's health, but not so much as to divert her from a continuing preoccupation with matchmaking, this time with the intention of settling the future of the Prince of Wales, whose shallowness had not been reversed by the social success of his trip to North America. Since Victoria was distracted by her mother's decline, the assignment to find Bertie a bride – almost certainly the future Queen – remained that of Vicky. Although she was situated where likely candidates existed, there were also Danish and Dutch possibilities; however, the Danish princess, though beautiful, seemed politically unacceptable as long as the dispute with Prussia over Schleswig and Holstein simmered.

Vicky had sent the Queen photographs, and Victoria responded about the Danish candidate, 'Princess Alexandra is indeed lovely!... What a pity she is who she is!' Albert's response to Victoria was more enthusiastic, although he might have been expected to be pro-German. 'From that photograph', he said, 'I would marry her at once.'

Bertie had been uncaged by the voyage to North America, but on 18 January 1861 he had been transferred from Christ Church, Oxford, to

LATEST FROM AMERICA.

*Punch* satirizing Bertie's social growth as a result of his American travels. His father is not amused.

Trinity College, Cambridge, both arrangements again implying matriculation rather than residence. Reports had come to Victoria and Albert that the Prince of Wales had often been seen with a cigar in his mouth, aping the more vulgar undergraduates, and remained gauche. At Cambridge he was housed with a staff appointed by his father at Madingley Hall, four miles from college, and cantered to campus on his horse or was driven in a phaeton. To bring him into closer contact with college life, Dr Whewell allotted to the young prince rooms at the Master's Lodge, where, Natty Rothschild discovered, 'the different Regius professors come and lecture to him'. Bertie was 'not allowed to take any notes but has to write out the lectures when he gets back to Madingley'. The eldest son of Lionel and Charlotte de Rothschild fancied that 'the little spirit [which the Prince of Wales] ever had is quite broken' from the strict regimen, yet Bertie played tennis – badly – every day, and was 'excessively fond of the chase' and of 'riddles and strong cigars'. His 'redeeming quality' was his excessive courtesy to every student without exception, but, Natty predicted, if the Prince could follow his own inclinations 'he would take to gambling and certainly keep away from the law lectures he is obliged to go to now'.

An early marriage, Albert hoped, would draw Bertie from bad company and bad habits, to both of which he was prone. The only university education which seemed to stick to him was extra-curricular and unhelpful. Any risk to foreign policy of a Danish bride seemed worth chancing.

Foreign affairs remained Albert's overwhelming concern. Regardless of the troubled area, he warned Palmerston, there were influential 'peace-at-any-price mongers'. To Disraeli, who had been at a Windsor dinner on 21 January, the Prince warned that Napoleon hoped for a 'Gladstone–Cobden' government to disarm the country, and 'Dizzy' promised the support of the Conservatives. 'What is the use of that?' said Albert candidly; 'the country is governed by newspapers, and you have not got a newspaper'. He copied down the gist of his conversation with Disraeli and sent it to Palmerston the next morning.

Though rushing from meeting to meeting, and overseeing the Queen's correspondence, the Prince was working at less than his usual efficiency. Well into February he was still suffering through nights made sleepless by a variety of aches and pains, and was seldom able to eat his dinner. Then he found himself forced to handle even more responsibilities. On 28 February, Sir George Couper, long the comptroller of the Duchess of Kent's household, died suddenly. Albert had to take those affairs in hand, a matter made more difficult by the weakened condition of the Duchess. At seventy-five, she was painfully crippled by erysipelas. An operation on her swollen right arm did nothing but hasten the end.

As 15 March waned into the next morning, Victoria went to the Duchess's room for the last time, to witness her first deathbed. 'I sat on a foot stool, holding her dear hand . . . I felt the end was fast approaching, as Clark went out to call Albert . . . Fainter and fainter grew the breathing. At last it ceased . . . The clock struck half-past nine at the very moment.'

Victoria was seized by paroxysms of grief that were in large measure feelings of guilt and remorse. When she began sorting her mother's papers after the funeral, her emotions gave way entirely. Her mother had saved every scrap of childhood memorabilia. She had really loved Victoria. All her villainy was long past and forgotten.

The Queen's mourning became so excessive that her family and the Court recognized that the hysterical indulgence in sorrow was a sign of a serious nervous collapse. She was now a 'poor orphan child', she wrote to Vicky. The Queen, Clarendon reported, 'was determined to cherish her grief & not be consoled'. For three weeks she took all her meals alone (the children were 'a disturbance'), and left Albert (in his words) 'well nigh overcome' with the Queen's business, the late Duchess's affairs, and those always left to his province. 'I hope this state of things won't last', Clarendon gossiped to the Duchess of Manchester, 'or she may fall into the morbid melancholy to wh[ich] her mind has always tended & wh[ich] is a constant cause of anxiety to P[rince] A[lbert].' In mid-April, Albert was still (to Clarendon) 'in a very melancholy tone', and when he confirmed to Palmerston that the Queen had approved of appointments or wished to comment about something, or was returning Dr Livingstone's 'interesting letter' from Africa, it seemed clear that her involvement in affairs remained minimal.

Recovery began with her agreeing, once more, to copy out in her hand such messages to the Prime Minister as suggested that she was overcoming her lassitude, but at the Royal Horticultural Show in South Kensington on 5 June, a pale, exhausted Prince Consort presided over the opening. The Queen was still unequal to public appearances, and

Albert brought his young family as if to compensate for her absence. Again his schedule was crowded. He had to hurry his return, in the rain, to Buckingham Palace in order to rush through dinner in time to go off again, eastward to John Adam Street, below the Strand, for a report to the Society of Arts on preparations for the 1862 reprise of the Great Exhibition. Next time, he had already cautioned the exhibition planners, he could not carry his former burdens. 'Am ill, feverish, with pains in my limbs, and feel very miserable', was a typical entry in his diary at the time.

Later in the month, King Leopold, now a gaunt seventy, made the Channel crossing to learn for himself about Victoria's breakdown, and found her not nearly as low as rumour had it; but he was disturbed by Albert's appearance, and wrote urgently to Stockmar. Returning a message via the King's agent, the Baron urged that Leopold use his good offices to end the morbid official Court mourning, which he suggested was a factor in undermining Albert's health. To Leopold's surprise, Albert declared that wearing black matched his mood, and that even half-mourning would be resisted by Victoria before the late Duchess's birthday in mid-August. The obsessive mourning – Victoria described herself as 'much shattered' – and the burden it had thrown upon a clearly ill Albert, had created, Leopold realized, serious strains between the Queen and Prince. He had little time to spare from the Queen's business to bring her out of her withdrawal from it.

To help, Princess Vicky was sent for, and her family visited for several weeks, much of which the Queen spent on marital plans for Bertie, almost her only therapy. Fortunately for Albert, the mausoleum on the Windsor grounds at Frogmore, where the Duchess had lived, was ready by her birthday for a visit by Victoria. Its 'repose and calmness', the Queen wrote to her daughter on August 17 – she had returned to Berlin – 'were most soothing. Beloved Papa is the cause of all this – he planned and designed it all!'

Externally, the anxieties for the Prince had also increased. The American Civil War had erupted that April. Eleven southern states had seceded and formed a Confederacy which the North was determined to undo, although the initial successes were all those of the slaveholding South. Palmerston's government had cautiously recognized the South not as a nation, but as a belligerent, a status reflecting the sea blockade of the Confederate States by the North. Concern rose about being drawn into the conflict, as Lancashire textile mills depended upon the

South's cotton. At the same time, the Queen and Prince were resisting efforts by Lord John Russell to furnish guarantees to Denmark, which denied Prussian claims to Holstein – 'a part of Germany' (the moribund Confederation), as a letter bearing Victoria's signature reminded her Foreign Minister.

Most sharply worded missives reflected Victorian emendations to Albert's more conciliatory language, and it may have been as true of her observations about the situation in North America as it was about Denmark and Prussia. Expectations in England were that the disunited States were likely to remain sundered, and that the North might attempt to repair its territorial losses at the expense of Canada. Rewriting Albert's draft, the Queen urged that Palmerston send additional artillery units to Canada rather than mere infantry, as 'the Colony' had no munitions industry. But, with no idea of Palmerston's Machiavellian designs to aid the South little short of war, Albert added, in Victoria's somewhat more caustic terms, 'The naval forces would, however, require strengthening even more. It is less likely that the remnant of the United States could send expeditions by land to the north while quarrelling with the South, than that they should commit acts of violence at sea.'

Near physical breakdown, Albert found himself nevertheless planning to go through with a trip to Ireland with the Queen, arranged to coincide with the Prince of Wales's ten weeks of army service there. An ambitious programme had been worked out to slide Bertie through the competency requirements of every officer grade – promoting him one rank every fortnight – until he could command a full battalion in view of the Queen and Prince when they visited the Curragh military grounds near Dublin in August. The reports from General Bruce, the Prince's governor, were discouraging. Meanwhile, Albert had to pull Victoria further out of her malaise so that royal guests could be met and entertained – the King of Sweden, the King of Belgium, her own son-in-law the Crown Prince of Prussia (and Vicky). These became more than mere protocol matters; European capitals were echoing with rumours that Victoria had suffered a breakdown so violent that she had to be restrained in a padded cell. Even Vicky had reported it – to her father – from Berlin. It was vital that Victoria be seen behaving like a queen.

That Bertie was unfit to command a company, let alone a battalion, was insufficient reason to call off the Irish visit. The Queen had not been there since 1849. Cancellation would give credence to the rumours of madness. The Queen and Prince came, visited the encampment at the Curragh on 24 August, and watched Bertie march past with a mere company of Grenadier Guards, his command a public airing of his non-progress. But Victoria's mind still dwelled self-indulgently only on her sorrows. In Ireland she was 'weak and very nervous', she wrote to Leopold; with her mother gone she felt (at forty-two!) 'as if we were no longer cared for'.

One member of the family thoroughly cared for was the Prince of Wales, who was overseen to absurdity. The other young officers, with whom he was ordered to have little to do, felt challenged to extract him from the royal cocoon. At a party before he left the Curragh, Bertie's brother subalterns conveyed into his bed Nellie Clifden, a young woman with a talent to amuse. The Prince of Wales saw to it that Nellie continued to amuse him. But no news of Nellie reached Victoria and Albert.

Only Scotland was perceived to have the healing qualities that the Queen felt she still needed. Albert carefully planned therapeutic expeditions away from Balmoral, including an incognito stay at the Ramsay Arms in Fettercairn, where the landlord and his wife – but no one else – were told in advance who their guests would be. Another outing took them to the inn at Dalwhinnie – where a maid recognized them. They went on daily walking tours. On their final expedition, they lunched on the Cairngorm heights, 'on a precipitous place, which made one dread anyone's moving backwards'. As they packed to leave, 'Albert wrote on a bit of paper that we had lunched there, put it into a Seltzer-water bottle, and buried it there, or rather stuck it in the ground'. Their Highland servant John Brown wished them well as they left, and added the hope that 'above all, you may have no deaths in the family'. The Queen took the bluff farewell as a reference to the Duchess of Kent. Later she wondered about second sight. She had forgotten her own remark to Vicky, on 7 October, after she and Albert had heard an Edinburgh minister preach a sermon that 'touched and enchanted us all', on a text from the Book of Amos, 'Prepare to meet thy God, O Israel'. The subject now affected her greatly, she wrote Vicky. 'I feel now to be so acquainted with death – and to be so much nearer that unseen world.'

# XVIII

## *Duty Done*

### *1861*

ALBERT'S SENSE OF fatality had intensified, and his nights, as he lay beside the sleeping Victoria, were troubled and waking. Confiding in the father-figure of his youth had often been his way of confronting adversity, even when he realized that his appeals would be unanswered prayers. The Prince's last letter to Baron Stockmar was dated 14 November 1861. 'I am fearfully in want of a true friend and counsellor', he wrote, 'and that *you* are the friend and counsellor I want, you will readily understand.' He knew that he was unlikely to receive any practical advice from Stockmar, and perhaps no response whatever. Infirm and reclusive, Stockmar would not leave Coburg.

On their return from Scotland, Windsor Castle had filled with invitees, and a band had played – the first time the Queen had permitted one since her mother's death – for Bertie's twentieth birthday on 9 November. The next day the Prince of Wales returned to his sham residency at Cambridge and Albert went off to London for a round of meetings, returning that night to pitch into his postponed paperwork. All of his schedule, including the birthday festivities, had been carried out in the gloom of his having discovered on the 6th that his cousin, Prince Ferdinand of Portugal, had died of typhoid fever, and that the ineffectual King Pedro, Ferdinand's elder brother, was dangerously ill. Soon he was dead, too, at twenty-five. The Saxe-Coburg-Kohary clan was ravaged. Albert was devastated. 'My Albert was very fond of him', Victoria wrote extravagantly of Pedro in her diary, 'and loved him like a son (as I did too), while he had unbounded confidence in Albert, and was worthy of him.'

The day before his plea to Stockmar, Albert had penned a lugubriously unconsoling letter to Vicky, who was also ill, closing with, 'Spare yourself, nurse yourself, and get completely well. The disaster in Portugal is another proof that we are never safe to refuse Nature her rights.' It was a startling reflection, indicative of the Prince's state of mind.

A calamity closer to home followed quickly. He should have realized months earlier that a young officer in the company of other moneyed young gentlemen in uniform would not acquire the facts of life from discreet fatherly confidences such as he had imparted to Princess Alice. A marriage was being arranged for her; Bertie, although older, had never been privy to such arcana. Now it was no longer necessary. On 16 November, two days after Albert's entreaty to Stockmar, he wrote to his son 'with a heavy heart upon a subject which has caused me the greatest pain I have yet felt in this life'. Lord Torrington, always attuned to gossip, had informed Albert of 'a story current in the Clubs' about Bertie's continuing involvement with Nellie Clifden, which explained his reluctance to consider the Danish betrothal scheme. A letter from Stockmar confirmed that allegations about an Irish 'actress' had already surfaced in Continental papers.

Too heartbroken to confront his son in person, Albert claimed, he had to protect Bertie, nevertheless, from the consequences of his misconduct, and urged him to tell all to General Bruce, who was, rather unsuccessfully, overseeing the Prince in Cambridge. In a second letter a few days later Albert forecast a melodramatic scenario of a future king compromised by blackmail and scandal. If the young woman were to become pregnant, Albert warned, there would be a press circus when the Prince of Wales was dragged into court to own up to his paternity. No particular of his 'profligacy' would escape 'the greedy Multitude' if Nellie Clifden herself were in the witness box to offer her own testimony. 'Oh horrible prospect, which this person has in her power, any day to realise! and to break your poor parents' hearts!' To channel such wanton impulses, he warned, Bertie would have to be hurried into an early marriage.

Victoria had already been told some of the circumstances, but not – she wrote later – 'the disgusting details'. Despite Bertie's contrite response, confessing that he had indeed yielded to temptation, but insisting that the affair was ended, she confided to her journal that she would never be able to look on her son again 'without a shudder'. Although Albert conceded to Bertie that further inquiries were useless, and that 'The past is past. You have to deal now with the future', he might not have informed the Queen in the first place had his head not reeled with illness, exhaustion, and agony over his proliferating problems. Given his caution, and his feelings about sheltering the monarchy from dishonour, he would have railed at his son in any case, although perhaps with less self-pity. He was at a low ebb physically, made worse by sleeplessness, and confessed to Victoria, '*Ich hange gar nicht am Leben; du hangst sehr daran...* [I do not cling to life; you do; but I set no store by it.]. 'I am sure that if I had a severe illness I should give up at once; I should not struggle for life. I have no tenacity of life.'

In retrospect, his fatalism appears more like self-diagnosis than prophecy. He was in no condition, mentally or physically, to fulfill a commitment to inspect the new buildings for the Staff College and Royal Military Academy at Sandhurst, long one of his goals, but he went anyway, on 22 November, despite a drenching rain – '*entsetzlicher Regen*' in his diary. He returned to Windsor wet and exhausted.

Still, Albert pushed himself further. When he returned from Sandhurst he was feeling too ill for the usual round of domestic activities that comprised much of the 'Court Circular' in the daily press, even failing to accompany the Queen on an afternoon walk. '*Bin recht elend*' – 'am very wretched' – he confessed in his diary on the 24th, but he had determined to have it out with his son, and ordered a special train to Cambridge for the next morning.

Rather than remain indoors for a heart-to-heart talk, he went out with Bertie despite a cold, intermittent rain and, although in no condition for an extended stroll, Albert had to go on longer than he anticipated because in the apparently emotional exchange they missed a turning. But Albert extracted assurances of appropriately princely conduct henceforth, and forgave his son, promising that there would be no investigation of the friends who had led him into wrongdoing. Remaining overnight at Madingley Hall, Albert returned on the 26th more exhausted than ever, admitting to pain in his back and legs, and to having slept little in two weeks of stress. The rheumatic symptoms, the

Queen suggested in her diary, were due to 'Bertie's mistaking the road during their walk'. Only on the 28th was Albert able to get about somewhat, although still suffering from pain and insomnia. That morning he learned of the *Trent* affair.

The first and worst diplomatic crisis of the American Civil War had begun on 8 November 1861 when the Confederate envoys (technically, 'Commissioners', as they had no diplomatic status) James Murray Mason of Virginia and John Slidell of Louisiana, were removed by force from the British West Indian mail packet *Trent* in the Caribbean. With their two aides, they had been taken aboard the American steam frigate *San Jacinto* commanded by Captain Charles Wilkes.

Secessionist president Jefferson Davis, frustrated by the failures of his agents in England and France to secure recognition of the Confederacy and eager to purchase ships and arms, had ordered Mason and Slidell to run the Union blockade to Cuba and find their way to Europe. Enemy communications were contraband of war. If the envoys carried nothing but oral instructions they could have been, legally, 'the embodiment of dispatches'.

*The Confederate commissioners removed from the British mail packet* Trent *(left) to the USS* San Jacinto. *(Engraving in the US Naval Historical Center, Washington, DC)*

Chasing the *Trent* down in the Old Bahama Channel, Wilkes ordered two warning shots to be fired across the ship's bow. The packet hove to, and Navy Lieutenant Donald M. Fairfax and a small detachment of marines boarded.

While Fairfax insisted upon custody of the Confederates, Mrs Slidell lectured him that Northerners were 'doing the very thing the South was hoping for – something to arouse England... Really, Captain Wilkes is playing into our hands!'

When the Americans returned to their frigate, Wilkes watched the *Trent* steam away rather than head to a Federal harbour with a prize crew. He may have wondered why his deputy, against orders, had let the packet go, but Wilkes did nothing about it. He had his prisoners, who would, he expected, serve out the war in a Northern cell.

The news reached England on 27 November. London newspapers the next morning seethed with indignation and demands for revenge. Historian Henry Adams, then unpaid additional secretary to his father, Charles Francis Adams, the courtly new American Minister, wrote later that if the Atlantic cable had been in operation, Britain would have gone to war with the North. The undersea link from Ireland to Newfoundland had operated briefly in 1858 before breaking apart. Only in 1868 was it finally in service again. In a climate of immediate communications, the hotheads might have prevailed.

Palmerston and Russell appear to have looked forward to a confrontation with the Union – possibly short of war – as a pretext to support the cotton-rich South. 'It is in the highest degree likely', the Prime Minister minuted Russell, 'that the North will not be able to subdue the South, and... if the Southern Union is established as an independent state, it would afford a valuable and extensive market for British manufactures. But the operations of the war have as yet been too inconclusive to warrant a [formal] acknowledgment of the Southern Union.' Palmerston was aware that a Union paddle-wheeler, the *James Adger*, had put into Southampton. He already knew that Mason and Slidell were planning to cross the Atlantic on a British steamer from St Thomas in the Virgin Islands, the *Trent*'s next destination. In the North it was thought that the emissaries had escaped the blockade of Charleston on the Confederate cruiser *Nashville* on a direct run to England, and Commander John Bonnett Marchand of the *James Adger* had left New York on 16 October in pursuit. The Prime Minister assumed that the *Adger*, coaling in Southampton harbour, was waiting for a packet flying the British White Ensign.

Although Palmerston had employed gunboat diplomacy against a weaker nation in the Don Pacifico affair, the pinnacle of his reputation for international truculence, on 11 November he called in his principal legal advisers for counsel. The United States was not puny Greece. What courses of action could England follow under international law, Palmerston asked, if a British vessel were accosted and the Southern envoys seized?

The question recalled the War of 1812, fought in part because the British claimed the right to board ships of other nations to remove Royal Navy deserters and to impress seamen claimed to be of British origin. That issue had been left unresolved by the Treaty of Ghent ending the war. A written opinion produced for Palmerston a day later concluded that the Americans had been right in 1812 and thus had no more lawful authority in 1861 to search a neutral vessel and remove passengers than the British did earlier. The document prompted the Prime Minister, who was anticipating (and possibly even welcoming) trouble, to summon Minister Adams. As the military fortunes of the Union had declined, and with them respect for him and his mission, Adams had endured a difficult year. American envoys were long considered to have substituted pallbearer's garb for Court dress because of State Department instructions that they be suited without aristocratic pretensions. When Adams had presented his credentials to the Queen and Prince on 19 May 1861, wearing traditional diplomatic costume, Victoria is said to have remarked tartly, 'I am thankful we shall have no more American funerals'.

With hardly more courtesy, Palmerston confronted Adams with the seaport rumour that the *James Adger* was awaiting an opportunity to intercept the Southern emissaries, warning, according to the Minister's report to Secretary of State William H. Seward, 'It would be regarded here very unpleasantly if the captain, after enjoying the hospitality of this country, [and] filling his ship with coals and other supplies, and filling his own stomach with brandy' – and here he laughed in his characteristic way – 'should, within sight of the shore, commit an act which would be felt as offensive to the national flag.'

Palmerston already knew that there would be no immediate difficulty from the American warship, as he had in his pocket a report from one of his operatives that the captain, 'having got very drunk this morning at Southampton with some excellent brandy, and find it blow heavily at sea', had decided not to weigh anchor. Not having the benefit of such up-to-date intelligence, Adams assured the Prime Minister that his apprehensions were groundless.

Adams's message to Seward about Palmerston's warning was still *en route* by sea to Washington when the *San Jacinto* docked in Norfolk on the evening of 15 November. (The Union controlled the chief ports of secessionist Virginia.) From there Secretary of the Navy Gideon Welles ordered Wilkes to take his prisoners to Fort Warren in Boston harbour. The news raced north quickly – that at noon on 8 November, a week earlier, the Southerners, then four thousand miles from the English Channel, had been encountered in waters north of Cuba, and taken captive.

The Queen and Prince learned of the anxieties in Whitehall on 13 November from Palmerston, who reviewed for them his conference at the Treasury. International law as accepted during the Napoleonic wars condoned a search, and the removal of the vessel to a harbour of the belligerent. Proceedings there for its seizure were justified 'if enemy dispatches were found on board, or any other contraband'. Palmerston had seen Adams, and assured him that the arrival of Slidell and Mason in England 'would have no more effect on the policy of her Majesty with regard to America than the presence of the three other Southern Deputies who have been here for many months'. Yet the Southerners had an informal legation in Suffolk Street, not far from the Houses of Parliament and Downing Street, had established contacts with MPs and sympathizers in the aristocracy, and were zealous in bargaining cotton for weapons.

In his distinctive third-person manner, Henry Adams recalled that on the afternoon of 27 November, while he languished in the American Legation in Mansfield Street, quiet during the absence of the Minister and Mrs Adams on a visit to Yorkshire, a Reuters telegram reporting the seizure of Mason and Slidell had come. The agency had facilities at Cork in Ireland, enabling Reuters to beat transatlantic news from ships arriving in Liverpool by several hours. 'All three secretaries, public and private, were there – nervous as wild beasts under the long strain on their endurance – and all three, though they knew it to be not merely their order of departure – not merely a diplomatic rupture – but a declaration of war – broke into shouts of delight. They were glad to face the end. They saw it and cheered it! Since England was waiting only for its own moment to strike, they were eager to strike first.'

Second Secretary Benjamin Moran, less elated than Adams, wrote anxiously in his diary, 'I am satisfied that the act will do more for the Southerners than ten victories, for it touches John Bull's honor, and the honor of his flag. I telegraphed the news at once to Mr Adams, and fear it has not added to his enjoyment of rural retirement.'

The Adamses were at Fryston Hall as guests of Richard Monckton Milnes, MP, soon to be Baron Houghton, who had arranged for the literary company of Froudes, Gaskells and Forsters to show England at its sophisticated best for the son and grandson of two American presidents. 'Telegram delivered to Mr Adams while he was inspecting Pomfret Castle announcing *the North* had captured Southerners off Eng. ship', Annabel Monckton Milnes jotted down in her pocket diary for 27 November 1861. To her sister she wrote, after the Americans had rushed back to London by train, 'This terrible threat of War in the far West is hanging over England! May God in his mercy avert such a calamity!... *Richee* and *all England* are feeling anxious about this American dispute...'

Adams expected to have his passport returned as soon as Whitehall learned the news, and was worried, as his hosts in Yorkshire had been, that war was inevitable. Even before he had arrived back in London, the Confederate commissioners there had rushed a memorandum to Russell and Palmerston contending that while envoys proceeding from an enemy port to a neutral one were subject to seizure, whatever the flag, if they were travelling from one neutral port to another, they were, under international law, to be conveyed unmolested, as were their dispatches. Only an admiralty tribunal, W.L. Yancey, P.A. Rost, and A. Dudley Mann wrote, could decide otherwise, and no such hearing had been held for the *Trent*. And they claimed for their imprisoned countrymen 'the full benefit of that protection to which every private person who seeks shelter under the British flag and demeans himself according to British law has heretofore ever before to be entitled'. A second letter from the trio would emphasize 'the great outrage upon the British flag'.

In Richmond, President Davis had already addressed the Confederate Congress on the *Trent* affair, declaring on 18 November, 'These gentlemen' – to the North they were rebel escapees – 'were as much under the jurisdiction of the British Government upon that ship and beneath its flag as if they had been on its soil, and a claim on the part of the United States to seize them in the streets of London would have been as well founded as to apprehend them where they were taken'.

The London press occupied itself with American belligerent rights at sea. Palmerston's own law officers advised that Captain Wilkes had illegally taken international law into his own hands – or had been instructed to do so by Washington. As Adams phrased it, ruefully, 'Great Britain would have been less offended if the United States had insulted her a good deal more'. By then Palmerston and everyone else had forgotten about the *James Adger*, which had slipped out of Southampton and into the Atlantic. But the irrelevant *Nashville* was never sighted, and Marchand would arrive in Hampton Roads, Virginia on 2 December, while the *Trent* imbroglio was still unsettled.

In Anthony Trollope's *Phineas Finn* (1867–69), the fictional Prime Minister asks the young MP, 'Have you seen the news from America?' 'Yes', says Finn, 'I have seen it but do not believe it.' Provoking the Empire seemed beyond comprehension.

Among the Queen's guests on 28 November, a Thursday, was the ambitious Chancellor of the Exchequer, W.E. Gladstone, whom Albert had wooed long and hard for military funding, and who was envisioned as a future Prime Minister. Earlier in the year the Prince had sent him a draft 'Law for Ministerial Responsibility' for Prussia, which Vicky had drawn up for her husband, 'intended to be called for by the opposition in that country and dreaded by many advisers of the King'. It appeared 'so well argued, that I made the Prince of Wales translate it from the German'. Clearly, Albert had a preliminary hand in it. In liberal but ill-conceived good will, he had been interfering in the internal affairs of another sovereign nation, and then displayed the evidence as a gesture of confidence in Gladstone. Only two weeks before the dinner, the Prince, whose activities had inevitably fallen off with his illness, had, as Master of Trinity House, honoured Gladstone with an appointment as an Elder Brother. Gladstone had already received from Albert a printed copy of his British Association address at Aberdeen, and an article from the *Revue des deux Mondes*, which Albert read regularly, on the financing of imperial France.

Returning to London from Windsor, Gladstone noted laconically in his diary, 'The Queen and Prince spoke much of the American news, &

in the anti-Northern sense.' The evening saw Albert's first attempt at
dinner in many days: news of the outrage had animated him. The next
day, 29 November, because of the crisis, the Queen went into London
without him to learn what she could of a Cabinet debate on the affair,
but had to return before it was ended. Although Albert had reported
himself as '*noch immer recht miserable*' – 'still extremely miserable' – he
was determined to show himself and avoid gossip about his health, and
had stood that morning for twenty minutes to watch two hundred Eton
College Volunteers pass in review. The weather was unseasonably mild,
but the Prince wore a coat with a fur lining and walked very slowly. '*Ich
muss leider dabei erscheinen*', he confided weakly in his diary – 'Unhappily I must put in an appearance'.

That Friday evening Gladstone was deputed back to Windsor, '&
reported to Q. & Prince'. Before dinner he sent a note to the Queen
'that the Cabinet is of opinion that reparation for the seizure of Messrs
Mason and Slidell ought to be asked from the Government of the
United States and that Lord Russell is to prepare a dispatch on which
the Cabinet will deliberate tomorrow, for submission to Your Majesty'.

Confined to his bedroom all afternoon, Albert left it to learn what
had happened. By then his initial wrath over the *Trent* affair had begun
to moderate. During the first years of his marriage he had been involved
in the movement to suppress the slave trade, and must have recalled that
the Royal Navy in the early 1840s had claimed the right to search
American vessels suspected to be slavers. It was known in England that
Slidell when a Senator in 1850 had helped to draft the notorious
Fugitive Slave Law. In *The Times* that morning had appeared letters,
signed 'Templar' and 'Senex', from readers conversant in international
law, warning of the tenuous grounds for demanding reparations from
Washington. 'There can be no reason of principle', 'Templar' argued,
'why persons other than military may not be contraband if they be in
fact engaged in furthering the military operations of the enemy.' 'Senex'
raised the point that 'You may stop the Ambassador of your enemy on
his passage, but when he has arrived and taken up himself the functions
of his office and has been admitted in his representative character, he
becomes...entitled to peculiar [diplomatic] privileges, as set apart for
the relations of amity and peace.' Further, 'Senex' recalled, a declaration
by the Queen on 15 April 1854, early in the Crimean War, contained the
passage (very likely Palmerstonian), 'It is impossible for Her Majesty to

forgo the exercise of her right of seizing articles [that are] contraband of war, and of preventing neutrals from carrying [the] enemy's despatches.' And newspapers had published reports of interviews with Mrs Slidell, who had now arrived with her daughter, seventeen-year-old Rosina, on the *Trent*, revealing that she had concealed her husband's contraband papers under her capacious crinoline.

Although Victoria had admired Harriet Beecher Stowe, read her *Uncle Tom's Cabin*, and even arranged to meet the lady who was the best-known foe of the Fugitive Slave Law, her emotions were now confused. To Vicky in Berlin, she wrote, 'The great and all absorbing event of the day is the American outrage. The Government have decided (and they could not do anything else – as the act is quite illegal) to ask reparation and if this is not given – we know what must follow. They are such ruffians!' Ill as he was, Albert had a conversion to attempt once the Queen's guests took their leave.

The next day, Foreign Minister Earl Russell (as Lord John had become) would draw up a Cabinet-approved memorandum to Lord Lyons, Minister to the United States, directing 'that the Washington Government' – the very term was truculent, implicitly recognizing a rival capital in Richmond, Virginia – 'should be told that what has been done is a violation of international law, and of the rights of Great Britain, and that Her Majesty's Government trust that the act will be disavowed and that the prisoners set free and restored to British protection; and that ... if this demand is refused, he' – Lyons – 'should retire from the United States'.

Reports from Unionists in London were much like that of George Francis Train in the *Boston Journal* – that 'the Army, the Navy, the Church, the Parliament, the Aristocracy, the Banker[s]', were supporting secession although ordinary people ('the pit and the gallery') were fearful of war and sympathetic with the Federal government. English vessels were shipping 'every sort of contraband to aid the rebellion', he claimed, and when Adams had protested to Palmerston, the Prime Minister had allegedly (so Train wrote) retorted, 'We know it; catch them if you can.'

Expecting that the *Trent* case would be a pretext for war, the *Boston Post* vowed 'Such a war will bring starvation to [British] doors. We have been their best customers; we have furnished them with bread, and we have bought their goods. The first hostile gun fired, and the doors of

Commerce will be slammed in the face of insolent Britannia. Not a bushel of grain – not a yard of cloth – shall cross the ocean.'

The enthusiasm of the Unionist press over the coup of the *San Jacinto* was interpreted in England to mean that Captain Wilkes had acted on the orders of Secretary of State Seward, to whom President Abraham Lincoln usually deferred in foreign relations matters. Seward and Lincoln now seemed captives of public opinion in the North. The shots across the bow of the *Trent* were not intended to provoke war with Britain – which should have been clear from a report in London that Fairfax had confided on boarding the *Trent* that his captain had acted on his own initiative. Yet the boarding of a ship flying the British flag seemed an insult to the empire. 'Bear this, bear all!' was the rallying cry in the London press. Eight thousand troops were ordered to Canada; warships were transferred to waters off the American coast; the sale of munitions to the North (but not to the South) was halted; arsenals in Britain were put on day-and-night shifts; and the Cunard steamer *Europa* sailed to New York with preliminary instructions to Lyons that could lead to a break in relations and possibly much more. On his own, he wrote on 19 November to Russell, 'I don't think it likely that they' – the North – 'will give in, but I do not think it impossible that they may do so, particularly if the next news from England brings a note of warlike preparation, and determination on the part of [our] Government and people.'

Having listened for two evenings to the Prince's moderating views on the *Trent* crisis, Gladstone wrote to Palmerston on Saturday morning, 30 November, after returning from Windsor on the 11.25 to Paddington. Later the same day, he noted in his diary 'Ld Russell's draft softened & abridged'. Revised Foreign Office drafts of instructions to Lyons arrived late on Saturday at Windsor while the Queen presided over yet another dinner for visiting dignitaries. The Prince, too ill to sit at the table, was absent. Yet he may not have been too ill to have seen that morning's *Times*, which would have been brought to him as usual. Prominent in it was another letter from a lawyer with an Inns of Court address, signed 'Justitia', which downgraded the seizure of the Confederate party to 'an irregularity...admitted even by those who are disposed to take the least inflammatory view of the subject'.

A Prize Court, the writer proposed, 'might have fairly taken the confession of Mr Slidell and his friends, that they were Southern

Commissioners, coupled with the occupation in which it is notorious that other Southern Commissioners are now engaged, as a sufficient proof of their mission. If the Court had come to such a decision, could the English Government have disputed their judgement as one in gross violation of law and justice? If not, it would have been binding on us, and the *Trent* would have been condemned as lawful prize.' Because the United States had not taken the *Trent* into port, the writer claimed that the act was illegal only in 'form', not in 'substance'.

The solution, 'Justitia' proposed, 'is this – what we are entitled beyond all question to demand is an apology for the illegal and irregular proceeding... and an undertaking that the offence shall not be re-peated... I cannot think that we are entitled to push our demand to the extreme point of requiring the restitution of the Commissioners. Such a demand would almost certainly be repelled. And England, before she can appeal to the arbitrament of arms, must have a quarrel good not only in *form*, but in substance.'

Whatever the legalities, another certainty was that a Palmerston government would not settle for less than the release of the Southerners. Albert had experienced enough confrontations with 'Pam' to realize that. The Prince had to reconcile, in any approach of his own, domestic needs with foreign policy pragmatism, and *The Times* had also held out the editorial hope that the seizure, as reported, was 'the act of the American commander, and was not expressly directed by his government'.*

Both Palmerston and Russell had prepared the Queen on Friday, 29 November, the day before, to receive a strong Cabinet draft, 'which will go to your Majesty about four o'clock tomorrow', and required '[no] loss of time', Russell urged, as the documents, in that pre-mechanical age, had to be recopied in time to make the Sunday evening mail packet

---

* Unknown yet in London was the congratulatory message from Secretary of the Navy Welles to Captain Wilkes – now promoted to Commodore – for his 'great public service' – but which also admonished him for failing to bring the *Trent* into port for adjudication. Not until 2 December would Congress pass an ill-considered joint resolution thanking Wilkes, and requesting President Lincoln to award Wilkes a special gold medal. 'I paid my respects to the President', Wilkes wrote in a memoir, '& had some conversation with him. He remarked that I had kicked up a breeze, but he intended to stand by me and rejoiced over the boldness, as he said, of my act.' But there was no gold medal, and despite his elevation in rank, no 'hearty welcome' from Welles when he visited the Navy Department in person.

to New York. Palmerston had been more inflammatory in his own preparatory letter, employing unsubstantiated allegations which suggested a reluctance to offer Washington anything it could honourably accept. The affair had been 'a gross outrage and [a] violation of international law has been committed'. The American response necessitated 'reparation and redress'.

Although Mrs Slidell had reported the boarding officer's admission of unilateral action, 'it was known', Palmerston claimed to the Queen, that the warship had put into St Thomas several weeks before 'and had there received communications from New York; and it is also said that General [Winfield] Scott, who has recently arrived in France, has said to Americans in Paris that he has not come on an excursion of pleasure, but on diplomatic business; that the seizure of these envoys was discussed in Cabinet at Washington, he being present, and was deliberately determined upon and ordered; that the Washington Cabinet fully foresaw that it might lead to war with England'. Further, Palmerston alleged, the elderly leader of the American war with Mexico (a doddering seventy-five) had been 'commissioned to propose to France in that case to join the northern States in war against England, and to offer France in that case restoration of [Quebec,] the French province of Canada'. Scott, he sneered, would 'find himself much mistaken', for the French government 'is probably thinking more about Cotton than about Canada'.

Palmerston seemed eager to raise the warlike hackles of a queen who had called herself 'a soldier's daughter'. England had been insulted, and America had been conspiring to draw her into war. In the Commons, Richard Cobden warned, 'Palmerston likes to drive the wheel close to the edge, and show how dexterously he can avoid falling over the precipice.'

Victoria brought the documents to Albert as he lay on a sofa awaiting the departure of her guests. He had already seen the Prime Minister's anticipatory invective, and now his ultimatum to the United States – it had that strident Palmerstonian tone – further agitated the Prince. 'This means war!' he warned.

As Albert lay, sleepless, into Sunday morning (1 December) – he had moved to a separate room days earlier to avoid disturbing Victoria – he pondered alternative approaches that could satisfy national pride and meet the government's minimum political requirements, yet might enable Washington to accede gracefully. Finally, in the lingering darkness that followed a December dawn he arose and struggled to draw up a response to the Cabinet for the Queen to re-draft and sign.

Palmerston and Russell, it was clear, had little expectation that Washington could afford, in the face of American public opinion, to submit to the British terms, even if Seward and Lincoln saw them as tolerable. While Adams waited for instructions from Washington, Seward was writing, too late to be of use, 'We have done nothing to anticipate the discussion [in Downing Street], and we have not furnished you with any explanations ... because we feel it is more prudent that the ground to be taken by the British government should first be made known to us here ...' Meanwhile, the Prime Minister expected – he wrote to Russell – that they would not get what they demanded from the United States 'without fighting for it', while *The Times* suggested that Seward wanted war in order to seize Canada as a replacement for the lost South. In Paris, the American consul, John Bigelow, saw British exploitation of the Mason–Slidell incident as an opportunity to split the Union. As Albert had told Disraeli, English newspapers orchestrated public opinion; indignation, with the lure of cotton in the background, and the salvage of industrial jobs, intensified daily, despite moral support in the Midlands for the anti-slavery North. 'That pink of modesty and refinement, *The Times*', Benjamin Moran seethed in his diary, 'is filled with such slatternly abuse of us and ours, that it is fair to conclude that all the Fishwives of Billingsgate have been transferred to Printing House Square to fill the ears of the writers there with their choicest phraseology'.

It was nearly eight o'clock when Albert shuffled to the Queen with his pages, confessing, as he handed them to her, '*Ich bin so schwach, ich habe kaum die Feder halten können*' – 'I am so weak, I have hardly been able to hold the pen'. In the margin of the manuscript Victoria would later note, 'This draft was the last the beloved Prince ever wrote ...' He could eat no breakfast, and returned to bed.

Setting her agitation about Albert aside, Victoria examined his response, making few alterations. 'The Queen returns these important Drafts', she wrote to Palmerston,

> which upon the whole she approves; but she cannot help feeling that the main Draft – that for communication to the American government – is somewhat meagre. She should have liked to have seen the

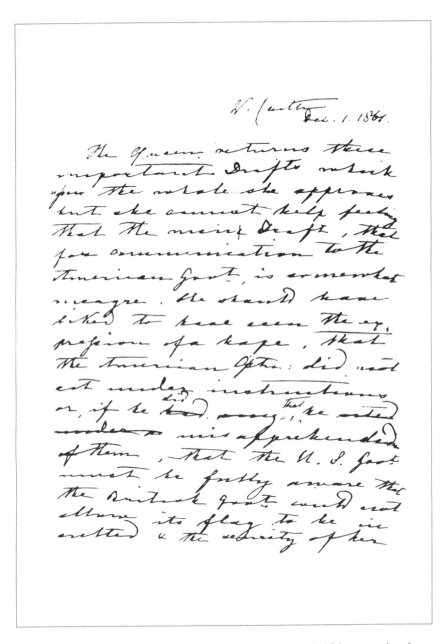

*Albert confessed that he was so weak that he could hardly hold his pen when he drafted his response to the Cabinet's* Trent *ultimatum on the morning of 1 December 1861.*

expression of a hope, that the American captain did not act under instructions, or, if he did, that he misapprehended them, – that the United States Government must be fully aware that the British Government could not allow its flag to be insulted, and the security of her mail communications to be placed in jeopardy; and Her Majesty's Government are unwilling to believe that the United States Government intended wantonly to put an insult upon this country, and to add to their many distressing complications by forcing a question of dispute upon us, and that we are therefore glad to believe that, upon a full consideration of the undoubted breach of International Law committed, they would spontaneously offer such redress as alone could satisfy this country, *viz*, the restoration of the unfortunate passengers and a suitable apology.

Palmerston read the Queen's message as he received further reports from New York – mail took ten to twelve days by sea to London – about the jubilation following Wilkes's exploit. The *New York Times* on 19 November had predicted, since it was 'such an exact imitation' of past English policy, that its government 'will [not] even remonstrate.' The *New York Tribune* suggested that English military assistance to the South was aimed at eliminating the United States as a commercial rival. Poet James Russell Lowell, later a much-admired American Minister to London, would capture public resentment of what seemed bullying from Britain in verses deploring,

> It don't seem hardly right, John,
> When both my hands was full,
> To stump me to a fight, John –
> Your cousin, *tu*, John Bull . . .

While Albert insisted on walking on the Castle terrace for half an hour, and, although looking pale and ill, to make a show – it was a Sunday – of attending Chapel with the Queen before returning to bed, Victoria's response on the *Trent* crisis was rushed by messenger to Whitehall. Refusing luncheon, Albert confessed to recurrent stomach pain and chills. Both Sir James Clark and Dr William Jenner came to see him but offered no new medication. The Prince also refused dinner and, shifting back and forth from sofa to bed, retired early but again could not sleep.

In London, Albert's expedient in the Queen's memorandum was immediately apparent to Palmerston and Russell. In a letter to Windsor on 29 November, which the Prince had read, Palmerston had acknowledged that the *San Jacinto* boarding-party had admitted to acting independently of Washington. The Prince preferred that explanation to the conspiratorial one attributed to ancient General Scott. Albert wanted Seward and Lincoln to have the opportunity, even if untrue, of denying responsibility for Captain Wilkes's breach of international law, and thereby to be able, without loss of dignity, to relinquish the Southerners. Despite the belligerence of the British press, Albert also saw no risk in removing from Palmerston's stipulations offensive expressions which might block a politic Federal retreat. *Punch*'s John Bull could warn Brother Jonathan – Uncle Sam's precursor – 'You do what's right, my son, or I'll blow you out of the water', but American honour precluded submitting to threats.

'Your Majesty's position is anyhow a good one', Palmerston (while still unaware how ill Albert was) conceded to the Queen. The conciliatory approach was not the one which the Prime Minister preferred, but Russell's instructions to Lord Lyons in Washington and the message he was to deliver to Seward reflected the temper of the Prince's draft, concluding,

> Her Majesty's Government, bearing in mind the friendly relations which have long subsisted between Great Britain and the United States, are willing to believe that the United States naval officer who committed this aggression was not acting in compliance with any authority from his Government, or that, if he conceived himself to be so authorised, he greatly misunderstood the instructions which he had received. For the Government of the United States must be fully aware that the British Government could not allow such an affront to the national honour to pass without full reparation; and Her Majesty's Government are unwilling to believe that it could be the deliberate intention of the Government of the United States unnecessarily to force into discussion between the two Governments a question of so grave a character, and with regard to which the whole British Nation would be sure to entertain such unanimity of feeling.

Her Majesty's Government therefore trust that, when this matter shall have been brought under the consideration of the United States, that Government will of its own accord offer to the British Government such redress as alone could satisfy the British nation, namely, the liberation of the four gentlemen, and their delivery to your Lordship, in order that they may again be placed under British protection, and a suitable apology for the aggression which has been committed.

Beneath the wooden diplomatic prose, the message was more tactful than Palmerston had intended. Frustrated in his pro-South subterfuges, he wrote hopefully to Russell on 6 December 1861 as their moderated provisos made their way on a mail packet to New York, 'It is difficult not to come to the conclusion that the rabid hatred of England which animates the exiled Irishmen who direct almost all the Northern newspapers, will so excite the masses as to make it impossible for Lincoln and Seward to grant our demands; and we must therefore look forward to war as the probable result . . . Republican nations or nations in which the masses influence or direct the destinies of the country are swayed much more by passion than by interest.'

When, on 19 December, the Foreign Minister received a surprisingly pacific reply from Seward, indicating that Mason and Slidell and their two aides would be released and put aboard a British steamer to Southampton, a decision confirmed by a Christmas Day Cabinet meeting, Palmerston suppressed the news until the press learned that the Southerners had actually sailed. Northerners were disgusted and unrepentant, but resigned. 'I had no right to object to the manner in which the Govt thought proper to act', Commodore Wilkes wrote, 'but when Mr Seward read me his dispatch to Lord Russell and asked my opinion of it, I frankly told him it was an act which I had not expected . . . I felt a glow of shame for my country . . .' In 'Donelson', Herman Melville compared 'The bitter cup / Of that hard Countermand / Which gave the Envoys up' to 'wormwood in the mouth'. To London publisher Frederic Chapman, Anthony Trollope wrote, 'So we are to have no war; I for one am very glad.'

It remains one of the intriguing *ifs* of the age that without Albert's intervention, the last political act of his life, in defusing the belligerent Palmerston–Russell ultimatum, there might have been an

Anglo-American war which could have drawn in France,* and irrevocably divided both Canada and the United States.

In the early days of December, Albert continued to deteriorate. His sleeplessness aggravated his fatigue. Food nauseated him; even soup with a bit of brown bread caused vomiting. Dr Jenner examined him and saw no cause for concern, although he thought that 'a long feverish indisposition' would be dangerous. Still, Albert's malaise and general discomfort had not been followed by fever, which encouraged Victoria to downplay the illness when Palmerston, sincerely anxious, asked to have another physician called in. In a few days it will 'pass off', she assured him. 'In addition to Sir James Clark, the Queen has the advantage of the constant advice of Dr Jenner, a most skillful Physician, and Her Majesty would be very unwilling to cause unnecessary alarm, where no cause exists for it, by calling in a Medical Man who does not upon ordinary occasions attend.'

The lack of alarm showed in the casualness of Albert's treatment – or lack of it. When he could, he paced about his dressing-room, and sometimes changed bedrooms. He could keep little food down, even tea, and alternated between wild incoherence and being a competent host to his children, who came to talk or to read to him. In an age when nurses functioned only in hospitals, the Prince was tended by such personal servants as Rudolf Löhlein, Court retainers, and Princess Alice. Eighteen, with no previous responsibility of any sort, she filled the vacuum as head nurse with instinctive authority, following her father when he padded restlessly about.

On 8 December, a Sunday, the doctors around Albert even told the Queen, because he seemed to be no worse, that he appeared somewhat better, a verdict made plausible when he asked to hear some music. Alice played, as he requested, the Lutheran chorale 'A Mighty Fortress Is Our God', but he soon murmured, '*Das reicht hin*' – 'That's enough'. Later, Alice was permitted to play several German songs that she knew were his favourites, and he asked to have his sofa moved closer to the window so that he could watch the clouds drift across the sky. When

---

* The French Minister in Washington, and, after the fact, the Foreign Minister, sided with the British, but words and war are very different matters, and the opportunistic Napoleon III may well have attempted to regain Quebec much as he tried, vainly, in 1863 to seat a puppet emperor on a throne he created for Prince Maximilian in Mexico.

Alice thought he had dozed off, she covered him with a blanket. He opened his eyes. 'Were you asleep?' she asked.

'No,' he said, with a wan smile, 'but my thoughts were so happy that I did not want to drive them away by moving.'

In the evening, Victoria read to him from Walter Scott's *Peveril of the Peak*, but he had her stop when he decided to change bedrooms again, and walked from her own to the 'King's Room' – the Blue Room, in which both George IV and William IV had died. He was apparently preparing for his own death, yet everything that his attending physicians could possibly conceive as a sign of improvement was so interpreted, and his renewed activity appeared to them positive and welcome.

The next day, the two envoys who had been on a condolence visit to Lisbon, Lord Methuen and General Seymour (Albert's companion in Italy in 1839), arrived, and Albert insisted upon seeing them. If they were carrying typhoid from Portugal, he may have thought the disease could hardly hurt him now. Also at Windsor was gouty Lord Palmerston, leaning on canes, to urge again that other medical opinions be sought. Again the Queen refused, although she was increasingly worried because Albert's mind was wandering and he insisted on calling her '*gutes Weibchen*' – 'good little wife' – and holding her hand.

Since a low fever had been confirmed, doctors now remained in attendance day and night. Jenner possessed considerable clinical experience of typhoid fever – often euphemistically referred to as 'gastric fever' – and finally thought he saw evidence of the characteristic pink rash of the disease. That it should have taken Jenner so long to identify Albert's ailment, if indeed he had, remains a mystery, for when he was a young physician in 1845 (he was now forty-six) he had published a paper establishing the clinico-pathologic distinction between typhus and typhoid fever. In any case, whatever he identified as typhoid, given his special reputation, was almost certain to be accepted as such by most other physicians – and by the Queen, who later knighted him. To her, he explained the implications of the disease in a dismissive manner. It would run its course in a month if there were no 'bad symptoms', as Victoria put it in her journal. The Prince was not to know any more than that he had a 'feverish cold'.

Nor was the public. The previous Sunday, two days earlier, a bulletin had been issued by his doctors declaring exactly that, adding that there were 'no unfavourable symptoms'. No new bulletin would be issued to the press identifying typhoid, and fresh releases on 11 December and 12 December would be equally uninformative except for the ominous implication of the signatures of additional physicians. No cases of typhoid appeared otherwise in the vicinity of Windsor, nor had any emerged at Sandhurst, where, in any event, Albert had arrived too ill to have luncheon, and had drunk nothing.

Tuesday, 10 December, found Albert too weak and listless to make any attempt to dress. To the Prince's aides, his condition seemed grave. They remembered Palmerston's repeated appeals for better medical advice. The Prince and the Prime Minister had often been at odds, but the elderly politician had come to respect Albert's abilities, and was concerned about losing him. Recalling the Flora Hastings embarrassment twenty-two years earlier, before the advent of the Prince, and the persistence at Court of the medical authority of that era, Sir James Clark, now seventy-three, Palmerston had earlier urged on Sir Charles Phipps the necessity of forestalling an even more tragic misdiagnosis. 'If it is unavoidable that the highest interests of the nation be sacrificed to personal and professional jealousy,' he warned, 'there is no help for it and so it must be. I could say much about the past, but my thoughts are wholly engrossed with the future.' There was still the risk of war with the United States. If that occurred, he wanted Albert available. The monarchy without him was almost inconceivable, and the instructions to Lord Lyons were on a mail packet due to arrive in New York the next day.

Beyond the Prince's family, the most distraught observer of the inevitable, his feelings complicated by unhappy medical insight and the helplessness of distance, was Baron Stockmar in Coburg. By early December he was disregarding information from the Court on Albert's condition as unreliable, and queried Squires, the royal chemists, to find out what medication had been prescribed. Peter Squire handed the letter to his head apothecary, David Williamson, telling him, he later recalled to his son, 'that if he liked he could reply to it, but that he must be on the side of extreme caution'. Very likely the actual preparations would have evidenced that the Prince was not being treated with anything intended to be curative.

On the morning of the eleventh, Albert sat up in bed to drink beef tea. When his aide, General Grey, also brought him some unwelcome and useless medicine, he managed a wry joke, raising the glass weakly and saying, 'Your very good health, Grey'. The gesture did not deceive the Queen, who was more frank than usual with Vicky, perhaps preparing herself as well as her daughter for the worst. The Court physicians remained satisfied with Albert's condition, she wrote – 'though he gets sadly thin. It is a dreadful trial to witness this, and requires all my strength of mind and courage not to be overcome – when I look at him...' They were so 'fortunate in the doctors', she insisted, but it was necessary 'to satisfy the public to have another eminent doctor to come and see him, which I own distressed me much...however I submitted'.

Despite some resentment from Clark and Jenner, Thomas Watson, one of the Physicians Extraordinary to the Queen, and the equally veteran Sir Henry Holland were called in, and the Queen clasped Holland's hands in hers and cried, 'Oh, you will save him for me, Dr Holland! You will save him for me, will you not?'

Both physicians accepted the minimal therapy in progress, but Sir Henry, recognizing that the public had to be prepared for what was beyond medicine, drew up a bulletin for the press, beginning, 'Hitherto there has been no anticipation of danger...' When his text was submitted to the Queen she was unable to face the implication, and struck out 'Hitherto'.

Neither Clark nor the septuagenarian Holland, Lord Clarendon deplored, 'were fit to attend a sick cat', but Sir Henry, at the least, was a realist. Once physician to George IV's estranged Queen Caroline, he dismissed the Prince's wandering mind as 'of no consequence, though very distressing'.

As Victoria suggested to her daughter in Berlin, the eminent Dr Watson, author of a textbook on medicine and later Sir Thomas Watson, was superfluous, but only because the Prince could not benefit from his pharmacopoeia. Had the Queen recalled Lord Melbourne's remark that 'English physicians kill you; the French let you die', she might have understood that Albert's doctors were applying, despite their Anglo-Saxon training, the humane French method. Sedated with brandy and given little else, Albert was failing rapidly.

On the twelfth, when another innocuous bulletin was issued by the four physicians in attendance, the Prince coughed up a large quantity of mucus. He shuddered with chills and with quickened breathing, although he was able, briefly, to lay his head affectionately on Victoria's shoulder as she knelt at his bedside. His temperature had risen, and he was often delirious. He imagined that he heard the birds singing at the Rosenau, and was consumed by absurd worries, even about cousins he had not seen for years. More lucidly, he asked Alice, now almost constantly present, whether Vicky knew about his illness. 'Yes,' said Alice truthfully. 'I told her you were very ill.'

'You did wrong. You should have told her that I am dying. Yes, I am dying.'

Alice had seen her father try to confide much the same recognition to the Queen, who resisted by breaking into sobs and forcing him into silence. Now he appeared to want to confide something further to his daughter, and she pulled a chair close to the bed. He struggled to say something, but she could not understand the words.

One wonders whether Albert, having accepted his imminent death, might have recalled songs he had composed in the inexperience of youth, when their melancholy was only appropriated from *Lieder* tradition. In '*Trauenlied*' ('Lament') the singer recalled pursuing

> a gleam of happiness
> which always seemed to lead me on,

and that when he followed its 'glimmering light' it 'did ever flee ahead', uncaptured.

> All of a sudden, I don't know how,
> I found I had to turn back to see it.
> It shone behind me like the twilight.
> How did I pass it without noticing?
> It must have happened in a dream.

There had also been his 'Last Words of a Bard', whose creative fires are 'extinguished', and whose 'torrent of songs' has ended. The wind stirs in him 'sounds from forgotten times', and from the window he sees the sinking sun throwing 'a last gleam of light for me'.

> The gentle lyre no longer sings
> At many a festival's high ceremony.
> Soon I will lie silent in my grave...

The 13th was a Friday. Jenner told the Queen that the Prince's condition was stable, and that she could take a morning walk, but by late afternoon it seemed urgent for the family to gather – a step that Alice had anticipated by summoning Bertie. 'The breathing was the alarming thing', Victoria recorded, 'it was so rapid. There was what they call a dusky hue about the face and hands, which I knew was not good.' She told Jenner, who appeared alarmed. Then she saw Albert begin to arrange his hair and fold his arms, 'just as he used to do when well and dressing...Strange! as though he were preparing for another and greater journey.'

The public knew almost nothing, other than that the Prince Consort was ill with a fever, although members of the Household from the Master of the Horse on down had begun to break through the wall of discretion. Mail from Windsor Castle to London and the Home Counties was often delivered the same day. Finally, at five o'clock the first bulletin suggesting a grave outcome was issued, recording that the patient had passed a restless night and confessing that 'the symptoms have assumed an unfavourable character during the day'. No specific malady was identified. The Queen was told that Albert was sinking fast.

When alone with Lady Augusta Bruce that evening, Victoria collapsed into hysterical tears and prayer. Recovering, she called for Sir Charles Phipps and collapsed again into uncontrollable grief. Then, bracing herself, she went to sit calmly by Albert's bed. He seemed now warm and comfortable, and managed to recognize her, kiss her, press her hand, and weakly call her *'gutes Fräuchen'*. Waiting for the inevitable, Albert's doctors continued drugging him with brandy every half-hour. He had taken no solid food for many days.

Phipps was instructed to send a messenger to Palmerston with the warning, 'I deeply grieve to say that the Prince's disease has taken a very unfavourable turn, and that the Doctors are in the *greatest anxiety* – they have even fears for the night.' When the Prince of Wales arrived late Friday evening, summoned, Natty Rothschild wrote to his parents from Cambridge, from a 'gay party', there was concern that his presence might upset his father, but Albert's eyes, when open, now stared fixedly. All that Bertie had known from Windsor before Alice's message had been the untruth that there was a gastric fever 'epidemic' at the Castle, and that the Prince Consort had fallen victim to it.

Once the Queen and the younger children had left the sickroom for the night, Colonel Biddulph, Master of the Household, with Generals Grey and Bruce, shifted Albert's bed from the window prospect that had given him pleasure to the centre of the room, in preparation for the end. To their surprise, the Prince was able to arise while the move was in progress, but he had to be helped back into bed.

On the bright early morning of 14 December, the growing group of doctors permitted themselves some renewed optimism. In the first sunlight of Saturday, Albert's gaunt face looked younger, and even radiant. Dr Henry Brown, who had been the Duchess of Kent's physician, even suggested to the Queen that 'there was ground to hope the crisis was over', prompting her to telegraph as much to the frantic and hopelessly remote Vicky. If the illness were typhoid, that was at least possible. If Albert's affliction, however, was a long, slow, debilitating one – probably stomach cancer, which fits many of his self-confessed symptoms over at least four years – he had no resources left. Had his physicians – even the obtuse Dr Clark – fathomed this earlier, they also knew that their skills offered no remedies. Victoria, too, seemed to have sensed something potentially catastrophic and to have pushed it away, uncertain as to whether her fragile equilibrium could absorb that much reality.

As the morning wore on, the doctors retreated from their fantasy that the Prince was rallying. 'Alas!' Phipps messaged to Palmerston, 'the hopes of the morning are fading away...' At midday, Albert was given a spoonful of brandy, but no attempt was made to raise his head. 'He is not worse', Dr Watson told Victoria without conviction; 'the pulse keeps up'. Then he confessed to being 'very much frightened, but [I] don't and won't give up hope'.

A bulletin at nine had indicated no change, but at 4.30 p.m. the patient was declared to be in a 'most critical state'.

In the darkened room, members of the Household gathered, stood uneasily, then slipped out. After her own exit, Lady Biddulph rushed to her husband's office in the castle to write to Earl Spencer, Groom of the Stole to Albert and thus titular head of his Establishment, 'VERY VERY bad news. All the Household have just been up to the Prince's room to see for the last time him who is *fast sinking*. The doctors say there is no hope not the slightest of His Royal Highness's life being spared, but none may say how long it may go on...'

Now and then one of the physicians checked the Prince's weakening pulse, but did little else. Alice remained at one side of the bed, where she had posted herself, when awake, for days. At the foot of the bed were Bertie and Helena, and, as the day wore on, Louise and Arthur.

Alfred was at sea; the haemophiliac Leopold was in France for his health and Beatrice, at four, was too young for such scenes. The Prince's rapid breathing had become alarming. Victoria hastened to the side of the bed across from Alice and whispered to Albert, '*es ist Fraüchen*'. Then she bent toward him and asked for '*einem Kuss*', and he kissed her. Then he dozed again. Victoria, with a terrible calm, held his thin, cold hand until her misery became overwhelming. She burst from the room and broke down.

The Queen's notes, written later when she could bear the recollection, suggest a somewhat quieter scene than that described immediately afterwards by Lady Augusta Bruce. At a quarter to eleven, when the Prince's breathing began to change, Alice whispered to Lady Augusta, 'That is the death rattle.' Calmly, she went for her mother.

'Oh, yes, this is death!' Victoria cried on seeing Albert. 'I know it. I have seen it before.' She fell upon the still, cold body, and called him by every endearing name she could recall from their life together. Then she allowed herself to be led away.

How should a Prince die? The once-irreverent and even uncharitable *Punch* would shortly, in chivalric terms, ask that. In battle, 'with red spur deep in [a] maddening charger's flank'? Ending a day of pleasure with 'painted goblet fully drained'? Albert, the lament acknowledged, had been 'graced with gentler powers' for a later day, and although he died 'too soon', one might measure his years by the 'wise, and bold, and Christian duties done'. And, *Punch* concluded,

> Him whom she loved we loved. We shared her joy,
> And will not be denied to share her grief.

# Afterword:
## Legacy

'WHY HAS THE earth not swallowed me up?' Vicky mourned when the dreaded news came.

'Oh, my poor child', the Queen returned, 'Why may the earth not swallow *us* up?... How am I alive after witnessing what I have done? Oh! I who prayed daily that we might die together and I never survive Him! I who felt, when in those blessed Arms clasped and held tight in the sacred Hours of the night, when the world seemed only to be ourselves, that nothing could part us. I felt so v[er]y secure.' She would, she insisted, live to do her duty and to follow Albert's wishes. 'But how I, who leant on him for all and everything – without whom I did nothing, moved not a finger, arranged not a print or photograph, didn't move to put on a gown or bonnet if he didn't approve it[,] shall go on, to live, to move, to help myself in difficult moments?'

The children, Albert's staff, Victoria's ministers, her Household officials, had all come forward in the Red Room once the Prince had breathed his last, to offer not only sympathy but pledges of support in the transition from dependence upon Albert to a reign without him. 'You will not leave or desert me now?' she had asked pathetically. Turning to Sir Charles Phipps, she said, 'There is no one to call me Victoria now.' Albert had been confidant, adviser, collaborator, spouse, even surrogate sovereign. A queen could have no close friends. She was now alone.

Exhausted by lack of sleep and numb with grief, she permitted herself to be led away, first to Beatrice, who was asleep, then to her own room and to bed. In shock, but unable to sleep and given no sedative, she dozed off only in the early hours of the morning.

With Victoria out of the room and unlikely to return for some hours, a death mask of the Prince was made, for the record and to facilitate the work of later sculptors. Albert had been staunchly against the practice, but the handling of a body in the absence of any legal injunctions to the contrary is always the option of the survivors. Told about the mask later, Victoria refused to look at it and would not 'allow that sacred cast . . . to go out of the house'.

As midnight approached, the dull boom of the great bell atop St Paul's announced that the royal family had been struck by death, and throughout Sunday the bells of London tolled. At Buckingham Palace, people queued quietly to sign a condolence book. Next to it, on a table in the reception room, was a statement that although she was in great tribulation, her Majesty bore her affliction with as much calmness and fortitude as could be supposed.

On Monday morning the war-scare newspaper placards about the *Trent* affair disappeared, replaced by particulars of the Prince Consort's death. While the bells still tolled, newspaper hawkers did a record business, and readers discovered posthumous and sweeping concessions in the press to Albert's value to the kingdom. Less than a decade after rumours had put him in the Tower for treason, the turnabout would have pleased the Prince's shade. 'Placed in a difficult position', said the *Observer*, 'Prince Albert knew how to deport himself so discreetly and so well, that he has died without leaving a single enemy, while his friends were a host . . . He was a man of elegant mind, of cultivated tastes, of a clear understanding, and of high and lofty aspirations for the public good . . . Peace to his ashes! A good husband, a good father, a wise prince, and a safe counsellor, England will not soon "look upon his like again".'

Similar feelings were common among ordinary Londoners. Novelist Mary Elizabeth Braddon wrote of 'the dull light of the December day . . . when rough omnibus drivers forgot to blaspheme at each other, and tied decent scraps of crape upon their whips'. Fellow novelist Elizabeth Gaskell recalled that her friend Mary Ewart had passed through London on the Monday after the Prince's death – the sixteenth – and found that 'all the little shops in Shoreditch were shut up – all blinds were down – up to Buckingham Palace'. With crowds of others she went to Buckingham Palace to put her name down in the mourning book, and found 'a room hung with black, & lighted with wax'. The fashionable shops, unlike those in the East End, were open, but 'people could not give their orders at Lewis' & Allonbys for crying'.

These were insignificant consolations for the Queen – if she knew about them – for beneath her initial surface equilibrium, after the first convulsive grief, was a dazed shock not uncommon to sorrowing spouses. Only on the Monday evening after – an interval of two days – could she begin her first post-Albert letter to Vicky. And not until the twentieth could she write to her uncle, addressing him as 'Dearest, kindest Father', and describing herself as the 'poor fatherless baby of eight months' (as she had been), now 'the utterly broken and crushed widow of forty-two' – as she indeed was:

> My *life* as a *happy* one is *ended*! the world is gone for *me*! If I *must* live on (and I will do nothing to make me worse than I am), it is henceforth for our poor fatherless children – for my unhappy country, which has lost *all* in losing him – and in *only* doing what I know and *feel* he would wish, for he *is* near me – his spirit will guide and inspire me! But oh! To be cut off in the prime of life ... is too awful, too cruel! And yet it *must* be for *his* good, his happiness! His purity was too great, his aspiration too *high* for this poor, miserable world! His great soul is now only enjoying *that* for which it *was* worthy!

Without instructions, the Lord Chamberlain's Department nevertheless began the necessary preparations, moving the Prince's body to the extra bedstead in the room where he had died. Löhlein and Albert's dresser, Macdonald, assisted. The Prince of Wales, next in authority to the Queen but only twenty and never called on before for advice, had to fix the date for the funeral. Consulting the Duke of Cambridge, he chose Monday, 23 December, nine days away. It was a brief interlude in which to organize a state ceremony, but it was crucial to keep the obsequies from colliding with Christmas – even with Christmas Eve, more important to many than the day itself.

The Lord Chamberlain's staff began with the assumption that the funeral of the Duchess of Kent, only months before, represented the wishes of the Queen as well as those of the Prince, and used that precedent for the arrangements. Although no equivalent panoply was called for, because Messrs Banting had been the undertakers at the

Duke of Wellington's funeral, they were called in as appropriate for Albert.

Dr Jenner filed a death certificate on 21 December, fixing the cause as 'typhoid fever; duration 21 days', the first time that the label was publicly applied; and although questions were raised in the *Lancet* and in the *British Medical Journal* about the discrepancies between the medical bulletins and the belated diagnosis, there was no autopsy. Instead, Jenner suggested to the Queen that death was 'due to the heart being over-strained by the Prince's heavy frame', and Clark added that three things had proved fatal – overwork, worry about the Prince of Wales's love affair, and 'exposure to chill when already sick'. In 1877 Jenner added further that '*no one* can diagnose typhoid at first'. Victoria underlined 'no one' in her memo of the conversation. Clark's 'when already sick' spoke further volumes.

Although Albert's own confidences about his failing health in his last years suggest stomach cancer – his mother had died of cancer at thirty, pointing to genetic predisposition – other possibilities unknown then to his doctors only emphasize their helplessness. In later decades, when physicians incorrectly attributed peptic ulcers to personality factors, Albert's stress-prone profile seemed ripe for chronic, wasting, ulcer disease. *Helicobacter pylori,* now known to cause peptic ulcers which can progress to stomach cancer, could have been involved. The bacterium was then unknown, as were curative antibiotics, and surgery was impossible – hopeless.

Calling the handling of Albert's illness, and his death, 'a national calamity of far greater importance than the public dream of', Lord Clarendon maintained to the Duchess of Manchester that the doctors had been contributing factors. 'Holland and Clark are not even average old women, and nobody who is really ill would think of sending for either of them. Jenner has had little [experience of] practice . . . Watson (who is no specialist in fever cases) at once saw that he had come too late to do any good.'

Early on Sunday morning, having rested for only a few hours, the Queen took the Duchess of Sutherland, Mistress of the Robes, into the Blue Room. Her doctors cautioned Victoria, citing the risk of infection, not to touch the body – a bit of nonsense, since she had embraced the dying Prince over and over again during his illness. She obeyed meekly, and instead embraced the clothes in which he was to be dressed. For years she would sleep with his nightshirt in her arms. Every night thereafter, she knelt at Albert's side of their bed before she put her head on her own pillow. In part, she would confide to Vicky, who had experienced the pleasures of the marital bed, the deprivations were profoundly sexual. 'My warm passionate loving nature', she confessed, '[remains] so full of that passionate adoration for that Angel whom I dared call mine. And at 42, all, all those earthly feelings must be crushed & smothered & the never quenched flame . . . *burns* within me & wears me out! . . . I am alas! not old – and my feelings are strong and warm; my love is ardent.'

To keep the sombre ambiance of the Blue Room from affecting her further, the Queen ordered that the room be cleaned and restored to usefulness, but not until the 'sad but lovely image' was photographed. She did not want it to remain as a *Sterbezimmer* – a death chamber – but intended to turn it into a room for her use that would nevertheless be a memorial. The 'sacred room', she wrote to Vicky, would have pictures and busts and china. Her precious cast of Albert's hand, made in happier days, would be kept in their bedroom, near her. In each of their homes, his dressing-room or study would be kept as it had been, even to the changing of linens, the daily replacement of towels and nightclothes, and – in the dressing-rooms – the bringing of hot water for shaving each morning, and a scouring of the unused chamber pot. Yet each room would continue to be used in some way by Victoria. At first her audiences in Albert's silent study or dressing-room were disconcerting in the extreme to her ministers.

In his diary on the sixteenth, Disraeli, having learned of the Curragh incident and its aftermath, wondered how the Prince of Wales would now fare. The matter was 'not seriously discreditable', Disraeli thought, 'but undignified'. The question about Bertie was 'into whose hands he may fall'. More crucial, with Albert gone, were the future influences upon the Queen, for she had 'long shown indications of a nervous or excitable disposition'. He recalled of Albert that 'nothing small or great was done but by his advice . . . I have myself . . . heard him at dinner, suggest to her in German to enquire about this, that, and the other: and the questions never failed to follow . . . The worst consequence possible is one, unluckily, not unlikely: that without being absolutely incapacitated for affairs, she may fall into a state of mind in which it will be difficult to do business with her, and impossible to anticipate what she will approve or disapprove.' The 'trying' situation he prophesied would quickly materialize. Victoria's sole immediate interest would be to embrace her grief.

Although the Queen, wearing her widow's cap, was hastened off to Osborne on the nineteenth, to be as far away from the funeral as was practical, her instructions for mourning fittings everywhere quickly exhausted supplies of black drapery throughout the kingdom. Dyeing establishments rushed to meet fresh orders. Christmas, following so soon after the funeral in Wolsey's Chapel, was darkened everywhere by official mourning. A grim extravaganza to parallel the Duke of Wellington's farewell, however, did not materialize. The Queen did not want it, and time was too short for ambitious preparations to proceed, or for many sovereigns or other state visitors to attend. From Osborne, Victoria sent word afterwards through Sir Charles Phipps that from reports she had received about the obsequies, everything had been conducted 'as she could have wished, with due solemnity and every mark of profound respect, and yet without any unnecessary form or state'.

Despite the insouciance he usually affected, Lord Torrington agreed with the assessment, writing to Delane, whose *Times* had set circulation records (an unprecedented 89,000 copies) on the Monday after the Prince's death, that the obsequies had been 'in every respect singularly well conducted – no confusion and no hurry. The music as fine as could be ... I am inclined to think that more real sorrow was evinced at this funeral than at any that has taken place *there* [at Windsor] for a vast number of years.' Reverting to form, he added that 'the champagne went briskly; but then the company had suffered extreme cold for at least an hour and a half ... Phipps looked his position, and ate a most excellent luncheon.' Disraeli's own private comment seemed not unreasonable in the circumstances: 'With Prince Albert we have buried our Sovereign. This German Prince has governed England for twenty-one years with a wisdom and energy such as none of our Kings have ever shown.'

On the dreariest Christmas Eve of her life, Victoria wrote again to her uncle from Osborne. She had been considering her future conduct as Queen.

I am ... anxious to repeat *one* thing, and *that one* is *my firm* resolve, my *irrevocable decision* ... that *his* wishes – *his* plans – about everything, *his* views about *every* thing are to be *my law*! And *no human power* will make me swerve from *what he* decided and wished . . . I am *also determined* that *no one* person, may *he* be ever so good, ever so devoted among my servants – is to lead or guide or dictate *to me*. I know *how he* would disapprove of it. And I live *on* with him, for him; in fact I am only *outwardly* separated from him, and only for a *time*.

The Prince of Wales had also been pondering appropriate responses. Albert had rejected the idea of a statue of himself in South Kensington to mark the Great Exhibition, and plans had been changed to make the principal figure that of the Queen. It had always been her wish, announced Albert Edward, that a likeness of the Prince Consort top the monument, and he would bear the cost. Executed by Joseph Durham and unveiled with great ceremony in June 1863, it faces, appropriately, the later Albert Hall.

Victoria would henceforth see everything through the lens of her bereavement. In that, she contributed nothing new to the vocabulary or symbolism of mourning. Oxford Street shops already existed for sable women's hats, sashed crêpe 'weepers' for men's tall hats, black armbands, deep purple clothes, black plumes for horses, and funeral accoutrements of every description. In Prussia or in Russia, the attention paid to the body of the deceased was greater; in France or Italy peasant women who became widowed, at whatever age, would wear black the rest of their lives; in England and Scotland, setting aside a room associated with the dead child or spouse, to keep it undisturbed as a document of the beloved's life, was commonplace. Few looked on such demonstrations as morbid. One indulged in what grief one could afford. Even Victoria's allegedly vicious uncle Ernest – King of Hanover after her accession – left the rooms of his queen, when she died in 1841, exactly as they had been. Night candles were lit, pages and dressers remained in attendance, and the King, who venerated her 'sweet and amiable character', went regularly to pray at the side of what had been her bed. In Prussia it was a royal custom to assemble on the anniversary of the death of an important member of the family for a religious ceremony in a room associated with the deceased.

The English poor could not afford the luxuries of such grief, and after the obsequies had to substitute the stiff upper lip. Still, in *David Copperfield*, Charles Dickens inveighed against the grotesque mummeries and extravagant expense of nineteenth-century lower-class funerals, and in 1903, Bernard Shaw wrote in the Devil's great speech in *Don Juan in Hell*, 'I saw a man die: he was a London bricklayer's labourer with seven children. He left seventeen pounds club money; and his wife spent it all on his funeral and went into the workhouse with the children the next day ... On death she spent all she had.' In the wide black edges on her handkerchiefs and writing paper, and in her widow's weeds, in the planned memorials to Albert and in his portrait in a locket around her neck or in the bracelet around her plump wrist, the Queen was not turning her back on life any more than did other widows of her time.

The 'easing of that violent grief', Victoria wrote in 1867, 'those paroxysms of despair and yearning and longing and of daily, nightly longing to die ... for the first three years never left me ... ' When Lord Canning, her Viceroy in India, died only six months after his wife (he was suddenly inconsolable, and had a nervous breakdown), Victoria wrote to his sister as if Canning had not been a flagrantly erring husband throughout the marriage, 'How enviable to follow so soon the partner of your life! How I pray that it be God's will to let me follow mine soon.' But she was Queen: there was civil war in America, into which her country might be drawn; there were conflicts brewing on the Continent nearby; there was social and political and religious agitation in England, and there were Fenian outbreaks in Ireland. Nothing of such external events emerges in Victoria's journal in early January, as she begins again to record her 'sad and solitary life'.

When Palmerston wrote to her on 9 January that the *Trent* affair had been concluded with the release of the Southerners to a British vessel, the Queen responded from Osborne the next day that 'the things of this world' were of no interest to her 'beyond the satisfaction she must experience if Peace is maintained and the country is in prosperity: for *her* thoughts are *fixed above*. She thinks with satisfaction, that the slight alterations in the draft to Lord Lyons, which the Queen suggested, and which was her precious husband's *last* work (which rendered it more easy for the American Government to comply with our request) have helped in bringing about this peaceful result, which she knows her dear Angel much wished for.'

To the Earl of Derby she wrote poignantly of herself (17 February 1862), 'She sees the trees budding, the days lengthening, the primroses coming out, but she *thinks* herself still in the month of December.' Victoria's desolation may have included a dimension of culpability – a result of a long and unconfessed realization of the presence of mortal illness, an unspoken secret she may have shared with her husband. Certainly Albert knew, and had attempted to make it known, although to deliberately deaf ears, and he had at times acted openly with a fatalistic acceptance. A denial of that reality during Albert's decline could only have added afterwards to Victoria's sense of complicity, a shameful thing sometimes put aside by blaming the deceased for the desolation in the survivor. She remained in seclusion, and the sovereign as symbol disappeared except from currency, coinage, postage stamps, and the *Court Circular* by which newspapers strained to see some meaningful activity by the Queen.

Mirroring her mourning, the Household, at the Queen's instruction, went about in black crêpe, broadcloth, and bombazine, underscoring the gloom. For a year after Albert's death, no member of her Household could appear in public except in mourning garb, a practice that might have continued indefinitely had her ladies not sunk so much in morale that Victoria relented sufficiently to permit 'semi-mourning' colours of white, mauve, and grey. Even royal servants were obliged to wear a black crêpe band on the left arm until 1869. At Windsor, Disraeli noted, the two guest books that existed, for the Queen and the Prince, were not discontinued – 'visitors write their names . . . as before – calling on a dead man'. Her efforts to recall him and memorialize him would be constant, although the cult of the Prince Consort was imposed rather than real. For many Englishmen he had been too German in his ways – too interested in science and education, in good works, in efficiency and energy.

Those who knew more than they read in the newspapers since 1840 had always had a different view. 'His character always comes out *honest*', novelist Emily Eden, daughter of the first Lord Auckland, had written to Mrs Drummond. 'I take it that he governs us really, in everything.' To John Scott Russell, who had worked with the Prince on the Great Exhibition and many later projects, Sir Charles Phipps shared thoughts on their loss, writing, 'I feel that I can never look on his like again. There was something in his character, an honesty, a straight-forwardness, a purity of motive, and an ameliorating consistency of action, which were quite unlike what I ever met in any other man . . .

This country does not know, as you know, deeply as they mourn, one-tenth of what he did for them.'

Having worked so intimately on the highest level with Albert over many years, Phipps realized that whatever influence the Crown exercised in England, and whatever regard it had acquired after the Hanoverian era, and especially its culmination with Victoria's sleazy uncles, George IV and William IV, was to the Prince's credit. He had salvaged the Crown as a pillar of the emerging constitutional state.

The modern constitutional and 'corporate' monarchy, worldwide, owes much to Albert's example. Yet his early death, and Victoria's prolonged retreat into mourning and seclusion, eroded his efforts to mould the monarchy into a conspicuous pulpit as well as a national symbol. Disraeli had seen past eulogy when he declared that England had lost a sovereign rather than a consort. Nevertheless it was unlikely that anything but Albert's death would have brought him England's love. For his being perceived as an unwelcome outsider, one must look rather to those emotional and intellectual qualities that separated him from his adopted countrymen. He was hardly more German in lineage than the five kings who had preceded him, or than Victoria herself.

Albert had a Germanic sentimentality that caused him to wear his emotions on his sleeve at a time when a chilly heartlessness was more the aristocratic mode. He was an internationalist when his countrymen were still insular. He valued art and science and technology – indeed, the entire world of the intellect – when men of power in England preferred traditional, if obsolescent, learning. He had a passion for reform when his peers, whatever the inexorability of change, distrusted anything but the *status quo*. He valued work with a more-than-Puritan propensity for it when the aristocratic establishment which had no personal need for productive labour lavished empty hours on unproductive pleasure. He promoted the importance of earnestness over its mere show, and hardly veiled his contempt for the religiosity that seemed to be replacing religion – which in any case he emptied of theology and like Victoria, emphasized good works. He realized that although he could never become what was, in the perception of his peers, an Englishman, his eldest son and heir would epitomize, to Albert, potentially the most appalling sort of Englishman.

The Prince had apparently intuited, as had Baron Stockmar, that he was suffering from an inoperable and incurable malignancy. That melancholy understanding had contributed to the despondent and workaholic states of his last years. Unwritten powers accrue to those who use them effectively. What he had accomplished for the monarchy, he realized, would inevitably be buried with him.

Gifted beyond most men, he was limited by his curious position which denied him opportunities his driven conscience sought. As a recent historian has summed him up, Albert did more than create Osborne and Balmoral and make Windsor Castle and Buckingham Palace operate more efficiently. 'He composed songs and sacred music, and was a competent sketcher and etcher; he patronized Winterhalter and Landseer and collected early German and Italian paintings. He ran model farms at Windsor and Balmoral, and exhibited his livestock at shows throughout the country. He rode to hounds with skill and verve, and was a competent shot. He believed in better housing for the workers, better education at Cambridge University (of which he was chancellor), and better weapons for the army. He was president or chairman of innumerable societies; he chaired one Royal Commission charged with the decoration of the Houses of Parliament; and he chaired another that planned the Great Exhibition of 1851. And all this was only in his spare time, in those odd moments of respite from the treadmill of public engagements and official correspondence.'*

Burdened by what he had to do, Albert nevertheless was one of his era's unsung great men because of what he managed to do beyond his duty. He helped thrust England's institutions and power structure into the dynamic century which, decades into it, the Establishment still distrusted. And his and Victoria's example of a domesticated, democratizing monarchy (despite Albert's attempt to retain some executive power for the Crown) seemed to temper the revolutionary ardour that elsewhere in Europe overturned thrones and generated continuing instability. He was not only seen – sometimes derisively in the press – as 'Albert the Good', he contributed concretely to the nation's good.

Albert remains, too, a hero figure who shared a romantic, troubled, moving love story and marriage that possessed the stuff of high drama,

---

* David Cannadine also observes that Prince Albert was no Thomas Jefferson, an Enlightenment figure who had independence of action as well as real genius (*The Pleasures of the Past*, 1989). Jefferson, however, was not handicapped by cultural transplantation, beginning life anew in a new language.

even classic tragedy. From student prince to uncrowned king, his life was without parallel. None of his descendants on the throne of his adopted country have taken the name of 'Albert', although many were christened with it. They recognized the risks.

The Prince's vision for the modern monarchy died with him. It could not have been sustained without his intellectual qualities and his intensity of purpose, and he left no such potential in his spouse or progeny. Although he would have deplored the glamorous, ornamental, impotent Crown that emerged in the next century, his life was a prototype invalidated by time. Windsor Castle as co-ordinate executive branch with Downing Street was an impossible dream. Driven by his sense of mission, he wanted to sustain more than a symbolic and ceremonial monarchy, but faced the tide of history. Had he lived a less abbreviated life, might something of his vision have been realized? On a rare occasion a single life makes a difference.

# Sources

The first reference to a source will be its fullest citation; further allusions will abbreviate the source. The published literature on Victoria and Albert is immense. Where facts are in common currency and found in a multiplicity of locations, no citation may be given below. Although many sources are cited in the notes, it can be assumed that the following books have been consulted at almost every stage: Charles Grey, *The Early Years of the Prince Consort*. Compiled for and annotated by Queen Victoria (1867); Theodore Martin, *Life of the Prince Consort*, 5 volumes (1875–1880), which include extracts from the diaries of both Queen and Prince; A.C. Benson and Viscount Esher, eds, *The Letters of Queen Victoria*, First Series, 3 volumes (1908); Kurt Jagow, ed., *Letters of the Prince Consort* (1938); Hector Bolitho, ed., *[Letters of] The Prince Consort and His Brother* (1933); Roger Fulford, *The Prince Consort* (1949); Elizabeth Longford, *Victoria R.I.* (1964); Cecil Woodham-Smith, *Queen Victoria, her life and times* (1972); Daphne Bennett, *King without a Crown* (1977); Hermione Hobhouse, *Prince Albert, His Life and Work* (1983); Robert Rhodes James, *Prince Albert* (1984); Stanley Weintraub, *Victoria* (1987; rev. 1996); Monica Charlot, *The Young Queen* (1991); and Hans-Joachim Neutzer, *Ein deutschen Prinz in England* (1992). In subsequent notes these may be referred to briefly by author/editor surname. Albert's post-marriage letters unless otherwise cited are from Jagow, Bolitho, Martin, the *Memoirs* of Ernest II, and Benson and Esher. Many sources not cited below may be inferred from the text itself.

## Preface

For details of the *Omphale and Hercules* painting at Osborne House, see chapter VIII. Tennyson's lines are from the Dedication to his *Idylls of the King* (1862). Since the outlines of the narrative are drawn from Malory's *Morte d'Arthur*,

Swinburne – whose politics were to the left of republicanism – thereafter referred to the *Idylls* as the *Morte d'Albert.*

## I Leaving for Good 1839–1840

Lady Wharncliffe's letter to Caroline Talbot is from *The First Lady Wharncliffe and Her Family*, ed. Caroline Grosvenor and Lord Stuart of Wortley (1927). Dickens's letters throughout are from the Pilgrim Edition (1959–). Extracts from Lord Clarendon's diaries are from George Villiers, *A Vanished Victorian. Being the Life of George Villiers Fourth Earl of Clarendon (1800–1870)* (1938). Grey furnishes the most details, as a participant and observer, on the partings at Gotha. Charles Greville's diaries and letters throughout are from Henry Reeve, ed., *The Greville Memoirs. A Journal of the Reigns of King George IV, King William IV, and Queen Victoria*, 8 vols (1896). John Wilson Croker's papers are from Louis Jennings, ed., *The Croker Papers. The Correspondence and Diaries of the Late Right Honourable John Wilson Croker*, 3 vols (1885). Stockmar's perspectives are from Ernst Stockmar, ed., *Memoirs of Baron Stockmar*, 2 vols (1872). Some of his correspondence with Albert is also in Jagow and Martin. Letters to and from Peel, other than from the Queen, are from Norman Gash, *Sir Robert Peel. The Life of Sir Robert Peel after 1830* (1972). Albert's bored doodling on his Windsor musical programme, saved by the Queen, is from RC/WPR, k-19 (f. 25). Disraeli's letters to his sister, Sarah, are from M.G. Wiebe *et al.*, eds., *Benjamin Disraeli. Letters: 1838–41* (1987), hereafter Wiebe.

## II Silver Spoon 1819–1831

Biographies (including letters) of Duchess Louise, Albert's mother, include D.A. Ponsonby, *The Lost Duchess. The Story of the Prince Consort's Mother* (1958); Paul von Ebart, *Luise. Herzogin von Sachsen-Coburg-Saalfeld. Ein Lebensbild nach Briefen derselben* (1903); and G. Holler, *Louise von Sachsen-Coburg – Ihr Kampf um Liebe und Glück* (1991). Details of the Rosenau and the Ehrenburg in Coburg are from visits by the author and from descriptive brochures at each location. The diaries of Henry Richard Vassall Fox, third Lord Holland, are in A.D. Kriegel, ed., *The Holland House Diaries 1831–1840* (1977). Disraeli papers are from Wiebe. Hector Bolitho writes about the Duchess from her original letters in a chapter of his *A Biographer's Notebook* (1950). He also explodes the canard of Albert's alleged Jewish extraction, first proposed in Max W.L. Voss's *England als Erzieher*, from which Lytton Strachey eagerly and erroneously picked it up for his *Queen Victoria* (1921). For an account of the Duke of Kent's illegitimate Adelaide Victoire see Mollie Gillen, *The Prince and His Lady* (1970), and S. Weintraub's *Victoria.*

## III The Student Prince 1832–1838

Anecdotes of Albert at Bonn University are from an unsigned biography in the London *Pictorial Times*, 1845 volume, p. 370. Albert's matriculation records at Bonn were furnished to me by Prof. Dr Rolf Lessenich, Universität Bonn. Reminiscences of Bonn by Prince Ernest are from his *Memoirs of the Duke of Saxe-Coburg-Gotha*, 4 vols (1888). Additional details about Albert at Bonn are in A. Rimmer, *Early Homes of Prince Albert* (1883). Thomas Raikes's diary is from *Portion of the Journal Kept by Thomas Raikes, Esq. from 1831 to 1847*, 2 vols (1858). Albert's education in Brussels is in part from Louis de Lichtervelde, *Léopold First* (1930), and also from Hans-Joachim Neutzer, *Ein deutschen Prinz* (1992), and from Stockmar. A biography of Pierre Bergeron is in C. van der Kindere, *L'Université Libre de Bruxelles 1834–1884* (1884). Count Mensdorff's reminiscences are in Ernest's *Memoirs* and in Bolitho's *Albert Prince Consort* (1932). Wordsworth quotes W. Schlegel on Albert's prospects in a letter of 28 November 1840 in Alan G. Hill, ed., *The Letters of William and Dorothy Wordsworth*, vol. 7 (1967). Victoria's letters to Albert, 30 June 1837 and 3 December 1837, are in the Royal Archives; her letter to Duke Ernest, that her marital intentions 'are still the same', is in Hector Bolitho, *The Reign of Queen Victoria* (London, 1949). The references to President Van Buren's marital interest in Victoria from Boston and Salem newspapers are from a report in the Plymouth, New Hampshire *Journal of Literature and Politics*, 5 August 1837.

## IV Courting a Husband 1838–1839

The future General Sir Francis Seymour's letters are quoted in Sir James Denham's *Memoirs of the Memorable* (1922). Identification of Ernst Platner was made by Professor Gerhard F. Strasser at the Herzog August Bibliothek, Wolfenbuettel. Albert's letters are from Martin, Jagow, and Duke Ernest II's *Memoirs*, as well as Benson and Esher. Metternich's snide dismissal of Albert as un-royal was delivered to the Earl of Aberdeen when he was Prime Minister, according to a letter of 3 April 1861 from Lord Clarendon to the Duchess of Manchester. His gossipy correspondence to her is in *My Dear Duchess*, ed. A.L. Kennedy (1956). Melbourne's warning to Victoria about creating Albert 'King Consort' is quoted by Lord George Russell in his anonymously published *Collections and Recollections* (1898).

## V *Serene Highness to Royal Highness 1840–1841*

For the Earl of Cardigan's 11th Dragoons see Richard Brett-Smith, *The 11th Hussars (Prince Albert's Own)* (1969), Cecil Woodham-Smith's *The Reason Why* (1954), and Piers Compton, *Cardigan of Balaclava* (1972). The quip from *John Bull* is quoted from his diary by Lord Malmesbury in his *Memoirs of an Ex-Minister*, 2 vols (1884). Princess Lieven to Lord Aberdeen is quoted from her *Correspondence* (1939). Her letters to Lady Palmerston are from the *Lieven–Palmerston Correspondence* (1943). Lady Palmerston's other letters are from *The Letters of Lady Palmerston*, ed. Tresham Lever (1957). Guizot's description of a boring evening at Windsor is from the London volume of his *Memoirs* (1862), *An Embassy to the Court of St James in 1840*. Victoria's reminiscences of her early years with Albert appear throughout her long correspondence with Princess Vicky, beginning in 1858 (6 vols, 1964–1990), the first five edited by Roger Fulford, the final one by Agatha Ramm. Thomas Carlyle's letters are from *The Collected Letters*, ed. Richard Charles Sanders (1970). Disraeli's letters are from Wiebe. Lady Charlotte Guest is quoted from the Earl of Bessborough, ed., *Lady Charlotte Guest. Extracts from Her Journal* (1950). Albert's letters to Lord Palmerston throughout are from the original correspondence at the University of Southampton.

Miss Barrett's letters are in Meredith B. Raymond and Mary Rose Sullivan, ed., *The Letters of Elizabeth Barrett Browning to Mary Russell Mitford 1836–1854*, 3 vols (1983). Monckton Milnes received the 'Prince Hallbert' song from Dickens; the letter to him from Robert Monteith is also quoted in James Pope-Hennessy, *Monckton Milnes. The Years of Promise 1809–1851* (1949). Albert's investiture as Fishmonger is recorded in the Bible awarded to him on the occasion, described in the Alan Rankin *Miscellany No. 45* catalogue, December 1995, Edinburgh, as item 19. The vicissitudes of the Gozlan farce about Victoria and Albert are described in the daily press and in Martha Katherine Loder, *The Life and Novels of Léon Gozlan* (1943). Sallie Stevenson's letters are in Edward Botkin, *Victoria, Albert, and Mrs Stevenson* (1957).

## VI *Taking Hold 1841–1843*

Carlyle's letter to Monckton Milnes is from vol. 13 of the *Collected Letters*. The letters of Dickens, Disraeli, Lieven, Melbourne, Palmerston and others are also from previously credited sources, as are the references to Greville, Peel, Aberdeen, Victoria, and Albert. Mendelssohn's visits to Windsor are described from his letters to his mother and to Ignaz Moscheles. Sallie Stevenson is again quoted from Boykin. The E.M. Ward episode is recorded in S.M. Ellis, ed., *A Mid-Victorian Pepys. The Letters and Memoirs of Sir William Hardman* (1923). Albert's marital difficulties with Victoria are easily inferred from her own diaries, and are described as well by Robert Rhodes James in *Prince Albert* (1984) from Anson's notes and Albert's memoranda in the Royal Archives. *Bell's Life* was a contemporary gossip sheet claiming to be a sporting newspaper. Baroness Bunsen's *Life and Letters*, ed. Augustus J.C. Hare (1880), reports of an intimate Victoria and Albert in the first decade of their marriage, will be quoted further in later chapters. Tom Moore is quoted from Wilfred S. Dowden, ed., *The Journal of Thomas Moore, vol. 5, 1836–1842* (1983).

## VII *The Goldfish-bowl 1843–1844*

G.P.A. Healy's memoirs are *Reminiscences of a Portrait Painter* (1894). For the couple's private life in general see S. Weintraub, *Victoria* (1987, 1996), and Clare Jerrold, *The Early Court of Queen Victoria* (1912). For Albert and Cambridge see especially John Willis Clark and Thomas McKenny Hughes, *The Life and Letters of the Reverend Adam Sedgwick* (1890). D.G.C. Allan's 'From Nobility to Royalty: The Background to Prince Albert's Election as President of the Society [of Arts]', in the *Journal* of the Royal Society for the Encouragement of Arts and Manufactures and Commerce, January 1986, is self-explanatory. A letter to the author from Dr David Painting, Law Librarian, University College of Swansea, 8 May 1994, explains the origin of 'the Prince Consort's Act' of 1843, Act 6 & 7 Vict. c. 36, known as the Scientific Societies Act. A letter from Bernard Shaw to Gilbert Murray, 3 December 1920, continued to refer to it under its Albertine connection. Albert's euphemistic allusion to the imminent birth of Princess Alice as 'an interesting event' occurs in a letter to Count Alphonse de Mensdorff-Pouilly, a Coburg cousin, quoted in the catalogue of the Sotheby (London) sale of 24 July 1995. The 'night-cap' verses appear as 'The Royal Riddles' in *The Satirist*, 15 January 1843. *Letters of the King of Hanover to Viscount Strangford* (1925) include some of the most hostile correspondence relating to Victoria and Albert, the King's niece and nephew, in print. The feeling was mutual.

## VIII *The Queen's Business 1845–1848*

For Albert's tastes and art purchases, as well as inadvertent purchases, reproductions and documentation see Christopher Lloyd, *The Queen's Pictures* (1991), David Robertson, *Sir Charles Eastlake and the Victorian Art World* (1978), Winslow Ames, *Prince Albert and Victorian Taste* (1968), Benedict Read, *Victorian Sculpture* (1982), and the many pictures owed to the Victoria-and-Albert years still hanging on royal walls, including the Anton von Gegenbaur *Omphale and Hercules*, a fresco in an iron chassis, 6 ft. 3½ in. high, signed and dated Rome 1830, bought by the Prince in 1844 and hanging since at Osborne House. Many pictures acquired from Prince von Oettingen-Wallerstein are now hanging in the National Gallery, where Christopher Brown, Chief Curator, kindly showed them to the author. The note co-signed by Albert (dated 1 June 1847) on behalf of the Bavarian prince as security for his Rothschilds loan is in the Rothschild Archive, as is the message from Albert's German secretary, Dr Mayer, dated 12 May 1847, inviting Lionel de Rothschild to Buckingham Palace the next morning to arrange with the Prince for his signature and to explain the nature of the obligation.

Albert's unwillingness to have the family embarrassed by public sales of his chronically debt-ridden brother's art is revealed by letters to Ernest in Bolitho.

The National Gallery Archive history files indicate that Henry Mogford, acting as agent for the Prince, once he was left with the pictures, offered them for sale to the Gallery on 8 August 1851 and again on 31 March 1852. The Trustees declined purchase on 5 April 1852. On 7 September 1862 Charles Eastlake reported to the Trustees that the Queen intended to present the pictures in which the Gallery had expressed an interest, still then at Kensington Palace, to the Gallery. The pictures now identified as Nos. 701–722 were accepted on 1 October 1862 and removed to the Gallery in February 1863 along with the addition of No. 622, an anonymous Netherlandish painting, and No. 1864, a Netherlandish Virgin and Child.

For the Royal couple at Stowe, see the Disraeli *Letters* and editorial notes in Wiebe, vol. IV. Albert's campaign for Chancellor at Cambridge is thoroughly detailed in the *Life and Letters*, largely a memoir, of Professor Adam Sedgwick (1890), also covered very fully, if satirically, in the pages of *Punch*, and fully and admiringly in Martin. Carlyle's acerbic comment of 26 February 1847 to Erskine is in the Carlyle *Letters* ; Wordsworth's ode, 15 March 1847, is in the *Letters of William and Dorothy Wordsworth*. Albert's dozens of letters to Palmerston in this period, briefly extracted in Brian Connell's *Regina vs. Palmerston* (1961), are at Southampton. Lord Frederic Hamilton's account of the Earl of Abercorn's children being presented to the Queen and Prince at Ardverikie is in his *The Days before Yesterday* (1920). A contemporary source for the Scottish visits is *The Illustrated London News*, which looks externally at what the Queen notes privately in her journals; her entries themselves are extracted at length in David Duff, ed., *Victoria in the Highlands* (1968). Albert's letter to his Aunt Julie about 'cold' Windsor is extracted from the Sophie Dupré (Calne, Wilts) catalogue 34 as item 33.

A useful and comprehensive source for the relations between Napoleon III and the Royal couple is Jasper Ridley, *Napoléon III and Eugénie* (1969); a more romantic perspective appears in Theo Aronson, *Queen Victoria and the Bonapartes* (1992).

## IX The Violent Year 1848

Letters and diary entries relating to the Queen, Albert, Ernest II, Palmerston, Peel, and Greville are from sources previously cited. Van der Weyer's story of his bringing the telegraphed news of the revolution in Paris to Albert is in Brison D. Gooch, *Belgium and the February Revolution* (1963). That Victoria and Albert discussed the revolutions spreading across Europe 'day by day and hour by hour' is recalled by the Queen in a letter of 11 August 1866 to Vicky. Albert's long memorandum on the future political composition of Germany and Europe is in the Palmerston Papers, Southampton. The letter from Julian Harney to Friedrich Engels alleging that Albert had 'bolted' from London is in *The Harney Papers*, ed. F.G. Black and R.M. Black (1969). The link of the proposed loan to Albert and the 'Jew Bill' is made by Richard Davis in *The English Rothschilds* (1983), quoting a letter of 10 May 1848 from Nathaniel de Rothschild to his brothers in London (RAL 109/73) in the Rothschild Archive, in which the idea is scoffed at as unrealistic. (Albert did keep an account with the Rothschilds, which his uncle, King Leopold, would supplement.)

Albert's letter to young Alice is reproduced in the Sophie Dupré catalogue 35 (1995), Calne, Wilts, as item 7. Victoria's handwritten prayer for the children, by which they were to recall their parents, is also from a manuscript catalogue. The Judge–Strange lawsuit by which Albert protected his and Victoria's rights to reproduce their own drawings was a long-running affair that dragged into 1849, and was covered in detail in the newspaper press, although afterwards long forgotten.

## X Master Mason 1849–1851

Aside from full reports in the newspaper press, Albert's activities furthering manufacturing and technology come from the minutes and associated documents preserved in the [Royal] Society of Arts in John Adam Street, which include the John Scott Russell papers. The minutes and account sheets of the Exhibition Commission are also at the Royal Society of Arts. Additional documents are printed in Cole. A lengthy document setting out the legal basis for the Exhibition, beginning in 1845, is the *Statement of Proceedings Preliminary to the Exhibition of Industry of All Nations, 1851*, prepared by John Scott Russell, and printed by the Society in January 1850. The report of the Queen's Commission for the Exhibition of 1851, *Great Exhibition of the Industry of All Nations, 1851*, dated 3 January 1850, is in the archives of the Royal Society of Arts. See also E.F. Armstrong, 'The Influence of the Prince Consort on Science', *Journal of the Royal Society of Arts*, 23 November 1945, pp. 4–14, and Henry Cole, *Fifty Years of Public Work*, 2 vols (1884), a rich source for Crystal Palace documentation through 1851, as is Violet Markham, *Paxton and the Bachelor Duke* (1935).

The texts of Albert's major speeches are from *Addresses delivered on Different Public Occasions by His Royal Highness the Prince Albert*. Published by the Society of Arts in 1857, when he was its President, it was augmented posthumously in 1862. Also published in 1862 was a small volume of extracts, also used here, *Prince Albert's Golden Precepts; or, The Opinions and Maxims of His Late Royal Highness The Prince Consort*.

The Palmerston Papers contain a long English translation of a memorandum on the Schleswig-Holstein question by Ernest, responding to Albert's own views. The Prince passed the document on to Palmerston, as he did most of his personal foreign policy correspondence. For documentation of Faraday's relations with Albert beyond press accounts, see Geoffrey Cantor, *Michael Faraday: Sandemanian and Scientist* (1991), and Frank A.J.L. James, ed., *The Correspondence of Michael Faraday* (in progress).

The Prince's conversation with Edward Stanley, later Lord Stanley and afterwards the fifteenth Earl of Derby, is part of the entry of 20 July 1850 in John Vincent, ed., *Disraeli, Derby and the Conservative Party. Journals and Memoirs of Edward Henry, Lord Stanley* 1849–1869 (1978). Thackeray's musings connecting *Hamlet* and the imagined death of Albert are part of a letter to Mrs Edward John Sartoris, completed 3 November 1850, in Edgar F. Harden, ed., *The Letters and Private Papers of William Makepeace Thackeray* (a supplement to the Gordon Ray edition), vol. I (1994). For Peabody's benefactions at the time of the Exhibition see Franklin Parker, *George Peabody. A Biography* (1971). Albert's difficulties with Birch, Bertie's High Church tutor, are described amusingly by Disraeli in a letter of 22 April 1850, in Wiebe, vol. 5. The Athanasian Creed attack on Albert, refuted by Dean Wellesley, appears in Peter Levi, *Edward Lear* (1995), as Gibbs had refuted the charge to Lear, quoting Wellesley. The scotched knighthood to Darwin is reported in Adrian Desmond and James More, *Darwin* (1991), based upon James Bunting, *Charles Darwin* (1974).

## XI *The Palace of Glass 1850–1851*

Facsimile reproductions of many items associated with the Crystal Palace, from a season ticket with Albert's signature to reproductions of pictures of the exhibits and souvenir-type ephemera, were published in 1971 as *Jackdaw No. 43, The Great Exhibition 1851* by Jackdaw Publications Ltd in London. Most were derived from the Victoria and Albert Museum. Albert commissioned two volumes of coloured lithographs of the exhibition areas, published as *Comprehensive Pictures of the Great Exhibition of 1851 from the originals painted...for H.R.H. Prince Albert* (1854). Minutes of the Crystal Palace Commissioners are in the Royal Society of Arts, as is a report of the success of the 'Public Waiting Rooms', this attached to the minutes of 23 June 1852.

Dickens's letters of the Crystal Palace period are in the *Letters 1850–1852* (Pilgrim edition), ed. Graham Storey, Kathleen Tillotson and Nina Burgis (1988). The comments by John Bright on the Exhibition are from his *Diaries*, ed. R.A.J. Walling (1931). For Lady Charlotte Guest's diaries, see V. Countess Granville's letter on the Exhibition, to Lady Rivers, was actually finished by a Mr Stuart, an old friend who had accompanied her, and appears in Susan H. Oldfield, *Some Records of the Later Life of Harriet, Countess Granville* (1901) as if by an amanuensis. Carlyle was quoted by George Eliot in a letter to Sara Sophia Hennell, 13 October 1851, in Gordon S. Haight, ed., *The George Eliot Letters* (1954). The children's illustrated book was *Aunt Busy-Bee's The Fine Crystal Palace the Prince Built*, published at sixpence (1851). The song 'How's Your Poor Feet?' was published at a penny by W.S. Fortey at Seven Dials, London (1851).

Albert's letter to the Prime Minister, Lord John Russell, 9 July 1851, recommending Exhibition Secretary Digby Wyatt for a new post was quoted in the Julian Browning (London) sale catalogue 14, 'The Nineteenth Century', as item 4.

## XII *From Glory to Grief 1852–1853*

Captain Inglefield's Arctic naming adventures are described by Francis Spufford in 'Traces in the Snow. Victorian relics of human purpose at the poles', *TLS*, 28 July 1995. Albert Smith's vicarious adventures in the lecture hall are described in Simon Schama, *Landscape and Memory* (1995). Lord Malmesbury's reminiscences and diaries are in his *Memoirs of an Ex-Minister* (1884). Proposed expenditures from Great Exhibition surpluses are reported in John Scott Russell's itemizing of Exhibition Committee correspondence with Albert and his secretaries in a fifteen-page handwritten descriptive index to the forty-seven letters from Albert, or for him, in the Society of Art archives. That the Queen and Prince used the private courier service of the Rothschild firm to carry confidential messages to Germany is validated by a thank-you note from Albert's private secretary, Anson, as early as 4 July 1845, in the Rothschild Archive. This arrangement continued into 1861.

Thomas Mulock's Irish backgrounds were researched for me in the National Library of Ireland by Sean Ronan, who also found other letters, such as one from D.W. Cahill, DD, in *The Freeman's Journal* of 30 December 1853, the original having been sent to Albert as the one who presumably ran the affairs of government. The Revd Dr Cahill wrote on 'the disastrous condition of Ireland', which he hoped the Prince could rectify. It was an indication of public perception – or misperception – of Albert's actual powers. According to the Royal Librarian, Thomas Mulock remained a staunch defender of the Queen even after the Prince's death, and Mulock's move to England in the 1860s, as he is recorded as a correspondent as late as April 1863.

## XIII Impeaching the Prince 1853–1855

Daphne Bennett's *King without a Crown* (1977) credits the letter under the initials 'M.P.' as having been written by Lord Maidstone, but Edward Stanley owns up to it in his diary entry for 3 January 1854. For Thomas Mulock, see XII. For broadsides of the time on the Prince, including 'Lovely Albert', published by E. Brown, Lower Street, London, see the bound volume of contemporary broadsides by contemporary printers in the British Library. Julian Osgood Field in his anonymously published *Uncensored Recollections* (1901) quotes the *Martin Chuzzlewit* perception about the Queen and the Tower as foreshadowing public ignorance in 1854. G.W. Dasent's *John Delane* (1908) quotes fully many letters of *The Times*'s editor, and Greville's diary furnishes Delane's conversations. Baroness Bunsen's are reported in the *Life and Letters of Baroness Bunsen*. Baron Charles Frederick Vitzthum von Eckstaedt's reminiscences, based upon his diaries, are published as *St Petersburg and London in the Years 1852–1864*, ed. Henry Reeve (1887). Many memoirs and histories already cited deal with the Crimean War, however the narrative more often referred to here aside from personal recollections is Cecil Woodham-Smith, *The Reason  Why* (1954), from which comes Disraeli's ironic quip on war aims.  Colonel Gordon's letters are quoted in the biography of his father, the Earl of Aberdeen.

## XIV Albert's War 1855–1856

Exhibition Commission papers are in the Royal Society of Arts archives, as is Scott Russell's correspondence with Albert. Robert Mallet's siege gun counterpart to Albert's weapon is described by Thomas F. Arnold in 'The Venerable Mortar', *Military History Quarterly*, 8 (Winter, 1996). Palmerston's relations with Albert are derived primarily from the Southampton archive and from *Regina vs. Palmerston*. The arranged marriage for Vicky is best described in Hanna Pakula, *An Uncommon Woman. The Empress Frederick* (1995), Daphne Bennett, *Vicky* (1983), and Richard Berkeley, *The Empress Frederick* (1956). Albert's appearance at the pre-Exposition private view is described in Robertson, *Sir Charles Eastlake*. Albert's reorganization of the army is outlined in his letters to Palmerston, who acquiesced. His letters to his future son-in-law, Prince Frederick, are quoted by Pakula. Albert's gift of a charger to Col. Alexander Gordon for use in the Crimea is recorded in *Lord Aberdeen*, the life of his father. The background of the purchase of Paton's *Home: The Return from the Crimea* is described in Lloyd, *The Queen's Pictures*. The song overheard by Theodor

Fontane ('Bad luck they say/to...the Cobugs...') is quoted by him in his diaries, trans. Dorothy Harrison, *Journeys to England in Victoria's Early Days 1844–1859* (1939).

## XV Managing Destiny 1856–1858

Tennyson's letter to Elizabeth Russell, 19 May 1856, on Albert's surprise visit to Freshwater, is in Cecil Y. Lang and Edgar F. Shannon, Jr, eds, *The Letters of Alfred Lord Tennyson, II, 1851–1870* (1987). George M. Dallas's letter to Lewis Cass, 24 April 1857, is in his *Diary*, ed. Susan Dallas (1892), as is his later letter on Napoleon III's visit to Osborne. Albert's letters to his daughter Vicky detail much of his activities. Albert's extensive memorandum of his long conversation on foreign policy with Napoleon III is reproduced in Martin, IV, and reported from his own conversation with Albert by Vitzthum. The Prince's address at the opening of the Art Treasures Exhibition at Manchester is published in the posthumous *Principal Speeches and Addresses*. Other sources were cited earlier or may be inferred from the text.

## XVI Corporate Personality 1858–1860

Bertie's Albertine education is laid out in letters from his father and in both George Dangerfield, *Victoria's Heir. The Education of a Prince* (1941) and Philip Magnus, *King Edward the Seventh* (1964). Vitzthum's diary records the affair of Prince George of Saxony's visit. E.F. Benson writes of Albert's relationship to Wellington College in *As We Were* (1930). The Humboldt letter that embarrassed Albert had been published in the *Letters of Alexander von Humboldt to Varnhagen von Ense from 1827 to 1858* (1859, trans. by Friedrich Kapp, 1860). The royal routine at this time, and precision of the railway arrangements for the Balmoral journeys, are described in detail in Benita Stoney and Heinrich C. Weltzien, eds., Sheila de Bellaigue, trans., *My Mistress the Queen. The Letters of Frieda Arnold, Dresser to Queen Victoria* (1994). The letters begin in 1855. Fräulein Arnold left the Queen's services in 1859. Both Albert's letters and recorded conversations, and Victoria's more guarded comments in her letters and journals, attempting to conceal from herself her fears about Albert's health, record his progressive deterioration. So do Stockmar's responses to Albert. Clarendon's letters here and later are from *My Dear Duchess*, including the 'Eliza and Joseph' code for Victoria and Albert.

## XVII  The Treadmill Donkey  1860–1861

For Albert's letter to Tennyson on *Idylls of the King*, see XV. Ernest II commented upon the Aldershot encampment in his memoirs. Albert's Statistical Congress speech was covered very fully in the press and published in his posthumous *Addresses*. The Queen's Scottish adventures are recounted as always in her journals and in shorter form in her *Leaves from the Journal of Our Life in the Highlands* (1868), ghost-edited by Arthur Helps. Details of how Bertie was managed at Cambridge, and how he evaded discipline, are described in a letter from Nathaniel de Rothschild to his mother, Charlotte, in an undated letter, but early 1860, in the Rothschild Archive. Albert's remarks to Disraeli about the political power of newspapers are in Lord Stanley's diaries. Clarendon's gossip, here as earlier, is in Kennedy. Albert's letters to Stockmar and to Ernest on his visions for Royal princes as ambassadors to the Empire are in Martin and in Ernest's memoirs. Albert's accident with the runaway four-in-hand is described, along with its aftermath, in Ernest's memoir. Lord Torrington's description of the family Christmas at Windsor is quoted from Dasent's *Delane*. Dr William Baly's death in a grotesque railway accident is recalled in the *British Medical Journal*, 26 January 1901.

## XVIII  Duty Done  1861

Albert's distraught letters to Bertie are quoted in Magnus. Sources for the *Trent* affair include George E. Baker, ed., *The Works of William H. Seward*, vol. V (1884); Norman B. Ferris, *The Trent Affair* (1977); Gordon H. Warren, *Fountain of Discontent: The Trent Affair and Freedom of the Seas* (1981); 'God's Hand against the Rebellion', *Living Age*, May 1862; 'The Exact Law of the Trent Case', *The Economist*, 21 December 1861; Richard E. Winslow III, *Constructing Munitions of War: The Portsmouth Navy Yard Confronts the Confederacy, 1861–1865* (1995); David F. Long, *Gold Braid and Foreign Relations. Diplomatic Activities of U.S. Naval Officers, 1798–1883* (1988); Richard Rush and Robert H. Woods, eds., *Official Records of the Union and Confederate Navies in the War of the Rebellion*, Series 1, vol. 1, 19 January 1861 to 31 December 1862 (1894); W.J. Morgan et al., eds, *Autobiography of Rear Admiral Charles Wilkes, U.S. Navy 1798–1877* (1978); Martin Duberman, *Charles Francis Adams 1807–1886* (1960); Lord Redesdale, *Memories*, vol. 1 (1915); Ridley, *Lord Palmerston*; Connell, *Regina vs. Palmerston*; Ephraim Douglas Adams, *Great Britain and the American Civil War*, vol. 1 (1925); Edward Chalfant, *Better in Darkness. A Biography of Henry Adams. His Second Life* (1994); Henry Adams, *The Education of Henry Adams* (1918); James Pope-Hennessy, *Monckton Milnes. The Flight of Youth 1851–1885* (1951); S.A. Wallace and F. E. Gillespie, eds, *The Journal of Benjamin Moran*, vol. 1 (1948);

Philip Guedalla, *The Queen and Mr Gladstone* (1933); N. John Hall, ed., *The Letters of Anthony Trollope, 1833–1870*, (1983); H.C.G. Matthew, ed., *The Gladstone Diaries*, vol. VI (1978); and the American and British periodical press. John Wheeler-Bennett's 'The Trent Affair: How the Prince Consort Saved the United States', *History Today*, December 1961, is in a class by itself in asserting, by ignoring Palmerston's own writings, reproduced here, that the Prime Minister, 'contrary to general belief, was not spoiling for a fight'. The title suggests on the basis of no evidence whatever that the Union would have lost any conflict with Britain.

Albert's terminal illness, albeit misdiagnosed, is detailed at length in the many biographies of the Queen and Prince, especially in Martin, and in the recollections of courtiers; but only Daphne Bennett speculates in a one-page appendix to her *King Without a Crown* that typhoid fails to account for Albert's symptoms, and suggests a 'wasting disease'. My survey of the clinical particulars as described by Albert himself over the years 1858–1861, when offered to medical specialists, has elicited considerable scepticism over the typhoid diagnosis, as indeed existed among contemporaries cited. G.C. Williamson, *Memoirs in Miniature* (1933) quotes his father on Stockmar and the Royal chemists. The anonymous *Notebooks of a Spinster Lady 1878–1903* (1919) quotes Sir Henry Holland on the Queen's plea to him. Lady Mary Biddulph's urgent note from Windsor to John Poyntz, 5th Earl Spencer, is in P. Gordon, ed., *The Red Earl. Papers of the Fifth Earl Spencer 1835–1885* (1982). Nathaniel de Rothschild's letter to his parents from Cambridge, 16–17 December 1861, is in the Rothschild Archive.

## *Afterword: Legacy*

Charles Phipps's letter to John Scott Russell, 11 January 1962 is in the archives of the Royal Society of Arts. Elizabeth Gaskell's description of London in mourning appeared in her letter to Marianne Gaskell, 26 December 1861, in J.A.V. Chapple and Arthur Pollard, eds, *Letters of Mrs Gaskell* (1967). Mary Elizabeth Braddon's observation appeared in the January 1862 instalment of her novel *Aurora Floyd*, in *Temple Bar* – obviously a timely addition to the text. Emily Eden's correspondence, ed. Eleanor Eden, was published as *Letters from India* (1972).

# Acknowledgements

Writing *Victoria* made writing this parallel biography almost inevitable – to examine one of the most famous marriages in history from the perspective of the other spouse. Thus my acknowledgement to persons and to archives in that book can be assumed to carry over to this one. Some names are repeated, however, when I convey my appreciation here to Lucy Addington, Richard Altick, Herbert Appeltshauser, Melanie Askey, Richard Atkins, Stephen Belcher, Christopher Brown, Harry P. Clark, Sarah Curtis, Alison Derrett, Frances Diamond, Robert C. Doyle, Vivian Elliot, Ken and Jenny Emrys-Roberts, Oliver Everett, Bonny Farmer, Roland Fleischer, Peter Funnell, Peter Gadsden, Victor Gray, John Halperin, Alan and Eileen Hanley-Browne, Bridget and Heinz Henisch, Jürgen Kamm, Marlene Eilers Koenig, Heinz Kosok, Rolf Lessenich, Elizabeth Longford, Bonnie McEwan, Tom McGarrity, M.D., Grant McIntyre, Charles W. Mann, George Mauner, Anne Michel, Patrick Middleton, David Painting, Michel Pharand, Franz-Josef Post, Shirley Rader, Sue Reighard, Sean Ronan, Barbara Ryan, Mina Schwalb, Sandra Stelts, Gerhard Strasser, Wendy Trewin, Elliot S. Vesell, M.D., Rodelle Weintraub, James L.W. West III, M.G. Wiebe, Richard Winslow III, Muriel Winterscheid.

I owe a special indebtedness to my research 'home' since 1970, the Institute for the Arts and Humanistic Studies at the Pennsylvania State University.

Stanley Weintraub

# The House of Coburg

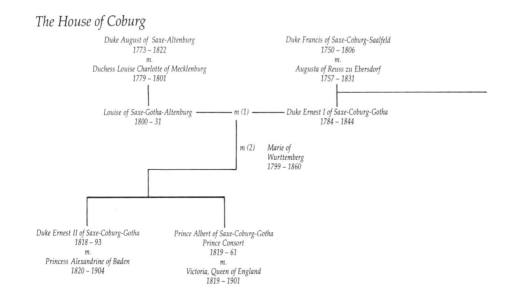

Duke August of Saxe-Altenburg
1773 – 1822
m.
Duchess Louise Charlotte of Mecklenburg
1779 – 1801

Duke Francis of Saxe-Coburg-Saalfeld
1750 – 1806
m.
Augusta of Reuss zu Ebersdorf
1757 – 1831

Louise of Saxe-Gotha-Altenburg ———— m (1) ———— Duke Ernest I of Saxe-Coburg-Gotha
1800 – 31                                                    1784 – 1844

m (2)   Marie of
Wurttemberg
1799 – 1860

Duke Ernest II of Saxe-Coburg-Gotha
1818 – 93
m.
Princess Alexandrine of Baden
1820 – 1904

Prince Albert of Saxe-Coburg-Gotha
Prince Consort
1819 – 61
m.
Victoria, Queen of England
1819 – 1901

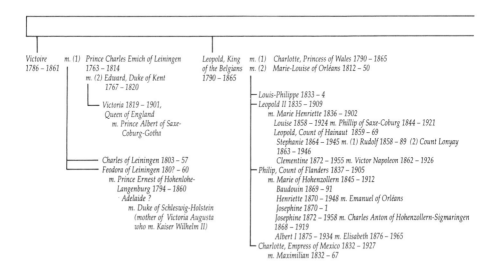

Victoire   m. (1)  Prince Charles Emich of Leiningen
1786 – 1861          1763 – 1814
                      m. (2) Edward, Duke of Kent
                            1767 – 1820

                            Victoria 1819 – 1901,
                            Queen of England
                            m. Prince Albert of Saxe-
                            Coburg-Gotha

                    Charles of Leiningen 1803 – 57
                    Feodora of Leiningen 180? – 60
                    m. Prince Ernest of Hohenlohe-
                       Langenburg 1794 – 1860
                        Adelaide ?
                          m. Duke of Schleswig-Holstein
                          (mother of Victoria Augusta
                          who m. Kaiser Wilhelm II)

Leopold, King   m. (1)  Charlotte, Princess of Wales 1790 – 1865
of the Belgians   m. (2)  Marie-Louise of Orléans 1812 – 50
1790 – 1865

    Louis-Philippe 1833 – 4
    Leopold II 1835 – 1909
        m. Marie Henriette 1836 – 1902
            Louise 1858 – 1924 m. Phillip of Saxe-Coburg 1844 – 1921
            Leopold, Count of Hainaut 1859 – 69
            Stephanie 1864 – 1945 m. (1) Rudolf 1858 – 89 (2) Count Lonyay
            1863 – 1946
            Clementine 1872 – 1955 m. Victor Napoleon 1862 – 1926
    Philip, Count of Flanders 1837 – 1905
        m. Marie of Hohenzollern 1845 – 1912
            Baudouin 1869 – 91
            Henriette 1870 – 1948 m. Emanuel of Orléans
            Josephine 1870 – 1
            Josephine 1872 – 1958 m. Charles Anton of Hohenzollern-Sigmaringen
            1868 – 1919
            Albert I 1875 – 1934 m. Elisabeth 1876 – 1965
    Charlotte, Empress of Mexico 1832 – 1927
        m. Maximilian 1832 – 67

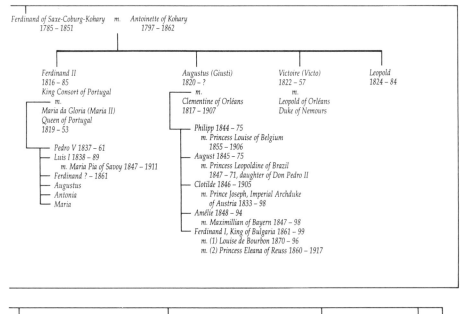

Ferdinand of Saxe-Coburg-Kohary    m.    Antoinette of Kohary
1785 – 1851                                    1797 – 1862

- **Ferdinand II** 1816 – 85 King Consort of Portugal
  m. Maria da Gloria (Maria II) Queen of Portugal 1819 – 53
  - Pedro V 1837 – 61
  - Luis I 1838 – 89 m. Maria Pia of Savoy 1847 – 1911
  - Ferdinand ? – 1861
  - Augustus
  - Antonia
  - Maria
- **Augustus (Giusti)** 1820 – ?
  m. Clementine of Orléans 1817 – 1907
  - Philipp 1844 – 75 m. Princess Louise of Belgium 1855 – 1906
  - August 1845 – 75 m. Princess Leopoldine of Brazil 1847 – 71, daughter of Don Pedro II
  - Clotilde 1846 – 1905 m. Prince Joseph, Imperial Archduke of Austria 1833 – 98
  - Amélie 1848 – 94 m. Maximillian of Bayern 1847 – 98
  - Ferdinand I, King of Bulgaria 1861 – 99 m. (1) Louise de Bourbon 1870 – 96 m. (2) Princess Eleana of Reuss 1860 – 1917
- **Victoire (Victo)** 1822 – 57 m. Leopold of Orléans Duke of Nemours
- **Leopold** 1824 – 84

---

- **Sophie** 1778 – 1850 m. Emmanuel, Count of Mensdorff-Pouilly of Austria 1777 – 1831
  - Alphonse 1810 – ?
  - Alexander 1813 – 71
  - Hugo 1816 – ?
  - Arthur 1818 – 1904
- **Antoinette** 1779 – 1824 m. Alexander, Duke of Wurttemberg 1771 – 1838
  - (Antoinette Frederika Augusta) Marie of Wurttemberg m. Ernest I
  - (Frederick Wilhelm) Alexander 1804 – 81 m. Marie of Valois, Princess of France
  - Philipp 1838 – 19? m. Maria Theresa, Princess of Austria
  - Ernest 1807 – 68
- **Juliana** 1781 – 1860 (Anna Feodorowna) m. Constantine, Grand Duke of Russia
- Marianne 1788 – 94
- **Maximillian** 1792 – 3

# The Descendants of Victoria and Albert

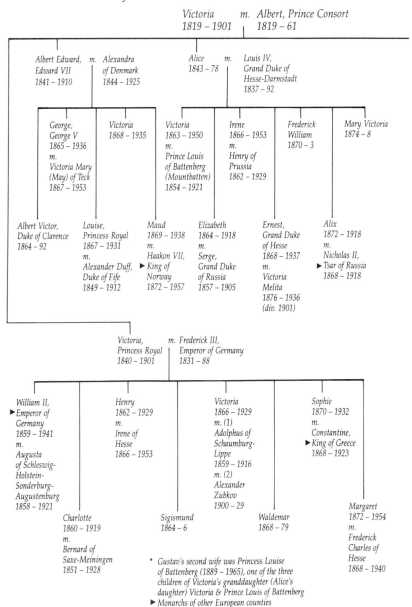

Victoria
1819 – 1901
m. Albert, Prince Consort
1819 – 61

Albert Edward,
Edward VII
1841 – 1910
m.
Alexandra
of Denmark
1844 – 1925

Alice
1843 – 78
m.
Louis IV,
Grand Duke of
Hesse-Darmstadt
1837 – 92

George,
George V
1865 – 1936
m.
Victoria Mary
(May) of Teck
1867 – 1953

Victoria
1868 – 1935

Victoria
1863 – 1950
m.
Prince Louis
of Battenberg
(Mountbatten)
1854 – 1921

Irene
1866 – 1953
m.
Henry of
Prussia
1862 – 1929

Frederick
William
1870 – 3

Mary Victoria
1874 – 8

Albert Victor,
Duke of Clarence
1864 – 92

Louise,
Princess Royal
1867 – 1931
m.
Alexander Duff,
Duke of Fife
1849 – 1912

Maud
1869 – 1938
m.
► Haakon VII,
King of
Norway
1872 – 1957

Elizabeth
1864 – 1918
m.
Serge,
Grand Duke
of Russia
1857 – 1905

Ernest,
Grand Duke
of Hesse
1868 – 1937
m.
Victoria
Melita
1876 – 1936
(div. 1901)

Alix
1872 – 1918
m.
► Nicholas II,
Tsar of Russia
1868 – 1918

Victoria,
Princess Royal
1840 – 1901
m. Frederick III,
Emperor of Germany
1831 – 88

William II,
► Emperor of
Germany
1859 – 1941
m.
Augusta
of Schleswig-
Holstein-
Sonderburg-
Augustenburg
1858 – 1921

Henry
1862 – 1929
m.
Irene of
Hesse
1866 – 1953

Victoria
1866 – 1929
m. (1)
Adolphus of
Schaumburg-
Lippe
1859 – 1916
m. (2)
Alexander
Zubkov
1900 – 29

Sophie
1870 – 1932
m.
Constantine,
► King of Greece
1868 – 1923

Charlotte
1860 – 1919
m.
Bernard of
Saxe-Meiningen
1851 – 1928

Sigismund
1864 – 6

Waldemar
1868 – 79

Margaret
1872 – 1954
m.
Frederick
Charles of
Hesse
1868 – 1940

* Gustav's second wife was Princess Louise
of Battenberg (1889 – 1965), one of the three
children of Victoria's granddaughter (Alice's
daughter) Victoria & Prince Louis of Battenberg
► Monarchs of other European counties

*and their marriages into the Royal Houses of Europe*

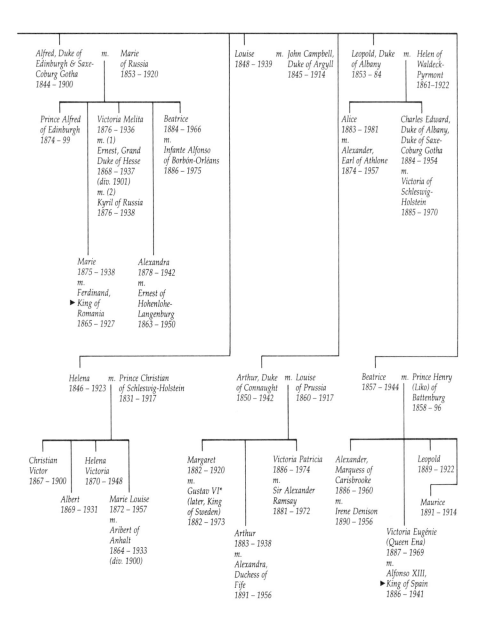

Alfred, Duke of
Edinburgh & Saxe-
Coburg Gotha
1844 – 1900

m.

Marie
of Russia
1853 – 1920

Louise
1848 – 1939

m. John Campbell,
Duke of Argyll
1845 – 1914

Leopold, Duke
of Albany
1853 – 84

m. Helen of
Waldeck-
Pyrmont
1861–1922

Prince Alfred
of Edinburgh
1874 – 99

Victoria Melita
1876 – 1936
m. (1)
Ernest, Grand
Duke of Hesse
1868 – 1937
(div. 1901)
m. (2)
Kyril of Russia
1876 – 1938

Beatrice
1884 – 1966
m.
Infante Alfonso
of Borbón-Orléans
1886 – 1975

Alice
1883 – 1981
m.
Alexander,
Earl of Athlone
1874 – 1957

Charles Edward,
Duke of Albany,
Duke of Saxe-
Coburg Gotha
1884 – 1954
m.
Victoria of
Schleswig-
Holstein
1885 – 1970

Marie
1875 – 1938
m.
Ferdinand,
▶ King of
Romania
1865 – 1927

Alexandra
1878 – 1942
m.
Ernest of
Hohenlohe-
Langenburg
1863 – 1950

Helena
1846 – 1923

m. Prince Christian
of Schleswig-Holstein
1831 – 1917

Arthur, Duke
of Connaught
1850 – 1942

m. Louise
of Prussia
1860 – 1917

Beatrice
1857 – 1944

m. Prince Henry
(Liko) of
Battenburg
1858 – 96

Christian
Victor
1867 – 1900

Helena
Victoria
1870 – 1948

Margaret
1882 – 1920
m.
Gustav VI*
(later, King
of Sweden)
1882 – 1973

Victoria Patricia
1886 – 1974
m.
Sir Alexander
Ramsay
1881 – 1972

Alexander,
Marquess of
Carisbrooke
1886 – 1960
m.
Irene Denison
1890 – 1956

Leopold
1889 – 1922

Albert
1869 – 1931

Marie Louise
1872 – 1957
m.
Aribert of
Anhalt
1864 – 1933
(div. 1900)

Arthur
1883 – 1938
m.
Alexandra,
Duchess of
Fife
1891 – 1956

Maurice
1891 – 1914

Victoria Eugénie
(Queen Ena)
1887 – 1969
m.
Alfonso XIII,
▶ King of Spain
1886 – 1941

# Index

# Index